Strong Arm Tactics

ALSO BY JOHN MAXYMUK

Uniform Numbers of the NFL:
All-Time Rosters, Facts and Figures
(McFarland, 2005)

Strong Arm Tactics

A History and Statistical Analysis
of the Professional Quarterback

JOHN MAXYMUK

McFarland & Company, Inc., Publishers
Jefferson, North Carolina, and London

Library of Congress Cataloguing-in-Publication Data

Maxymuk, John.
Strong arm tactics : a history and statistical analysis of the professional
quarterback / John Maxymuk.
p.   cm.
Includes bibliographical references and index.

ISBN-13: 978-0-7864-3277-6
illustrated case binding : 50# alkaline paper ∞

1. Quarterbacks (Football)— History.   2. Quarterbacks
(Football)— Statistics.   I. Title.
GV938.M39   2008   796.332'25 — dc22   2007031867

British Library cataloguing data are available

Cover photograph: Indianapolis Colts quarterback Peyton Manning,
center, drops back to pass against the Chicago Bears during Super Bowl XLI
on Sunday, Feb. 4, 2007 (AP Photo/Amy Sancetta)

Manufactured in the United States of America

*McFarland & Company, Inc., Publishers
Box 611, Jefferson, North Carolina 28640
www.mcfarlandpub.com*

For Suzanne, Katie and Juliane:
the stars of my backfield

Acknowledgments

In addition to my family and my coworkers at the Robeson Library on the Camden campus of Rutgers University, I would like to thank Saleem Choudhry and the staff at the Pro Football Hall of Fame who, as always, were happy to lend email assistance on thorny questions. A special thanks also to Dr. Ken Leistner who graciously looked over parts of the manuscript and made suggestions for improvements.

Table of Contents

Acknowledgments   vi
Preface   1
Introduction   5

I. Quarterbacks in Context   11

1. More Than Just a Live Arm   11
   Physical Attributes   11
   Attitude   16
   Playing Style   18
   Team Role   21

2. The Ongoing Search   24
   Football Factories   24
   The Draft   25
   Undrafted Free Agents   28
   Trades   29
   Unrestricted Free Agency   31
   Competitor Leagues   32

3. Career Arc   35
   Youth   35
   Prime Years   38
   Relationships with Coaches   39
   Injuries   42
   Age   45
   Coaching Careers   46
   Playing Outside the NFL   47

4. Glory   48
   Winning   48
   Fourth Quarter Comebacks   54
   The Playoffs   57

5. Measures and Rankings   60
   Statistical Measures   60
   Honors, Awards and the Hall of Fame   65
   All Time Rankings   66

6. Of Passing Interest: Miscellaneous Notes   71
   Passing Tailbacks   71
   The Halfback Option Play   71
   Quarterback Brothers   72
   Quarterback Fathers and Sons   72
   Quarterbacks and Professional Baseball   73
   Head-to-Head Duels   73
   Following a Legend   74
   Interceptions   75
   Fumbles and Turnovers   76

II. Quarterbacks in Time   79

7. 1920–1932: Grounded   79
8. 1933–1945: The Emerging T   89
9. 1946–1949: The All America Football Conference   102

10. 1946–1959: Taking Flight   107
11. 1960–1969: The American
        Football League   122

12. 1960–1977: Ball Control   133
13. 1978–1993: Full Throttle   151
14. 1994–2006: Air Time   169

III. Quarterbacks by Team   185

15. Arizona Cardinals   185
16. Atlanta Falcons   189
17. Baltimore Ravens   192
18. Buffalo Bills   194
19. Carolina Panthers   197
20. Chicago Bears   199
21. Cincinnati Bengals   203
22. Cleveland Browns   206
23. Dallas Cowboys   210
24. Denver Broncos   213
25. Detroit Lions   217
26. Green Bay Packers   221
27. Houston Texans   225
28. Indianapolis Colts   226
29. Jacksonville Jaguars   230
30. Kansas City Chiefs   232

31. Miami Dolphins   235
32. Minnesota Vikings   239
33. New England Patriots   242
34. New Orleans Saints   246
35. New York Giants   249
36. New York Jets   253
37. Oakland Raiders   257
38. Philadelphia Eagles   260
39. Pittsburgh Steelers   265
40. St. Louis Rams   269
41. San Diego Chargers   274
42. San Francisco 49ers   277
43. Seattle Seahawks   281
44. Tampa Bay Buccaneers   284
45. Tennessee Titans   287
46. Washington Redskins   291

Appendix A: Records (through 2006)   297
    Passing   297
    Passer Rating   297
    Attempts   297
    Completions   298
    Completion Percentage   298
    Yards Gained   299
    Average Gain   300
    Touchdowns   300
    Had Intercepted   301
    Lowest Percentage Intercepted   302
    Times Sacked   302
    Fumbles   302

Appendix B: Extended Passing Data   304
    League Passing Rates   304
    Basic League Passing Data   306
    Career Relative Passer Rating   307
    Won-Lost Records   313
    Estimated Won-Lost Records   315

    4th Quarter Game Winning
        Drives   315
    Comeback Leaders by Decades   317
    Postseason Data for All Passers   318
    Playoff Rushing by Quarterbacks   322
    Head to Head Matchups of Top
        Five Quarterbacks   323
    300-Yard Games   323
    Black Quarterbacks   325
    Running Quarterbacks   326

Appendix C: Drafts, Trades, Awards,
Numbers   328
    Quarterbacks and Passing
        Tailbacks Drafted in the
        First Round   328
    Table of Quarterback Trades   329
    Quarterback Award Winners   335
    Uniform Numbers of Top Passers   336

Bibliography   341
    Index   343

Preface

There are three things that football broadcasters do on a regular basis that drive me crazy. The first is that they chatter endlessly about irrelevant nonsense. The second is that they do not keep track of who is on the field and what formations the teams are aligned in. The third is that they usually provide statistics without any context for comparison. For example, they might say that Jake Plummer has 69 wins. OK, so what. How does that compare to other active players? How many losses does he have? How does his winning percentage compare to that of his peers? How do his numbers compare to quarterbacks from other time periods? No player exists in a vacuum, but the way numbers are tossed out on television, it sometimes seems that way.

I always have had a love for football history and statistics and am always seeking meaningful and comprehensible ways to compare and rank quarterbacks, because quarterback is the most complex and interesting position in this most complicated of team games. Sports statistics have expanded exponentially in recent decades, but they are not always transparent in meaning. The numbers wizards at Football Outsiders have created some amazing statistical measures to try to determine how effective particular players are within a game in which all statistics are wholly dependent on how well your 10 teammates perform. I find their work well written, convincing and informative, but the statistics are so complicated and seemingly removed from the game itself that I don't really understand what they are measuring. That's why in this book I deal only in basic statistics and comparative percentages; I think there is still much that can be learned from examining these types of numbers with the right perspective.

The book is divided into three sections. The first section offers a narrative study of the quarterback position through professional football history. I try to look at quarterbacks from a variety of perspectives. I classify major quarterback types according to physical attributes, attitude, playing style and role on a team. I examine where quarterbacks come from and the arc of their careers. I look at the greatest winners and the worst losers, and I try to cumulate various measures and rankings to discern who were the very best quarterbacks ever.

This section is filled with tables that provide a variety of views of quarterbacks. There are tables of black quarterbacks, running quarterbacks and rookie quarterbacks. There are tables listing won-lost records and fourth quarter comebacks for signal callers going all the way back in history, in addition to full postseason records for all quarterbacks and relative passer ratings to compare quarterbacks across eras. In most cases, the tables in the narrative are abbreviated, with complete tables either included in the appendices or on my website (http://www.rci.rutgers.edu/~maxymuk/home/home.html). The won-lost records and comeback tallies were accumulated by hand, largely by going through old newspaper accounts. Won-lost records prior to 1950 are merely estimates due to the way players were used in those days. Data from the 1950s and for the earliest years of the AFL were hard to come by and required some intuition at times in deciphering just who the starting quarterback was. These numbers are probably not flawless, but they represent as accurate a reading as I could compile, and they do provide context to the published records of current quarterbacks.

The second section is a study of the quarterback within his own time period. I divided pro football history into six eras that seemed to indicate significant change and provided separate sections on the All America Football Conference (AAFC) and the American Football League (AFL). The first era, from 1920 to 1932, was a time of infrequent passing and no official records, although I have used the incomplete and unofficial data culled from newspaper accounts for the Neft, Cohen and Korch *Football Encyclopedia*. Rule and equipment changes ushered in a new era in 1933, and this was an era in transition from the single wing to the Modern T formation. The postwar era that began in 1946 exhibited the wide-open passing possibilities of the Modern T and of two-platoon, free substitution football that marked the beginnings of the NFL's vast growth in popularity. Another transitional era began in 1960 with greater and greater emphasis placed on ball control offense and sturdy defense. As a result, the league repeatedly tinkered with the rules throughout the 1970s until they finally amended the rules on pass defense so radically that a new era began: the contemporary era, in 1978. It has been onward and upward with passing ever since, and further changes in 1994 completely created the coach's game that flourishes today.

There are certainly other ways that pro football could be divided into quarterback eras, but these made the most sense to me. The point is to be able to compare meaningfully the basic statistics of quarterbacks. Johnny Unitas' statistics don't look so hot compared to Peyton Manning's, but compared to the quarterbacks he competed against, he is clearly at the top. In this second section, I include statistics for the leading quarterbacks of the period and a description of the characteristics of the game at that time. For each season, there is a summary of rule and equipment changes, top rookies, best and worst performances and postseason notes. Statistics for the league and for the top quarterbacks are given. "Top" quarterbacks for each year are defined as those who finished in the top five of any of these categories: completion percentage, yards, touchdowns, or passer rating.

The third section breaks down quarterbacks by team. For each current team, statistics are detailed for the top 10–20 quarterbacks. Other team information is given in self-explanatory categories, such as Best and Worst Starters, Best Leader, Most Accurate, Tallest, Smallest, Oldest, Quarterback Controversy, Nicknames, and Off the Field. Each chapter in the section includes a bibliography of books by and about that team's quarterbacks.

There are also three appendices. Appendix A details passing records. Appendix B features a dozen data tables, more complete than the excerpts included in the text. Appendix C consists of four listings for quarterbacks: first round draft picks, trades, award winners and uniform numbers worn.

My hope is that this work will be useful to any football fan who wants to know more about professional quarterbacks — how they have changed the game and how the game has changed the position.

Team abbreviations are as follows. Three character abbreviations are used for current teams. Four-character abbreviations beginning with X are for NFL teams that failed; four character abbreviations beginning with Z are for defunct AAFC teams.

ARZ	Arizona, Phoenix, St. Louis and Chicago Cardinals
ATL	Atlanta Falcons
BAL	Baltimore Ravens
BUF	Buffalo Bills
CAR	Carolina Panthers
CHI	Chicago Bears, Chicago Staleys, Decatur Staleys
CIN	Cincinnati Bengals
CLE	Cleveland Browns
CIN	Cincinnati Bengals
DAL	Dallas Cowboys
DEN	Denver Broncos
DET	Detroit Lions, Portsmouth Spartans
GBP	Green Bay Packers
HOU	Houston Texans
IND	Indianapolis Colts, Baltimore Colts
JAX	Jacksonville Jaguars
KCC	Kansas City Chiefs, Dallas Texans
MIA	Miami Dolphins
MIN	Minnesota Vikings
NEP	New England Patriots, Boston Patriots
NOS	New Orleans Saints
NYG	New York Giants
NYJ	New York Jets, New York Titans
OAK	Oakland Raiders, Los Angeles Raiders
PHL	Philadelphia Eagles
PIT	Pittsburgh Steelers, Pittsburgh Pirates
STL	St. Louis Rams, Los Angeles Rams, Cleveland Rams
SDC	San Diego Chargers, Los Angeles Chargers
SFF	San Francisco 49ers
SEA	Seattle Seahawks
TBB	Tampa Bay Buccaneers
TEN	Tennessee Titans, Tennessee Oilers, Houston Oilers
WSH	Washington Redskins, Boston Redskins, Boston Braves
XAKR	Akron Pros
XBAL	Baltimore Colts (1950)
XBST	Boston Bulldogs
XBOS	Boston Yanks
XBRK	Brooklyn Dodgers, Brooklyn Tigers
XBUF	Buffalo All Americans, Buffalo Bisons, Buffalo Rangers
XCAN	Canton Bulldogs
XCIN	Cincinnati Reds
XCLE	Cleveland Bulldogs
XCOL	Columbus Panhandles, Columbus Tigers
XDAL	Dallas Texans (1952)
XDAY	Dayton Triangles
XDET	Detroit Panthers, Detroit Wolverines
XDUL	Duluth Eskimos

XFRA	Frankford Yellow Jackets
XMIL	Milwaukee Badgers
XNYB	New York Bulldogs, New York Yanks
XNYY	Red Grange's New York Yankees
XOOR	Oorang Indians
XPOT	Pottsville Maroons
XPRV	Providence Steam Roller
XRAC	Racine Legion, Racine Tornadoes
XROC	Rochester Jeffersons
XRIII	Rock Island Independents
XSTL	St. Louis All Stars
XSIS	Staten Island Stapletons
XTOL	Toledo Maroons
XWAS	Washington Senators
ZBAL	Baltimore Colts
ZBRK	Brooklyn Dodgers
ZBUF	Buffalo Bills, Buffalo Bisons
ZCHI	Chicago Rockets, Chicago Hornets
ZLAD	Los Angeles Dons
ZMIA	Miami Seahawks
ZNYY	New York Yankees

Introduction

In the beginning there was college football, and it was a rugged game of brutal scrums and dirty play, so violent that 18 players died during 1905. This prompted President Theodore Roosevelt to get involved to reform football just as he reformed big business. TR actually loved football — several of his Rough Riders were college football players — and he once wrote in a boys' magazine, "In life, as in football, the principle to follow is: Hit the line hard; don't foul and don't shirk, but hit the line hard." Roosevelt had athletic leaders from the major universities of the day form a commission to clean up the game. This commission would form the basis of the National Collegiate Athletic Association, and it promulgated several new rules for football: mass formations like the flying wedge and gang tackling were banned; first down yardage was increased from five to 10 yards; and passing the football was permitted. Yes, it took the intervention of the president of the United States to introduce the forward pass to football in 1906.

The main offensive formation of the time was the T formation, which actually went back to the legendary Walter Camp at Yale in the early 1880s. The main proponent of the T was Amos Alonzo Stagg, a former star player at Yale and the head coach at the University of Chicago for 41 years from 1892 through 1932. In the early version of the T, linemen were shoulder to shoulder with no gaps and the backfield consisted of the quarterback about a yard behind the center, two halfbacks stationed behind the quarterback and the fullback stationed behind the halfbacks. Thus, in the original T, the names of the backfield positions were fairly literal, unlike today, when on the rare occasion a team even employs a fullback, he will most likely be stationed closer to the line than the running back.

In the early years of the 20th century, at the Carlisle Indian Institute, Glenn "Pop" Warner came up with an alternative formation: the single wing. In Warner's single wing, the line was unbalanced; that is, either both guards or both tackles were on the same side of the center to offer greater blocking power at the point of the rushing attack. Football was a ground-oriented game, and the single wing was a running formation ideal for the time. The quarterback was a blocking back who often called signals and was stationed behind a guard. To his right or left was the wingback, stationed behind the end's outside shoulder. Further behind the quarterback was the fullback, and beyond the fullback was the tailback set about seven yards behind the center and ready to take the long snap. A decade or so later at Stanford, Warner developed the double wing in which the fullback usually took the long snap and the tailback was set as a second wingback on the opposite side.

By the time that the scattered midwestern dreamers playing professional football got organized enough to form the American Professional Football Association, the precursor to the NFL, in 1920, almost everyone was running some variation of Pop Warner's single wing formation. Like the college sport, pro football was a running game, and the wing formations seemed to offer the best option for rushing. Hall of Famers Curly Lambeau and George Halas went in different directions.

Lambeau had attended Notre Dame under Knute Rockne, and he used the Notre Dame Box throughout the 1920s. In the Box, the line was balanced and the backfield lined up in a T formation and then shifted to one side or the other before the play was run with the quarterback behind a guard, the wingback behind an end, and the tailback and fullback lined up similarly to how they would be lined up in the single wing.

Halas had attended Illinois and played under Bob Zuppke, who used the T. Like Lambeau, Halas brought his college formation to the pros. Halas coached the Bears for forty years, but took a break from coaching every 10 years or so. His first sabbatical came in 1930 when he hired Ralph Jones to coach the team. Jones wrought some changes to the Bears' hoary T. He introduced a man-in-motion to the backfield and may have spread out his linemen some. Halas returned in 1933, the same year that Amos Stagg was forced to retire from the University of Chicago due to age. With Stagg's replacement, Clark Shaughnessy, Halas struck up a friendship that would pay dividends by the end of the decade. The irony is that Stagg hated pro football as an immoral "menace" to his beloved college game, but his successor at Chicago designed changes to the venerable T that opened up the offense and allowed the pros to develop their own devoted following and eventually outstrip the college game. Shaughnessy moved the linemen further apart to open gaps in the defense and moved the quarterback directly under the center so he could take a hand-to-hand snap. These changes made the Bears offense faster than any defense of the time and made the quarterback the central point of the offense.

In Shaughnessy's updated T, the quarterback took the snap and quickly handed off to a back moving at full speed into the line or faked a handoff and passed the ball to a receiver. Because the runner was hitting the line so fast on dives and slants and counters, all the linemen had to do was briefly brush block or shield the defender from the play. The quarterback's ball handling and faking skills became paramount, and Halas picked Sid Luckman from Columbia to be his prototype modern T formation quarterback.

After the Bears annihilated the Redskins 73–0 for the 1940 championship, it was only a matter of time before all pro teams switched to the more versatile and explosive modern T. By 1948, all NFL teams but the Steelers had converted to the T, and Shaughnessy was then the coach of the Rams, where he tweaked the T further by making the halfback-in-motion a second wide receiver, lined up in the slot to form the Slot T or out on the flank to form what became known as the Pro Set, which has dominated both the pro and college game ever since. Shaughnessy's high-scoring Rams became experts at the deep pass.

Meanwhile in Cleveland, Paul Brown took several steps to create the modern passing offense on the "new" T formation. Originally, most pass plays in the T involved play action fakes since football was still a running game in the 1940s. In that 73–0 title game, the Bears ran for 390 yards and passed for just 138. Brown organized a pass-blocking scheme to form a protective cup around quarterback Otto Graham and dubbed it the "pocket." Cleveland linemen would break from the huddle, shouting their Otto motto, "Nobody touches Graham!" With the pocket, Brown incorporated many straight, drop-back pass plays with no play action fakes. Moreover, the Browns brought a playbook's worth of regular patterns to the passing game, especially timing patterns like outs, comebacks and slants. The Browns routed the vaunted NFL champion Eagles on opening day of the 1950 season, and all the elements of modern passing were in effect.

From here on there really was no longer a pure T formation, but instead endless variations on variations. We have seen the Wing T, the I formation, the Wishbone, the Shotgun, and a plethora of Spread formations over the past 50 years. The overall tendency has been for the offense to spread out further and further and open up gaps in the defense to exploit. Most teams employ variations of all of these formations in their offense, even if their base set is still Shaughnessy's Pro Set. More important than the formation is the overall offense. The strategies we see today are the descendants of a handful of groundbreaking offensive minds.

Vince Lombardi developed an offense in which the passing game is secondary to a power running game. Lombardi brought the idea of option blocking with him from West Point to the pros. In option blocking, the blocker rides the defender in the direction the defender wants to go so that the runner must read the blocks, find the hole and "run to daylight," in Lombardi's memorable phrase. The base play in his offense was the power sweep featuring two pulling guards; this was an updated version of the cutback play in the single wing. Once again, the runner would find the hole and shoot through it. Similarly, Lombardi's passing game relied on receivers' reading the defenders and adjusting their routes accordingly. Lombardi's playbook was very small, but the plays themselves had many options built in depending on how the defense reacted. A strong running attack tended to open up the passing game, and Lombardi's quarterback Bart Starr was famous for reading defenses. His signature play was to fake a run on third or fourth and short and throw long instead because the defense was bunched closely at the line of scrimmage to stop the expected run.

Sid Gillman, who started in pro football with the Rams before fully working out his schemes with the Chargers in the AFL, is the father of the deep passing attack. His offense was pass-oriented and featured long bombs to the post and to the corners and deep, timed crossing routes to speedy wide receivers. He also liked to get his backs into patterns that isolated them on slower linebackers. On the Chargers, this meant Jack Kemp, Tobin Rote and John Hadl throwing bombs to Lance Alworth and Gary Garrison and underneath routes to Paul Lowe and Keith Lincoln. Gilman's end coach Al Davis took this concept to Oakland and called it his "vertical passing game" with bombers like Daryle Lamonica and Jim Plunkett throwing to Warren Wells and Cliff Branch. Don Coryell was coaching at San Diego State in the early 1960s and brought the offense to the Cardinals and Chargers in the 1970s and 1980s. Coryell liked to run the offense with one back and two tight ends. Coryell's assistant Joe Gibbs brought it to Washington and added a heavy reliance on the ground game. Norv Turner ran a run-oriented variation of it Dallas, and Mike Martz ran a spectacular version in St. Louis.

Gillman follower Bill Walsh came to Paul Brown's staff on the expansion Bengals from the Raiders. With strong-armed rookie quarterback Greg Cook under center, Walsh initially favored a downfield passing game. When Cook got hurt, though, the Bengals had to switch to smart but weak-armed backup Virgil Carter. Walsh had to change the offense to negate the Bengals' lack of a deep threat and deficient running game. He had Carter throw short, high-percentage passes to wide receivers and backs, emphasizing ball control. The offense was designed to have the quarterback quickly go through a progression of reads, hit the open man in stride, and let the receiver gain yards after the catch. Because the Bengals weren't a great team, the offense did not attract much notice at the time. However, when Walsh got to San Francisco, Joe Montana and Steve Young showed how explosive the approach could be, and it began to be called the West Coast Offense, although the Gillman offense deserves that appellation more. From the 1980s on, the West Coast offense has spread so widely that roughly half of NFL teams run some version of it today.

The most radical offense tried was the Run & Shoot high scoring, pass-happy attack that detractors like defensive coach Buddy Ryan dubbed the Chuck & Duck. Mouse Davis popularized the offense at Portland State and sent quarterbacks June Jones and Neil Lomax to the pros from the Run & Shoot. The Run & Shoot employed four wide outs, often of the smallish variety, and one running back. It required the quarterback to get rid of the ball quickly because he had no blocking help for blitzes. The first pro team to try the Run & Shoot was the Houston Gamblers of the USFL with Jim Kelly as quarterback. Kelly would run this offense at times with Buffalo after he moved on to the NFL in the late 1980s. Jerry Glanville brought the Run & Shoot to the NFL fulltime when he used it as his offense first with the Oilers and then the Falcons. The Lions also used this as their primary offense in the late 1980s. We still see Run & Shoot variations, but they are part of a team's offense and not the whole thrust.

Throughout the history of professional football, the cyclical pattern is for offensive innovations to lead to defensive counter measures. When these counter measures become too effective and onerous, rules are changed and more innovations flow from the offense. With every offense and every variation, the defense has countered with its own inventions. Shaughnessy's T led to Greasy Neale's 5-2 Eagle Defense. Paul Brown's open passing attack led to Steve Owen's Umbrella Defense and then Tom Landry's basic 4-3 with the middle linebacker as the focus. Safety blitzes, nickel and dime packages, bump-and-run coverage, zone coverage, cover 2, the 3-4 defense, the 46 defense ... complexity after complexity as the game continues to evolve. As with offense, the defensive base set means nothing today. Formations and strategies change on every down as clever defensive coordinators attempt to confuse the quarterback and disrupt the play. When Fritz Shurmer was coaching the Rams defense, he beat the Eagles in a 1989 playoff game by running a zone with five linebackers and six defensive backs on passing plays. Three-time Super Bowl winner Bill Belichick is famous for his imaginative schemes and odd personnel deployments. While Belichick's schemes may aim at shutting down a particular weapon — as, for example, when the Patriots focused on Brian Westbrook, not Terrell Owens, in Super Bowl 38 — the ultimate aim is to baffle the opposing quarterback.

No matter what formation is run or what offense employed, there is one man in charge on the field, and that is the quarterback. The quarterback gets the ball on every play and decides what to do with it. It's a fact that in today's complicated, coaches' chess match quarterbacks rarely call their own plays anymore, but they still have the ball and the game in their hands. The quarterback chooses whether to audible to another play and where to throw the ball. The offense is his responsibility. As Johnny Unitas once put it, "A quarterback doesn't come into his own until he can tell the coach to go to hell." That is still true today. A quarterback must assert himself and command the offense. He is there to lead the team. That is why the quarterback gets the blame when his team loses and the credit when his team wins. It is why he gets famous. It is why he gets rich.

With the fame and riches come duties and burdens that require him to be as tough mentally as he is physically. Football players do not play in a vacuum or on a sound stage; they perform in front of packed stadiums and hyperanalytical media. Don Strock said after his first NFL start that he hadn't faced so many questions "since my mother caught me drinking in high school." Bill Parcells once told Phil Simms after a tough game, "Don't buy the papers tomorrow, you're not going to like what you read." A quarterback cannot afford to be too sensitive. Moreover, there are the fans. While some cities like Philadelphia, New York and Boston are especially notorious for having impatient, vocal and aggressive fans, every town boos the quarterback at some point. Bobby Layne claimed, "I got booed in the men's room." Sonny Jurgensen likened playing quarterback to "holding group therapy for 50,000 people a week." His teammate Billy Kilmer agreed on the need for a thick skin: "If I let that bother me, I'd have to go back pressing pants with my old man."

Quarterback is the toughest, most pressure-packed, most visible, most lauded, most villified and most fascinating position in sports. Let's take a closer look at the man who directs the offense, generates the scoring and facilitates the victory on the football field—the field general, the signal caller, the *quarterback*.

1

More Than Just a Live Arm

Throughout the history of the NFL, the passing game has steadily increased in importance. The offensive strategies and tactics are ever evolving and require a quarterback with a broad mix of skills. Charlie Tate, who coached the University of Miami in the 1960s, once said, "Having a pro offense with great receivers but no first-rate quarterback is like having a new limousine with a chimpanzee at the wheel." While the skill set of every quarterback will differ, there are a number of broad areas in which there are similarities. In general, we can catalogue quarterbacks in at least four different ways — by their physical attributes, their attitude, their playing style and their role on the team. These classes and the 20 types under them are by no means exclusive; each quarterback may fit into more than one category. Think of this as a way to compare the abilities, styles and roles of some of the most significant figures to have played this most prominent position.

Physical Attributes

Mighty Mites

Mighty Mites are quarterbacks who have had to overcome the stigma and disadvantage of being small in stature in a big man's game. The smallest player ever to be listed as a quarterback and probably the smallest NFL player ever was Jack Shapiro of the Staten Island Stapletons who was listed at 5'1" and 119 pounds, but he only played one game in 1929 and was not really a passer anyway. Two slight former Michigan Wolverines were prominent passing tailbacks for the Giants in the 1920s and 1930s; Benny Friedman and Harry Newman stood 5'10" and 5'8" respectively. However, the smallest regular passer was Davey O'Brien, a single wing tailback for Philadelphia in 1939 and 1940 at 5'7" and 150 pounds. When he wasn't running for his life behind the awful Eagle line, he managed to lead the NFL in passing yards as a rookie and attempts and completions the next year. During World War II, the Cardinals used a 5'8" 150-pound passing tailback named Ronnie Cahill, but he threw only 3 touchdowns to 21 interceptions and was gone after one season.

In the late 1940s amongst a slew of 5'10" quarterbacks such as Boley Dancewicz, George Cafego, Albie Reisz, Allie Sherman, Dwight Sloan, Al Dekdebrun, Sam Vacanti, George Terlep, Scott Gudmundson and Jesse Freitas, Sr. emerged the next miniature star quarterback, Frankie Albert. The 5'10" 166-pound Albert had learned the T-formation under innovator Clark Shaughnessy at Stanford and was drafted by the Bears, but chose to sign with the 49ers in the rival All America Conference after the War instead. He was noted for his ball-handling and faking skills, but was also a deadly passer and elusive runner, and he led San Francisco into the NFL as the second best team in AAFC four years later when the leagues merged.

As Albert retired, Eddie LeBaron of the Redskins and, later, Cowboys, took up his mighty mite mantle. LeBaron was listed at 5'9" and 168 pounds, but was most likely 5'8" at best.

Again, he was noted for ball-handling and faking skills, which seems to be a pattern for smaller quarterbacks. He honed those skills as a 16-year-old prodigy under ancient college coach Amos Alonzo Stagg at the College of the Pacific. As if competing against the behemoths of professional football were not proof enough of his toughness, LeBaron was also a former Marine who had been wounded in Korea. Although he played on generally awful teams and amassed mediocre statistics, he played in four Pro Bowls. The other short quarterbacks of the 1950s and 1960s were less successful and stood at 5'10". They include Bob Celeri, Ted Marchibroda, Travis Tidwell, Harry Theofiledes and Marlin Briscoe.

Although Pat Haden, Jerry Rhome, Bob Griese, Fran Tarkenton and Joe Theismann all appear to belong in this grouping, each claimed to be at least 5'11". The only quarterback officially less than 5'11" since LeBaron retired in 1963 has been Doug Flutie who claimed to 5'10", but that was probably about an inch on the optimistic side. The Heisman Trophy winner was most famous for his 47-yard last-play Hail Mary touchdown pass to beat Miami. Flutie flunked brief trials in Chicago and New England and had to go prove himself in Canada before he could get a real opportunity to play and excel in the NFL in the late 1990s. By the time Buffalo gave the six-time CFL MVP a real shot, he was 35 years old, but he put together five good seasons in the NFL. As impressive as O'Brien, LeBaron and Albert were, it's important to remember that the average defensive lineman at the end of Doug's career was 170 percent heavier than he was. The percentages for O'Brien, Albert and LeBaron come out to 152 percent, 146 percent and 155 percent respectively. How we define Mighty Mite in the NFL continues to inch upwards. Among current quarterbacks, there are only four under 6'1": Seneca Wallace at 5'11" and Drew Brees, Michael Vick and Tim Rattay all at 6'.

Hulks

At the opposite end of the spectrum are the Hulks, the biggest quarterbacks. It is interesting to note that when Sammy Baugh started in 1937 he was considered very tall at 6'2". The only passer taller up to that point was Bernie Masterson of the Bears who was 6'3". The first passer to reach 6'4" was Glenn Dobbs, a tall, thin, star passer and punter and the AAFC's answer to Sammy Baugh. Forgettable 6'4" Steeler Joe Gasparella was next in the late 1940s. Into the 1960s, 6'4" still was considered as very tall for a quarterback including such famous passers as Norm Snead, Craig Morton and Greg Landry. A new height mark was set when the Cowboys drafted the 6'7" Sonny Gibbs in the second round of the 1962 NFL draft, but he couldn't beat out veteran Eddie LeBaron, almost a foot shorter, for a spot on the team.

The quarterback ahead of the trend at the time was 6'5" Roman Gabriel who proved that someone that size did not have to be stiff, immobile, geeky and injury-prone as other 6'5" quarterbacks from the 1960s and 1970s were. These brittle beanpoles include Dick Wood, Ron Smith, Steve Tensi, Al Woodall, Scott Bull, Bill Troup and Don Strock. Strock at least was a reliable backup, but it wasn't until the 1980s that 6'5" became a desirable height with such stars as Boomer Esiason, Bernie Kosar, Jim Everett and Vinny Testaverde. They have since been joined by more stars like Drew Bledsoe, Peyton Manning, Brad Johnson, Kerry Collins, Byron Leftwich, Ben Roethlisberger and Philip Rivers.

The new frontier is 6'6". The first to reach that height were Marc Wilson and replacement player Brian McClure in the 1980s, and they have been joined in recent years by Scott Mitchell, Jonathan Quinn, Gibran Hamdan, John Navarre and Derek Anderson, but none yet have been very successful. The record-setting Gibbs was equaled in the 1970s by the 6'7" sometime tight end Frank Patrick and surpassed by the 6'8" draft bust Dan McGwire in the 1980s. However as defensive lineman continue to grow bigger, it is likely that quarterbacks will as well. We certainly see that in weight where stout bodies like Daunte Culpepper, Donovan McNabb and Byron Leftwich would have played different positions had they been active in earlier generations. The Jabba the Hut Award, though, goes to 285-pound backup Jared Lorenzen of the Giants, sometimes referred to as the "Pillsbury Throwboy" and the "Round Mound of Touchdown."

Lefthanders

While lefthanded quarterbacks continue to be out of the ordinary, they were once as rare as Republicans in Hollywood. Allie Sherman of the 1943 Steagles was the first left-handed professional quarterback. He would play four more years as a backup with the Eagles and later coach the New York Giants in the 1960s. The first star left-hander was Frankie Albert of the 49ers who was known for his crafty play and threw 88 touchdown passes in the four seasons of the AAFC. UCLA's southpaw Ernie Case played briefly for the Colts in the AAFC as well.

Although Cleveland drafted Harry Agannis of Boston College in the second round in 1952, this lefty signed to play baseball with the Red Sox instead and then tragically died young. Finally ten years after Albert retired, another lefty, Heisman Trophy winner Terry Baker, was drafted by the Rams, but he flopped as a pro. At the end of the decade, Bobby Douglass joined the Bears, but was better noted for setting a quarterback rushing record with 968 yards in 1972 than for his woefully inaccurate passing arm. The 1970s welcomed the very accurate All Pro Ken Stabler, the footloose Jim Zorn, the forgettable David Humm and the regrettable mutton-chopped Jim Del Gaizo.

Hall of Famer Steve Young turned pro in the 1980s and was accompanied by All Pro Boomer Esiason and journeyman Paul McDonald. The 1990s brought a star in Mark Brunell as well as stiffs Todd Marinovich, Scott Mitchell, Tony Graziani, Will Furrer and Erik Wilhelm. Currently, we can watch lefthanders Michael Vick, Chris Simms, Matt Leinart, Dave Ragone and Hefty Lefty Jared Lorenzen try to make their mark in a right-handed league.

The Black Quarterback

The 1999 draft was remarkable for quarterbacks with five being selected in the first round. Even more remarkable is the fact that three of those five were black quarterbacks; it was the first time more than one black quarterback was drafted in the first round of the NFL draft. At the top of the list was Donovan McNabb who was selected in the second slot, the highest ever for a black quarterback. Two years later Michael Vick would become the first black quarterback selected with the top pick in the draft.

At long last, we can relegate the NFL's dismal treatment of black signal callers to the past. 1999 was also the first season in which ten black quarterbacks were the primary starters of their teams. One of those ten starters was the rookie Donovan McNabb. The strange thing about McNabb is how frequently he has been caught in racial questions despite playing in an era when the restrictions on black quarterbacks have disappeared. When negotiating his first contract, he and his agent grumbled that he was being treated differently because of his race about a sticking point on voidable years. There has been constant tension between McNabb and local fans and media over his deemphasis on running in his desire to be seen as a pocket passer because he views "running quarterback" as a pejorative term for a black quarterback. He discounts the fact that his running ability is a great asset that makes his passing more effective. In 2003, Rush Limbaugh made his famous comment that the struggling McNabb's failings as a quarterback were ignored by the media because of his race. Then, in 2005, McNabb responded to the petty comments of egomaniacal wide receiver Terrell Owens that the Eagles would be better off with Brett Favre at quarterback by claiming this was an example of "black-on-black crime." McNabb would benefit by understanding how far the league has come from its past disreputable practices towards African American quarterbacks.

In the early years of single wing football in the NFL, Hall of Famer Fritz Pollard was the first black quarterback as well as the first black head coach with the Akron Pros. Only one other black passer emerged before the unofficial color ban bleached the NFL lily white in 1934, and that was Oregon tailback Joe Lillard of the Chicago Cardinals who completed just 28 percent of his passes in his brief career, but was the star back of the team as a runner and returner. The NFL slowly began to sign black players again in the post–World War II era, but T-Formation quarterback was not a position blacks were deemed qualified to assume. The Los Angeles Dons of the rival All America Conference did employ black single wing tailback George Taliaferro in 1949, but the first black quarterback in the NFL was Michigan State's Willie Thrower who got to toss just 8 passes for the 1953 Chicago Bears. Also in 1953, George Taliaferro, now a T-Formation quarterback, got to start two games with the brand new Baltimore Colts. Two years later, the Green Bay Packers drafted Praire View's shotgun-armed Charlie "Choo Choo" Brackins in the 16th round, and he got to throw two passes as Tobin Rote's backup. He was cut for disciplinary reasons the following season.

The next milestones would not come until 1968 when the Oakland Raiders made Tennessee State's Eldridge Dickey the first black quarterback taken in the first round of the draft. That same year, fellow rookie Marlin "the Magician" Briscoe started six games and appeared in five others for the Denver Broncos. However, these two were not given a real chance at quarterback. Dickey was converted to wide receiver as a rookie. Moreover, Briscoe was cut the next season despite showing promise as a quarterback. Marlin was switched to wideout by the Bills in 1969, the same year they drafted Grambling's James Harris in the seventh round. Harris would eventually win the starting job with the Rams in 1974 and become the first black quarterback to start a playoff game that year and the first black quarterback named MVP of the Pro Bowl. 1974 also marked the first season that more than one team started a black quarterback when another Tennessee State alumnus, Joe Gilliam, who was tall, spindly and elusive with a whip arm, started six games for the Steelers. Harris would go on to have an 11-year NFL career, but the career of flashy Jefferson Street Joe was derailed by drugs, and he died at age 49.

Small steps were being achieved in the 1970s as nine African Americans would play quarterback in the NFL during the decade. The most prominent was Doug Williams, drafted in the first round by the expansion Tampa Bay Bucs in 1978 and handed the starting job on an awful team. Within two years, the Bucs were in the playoffs although they would not have many years of success, and Williams would end up in the USFL after a bitter salary dispute. While the situation slowly improved, several black college quarterbacks chose to go to the Canadian Football League rather than be forced to switch positions in the NFL in the 1970s — Chuck Ealey, Cornelius Greene, Jimmy Streeter, J.C. Watts, Condredge Holloway and Warren Moon to name the most prominent.

Hall of Famer Warren Moon made it very clear before the 1978 NFL draft he had no intention of switching positions and instead signed with Edmonton in the CFL to preclude the possibility of a position switch. He was not drafted despite quarterbacking the Washington Huskies to the Rose Bowl title in 1978. After six spectacular seasons and five championships in the CFL, Moon signed with the Oilers as a free agent in 1984 and became the first black quarterback star. Two years later, Randall Cunningham, the "Ultimate Weapon," won the Eagles starting quarterback job, and the prejudices of NFL talent evaluators began to crumble as Moon and Cunningham demonstrated that black quarterbacks could lead their teams to victory as well as any other quarterback. The final proof was delivered in Super Bowl XXII when the resurrected Doug Williams led the Redskins to a 42–10 win over Denver, highlighted by an otherworldly second quarter in which Williams threw for 228 yards and four touchdowns as Washington blew the game apart. There were three black starting quarterbacks in 1987 (Moon, Cunningham and Williams), four in 1992, five in 1996, seven in 1997, eight in 1998 and ten in 1999. The total dipped back to eight in 2006, but the result is clear — quarterbacks today are judged by winning and losing, not by black and white.

Although it is time to bury the term "black quarterback" in today's NFL, for the historical record the following table lists the career passing records of black quarterbacks who passed for at least 10,000 yards. The full table of African Americans who played quarterback in the NFL 1920–2006 is in Appendix B.

Name	1st Year	Att	Comp	%	Yards	Y/Att	Y/Comp	TD	Int	Rating
Moon, Warren	1984	6823	3988	58.4%	49325	7.2	12.4	291	233	80.9
McNair, Steve	1995	4339	2600	59.9%	30191	7.0	11.6	172	115	83.2
Cunningham, Randall	1985	4289	2429	56.6%	29979	7.0	12.3	207	134	81.5
McNabb, Donovan	1999	3259	1898	58.2%	22080	6.8	11.6	152	72	85.2
Blake, Jeff	1992	3241	1827	56.4%	21711	6.7	11.9	134	99	78.0
Culpepper, Daunte	1999	2741	1759	64.2%	21091	7.7	12.0	137	89	90.8
Brooks, Aaron	1999	2963	1673	56.5%	20261	6.8	12.1	123	92	78.5
Williams, Doug	1978	2507	1240	49.5%	16998	6.8	13.7	100	93	69.4

Name	1st Year	Att	Comp	%	Yards	Y/Att	Y/Comp	TD	Int	Rating
Peete, Rodney	1989	2346	1344	57.3%	16338	7.0	12.2	76	92	73.3
Banks, Tony	1996	2356	1278	54.2%	15315	6.5	12.0	77	73	72.4
Stewart, Kordell	1995	2358	1316	55.8%	14816	6.3	11.3	77	84	70.8
Vick, Michael	2001	1730	930	53.8%	11505	6.7	12.4	71	52	75.7

The next table lists black quarterbacks who gained at least 1,000 rushing yards through 2006.

Name	Rush Att	Rush Yds	Rush Ave	Rush TD
Cunningham, Randall	681	4435	6.5	32
Vick, Michael	529	3859	7.3	21
McNair, Steve	659	3558	5.4	37
Stewart, Kordell	560	2874	5.1	38
McNabb, Donovan	447	2726	6.1	24
Culpepper, Daunte	464	2496	5.4	30
Blake, Jeff	418	2027	4.8	14
Taliaferro, George	403	1794	4.5	10
Moon, Warren	543	1736	3.2	22
Brooks, Aaron	362	1534	4.2	13
Peete, Rodney	270	1139	4.2	16
Evans, Vince	212	1129	5.3	14

Here is the roll call for all Black quarterbacks listed by their rookie years (r = replacement player, x = never appeared in NFL game):

Name	Rookie Year	Name	Rookie Year	Name	Rookie Year
Pollard, Fritz	1920	Gillus, Willie	1987r	Bonner, Sherdrick	1999x
Lillard, Joe	1932	Miller, Larry	1987r	Wynn, Spergon	2000
Taliaferro, George	1949 AAFC	Blount, Ed	1987r	Bishop, Michael	2000
		Briggs, Walter	1987r	Craig, Dameyune	2000
Thrower, Willie	1953	Jordan. Homer	1987x	Hamilton, Joe	2000
Brackins, Charlie	1955	Tipton, Greg	1987x	Vick, Michael	2001
Briscoe, Marlin	1968	McPherson, Don	1988x	Carter, Quincy	2001
Harris, James	1969	Peete, Rodney	1989	Jackson, Jarious	2001
Lewis, Dave	1970	Ware, Andre	1990	Martin, Tee	2001
Douglass, Karl	1971x	Mitchell, Brian	1990	Woodbury, Tory	2001
Gilliam, Joe	1972	Slack, Reggie	1990x	Garrard, David	2002
Jones, John	1975	Blake, Jeff	1992	Davey, Rohan	2002
Mays, Dave	1976	Moore, Shawn	1992	Leftwich, Byron	2003
Walton, Johnnie	1976	McNair, Steve	1995	Wright, Anthony	2003
Dickinson, Parnell	1976	Stewart, Kordell	1995	Wallace, Seneca	2003
Evans, Vince	1977	Banks, Tony	1996	Marquel Blackwell	2003x
Dungy, Tony	1977	Lucas, Ray	1996	Gray, Quinn	2005
Williams, Doug	1978	Walker, Jay	1996	Campbell, Jason	2005
Moon, Warren	1984	Batch, Charlie	1998	Lemon, Cleo	2005
Cunningham, Randall	1985	Richardson, Wally	1998	Adrian McPherson	2005x
Ransom, Brian	1985x	Culpepper, Daunte	1999	Vince Young	2006
Collier, Reggie	1986	McNabb, Donovan	1999	Jackson, Tarvaris	2006
Totten, Willie	1987r	Brooks, Aaron	1999	Shockley, D.J.	2006x
Robinson, Tony	1987r	King, Shaun	1999	Printers, Casey	2006x
Stevens, Mark	1987r	Smith, Akili	1999	Jacobs, Omar	2006x
Quarles, Bernard	1987r	White, Ted	1999x	Boyd, Shane	2006x

Attitude

Fiery Leaders

This is the hot-tempered class of quarterbacks, signal callers who like to get in the face of their teammates to inspire them to greater performances. The prototypical Fiery Leader was Norm Van Brocklin whose head coach Hampton Pool once said of him, "Soon he'll break every existing record — if some lineman doesn't break his neck first." Pool was referring to Van Brocklin's fellow Ram linemen, not the opponents in that comment. Van Brocklin also is said to have gotten back at a fast-charging defender on at least one occasion by deliberately drilling him in the face (pre-facemask days) with a hard pass at short range. As an Eagle, Norm is also given credit for turning former running backs Tommy McDonald and Pete Retzlaff into star receivers and for leading a rather mediocre 1960 club to the world championship in his final year.

Van Brocklin's contemporary Bobby Layne was the same way on the field, bawling out linemen who let in pass rushers, but Bobby took care of his teammates off the field by paying for their drinks since he was the highest-paid player on the team and the unquestioned leader of the champion Lions of the 1950s. Other Fiery Leaders over the years include Tommy Thompson of the Eagles, Billy Kilmer of the Redskins, Brian Sipe of the Browns, Roger Staubach, Dan Fouts of the Chargers, Dan Marino of the Dolphins, John Elway of the Broncos, Rich Gannon of the Raiders, Brett Favre of the Packers, Jake Delhomme of the Panthers and Peyton Manning of the Colts. Staubach and Manning in particular proved you didn't have to be foul-mouthed to be a Fiery Leader. What these quarterbacks have in common above all else was they were winners who never quit, pulling out many games at the end.

Cool Surgeons

The opposite in demeanor to the Fiery Leader is the Cool Surgeon who does not express his passion for the game so overtly, but is just as dedicated to winning. The clearest examples of this have been Johnny Unitas and Joe Montana. Both were always cool under pressure and pulled off some of the most memorable comebacks in league history. Unitas was famous for his old school high-top shoes, crewcut and expressionless face. When he threw a touchdown pass, even a game-winner, he simply turned away and walked off the field. Just another day at the office. He was the Gary Cooper of the gridiron.

Montana was known as Joe Cool, but he did show more emotions than Unitas. He would sometimes signal a touchdown pass with his arms and even break out in a smile. However, the fire that drove him to four championships was never visible on the field. It is no wonder that Montana and Unitas are usually listed in the top three of all-time quarterbacks. Others who maintained their cool demeanor under fire include Otto Graham of the Browns, Bart Starr of the Packers, Ken Anderson of the Bengals, Sid Luckman of the Bears, Charley Conerly of the Giants, Bob Waterfield of the Rams, Len Dawson of the Chiefs and Warren Moon of several franchises. The current player who most exemplifies this spirit is Tom Brady, the three-time Super Bowl champion of the Patriots.

Role Models

Although athletes often say they do not want to be seen as role models for their young fans, that is the way they are perceived. As the central player on the football field, quarterbacks take on a heroic role, and some continue that in the way they live their very public lives. Otto Graham was an All American both on and off the field, a milk drinker in a world of whiskey drinkers. It would be a mistake to underestimate his competitive drive and toughness between the lines, however. At the same time, he felt that football taught him discipline, cooperation, loyalty and appreciation, a feeling he shared with so many other star players. Davey O'Brien claimed his most prized accomplishment was winning the Best All Around Camper award when he was a school boy struggling to overcome a bad temper. Sid Luckman was a thoughtful and generous man. Bob Waterfield was a golden boy who married a movie star. Bart Starr was noted for his honesty and decency. Roger Staubach graduated from the Naval Academy and fulfilled his four-year military obligation after that before even getting a chance to begin his career as the quarterback of America's Team. Dan Marino was a great family man. Other fine role models include Bob Griese, Phil Simms, John Elway, Steve Young, Mark Brunell Kurt Warner and Troy Aikman. In today's game, Tom Brady embodies many fine qualities with his commitment to the virtues of teamwork and community.

Party Boys

Party Boys are always looking for a good time, trying to get this party started. Often that leads them into bars and the company of people of dubious character. Bobby Layne lived this wild life fuller than most. As the leader of both the Lions and Steelers, he conducted court from the local saloon. As one teammate put it, "when Bobby said drink, you drank." His most prominent follower was Joe Namath who took Layne's high-living to a higher plane by pursuing the same pleasures in New York rather than Detroit and Pittsburgh. He even titled his autobiography *I Can't Wait Until Tomorrow ... 'cause I Get Better Looking Every Day*. Namath helped establish both the Jets franchise and the American Football League with his much-larger-than-life persona and yet almost threw it all away by retiring six months after winning Super Bowl III rather than selling his interests in Bachelors III, a bar frequented by gamblers. A month later, Namath reconsidered that ill-advised move.

Party Boys are fun when they can still perform on the field despite their extracurricular activities like Sonny Jurgensen, Billy "Whiskey" Kilmer, Dandy Don Meredith and Kenny "Snake" Stabler. As the Snake put it, "There's nothing wrong with reading the game plan by the light of a jukebox." For others, it has serious consequences. Kerry Collins had to get control of his alcohol problem before he was able to achieve success in the NFL. Jake Plummer has never fulfilled his potential. Richard Todd stuffed a smaller reporter into a locker. Dan Pastorini shoved a reporter through a door. Cade McNown and Ryan Leaf both blew out of the league in a couple of years because they would not dedicate themselves to their profession.

Goof Balls and Flakes

Like Party Boys, Goof Balls can be a positive or negative influence on a team. An anti-establishment leader like Jim McMahon or Joe Kapp can rally a team behind him. A loose cannon backup quarterback like colorful author George Ratterman or Koy Detmer can be an entertaining pressure reliever. However, a space cadet like Randall Cunningham does not gain the full respect and loyalty of his teammates easily. It took Terry Bradshaw several seasons to prove himself to the Steelers. Frank Ryan wasn't really flaky, but he was very smart, eventually earning a PhD. in mathematics, and this did not endear him to some coaches and teammates.

Most times, though, flakes are players of limited talent and limitless ego. Jim "King" Corcoran thought he was the second coming of Joe Namath with white shoes, expensive tastes and a big arm, but spent the majority of his career with the semipro Pottstown Firebirds. Jim Del Gaizo seemed more intent on cultivating the longest sideburns in the league than on developing his talent. Backups Lee Grosscup and Marty Domres both wrote books, during their lackluster careers. Grosscup's was a thoughtful and wry take on his mediocre career, while Domres focused on his exciting life as a horny bachelor.

Coach Killers

Coach Killers are quarterbacks whose underachievement undermines their teams and costs the coaches their jobs. In 2006, former coach Jim Mora called Michael Vick a Coach Killer on the NFL Network, and it was a big story because Vick's coach at the time was Mora's son Jim Jr. It was not the smartest thing to say in public, but it proved to be prophetic a few weeks later when Mora Jr. was canned. Vick is reminiscent of Randall Cunningham in his running ability, his big passing arm, his fluctuating accuracy and his uncoachability.

Probably the king of Coach Killers was Jeff George who went from franchise to franchise, exhibiting his athletic talent as well as his inability to play within a system and win. Others who didn't have the maturity to respond to coaching like Vick, George and Cunningham, include Tony Banks, Kordell Stewart and Jay Schroeder. Some just have enormous egos that they can't subjugate to anyone like Benny Friedman and Lamar McHan. Sometimes a quarterback has serious conflicts with a coach like Fran Tarkenton with Norm Van Brocklin, Bernie Kosar with Bill Belichick or Terry Bradshaw in the early years with Chuck Noll. For other Coach Killers, an outside influence leads them astray. Art Schlichter was addicted to gambling. Frank Filchock was implicated in a gambling scandal. Joe Gilliam and Todd Marinovich had drug problems. Finally, some just make too many dumb mistakes on the field with key interceptions or fumbles; examples include Jake Plummer, Jim Everett and Richard Todd.

Playing Style

Game Manager

The essence of a good Game Manager is a quarterback who will not lose a game with bad decisions, fumbles and interceptions. Instead, he will rely on the team's defense and running game to prevail and won't try to win the game with his arm. As Ravens linebacker Ray Lewis told quarterback Elvis Grbac, "You don't have to win it, just don't lose it." If the team's defense is good enough, a Game Manager may even win a championship, but that is rare. The epitome of the Game Manager was Bill Wade who won a title with the 1963 Bears that set a record for fewest points allowed that season. The Bears beat the Giants for the title that year 14–10 on two quarterback sneaks by Wade that were set up by the defense. In a similar role, Trent Dilfer won a title with the 2000 Baltimore Ravens, and Brad Johnson followed suit with the 2002 Tampa Bucs.

Most teams with a Game Manager as their quarterback won't get that far because the defense has to truly be dominating for this to work. Game Managers like Joe Ferguson or Bobby Hebert or Steve Walsh or Rodney Peete were able to get into the playoffs, but not very deep. Some might call Bart Starr and Troy Aikman Game Managers because that was their preferred style; they liked to rely on the run game and the defense. However, both were talented enough passers to win with their arms when necessary. Many forget that the Packers' running attack for their two Super Bowl wins was nowhere near what it had been for their first titles five years before. Instead the team relied on Starr's passing to win. Aikman had a strong, accurate arm, but a selfless, team-oriented attitude. The two won eight championships between them.

Pinpoint Passers

These are the most reliably accurate quarterbacks, and Otto Graham was the epitome. Graham was known as "Automatic Otto" because of the accuracy of his passing, and was especially deadly on short passes and timing patterns which the Browns essentially invented. You cannot simply look at the completion percentage statistics for this category, though, because that may be tricked up by too many dink passes to running backs and not reflect how well a passer hits his targets downfield. For a few years before he got hurt and old, Kurt Warner was the best at hitting his receivers in stride 20 yards downfield. He was reminiscent of Sammy Baugh, Y.A. Tittle, Bart Starr, Len Dawson, Ken Stabler, Dan Fouts, Joe Montana, Steve Young and Troy Aikman. Of Aikman, it was said that there were days in practice that none of his passes hit the ground; everything was right on target. Today, Peyton Manning and Tom Brady are the most accurate passers in the league and the best quarterbacks.

Long Range Bombers

The earliest bomber of note was Arnie Herber who cradled the ball in his small right hand and heaved it downfield to Don Hutson. Sid Luckman was a deadly bomber in the wide open Chicago offense of the 1940s, and he was superseded by Bob Waterfield and Norm Van Brocklin of the Rams in the 1950s. The 1960s featured long-ball specialists Sonny Jurgensen, Y.A. Tittle, Don Meredith and Charley Johnson in the NFL, but the AFL was especially known for the bomb.

The AFL focused on long passes right from the start with such imaginative, offensive-minded coaches as Sid Gillman and Hank Stram. The Raiders' Vertical Passing Offense that relied on the quick strike from anywhere on the field found its perfect operator in Daryle Lamonica, who was known as the "Mad Bomber" for his deep passing. An attack offense was the essence of the old AFL, which featured such bombers as Tobin Rote, John Hadl, George Blanda, Jack Kemp and Joe Namath. After the leagues merged, the 1970s brought big-armed Steve Bartkowski and Terry Bradshaw, while the 1980s introduced the strong arms of Randall Cunningham, John Elway, Dan Marino and

Vinny Testaverde. In recent years, Drew Bledsoe, Brett Favre and Peyton Manning have had live arms, but Carson Palmer probably throws the best deep ball today.

Gamblers

After throwing six interceptions in a playoff game against the Rams, Brett Favre commented succinctly on his gambling style, "No risk; no reward." Two other modern quarterbacks threw six picks in a playoff game, Bobby Layne and Norm Van Brocklin. They were both gamblers as well who sometimes tried to force a ball into too tight a spot. Each of the three won at least one championship. The most celebrated gambler was Johnny Unitas who fearlessly would throw any pass at any time if he felt it would succeed, even throwing a dangerous quick out at the goal line in the winning drive of the Sudden Death championship win over the Giants in 1958. The stealthiest gambler, though, was Bart Starr who made a habit of throwing deep on third or fourth and short plays when the defense would bunch up to stop the expected run.

The gamblers we remember tend to be the successful ones like Joe Namath guaranteeing a win in Super Bowl III and backing it up, Kenny Stabler throwing the Sea of Hands winning touchdown pass against the Dolphins in the playoffs, Roger Staubach inventing the Hail Mary to beat the Vikings in the playoffs, Terry Bradshaw's long touchdowns to Swann and Stallworth in the Super Bowl, not to mention Dan Fouts, Joe Montana, Dan Marino and John Elway. By contrast, gamblers who crap out regularly don't last long.

Running Quarterbacks

In the 1950's, Paul Brown foresaw that defensive linemen were getting steadily bigger and faster and rushing the passer with growing determination. In "I Watch the Quarterback" for the October 28, 1955 issue of *Colliers*, he concluded, "The new development in pro football, therefore, will have to be the running quarterback."

Paul Brown is also the coach credited with inventing the pocket, that is, teaching his linemen to form a protective cup insulating their quarterback from the pass rush. His own quarterback, Otto Graham, had been a running tailback in college, but adapted to being the first pocket quarterback in the pros. Graham was still a mobile quarterback, adept at stepping up in the pocket to avoid edge rusher, and still holds the all-time record for touchdowns by a quarterback with 44.

While Brown made that prediction in 1955, he never really had a running quarterback even though he coached until 1975. Instead, he had mobile quarterbacks with quick feet. It worked for Graham in Cleveland, and it also worked for Greg Cook and Kenny Anderson in Cincinnati. In fact, simply being able to take a couple of nimble steps to avoid the rush and get off a perfect pass has worked for a number of great quarterbacks from Bart Starr to Joe Montana to Tom Brady today. Still, Brown was correct that there is another way, and that way is running.

There are two types of running quarterbacks: scramblers who run around trying to buy time to find an open receiver and runners who put the ball under their arm and take off at the first sign of danger. These are not mutually exclusive categories — scramblers sometimes run and runners sometimes scramble — and they often change over time, but they define the general approach of the quarterback. This approach was summed up by the itinerant backup quarterback Jack Thompson, "It's amazing what the human body can do when chased by a bigger human body."

The first and most famous scrambler is usually considered to be Fran Tarkenton who scrambled for his life behind the weak offensive lines of the expansion Vikings. The term scrambler had been used before, however. In 1960, the *Los Angeles Times* referred to the veteran 49ers quarterback Y.A. Tittle as a scrambler, adding that when you think you have him cornered, he'll break away to throw a completed pass or run for a first down." While Tittle had been a running tailback at LSU 15 years before, his scrambling was nothing like Tarkenton's. Tarkenton took scrambling to a whole new level as he weaved around in circles behind the line of scrimmage, sometimes as far as 40 yards into the backfield. Tarkenton's coach was Norm Van Brocklin who had no running ability of any kind as a player and was quoted as saying, "Quarterbacks should never run except from terror." Not surprisingly, the two, who were both bull-headed as well, often clashed and both left Minnesota in the same year.

Success of course breeds imitation, whether it come from scrambling nonentities like Pete Beathard and Gary Wood or from talented scrambling quarterbacks like Roger Staubach, Bob Griese, Joe Theismann, Doug Flutie and Jake Plummer. Griese exhibited the downside for scrambling in Super Bowl VI when he got caught by the Cowboys Bob Lilly for a 29-yard loss on a failed scramble, but he won the next two Super Bowls.

Some of those scramblers liked to run the ball on occasion as well, but a good way to tell who was a running quarterback is to look at the following table of passers who have run for 100 yards in a game.

Quarterback	100 Yd Games
Michael Vick	8
Billy Kilmer	3
Bobby Douglass	3
Randall Cunningham	3
Tobin Rote	3
Bill Shepherd	2
Donovan McNabb	2
Frankie Sinkwich	2
John Grigas	2
Kordell Stewart	2
Parker Hall	2
Aaron Brooks	1
Ace Parker	1
Cecil Isbell	1
Dutch Clark	1
Ed Danowski	1
Frank Filchock	1
Harry Newman	1
Bobby Layne	1
Jack Concannon	1
Norris Weese	1
Steve Grogan	1
Steve Young	1
Vinny Testaverde	1

This has been achieved 45 times in NFL history. We can throw out the names of pre–T Formation tailbacks Shepherd, Sinkwich, Grigas, Hall, Isbell, Clark, Danowski and Filchock and Newman. Billy Kilmer is also a question because he achieved his performance in three straight games as the running option quarterback in the 49ers 1961 experimental Shotgun Formation. Weese and Concannon were back-ups and Testaverde is an anomaly. That leaves us with this group: Michael Vick, Bobby Douglass, Randall Cunningham, Tobin Rote, Donovan McNabb, Kordell Stewart, Aaron

Brooks, Steve Grogan and Steve Young. To which we should add Greg Landry, Rich Gannon, Daunte Culpepper and Vince Young as the most prominent running quarterbacks. Another way to identify these quarterbacks is a list of the 24 times quarterbacks achieved 500-yard rushing seasons. John Elway, Mark Brunell and Steve McNair are the only three modern quarterbacks that appear on neither list, but were top running quarterbacks.

Quarterback	500 Yd Seasons
Randall Cunningham	6
Michael Vick	4
Bobby Douglass	2
Greg Landry	2
Steve McNair	2
Tobin Rote	1
Steve Grogan	1
Steve Young	1
Kordell Stewart	1
Rich Gannon	1
Donovan McNabb	1
Daunte Culpepper	1
Vince Young	1

The earliest running quarterbacks were Frankie Albert and Johnny Lujack, but the best running quarterback of the post–War era was the Packers' Tobin Rote. Rote was a throwback single wing tailback in his talents and a throwback in general for his toughness. In one game, he had his nose broken, left the field, and then came back for the next play with blood streaming down his face. He could run more consistently than he could throw, and he had a long successful career in the NFL, AFL and Canada. In the early 1950s, his career rushing total ran neck and neck with Bobby Layne, but Rote passed Layne in 1955 and held the record for rushing yards by a quarterback until 1972 when scrambling Fran Tarkenton passed him. Randall Cunningham, whom *Sports Illustrated* dubbed the Ultimate Weapon, exceeded Tarkenton's total in 1992 and still holds the career mark, but Michael Vick might someday pass him.

Vick already holds the single game mark of 173 yards that bettered Tobin Rote's 150 yards. In 2006, Vick also surpassed Bobby Douglass' seasonal mark of 968 yards with a total of 1,039. Cunningham and Vick have been especially scary to defenses because of their combination of great speed, elusive running and big arms. However, both have had similar drawbacks — a tendency to make mistakes and a resistance to coaching. Steve Young is probably the greatest running quarterback in history because of how he learned to balance his skills for the good of the team. Balancing your skills is necessary because just like major league pitchers have to adjust to losing speed from their fastball, running quarterbacks will slow down due to age or injuries. Steve McNair

learned this lesson, but Kordell Stewart never did. Randall Cunningham was never the same after a couple of injuries, while Steve Young, John Elway and Tobin Rote all won championships after their best running days were behind them.

The following table lists the quarterbacks with the top 15 rushing totals. A longer table for all quarterbacks with at least 1,500 rushing yards is in the appendix.

Name	Games	Pass Yards	Rush Att	Rush Yards	Avg	TD
Cunningham, Randall	161	29979	775	4928	6.4	35
Young, Steve	169	33124	722	4239	5.9	43
Vick, Michael	74	11505	529	3859	7.3	21
Tarkenton, Fran	246	47003	675	3674	5.4	32
McNair, Steve	155	30191	659	3558	5.4	37
Elway, John	234	51475	774	3407	4.4	33
Rote, Tobin	149	18850	635	3128	4.9	37
Stewart, Kordell	126	14816	560	2874	5.1	38
Harbaugh, Jim	177	26288	560	2787	5.0	18
McNabb, Donovan	104	22080	447	2726	6.1	24
Landry, Greg	147	16052	430	2655	6.2	21
Douglass, Bobby	89	6493	410	2654	6.5	22
Culpepper, Daunte	85	21091	464	2496	5.4	30
Layne, Bobby	175	26768	611	2451	4.0	25
Gannon, Rich	157	28743	521	2449	4.7	21

Team Role

Kickers and Punters

Before enlarged rosters and rampant specialization made professional football a coach's game, quarterbacks had to have additional skills to ball handling and passing. They had to call their own plays; they were usually called on to hold for placekicks; and they sometimes doubled as the team's punter or placekicker.

Most commonly, they were used as punters. On the following table of the 15 quarterbacks who punted for at least 10,000 yards, sorted by punting average, I would make these notes. Sammy Baugh and Glenn Dobbs were great passers as well as punters. Dobbs scored the NFL first for the AAFC and then for Canada. Randall Cunningham was built similarly to those two and averaged 44.7 yards on just 20 punts in his career. Danny White in 1984 and Dan Pastorini in 1975 are the last two regular quarterbacks to double as a team's punter. Tom Tupa did not begin punting till after he washed out of the league as a quarterback. Jug Girard spent most of his career as an all-purpose

back, only playing quarterback in his first two seasons.

Quarterback	Punts	Yards	Avg
Dobbs, Glenn	231	10721	46.4
Baugh, Sammy	338	15178	44.9
Tupa, Tom	873	37862	43.4
Albert, Frankie	299	12866	43.0
Van Brocklin, Norm	523	22413	42.9
Waterfield, Bob	315	13380	42.5
Hill, King	368	15181	41.3
Burk, Adrian	474	19365	40.9
Brown, Ed	493	19994	40.6
White, Danny	610	24509	40.2
Girard, Jug	397	15927	40.1
Zimmerman, Roy	278	11065	39.8
Pastorini, Dan	316	12530	39.7
Yewcic, Tom	376	14553	38.7
Davidson, Cotton	280	10679	38.1

Less frequently, quarterbacks have been called on to kick extra point and field goals. The most prominent and recent was the ageless George Blanda whose career ended in 1975. The following table lists the 12 quarterbacks who have done any significant placekicking, plus the record of passing tailback Benny Friedman for good measure.

Quarterback	FG	FG Att	XP	XP Att	TD	Points
Blanda, George	335	637	943	959	9	2002
Waterfield, Bob	60	110	315	336	13	573
Layne, Bobby	34	50	120	124	25	372
Lujack, Johnny	4	9	130	136	21	268
Zimmerman, Roy	18	42	133	145	7	229
Friedman, Benny	2	0	71	110	18	185
Parker, Ace	1	5	25	32	20	148
Plum, Milt	6	16	16	16	13	112
Snyder, Bob	8	16	78	83	1	108
Davidson, Cotton	2	5	31	32	11	103
Kerkorian, Gary	10	21	47	55	2	89
Sinkwich, Frankie	2	9	24	30	8	78
Held, Paul	3	5	14	16	0	23

This final table lists the top 20 scoring quarterbacks. Otto Graham scored the most touchdowns with 44, and Steve Young is right behind with 43.

Quarterback	FG	XP	TD	Points
Blanda, George	335	943	9	2002
Waterfield, Bob	60	315	13	573
Layne, Bobby	34	120	25	372
Lujack, Johnny	4	130	21	268
Graham, Otto	0	0	44	264
Young, Steve	0	0	43	258
Kemp, Jack	0	2	40	242
Tittle, Y.A.	0	0	39	234
Zimmerman, Roy	18	133	7	229
Rote, Tobin	0	0	38	228
Stewart, Kordell	0	0	38	228
McNair, Steve	0	0	37	222
Grogan, Steve	0	0	36	216
Elway, John	0	2	33	200
Cunningham, Randall	0	0	32	192
Tarkenton, Fran	0	0	32	192
Gabriel, Roman	0	0	30	180
Culpepper, Daunte	0	0	30	180
Bradshaw, Terry	0	0	28	168
Albert, Frankie	0	1	27	163

Relief Pitchers

Relief pitchers are common in baseball where the pitcher rarely pitches a full game and an ineffective pitcher can give up so many runs that it would be nearly impossible to catch up. Football is a different story. The quarterback is an offensive player who could find his rhythm at any moment and turn around an ineffective attack. Most coaches have been hesitant to mess with the psyches of sensitive quarterbacks by pulling them midway through a game except in the event of an injury. The most acclaimed example was George Blanda on the Raiders in the late 1960s and 1970s. Blanda frequently would come in late if starter Daryle Lamonica was struggling and even won a league MVP trophy by pulling out several games with his passing and kicking in the 1970 season. Ironically, another outstanding relief pitcher was Lamonica himself who regularly relieved starter Jack Kemp in Buffalo in the mid–1960s.

Norm Van Brocklin and Bob Waterfield would relieve each other in Los Angeles; in fact, Van Brocklin won the 1951 championship when he was brought in as a fourth quarter relief pitcher and threw a 73-yard game-winning touchdown pass. Don Shula was involved in two well-known post-season relief decisions. In Super Bowl III, he waited too long to lift ineffective Earl Morrall for wounded Johnny Unitas, but five years later quickly lifted Morrall for the returning Bob Griese in a playoff win over Pittsburgh in the 17–0 season. John Brodie started out relieving Y.A. Tittle and later was relieved by George Mira and Steve Spurrier. Tittle relieved Charlie Conerly, and Conerly relieved Tittle. Sonny Jurgensen, Don Strock, Steve Grogan and Steve Young also performed well as relief pitchers. Angry fans frequently call for the backup to relieve the starter, but coaches rarely do so. Relief pitchers are viewed with fear and distrust in pro football.

Career Backups

The Career Backup is good enough to play in the NFL, but not good enough to start. Jeff Garcia in 2006 proved again how nice it is for a team to have a tested backup as he led the Eagles to five straight wins and another in the playoffs. That run salvaged the Eagles' season, but there are limits; the skittish, weak-armed Garcia was not going to bring home the Vince Lombardi Trophy. Earl Morrall got chances to start in six cities, but was most useful as a reliable backup. Morrall won a league MVP trophy in 1968 when he stepped in for Johnny Unitas in Baltimore, but choked in the Super Bowl against the Jets. He did manage to win a Super Bowl three years later relieving an injured Unitas in a sloppy win over the Cowboys, but two years after that he was pulled in the playoffs after guiding the Dolphins for over half of their undefeated season. Don Strock lasted 14 years as a backup quarterback in Miami and was generally solid when called upon to play. Steve DeBerg played in six cities and was a starter in four. He was beaten out by Joe Montana in San Francisco, John Elway in Denver and Steve Young in Tampa. In the course of a 17-year career, he threw for over 30,000 yards and 196 touchdowns. Of him, 49ers coach Bill Walsh reportedly uttered the epitaph for all career backups, "he's just good enough to get you beat." Others who spent most of their careers holding a clipboard include George Ratterman, Jim Ninowski, Zeke Bratkowski, Mike Tomczak, Frank Reich, Pat Ryan, Gary Kubiak, Jason Garrett, Bob Lee, Turk Schonert, Don Heinrich, Harry Gilmer, Jamie Martin, Gus Frerotte, Steve Spurrier, King Hill, Terry Hanratty and the brothers Detmer, Ty and Koy.

Overrated Understudy

The Overrated Understudy is a young backup quarterback who has seen little playing time, but whose potential inspires other teams to offer number one draft picks to acquire this inexperienced phenom. There have been only three such quarterbacks who have ever proved worth it: Joe Theismann who refused Miami for Canada to prove himself; Brett Favre who drank his way out of Atlanta; and Bobby Layne who was lodged behind Sid Luckman and Johnny Lujack in Chicago.

The prototype here is Gary Cuozzo who was Johnny Unitas' backup for four years, getting to throw just over 200 passes in that time. The fledgling Saints gave the Colts the first pick in the 1967 draft who turned out to be Bubba Smith for Cuozzo. After one unimpressive season in the Big Easy, Cuozzo was traded to the Vikings for another number one pick. Cuozzo then spent four lackluster seasons with the

Vikings and was traded once again to the Cardinals who mysteriously gave up a second round pick for this proven mediocrity.

Jim Hardy of the Rams was the first overrated understudy to draw a first round draft choice in a 1950 trade with the Cardinals. He was followed by the Giants trading for Arnold Galiffa in 1953, the Redskins trading for Rudy Bukich in 1957, the Giants trading for George Shaw in 1959, the Lions trading for Jim Ninowski in 1960, the Eagles trading for King Hill in 1961, the Broncos giving up two number ones for Steve Tensi in 1967, the Oilers trading a number one and two players for Pete Beathard in 1967, the Bengals trading for John Stofa in 1968, the Colts trading for Marty Domres in 1971, the Eagles trading for Mike Boryla in 1974, the Chargers trading a one and a two for Clint Longley in 1976, the Bucs trading for Jack Thompson in 1982, the Broncos trading for Matt Robinson in 1980, the Saints trading for Steve Walsh in 1990 and the Bucs trading for Craig Erickson in 1996. The most recent example was the Bills trading a one and a four for the lackadaisical Rob Johnson in 1998. In 2006, the untested backup that teams were slobbering over was Matt Schaub, Michael Vick's backup in Atlanta. History would advise against giving up a high draft pick for Schaub.

Luckless Pedestrians

Luckless Pedestrians come in two basic types: those stuck on lousy teams with bad coaches for most or all of their careers and those whose careers are continually derailed by injuries. Archie Manning is the patron saint for the former after suffering so many losing years in New Orleans and then moving on to Houston and Minnesota, but never experiencing a winning season anywhere. Similarly, Norm Snead, Jim Hart, Jim Zorn and Steve DeBerg also played for mostly losing teams for long careers. Tobin Rote, John Brodie, Sonny Jurgensen and Vinny Testaverde also played for a lot of awful teams, but all got to experience some success at the ends of their careers. If Brett Favre had stayed in Atlanta and not met up with Mike Holmgren, would we have ever heard of him or would he have just been another flop? Luck can play just as large a part in a player's success as hard work.

Staying healthy and upright is more good

fortune. Injuries can irreparably alter a career; the frequently-dinged Chris Chandler is one good example, but we can't forget the knees of Joe Namath, Lynn Dickey and Bill Nelsen, the shoulders of Sonny Jurgensen, Greg Cook, Steve Bartkowski, Bert Jones, Don Majkowski and Chad Pennington, the concussions of Steve Young and Troy Aikman, and the overall battering of Len Dawson, Dan Pastorini and Jim McMahon. Recently, Byron Leftwich, Donovan McNabb and Rex Grossman seem to have trouble staying on the field. Football is a "collision sport" according to Vince Lombardi, and injuries are inevitable. Some quarterbacks are more susceptible than others to injuries and this helps to contribute to teams continually being on the hunt for new passing talent.

2

The Ongoing Search

Vikings coach Bud Grant spoke of the basics for success, "A good coach needs a patient wife, a loyal dog and a great quarterback, but not necessarily in that order." When a team is looking for a young quarterback, they look first to college football, the NFL's de facto minor leagues. They might obtain veterans through a trade, free agency or even the scrap heap of quarterbacks who were cut from their original team. Being successful at selecting a college quarterback who can perform well at the professional level, though, is a dicey proposition that often leaves a team undermanned at the most critical position on the field. There is so much to be thoroughly analyzed for each prospect. Is his arm strong enough to throw the deep ball? Is he accurate enough to hit receivers in stride? Are his footwork and throwing mechanics sound? Is he receptive to coaching? Is he big enough to see downfield over a hard-charging rush? Is he elusive enough to avoid the rush and extend a play when things break down? Is he tough enough physically to withstand the pounding he will take at times? Is he tough enough mentally to stay poised at the critical point of the game? Is he mature enough to learn from inevitable mistakes and not dwell on them? Is he so confident in his abilities that he won't wilt when the fans boo? Is he smart enough to master the playbook and make the proper audibles? Does he have the football sense to make good fast decisions on where to go with the ball? Is he dedicated enough that he will do whatever it takes on and off the field to win on Sunday? Is he a good teammate? Is he a leader that teammates will follow? None of these questions can be answered with a simple yes or no; rather, they are answered in degrees, and the whole package for each quarterback is evaluated as a whole. While the ultimate results may appear to be clear in hindsight, the trick is in the projection.

Football Factories

Are some colleges more adept than others at turning out professional quarterbacks than others? Of course, but it depends on how you measure success. What schools pop into your head first as molders of pro quarterbacks? Miami with Jim Kelly, Bernie Kosar, Vinny Testaverde, Steve Walsh, Craig Erickson and Gino Torretta? Alabama with Bart Starr, Joe Namath, Steve Sloan, Ken Stabler, Scott Hunter, Richard Todd and Jeff Rutledge? Michigan with Elvis Grbac, Todd

Collins, Brian Griese, Tom Brady, Drew Henson and John Navarre? Brigham Young with Gifford Nielsen, Marc Wilson, Jim McMahon, Steve Young and Ty Detmer? None of them are among the dozen schools that have produced at least 12 quarterbacks who played in the NFL:

Notre Dame	26
Stanford	16
USC	16
UCLA	15
Tulsa	14
Boston College	13
Washington	13
Maryland	13
California	13
Purdue	12
Oregon	12
Penn State	12

There are a couple of surprises on that list, partly due to the fact that it goes all the way back to the pre-draft period in NFL history. Most observers would not think of Tulsa and Penn State as being likely places to find the next hot quarterback, for example, but they were once fairly prolific.

The list changes a bit if we limit it to quarterbacks who began their career in more recent years, say 1978 when the passing game was fully opened up in the NFL.

UCLA	11
Washington	11
Stanford	9
Notre Dame	8
USC	8
California	8
Miami	8
Maryland	7
Michigan	7
Arizona State	7
Ohio State	7

Other schools just off the list with six include LSU whose JaMarcus Russell will likely be their seventh modern quarterback in 2007, Boston College, Oregon, Florida State, Washington State and Virginia.

But who has produced the best talent? Five teams have produced two Hall of Famers including Purdue (Bob Griese and Len Dawson), Oregon (Norm Van Brocklin and Dan Fouts), Alabama (Bart Starr and Joe Namath), UCLA (Troy Aikman and Bob Waterfield) and Duke (Ace Parker and Sonny Jurgensen). Broadening our definition of talent to include All Pros and just everyday regular starting quarterbacks, Notre Dame and USC are atop the list with nine apiece. Notre Dame has had more at the very top, while USC has specialized in functioning starters like Bill Nelsen, Pat Haden, Rodney Peete and Rudy Bukich. USC's only star has been Carson Palmer, while Notre Dame can boast of Joe Montana, Joe Theismann, Daryle Lamonica and Johnny Lujack. Behind those two schools are Purdue with seven and Michigan, UCLA and BYU with six each. However, quarterback alumni of these schools also feature many failures — those who never became regulars or those drafted who never even played. Of Notre Dame's 26 NFL quarterbacks, 17 were never more than backups like John Huarte, George Izo or Ralph Guglielmi or failed starters like Terry Hanratty, Angelo Bertelli and Bobby Williams. These are the success rates of the leading factories:

Notre Dame	9 of 26
Stanford	5 of 16
USC	9 of 16
UCLA	6 of 15
Tulsa	5 of 14
Boston College	5 of 13
Washington	6 of 13
Maryland	3 of 13
California	4 of 13
Purdue	7 of 12
Oregon	5 of 12
Penn State	2 of 12

In short, while USC, Purdue, Washington and Oregon are the best bets, be careful with Penn State, Maryland, California and Notre Dame whose quarterbacks tend to be overrated. Furthermore, while Troy Smith may prove to be an exception, it has generally been a waste of time to draft an Ohio State quarterback. The best two OSU pros have proven to be decidedly mediocre long-time backups Kent Graham and Mike Tomczak. Ohio State also has the largest number of quarterbacks drafted who never played the position in the pros with eight, including Rex Kern and Les Horvath who were converted to other positions in the NFL. Iowa has had six such draft washouts and Nebraska five.

The Draft

As is clear from looking at the record of players drafted from the most successful college programs, the draft is much more of an art than a science as scouts, coaches and general managers struggle to judge untested quarterbacks. Moving beyond looking at the flop rate from individual colleges, let's look at the pros' success/failure rate on drafting quarterbacks in the first round.

The first group consists of the quarterbacks judged to be so excellent that they were selected with the top pick in the NFL draft. There have been 31 such signal callers in the last 70 years, including seven in the last nine years. In that 31, I have included Steve Young who was the top pick in the 1984 USFL draft and may have been the top pick in the regular draft if he had not signed with the USFL first. This group runs from George Cafego in 1940 to Alex Smith in 2005. I assigned a grade to each quarterback's NFL career: 4 for Hall of Famer, 3 for All Pro, 2 for regular starter and 1 for anything less, a flop. Of the 31 top picks, 11 were flops, five were starters and 15 were stars. Most of the flops were from more than 40 years ago, however. The only recent quarterback to flop was Tim Couch in 1999. While the jury is still out on such recent picks as Michael Vick, David Carr, Eli Manning and Alex Smith, all appear to be functioning NFL starters at least. They may prove to be disappoints as top picks, but not utter flops. The last flop before Couch was Heisman Trophy winning tailback Terry Baker in 1963 who could not find a position with the Rams. He joined previous flops Randy Duncan who only played in Canada and the AFL, King Hill, a lifelong backup, Gary Glick who was switched to defense, George Shaw who was beaten out by on different teams Johnny Unitas, Fran Tarkenton and Frank Tripucka, Bobby Garrett who stuttered so badly that he couldn't call signals, Harry Gilmer who later became an unsuccessful head coach, and two from Notre Dame Boley Dancewicz and Angelo Bertelli who were both picked by the Boston Yanks within two years of one another. Some of these top pick quarterbacks flopped with their original teams, but later developed elsewhere in the league like Jim Plunkett and Vinny Testaverde. The toughest call to make was Jeff George who created problems wherever he went, yet was a functioning starter and thus not a flop but instead a major disappointment as the top pick in 1990.

The second group to examine is top 10 picks, quarterbacks selected within the first ten picks of the draft. When the draft first started in 1936, there were only 10 teams so the top 10 was the entire first round. Today, there are 32 teams so the top ten is less than one third of the first round. There have been 80 quarterbacks taken in picks two through 10, including quarterbacks drafted in sporadic supplemental drafts from 1981–1992 (Dave Wilson, Bernie Kosar, Steve Walsh, Timm Rosenbach and Dave Brown). Riley Smith of Alabama was taken second by the Redskins in 1936 and was the first quarterback ever drafted. He was more of a blocking back who only threw 46 passes in his career, but he did call signals for Washington. The following year, the Redskins selected the first pure passer in draft history when they took Sammy Baugh with the sixth pick.

Of the 80 quarterbacks taken two through 10, 35 were flops, 12 were regular starters and 33 were stars. Unlike the top pick in the draft where improved scouting has made complete flops very rare in recent decades, modern flops in this group include Oregon Ducks Joey Harrington and Akili Smith, the third picks in 2002 and 1999, and two sloppy seconds picks — Ryan Leaf in 1998 and Rick Mirer in 1993. Leaf was picked second by the Chargers after the Colts took Peyton Manning number one, and Mirer was taken second by Seattle after New England took Drew Bledsoe number one. On two other occasions, quarterbacks have been taken one and two in the draft, and twice they have gone 1–2–3. In 1954, the Browns took Bobby Garrett with the Bonus Pick, and the Cardinals then took Lamar McHan. In 1956, the Steelers took Gary Glick with the Bonus Pick, and the 49ers followed with Earl Morrall. In 1971, the Patriots took Jim Plunkett, and the Saints followed with Archie Manning, and then the Oilers took Dan Pastorini. In 1999, the Browns took Tim Couch number one, then the Eagles took Donovan McNabb with number two, then the Bengals took Akili Smith with number three, making McNabb the meat in a flop sandwich.

The Redskins have had the sorriest record drafting in this group. After having great success with Baugh, Washington spent the 1950s and early 1960s fruitlessly trying to find his replacement. In 1952, they used the seventh pick on Larry Isbell. Then, they took Jack Scarbath with the third pick in 1953, Ralph Guglielmi with the fourth pick in 1955, Don Allard with the fourth pick in 1959, Richie Lucas with the fourth pick in 1960 and finally Norm Snead with the second pick in 1961. Oddly, the same year they drafted Snead, they traded the Notre Dame's Guglielmi to the Cardinals for Notre Dame's George Izo who had been the second pick of the 1960 draft. That left the Redskins with four top ten quarterbacks in three years. Snead was inconsistent, but at least had a long career as an NFL starter. Allard went to Canada and the AFL; Lucas played in the AFL mostly as a defensive back and Izo was never more than a backup. As for the earlier picks, Isbell went to Canada, local favorite Scarbath completed just 36 percent of his passes and Guglielmi threw more than twice as many interceptions as touchdowns.

The only other teams to invest so heavily in the quarterback position in so short a time were the Packers and the Rams. Green Bay took Ernie Case with the seventh pick in 1947 and lost him to the AAFC. They took Jug Girard with the seventh pick in 1948, and he ended up a defensive back. They took Stan Heath fifth in 1949, and he completed 24 percent of his passes and went to Canada. Finally in 1950, they took Tobin Rote as the 17th pick which fell in the second round, and he proved to be a good, but inconsistent quarterback. For competition, they brought in Babe Parilli with the fourth pick in 1952, but he had little success in Wisconsin. As for the Rams, they selected an excellent quarterback, Roman Gabriel, with the second pick in 1962, but then hedged their bets by taking Terry Baker with the top pick in 1963 and Bill Munson with the seventh pick in 1964. In three years, Baker was out of football; in four, Munson was in Detroit.

To complete our look at first round quarterbacks, 36 quarterbacks have been taken with picks 11 through 32 when those picks fell in the first round. In other words, Hall of Famer Ace Parker, taken 13th in the second round in 1937, does not count here, but Patrick Ramsey, taken 32nd in 2002, does. Of these 36, 15 flopped, 15 became regular starters and 6 became stars. While the flop rate of 42 percent is essentially the same as the 41 percent flop rate of the top ten, what is interesting is the 42 percent rate of regular starters. Of particular note here are the stars—Billy Kilmer, Daunte Culpepper and Ben Roethlisberger all taken 11th, Hall of Famer Joe

Namath taken 12th by the Cardinals although he was the top pick in the AFL draft in 1965 and signed with the Jets, Hall of Famer Jim Kelly taken 14th in 1983 and Hall of Famer Dan Marino taken 27th in 1983. A complete list of quarterbacks drafted in the first round can be found in the appendix.

Besides Namath, the American Football League signed three other quarterbacks who they drafted in the first round: Sandy Stephens, Pete Beathard and Rick Norton. Stephens was an exciting black quarterback from Minnesota who had to go to Canada to get a chance to play; Beathard threw almost twice as many interceptions as touchdowns; Norton threw four times as many interceptions as touchdowns. The earlier All America Conference had even less luck with first round quarterbacks. They drafted nine and signed just three (Ernie Case, Bob Chappuis and George Taliaferro). Only the versatile black tailback Taliaferro was any good as a pro. However, the AAFC did sign wartime NFL number one picks Otto Graham, Glenn Dobbs and tailback Spec Sanders who all became stars in the new league. The only other number one picks the NFL lost to a rival were the previously noted Larry Isbell and Randy Duncan who both went north of the border to the CFL,

Ace Parker's group, those who were drafted between 11 and 32 before those slots fell in the first round, is made up of 30 quarterbacks. Six of them were stars (Parker, Paul Christman, Tobin Rote, Fran Tarkenton, Don Meredith and Drew Brees), two (Al Dorow and Milt Plum) were regular starters, and the other 22 were flops as quarterbacks. Ace's other peer group, Hall of Famers, consists of 26 quarterbacks in the postdraft years. Of these 26, 14 were first round picks, 11 were picked in a later round, and one, Warren Moon, went undrafted altogether. Though Moon was ignored, Y.A. Title was picked in the first round twice. The Lions took him with the sixth pick in 1948, but he signed with the AAFC Colts instead. After the original Baltimore Colts disbanded, the 49ers took him with the third pick in the 1951 draft. Besides Parker in round two and Tarkenton in round three, the rest of the late round Hall of Famers are Dan Fouts and Joe Montana in round three, Norm Van Brocklin and Sonny Jurgensen in round four, Bob Waterfield in round five, Johnny Unitas in round nine, Roger Staubach in round 10, George Blanda in round 12 and Bart Starr in round 17. Unitas was the 102nd player drafted, Blanda the 119th, Staubach the 129th and Starr the 200th. Probable Hall of Famers Brett Favre and Tom Brady were taken with the 33rd pick (second round) and 199th pick (sixth round) respectively.

The latest draft pick who ever became an NFL quarterback was Bob Lee, the 441st pick in the 17th round of 1968. Three other 17th rounders went even later in 1976, but none ever played in the league. The latest an All Pro was ever selected was Brian Sipe in the 13th round of 1972, the 330th pick. Other stars picked after the above noted Brady and Starr were Jack Kemp, 17th round, 1957, 203rd pick; Joe Kapp, 18th round, 1959, 209th pick; Wade Wilson, 8th round, 1981, 210th pick; Trent Green, 8th round, 1993, 222nd pick; Brad Johnson, 9th round, 1992, 227th pick; Don Majkowski, 10th round, 1987, 255th pick; and Doug Flutie, 11th round, 1985, 285th pick.

The most fabled quarterback draft was in 1983 when six QBs were selected first — a record three of whom (Marino, Kelly and Elway) have gone into the Hall of Fame. Second to that was 1999 with five quarterbacks in the first round (Couch, McNabb, Akili Smith, Daunte Culpepper and Cade McNown). The only other drafts that have included as many as four QBs in the first round were 1959, 1987, 2003 and 2004. None of the four from 1959 (Randy Duncan, Don Allard, Dave Baker and Lee Grosscup) ever became a starting quarterback in the NFL. The 1987 group included three starters (Vinny Testaverde, Chris Miller and Jim Harbaugh and one flop (Kelly Stouffer). The more recent drafts featured Carson Palmer, Byron Leftwich, Kyle Boller and Rex Grossman in 2003 and Eli Manning, Philip Rivers, Ben Roethlisberger and J.P. Losman in 2004. The most college quarterbacks ever drafted in one year was 25 in 1976, followed by 23 in 1971, 22 in 1968 and 1973, 21 in 1967 and 20 in 1956, 1975 and 1992. The most professional quarterbacks to emerge from any draft was 13 in 1992 and 2003. There were 12 who surfaced in 1968, 1983 and 2005. The best draft success rate was achieved in 2003 when all 13 quarterbacks drafted found work in the NFL. Since 1999, the percentage of drafted quarterbacks making a roster has been over 80 percent every year except 2002 and 2004. The highest percentages in earlier years were 74 percent in 1964 and 75 percent in 1983. For top talent, the only "Year of the Quarterback" draft that approaches 1983 was 1971 when Jim Plunkett, Archie Manning, Dan Pastorini were picked in the first round, Ken Anderson and Lynn Dickey were picked in the third round, and Joe Theismann went in round four.

One final thing that can go wrong in drafting a quarterback number one is that they might refuse to sign with that team. This has happened three very prominent times. John Elway in 1983 forced Baltimore to trade his rights. Kelly Stouffer did the same to the Cardinals in 1987, and Eli Manning jilted San Diego in 2004. Only Elway was worth holding on to. One other famous "refusenik" was Harry Agganis, a big sports star from Boston who signed to play baseball with the hometown Red Sox rather than football with the Browns. Agganis played briefly in the majors and then tragically died young from a pulmonary embolism in 1955.

Undrafted Free Agents

The opposite of a refusenik is an undrafted free agent. These quarterbacks were first rejected by the NFL, and face a much more arduous route to prove that they belong in the league. In 2006, Tony Romo became the latest undrafted free agent to make a splash and was one of four prominent undrafted quarterbacks active that year. Historically, he may join the 14 undrafted free agent quarterbacks who gained over 10,000 yards passing. They are listed on the following page.

Most of these players came out of small schools, which is the main reason they went undrafted. Warner went to Northern Iowa, Hart to Southern Illinois and Romo to Eastern Illinois. Delhomme went to Louisiana-Lafayette and Hebert to Northwestern State Louisiana. Jay Fiedler went to Dartmouth and Krieg to Milton. Jim Zorn went to Cal-Poly, Tom Flores to Pacific and Jeff Garcia to San Jose. Purdue's Gary Danielson signed instead with the World Football League. George Ratterman was Heisman Trophy winner Johnny Lujack's backup at Notre Dame and declared himself a free agent in 1947 at age 20 and signed with Buffalo of the AAFC. He actually was drafted a year later by the Boston

Quarterback	Years	Games	Attempts	Comp	%	Yards	Y/Att	TD	Int	Rating
Tommy Thompson	1940–50	96	1424	732	51.4	10385	7.3	91	103	66.5
George Ratterman	1947–56	92	1396	737	52.8	10473	7.5	91	96	70.4
Tom Flores	1960–69	111	1715	838	48.9	11959	6.97	93	92	67.6
Jim Hart	1966–84	201	5076	2593	51.1	34665	6.8	209	247	66.6
Gary Danielson	1976–88	102	1932	1105	57.2	13764	7.1	81	78	76.6
Jim Zorn	1976–87	140	3149	1669	53	21115	6.7	111	141	67.3
Dave Krieg	1980–98	213	5311	3105	58.5	38147	7.2	261	199	81.5
Warren Moon	1984–2000	208	6823	3988	58.4	49325	7.2	291	233	80.9
Bobby Hebert	1985–96	120	3122	1840	58.9	21693	7.0	135	124	78
Mike Tomczak	1985–99	185	2337	1248	53.4	16079	6.88	88	106	68.9
Jay Fiedler	1998–2005	76	1717	1008	58.7	11844	6.9	69	66	77.1
Kurt Warner	1998–2006	80	2508	1645	65.6	20591	8.2	125	83	93.8
Jake Delhomme	1998–2006	67	1934	1151	59.5	13965	7.2	80	92	84
Jeff Garcia	1999–2006	99	2973	1811	60.9	20385	6.9	136	73	86.4

Yanks in the 16th round of the 1948 NFL draft. Rose Bowl champion Warren Moon of Washington went to Canada because he was not willing to change positions, and therefore was not even drafted. As a black quarterback, he had to prove himself before signing with the Oilers as a free agent six years later.

The most interesting case, though, is the first undrafted quarterback on the list, Tommy Thompson. Despite being blind in one eye, Tommy was an All Missouri Valley Conference selection at Tulsa in 1938, but left school in 1939 with a year of eligibility remaining. Tulsa had a rule against married athletes, and Tommy was secretly married that spring. When word got out about his marriage, he was ruled ineligible to play football. Two weeks later, his wife swallowed poison and committed suicide during a party, possibly because she was upset that her marriage was costing Thompson his senior season. Tulsa declared Tommy eligible for football once again, but he signed instead with the Chicago Cardinals even though he could not play in the NFL for another year until his class graduated. In the interim, he joined the St. Louis Gunners of the minor league AFL for the 1939 season. In 1940, the Cardinals released Thompson, but Pittsburgh signed him 10 days later. In the 1941 franchise swap of Pittsburgh and Philadelphia, Thompson ended up a Philadelphia Eagle under new coach Greasy Neale who was installing the T Formation that the strong-armed Thompson was perfect to direct. He would lead the Eagles to three straight championship games and two titles in the decade.

Almost as low as the undrafted free agent are those on the once-drafted-and-now-cut scrap heap from which the Colts dredged up Hall of Famer Johnny Unitas. After the Steelers cut him, Johnny bided his time playing semipro football until Baltimore gave him the chance Pittsburgh had not. Lesser mortals uncovered this way include Jeff Blake by the Bengals, Trent Green by the Redskins and Marc Bulger by the Rams. A more common way for a devalued player to bounce from one team to another is through trades.

Trades

Among the most frequently traded quarterbacks in NFL history, it's not surprising that you find inconsistent starters and career back ups like Norm Snead, Steve DeBerg, Earl Morrall, Zeke Bratkowski and Dick Shiner who all were traded four times in their careers. The name on this list that is surprising is Bobby Layne. The Bears acquired his draft rights in 1948 for Ray Evans and then traded him for a number one pick in 1949 to the Bulldogs who then traded him in 1950 to Detroit where he led the Lions to three title games before being traded in 1958 to the Steelers for Earl Morrall and others. In his series of trades, Layne was involved in all the most interesting types of quarterback trades — trading a quarterback for a number one draft pick, trading a quarterback for another quarterback, acquiring a quarterback to win a title and acquiring a Hall of Fame quarterback.

In chapter one, we noted that Layne was one of only a handful of untested backup quarterbacks traded for a number one draft choice that proved to be worth it. Number one picks are bandied about to acquire established quarterbacks who have outworn their welcome in their current cities as well. The most renowned case was when Joe Montana was asked to take his four Super Bowl rings elsewhere by the 49ers and was traded to the Chiefs along with David Whitmore and a number three pick for a number one. This is one of only three instances where this type of trade has worked out. The Eagles gave up a number one in addition to tackle Buck Lansford and defensive back Jimmy Harris for Norm Van Brocklin, and the Chiefs gave the Rams a number one to acquire Trent Green and a number five pick. A case could be made that Drew Bledsoe was worth the number one pick the Bills gave up for him in 2002, but there is usually a very good reason a team is willing to jettison its starter: his shortcomings on or off the field have been exposed. In the nine similar deals involving a number one pick, the Steelers traded for aged Ed Brown in 1962, the Raiders traded for aging Cotton Davidson in 1962, the Giants traded for free spirited Craig Morton in 1974, the Bears traded for turnover machine Mike Phipps in 1977, the Rams traded for broken down Bert Jones in 1982, the Saints traded for dissipated Richard Todd in 1984, the Bucs traded for injury prone Chris Chandler in 1990, the Bears traded for shaky Rick Mirer in 1994 and the Redskins obtained quiet game manager Brad Johnson in 1999. The only team even to make the playoffs with their new quarterback, aside from the Chiefs with Montana and Green, were the Redskins with Johnson and the defensively-minded Bears with Phipps who were both pushed aside soon after.

An even worse trend started in the late 1960s when some teams decided that blowing off one top draft pick wasn't enough and gave up multiple picks for a quarterback on the downside. This happened five times. In 1967, the Vikings traded a disgruntled Fran Tarkenton to the Giants for two number ones and a number two. Five years later, they sent Tarkenton back to Minnesota for a number one, a number two, Norm Snead and two other players. Strangely, the Vikings got the best of both deals as Tarkenton had his greatest success in the last third of his career. In 1973, the Eagles gave the Rams Harold Jackson, Tony Baker, two number one picks and a number three to acquire Roman Gabriel who had one terrific year before

fading quickly due to age and injuries. The following season, the Packers gave the Rams two number ones, two number twos and a number three for Gabriel's replacement John Hadl. It was known in Green Bay as the Lawrence Welk trade — a one and a two and a three ... Is it any wonder that the Rams were a perennial playoff team in the 1970s while the Packers and Eagles were not? Perhaps the worst transaction was the 49ers giving the Patriots three number ones, a number two and backup quarterback Tom Owen for a shell-shocked Jim Plunkett in 1976. No one has sunk to such lunacy since then.

The 49ers throwing in backup Tom Owen in the Plunkett deal is a common practice in quarterback trades. The idea is to add a quarterback of lesser value for some sort of positional balance. There have been several trades of quarterbacks of more equal stature as well. The most notorious, at least in Philadelphia, was the 1963 deal that sent future Hall of Famer Sonny Jurgensen and a defensive back to the Redskins for sturdy, mediocre, younger Norm Snead and a defensive back. When questioned about it, quotable Eagles coach Joe Kuharich replied, "It's quite rare but not unusual." Jurgensen seemed to take special pleasure in saving his best games for the Eagles each year, while Snead had seven up-and-down seasons in Philadelphia before moving on again.

One of the earliest QB-for-QB trades had two unusual aspects. In 1954, the Packers traded Babe Parilli and a lineman to the Browns for Bobby Garrett and three other players. Parilli went into the Army for two years and then played briefly for Cleveland in 1956. In 1957, the Browns traded Parilli and five others back to Green Bay for Garrett, who had never appeared in a Packer game, and Roger Zatkoff. In addition to the strangeness of two players being traded again for each other, the eight player deal is the second largest ever to involve a quarterback. The largest deal was a 1953 15-player trade between the Browns and Colts in which the rights to Harry Agganis went to Baltimore. Parilli was again involved in a straight up deal in 1968 when the Patriots traded the elderly Babe for the Jets' young backup Mike Taliaferro. Babe went to the Super Bowl as Joe Namath's backup. Namath himself got to New York through a trade of draft rights. The Jets held the draft rights to Tulsa's Jerry Rhome and traded them to the Oilers for the top pick in the 1965 AFL draft that they used to snag Namath. Rhome signed with the Cowboys, and Houston ended up with nothing.

Another AFL trade in which there was a big winner occurred in 1967 when the Bills sent a young Daryle Lamonica and receiver Glen Bass to Oakland for veteran Tom Flores and receiver Art Powell. Buffalo was looking for a big-time receiver, but quickly found that the aging Powell was washed up. Lamonica blossomed as the Raiders' Mad Bomber and led them to a Super Bowl. The Raiders were also involved in a *mano a mano* deal that looked to be reminiscent of Jurgensen/Snead when they traded their star Ken Stabler straight up for Oiler younger starter Dan Pastorini who had a bigger arm but less accuracy and durability. As it turned out, Stabler hung on with the Oilers and Saints for a few unproductive years, while Pastorini broke his leg and was beaten out by Jim Plunkett.

The most recent example of this type of trade was the 2004 draft day trade of the rights to Philip Rivers going to the Chargers and the rights to Eli Manning going to the Giants. How that works out ultimately will be fun to watch, especially if either leads his team to a title. A championship is what all teams are trying to get closer to when they trade for a quarterback, and it has happened many times, although not always immediately. The Giants obtained Charlie Conerly in 1948 and won a title in 1956; the Lions obtained Bobby Layne in 1950 and won titles in 1952 and 1953; the Eagles obtained Norm Van Brocklin in 1958 and won a title in 1960; the Bears obtained Bill Wade in 1961 and won a title in 1963; the Browns obtained Frank Ryan in 1963 and won a title in 1964; the Colts obtained Earl Morrall in 1968 and won a title in 1971; the Broncos obtained the rights to John Elway in 1983 and won titles in 1997 and 1998; the 49ers obtained Steve Young in 1987 and won a title with him at quarterback in 1994. Trades brought Fran Tarkenton and Craig Morton to franchises that they took to the Super Bowl although they did not win the ultimate game.

On rare occasions, starting quarterbacks are traded for non-quarterbacks. Tackle Lou Cordileone reacted with disbelief when he heard the Giants had swapped him to the 49ers for an All Pro quarterback, "They traded me for Tittle? Just me?" However, some big quarterback names have changed teams this way. The Giants traded fullback Howie Livingston to the Redskins for Charlie Conerly, and the Lions traded end Bob Mann to the Bulldogs for Bobby Layne. Charger John Hadl was traded to the Rams for defensive end Coy Bacon and runner Bobby Thomas. Ron Jaworski was traded from the Rams to the Eagles for tight end Charlie Young, and Archie Manning was traded from the Saints to the Oilers for tackle Leon Gray.

Quarterbacks have also been involved in a number of very strange deals. In 1929, the Giants bought the entire Detroit Wolverine franchise primarily to obtain passer Benny Friedman. In 1949, the Eagles drafted Notre Dame's Frank Tripucka with their number one pick, but then simply waived him to the Lions in midseason. In 1950, the Bears included George Blanda with four other players in a deal with the Colts for All Pro guard Dick Barwegen. One week later they bought Blanda back for cash. In 1951, the Rams sent Bobby Thomason to Green Bay for conditional number one and two picks. If Thomason were still a Packer on December 31, 1951, then the Packers owed the Rams the picks. At the end of the season, Green Bay decided that the efficient Thomason wasn't worth that much and returned him to Los Angeles which in turn traded him for good to Philadelphia. In 1960, the Bears traded Rudy Bukich to the Steelers for future considerations that in 1962 turned out to be Rudy Bukich returning to Chicago. He had been traded for himself. In 1964, the Oilers sent Jacky Lee on a two-year loan to Denver for Bud McFadin and a number two pick; in 1966, Lee returned to Houston. Full details on all of these deals and all other major quarterback trades can be found in the Trade Register in the Appendix.

Unrestricted Free Agency

Another way to look for that championship quarterback is through free agency although Trent Dilfer and Brad Johnson are the only free agents to win titles with their new teams through 2006. True free agency is a fairly recent development in the NFL. Teams always had the opportunity to pick up a released veteran off the scrap heap and see what he had left. The Giants did this in 1944 with Arnie Herber who took them to the championship game. The Raiders picked up George Blanda when the Oilers cut him in 1967, and he kicked and served as a relief pitcher for them for nine years. In 1980, Oakland signed a forgotten Jim Plunkett, and he led them to two Super Bowl titles in seven years. Another whiff of free agency was when the AFL began in 1960 and such former NFL quarterbacks as George Blanda, Babe Parilli, Jack Kemp, Frank Tripucka, Cotton Davidson, Len Dawson and Tobin Rote found a second act to their careers. In theory, players also could play out their options to become "free agents" in that era, but compensation was required and was decided by the league. Thus, when Viking quarterback Joe Kapp played out his option in Minnesota and signed with the Patriots, the Vikings received a number one pick and a player in return for a Kapp who was out of the league a year later.

The first version of real free agency in the NFL was Plan B Free Agency, which was in force from 1989–92 and was set up mostly for lesser players to be able to sign with another team to get a better chance to start. Under Plan B, each team could protect 37 players on its roster with the unprotected players being free to seek a better deal elsewhere. Quarterbacks who took advantage of this were retreads like Jim McMahon in 1990, Erik Kramer and Mike Tomczak in 1991, and Dave Krieg, Steve DeBerg and Mike Tomczak in 1992. This plan was struck down by the courts in 1993 and true free agency was instituted for all players.

The teams most active in signing free agent quarterbacks in the last 14 years have been the Cardinals with eight, the Bears, Raiders and Eagles with seven and the Jets, Dolphins, Redskins and Vikings with six. However, the number of championships those teams have won in that same period is 0. The most frequently signed quarterbacks have been Dave Krieg, Jeff Blake and Vinny Testaverde who have each signed with five teams in the effort to keep their fading careers alive. Trent Dilfer, Gus Frerotte and Bubby Brister each signed with four teams.

There have been good signings over the years, though. Game managers Dilfer and Brad Johnson won titles with the dominating Ravens and Bucs defenses respectively. Kerry Collins, Rich Gannon and Jake Delhomme solidified the quarterbacking in New York, Oakland and Carolina and took their teams to the Super Bowl as well. The first Collins and Gannon signings came in 1999, probably the best free agent quar-terback year with Trent Green signing with the Rams as well. Johnson and Gannon reflect the best types of quarterbacks that can be found via this method: game managers and unproven backups. Kerry Collins demonstrates another common type — the head case looking for another chance. The Giants got lucky with the second chance Collins — usually those players don't work out.

Drew Brees to the contrary, a team is not likely to find a franchise quarterback this way, but it can find an effective player for your offensive system. These signings can lead to playoff berths as happened with Boomer Esiason with the Jets and Vinny Testaverde with Cleveland in 1993, Erik Kramer with Chicago and Scott Mitchell with Detroit in 1994, Rodney Peete with Philadelphia in 1995, Ty Detmer with Philadelphia in 1996, Randall Cunningham with Minnesota and Elvis Grbac with Kansas City in 1997, Doug Flutie with Buffalo and Vinny Testaverde with the Jets in 1998, Jim Miller with Chicago and Jeff George with Minnesota in 1999 (in addition to the three noted above), Trent Dilfer with Baltimore and Jay Fiedler with Miami in 2000, Brad Johnson with Tampa and Elvis Grbac with Baltimore in 2001, Jake Plummer with Denver and Jake Delhomme with Carolina in 2002 and Jeff Garcia with Philadelphia in 2006.

Competitor Leagues

One final way to find a quarterback is to pluck one from another professional league. The NFL has had a steady stream of competitors over the years, some more serious than others, and has drawn signal callers from most of them. The first competitor of significance was the All America Conference from 1946 until it merged with the NFL in 1950. With the merger three teams entered the NFL wholesale with the players from the disbanded teams dispersed through drafts and other arrangements that precluded free agency. The AFL of the 1960s that also merged with the NFL lost no quarterback talent to the older league. In fact, it was when the AFL started raiding the NFL and signing such stars as Roman Gabriel and John Brodie to big contracts that peace talks got serious. The Canadian Football League, though, dates to the post World War II period and has supplied the NFL with a good number of quarterbacks ever since.

It is interesting to compare the statistics of some of the more prominent NFL players who got their start in the CFL. These quarterbacks include Sam Etcheverry who came down to the Cardinals with much fanfare in 1960, Joe Kapp who came south to Minnesota with his coach Bud Grant, and Joe Theismann, Dieter Brock, Warren Moon, Erik Kramer and Jeff Garcia who were not taken seriously as quarterback prospects by the NFL until they first showed their skills in Canada. Theismann, Moon and Garcia were the biggest prizes. The NFL and CFL stats of each of these players are presented in the following table:

Name	League	Years	Att	Comp	%	Yards	Y/Att	TD	Int	Rating
Sam Etcheverry	CFL	1952–60	2829	1630	57.6%	25582	9.0	183	163	85.3
Sam Etcheverry	NFL	1961–62	302	154	51.0%	1982	6.6	16	21	60.6
Sam Etcheverry Total			**3131**	**1784**	**57.0%**	**27564**	**8.8**	**199**	**184**	**82.9**
Joe Kapp	CFL	1959–66	2709	1476	54.5%	22725	8.4	136	130	79.2
Joe Kapp	NFL	1967–70	918	449	48.9%	5911	6.4	40	64	55.1
Joe Kapp Total			**3627**	**1925**	**53.1%**	**28636**	**7.9**	**176**	**194**	**73.1**
Joe Theismann	CFL	1971–73	679	382	56.3%	6092	9.0	40	34	85.1
Joe Theismann	NFL	1974–85	3602	2044	56.7%	25206	7.0	160	138	77.4
Joe Theismann Total			**4281**	**2426**	**56.7%**	**31298**	**7.3**	**200**	**172**	**78.6**
Dieter Brock	CFL	1974–84	4535	2602	57.4%	34830	7.7	210	98	88.3
Dieter Brock	NFL	1985	365	218	59.7%	2658	7.3	16	13	82.0
Dieter Brock Total			**365**	**218**	**59.7%**	**2658**	**7.3**	**16**	**13**	**82.0**
Warren Moon	CFL	1978–83	2382	1369	57.5%	21228	8.9	144	77	93.8
Warren Moon	NFL	1984–00	6823	3888	57.0%	49325	7.2	291	233	79.7
Warren Moon Total			**9205**	**5257**	**57.1%**	**70553**	**7.7**	**435**	**310**	**83.3**
Erik Kramer	CFL	1988	153	62	40.5%	964	6.3	5	13	37.6
Erik Kramer	NFL	1987r, 1991–99	2299	1317	57.3%	15337	6.7	92	79	76.6
Erik Kramer Total			**2452**	**1379**	**56.2%**	**16301**	**6.6**	**97**	**92**	**74.2**
Jeff Garcia	CFL	1994–98	2024	1249	61.7%	16449	8.1	111	52	94.9
Jeff Garcia	NFL	1999–05	2785	1695	60.9%	19076	6.8	126	71	85.8
Jeff Garcia Total			**4809**	**2944**	**61.2%**	**35525**	**7.4**	**237**	**123**	**89.6**

Many quarterbacks have tried a stint in the CFL in the middle of their careers before returning to the NFL such as Frankie Filchock, Eddie Lebaron, Pete Liske, Tom Clements, Vince Ferragamo, Jack Kemp, Babe Parilli and Frank Tripucka. Two others who had impressive numbers in both leagues were Tobin Rote and Doug Flutie. Flutie also played in the USFL. Their statistics are in the following table:

Name	League	Years	Att	Comp	%	Yards	Y/Att	TD	Int	Rating
Doug Flutie	USFL	1985	281	134	47.7%	2109	7.5	13	14	67.8
Doug Flutie	NFL	1986–89, 1998–05	2151	1177	54.7%	14715	6.8	86	68	76.3
Doug Flutie	CFL	1990–97	4854	2975	61.3%	41355	8.5	270	155	93.9
Doug Flutie Total			**7286**	**4286**	**58.8%**	**58179**	**8.0**	**369**	**237**	**87.7**
Tobin Rote	NFL/AFL	1950–59, 1963–64, 1966	2907	1329	45.7%	18850	6.5	148	191	56.8
Tobin Rote	CFL	1960–62	1187	662	55.8%	9672	8.1	66	58	80.7
Tobin Rote Total			**4094**	**1991**	**48.6%**	**28522**	**7.0**	**214**	**249**	**63.7**

In the 1970s, the World Football League started up with much fanfare, signing stars away from the NFL for big contracts. Within two years, the WFL was bankrupt and kaput. The WFL, though, gave future NFL quarterbacks Danny White, Gary Danielson, Pat Haden, Norris Weese, Tony Adams and Johnny Walton a start in professional football. White, Danielson and Haden had solid NFL careers; their comparative statistics are in the following table:

Name	League	Years	Att	Comp	Comp %	Yards	Y/Att	TD	Int	Rating
Gary Danielson	WFL	1974–75	75	37	49.3%	412	5.5	1	2	59.4
Gary Danielson	NFL	1976–88	1932	1105	57.2%	13764	7.1	81	78	76.6
Gary Danielson Total			**2007**	**1142**	**56.9%**	**14176**	**7.1**	**82**	**80**	**75.9**
Danny White	WFL	1974–75	350	183	52.3%	2635	7.5	21	17	76.8
Danny White	NFL	1976–88	2950	1761	59.7%	21959	7.4	155	132	81.7
Danny White Total			**3300**	**1944**	**58.9%**	**24594**	**7.5**	**176**	**149**	**81.2**
Pat Haden	WFL	1975	163	98	60.1%	1404	8.6	11	9	87.6
Pat Haden	NFL	1976–81	1363	731	53.6%	9296	6.8	52	60	69.6
Pat Haden Total			**1526**	**829**	**54.3%**	**10700**	**7.0**	**63**	**69**	**71.5**

In the 1980s, the new challenger was the USFL which started as a spring league and did fairly well until they tried to shift to a fall schedule after two years. They eventually went belly up, won their antitrust court case against the NFL but were awarded just one dollar in damages and vanished. While Doug Williams, Greg Landry, Vince Evans and Chuck Fusina jumped from the NFL to the USFL and would later return to the established league, four star quarterbacks got their starts in the USFL. The numbers of Doug Flutie are noted above, but the comparative numbers of Hall of Famers Steve Young and Jim Kelly as well as Bobby Hebert are in the following table:

Name	League	Years	Att	Comp	Comp %	Yards	Y/Att	TD	Int	Rating
Steve Young	USFL	1984–85	560	316	56.4%	4402	7.9	16	22	75.0
Steve Young	NFL	1985–99	4149	2667	64.3%	33124	8.0	232	107	96.8
Steve Young Total			**4709**	**2983**	**63.3%**	**37526**	**8.0**	**248**	**129**	**94.2**
Bobby Hebert	USFL	1983–85	1407	773	54.9%	11137	7.9	81	58	82.9
Bobby Hebert	NFL	1985–96	3121	1839	58.9%	21683	6.9	135	124	78.0
Bobby Hebert Total			**4528**	**2612**	**57.7%**	**32820**	**7.2**	**216**	**182**	**79.5**
Jim Kelly	USFL	1984–85	1154	730	63.3%	9842	8.5	83	45	98.1
Jim Kelly	NFL	1986–96	4779	2874	60.1%	35467	7.4	237	175	84.4
Jim Kelly Total			**5933**	**3604**	**60.7%**	**45309**	**7.6**	**320**	**220**	**87.1**

The ultimate legacy of the USFL may be Arena Football, which was started by a former USFL official. This fast-paced, indoor, eight-man game has been the haven of a number of failed NFL quarterbacks, but also served as the training ground for an NFL star, Kurt Warner. The only other competitor league to materialize was the ridiculous XFL produced by NBC and the World Wrestling Federation in 2001. Its only importance in professional football history is that it restarted the career of Tommy Maddox who resurfaced in Pittsburgh after that. Finally, there was NFL Europe, the league's developmental minor league. While most of the quarterbacks assigned by NFL teams to play in NFL Europe turned out to be backups at best like Jason Garrett, Stan Gelbaugh, Doug Pederson, Kurt Kittner and Dave Ragone, a few starters emerged. Sometime starters Scott Mitchell, Jon Kitna and Damon Huard all spent time in Europe, but the biggest success has been Jake Delhomme who won the World Bowl championship there and took Carolina to the Super Bowl as well.

3

Career Arc

According to Hall of Famer Joe Montana, "Having a long NFL career is an accomplishment in itself" because quarterback is not an easy job. An NFL quarterback's career is marked by a series of ups and downs affected by not only his own talent, but by the talents of his teammates, injuries, coaching and age. From his rookie season to his last, even the greatest quarterback will have stretches in which fans, teammates and coaches openly question whether he is still the man to lead the team. For ordinary and below average quarterbacks, that doubt is a constant. Most careers, though, follow the same general pattern of the exuberant mistakes of youth, the prime seasons of experienced professionalism and the inevitable decline of age.

Youth

Rookies are often in the best physical shape of their lives, but are ill-equipped to use their skills to the fullest due to their lack of experience. There is so much to learn and so much to comprehend that there are two schools of thought as to how to best break in a rookie quarterback — sit him for a season or play him immediately. Because of the big money invested in high draft picks in the free agency era, most top prospects find themselves behind center by midseason of their rookie years, learning on the run. As Phil Simms, who was sacked 39 times and threw 13 touchdowns as a rookie, put it, "Name me the quarterback whose confidence was ruined because he played as a rookie, and I'll show you a quarterback who had no business playing at all." Taking a look at the roughly 180 passers who threw at least 100 passes in their rookie seasons, we find quarterbacks who completed a measly 50.3 percent of their passes for a substandard 6.5 yards per pass and completed just 3.9

percent of their passes for touchdowns while throwing 5.5 percent of their passes for interceptions. In short, they fall shy of the average league performance in all categories. In recent years, rookie completion percentages are better because of the nature of the modern short passing game, but still fall significantly short of the contemporary league average.

Peyton Manning's 1998 rookie season is a good example. He is one of four quarterbacks to throw for over 300 yards in his very first game along with Mark Rypien, Ryan Fitzpatrick of the Rams and replacement player Ed Rubbert. Peyton threw for a rookie record of 3,739 yards and 26 touchdowns, but also set the rookie mark with 28 interceptions and averaged just 6.5 yards per pass. Despite some big numbers, his passer rating of 71.2 was only 91 percent of the league average. Most of the passers who performed well above the league average in passer rating played in the 1930s and 1940s when there was a much greater disparity among the best and worst passers. Sid Luckman and Otto Graham both achieved passer ratings more than double the league average in their first seasons. Luckman only threw 53 passes in 1939, but averaged 12.5 yards per attempt; Graham's 112.1 rating in 1946 is the highest ever achieved by a rookie. The only other freshman quarterback to score over 100 was Marc Bulger who in half a season racked up a 101.5 rate in 2002. He and Dan Marino both achieved a rating 126 percent of the league average — the two highest rankings since 1978.

Among the names of quarterbacks who scored at least 10 percent better than the league average in passer rating are such stars as Luckman, Graham, Marino, Sammy Baugh, Bob Waterfield, Y.A. Tittle, Charlie Conerly, Johnny Unitas, Ace Parker, Joe Namath, Ben Roethlisberger, Ken Anderson and Jim Kelly. Roethlisberger set the completion percentage mark for rookies in 2004 with 66.4 percent and won 13 straight games. Y.A. Tittle, Charlie Conerly and Sammy Baugh are often noted for their excellence at their final years, but were great right from the start. Dan Marino may have been the most impressive of all. He threw 20 touchdowns to just six interceptions, led his team to the playoffs and started in the Pro Bowl. His rookie year led seamlessly to a sophomore season in which he set new league records for yards and touchdowns while taking the Dolphins to the Super Bowl. Although he would be consistently among the top three quarterbacks for the rest of his record-setting career, he would never quite match that beginning. However, in this group you'll also find such flashes in the pan as Irv Comp, Greg Cook, Pat Haden, Mike Boryla, Tom Flores, Tom Kennedy, Clyde LeForce and Aaron Brooks. Just because a quarterback plays well in his first season does not mean he will continue to stay healthy, develop and get better.

Even if we narrow the group to quarterbacks who threw at least 250 passes and topped the league average in quarterback rating, as in the following table, we still get a mix of greats and ordinary quarterbacks:

Name	Year	Age	Games	Att	Comp	%	Yards	Y/Att	TD	Int	Rating	Rel Rate
Tittle, Y.A.	1948	22	14	289	161	55.7	2522	8.7	16	9	90.3	141
Conerly, Charlie	1948	27	12	299	162	54.2	2175	7.3	22	13	84	140
Marino, Dan	1983	22	11	296	173	58.4	2210	7.5	20	6	96	126
Dobbs, Glenn	1946	26	13	269	135	50.2	1886	7.0	13	15	66	119
Namath, Joe	1965	22	13	340	164	48.2	2220	6.5	18	15	68.8	118
Roethlisberger, Ben	2004	22	14	295	196	66.4	2621	8.9	17	11	98.1	118
Flores, Tom	1960	23	14	252	136	54	1738	6.9	12	12	71.8	116
Songin, Butch	1960	36	14	392	187	47.7	2476	6.3	22	15	70.9	114
Kelly, Jim	1986	26	16	480	285	59.4	3593	7.5	22	17	83.3	112
Brock, Dieter	1985	34	15	365	218	59.7	2658	7.3	16	13	82	111
Plunkett, Jim	1971	23	14	328	158	48.2	2158	6.6	19	16	68.6	110
Tarkenton, Fran	1961	21	14	280	157	56.1	1997	7.1	18	17	74.7	109
Batch, Charlie	1998	23	12	303	173	57.1	2178	7.2	11	6	83.5	107
O'Donnell, Neil	1991	25	12	286	156	54.5	1963	6.9	11	7	78.8	103
Moon, Warren	1984	27	16	450	259	57.6	3338	7.4	12	14	76.9	101
Garcia, Jeff	1999	29	13	375	225	60	2544	6.8	11	11	77.9	101

Conversely, a rough start does not mandate a lost career. Terry Bradshaw is a great case in point. Bradshaw had one of the very worst rookie campaigns in league history in 1970. He was so far over his head in his first year that he completed just 38 percent of his passes for six touchdowns and 24 interceptions. His passer rating was just 46 percent of the league average, yet he went on to have a Hall of Fame career. Meanwhile, quarterback Dennis Shaw was Rookie of the Year in 1970, but was out of the league when Bradshaw won his second Super Bowl. Included among the quarterbacks who completed less than 40 percent of their passes as rookies are Bradshaw, Bert Jones, Doug Williams and Tobin Rote; all but Jones won championships and Bert went to the playoffs more than once. Furthermore, the touchdown-interception ratios for Hall of Famers John Elway, Steve Young and Troy Aikman as rookies were 7:14, 3:8 and 9:18 respectively. The combination of an inexperienced rookie quarterback playing on a weak team with a high draft slot can lead to discouraging beginnings as the rookie takes his lumps.

Of course, lowly rookie stats often do indicate a flop. The worst rookie season ever was turned in by Stan Heath of the Packers in 1949 who set rookie marks by completing just 24.5 percent of his passes for 3.5 yards per pass, a touchdown-interception ratio of 1:14 and a passer rating of 9. This number one draft choice was in Canada the following year. Among quarterbacks who threw at least 200 passes as rookies and averaged more than 20 percent below the league average in passer rating, only Bradshaw, Rote, Steve DeBerg, Dan Pastorini, Elway, Aikman, John Hadl, Kerry Collins and Donovan McNabb had significant success in their careers. The legacy of most was more like that of Ryan Leaf, Lamar McHan, Bud Schwenk and Chris Weinke in the table on the following page.

There have been a number of success stories like Carson Palmer, Ken O'Brien and Mark Rypien who did not play at all in the year they

Name	*Rookie Yr*	*Att*	*Comp*	*%*	*Yards*	*Y/Att*	*TD*	*Int*	*Rating*	*Rel Rate*
Bradshaw, Terry	1970	218	83	38.1	1410	6.5	6	24	30.4	46
Leaf, Ryan	1998	245	111	45.3	1289	5.3	2	15	39	50
Rote, Tobin	1950	224	83	37.1	1231	5.5	7	24	26.7	50
McHan, Lamar	1954	255	105	41.2	1475	5.8	6	22	32.4	52
Darragh, Dan	1968	215	92	42.8	917	4.3	3	14	33	53
DeBerg, Steve	1978	302	137	45.4	1570	5.2	8	22	40	62
Schwenk, Bud	1942	295	126	42.7	1360	4.6	6	27	25.5	63
Pisarcik, Joe	1977	241	103	42.7	1346	5.6	4	14	42.3	69
Pastorini, Dan	1971	270	127	47	1702	6.3	7	21	43.8	70
Johnson, Randy	1966	295	129	43.7	1795	6.1	12	21	47.8	71
Walter, Andrew	2006	276	147	53.3	1677	6.1	3	13	55.8	71
Trudeau, Jack	1986	417	204	48.9	2225	5.3	8	18	53.5	72
Elway, John	1983	259	123	47.5	1663	6.4	7	14	54.9	72
Sherman, Tom	1968	226	90	39.8	1199	5.3	12	16	45.6	73
Zorn, Jim	1976	439	208	47.4	2571	5.9	12	27	49.5	74
Harrington, Joey	2002	429	215	50.1	2294	5.4	12	16	59.9	74
Orton, Kyle	2005	368	190	51.6	1869	5.1	9	13	59.7	74
Aikman, Troy	1989	293	155	52.9	1749	6.0	9	18	55.7	74
Nix, Kent	1967	268	136	50.7	1587	5.9	8	19	49.5	74
Snead, Norm	1961	375	172	45.9	2337	6.2	11	22	51.6	75
Komlo, Jeff	1979	368	183	49.7	2238	6.1	11	23	52.8	75
Hadl, John	1962	260	107	41.2	1632	6.3	15	24	43.3	75
Whelihan, Craig	1997	237	118	49.8	1357	5.7	6	10	58.3	75
Shuler, Heath	1994	265	120	45.3	1658	6.3	10	12	59.6	76
Carr, David	2002	444	233	52.5	2592	5.8	9	15	62.8	78
Collins, Kerry	1995	433	214	49.4	2717	6.3	14	19	61.9	78
McNabb, Donovan	1999	216	106	49.1	948	4.4	8	7	60.1	78
Weinke, Chris	2001	540	293	54.3	2931	5.4	11	19	62	79
Fuller, Steve	1979	270	146	54.1	1484	5.5	6	14	55.8	79
Boller, Kyle	2003	224	116	51.8	1260	5.6	7	9	62.4	79
Munson, Bill	1964	223	108	48.4	1533	6.9	9	15	56.5	79

were drafted and then had a breakout "rookie" season the next year. Similarly, some of the best rookie seasons have been achieved by quarterbacks who first got experience in a rival league such as Pat Haden in the WFL, Jim Kelly in the USFL and Warren Moon and Jeff Garcia from the CFL. Others like Joe Montana and Tom Brady threw just a handful of passes in their rookie years and then were ready to go in their second year. Philip Rivers and Chad Pennington didn't really get a chance to play until their third years. The following table gives the statistics of the best "sophomore" rookies who threw fewer than 50 passes in their actual rookie years:

Name	*Year*	*Age*	*Att*	*Comp*	*%*	*Yards*	*Y/Att*	*TD*	*Int*	*Rating*	*Rel Rate*
Layne, Bobby	1949	22	299	155	51.8	1796	6.0	9	18	55.3	103
Van Brocklin, Norm	1950	24	233	127	54.5	2061	8.9	18	14	85.1	161
Starr, Bart	1957	23	215	117	54.4	1489	6.9	8	10	69.3	110
Johnson, Charley	1962	23	308	150	48.7	2440	7.9	16	20	65.9	91
Hart, Jim	1967	23	397	192	48.4	3008	7.6	19	30	58.4	88
Montana, Joe	1980	24	273	176	64.5	1795	6.6	15	9	87.8	119
Favre, Brett	1992	23	471	302	64.1	3227	6.9	18	13	85.3	113
Brunell, Mark	1995	25	346	201	58.1	2168	6.3	15	7	82.6	104
Green, Trent	1998	28	509	278	54.6	3441	6.8	23	11	81.8	105
Warner, Kurt	1999	28	499	325	65.1	4353	8.7	41	13	109.2	142
Griese, Brian	1999	24	452	261	57.7	3032	6.7	14	14	75.6	98
Culpepper, Daunte	2000	23	474	297	62.7	3937	8.3	33	16	98	126
Brady, Tom	2001	24	413	264	63.9	2843	6.9	18	12	86.5	110
Brees, Drew	2002	23	526	320	60.8	3284	6.2	17	16	76.9	96
Pennington, Chad	2002	26	399	275	68.9	3120	7.8	22	6	104.2	130

Name	Year	Age	Att	Comp	%	Yards	Y/Att	TD	Int	Rating	Rel Rate
Rivers, Philip	2006	24	460	284	61.7	3388	7.4	22	9	92	117
Romo, Tony	2006	25	337	220	65.3	2903	8.6	19	13	95.1	121

As to the ultimate team success, six rookies found themselves in the league championship game with Ed Danowski, Sammy Baugh, Bob Waterfield and Otto Graham winning it all and Harry Newman and Cecil Isbell losing close games. Isbell won a title in his second season as did Sid Luckman, Tom Brady and Ben Roethlisberger, while Dan Marino made his only Super Bowl appearance as a sophomore. Bob Waterfield's 1945 rookie campaign with the Cleveland Rams was the most spectacular as he was named Most Valuable Player for the NFL as well. The Rams moved to Los Angeles, but remarkably the Browns won the AAFC title in 1946 behind rookie Otto Graham who finished second to fellow rookie Glenn Dobbs as MVP.

Prime Years

Youthful phenoms are rarities, however, as NFL quarterbacks tend to get better with experience. It's sometimes said in sports that an athlete's prime seasons run from around 28 to 32, but that often seems to be the optimistic spin of a 29-year old player trying to win a big contract for years of decline. The physical pounding that football players take in addition to the need for speed in the modern game has led some teams to set a policy against signing players over 29. With most positions, that seems sensible, but what about quarterback?

I conducted a small study to try to determine the prime age for NFL quarterbacks. I looked at 10-year veterans, both retired and active. For the statistical categories of touchdown passes, yards passing and passer rating, I recorded the quarterback's age when he achieved his best in each category and for when he began his best four-year run for each category. I then broke the results in half according to whether the quarterback was above average or below average according to career passer rating.

For single season bests, the average age for best performance was 29 for TD passes, 29 for yards and 30 for rating. The subset results for the above average and below average quarterbacks was virtually identical with the only difference being that the better quarterbacks threw for the most yards at age 30 on average rather than 29. In fact, 29 is the average age at which quarterbacks win championships, although 27 is the most common age to do so.

For the four-year prime period, the average age range for touchdown passes and yards was 27.5 to 31.5, while the average range for passer rating was 28 to 32. In each of these three categories, the prime years for the better quarterbacks began about a year later — 28–31 rather than 27–30 — than the lesser quarterbacks. This is probably due to the fact that better quarterbacks will remain starters longer in their careers. Nevertheless, it is a slight difference, and 27–32 seems to be the range that most quarterbacks experience their greatest success, no matter what its level. This bears out Weeb Ewbank's contention that, "There are two kinds of daring in quarterbacks: The experienced guy who does smart things and the young guy who does stupid things."

Some of the outlying extremes in this study were interesting. Randy Johnson hit his best in touchdown passes at 22; Bernie Kosar at 23, and Joe Namath at 24. Johnson, Kosar and Drew Bledsoe all threw for the most yards when they were 22, while Dan Marino did so at 23 and Joe Namath at 24. Marino, Pat Haden, Lamar McHan and Frankie Filchock all had their best years for passer rating at 23. As for four-year periods for touchdown passes, Kosar, Johnson and McHan all were best from 22–25, with Marino, Bert Jones, Bobby Layne, Charlie Johnson and Greg Landry all at their best from 23–26. In yards, Marino, Bledsoe, Kosar and Randy Johnson were all at their bests from 22–25. In passer rating, Marino's best was from 22–25, Bert Jones and Bledsoe from 23–26 and Namath, Haden, McHan, Jim McMahon, Jeff Blake, Rodney Peete and Bobby Douglass and Frankie Filchock all peaking from 24–27.

These quarterbacks who had their best years earliest in their careers did so for a variety of reasons. Joe Namath, Bernie Kosar, Bert Jones and Jim McMahon were clearly affected by injuries. Randy Johnson, Bobby Douglass and Lamar McHan were never that good to begin with. Drew Bledsoe, Charlie Johnson and Pat Haden never seemed to develop into what they could have been. Marino and Bobby Layne, though, were Hall of Famers right from the start who had long careers of slow decline as they accumulated impressive career totals.

Then there are the quarterbacks who had their best performances in most things at an early age, but had a revival late in life. Tobin Rote's best four-year period in all three categories was from 27–30, but his greatest season came at age 35 when he returned from Canada to lead the Chargers to the title in 1963. Rodney Peete had a career year in touchdowns and yards at age 36, but his peak was from 23 to 27. Late starter Steve Young's prime was from 31 to 34, but his highs in touchdowns and yards came at age 37. Roman Gabriel set a personal record for yards at age 33, three years after his prime seasons; Fran Tarkenton reached his high in yards at 38, eight years after his prime years. Boomer Esiason and Dave Krieg both had their best passer ratings at age 36, but their prime seasons were from 24 to 28. Jim Plunkett's prime for touchdowns and yards was from 23 to 26, but his best season was at 35, and that was the season that he began his prime in passer rating, relying on his smarts to be a more effective veteran signal caller. Craig Morton went the other way. His best season for touchdowns was at 26, but his prime was from 35 to 38. Morton and Plunkett stand as two good examples that a quarterback's experience can make the aging quarterback a smarter and better performer.

Relationships with Coaches

Another factor in a quarterback's development is coaching. In order for a quarterback to be successful on the field, he needs to understand what he sees in the opposing defense. A good coach will prepare his quarterback as to what he is most likely to encounter on the field. A good coach will work out any mechanical problems with his quarterback's footwork and throwing motion. A good coach will help his quarterback make smart decisions during a game. A good coach will study how defenses are playing his quarterback and work to improve his weak points. A good coach will communicate and connect with his quarterback in whatever way is most effective, a kick in the pants or a pat on the back. A good coach will bring the best out in a player.

The most intense quarterback-coach relationships have been ones in which the two are bound together for success or failure. Terry Bradshaw played for only Chuck Noll throughout his entire 14-year career. He has spoken and written several times about how difficult that relationship was and how long it took for him to understand Noll at all. Three other quarterbacks had decade-long careers with only one coach: Danny White, 13 years with Tom Landry; Roger Staubach, 11 years with Tom Landry and Otto Graham, 10 years with Paul Brown. Oddly, Bradshaw was the only one of these signal callers who got to engage in the now nearly abandoned practice of calling his own plays. There have been 16 quarterbacks who spent at least a decade with a head coach including the four purely monogamous relationships just noted:

Quarterback	Coach	Years
Terry Bradshaw	Chuck Noll	14
Don Strock	Don Shula	14
Dan Marino	Don Shula	13
Len Dawson	Hank Stram	13
Danny White	Tom Landry	13
Bobby Layne	Buddy Parker	12
Roger Staubach	Tom Landry	11
Jim Kelly	Marv Levy	11
Arnie Herber	Curly Lambeau	11
Bob Griese	Don Shula	11
Steve McNair	Jeff Fisher	11
Otto Graham	Paul Brown	10
Craig Morton	Tom Landry	10
John Elway	Dan Reeves	10
Tommy Thompson	Greasy Neale	10
Joe Montana	Bill Walsh	10

Strock is an anomaly here because he was a backup for his entire career, but the other 15 starters won 28 championships in their time with these coaches. While the relationships were sometimes strained as with Bradshaw-Noll and Elway-Reeves, there were also devoted marriages as with Dawson-Stram and Layne-Parker. Buddy Parker quit as the Lions' coach, and when he caught on with the Steelers, he soon made a trade to reunite him with his veteran, hard-drinking, on-the-field leader. One of the most interesting aspects of Shula's long, successful run as coach is his string of quarterbacks. He inherited Johnny Unitas for seven years with the

Colts, then went to Miami where he straightened out struggling fourth-year pro Bob Griese for an 11-year stretch, and then after a two-year gap, drafted Marino for the last 13 years of his coaching career. Add in 14 years of Don Strock in Miami and eight years of Earl Morrall in both cities, and you might say that Don Shula had an unparalleled stable quarterbacking situation for over 30 years. The only coach who came close was Tom Landry in Dallas who went from nine years of Don Meredith to 10 years of Craig Morton overlapping with 11 of Roger Staubach that overlapped with 13 of Danny White for 29 years of fairly stable quarterbacking.

Good coaches develop young talent. Buddy Parker developed Layne. Sid Gillman developed John Hadl. Bill Parcells developed Phil Simms. Mike Holmgren developed Brett Favre. Bill Walsh developed Ken Anderson as an assistant coach and Joe Montana as a head coach. Weeb Ewbank developed Johnny Unitas and Joe Namath. Tom Landry developed Meredith, Morton, Staubach and White.

Good coaches can also rescue talented veterans who have not reached their potential. Bart Starr was struggling without confidence until Vince Lombardi came along. Frank Ryan was frustrated by the lack of coaching that former quarterback Bob Waterfield provided on the Rams. After being traded to the Browns, Ryan thrived under Blanton Collier. Collier then worked his magic on Steelers refugee Bill Nelsen. Tommy Thompson was a failed single wing tailback because he had limited running skills, but Greasy Neale converted him to a star T formation quarterback in Philadelphia. Len Dawson was a number one draft choice whose confidence and mechanics were both completely shot after five years on the bench in Cleveland and Pittsburgh before he signed with the Chiefs, and Hank Stram helped resurrect his Hall of Fame career. Don Coryell turned around the floundering careers of Jim Hart with the Cardinals and Dan Fouts with the Chargers. Tom Flores reinvigorated Jim Plunkett in Oakland after he had been cut by the 49ers. Mike Shanahan finetuned the final years of John Elway so that they were the very best ones of his career.

Proponents of Randall Cunningham and Vinny Testaverde make the point that a big reason that these two quarterbacks never fulfilled their potential was that they did not receive adequate coaching. Buddy Ryan's idea of offense when he was coaching the Eagles was that Randall should come up with a couple of spectacular plays to augment his defense. Vinny was bounced from coach to coach, playing under eight different coaches in his long career, an unpromising fate for a professional. Fifteen other quarterbacks suffered under at least 8 different head coaches in the NFL:

Quarterback	Coaches
George Blanda	10
Archie Manning	10
Steve DeBerg	10
Chris Chandler	10
Marty Domres	9
Sammy Baugh	8
Jeff Blake	8
Steve Beurelein	8
Jeff George	8
Sonny Jurgensen	8
Greg Landry	8
Bill Munson	8
Dick Shiner	8
Norm Snead	8
Vinny Testaverde	8
Dave Krieg	8

While the 16 quarterbacks in the first table won 28 championships, the 16 in this table won just six. Two of them were by Sammy Baugh under Hall of Fame coach Ray Flaherty who led the Redskins for Baugh's first six seasons. In the last 10 years of his career, Sammy had seven coaches and no titles. George Blanda's long career was divided into thirds. He had two coaches in his first 10 years in Chicago where he was a backup on a championship team. He also had two coaches in his final nine years as mostly a kicker in Oakland. In the middle, he quarterbacked the Oilers to two AFL titles in seven years under six coaches. Sonny Jurgensen won the other title for this group when he was a benchwarmer for the 1960 Eagles.

Mostly what this group experienced in the NFL was losing, and that frequently leads to a quarterback controversy. All of the 16 quarterbacks on the latter list were involved in at least one quarterback controversy in their careers. In fact, most of the 16 on the former list were as well. Quarterback controversies are almost inevitable in every quarterback's career, but losing teams and coaching changes exacerbate the situation. There have been some job sharing arrangements for two quarterbacks that have worked, but these were mostly far in the past. Even Hall of Famer Sid Luckman shared his job in the days of two-way players. His coach, George Halas, liked to keep his backs fresh by rotating them so that even though Luckman played most of the time, there was still playing time in each game for Charlie O'Rourke or Bob Snyder or Gene Ronzani to spell Luckman. In Washington at that time, Sammy Baugh and Frankie Filchock regularly platooned at tailback. When the Redskins went to the T formation in 1944, Baugh struggled with it at first so Washington sometimes put Filchock at quarterback and Baugh at tailback at the same time with either likely to take the snap. In Green Bay, Curly Lambeau always had more than one passer — Arnie Herber and Bob Monnett in the early 1930s and Herber and Cecil Isbell in the late 1930s.

In the 1950s, there were several notable job-sharing situations. Hall of Famers Bob Waterfield and Norm Van Brocklin ended up alternating quarters for the Rams in the early 50s, and in one game in 1953, Rams coach Hampton Pool had Van Brocklin and Rudy Bukich alternating plays. The following preseason, Pool tried sending his backup quarterbacks, Bill Wade and Rudy Bukich, to the huddle to relay the play and then racing right back off the field. Commissioner Bert Bell outlawed that plan immediately. Paul Brown switched from messenger guards to quarterbacks for one game and shuttled Milt Plum and Jim Ninowski in a 1958 loss to the Giants. Bobby Layne and Tobin Rote each played every game in 1957 until Layne broke his leg for the title-bound Lions. Bobby Thomason and Adrian Burk shared the job in Philadelphia throughout the decade. Giants offensive coach Vince Lombardi instituted a practice in the mid–1950s whereby backup Don Heinrich would start each game and play for a few series, testing the opposing defense so that real starter Charlie Conerly could come in and try to exploit the weaknesses that Heinrich uncovered. If nothing else, the practice probably extended the career of the aging and battered Conerly, and the Giants did win a title in 1956 and go to the championship game in 1958 and 1959.

Since then, there have been few such arrangements. Tom Landry brought Don Meredith along slowly by having him share time with veteran Eddie LeBaron, even having the two alternate plays at one point. After Meredith retired, Landry had a difficult time deciding between Craig Morton and Roger Staubach and went back and forth between them for a couple of years — again even having them alternate plays in one game in 1971. Don Shula went to a Super Bowl with the quarterback tandem of "Wood-Strock," David Woodley and Don Strock, but Dan Marino quickly brought that era to a close. Finally, former Cowboy Dan Reeves revived the alternating quarterbacks practice for one game in 1992 when an injured John Elway forced Reeves to rely on rookies Tommy Maddox and Shawn Moore. Alternating quarterbacks was never popular or successful anywhere.

Quarterback controversies are always difficult. The rarest type is the ménage à trois, involving three quarterbacks. The Bears tried this twice in 10 years with three "L's" and then three "B's." In 1948, rookies Johnny Lujack and Bobby Layne supplemented aging Sid Luckman. The Bears traded Layne in 1949 and awarded the starter's job to Lujack who looked to be a star until a shoulder injury ended his career. By 1954, Chicago added rookies Ed Brown and Zeke Bratkowski to holdover George Blanda, and the three competed through the 1958 season when Blanda retired. Brown slowly gave way to Bratkowski by 1961 and was traded. Bratkowski was traded to the Rams in 1962 for Billy Wade who took the Bears to a title.

Another franchise to experiment with a threesome was the Rams in the 1970s who continually had one quarterback coming, one starting and one going, whether it was John Hadl-James Harris-Ron Jaworski, James Harris-Ron Jaworski-Pat Haden or Haden-Joe Namath-Vince Ferragamo. The Steelers in the early 1970s had a threesome of young quarterbacks with Terry Hanratty beginning in 1968, Terry Bradshaw in 1970 and Joe Giliam in 1972. Each had a crack at trying to lead the Steel Curtain's offense before Bradshaw finally claimed the job for good in 1974.

Several other teams have had to make the tough choice between two young starters. The Cowboys twice chose the Hall of Famer, picking Staubach over Craig Morton and Troy Aikman over Steve Walsh. Similarly, the Rams picked All Pro Roman Gabriel over also-ran Bill Munson. In fact, Terry Baker was briefly involved in this trifecta of young talent as well. The Jets took the sometimes-spectacular Richard Todd over the woeful Matt Robinson. The Oilers chose first round pick Dan Pastorini over second round pick Lynn Dickey, partly because Dickey kept getting hurt. When Dickey finally got healthy in Green Bay, he put up the better numbers of the two. Finally in 1958, Paul Brown had 22-year-old Jim Ninowski and 23-year old Milt Plum. Plum won the job, and Ninowski was traded to Detroit in 1960. After two horrible years as the Lions' starter, Ninowski was reacquired by Cleveland for Plum with whom Brown could not get along. While sifting through those two mugs, Brown let Hall of Famer Len Dawson get away.

Youth is generally served in these quarterback competitions, even when it's two veterans like elderly Y.A. Title (35) and ancient Charlie Conerly (39) or Billy Kilmer (32) and Sonny Jurgensen (37) or Rudy Bukich (32) and Billy Wade (35) or Jeff Hostetler (30) and Phil Simms (35) although Simms did win his job back in 1993 at age 37 for one last year. When it is clearly a case of old versus young, the young quarterback always wins out in the end. Sid Luckman was succeeded by Johnny Lujack; Ron Jaworski was succeeded by Randall Cunningham; Charlie Johnson was succeeded by Jim Hart; Jim Zorn was succeeded by Dave Krieg, Bob Waterfield was succeeded by Norm Van Brocklin who was then succeeded by Billy Wade. Kurt Warner was succeeded by Marc Bulger. Drew Bledsoe was succeeded by Tom Brady. Frankie Albert was succeeded by Y.A. Tittle who was succeeded by John Brodie. Joe Montana was succeeded by Steve Young who was succeeded by Jeff Garcia. While in some cases the supplanted older quarterback in this constant carousel moves on to another team, all that's left for some is retirement.

Injuries

One reason that teams are constantly recruiting for the quarterback of the future is the frequency of injuries in football. Any starting quarterback is always just one play away from a career altering injury. The defense targets the quarterback to either shake him up or knock him out. Giants coach Steve Owen once boiled the game down to, "Football is a game played in the dirt and always will be." In November 1977,

eight quarterbacks were knocked out of the game on one Sunday, including Fran Tarkenton, Lynn Dickey and Bill Munson all suffering broken legs. In 1986, seven starting quarterbacks were knocked out during the seventh week of the season. In 1990, six starters were kayoed in successive weeks, 12 quarterback kills in two weeks. That was also the season of the infamous Body Bag Game in which the Eagles' defense hit the Redskins so hard that it seemed they were being carted out in body bags. Eleven Redskins were knocked out of the game, including both quarterbacks, so that Washington had to finish the game with kick returner Brian Mitchell calling signals.

Killing the quarterback is nothing new. Sammy Baugh would get hit on every play whether he had the ball or not because the rules allowed passers to be hit until the whistle blew. Passers gained some protection when that rule was changed, but defenders still made their reputations by nailing the quarterback. Defensive end Ed Sprinkle of the Bears was notorious for questionable hits; he bruised Bob Waterfield's jaw in 1947 and broke Otto Graham's nose in 1951. Charlie Conerly was driven from a game in which the Eagles sacked Giants quarterbacks 14 times in 1952, and Arnold Galiffa had his back broken in another Giants-Eagles game in 1953. Y.A. Tittle's cheek was fractured by the Lions in 1953, and Bobby Layne was given a severe concussion when he was speared from the blind side by Ed Meadows of the Bears in 1956. The Raiders' Ben Davidson was another infamous quarterback hunter. In 1967, he broke Joe Namath's cheekbone and in 1970 speared a prone Lenny Dawson in the back. Namath said of Davidson at the time, "It's one thing to give a guy a good lick and he gets hurt. That's the game. But it's another to twist my leg in a pile-up like Davidson did when I was a rookie." In 1980, Ron Jaworski was speared from the blind side by Mike Hartenstine of the Bears, but it was Bear quarterback Jim McMahon who took perhaps the nastiest hit of all when Charles Martin of the Packers picked him up and drove him into the ground on his bad shoulder in 1986.

Hits like these can change a team's season. The game that Layne was driven out of by Meadows in the second quarter clinched the division for Chicago. The Eagles lost two seasons in the 1990s to Randall Cunningham going down to leg injuries in the first four games. The brutality can also provide an opportunity for the backup quarterback. Late in 1934, the Bears broke two bones in Giants passer Harry Newman's back, but rookie Ed Danowski replaced Newman and had the last laugh by leading New York to the title over Chicago. Giants starter Phil Simms, 56 years later, went down late in the season and was replaced by Jeff Hostetler who led the team to a Super Bowl win. Trent Green signed as a free agent with the Rams, went down to a knee injury and was replaced by unknown Kurt Warner who led the Rams to the title in 1999. Drew Bledsoe was knocked out of the second game of the year with an injured sternum and never got his job back as Tom Brady took the Patriots to their first improbable title in 2001.

Momentous hits happen in the playoffs as well. Sammy Baugh suffered a concussion in punt coverage when he was tackling returner Sid Luckman in the 1943 title game and missed much of the loss to the Bears; two years later, a hard hit bruised his ribs in the title match against the Rams, and again the Redskins lost. In 1963, the Bears crumpled Y.A. Tittle's knee and won the championship while Tittle gamely struggled to finish the game. In 1965, Bart Starr badly bruised his ribs trying to make a tackle on the first play of a playoff against the Colts and missed the rest of the game. The Colts had lost both Johnny Unitas and Gary Cuozzo that season and were using runner Tom Matte at quarterback. Backup Zeke Bratkowski led Green Bay to an overtime win, and then Starr returned heavily bandaged to lead the Packers over the Browns for the title the next week. Joe Montana was crushed by Jim Burt in the first quarter of a 49–3 loss to the Giants in 1987 and missed the rest of the game with a concussion.

Crushing playoff hits can have other consequences, too. Tony Siragusa was fined $10,000 for driving the Raiders' Rich Gannon into the ground in 2001, and the Eagles' Hugh Douglass was fined $35,000 for slamming down the Bears' Jim Miller after an interception in 2002. In 2006, Steeler Kimo Von Oelhoffen hit Carson Palmer's knee on the Bengals' first pass play and drove him from the game. The result was a new rule forbidding defensive linemen from hitting quarterbacks below the knee.

Injuries often shape a quarterback's career. Joe Namath's knees lessened his overall ability as a professional. Sonny Jurgensen took two years to recover from a severe shoulder separation. Phil Simms missed two of his first five seasons with knee and thumb injuries. Lynn Dickey missed 53 games in his first nine seasons to hip, knee, leg and shoulder injuries. Joe Montana injured his elbow in training camp in 1991 and missed nearly two complete seasons. Kurt Warner's brilliant career was derailed by thumb injuries. Injuries can also end a career. Johnny Lujack and Greg Cook both had to retire as young men because of shoulder injuries. Neil Lomax had an arthritic hip that ended his career. The most brutal and shocking ending was Joe Theismann having his leg snapped like a twig from a tackle by Lawrence Taylor on Monday Night Football in 1985.

Although the Theismann injury made for gory TV, concussions are scarier still. The 2002 rule outlawing helmet-to-helmet hits was motivated by a desire to minimize concussions, especially to quarterbacks. Ron Jaworski claims to have suffered 32 concussions in his career although that is hard to believe. Concussions caused Chris Miller to stop playing for three years before trying again in Denver, and then he was stymied again by another concussion. Roger Staubach's career was brought to an end by two severe concussions in his last year. Steve Young had eight total concussions, including four in his last three years. The final one dealt by Aeneas Williams ended his career. Troy Aikman suffered 10 concussions; the last by LaVar Arrington finished his playing days as well.

New helmets with longer jaw lines were introduced in the past few years to help with the concussion problem, but they offer limited protection. This helmet advance is the latest in a number of equipment changes instigated by quarterback injuries over the years, but safety changes sometimes are greeted with derision. Linebacker Jack Lambert once stated that they should just put dresses on quarterbacks, and Roger Staubach himself asked, "Do they want me to wear a little red flag on my hip?" when the in-the-grasp rule was put into place in 1979. Helmets themselves weren't mandatory till 1943, and Arnie Herber is thought to be the last passer to play without one in 1940. Facemasks originated in the late 1940s, but at first were brittle and ineffective. After severe facial injuries to Otto Graham, Y.A. Tittle and Jim Finks forced them to wear makeshift masks in 1953, facemasks were made mandatory for all players in 1954, with some exceptions. Finks was injured again in 1954 and wore a mask that UPI reported made him look like a "man from Mars." Paul Brown is credited with getting the facemask perfected for Graham in 1955. Bobby Layne was the last quarterback to play without a facemask in 1962.

Two pieces of quarterback equipment were particularly unusual. In the 1930s, Cecil Isbell of the Packers dislocated his left shoulder so regularly that he wore a leather harness in which a chain ran from his torso to his arm to keep him from raising it too high. In the 1977, Bob Griese became the first NFL quarterback to wear eyeglasses, which he had trouble with fogging up on humid days. Advances in knee braces were brought about to keep passers like Joe Namath, Bill Nelsen and Dick Wood on the field in the 1960s. In the 1970s, quarterbacks began wearing flak jackets to protect their ribs after an inventor brought one to Dan Pastorini as Dan was recovering from broken ribs in his hospital room. Dan wore one successfully into the playoffs that year.

Even when they manage to stay upright, quarterbacks take a beating, whether they are scramblers or pure pocket passers. Both types are represented on the list of quarterbacks who have been sacked the most since the mid 1960s when "sacked" began to be counted. When we add in some unofficial numbers from the early 1960s, slightly built Fran Tarkenton, who surprisingly didn't miss a game due to injury until he broke his leg in his 17th NFL season, is at the top.

Quarterback	Sacked	Passes	Sacked %
Fran Tarkenton	572	6467	8.1%
John Elway	516	7250	6.6%
Dave Krieg	494	5311	8.5%
Randall Cunningham	484	4289	10.1%
Phil Simms	477	4647	9.3%
Drew Bledsoe	467	6717	6.5%
Warren Moon	458	6823	6.3%
Brett Favre	424	8223	4.9%
Vinny Testaverde	408	6529	5.9%
Craig Morton	405	3786	9.7%

Quarterbacks are sacked because they have a weak line or they cautiously hold the ball too long or they try to scramble around before their receivers are open. This table lists quarterback who were sacked the greatest percentage of pass plays with a minimum of 100 sacks.

Quarterback	Sacked	Passes	Sacked %
Rob Johnson	140	806	14.8%
Bob Berry	193	1173	14.1%
Steve Fuller	152	1066	12.5%
Tony Banks	327	2356	12.2%
Hugh Millen	126	926	12.0%
Greg Landry	310	2300	11.9%
Bart Starr	235	1847	11.3%
Joe Pisarcik	112	898	11.1%
David Carr	249	2070	10.7%
Aaron Brooks	235	1963	10.7%

Most of those quarterbacks were fairly mobile. By contrast, the lowest sacked percentage in history was attained by fairly immobile Dan Marino and his quick release. He was sacked only 270 times on over 8,600 pass plays, a percentage of 3.1. The only other quarterback under 4 percent is fairly immobile but quick on the draw Peyton Manning with 3.4 percent. Those who are the most durable soldier on through the pain. Bobby Layne once asserted he proved he was tough enough to be a quarterback when he played for the atrocious New York Bulldogs in 1949 and learned he could stay in the pocket and get hit without it bothering him. Toughness is Johnny Unitas throwing the winning 39-yard touchdown against the Bears in the last 17 seconds after Doug Atkins and Bill George gashed his mouth and nose so badly that he had to slap mud on his face to stop the bleeding in 1960. Toughness is Terry Bradshaw throwing the 75-yard winning touchdown to Lynn Swann in the Super Bowl as he was being knocked unconscious by D.D. Lewis of the Cowboys. Brett Favre further defined toughness to USA Today as, "To play every week and to be someone that your teammates can rely on to be there for them." He would know, he played through severe ankle sprains, knee ligament problems, broken thumbs, and the death of his father and tops the list of consecutive quarterback starts:

Quarterback	Consecutive Starts
Brett Favre	237
Peyton Manning	144
Ron Jaworski	116
Joe Ferguson	107
Otto Graham	99
Dan Marino	95
Tom Brady	94
Johnny Unitas	92
Roman Gabriel	89

Quarterback	Consecutive Starts
Jim Everett	87
Richard Todd	86
Aaron Brooks	82
Trent Green	82
Frankie Albert	79
Steve Grogan	78
Fran Tarkenton	73
John Hadl	73
Trent Dilfer	72
Rich Gannon	71
Joe Theismann	71
Dan Fouts	69
Drew Bledsoe	64
Jim Hart	63
Jeff Garcia	61
Jake Delhomme	59
Babe Parilli	58

The first NFL quarterback to top 50 consecutive starts was Bobby Layne who had a streak of 54 in the 1950s. However, Frankie Albert never missed a game in the AAFC and then played in his first 25 games in the NFL to set the high mark for pro football with 79. He was quickly surpassed by Otto Graham who never missed a game in 10 years, although he did not start two. The first was the very first Browns game in 1946 when Graham gentlemanly stepped aside to let Cleveland-local Cliff Lewis start. The other was when George Ratterman started a game for Graham late in 1953 since the Browns had already clinched the division. Johnny Unitas took the unofficial NFL record in the 1960s with 92 although he never passed Graham's 99. In the 1980s, Ron Jaworski and Joe Ferguson each had a streak running concurrently and both passed Unitas together. Jaworski continued on for nine games past Ferguson's 107. Favre then passed Jaworski in 1999 and has doubled it since then. Peyton Manning is six seasons behind the seemingly indestructible Favre. If the three strike replacement games are not counted, then Dan Marino would have had a streak of 145 games in the 1980s.

Age

If nothing else brings down Favre, age will. Age brings about the destruction of all things, and time is the enemy of every athlete. Injuries, age and declining skills halt every quarterback's career. Late in his career, Dan Marino told one of his receivers, "Get more open — I'm getting old." On average, a quarterback's prime seasons are finished by the time he reaches 33. At the ages of 33 and 34 there were roughly 100 quarterbacks who played in the league. Before the 1960s, only Arnie Herber, Sammy Baugh and Charlie Conerly had played on past 34. The 1960s saw the first influx of 35 year olds like Y.A. Tittle, George Blanda, Bobby Layne, Ed Brown, Babe Parilli and Tobin Rote, although there is still a decline at that age. At 35, there were 78 quarterback-seasons and only 55 of them were by quarterbacks who threw at least 100 passes. Randall Cunningham threw for the most touchdowns at 35 in 1998 with 34, and Brett Favre had the most yards in 2004 with 4,088. At 35, Babe Parilli threw for 31 touchdowns in 1964; John Elway threw for 26 touchdowns in 1995; Fran Tarkenton in 1975 and Lynn Dickey in 1984 threw for 25 touchdowns; and John Brodie in 1970 and Joe Theismann in 1984 threw for 24. Tobin Rote led the Chargers to the AFL title in 1963 with a passer rating 133 percent of the league average. Charlie Conerly and Roger Staubach also won titles at 35. Quarterbacks who jumped the shark at 35 include George Blanda who threw 42 interceptions to 27 touchdowns in 1962; Bobby Layne who threw 17 interceptions to 9 touchdowns also in 1962; John Hadl who threw 21 interceptions to 6 touchdowns in 1975; Jim Hart who threw 20 interceptions to 9 touchdowns in 1979; and Dan Fouts who threw 22 interceptions to 16 touchdowns in 1986.

At age 36, there were just 71 quarterback-seasons and only 54 with at least 100 attempts. Y.A. Tittle set the mark for touchdowns with 33, followed by 26 by John Elway in 1996 and Rich Gannon in 2002, as well as 25 by Roger Staubach in 1978. Gannon passed for an amazing 4,689 yards in the Raiders run to the Super Bowl in 2002. Y.A. Tittle, Roger Staubach, Steve DeBerg, Steve Young, Brett Favre and Vinny Testaverde all exceeded 3,000 yards as well. Favre and Testaverde were spent, however, as were Babe Parilli, Lynn Dickey and Jim Kelly. Favre threw 29 interceptions to 20 touchdowns in 2004; Testaverde went 25 to 21 in 2000; Parilli went 26 to 18 in 1965; Dickey went 17 to 15 in 1985; and Kelly went 18 to 14 in 1996. At 36, though, Earl Morrall won a title with the Colts in 1970, and Jim Plunket won one with the Raiders in 1983.

Age 37 brings further decline, with only 54 quarterback seasons and 34 with at least 100 pass attempts. High achievers again include Y.A. Tittle with 36 touchdowns and 3,145 yards in 1963, Steve Young with 36 touchdowns and 4,170 yards in 1998 and Warren Moon with 4,264 yards in 1994. John Elway won his first Super Bowl in Denver with 27 touchdowns and 3,635 yards, and Johnny Unitas won his last title in Baltimore in 1970. Roger Staubach retired on the strength of 27 touchdowns and 3,586 yards in 1979, while Sammy Baugh was washed up in 1951 with seven touchdowns and 17 interceptions.

Thirty-eight is the oldest age that any quarterback ever won a title. That was accomplished by two of the 39 quarterbacks who played at that age. Just 21 of them threw at least 100 passes, including backup Earl Morrall of the undefeated Dolphins in 1972 and John Elway of the champion Broncos in 1998. Warren Moon had the big numbers with 33 touchdowns and 4,228 yards in 1995, while Charlie Conerly led the NFL in passing in 1959, and Craig Morton had one last fling in 1981 with 21 touchdowns and 3,195 yards. Fran Tarkenton finished his career in 1978 throwing for 25 touchdowns and 3,468 yards, but also 32 interceptions. Dan Marino went out gasping with 12 touchdowns and 17 interceptions.

At 39, only nine of 20 quarterbacks threw at least 100 passes. The most significant season was Doug Flutie's 2001 with 15 touchdowns, 18 interceptions and 3,464 yards. George Blanda threw 17 touchdowns and 21 interceptions in 1966, and Len Dawson threw 7 touchdowns and 13 interceptions in 1974. Charlie Conerly, John Unitas, and Sonny Jurgensen all saw spot duty at 39. After 40, the leadership positions are all Warren Moon who threw for 25 touchdowns and 3,678 yards at 40 and 11 touchdowns and 1,132 yards at 41. Sonny Jurgensen had a very nice year at 40 with 11 touchdowns, 5 interceptions and a passer rating 147 percent of the league average. There are only 15 quarterback seasons at age 40, five at 41 and 42, three at age 43 (Blanda, Moon and Flutie), two at 44 (Blanda and DeBerg) and one in each year from 45 to 48 (all Blanda). Blanda even won an MVP award on his kicking and 55 pass attempts in 1970 at 43. Of this he said, "I have to keep playing so that people over 40 will have somebody to root for on Sunday afternoons." The career arc of most quarterbacks ends by age 35. The healthiest and cleverest may continue on through age 38, but only freaks of nature like Blanda, Moon and Flutie go much beyond that, and no one past 38 has ever led his team to a championship.

Coaching Careers

In their post-playing careers, quarterbacks have assumed many guises. Carlos Brown went into acting. Jack Kemp and Heath Shuler were elected to the U.S. Congress. tailback Whizzer White served on the U.S. Supreme Court. Paddy Driscoll, Davey O'Brien, Adrian Burk, Dean Look, Gary Lane and Pete Liske became NFL referees. Several former quarterbacks became assistant coaches, everyone from Sid Luckman and Kenny Anderson to John Hufnagle and Jason Garrett. 20 former T formation quarterbacks have become NFL head coaches, but they lost more games than they won; passing tailbacks like Benny Friedman, Paddy Driscoll, Cecil Isbell and Curly Lambeau are excluded from this table:

Coach	Years	Teams	Wins	Losses	Ties	%	Post Wins	Post Losses	Titles
Albert, Frankie	1956–58	SFF	19	16	0	.543	0	1	
Baugh, Sammy	1960–61, 1964	NYJ, TEN	18	24	0	.429	0	0	
Filchock, Frank	1960–61	DEN	7	20	1	.268	0	0	
Flores, Tom	1979–87, 1992–94	OAK, SEA	97	87	0	.527	8	3	1980, 1983
Gilmer, Harry	1965–66	DET	10	16	2	.393	0	0	
Jones, June	1994–96, 1998	ATL, SDC	22	36	0	.379	0	0	
Kubiak, Gary	2006	HOU	6	10	0	.375	0	0	
Marchibroda, Ted	1975–79, 1992–98	IND, BAL	87	98	1	.470	2	4	
Molesworth, Keith	1953	IND	3	9	0	.250	0	0	

Coach	Years	Teams	Wins	Losses	Ties	%	Post Wins	Post Losses	Titles
Payton, Sean	2006	NOS	10	6	0	.625	1	1	
Rauch, John	1966–70	OAK, BUF	40	28	2	.586	2	2	
Ronzani, Gene	1950–53	GBP	14	31	1	.315	0	0	
Sherman, Allie	1961–69	NYG, XBRK	63	59	4	.516	0	3	
Snyder, Bob	1947	STL	6	6	0	.500	0	0	
Spurrier, Steve	2002–03	WSH	12	20	0	.375	0	0	
Starr, Bart	1975–83	GBP	52	76	3	.408	1	1	
Stephenson, Kay	1983–85	BUF	10	26	0	.278	0	0	
Van Brocklin, Norm	1961–74	MIN, ATL	66	100	7	.402	0	0	
Waterfield, Bob	1960–62	STL	9	24	1	.279	0	0	
Wyche, Sam	1984–95	CIN, TBB	84	107	0	.440	3	2	
Totals			635	699	71	.476	17	18	

Playing Outside the NFL

Some NFL quarterbacks have ended their long careers in another league. Glenn Dobbs, Jack Jacobs and Pete Liske finished their careers in Canada. These quarterbacks ended up in the failed WFL.

Quarterback	League	Years	Att	Comp	%	Yards	Y/Att	Y/Comp	TD	Int	Rating
George Mira	NFL	1964–71	346	148	42.8%	2110	6.1	14.3	19	20	57.4
George Mira	WFL	1974–75	567	278	49.0%	3923	6.9	14.1	29	26	69.7
George Mira Total			913	426	46.7%	6033	6.6	14.2	48	46	65.0
Pete Beathard	NFL/AFL	1964–73	1284	575	44.8%	8243	6.4	14.3	43	86	49.4
Pete Beathard	WFL	1974–75	381	188	49.3%	2133	5.6	11.3	9	18	54.7
Pete Beathard Total			1665	763	45.8%	10376	6.2	13.6	52	104	50.6
Bob Davis	NFL	1967–73	324	133	41.0%	1553	4.8	11.7	14	23	41.1
Bob Davis	WFL	1974–75	608	322	53.0%	4193	6.9	13.0	28	35	66.3
Bob Davis Total			932	455	48.8%	5746	6.2	12.6	42	58	57.5
Edd Hargett	NFL	1969–73	437	205	46.9%	2727	6.2	13.3	11	10	66.0
Edd Hargett	WFL	1974–75	398	209	52.5%	2663	6.7	12.7	20	18	71.6
Edd Hargett Total			835	414	49.6%	5390	6.5	13.0	31	28	68.7
Mike Taliaferro	NFL	1964–72	966	419	43.4%	5241	5.4	12.5	36	63	46.1
Mike Taliaferro	WFL	1974	143	74	51.7%	833	5.8	11.3	5	8	57.8
Mike Taliaferro Total			1109	493	44.5%	6074	5.5	12.3	41	71	47.6
Don Trull	NFL	1964–69	637	276	43.3%	3980	6.2	14.4	30	28	61.6
Don Trull	WFL	1974	31	16	51.6%	117	3.8	7.3	2	4	42.7
Don Trull Total			668	292	43.7%	4097	6.1	14.0	32	32	60.1
John Huarte	NFL	1966–72	48	19	39.6%	230	4.8	12.1	1	5	22.4
John Huarte	WFL	1974–75	373	192	51.5%	2966	8.0	15.4	28	18	83.0
John Huarte Total			421	211	50.1%	3196	7.6	15.1	29	23	75.7
Don Horn	NFL	1967–74	465	232	49.9%	3369	7.2	14.5	20	36	55.9
Don Horn	WFL	1975	272	158	58.1%	1742	6.4	11.0	11	12	72.3
Don Horn Total			737	390	52.9%	5111	6.9	13.1	31	48	62.0
Daryle Lamonica	NFL	1963–74	2601	1288	49.5%	19154	7.4	14.9	164	138	72.9
Daryle Lamonica	WFL	1975	19	9	47.4%	90	4.7	10.0	1	3	39.3
Daryle Lamonica Total			2620	1297	49.5%	19244	7.3	14.8	165	141	72.5
King Corcoran	NFL	1968	7	3	42.9%	33	4.7	11.0	0	3	17.9
King Corcoran	WFL	1974–75	645	325	50.4%	4072	6.3	12.5	34	36	64.7
King Corcoran Total			652	328	50.3%	4105	6.3	12.5	34	39	62.7

While Jim Druckenmiller, Jeff Brohm and Casey Weldon ended their abysmal careers in the frightful XFL, some memorable quarterbacks finished in the USFL.

Quarterback	League	Years	Att	Comp	%	Yards	Y/Att	Y/Comp	TD	Int	Rating
Matt Robinson	NFL	1977–82	523	244	46.7%	3519	6.7	14.4	18	38	50.2
Matt Robinson	USFL	1984–85	545	281	51.6%	3869	7.1	13.8	22	32	63.6
Matt Robinson Total			**1068**	**525**	**49.2%**	**7388**	**6.9**	**14.1**	**40**	**70**	**57.0**
Brian Sipe	NFL	1974–83	3439	1944	56.5%	23713	6.9	12.2	154	149	74.8
Brian Sipe	USFL	1984–85	413	247	59.8%	3225	7.8	13.1	21	17	84.3
Brian Sipe Total			**3852**	**2191**	**56.9%**	**26938**	**7.0**	**12.3**	**175**	**166**	**75.8**
Mike Rae	NFL	1976–79	249	124	49.8%	1536	6.2	12.4	12	14	61.9
Mike Rae	USFL	1985	319	175	54.9%	1964	6.2	11.2	11	10	71.9
Mike Rae Total			**568**	**299**	**52.6%**	**3500**	**6.2**	**11.7**	**23**	**24**	**67.5**
Bobby Scott	NFL	1973–81	500	237	47.4%	2781	5.6	11.7	15	28	51.4
Bobby Scott	USFL	1983	374	210	56.1%	2813	7.5	13.4	11	19	68.9
Bobby Scott Total			**874**	**447**	**51.1%**	**5594**	**6.4**	**12.5**	**26**	**47**	**58.9**
Joe Gilliam	NFL	1972–75	331	147	44.4%	2103	6.4	14.3	9	17	53.2
Joe Gilliam	USFL	1983	102	40	39.2%	673	6.6	16.8	5	12	39.0
Joe Gilliam Total			**433**	**187**	**43.2%**	**2776**	**6.4**	**14.8**	**14**	**29**	**47.7**
Ed Luther	NFL	1980–84	460	245	53.3%	3187	6.9	13.0	12	23	63.2
Ed Luther	USFL	1985	400	240	60.0%	2792	7.0	11.6	15	21	71.8
Ed Luther Total			**860**	**485**	**56.4%**	**5979**	**7.0**	**12.3**	**27**	**44**	**67.2**

4

Glory

As great as John Elway had played in his first 15 years in the NFL, he still had one last hurdle to clear in 1997: winning the Super Bowl. Even though he hauled three mediocre Bronco teams to the Super Bowl in the 1980s, won more games than any other quarterback in history and led more fourth quarter game-winning drives than anyone else, some critics still maintained Elway was a fraud who could not win the big one. Once he won not just one but two Super Bowls, though, all doubt was removed that Elway belonged in the football pantheon. Pro football players are paid to win, not just play, and that is truest of all for quarterbacks.

Winning

Three of the four major team sports rank individual players by wins and losses; only basketball does not. In baseball and hockey, wins and losses are attributed to the main defensive player on the team — the pitcher in baseball and the goalie in hockey. In football, however, wins and losses are attributed to the offensive player with the ball in his hands, the player commonly judged to have the greatest effect on the outcome of this ultimate team sport, the quarterback. The most obvious shortcoming to ranking quarterbacks this way is the fact that football is such a team game that individual heroics are much less distinguishable than in a sport like baseball where so much depends on the man-on-man battle of pitcher and batter. In addition, the method by which wins are assigned is overly simplistic; the starting quarterback gets the win or loss no matter how much he played or how much he had to do with the result. A quarterback could get hurt in the first quarter or be benched because his team was down by 21 points, and if his team wins, he gets a victory. Like every other measure of quarterback effectiveness, wins and losses should be viewed in the context of other factors.

The list of active players' won-lost records is readily available from the annual *NFL Record & Fact Book*, but the numbers for pre–1980s records are nowhere to be found. I went back through 50 years of newspaper accounts to accumulate these listings and supplemented this research with team media guides on the rare occasions when starting quarterback information was provided. In older newspaper accounts, it was often difficult to ascertain the starting quarterback. The most difficult period was the first few years of the AFL when press coverage was very sparse so that sometimes I had to make an educated guess as to the starter. I did not attempt to do much with records prior to 1950 for two reasons. First, the T formation was just supplanting the single-wing in the 1940s so it was not always clear who the team's signal caller was. Second, 1950 marks the full transition to two-platoon football where the modern quarterback emerges, with his skills no longer diminished by spending half his time playing safety on defense.

Certain exceptions were made in the 1950s data due to the odd ways some teams used their quarterbacks. As noted earlier, the Rams used Hall of Famers Bob Waterfield and Norm Van Brocklin in alternating quarters, the Packers played both Tobin Rote and Babe Parilli, the 1957 Lions played both Rote and Bobby Layne and the Giants used both Charlie Conerly and Don Heinrich in most games in the later years of the decade. In all of these instances, I attributed the wins and losses to both quarterbacks as long as they both played because of the regularity of the way the team used its passers.

With that said, the 30 quarterbacks who have won at least 84 starts through 2006 are:

Name	Wins	Losses	Ties	Percentage
Elway, John	148	82	1	.643
Favre, Brett	147	90	0	.620
Marino, Dan	147	93	0	.613
Tarkenton, Fran	125	106	6	.540
Unitas, John	119	57	4	.672
Montana, Joe	117	47	0	.713
Bradshaw, Terry	107	51	0	.677
Graham, Otto	103	17	4	.847
Moon, Warren	102	100	0	.505
Kelly, Jim	101	59	0	.631
Krieg, Dave	98	77	0	.560
Bledsoe, Drew	98	95	0	.508
Stabler, Ken	96	49	1	.661
Griese, Bob	95	56	3	.627
Dawson, Len	95	58	8	.615
Simms, Phil	95	64	0	.597
Young, Steve	94	49	0	.657
Baugh, Sammy	94	50	7	.646
Starr, Bart	94	59	5	.611
Aikman, Troy	94	71	0	.570
Manning, Peyton	92	52	0	.639
Anderson, Ken	91	81	0	.529
McNair, Steve	89	58	0	.605
Testaverde, Vinny	88	119	1	.425
Tittle, Y.A.	87	70	3	.553
Hart, Jim	87	87	5	.500
Staubach, Roger	86	29	0	.748
Gabriel, Roman	86	65	7	.566
Fouts, Dan	86	83	1	.509
Layne, Bobby	84	60	4	.581

This list is heavily dotted by recent quarterbacks who played more games because seasons are longer and, in many cases, careers last longer. Dan Marino heads the list of most starts with 240, and only three quarterbacks who played before 1978 make the top 10 in starts: Fran Tarkenton with 237, Johnny Unitas with 180 and Jim Hart with 179. When the league switched from a 12 to a 14 game season in 1961, just seven quarterbacks had won at least 50 games: Otto Graham 103, Charlie Conerly 77, Bobby Layne 75, Norm Van Brocklin 75, Bob Waterfield 58, Y.A. Tittle 55 and Frankie Albert 52. Seventeen years later when the NFL went to a 16-game schedule in 1978, all but Waterfield and Albert still ranked in the top 15 of quarterback wins that went from Unitas' 118 wins to Sonny Jurgensen's 68 wins. Today, only Graham, Tittle and Layne from 1961 remain in the top 30 in wins, while only 10 of the 1978 top 15 remain in the top 30 as game and victory totals continue to grow.

As an imperfect comparison because of the nature of the pre–1950 game, the following table lists the top 10 of estimated wins for early passers and signal callers. Six of these 11 field generals are in the Hall of Fame, including the first four:

Name	Est Wins	Est Losses	Est Ties	Percentage
Baugh, Sammy	94	50	7	.646
Herber, Arnie	81	41	6	.656
Luckman, Sid	72	23	2	.753
Driscoll, Paddy (tailback)	70	36	13	.643
Dunn, Red	68	27	8	.664
Smyth, Lou (tailback)	57	26	9	.668
Friedman, Benny	56	30	5	.643
Brumbaugh, Carl	55	18	3	.743
Leemans, Tuffy (tailback)	53	27	8	.648
Presnell, Glenn (tailback)	48	20	6	.689
McBride, Jack (tailback)	48	39	11	.546

To get a better idea of the biggest winners, however, we need to add some perspective. For quarterbacks with at least 50 starts, 15 winners won at least 65 percent of their starts. Most of these names are familiar winners. The surprises on the following table include Daryle Lamonica, Frank Ryan and Danny White who all were top quarterbacks for excellent teams, but are largely forgotten today. Lamonica was overshadowed by his 40-year-old relief man George Blanda and by his successor Kenny Stabler. White was seen widely as his predecessor Roger Staubach's "little brother." Neither won a title. Ryan won a championship, but was eclipsed by the greatest runner in history, Jim Brown. The shocker in the group is David Woodley, who was not very good as a quarterback, but was very lucky for a short period on a talented Dolphins team.

Name	Wins	Losses	Ties	Percentage
Graham, Otto	103	17	4	.847
Lamonica, Daryle	66	15	6	.793
Staubach, Roger	86	29	0	.748
Brady, Tom	70	24	0	.745
Montana, Joe	117	47	0	.713
McMahon, Jim	67	30	0	.691
Waterfield, Bob	58	26	4	.682
Bradshaw, Terry	107	51	0	.677
White, Danny	62	30	0	.674
Unitas, John	119	57	4	.672
Ryan, Frank	56	27	3	.669

Name	Wins	Losses	Ties	Percentage
Woodley, David	34	17	1	.663
McNabb, Donovan	65	33	0	.663
Stabler, Ken	96	49	1	.661
Young, Steve	94	49	0	.657

While seven of those 15 are in the Hall of Fame, only Sid Luckman, tailback Dutch Clark and Arnie Herber made the Hall from the early field generals whom I estimate to have won at least 65 percent of their games:

Name	Est Wins	Est Losses	Est Ties	Percentage
Molesworth, Keith	45	10	8	.778
Isbell, Cecil	41	12	2	.764
Luckman, Sid	72	23	2	.753
Brumbaugh, Carl	55	18	3	.743
Dunn, Red	68	27	8	.699
Masterson, Bernie	38	16	3	.693
Presnell, Glenn	48	20	6	.689
Clark, Dutch	38	16	6	.683
Danowski, Ed	45	20	5	.679
Stockton, Hust	44	20	7	.669
Smyth, Lou	57	26	9	.668
Herber, Arnie	81	41	6	.656

The most remarkable name at the top of both the list of most wins and the list of best percentage is the Cleveland Browns' Hall of Famer Otto Graham. Everyone else in the top ten for career victories played several more seasons and many more games than Graham. That is why he tops the list of highest winning percentage by over 50 points with an unassailable .847 winning percentage over his ten seasons in professional football. Even if we limited his record to the six seasons he spent in the NFL and eliminated his four years in the All America Conference, his won lost record of 57–13–1 would still represent the all-time top winning percentage with .810. Cleveland coach Paul Brown said of him that "the test of a quarterback is where his team finishes. By that standard, Otto was the best of them all."

Graham went to Northwestern where he was named All American in both basketball and football. As a single-wing tailback on a weak team, he caught the eye of Ohio State coach Paul Brown by leading the Wildcats to two upset victories over the Buckeyes before going into the Navy. Although he was drafted by the Detroit Lions, Graham chose to sign with Paul Brown of the new Cleveland Browns of the upstart All

America Conference who agreed to pay Otto a stipend for the extent of his war service. Before he joined the Browns, though, he spent a season with the Rochester Royals of the National Basketball League and, to foreshadow his football career, won the championship.

Otto Graham was known as "Automatic Otto" because of the accuracy of his passing, and was especially deadly on short passes and timing patterns. He was a steady, consistent and durable leader who was cool under all circumstances. Perhaps his two most memorable games bookended the 1950 season. On opening day, the AAFC champion Browns played the NFL champion Eagles in Philadelphia and dismantled the Birds 35–10 as Graham picked Philadelphia's secondary apart in a game some refer to as the first Super Bowl. Three months later in the title game against the Rams, Graham drove the Browns 60 yards in the last 1:48 to set up Lou Groza's 16-yard game-winning field goal. In that game, Graham completed 22 of 33 passes for 298 yards, 4 touchdowns and only 1 interception. In addition, he ran the ball 12 times for 99 more yards. The only thing he didn't do in his career was call the plays because Brown would not allow that, but Graham proved that he would do whatever it took to win.

In 10 seasons as a professional quarterback, Otto led the Browns to 10 title games and won seven of them; he was four for four in the All America Conference and three for six in the NFL. Three times he was the MVP in the AAFC and twice in the NFL. He led the AAFC in passer rating three times, touchdown passes twice and passing yards three times, while he led the NFL in passer rating twice, TD passes once and passing yards twice. When he died at age 82 in 2003, Otto Graham, the ultimate winner, was still commonly considered one of the top 3–5 quarterbacks in history nearly 50 years after he finished playing.

Not every quarterback is as lucky as Graham was in landing on the perfect team with the perfect coach at the perfect time to maximize his already formidable skills. Joe Montana felt it was more than just luck and said that, "the only thing that separates chumps from champions is the individual's competitive drive." That's all fine for a four-time Super Bowl winner to claim, but what about an overwhelmed young quarterback on an awful team like Dan Pastorini who lost a

record 23 straight starts on the early 1970s Oilers? For the rest of his career, Pastorini won 56 percent of his starts, but could not undo his horrible start and ended up with a losing record for his career. Does that make him a failure? No, but ultimately in every game there is a loser as well as a winner, and here are the most prolific losers in NFL history:

Name	Wins	Losses	Ties	Percentage
Testaverde, Vinny	88	119	1	.425
Tarkenton, Fran	125	106	6	.540
Manning, Archie	36	105	3	.260
Snead, Norm	51	101	7	.343
Moon, Warren	102	100	0	.505
Bledsoe, Drew	98	95	0	.508
Esiason, Boomer	80	93	0	.462
Marino, Dan	147	93	0	.613
Ferguson, Joe	79	92	0	.462
Favre, Brett	147	90	0	.620
Everett, Jim	64	89	0	.418
Hart, Jim	87	87	5	.500
DeBerg, Steve	53	86	1	.382
Chandler, Chris	67	85	0	.441
Fouts, Dan	86	83	1	.509
Collins, Kerry	66	82	0	.446
Elway, John	148	82	1	.643
Anderson, Ken	91	81	0	.529

Some of those quarterbacks are all-time greats who only lost a lot of games because they played in so many. Tarkenton, Moon, Marino, Fouts and Elway are in Canton; Favre will go and Anderson isn't that far removed. Others like Esiason and Hart played on too many lousy teams. It's hard to imagine any struggling quarterback in the future sticking around as long as Vinny Testaverde who lost an astounding number of games in his 20-year career. A more informative losers' table is of the quarterbacks with the lowest winning percentage (minimum of 30 games):

Name	Wins	Losses	Ties	Percentage
Wright, Randy	7	25	0	.219
Johnson, Randy	11	37	1	.235
Manning, Archie	36	105	3	.260
Enke, Fred	9	24	0	.273
Douglass, Bobby	15	37	1	.292
Carr, David	22	53	0	.293
Tolliver, Billy Joe	15	32	0	.319
Pagel, Mike	17	36	1	.324
Tensi, Steve	10	21	1	.328
McHan, Lamar	23	46	1	.336
Tripucka, Frank	19	38	1	.336

Name	Wins	Losses	Ties	Percentage
Friesz, John	13	25	0	.342
Snead, Norm	51	101	7	.343
Harrington, Joey	23	43	0	.348
Mirer, Rick	24	44	0	.353
Taliaferro, Mike	12	22	0	.353
Davidson, Cotton	19	35	1	.355
Spurrier, Steve	13	24	1	.355
Evans, Vince	14	25	0	.359
Miller, Chris	34	58	0	.370

At the very bottom is Randy Wright, a sixth round draft pick who once fainted in the huddle in a game against the Vikings and never should have been given 32 chances to prove how poor he was. In the bottom three of both of these lists is Archie Manning, who never played on a winning team in his 14-year career. Archie was so far in the hole that for his two sons to bring family Manning over .500 would take at least three more seasons of Peyton going 12–4 and Eli 9–7. Archie was one of 10 first round draft picks on this bottom 20 list, including Johnson, Carr, McHan, Tripucka, Snead, Harrington, Mirer, Spurrier and Miller. It's startling that two of these losers had longer careers than Archie, but Vince Evans played for 15 lousy years and Norm Snead lasted 16 mostly terrible seasons. Then there is the still lesser category of lowest winning percentage for quarterbacks who weren't good enough to get 30 starts, but did start at least 10 games:

Name	Wins	Losses	Ties	Percentage
Norton, Rick	1	11	0	.083
Gelbaugh, Stan	1	11	0	.083
Stenstrom, Steve	1	9	0	.100
Weinke, Chris	2	17	0	.105
O'Brien, Davey	2	19	1	.114
Komlo, Jeff	2	13	0	.133
Whelihan, Craig	2	12	0	.143
Darragh, Dan	1	8	1	.150
Campbell, Scott	2	11	0	.154
Slaughter, Mickey	2	15	2	.158
Klingler, David	4	20	0	.167
Herrmann, Mark	2	10	0	.167
Golsteyn, Jerry	2	10	0	.167
Pederson, Doug	3	14	0	.176
Smith, Akili	3	14	0	.176
Johnson, Doug	2	9	0	.182
Adams, Tony	2	9	0	.182
Reaves, John	3	13	0	.188
Thompson, Jack	4	17	0	.190
Leaf, Ryan	4	17	0	.190
Long, Chuck	4	17	0	.190

What separates Rick Norton from Stan Gelbaugh at the bottom of this list is that he was a number one draft pick — perhaps the worst ever. After all, Norton's 4.6 yards per pass and touchdown to interception ratio of 6:30 makes Gelbaugh's 5.4 and 10:22 look positively laudable. In fact, eight of these 21 ultraflops were number one picks, including Norton, O'Brien, Klingler, Smith, Reaves, Thompson, Leaf and Long. In addition, Mark Herrmann was the quarterback the Broncos sent to the Colts in the deal for the rights to John Elway in 1983. Weinke held the bottom spot securely since his 2001 rookie season when he won his first start and then lost his next 15. For some unexplainable reason, he was still the Panthers' backup in 2006 when Jake Delhomme went down. Weinke predictably lost his first two starts but then blew his chance at immortality by winning what will likely be his final start to bookend his career with wins. An asterisk should be attached to that last win, though. In it, the Panthers beat Atlanta 10–3 with Weinke throwing just seven passes and being removed from the game on each third down play to let a running back take a direct snap instead. Weinke deserves to be remembered as the worst starter ever.

One other way to approach how much a particular quarterback has to do with a team's success is to compare his won-lost record as a starter with his team's record in games he didn't start. I compiled the following tables by taking certain mitigating factors into account. For instance, if a quarterback didn't play or threw just a handful of passes in his first year or two, those years were not compared to his record because he had not had a chance to establish a playing level. Similarly, if a quarterback was merely a third quarterback who never played in his final years, like ancient Oakland placekicker George Blanda, those years were not counted either. Other factors that must be noted are that if a quarterback doesn't miss any games like Brett Favre or Peyton Manning, this process will provide no reading. By contrast, if the team's backup quarterback is truly awful like Chris Weinke, that steep drop off could give a false reading as well. Furthermore, it is easier for a good quarterback to have a much better record than his backup on a bad team, such as Tom Flores on the early Raiders, than for a great quarterback on a great team to show such a differential because a great team will go on winning with any competent quarterback against most opponents. The following table lists the quarterbacks whose winning percentage is at least .050 greater than that of the team, i.e., the quarterbacks who may claim to have the biggest impact on their team's success:

Quarterback	Wins	Losses	Ties	Percentage	Team Wins	Team Loss	Team Ties	Team %	Difference
Meredith, Don	46	32	1	.589	56	63	5	.472	.117
Ryan, Frank	56	27	3	.669	76	57	3	.570	.099
Jones, Bert	47	49	0	.490	58	85	0	.406	.084
Flores, Tom	31	32	3	.492	44	64	4	.411	.082
Vick, Michael	38	28	1	.575	47	48	1	.495	.080
Schroeder, Jay	62	37	0	.626	87	72	0	.547	.079
Montana, Joe	117	47	0	.713	137	78	1	.637	.077
Baugh, Sammy	94	50	7	.646	99	74	7	.569	.076
Gabriel, Roman	86	65	7	.566	98	102	10	.490	.076
Humphries, Stan	47	29	0	.618	61	51	0	.545	.074
Brown, Ed	54	32	4	.622	82	67	5	.549	.074
McMahon, Jim	67	30	0	.691	109	67	0	.619	.071
Rypien, Mark	47	31	0	.603	77	67	0	.535	.068
Flutie, Doug	38	28	0	.576	82	77	0	.516	.060
Unitas, John	119	57	4	.672	154	96	6	.613	.059
Nelsen, Bill	40	31	3	.561	62	61	3	.504	.057
Parilli, Babe	47	41	10	.531	70	78	10	.475	.056
Frerotte, Gus	36	42	1	.462	71	104	1	.406	.056
Majkowski, Don	26	30	1	.465	39	56	1	.411	.053
Johnson, Charley	62	56	8	.524	93	105	11	.471	.053
Harrington, Joey	23	43	0	.348	19	45	0	.297	.052
Grogan, Steve	75	60	0	.556	122	120	0	.504	.051
Woodley, David	34	17	1	.663	54	34	0	.614	.050

The biggest surprises, aside from how high Don Meredith and Frank Ryan rank in this list, are the presence on the list of mediocrities like Jay Schroeder, Gus Frerotte, Joey Harrington and David Woodley. However, their backups, including Todd Marinovich, Vince Evans, Heath Shuler, Mike McMahon and Mark Malone, were extremely bad. On the other side of the coin are the quarterbacks whose winning percentage was at least .030 lower than their teams' percentage:

Quarterback	Wins	Losses	Ties	Percentage	Team Wins	Team Loss	Team Ties	Team %	Difference
Wright, Randy	7	25	0	.219	29	49	1	.373	-.155
McHan, Lamar	23	46	1	.336	50	64	2	.440	-.104
Davidson, Cotton	19	35	1	.355	41	52	3	.443	-.088
Johnson, Randy	11	37	1	.235	43	93	4	.321	-.087
Pagel, Mike	17	36	1	.324	74	108	2	.408	-.084
Grbac, Elvis	40	30	0	.571	82	46	0	.641	-.069
Livingston, Mike	31	44	1	.414	71	78	5	.477	-.063
Blanda, George	53	60	2	.470	81	72	1	.529	-.060
Malone, Mark	23	30	0	.434	54	57	0	.486	-.053
Morton, Craig	81	60	1	.574	150	90	2	.624	-.050
Wade, Bill	43	47	2	.478	85	76	7	.527	-.049
Williams, Doug	38	42	1	.475	62	57	1	.521	-.046
Tolliver, Billy Joe	15	32	0	.319	52	92	0	.361	-.042
Kosar, Bernie	53	54	1	.495	93	81	1	.534	-.039
Green, Trent	56	51	0	.523	69	54	0	.561	-.038
George, Jeff	46	78	0	.371	78	114	0	.406	-.035
Jurgensen, Sonny	68	74	7	.480	120	114	10	.512	-.032
Hadl, John	82	78	9	.512	124	104	10	.542	-.030
Mirer, Rick	24	44	0	.353	49	79	0	.383	-.030

Quarterback	Wins	Losses	Ties	Percentage	Team Wins	Team Loss	Team Ties	Team %	Difference
Beuerlein, Steve	47	55	0	.461	102	106	0	.490	–.030
Zorn, Jim	43	62	0	.410	72	92	0	.439	–.030

Once again we find the familiar name of Randy Wright at the bottom and are even more baffled as to why he got 32 starts. In general, this is a mix of outright bunglers like Lamar McHan, Mike Pagel, Randy Johnson and Billy Joe Tolliver, good quarterbacks beaten out by great ones like Craig Morton and Trent Green and aging pros who were pushed aside on a very good team like Sonny Jurgensen on George Allen's Redskins, John Hadl on the Rams and Bernie Kosar on the Cowboys and Dolphins. Hall of Famer George Blanda makes the list mostly because he was very unimpressive during his decade with a very decent Bears team in the 1950s. In his later years as a Raider, he found his niche as an unruffled relief pitcher off the bench who captained several exciting last-minute victories.

Fourth Quarter Comebacks

Any game, no matter how sloppy or dull, can be salvaged by an exciting conclusion. A lead change in the closing minutes makes for a memorable contest, especially when the winning score is set up by a methodical drive down the field led by a confident quarterback. As the following table indicates, late comebacks were rare in the early days of pro football. However, as increased passing loosened up the offense in subsequent decades, there has been a nearly unbroken swell in fourth quarter heroics to the point where nearly one third of all regular season games today are not decided until the last quarter.

Decade	Comebacks	Games	%	Playoff Comebacks	Playoff Games	Playoff %
1920s	78	817	9.5%	0	0	NA
1930s	87	579	15.0%	2	7	28.6%
1940s	125	811	15.4%	4	21	19.0%
1950s	170	726	23.4%	8	15	53.3%
1960s	241	1001	24.1%	7	39	17.9%
1970s	495	1932	25.6%	19	74	25.7%
1980s	636	2128	29.9%	27	96	28.1%
1990s	704	2328	30.2%	27	110	24.5%
2000s	566	1776	31.9%	21	77	27.3%
Total	3102	12098	25.6%	115	439	26.2%

What I am calling a fourth quarter comeback is more accurately described as a fourth quarter game-winning drive. In my survey of NFL line scores, I counted games in which the winning team was tied or behind in the fourth quarter and won the game because of an offensive drive of any length. Games won on returns were not counted here because we are comparing the effectiveness of quarterbacks in rallying their teams at crunch time.

The leading comeback artists in the first two decades of the NFL were Benny Friedman with eight, and Red Dunn, Arnie Herber and Dutch Clark with seven each. The first three were probably the top three passers of the time. They were succeeded by Sammy Baugh, the first truly great passer, who recorded 12 comebacks in the 1940s to surpass the eight led by fellow

Hall of Famers Sid Luckman and Bob Waterfield in that decade.

By the 1950s, nearly one quarter of the games were decided in the last quarter. Otto Graham opened the decade with a spectacular last-minute drive to win the 1950 title and things expanded from there. The man with the biggest reputation for late wins was Graham's nemesis, Bobby Layne. Layne brought the Lions offense on the field with 4:10 left in the 1953 championship against the Browns, down 16–10 with 80 yards to go. He implored his teammates in the huddle to block for him so that, "ol' Bobby will pass you to the championship." Completing four of six passes including a 33-yard touchdown to Jim Doran, he did just that. Y.A. Tittle had the most comebacks, 19, for the decade. Layne and Charlie Conerly both had 14 in the regular season, and Conerly set a single season record in 1950 with four. That was broken in 1953 by little Eddie LeBaron who achieved five of the Redskins' six wins by engineering fourth quarter drives.

A more ball-control orientation took hold in the 1960s, but the leader in comebacks for the decade was Johnny Unitas who perfected the two-minute drill in the 1950s, most notably in the 1958 Sudden Death championship win over the Giants in which he led the Colts on a 73-yard drive to tie the game with seven seconds left and then led a 80-yard drive to win the championship in overtime. Unitas had 23 comebacks in the sixties, while Fran Tarkenton had 18, and Bart Starr had 17. Starr had one that was unforgettable in the postseason as well. In the Ice Bowl NFL championship against the Cowboys in 1967, Starr led the Packers on a 12-play, 68-yard march to the winning touchdown when the temperature was -13 degrees with a -46 degree windchill.

Roger Staubach became known as Captain Comeback in the 1970s for such fantastic finishes as leading the Cowboys to 17 fourth quarter points to overcome a 28–13 49er lead in the 1972 divisional round and beating the Vikings in the 1975 divisional match on his 50-yard "Hail Mary" pass to Drew Pearson. Staubach had 21 regular season comebacks to top the decade and was trailed by Snake Stabler's 20, Fran Tarkenton's 18 and Terry Bradshaw's 16. Bradshaw added four more in the postseason. In 1978, Dan Pastorini, Steve Bartkowski and Steve Grogan each had a new-record six comebacks during the season, and Pastorini and Bartkowski each added a seventh in the playoffs. The following year, Brian Sipe, the leader of Cleveland's Kardiac Kids, extended the regular season mark to seven.

Joe Montana, John Elway and Dan Marino set the comeback standard in the 1980s. Montana had 21 regular season comebacks that decade, while Elway had 17 and Marino had 16. They were joined by unheralded Ron Jaworski's 17 and much-denigrated Steve DeBerg's 16. Of course, Montana and Elway are most famous for their postseason work. Montana capped an 89-yard drive in the closing minute of the 1981 NFC Conference championship against the Cowboys by hitting Dwight Clark in the back of the endzone on a play known simply as The Catch. Joe Cool later concluded the 49ers' third Super Bowl win in 1989 by leading a 92-yard drive in the closing three min-

utes with the winning points coming on a 10-yard bullet to John Taylor with 34 second remaining. Elway's greatest moment came during the 1987 AFC championship against the Browns and is known as The Drive. Elway led a 15-play, 98-yard drive to tie the game with 39 seconds remaining and then led the game winning drive in overtime. Don Majkowski of the Packers equaled the seasonal record of seven comebacks in his Majik Man season of 1989.

Marino and Elway continued in the 1990s with 26 and 25 regular season comebacks and three postseason comebacks apiece. They were joined by Warren Moon's 23, Jim Kelly's 21 and Jim Harbaugh's 19. The most famous comeback was led by Jim Kelly's backup Frank Reich who brought the Bills back from a 35–3 deficit in the second half of a playoff win over the Oilers. Most of the comeback took place in the third quarter, but the Bills did not take the lead till the fourth quarter, and then were tied by the Oilers to force overtime. In overtime, Reich led one more drive to set up a game-winning field goal. The seasonal record of seven comebacks was tied twice in the decade by Jake Plummer in 1998 and Peyton Manning in 1999.

Since the retirements of Elway and Marino, the most prolific comeback artists currently are Tom Brady and Peyton Manning. Brady, in particular, has specialized in the playoffs. He led the Patriots to an overtime win over the Raiders in the snow in 2001, and then topped that by setting up the game-winning field goal on the last play of the Super Bowl against the Rams. In 2003, Jake Delhomme tied the seasonal comeback mark with seven and had an eighth in the playoffs. He actually had a ninth in the Super Bowl by driving the Panthers to take the lead in the last minute, but that was wiped out by a patented close-out drive by Tom Brady for the Patriots second championship. The following table lists the 20 quarterbacks with at least 24 regular season comebacks.

Name	Regular Season
Elway, John	42
Marino, Dan	42
Unitas, John	37
Tarkenton, Fran	36
Moon, Warren	35
Favre, Brett	33
Testaverde, Vinny	33

Name	Regular Season
Krieg, Dave	31
Bledsoe, Drew	31
Montana, Joe	29
Kelly, Jim	29
Plummer, Jake	29
Johnson, Brad	29
Manning, Peyton	28
Stabler, Ken	25
Brunell, Mark	25
Bradshaw, Terry	24
Esiason, Boomer	24
Ferguson, Joe	24
Tittle, Y.A.	24

As for frequency, eight quarterbacks had fourth quarter comebacks in at least 20 percent of their starts: Brad Johnson 24.1 percent, Doug Williams 23.5 percent, Aaron Brooks 22 percent, Jake Plummer 21.6 percent, Brian Sipe 20.9 percent, Daryle Lamonica 20.7 percent, Johnny Unitas 20.6 percent and Jon Kitna 20.3 percent. Nine quarterbacks had fourth quarter comebacks in at least 40 percent of their wins: Doug Williams 50 percent, Aaron Brooks 47.4 percent, Jon Kitna 44.4 percent, Jeff Blake 43.6 percent, Jake Plummer 43.5 percent, Lynn Dickey 42.2 percent, Steve DeBerg 41.5 percent, Brian Sipe 41.1 percent and Brad Johnson 40 percent. Since most of the quarterbacks on these two lists are underrated to say the least, these numbers, if anything, indicate a general inconsistency in their quarterbacking or in their teams.

If we add playoff comebacks to the totals, we get a slightly different list of quarterbacks with at least 24 comebacks. The following table adds in such familiar names as Tom Brady, Dan Fouts, Joe Theismann and Randall Cunningham. It should also be noted that my total for John Elway is one greater than the official total because I include a game from September 23, 1990 in which the winning drive came in overtime.

Name	Regular Season	Wins	Post-Season	Total
Elway, John	42	148	6	48
Marino, Dan	42	147	4	46
Unitas, John	37	119	2	39
Tarkenton, Fran	36	125	1	37
Moon, Warren	35	102	2	37
Favre, Brett	33	147	2	35
Montana, Joe	29	117	5	34
Testaverde, Vinny	33	88	0	33
Krieg, Dave	31	98	1	32
Bledsoe, Drew	31	98	0	31
Kelly, Jim	29	101	1	30
Manning, Peyton	28	92	1	29
Johnson, Brad	29	71	0	29
Plummer, Jake	29	69	0	29
Bradshaw, Terry	24	107	4	28
Stabler, Ken	25	96	2	27
Fouts, Dan	23	86	3	26
Brunell, Mark	25	79	1	26
Cunningham, Randall	23	82	2	25
Theismann, Joe	23	76	2	25
Tittle, Y.A.	24	87	0	24
Esiason, Boomer	24	80	0	24
Ferguson, Joe	24	79	0	24
Jaworski, Ron	23	72	1	24
Brady, Tom	18	70	6	24
Bartkowski, Steve	23	59	1	24

The leading playoff comeback artists are John Elway and Tom Brady with six, Joe Montana with five, Dan Marino and Terry Bradshaw with four, and Dan Fouts and Otto Graham with three. Graham, that ultimate winner, can never be ignored. Playoff comebacks are the most exciting because those are the games with the most at stake and in which the quarterbacks must perform under the most pressure. Under such extreme pressure great quarterbacks have turned in some performances that sparkled like diamonds.

The Playoffs

The pressure-packed playoffs can make or break a quarterback's reputation, especially with the increased spotlight of the Super Bowl. Is there any greater reminder that football is a team game than the fact that Hall of Famer Y.A. Tittle lost all five of his postseason starts and never won a championship, while glorified backup Trent Dilfer compiled a 5–1 postseason record with a Super Bowl ring on his finger? No one would choose as quarterback Dilfer in his prime over Tittle in his dotage, but game manager Dilfer won a title behind the Ravens' dominating defense while Tittle was done in by bad weather, feeble defense and injuries. Yet, winning championships will always be a factor of great magnitude in ranking quarterbacks.

Since the inception of the Super Bowl, more rounds and games have been added to the postseason, giving quarterbacks increased opportunities to shine. The following table lists the top 20 quarterbacks ranked by postseason passing yards. Only Otto Graham, ever the exception, played before the first Super Bowl.

Quarterback	Attempts	Complete	Percent	Yards	Y/ Att	Y/ Cmp	TD	Ints	Rating
Montana, Joe	732	463	63.3%	5772	7.9	12.5	44	20	96.3
Elway, John	650	355	54.6%	4964	7.6	14	25	21	78.8
Favre, Brett	663	401	60.5%	4902	7.4	12.2	34	26	84
Marino, Dan	687	385	56%	4512	6.6	11.7	32	24	77.1
Kelly, Jim	545	322	59.1%	3863	7.1	12	21	28	72.3
Aikman, Troy	502	320	63.7%	3849	7.7	12	24	17	89
Bradshaw, Terry	456	261	57.2%	3832	8.4	14.7	30	26	83
Manning, Peyton	475	290	61.1%	3495	7.4	12.1	18	15	83.1
Young, Steve	471	292	62%	3326	7.1	11.4	20	13	85.8
Brady, Tom	486	295	60.7%	3217	6.6	10.9	20	10	85.4
Moon, Warren	403	259	64.3%	2836	7	10.9	17	14	84.5
Staubach, Roger	410	224	54.6%	2827	6.9	12.6	24	19	76.5
Stabler, Kenny	351	203	57.8%	2641	7.5	13	17	15	80
McNabb, Donovan	412	245	59.5%	2524	6.1	10.3	17	12	78.8
Cunningham, Randall	365	192	52.6%	2426	6.6	12.6	13	10	74.1
Plunkett, Jim	272	162	59.6%	2296	8.4	14.2	10	12	80.8
White, Danny	359	206	57.4%	2284	6.4	11.1	15	16	71.8
Warner, Kurt	268	169	63.1%	2221	8.3	13.1	15	10	92.3
Graham, Otto	301	159	52.8%	2101	7	13.2	14	17	67.2
Fouts, Dan	286	159	55.6%	1991	7	12.5	12	18	65.2

Joe Montana started more playoff games than any other quarterback and holds several career marks, including most attempts, 732; most completions, 463; and most touchdowns, 44. Despite the championships of Otto Graham, Bart Starr and Sid Luckman, it's no wonder that Montana is often considered the game's greatest winner. It started at Notre Dame where Montana established a legendary ability to pull games out at the end, even though his coach Dan Devine was reluctant to make Montana the starter. Joe won the National Championship in college and is the only quarterback besides Alabama's Joe Namath to lead his team to the title in both college and the NFL. Once he got to San Francisco under Coach Bill Walsh, Montana became a national hero known for his intelligence and coolness under pressure in continually leading the 49ers into the playoffs and winning four Super Bowls in the 1980s. Even in the last two years of his career in Kansas City, he had enough smarts and just enough arm to get the Chiefs into the playoffs. His peers in the top 10 in postseason touchdown passes are all Hall of Famers, present or future:

Quarterback	TD	Quarterback	TD
Montana, Joe	44	Aikman, Troy	24
Favre, Brett	34	Staubach, Roger	24
Marino, Dan	32	Kelly, Jim	21
Bradshaw, Terry	30	Young, Steve	20
Elway, John	25	Brady, Tom	20

These 10 quarterbacks won 20 of the 31 Super Bowls they started. The new face in the crowd is Tom Brady of the Patriots. An unheralded Michigan quarterback who was drafted in the sixth round by New England, he stepped in when Drew Bledsoe went down to injury and never relinquished his job. Under his cool leadership reminiscent of the style of his boyhood idol Joe Montana, the Patriots have been the team of the new millennium. As for yards per attempt and yards per completion, Carson Palmer tops both categories with an average of 66 yards — of course he only threw one postseason pass before being injured so that average will come down when he can get the Bengals back to the playoffs. Of those who have thrown at least 200 passes, the leader in yards per attempt with 8.4 is still Terry Bradshaw of the Steelers' dynasty of the 1970s. Bradshaw took five years to

begin to settle in at quarterback, but once he felt comfortable, Pittsburgh won four Super Bowls in six years behind Bradshaw's bombs to Lynn Swann and John Stallworth. Another quarterback who won four NFL titles, Sid Luckman, was also a master of the deep pass and averaged 8.5 yards per pass, but only threw 86 passes in his six postseason starts. Luckman was the first quarterback to operate out of the modern T formation and had defenses dumbfounded in the 1940s with his passing, ball handling and play calling.

The postseason leader in completion percentage for at least 200 passes is Warren Moon at 64.3 percent; for at least 500 passes, it's Troy Aikman at 63.7 percent; and for at least 600 passes, it's Montana at 63.3 percent. The top 10 in passer rating of those who threw at least 200 postseason passes is in the following table:

Quarterback	Attempts	Complete	Percent	Yards	Y/ Att	Y/ Cmp	TD	Ints	Rating
Starr, Bart	213	130	61%	1753	8.2	13.5	15	4	102.9
Montana, Joe	732	463	63.3%	5772	7.9	12.5	44	20	96.3
Warner, Kurt	268	169	63.1%	2221	8.3	13.1	15	10	92.3
Theismann, Joe	211	128	60.7%	1782	8.4	13.9	11	7	91.4
Aikman, Troy	502	320	63.7%	3849	7.7	12	24	17	89
Young, Steve	471	292	62%	3326	7.1	11.4	20	13	85.8
Brady, Tom	486	295	60.7%	3217	6.6	10.9	20	10	85.4
Gannon, Rich	240	154	64.2%	1691	7	11	11	9	84.6
Moon, Warren	403	259	64.3%	2836	7	10.9	17	14	84.5
Favre, Brett	663	401	60.5%	4902	7.4	12.2	34	26	84

At the top of this list is the greatest winner in NFL history, Bart Starr, who won five NFL titles, including the first two Super Bowls and first two Super Bowl MVP trophies. Starr was another unheralded college quarterback, a 17th round pick, who blossomed under Vince Lombardi and led the Packers with unflappable precision in the 1960s.

Running quarterbacks have also been successful in the playoffs. These 11 quarterbacks have topped 200 yards rushing:

Quarterback	Rush Att	Yrds	Ave	Rush TD
Young, Steve	96	535	5.6	7
Elway, John	94	461	4.9	6
Staubach, Roger	76	432	5.7	0
McNabb, Donovan	63	362	5.7	3
Graham, Otto	73	362	5.0	6
McNair, Steve	55	355	6.5	6
Montana, Joe	64	300	4.7	2
Bradshaw, Terry	51	288	5.6	3

Quarterback	Rush Att	Yrds	Ave	Rush TD
Cunningham, Randall	46	254	5.5	1
Stewart, Kordell	45	250	5.6	2
Vick, Mike	28	239	8.5	0

The leader in rushing average is Michael Vick with 8.5, while Steve Young scored the most touchdowns with seven.

While I highlighted the biggest champions above, there have been 23 quarterbacks who have led their teams to more than one title:

Quarterback	Titles	Quarterback	Titles
Otto Graham	7	Tobin Rote	2
Bart Starr	5	Len Dawson	2
Sid Luckman	4	Ed Danowski	2
Terry Bradshaw	4	Tommy Thompson	2
Joe Montana	4	Bob Waterfield	2
Johnny Unitas	3	Norm Van Brocklin	2
Troy Aikman	3	Bobby Layne	2

Quarterback	Titles
Tom Brady	3
Arnie Herber	2
Sammy Baugh	2
George Blanda	2
Jack Kemp	2
Bob Griese	2
Roger Staubach	2
Jim Plunkett	2
John Elway	2

Quarterback	Wins	Losses	%
Starr, Bart	9	1	90.0%
Brady, Tom	12	2	85.7%
Roethlisberger, Ben	5	1	83.3%
Luckman, Sid	5	1	83.3%
Dilfer, Trent	5	1	83.3%
Plunkett, Jim	8	2	80.0%
Morrall, Earl	4	1	80.0%
Hostetler, Jeff	4	1	80.0%
Graham, Otto	9	3	75.0%
Theismann, Joe	6	2	75.0%
Unitas, Johnny	6	2	75.0%

In this table, I have included Otto Graham's four AAFC titles and the pre-merger AFL titles won by Blanda, Kemp, Dawson and Rote.

As for postseason wins in general, there have been 75 quarterbacks who started at least five playoff games in their careers. 49 of them won at least half their playoff games, proving either that experience wins or that only the best quarterbacks get to move on in the playoffs. The top 10 in postseason wins include only Starr and Graham of passers who at least partly predate the Super Bowl:

Quarterback	Wins	Losses	%
Montana, Joe	16	7	69.6%
Bradshaw, Terry	14	5	73.7%
Elway, John	14	8	63.6%
Brady, Tom	12	2	85.7%
Aikman, Troy	11	5	68.8%
Staubach, Roger	11	6	64.7%
Favre, Brett	11	9	55.0%
Starr, Bart	9	1	90.0%
Graham, Otto	9	3	75.0%
Young, Steve	9	7	56.3%
Kelly, Jim	9	8	52.9%

In the top 10 in winning percentage, we find a host of new names, both celebrated like Sid Luckman and Johnny Unitas and merely fortunate like Trent Dilfer and Jeff Hostetler.

The 26 quarterbacks with at least five postseason starts and a losing record include four

Hall of Famers: Dan Marino 8–10; Dan Fouts 3–4; Warren Moon 3–7; and Y.A. Tittle 0–5. None of these greats ever won a title, and all have had to deal with critics questioning their greatness because they never won a ring. In fact, the only quarterback in the lower 26 who did win it all was underrated Charlie Conerly of the Giants who went 2–3 in playoff games, but won the 1956 championship over the Bears. The 17 Hall of Famers in the upper 49 won 48 titles among them, even though they include three-time loser Fran Tarkenton and four-time loser Jim Kelly. Furthermore, the six Hall of Famers not on this list because they played in fewer than five postseason games (Bobby Layne, George Blanda, Arnie Herber, Joe Namath, Ace Parker and Sonny Jurgensen) won another seven titles. Only Duke graduates Parker and Jurgensen of that group never won anything, and Jurgy never even started a postseason game.

What makes the postseason such a great crucible for top quarterbacks is that those are the games played among the upper division teams and against the best defenses. Quarterbacks who perform at their best against the best are usually considered the paragons of their profession. To have never won the game's ultimate prize is a source of endless personal frustration that weighs heavily on history's rankings.

5

Measures and Rankings

If you want to start an argument, walk into a sports bar and ask who the best quarterback in the game was this year. Because there are so many valid but incomplete ways to judge quarterbacks, there are always several strong candidates. Even in Dan Marino's otherworldly 1984 season of 5,084 yards and 48 touchdowns, a case could be made for Joe Montana's 3,630 yards and 28 touchdowns, especially since Montana's 49ers convincingly defeated Marino's Dolphins in the Super Bowl that year. Trying to rank the relative merits of quarterbacks from different eras is even more daunting so that selecting an all time top 10 or 20 or 50 may even start a brawl. Here is my attempt at cobbling together flawed statistical measures and subjective reputation-based achievements and honors to arrive at the best of the best.

Statistical Measures

Nine different systems were used to rank quarterbacks first 41 years that passing statistics were officially kept. The systems could be divided into two types that each held sway for roughly half the time — the passing leader was awarded either according to a single category such as Passing Yards or Completion Percentage or by a system of inverse rankings across several categories in which each passer is awarded points in comparison to all other passers in every category. One style was simple, and the other was cumbersome, but neither was desirable. In 1971, Commissioner Pete Rozelle charged a committee led by Don Smith from the Hall of Fame to come up with a new and equitable system. Smith devised a calculation based on standards of achievement, and the current Passer Rating system was adopted in 1973.

The NFL's passer rating system is a complex calculation that awards points for a quarterback's performance in four percentage-based categories.

NFL Passing Leadership Criteria

1932–37	*Most Yards*
1938–40	*Best Completion Percentage*
1941–43	Inverse ranking point system based on *completions and completion percentage*
1944–48	Inverse ranking point system based on *completions, completion percentage, yards, TD, interceptions and interception percentage*
1949	Inverse ranking point system based on *completions, completion percentage, yards, TD and interception percentage*
1950–59	*Best Yards per Attempt*, minimum of 100 attempts
1960–61	Inverse ranking point system based on *completions, completion percentage, yards, TD, yards per attempt and interception percentage*
1962–71	Inverse ranking point system based on *completion percentage, TD, yards per attempt and interception percentage*
1972	Inverse ranking point system based on *completion percentage, TD percentage, yards per attempt and interception percentage*
1973–2006	Passer Rating calculation based on *standards of 50% completions, 7 yards per attempt, 5% touchdowns and 5.5% interceptions*

The standards for each of these categories were set according to the league average at the time the system was devised, the early 1970s. Thus, if a quarterback completes 50 percent of his passes, he gets one point; if he completes 70 percent, he gets 2 points; if he completes 30 percent, he gets zero. All percentages in between would receive a proportional score. The total score for the four categories is then multiplied by 100 and divided by 6 so that a perfectly average performance would merit a 66.7 rate, and a rate of 100 would be the gold standard of passing efficiency — although an actual perfect score would come out to the oddball number of 158.2.

Don Smith, who came up with the formula, thought that it would allow quarterbacks to be compared easily to one another even across time. In the ensuing years, the passer rating system has engendered a great deal of criticism because it has clear faults. It does not measure which quarterbacks are most effective at leading scoring drives or winning games. It does not measure other skills that quarterbacks may bring to the game such as a talent for running or the ability to escape a pass rush. Furthermore, passing attacks have changed so much in the past 30 years, it does not allow for easy comparison between eras. What it does do, and do fairly well, is measure passing efficiency for quarterbacks at a particular time.

The end of the 1970s was a watershed time for passing in the NFL. On the one hand, defenders were forced to adhere to a much stricter set of rules regarding pass defense; on the other, Bill Walsh brought his West Coast Offense of short, high percentage, low risk passes to San Francisco and perfected it so that it spread quickly throughout the league. If we look at the top 100 seasonal performances in completion percentage, pass yardage per game and interception percentage, we find the great bulk have occurred since 1978. Ninety of the top 100 performances in completion percentage, 88 of the top 100 performances in pass yardage per game and 86 of the lowest 100 performances in interception percentages happened since 1978. Conversely, only 24 of the top 100 performances in average gain per pass have happened since 1978.

Paul Zimmerman of *Sports Illustrated* has objected to all the ratios in the calculation being based on the attempt rather than the completion. For one thing, this tends to reward the dinkers over the bombers. If a quarterback leads his team on a 72-yard drive in which he completes eight of nine passes for nine yards each, his passer rating is 137. If another quarterback throws two incompletions and then throws a 72-yard touchdown pass, his rating is 121.6. Both led their team to points and both received high rates, but the bomber receives less credit. Yards per completion is a stat that is not even kept by the NFL, but it gives a better picture than yards per attempt as to which quarterbacks is good at throwing the ball downfield. If we look at the all time top 20 quarterbacks in yards per completion (minimum 1,000 attempts), we find such well known bombers as Sid Luckman, Norm Van Brocklin, Daryle Lamonica and Joe Namath.

Quarterback	Att	Comp	%	Yards	Y/ Att	Y/ Comp	TD	Int	Rate
Herber, Arnie	1175	481	40.9%	8041	6.8	16.7	82	106	50.4
Brown, Ed	1987	949	47.8%	15600	7.9	16.4	102	138	62.8
Luckman, Sid	1744	904	51.8%	14685	8.4	16.2	137	132	75.0
Graham, Otto	2626	1464	55.8%	23584	9.0	16.1	174	135	86.6
McHan, Lamar	1442	610	42.3%	9449	6.6	15.5	73	108	50.3
Davidson, Cotton	1751	770	44.0%	11760	6.7	15.3	73	109	54.7
Van Brocklin, Norm	2895	1553	53.6%	23611	8.2	15.2	173	178	75.1
Morrall, Earl	2689	1379	51.3%	20809	7.7	15.1	161	148	74.1
LeBaron, Eddie	1796	898	50.0%	13399	7.5	14.9	104	141	61.4
Lamonica, Daryle	2601	1288	49.5%	19154	7.4	14.9	164	138	72.9
Kemp, Jack	3073	1436	46.7%	21222	6.9	14.8	114	183	57.4
Layne, Bobby	3700	1814	49.0%	26768	7.2	14.8	196	243	63.4
Ryan, Frank	2133	1090	51.1%	16042	7.5	14.7	149	111	77.6
Nelsen, Bill	1905	963	50.6%	14165	7.4	14.7	98	101	70.2
Meredith, Don	2308	1170	50.7%	17199	7.5	14.7	135	111	74.8
Namath, Joe	3762	1886	50.1%	27663	7.4	14.7	173	220	65.5
Parilli, Babe	3330	1552	46.6%	22681	6.8	14.6	178	220	59.6
Waterfield, Bob	1617	814	50.3%	11849	7.3	14.6	97	128	61.6
Christman, Paul	1140	504	44.2%	7294	6.4	14.5	58	76	54.8
Beathard, Pete	1284	575	44.8%	8243	6.4	14.3	43	86	49.4

Unfortunately, we also find such lesser lights as Ed Brown, Lamar McHan, Cotton Davidson and Pete Beathard in this ranking, and no one who played past 1977 is anywhere to be found. Since 1932, just 53 quarterbacks who threw at least 1,500 passes averaged 13 yards per completion or more, and only 10 of them played past 1978 (Steve Grogan, Jay Schroeder, Terry

Bradshaw, Doug Williams, Craig Morton, Roger Staubach, James Harris, Lynn Dickey, Jim Plunkett and Dan Fouts). Of the modern quarterbacks, only the gritty Grogan at 14.3 and the erratic Schroeder at 14.1 exceeded 14 yards per completion. In fact, the highest active player is Trent Green at a mere 12.7 yards per completion. Yards per Completion hearkens to a time when passers worried less about dumping the ball off to a short receiver than about trying for a big play. Of course, the short passing offense has been effective, and there is something to be said for an offense that can generate long drives to wear out the opposing defense and give yours a rest.

Ranking quarterbacks over time is another weakness of the passer rating system. Because the standards in the calculation have not changed while the game has, 70 of the top 100 seasonal performances in passer rating have come since 1978. The all time list of passer rating includes such immortals as Marc Bulger sixth, Matt Hasselbeck ninth, Brian Griese 15th and Jake Delhomme 17th while true immortals like Bart Starr, Dan Fouts, Johnny Unitas, Norm Van Brocklin, Sid Luckman and Y.A. Tittle are 37th, 42nd, 53rd, 76th, 78th and 82nd respectively. A better way to compare quarterbacks throughout NFL history using the passer rating is to make the ratings relative to contemporaries. I compared the passer ratings for each quarterback to the league average passer rating during the years they were active. The result was a relative career passer rating that better expresses how each quarterback compared to his peers and seems to be a more effective way to rank great performances. With a minimum of 1,500 pass attempts, the following table lists the top 20 all time in relative passer rating:

Name	Years	Pass Rate	L Pass Rate	Relative Pass Rate
Sid Luckman	1939–50	75.2	47.6	158%
Sammy Baugh	1937–52	72.2	47.4	152%
Otto Graham	1946–55	86.6	57.6	150%
Len Dawson	1957–75	82.6	63.8	129%
Frankie Albert	1946–52	73.5	57.6	128%
Roger Staubach	1969–79	83.4	65.5	127%
Norm Van Brocklin	1949–60	75.1	59.2	127%
Steve Young	1985–99	96.8	76.5	127%
Sonny Jurgensen	1957–74	82.6	66.9	123%
Joe Montana	1979–94	92.3	75.3	123%
Fran Tarkenton	1961–78	80.4	66.5	121%
Bart Starr	1956–71	80.5	67.2	120%
Peyton Manning	1998–06	94.4	78.9	120%
Kurt Warner	1998–06	93.8	78.9	119%
Y.A. Tittle	1948–64	74.3	63.3	117%
Johnny Unitas	1956–73	78.2	66.9	117%
Ken Anderson	1971–86	81.9	70.1	117%
Daryle Lamonica	1963–74	72.9	63.2	115%
Daunte Culpepper	1999–06	90.8	79	115%
Bob Griese	1967–80	77.1	67.1	115%
Marc Bulger	2002–06	91.3	79.6	115%

Matt Hasselbeck and Jake Delhomme have dropped out of this list. The only Griese to be found is Brian's Hall of Fame father Bob who is tied at 20th with Marc Bulger, a pretty effective quarterback after all. Starr, Unitas, Van Brocklin, Luckman and Tittle have all moved into the top 20 and Dan Fouts is ranked 29th on this list, up from 42nd.

We can also look at the seasonal components of relative passer rate. For this, I looked at each season in which a quarterback threw at least 100 passes and counted it in one of two categories — 1) at or above the league average or 2) below the league average. I made a second count for extreme seasons at least 10 percent better or worse than the league average to get a feel for quarterbacks who truly excelled or were truly disastrous. Fran Tarkenton had 17 seasons at or above the league average with only one season below, and Dan Marino had 16 above and one below. Seven quarterbacks with at least seven full seasons never had a passer rating below the league average: Len Dawson 14, Joe Montana 13, Otto Graham 10, Arnie Herber 10, Sid Luckman 9, Roger Staubach 8 and Daryle Lamonica 7. Sammy Baugh had the most exceptional seasons at least 10 percent above the league average with 14, while Marino had 13, Tarkenton and Y.A. Tittle both had 12 and Dawson, Montana and Ken Anderson each had 11. The following table lists quarterbacks with at least 10 seasons at or above the league average passer rating.

Name	>=100%	<100%	10%-10%	
Fran Tarkenton	17	1	12	0
Dan Marino	16	1	13	1
Len Dawson	14	0	11	0
Sammy Baugh	14	1	14	1
Joe Montana	13	0	11	0
Bob Griese	13	1	10	1
Y.A. Tittle	13	4	12	2
Ken Anderson	12	2	11	1
Johnny Unitas	12	4	10	2
Phil Simms	11	2	5	1
Bart Starr	11	3	10	1
Charlie Conerly	11	3	10	3
Roman Gabriel	11	3	7	1
Brett Favre	11	4	9	1
Dave Kreig	11	4	6	0
Otto Graham	10	0	10	0
Arnie Herber	10	0	9	0
Norm Van Brocklin	10	1	7	0
Jim Kelly	10	1	5	0
Mark Brunell	10	1	4	1
Sonny Jurgensen	10	2	9	0
Craig Morton	10	3	6	1
Bobby Layne	10	4	6	2
Dan Fouts	10	5	10	1
John Elway	10	6	5	2
Steve DeBerg	10	6	2	3

On the flip side, Rick Mirer never met the league average in any season; he not only had 7 below average seasons, but each was at least 10 percent below average. Mike Pagel and Bobby Douglass also never met the league average, while each had 6 below average years. Two quarterbacks had 6 seasons at least 10 percent below average, but Babe Parilli had 5 above average, including three at 10 percent above, and Dan Pastorini had four above, including one at 10 percent above. Overall, Vinny Testaverde had the most negative seasons by far. The following

table lists quarterbacks with at least seven seasons below the league average in passer rating.

Name	>=100%	<100%	10%	-10%
Vinny Testaverde	5	12	5	5
Jim Hart	7	8	3	5
Jim Harbaugh	5	8	2	1
Drew Bledsoe	5	8	1	3
Kerry Collins	3	8	0	5
Jay Schroeder	2	8	1	4
Mike Tomczak	2	8	0	5
Boomer Esiason	7	7	6	2
Norm Snead	7	7	3	5
Steve Grogan	7	7	4	4
Joe Ferguson	7	7	2	5
Babe Parilli	5	7	3	6
Tobin Rote	5	7	3	5
Charley Johnson	4	7	4	1
Rodney Peete	4	7	1	4
Dan Pastorini	4	7	1	6
Richard Todd	2	7	2	3
Trent Dilfer	2	7	1	3
Rick Mirer	0	7	0	7

Three Hall of Famers had as many as six negative seasons. George Blanda made the Hall primarily as a kicker so we'll set him aside. The other two, though, are instructive about the care and feeding of quarterbacks. John Elway's first 10 seasons in the league were spent under Coach Dan Reeves with whom he didn't get along. In that time, he was usually a few percentage points on either side of average, and then Reeves was fired. For the last six years of Elway's career, he was at least 9 percent above the league average each season as he blossomed under his former college coach, Jim Fassell, and then the West Coast master Mike Shanahan. Terry Bradshaw simply took an eternity to develop into a pro quarterback. He was below average for his first five and six of his first seven seasons. Once things clicked, however, he had six straight positive seasons, including four at least 10 percent above average. Dan Fouts, who had five negative seasons, was another quarterback who took several struggling seasons to develop, while Joe Namath, who also had five in the red, serves as an example of what injuries can do to a Hall of Fame career.

One thing Namath was undeniably good at was putting points on the board. The aim of each player is to win the game, and the best way a quarterback can help his team win is by leading his offense to scores. Scoring is another way we can examine a quarterback's performance relative to the league average. I looked at every quarterback who was the predominant starter on his team in at least five seasons and compared the team's point totals to the league average in those seasons. Admittedly, this is a quick and dirty study. Some teams are better at scoring via defense and special teams than others, and that is not taken into account here. In addition, it's easier to lead your team to scoring drives if you have Jerry Rice and John Taylor to throw to as Joe Montana and Steve Young did rather than Lionel Manuel and Phil McConkey as Phil Simms did. With those caveats in mind, the following table lists the top 20 quarterbacks in scoring above the league average:

Name	Years as Starter	Points	League Points per Team	Relative Scoring Offense
Frank Filchock	1939–41, 1944–46	1881	1089	173%
Benny Friedman	1927–33	1328	790	168%
Sid Luckman	1940–48	2790	1851	151%
Cecil Isbell	1938–42	1252	858	146%
Arnie Herber	1932–40, 1944–45	2236	1600	140%
Bob Waterfield	1945–52	2674	2011	133%
Daryle Lamonica	1967–72	2307	1748	132%
Steve Young	1986, 1991–98	3805	2898	131%
Bob Griese	1967–79	4041	3086	131%
Otto Graham	1946–55	3545	2725	130%
Norm Van Brocklin	1950–60	3569	2845	125%
Trent Green	1998, 2000–06	3347	2678	125%
Peyton Manning	1998–06	3759	3011	125%
Kurt Warner	1999–02, 2004–05	2468	2006	123%
Frankie Albert	1946–51	2013	1687	119%
Joe Montana	1980–90, 1993–94	4848	4125	118%
Tom Brady	2001–06	2302	2006	115%
Terry Bradshaw	1970–82	4133	3602	115%
Brett Favre	1992–06	5651	4936	114%
Drew Brees	2002–06	1923	1683	114%
Danny White	1980–87	2877	2526	114%
Randall Cunningham	1986–90, 1992, 1994, 1998–99	3327	2925	114%

Seven of the top 10 are in the Hall of Fame and two others spent part of their careers sharing time with a Hall of Famer — Filchock with Sammy Baugh and Isbell with Arnie Herber. The only Hall of Famers below 105 percent of the league average were Troy Aikman and Y.A. Tittle at 104 percent, Sonny Jurgensen at 103 percent and Ace Parker way down at 91 percent. There are no surprises at the bottom of the list. Tim Couch is at the bottom as his Browns scored just 76 percent of the league average in points in his five seasons. He is joined by Mike Pagel, Bobby Douglass, David Carr, Gary Hogeboom, Archie Manning, Dave Brown, Jack Trudeau, Billy Joe Tolliver and Adrian Burk. While Manning and Burk had some spectacular moments,

these were bad quarterbacks on terrible teams or vice versa.

As for Namath, he ended up at 107 percent in this measure, but before he went down to a season-ending injury for the third time in four seasons in 1973, he was at 116 percent. Had he quit football at that point, he would be among the top scorers over the league average. For the rest of his injury-racked career, Namath would throw just 47 touchdowns but 77 interceptions. At the end of 1972, he was also at 110 percent in relative passer rating, but would end up a much more pedestrian 103 percent. By hanging on well past when he could perform, a great quarterback seriously damaged his reputation and lessened his Hall of Fame legacy.

Honors, Awards and the Hall of Fame

Since even the best statistical measures fail to reveal a quarterback's full value in this greatest of all team sports, let's look at how a quarterback gains renown. One way to measure the reputations of quarterbacks is to see how many times they were honored by being named either an All Pro or to the Pro Bowl. The two quarterbacks with the most honored seasons are Johnny Unitas and Fran Tarkenton with 11 apiece. Right behind them with 10 are Otto Graham and Dan Marino. The list of quarterbacks who were honored in at least five seasons includes 24 Hall of Famers and seven others. Among the others are Jack Kemp, whose substandard statistics belie the fact that he was regularly a winner and an All Pro in the AFL; John Hadl and Jim Hart, a couple of big arms and inconsistent talents; and the solid but dull Dave Krieg. Also highly honored were the underrated pair of Ken Anderson and Daryle Lamonica and short-termer Cecil Isbell.

Four Hall of Famers had fewer than five honored seasons—Arnie Herber, Ace Parker, Terry Bradshaw and George Blanda. Bradshaw had more Super Bowl wins (4) than honored seasons (3); he didn't really get the respect he deserved, possibly because he played with such a talented cast in Pittsburgh. The other one of interest in this group is Ace Parker who was an unlikely choice for Canton. His brief career (1937–41, 1945–46) was interrupted by World War II and ran parallel to that of Sammy Baugh, Sid Luckman and the above-noted Cecil Isbell who only played five years before quitting to go into coaching. The surprising thing is if you compare the first five seasons of the four, Isbell was first in touchdowns and interception percentage, second in yards and yards per attempt and third in completion percentage, while Sid Luckman was first in yards and yards per attempt, second in completion percentage and touchdowns and fourth in interception percentage. Baugh was third in four of the five categories, while Parker was fourth in four of the categories. Cecil Isbell also ran for more yards than any of the others. His career was too short for the Hall of Fame, but he is a neglected figure in NFL history.

Another honor frequently given to quarterbacks is the Most Valuable Player award. MVP awards have been given out by various organizations and publications in all years since 1938 except for 1950–52, and quarterbacks have been given at least one of these awards in 50 of those 66 seasons. Otto Graham received awards in a record four seasons, two in the AAFC and two in the NFL. Johnny Unitas, Y.A. Tittle, Randall Cunningham and Brett Favre each won MVP awards in three seasons. Favre's were consecutive. Fourteen quarterbacks have won an MVP trophy in two seasons, including two who won the second time in a relief role—the Raiders' George Blanda in 1970 and Earl Morrall in the Dolphins' undefeated 1972. Although Archie Manning and Mark Rypien each had an MVP–winning year, Hall of Famers Sammy Baugh, Bobby Layne, Sonny Jurgensen, Len Dawson, Jim Kelly and Troy Aikman never did.

An honor achieved much less frequently by quarterbacks is Rookie of the Year. Because the position is so difficult to master, only 10 quarterbacks have been so honored in the 42 years that awards have been given. Of these 10, Dan Marino was the only unqualified success. Dennis Shaw of the Bills was selected as Rookie of the Year by all four organizations in 1970, but turned out to be a flop just like the Seahawks' Rick Mirer 23 years later. Greg Cook, Joe Namath and Jim McMahon all had their careers shortened and/or destroyed by injuries, while Jim Plunkett and Steve Bartkowski had careers featuring highs and lows. Ben Roethlisberger and Vince Young are still building their careers and reputations at this time.

The ultimate honor for a pro football player is to be elected to the Hall of Fame, and 28 quarterbacks have received this accolade; 23 are from the modern era of post–1950, two-platoon football, while Benny Friedman, Arnie Herber, Ace Parker, Sammy Baugh and Sid Luckman are from the earlier era of two-way players. The election of the revolutionary passer Friedman in 2005 removed the last clearly overqualified quarterback from the waiting list. Because quarterback is such a glamour position, there are more quarterbacks in the Hall than any position other than running back, yet they aren't really overrepresented. The problem with Canton isn't that there are too many quarterbacks, but that there are too few guards and tackles.

Of the 28 enshrined quarterbacks, the five

most questionable are George Blanda, Joe Namath, Warren Moon, Bob Griese and Ace Parker. George Blanda played pro football for 26 years and left the game having scored more points than any other player; he was deservingly elected for his placekicking, longevity and irascible personality. Joe Namath was a great talent who changed the game. Namath signed with the Jets in 1965 for more money than anyone had imagined at the time and had an immediate impact as an on-the-field bomber and as an off-the-field celebrity. He helped establish the AFL's struggling New York franchise and then led that team to a shocking Super Bowl win over the Colts that put the upstart AFL on par with the traditional NFL. And he did all this bravely on two injury-ravaged knees that rendered him nearly immobile. His peak was short, his career statistics unimpressive, but he belongs in the Hall. Warren Moon went to Canada for six seasons to establish that he could play because no NFL team would draft this proud black quarterback. His career had its ups and downs, but he played until he was 44 and accumulated impressive lifetime statistics while proving to the league that there was no room for racism at the quarterback position. Bob Griese was steady, smart and the leader of back-to-back Super Bowl champions. He did not have to pass much in the Dolphins run-heavy offense, but he was a respected winner who won two MVP's as well. Ace Parker is probably the least qualified quarterback in the Hall, but his career was interrupted by war and his relative passer rating was a healthy 31 percent better than the league average. It's just that Sammy Baugh was 52 percent better, Sid Luckman was 58 percent better and the forgotten Cecil Isbell was 88 percent better.

To qualify for the Hall of Fame, a quarterback should have been among the top two or three passers in the league at some point in his career. Each enshrinee can make that argument. The most deserving names of those outside the Hall have a tougher time making their cases. Charlie Conerly won an NFL title and had 10 seasons 10 percent better than the league. For his career, he was 13 percent better than the league had a won-lost record of 79–52. Unfortunately, he also played in a decade already represented by six Hall of Famers. Ken Stabler had a 96–49 won-lost record, won a Super Bowl and two MVP awards, had a relative rating 9 percent

greater than the league, had five seasons at least 10 percent greater than the league and had four honored seasons. He also had four seasons below the league average in passer rating and threw 28 more interceptions than touchdowns. Ken Anderson had 11 seasons 10 percent better than the league, had five honored seasons and was 17 percent better than the league for his career. Playing for a lot of mediocre teams, his won-lost record was 91–81. He was intelligent, consistent and accurate, but was not lucky enough to play on great teams. Four times he led the league in passing. Phil Simms had a 95–64 won-lost record, won a Super Bowl, had five seasons 10 percent better than the league, had three honored seasons and only two negative seasons. But he never had top-flight receivers and worked primarily in an offense that emphasized running. Randall Cunningham never got to a Super Bowl, but won three MVP awards as the Ultimate Weapon who was equally talented at running and throwing. He had five seasons 10 percent better than the league and an 82–52 won-lost record. He was also known for melting under pressure and was just 3–6 in the playoffs.

The Hall of Fame chances of these quarterbacks are also affected by quarterbacks yet to retire. Among active players, Brett Favre, Peyton Manning and Tom Brady seem to have the clearest path to Canton as quarterbacks whose careers demonstrate a good balance of both peak and extended value. While the first half of Terry Bradshaw's career was awful, he made the Hall on the basis of the high peaks he achieved in the second half. By contrast, Warren Moon made a stronger case of his value over his entire extended career. The best of the best stake a claim to both types of value; Otto Graham, Johnny Unitas and Joe Montana were at the top of the game for most of their long careers and usually are ranked in the top three of all quarterbacks in history.

All Time Rankings

Although membership in the Hall of Fame would seem to be a prerequisite for being included in discussions ranking the greatest quarterbacks ever to play, that is not always the case. A number of prominent commentators over the years have attempted to rank the top quarterbacks in NFL history, and they sometimes have some eccentric choices. Sportswriter Murray Olderman wrote *The Pro Quarterback* in 1968 and selected his top 10:

1	Otto Graham	6	Norm Van Brocklin
2	John Unitas	7	Y.A. Tittle
3	Bobby Layne	8	Bob Waterfield
4	Sammy Baugh	9	Bart Starr
5	Sid Luckman	10	Charley Conerly

When Olderman wrote that book, the NFL was not quite 50 years old, and the modern T-formation was only around 20 so his range of quarterback choices was somewhat limited. In 1982, Hall of Fame coach George Allen wrote *Pro Football's 100 Greatest Players* and selected his top 14 quarterbacks from a broader population, but eight of Olderman's 10 were in Allen's top 10 as well. Allen replaced Conerly and Tittle with Terry Bradshaw and Roger Staubach:

1	Sammy Baugh	8	Bobby Layne
2	Sid Luckman	9	Norm Van Brocklin
3	Johnny Unitas	10	Bob Waterfield
4	Terry Bradshaw	11	Arnie Herber
5	Bart Starr	12	Fran Tarkenton
6	Otto Graham	13	Ken Stabler
7	Roger Staubach	14	Joe Namath

Thirty years after Olderman, there were many more qualified names to choose from, and several top 50 lists began to appear. The editors of *Total Football* compiled their unranked list of the top 50 in 1998, while NFL Films produced a video that ranked their top 50, including this top 10:

NFL Films (1998)

1	Joe Montana	6	John Elway
2	John Unitas	7	Sammy Baugh
3	Dan Marino	8	Roger Staubach
4	Terry Bradshaw	9	Brett Favre
5	Otto Graham	10	Bart Starr

Four of Olderman's choices and six of Allen's made the top quintile of the NFL Films list, but only three of Olderman and five of Allen would make the crest of *Sports Illustrated's* Peter King's top 50 in his 1999 book *Greatest Quarterbacks*.

Peter King (1999)

1	Otto Graham	6	Dan Marino
2	Joe Montana	7	Steve Young
3	John Unitas	8	Terry Bradshaw
4	Sammy Baugh	9	Brett Favre
5	John Elway	10	Roger Staubach

Veteran sportswriter Jonathan Rand ranked his top 25 quarterbacks in *The Gridiron's Greatest Quarterbacks* (2004) and included at the top five from Olderman's original list and seven from Allen's.

Jonathan Rand (2004)

1	Joe Montana	6	Terry Bradshaw
2	Otto Graham	7	Dan Marino
3	John Unitas	8	Roger Staubach
4	Sammy Baugh	9	Bart Starr
5	John Elway	10	Sid Luckman

Three more compilations came in 2005. *Sports Illustrated* listed its unranked top 25 quarterbacks in *The Football Book*, and in the same book included Paul Zimmerman's All Decade teams that included 21 generally familiar quarterbacks. The *Sporting News* ranked its top 50 that same year in *Pro Football's Greatest Quarterbacks*. Once again, four of Olderman's choices make the *Sporting News* top 10 while six of Allen's list are included.

Sporting News (2005)

1	John Unitas	6	Dan Marino
2	Joe Montana	7	Brett Favre
3	Otto Graham	8	Terry Bradshaw
4	John Elway	9	Roger Staubach
5	Sammy Baugh	10	Bart Starr

Each of the four top 50 lists has some idiosyncratic selections not found on any other list. NFL Films includes Dandy Don Meredith, pioneer Doug Williams and Buffalo's Joe Ferguson. Peter King includes little guys Doug Flutie and Eddie LeBaron, lefties Frankie Albert and Mark Brunell, injury-prone Jim McMahon and Greg Cook, and rooted trees Drew Bledsoe and Bernie Kosar. The *Sporting News* included old timers Paddy Driscoll and Dutch Clark as well as current players Steve McNair and Kurt Warner. *Total Football* included underrated Cecil Isbell, blood and guts Billy Kilmer, overrated Neil Lomax and super sub Earl Morrall. Altogether in these lists there are 71 names, 72 if you add in *Sports Illustrated's* inclusion of non-passer Fritz Pollard. To find the consensus ranking among these groups, I assigned 50 points for a number one rank 49 for number two and so on. The following table lists the consensus top 26:

	NFL Films (1998)	Peter King (1999)	Sporting News (2005)	Jonathan Rand (2004)	Total
Joe Montana	50	49	49	50	198
John Unitas	49	48	50	48	195
Otto Graham	46	50	48	49	193
John Elway	45	46	47	46	184
Sammy Baugh	44	47	46	47	184
Dan Marino	48	45	45	44	182
Terry Bradshaw	47	43	43	45	178
Roger Staubach	43	41	42	43	169
Brett Favre	42	42	44	40	168
Bart Starr	41	38	41	42	162
Steve Young	40	44	38	37	159
Sid Luckman	35	40	37	41	153
Fran Tarkenton	37	36	40	39	152
Troy Aikman	39	37	39	36	151
Bobby Layne	34	33	35	38	140
Dan Fouts	29	34	36	35	134
Joe Namath	32	39	28	34	133
Jim Kelly	36	32	32	31	131
Sonny Jurgensen	30	35	33	32	130
Y.A. Tittle	38	29	31	30	128
Norm Van Brocklin	33	27	34	33	127
Len Dawson	31	26	30	28	115
Bob Griese	28	28	29	29	114
Warren Moon	22	24	27	26	99
Ken Stabler	24	25	21	27	97
Phil Simms	26	31	24	0	81

Eight of Olderman's original choices are still in the top 21 of the merged list. The other two, Bob Waterfield and Charlie Conerly, dropped to 31st to 43rd respectively. Twelve of George Allen's top 14 are on this list as well. Missing are Bob Waterfield again, and early tailback Arnie Herber. Montana, Unitas and Graham are clearly the consensual choices as the greatest ever in this approach.

The editors of *The Hidden Game of Football* (1998) took another approach to rank players. In thinking about the Hall of Fame, they came up with a method to rank linemen and others with little or no statistics — use their All Pro and Pro Bowl selections. They awarded eight points for each year as a consensus selection, five points for each year as a first team or Pro Bowl selection and three points for each year as a second team selection. They then applied this to all positions, including the statistics-rich quarterback slot. I have updated their data through 2006 and applied it to the 26 quarterbacks above, plus current stars Peyton Manning and Tom Brady. We can call this the Hall of Fame Predictor Method:

Name	Consensus	1st Team	2nd Team	Points
Otto Graham	9	1	0	77
Johnny Unitas	5	6	0	70
Sammy Baugh	5	4	0	60
Dan Marino	3	6	1	57
Fran Tarkenton	1	9	1	56
Sid Luckman	5	1	2	51
Brett Favre	3	5	0	49
Joe Montana	2	6	0	46
John Elway	0	9	0	45
Warren Moon	0	9	0	45
Steve Young	3	4	0	44
Y.A. Tittle	3	4	0	44
Norm Van Brocklin	1	7	0	43
Bob Griese	2	4	1	39
Peyton Manning	3	3	0	39
Roger Staubach	4	1	0	37
Len Dawson	2	4	0	36
Dan Fouts	2	4	0	36
Bobby Layne	1	4	1	31
Joe Namath	2	2	1	29
Sonny Jurgensen	1	4	0	28
Jim Kelly	1	4	0	28
Bart Starr	1	3	1	26
Ken Stabler	2	2	0	26
Troy Aikman	0	5	0	25
Terry Bradshaw	1	2	0	18

Name	Consensus	1st Team	2nd Team	Points
Tom Brady	0	3	0	15
Phil Simms	0	3	0	15

Montana falls back into the pack a bit because he didn't quite get the All Pro recognition of some others. Of course, there was no greater champion than Montana so that should be taken into account. *The Hidden Game* editors listed championship game results in their tables, but did not assign points for them. I have given eight points for a Super Bowl or title game MVP, five points for winning a Super Bowl or league title and three for just starting in one. For roughly 10 years before the Super Bowl, *Sport Magazine* would give a Corvette to the NFL Championship MVP. I have counted that here and retroactively given title game MVPs in several earlier years if the quarterback was the main factor in his team winning the game.

Name	All Pro Points	Title Game Won-Lost	SB MVP	Title Points	Total
Otto Graham	77	7–3	4	56	133
Johnny Unitas	70	2–3	2	25	95
Sid Luckman	51	4–1	3	32	83
Sammy Baugh	60	2–3	1	22	82
Joe Montana	46	4–0	3	29	75
Norm Van Brocklin	43	2–3	2	25	68
John Elway	45	2–3	1	22	67
Fran Tarkenton	56	0–3		9	65
Bart Starr	26	5–1	2	34	60
Dan Marino	57	0–1		3	60
Brett Favre	49	1–1		8	57
Roger Staubach	37	2–2	1	19	56
Y.A. Tittle	44	0–3		9	53
Bobby Layne	31	3–1	1	21	52
Len Dawson	36	2–1	1	16	52
Bob Griese	39	2–1		13	52
Steve Young	44	1–0	1	8	52
Peyton Manning	39	1–0	1	8	47
Warren Moon	45	0–0		0	45
Terry Bradshaw	18	4–0	2	26	44
Troy Aikman	25	3–0	1	18	43
Jim Kelly	28	0–4		12	40
Joe Namath	29	1–0	1	8	37
Tom Brady	15	3–0	2	21	36
Sonny Jurgensen	28	1–1		8	36
Dan Fouts	36	0–0		0	36
Ken Stabler	26	1–0		5	31
Phil Simms	15	1–0	1	8	23

Otto Graham tightened his grip on the top spot, while Joe Montana rose three spots with championship points, as did another great champion, Sid Luckman. However, Bobby Layne jumped five spots, Terry Bradshaw six, Norm Van Brocklin seven and Bart Starr nine. Moving down were quarterbacks who weren't as successful in the postseason. Fran Tarkenton dropped three spots, Dan Marino and Steve Young six and Warren Moon nine. Now, let's give some value to passing skills by adding four points for each season one of these quarterbacks led the league in passer rating.

Name	All Pro Points	Title Points	Leader Points	Total
Otto Graham	77	56	24	157
Sammy Baugh	60	22	24	106
Johnny Unitas	70	25	0	95
Joe Montana	46	29	20	95
Sid Luckman	51	32	4	87
Dan Marino	57	3	20	80
Norm Van Brocklin	43	25	8	76
Roger Staubach	37	19	20	76
Steve Young	44	8	24	76
John Elway	45	22	8	75
Bart Starr	26	34	12	72

Name	All Pro Points	Title Points	Leader Points	Total
Fran Tarkenton	56	9	4	69
Len Dawson	36	16	16	68
Brett Favre	49	8	4	61
Bob Griese	39	13	8	60
Peyton Manning	39	8	12	59
Y.A. Tittle	44	9	4	57
Warren Moon	45	0	8	53
Bobby Layne	31	21	0	52
Terry Bradshaw	18	26	4	48
Sonny Jurgensen	28	8	12	48
Jim Kelly	28	12	4	44
Troy Aikman	25	18	0	43
Dan Fouts	36	0	4	40
Ken Stabler	26	5	8	39
Joe Namath	29	8	0	37
Tom Brady	15	21	0	36
Phil Simms	15	8	0	23

Otto Graham stays at the top no matter what criteria are used. He was an accurate, efficient passer, revered in his time, and the ultimate winner. With the passing leader data added, Dan Marino, Roger Staubach and Sonny Jurgensen all rose four spots, while Steve Young jumped up eight. Fran Tarkenton continued to drop, going down another four along with Y.A. Tittle, while Bobby Layne fell five spots back to where he started.

Comparing the final results from the Hall of Fame Predictor to the Expert Rankings, some quarterbacks are treated diametrically differently. The experts rank Terry Bradshaw 13 spots higher than the method does. Similarly, Troy Aikman and Joe Namath are ranked nine spots higher, Dan Fouts eight spots and John Elway six. Meanwhile, the method raises Norm Van Brocklin 14 spots, Len Dawson nine, Bob Griese eight, Sid Luckman seven and Warren Moon six. With the method, we can see what is being measured and how things are weighted. With the experts, the weighting changes from case to case. Terry Bradshaw is ranked seventh by the experts on the basis of his four Super Bowl wins, but Bart Starr with five titles is 10th, Sid Luckman, with four titles is 12th and Norm Van

Brocklin with three titles is 21st. Joe Namath is ranked 17th by the experts because of his raw talent that injuries prevented him from fully expressing and for the impact of his guaranteed win in Super Bowl III. Actually, Namath is outperformed in the method by three Hall of Famers who didn't even make the experts' cut—Arnie Herber, Bob Waterfield and Benny Friedman—as well as by non-enshrinees Ken Anderson, Jack Kemp and John Hadl. As a matter of fact, all retired players who scored at least 60 by the method are in Canton except for Anderson, Kemp and Hadl. Kemp and Hadl threw a lot of interceptions, completed a poor percentage of their passes and had their roots in the early days of the AFL. They will never be elected to the Hall, but Ken Anderson remains on the ballot.

Quarterback is such a multifaceted position that to rank quarterbacks becomes a very personal enterprise according to what you value most. If you value wins, maybe you'll go with Elway or Favre; if you favor winning percentage, you'll go with Graham; if you favor spectacular postseasons, maybe you'll pick Montana or Bradshaw; if you favor championships, you might pick Starr or Graham; if you favor passer rating, you could take Young or Montana; if you favor relative passer rating, you'll lean to Baugh and Luckman; if you favor touchdown passes, maybe you go with Marino or Unitas. Each element represents a part of the perfect quarterback, but no great quarterback is without flaws.

We've looked at several ways to rank quarterbacks, yet none of them totally satisfy me. Here's another way to look at the question of who is the greatest of all quarterbacks—the one game test. If you had one game to win, whom would you want behind center? I would take Bart Starr who has the highest postseason passer rating (102.9) and lowest postseason interception rate (1.88) of any quarterback who started at least 10 playoff games. He never had a bad game when it counted, and, to me, that it is what is all about.

Of Passing Interest: Miscellaneous Notes

Passing Tailbacks

Before the T-Formation, triple threat tailbacks did most of the passing. Sammy Baugh's career was split almost exactly in half between playing tailback and quarterback. The breakdown of his statistics looks like this:

Name	Games	Att	Comp	%	Yards	Y/Att	TD	Int	Rating
Baugh, Sammy as QB	87	1620	932	57.5%	12658	7.8	103	102	77.5
Baugh, Sammy as TB	80	1375	761	55.3%	9228	6.7	84	101	65.9

The following table lists the 18 tailbacks that passed for at least 2,500 yards. Two notes: pre–1933 numbers Friedman, Dunn, Lambeau, Nevers and McBride are incomplete and suspect; Bob Hoernschemeyer was a tailback in the AAFC, but switched to halfback when he joined the NFL

Name	Att	Comp	%	Yards	Y/Att	TD	Int	Rating
Baugh, Sammy as TB	1375	761	55.3%	9228	6.7	84	101	65.9
Herber, Arnie	1216	496	40.8%	8324	6.8	81	109	49.5
Friedman, Benny	875	470	53.7%	7650	8.7	68	68	73.9
Isbell, Cecil	818	411	50.2%	5945	7.3	61	52	72.6
Dobbs, Glenn	934	446	47.8%	5876	6.3	45	52	61
Filchock, Frank	677	342	50.5%	4921	7.3	47	79	58
Parker, Ace	718	335	46.7%	4701	6.5	30	50	53.2
Dunn, Red	620	275	44.4%	4641	7.5	48	63	56.5
Lambeau, Curly	700	278	39.7%	4493	6.4	24	78	33.8
Hoernschemeyer, Bob as TB	688	308	44.8%	4109	6.0	32	51	48.9
Hall, Parker	721	329	45.6%	4013	5.6	29	67	38
Nevers, Ernie	573	257	44.9%	4012	7.0	25	61	43.6
Danowski, Ed	637	309	48.5%	3817	6.0	38	43	59.2
Comp, Irv	519	213	41.0%	3354	6.5	28	52	41.6
Clement, Johnny	442	192	43.4%	3226	7.3	20	39	47
McBride, Jack	402	206	51.2%	3123	7.8	31	57	63.3
Sanders, Spec	418	204	48.8%	2771	6.6	23	37	51.8
O'Brien, Davey	478	223	46.7%	2614	5.5	11	34	41.8

The Halfback Option Play

One other group of passers that should not be ignored is the running backs. Particularly in the 1950s and 1960s, the halfback option play where the runner takes the handoff and has the option of running or passing was a popular and successful ground gainer. Specialists included Frank Gifford, Paul Hornung and Dan Reeves. In the years since, Walter Payton and Marcus Allen were good at running the play, but it is used much less frequently now. The two current specialists are Ladainian Tomlinson who has completed 7 of 10 passes for 6 touchdowns and Antwaan Randle El whose amazing near-perfect performance appears on this table of runners and receivers who have gained at least 200 yards through the air, sorted by yards.

Name	Attempts	Comp	%	Yards	Y/Att	TD	Int	Rating
Tracy, Tom	67	24	35.8%	854	12.7	6	5	82.8
Gifford, Frank	63	29	46.0%	823	13.1	14	6	92.5
Crow, John David	70	33	47.1%	759	10.8	5	5	80.6
Hoak, Dick	40	20	50.0%	427	10.7	4	3	90.3
Hornung, Paul	55	24	43.6%	383	7.0	5	4	67.5
Moore, Tom	19	13	68.4%	383	20.2	5	1	128.8
Reeves, Dan	32	14	43.8%	370	11.6	2	4	68
Payton, Walter	34	11	32.4%	331	9.7	8	6	69.6
Lowe, Paul	21	10	47.6%	326	15.5	1	1	89.9
Allen, Marcus	27	12	44.4%	282	10.4	6	1	106.8
Matte, Tom	42	12	28.6%	246	5.9	2	2	47.5
Foster, Gene	19	11	57.9%	245	12.9	1	0	127.1
Lincoln, Keith	17	8	47.1%	240	14.1	5	1	108.5
Barnes, Billy	25	10	40.0%	233	9.3	4	4	74.3
Randle El, Antwaan	19	16	84.2%	216	11.4	3	0	153.6
Hill, Calvin	13	5	38.5%	204	15.7	3	1	93.8
Mingo, Gene	18	6	33.3%	200	11.1	2	1	90

Quarterback Brothers

If you are preparing to sign one of two quarterbacking brothers, always pick the older one. There have been six pairs of brothers to play quarterback in the NFL — not counting Dutch and Joey Sternaman from the 1920s Chicago Bears who weren't really modern quarterbacks. In each case, the older brother was better, usually by a significant margin. In this table, the older brother is listed first:

Name	Games	Att	Comp	%	Yards	Y/Att	TD	Int	Rating
Bradshaw, Terry	168	3901	2025	51.9%	27989	7.2	212	210	70.9
Bradshaw, Craig	2	0	0	0	0	0	0	0	0
Detmer, Ty	54	946	546	57.7%	6351	6.7	34	35	74.7
Detmer, Koy	103	354	184	52.0%	1944	5.5	10	14	61.2
Hasselbeck, Matt	119	2576	1552	60.2%	18367	7.1	114	72	85.1
Hasselbeck, Tim	11	177	95	53.7%	1012	5.7	5	7	63.6
Huard, Damon	48	533	318	59.7%	3569	6.7	20	9	85.2
Huard, Brock	8	107	60	56.1%	689	6.4	4	2	80.3
Manning, Peyton	144	4890	3131	64.0%	37586	7.7	275	139	94.4
Manning, Eli	41	1276	690	54.1%	8049	6.3	54	44	73.2
McCown, Josh	35	862	498	57.8%	5431	6.3	25	29	72.1
McCown, Luke	5	98	48	49.0%	608	6.2	4	7	52.6

Twelve more quarterbacks had brothers who played in the NFL at another position:

Randall Cunningham and FB Sam Cunningham
Joe Duffek and LB Don Duffek
Tony Eason and DB Bo Eason
Doug Flutie and WR Darren Flutie
John Fourcade and LB Keith Fourcade
Jason Garrett and WR John Garrett
Don McPherson and DB Miles McPherson
Moses Moreno and LB Zeke Moreno
Steve Pelluer and LB Scott Pelluer
Bob Reinhard and G Bill Reinhard
Mike Shula and WR David Shula
Leo Stasica and HB Stan Stasica

Quarterback Fathers and Sons

There have been seven quarterbacks in NFL history who had sons play in the NFL. The father is listed first in each of these families:

Name	Games	Att	Comp	%	Yards	Y/Att	TD	Int	Rating
Freitas, Jesse	31	253	123	48.6%	1884	7.4	21	27	61.7
Freitas, Jesse Jr.	13	219	98	44.7%	1244	5.7	8	13	50.5
Griese, Bob	161	3429	1926	56.2%	25092	7.3	192	172	77.1
Griese, Brian	81	2350	1481	63.0%	16564	7.0	104	80	84.5
Kemp, Jack	121	3073	1436	46.7%	21232	6.9	114	183	19.9
Kemp, Jeff	97	916	479	52.3%	6230	6.8	39	40	70
Simms, Phil	164	4647	2576	55.4%	33462	7.2	199	157	78.5
Simms, Chris	19	492	291	59.1%	3087	6.3	12	17	71.2
Nix, Emery	16	72	34	47.2%	546	7.6	5	3	78.8
Nix, Kent	45	652	301	46.2%	3644	5.6	23	49	44.3
Manning, Archie	151	3642	2011	55.2%	23911	6.6	125	173	67.1
Manning, Peyton	144	4890	3131	64.0%	37586	7.7	275	139	94.4
Manning, Eli	41	1276	690	54.1%	8049	6.3	54	44	73.2
David Whitehurst	54	980	504	51.4%	6205	6.3	28	51	59.2
Charlie Whitehurst	2	0	0	0	0	0	0	0	0

No quarterback ever had a son who played any other position than quarterback, probably because to play any other position would be slumming. Fourteen NFL players, though, have had sons who played quarterback.

The sons of three backs: Mike Shula, Danny White and Bert Jones

The sons of two linebackers: Todd Marinovich and Bradlee Van Pelt

The sons of four linemen: Brian Clark, Bill Kenney, Craig Kupp and Marquess Tuiasosopo

The sons of five ends: Scott Campbell, Matt and Tim Hasselbeck, Greg Knafelc, Kyle Mackey and George Wilson Jr.

In addition, Anthony Dilweg was the grandson of the great 1920s Packers end Lavvie Dilweg, while Rex Grossman's grandfather Rex was a fullback on the original Baltimore Colts and his uncle Terry Cole was a runner for the Colts in 1968.

Quarterbacks and Professional Baseball

Passing tailbacks who played major league baseball include infielder Paddy Driscoll who hit .107 in 1917 and pitcher Ernie Nevers who won 6 and lost 12 from 1926–28, while Joe Lillard played extensively in the Negro Leagues. These quarterbacks also made the majors

Infielder Ace Parker hit .179 in 1937–38.
Catcher Tom Yewcic hit .000 in 1957.
Outfielder Dean Look hit .000 in 1961.
Third Baseman Josh Booty hit .269 in 1996–98.

Quarterbacks who played in the minor leagues include Sammy Baugh, Bubby Brister, Adrian Burk, Quincy Carter, John Elway, Jug Girard, Drew Henson, Chad Hutchinson, Doug Johnson, Bobby Layne, Keith Molesworth, Jay Schroeder, Akili Smith, Charlie Trippi and Chris Weinke. It may also be noted that superstar Tom Brady was drafted as a catcher in the 18th round in 1995.

Head-to-Head Duels

The dramatic annual showdowns between the two top quarterbacks in football, Peyton Manning and Tom Brady, have produced nine charged battles in the past six years. The first six went to Brady on his way to three Super Bowls, but Manning has won the last three and a Super Bowl of his own. The competition is reminiscent of the pitched battles between Bart Starr's Packers and Johnny Unitas' Colts in the 1960s. That competition ended in an 8–8 draw. I went through each half decade and selected the top five quarterbacks subjectively and compared how they did when they went head to head.

A few of the most celebrated pairings are not included because the two met all too rarely — Dan Marino and John Elway met only three times in 16 years; Terry Bradshaw and Roger Staubach met only four times. Joe Namath and Johnny Unitas only met two times after Super Bowl III, but the last time, on September 24, 1972, was an unforgettable shootout that set a league record with 892 combined passing yards. Unitas completed 26 of 44 for 376 yards and two touchdowns, but Namath completed 15 of 28 for 496 yards and six touchdowns, including scoring strikes of 65, 67, 79 and 80 yards. The Jets won 44–34, and the two master quarterbacks never met again.

Some of the best rivalries such as Terry Bradshaw and Dan Pastorini or Dan Marino and

Ken O'Brien I did not include because only one of the two was truly an elite quarterback. Thus, there have been just 10 such Olympian face offs that had as many as 10 meetings; the results are detailed in the following table. Brady and Manning will meet for the 10th time in 2007.

%	Quarterback	Wins	Opponent	Wins	Ties
.727	Otto Graham	8	Frankie Albert	3	0
.679	Norm Van Brocklin	9	Y.A. Tittle	4	1
.667	Jim Kelly	14	Dan Marino	7	0
.600	Sid Luckman	6	Sammy Baugh	4	0
.571	Y.A. Tittle	8	Bobby Layne	6	0
.565	Bobby Layne	13	Norm Van Brocklin	10	0
.563	Terry Bradshaw	9	Ken Anderson	7	0
.500	John Unitas	8	Bart Starr	8	0
.500	Len Dawson	6	Daryle Lamonica	6	2
.500	Otto Graham	5	Charlie Conerly	5	1

Following a Legend

How do you replace a Hall of Fame quarterback? Usually not very successfully. On four occasions, one Hall of Famer has been succeeded by another: Bob Waterfield by Norm Van Brocklin; Norm Van Brocklin (in Philadelphia) by Sonny Jurgensen; Johnny Unitas (in San Diego) by Dan Fouts and Joe Montana by Steve Young. Unitas is interesting because he was succeeded by Marty Domres and Bert Jones on the 1973 Colts and by Fouts on the 1974 Chargers. Warren Moon was replaced in three different cities.

Hall of Famers have sometimes been part of a string of three or more quality quarterbacks: Bob Waterfield, Norm Van Brocklin and Billy Wade with the Rams; Frankie Albert, Y.A. Tittle and John Brodie with the 49ers; Charlie Conerly, Y.A. Tittle and Earl Morrall with the Gi-

ants; Don Meredith, Craig Morton, Roger Staubach and Danny White with the Cowboys; Sonny Jurgensen, Billy Kilmer and Joe Theismann with the Redskins; Daryle Lamonica, George Blanda, Kenny Stabler and Jim Plunkett with the Raiders; and Joe Montana, Steve Young and Jeff Garcia with the 49ers.

In the following table, I compare the Hall of Famers and their followers by career relative passer rating. In short, a quarterback's career passer rating is compared to the league average passer rating during his career. The differences in this table are interesting, but there are failings as well. John Elway never scored well on passer rating, while his successor Brian Griese did, but no one would ever put Griese on the same plane as the all-time great Elway. Thus, this table is for amusement purposes only.

Hall of Famer	HOF Rel Rate	Followed by	Follower Rel Rate	Difference
Sammy Baugh	152	Eddie LeBaron	96	-56
Otto Graham	150	Tommy O'Connell	97	-53
Sid Luckman	158	Johnny Lujack	118	-40
Bart Starr	120	Scott Hunter	84	-36
Johnny Unitas	117	Marty Domres	83	-34
Len Dawson	129	Mike Livingston	97	-32
Dan Fouts	112	Mark Malone	83	-29
Bob Griese	115	David Woodley	87	-28
Terry Bradshaw	104	Cliff Stoudt	78	-26
Joe Montana (KCC)	123	Steve Bono	98	-25
Fran Tarkenton	121	Tommy Kramer	99	-22
Jim Kelly	110	Todd Collins	89	-21
Norm Van Brocklin (STL)	127	Billy Wade	107	-20
Warren Moon (TEN)	106	Billy Joe Tolliver	88	-18

Hall of Famer	HOF Rel Rate	Followed by	Follower Rel Rate	Difference
Steve Young	127	Jeff Garcia	109	-18
Troy Aikman	105	Quincy Carter	90	-15
Sonny Jurgensen	123	Billy Kilmer	108	-15
Dan Marino	113	Jay Fiedler	98	-15
Roger Staubach	127	Danny White	113	-14
Bobby Layne (PIT)	103	Ed Brown	93	-10
Y.A. Tittle (SFF)	117	John Brodie	108	-9
Warren Moon (SEA)	106	Jon Kitna	97	-9
Joe Namath	103	Richard Todd	94	-9
Bobby Layne (DET)	103	Tobin Rote	95	-8
Y.A. Tittle (NYG)	117	Earl Morrall	111	-6
Johnny Unitas (SDC)	117	Dan Fouts	112	-5
Norm Van Brocklin (PHL)	127	Sonny Jurgensen	123	-4
Johnny Unitas (IND2)	117	Bert Jones	114	-3
Warren Moon (MIN)	106	Brad Johnson	105	-1
John Elway	105	Brian Griese	107	2
Joe Montana (SFF)	123	Steve Young	127	4
Bob Waterfield	113	Norm Van Brocklin	127	14
Arnie Herber	147	Cecil Isbell	188	41

Interceptions

The negative statistic of pass interceptions is often more indicative of a quarterback's success or failure than all the many positive ones, especially in the playoffs. Yet, roughly half of the quarterbacks who threw more than 200 interceptions were Hall of Famers, including such gunslingers as Johnny Unitas, Joe Namath, Terry Bradshaw, Dan Marino, Y.A. Tittle and Dan Fouts. In the 75 years that the NFL has kept official passing statistics, there have been just four passers who have held the dubious distinction of throwing the most career interceptions: Arnie Herber, Sammy Baugh, Bobby Layne and George Blanda. Brett Favre will become the fifth in 2007 and may never relinquish the crown. Blanda also holds the single season record of 42 in a 14-game season. All but Herber are among the 24 quarterbacks in the following table who threw more than 200 interceptions lifetime:

Name	Interceptions	Int/Pass
Blanda, George	277	6.91%
Favre, Brett	273	3.32%
Marino, Dan	271	3.24%
Hadl, John	268	5.72%
Tarkenton, Fran	266	4.11%
Testaverde, Vinny	261	4.00%
Snead, Norm	257	5.90%
Unitas, Johnny	253	4.88%
Tittle, Y.A.	248	7.30%
Hart, Jim	247	4.87%
Layne, Bobby	243	6.57%

Name	Interceptions	Int/Pass
Fouts, Dan	242	4.32%
Moon, Warren	233	3.41%
Elway, John	226	3.12%
Brodie, John	224	4.99%
Stabler, Ken	222	5.85%
Namath, Joe	220	5.85%
Parilli, Babe	220	6.61%
Bradshaw, Terry	210	5.38%
Ferguson, Joe	209	4.62%
Grogan, Steve	208	5.79%
Bledsoe, Drew	206	3.07%
DeBerg, Steve	204	4.06%
Baugh, Sammy*	203	6.78%

As modern passing offenses placed more emphasis on shorter, safer passes, the percentage of interceptions decreased drastically. The first passer to hold the lowest career interception percentage was Sammy Baugh whose percentage was 6.78. By 1995, the record was held by virtual nonentity Neil O'Donnell with a percentage of 2.11. Only 14 of the top 100 career percentages were by quarterbacks who retired before 1978, and the worst was the Chiefs' career backup Mike Livingston at 4.75 percent. Furthermore, four quarterbacks who threw at least 50 interceptions also had an interception percentage over 10 percent — Frank Filchock, Charlie O'Rourke, Irv Comp and Roy Zimmerman. Of quarterbacks who threw at least 100 interceptions, 26 had an interception percentage higher than the standard of 5.5 percent inherent in the passer rating system, and they are listed in the following table.

Name	Interceptions	Int/Pass
Herber, Arnie	106	8.72%
Bratkowski, Zeke	122	8.22%
Waterfield, Bob	128	7.92%
LeBaron, Eddie	141	7.85%
Luckman, Sid	132	7.57%
McHan, Lamar	108	7.49%
Tittle, Y.A.	248	7.30%
Thompson, Tommy	103	7.23%
Tripucka, Frank	124	7.11%
Brown, Ed	138	6.95%
Blanda, George	277	6.91%
Baugh, Sammy	203	6.78%
Parilli, Babe	220	6.61%
Rote, Tobin	191	6.57%
Layne, Bobby	243	6.57%
Davidson, Cotton	109	6.23%
Van Brocklin, Norm	178	6.15%
Phipps, Mike	108	6.00%
Kemp, Jack	183	5.96%
Snead, Norm	257	5.90%
Conerly, Charlie	167	5.89%
Stabler, Ken	222	5.85%
Namath, Joe	220	5.85%
Grogan, Steve	208	5.79%
Dickey, Lynn	179	5.73%
Hadl, John	268	5.72%

Fumbles and Turnovers

Fumbles began to be counted officially in 1945, and the career leader has always been a quarterback from Paul Christman to Sammy Baugh to Bobby Layne to Johnny Unitas to Roman Gabriel to Dan Fouts to Dave Krieg to Warren Moon. That is not surprising since quarterbacks handle the ball on nearly every play. The seasonal record of 23 fumbles is held by Kerry Collins in 2001 and Daunte Culpepper in 2002. Eight of the 20 most butter-fingered quarterbacks were Hall of Famers.

Name	Fumbles
Moon, Warren	161
Krieg, Dave	153
Favre, Brett	138
Elway, John	137
Bledsoe, Drew	123
Esiason, Boomer	123
Collins, Kerry	117
Testaverde, Vinny	114
Marino, Dan	110
Fouts, Dan	106
Cunningham, Randall	105
Gabriel, Roman	105
Chandler, Chris	98

Name	Fumbles
Unitas, Johnny	95
Simms, Phil	93
McNair, Steve	91
Bradshaw, Terry	84
Tarkenton, Fran	84
Dawson, Len	84
Kitna, Jon	83
DeBerg, Steve	83

To put this in some perspective, we can compare fumbles to games played. Seven quarterbacks who played at least 150 games fumbled at a rate of 25 percent of games or less: Daryle Lamonica, Mike Tomczak, Sonny Jurgensen, Joe Namath, John Brodie, Earl Morrall and Joe Theismann. Daryle Lamonica's 21 percent on 32 fumbles in 150 games is the best figure. At the other end, we have 17 quarterbacks with at least 50 fumbles who fumbled in more than 60 percent of their games. Daunte Culpepper is four fumbles from averaging one bobble per game. Only Warren Moon from this group is in the Hall of Fame.

Name	Fumbles	Games	F/Game
Culpepper, Daunte	81	85	0.95
Carr, David	66	76	0.87
Warner, Kurt	66	80	0.83
Trudeau, Jack	52	67	0.78
Moon, Warren	161	208	0.77
Kitna, Jon	83	108	0.77
Banks, Tony	73	97	0.75
Collins, Kerry	117	156	0.75
Vick, Michael	55	74	0.74
Krieg, Dave	153	213	0.72
Meredith, Don	71	104	0.68
Brooks, Aaron	63	93	0.68
Peete, Rodney	71	106	0.67
Esiason, Boomer	123	188	0.65
Cunningham, Randall	105	161	0.65
Kemp, Jack	78	121	0.64
Majkowski, Don	59	93	0.63
Bledsoe, Drew	123	194	0.63

Another approach to apply perspective is to compare fumbles to plays. Total snap data are not available, but we can count passes, rushes and times sacked for quarterbacks of the modern era when sacks began to be counted. Of quarterbacks who fumbled at least 50 times, 19 fumbled on at least 2 percent of plays. Jack Trudeau who was fourth in per-game data, takes the bottom rung here. Again, only Warren Moon from this group is in the Hall of Fame.

Name	Fumbles	F/Plays
Trudeau, Jack	52	2.82%
Banks, Tony	73	2.74%
Carr, David	66	2.55%
Majkowski, Don	59	2.54%
Meredith, Don	71	2.53%
Peete, Rodney	71	2.48%
Krieg, Dave	153	2.46%
Culpepper, Daunte	81	2.35%
Warner, Kurt	66	2.34%
Vick, Michael	55	2.25%
Kemp, Jack	78	2.21%
Kitna, Jon	83	2.12%
Beuerlein, Steve	82	2.11%
Dilfer, Trent	72	2.10%
Gabriel, Roman	105	2.06%
Chandler, Chris	98	2.06%
Esiason, Boomer	123	2.06%
Morrall, Earl	63	2.06%
Moon, Warren	161	2.06%

Name	Fumbles	F/Plays
White, Danny	68	2.03%
Collins, Kerry	117	2.02%
Dawson, Len	84	2.00%

Finally, if we combine the fumble and interception data and look at quarterbacks who had at least 100 combined fumbles and interceptions, the bottom 20 of quarterbacks losing control of the ball includes Hall of Famers Dan Fouts, Bobby Layne, Bob Waterfield, Joe Namath and Terry Bradshaw as well as failures like Jack Trudeau, Jon Kitna, Al Dorow and Richard Todd. Although he did not stick in the NFL long enough to reach 100 combined fumbles and interceptions, head case Ryan Leaf had the worst record with 24 fumbles and 36 interceptions in 25 games, 2.4 turnovers per game.

Name	Fumbles	Interceptions	Fum + Int	Turn/ game
Kemp, Jack	78	183	261	2.16
Trudeau, Jack	52	89	141	2.10
Tripucka, Frank	21	124	145	2.01
Culpepper, Daunte	81	89	170	2.00
Grogan, Steve	81	208	289	1.94
Kitna, Jon	83	126	209	1.94
Fouts, Dan	106	242	348	1.92
Moon, Warren	161	233	394	1.89
Warner, Kurt	66	83	149	1.86
Collins, Kerry	117	172	289	1.85
Layne, Bobby	80	243	323	1.85
Christman, Paul	35	76	111	1.82
Waterfield, Bob	36	128	164	1.80
Dorow, Al	31	93	124	1.80
Namath, Joe	33	220	253	1.78
Snead, Norm	60	257	317	1.78
Todd, Richard	50	161	211	1.77
Meredith, Don	71	111	182	1.75
Bradshaw, Terry	84	210	294	1.75
Rote, Tobin	67	191	258	1.73
Carr, David	66	65	131	1.72

7

1920–1932: Grounded

In the beginning of professional football, there was no one resembling a modern passing quarterback. Football was a low scoring, brute force, running game, and most teams eschewed the pass unless they were desperate. It was a game of field position where punting on third down was a conventional strategy in order to try to provoke a game-changing turnover. Players played both offense and defense, and there were no "special teams" or specialists. Punting and kicking, often of the drop-kicking variety, was handled by the regular players. Padding was slight, helmets were made of leather and not everyone wore one. Players made their own decisions because coaching from the bench was not permitted. Daly and O'Donnell pointed out in *The Pro Football Chronicle* that two-thirds of all games in the 1920s were shutouts, and even 0–0 ties were far from unusual. It was no wonder that professional football provided no competition to college football for most football fans.

The deck was stacked against passing in the early pro game. A passer had to be at least five yards behind the line of scrimmage to legally throw a pass, and if he threw an incomplete pass into the end zone, his team lost possession of the ball on a touchback. There were no hashmarks on the field so when a ball carrier was tackled near the sideline, that's where the ball was snapped on the next play. Often that meant the entire offense was forced to be on one side of the misnamed center. The ball itself was fatter and harder to throw, leading to an interception to touchdown pass ratio of 3:1.

The NFL itself started out as a loose con-

federation of former town teams, mostly from the Midwest. Schedules were at the teams' discretion and often included exhibition clashes with non-league semi-pro outfits. The season had no official starting or ending dates, and roster limits were not established till the mid–1920s. Furthermore, there were no official statistics collected until 1932. Therefore, the numbers for this period are to be taken with a grain of salt. They are incomplete and were collected after the fact from newspaper accounts by the diligent researchers who put together the Neft, Cohen and Korch *Football Encyclopedia*. In that work, they separated complete game statistics from incomplete game statistics, but here I have combined them for the sake of simplicity, although that makes any percentage stats even less reliable. While the dubious accuracy of the statistics from this period makes it impossible to compare them with other eras, they do allow us to make comparisons of passers within this early period and gives a general sense of how much passing was going on and who were the best passers of the time.

The earliest and most consistent proponent of the passing game was Curly Lambeau, the founder, coach and tailback of the Green Bay Packers. Under Lambeau, the Packers were the leader in passing yards for most seasons in the early period and never finished lower than third. Lambeau threw 24 touchdown passes and scored 110 points and was a second team All League selection three times as a player. As a coach, his teams played a fast and exciting brand of football, emphasizing speed and trickery as the great equalizer against bigger and stronger opponents. He was one of the first coaches to hold daily practices and an early advocate of the use of game films for preparation and planning.

Lambeau was one of just five early passers who threw at least 500 passes in this period, and they played in various styles of the single wing attack. Lambeau had learned the Notre Dame Box from his one year under Knute Rockne at Notre Dame and ran that in Green Bay with himself as the tailback who might receive the long snap from center. In the Box, though, the quarterback who lined up behind one of the guards might take a short snap from center as well. The Packers' championship teams from this time featured Red Dunn as their quarterback and leading passer, and Dunn was second only to Hall of Famer Benny Friedman in touchdown passes

and yards passing for the era. Friedman was a tailback in a classic single wing offense; he was an adept runner as well as the finest passer of his time. The only player with a similar balance of skills was Ernie Nevers, a fullback who took most of the long snaps in the double wing, who was a star runner and a now-forgotten passer. The fifth most prolific passer of the time was Ken Mercer who played quarterback, tailback and fullback for the Frankford Yellow Jackets at the end of the 1920s.

The aggregate, league-wide, *incomplete and unofficial* passing data for the period from 1920 through 1932 in the NFL reflect the embryonic stage of the passing offense. Even by 1932, there were three times as many runs as passes and two times as much rushing yardage as passing yardage.

Att	Comp	%	Yards	Y/Att	Y/Comp	TD	Int	Rating
15449	6272	40.6%	100572	6.5	16.0	757	2040	39.8

Just 14 passers threw for at least 1,500 yards during this era. Only Benny Friedman, by far the greatest passer of the age, may have thrown more touchdowns than interceptions. His closest competitor, Red Dunn, had only two-thirds the yards and three-fourths the touchdown

passes of Friedman. Friedman was the first passer to reach 2,000 yards and 20 touchdowns in a season. Lambeau had been the first to reach 1,000 yards, but threw more interceptions than any other passer of the time. The 14 1,500-yard passers ranked by yards:

Name	Attempts	Comp	%	Yards	Y/Att	Y/Comp	TD	Int	Rating
Benny Friedman	782	393	50.3%	7040	9.0	17.9	63	59	76.9
Red Dunn	620	275	44.4%	4641	7.5	16.9	48	63	56.5
Curly Lambeau	700	278	39.7%	4493	6.4	16.2	24	78	33.8
Ernie Nevers	573	257	44.9%	4012	7.0	15.6	25	61	43.6
Ken Mercer	516	201	39.0%	2961	5.7	14.7	29	46	40.0
Jack McBride	375	192	51.2%	2948	7.9	15.4	28	55	62.8
Hust Stockton	272	115	42.3%	2406	8.8	20.9	14	49	51.7
Jack Ernst	464	187	40.3%	2357	5.1	12.6	14	60	27.3
Jimmy Conzelman	316	151	47.8%	2205	7.0	14.6	12	37	44.1
Wildcat Wilson	298	130	43.6%	2202	7.4	16.9	12	40	43.1
Paddy Driscoll	248	96	38.7%	2100	8.5	21.9	16	33	51.5
Frank Kirkleski	252	108	42.9%	2068	8.2	19.1	23	27	62.8
Vern Lewellen	334	121	36.2%	2040	6.1	16.9	6	41	24.1
Lou Smyth	245	83	33.9%	1679	6.9	20.2	12	36	35.6

Overall, the quarterbacks who led the league the most times in passing categories over this era were:

Yards	Benny Friedman	5
TD	Benny Friedman	4
Interceptions	Curly Lambeau	2

1920

The American Professional Football Association was formed in 1920 in Canton, Ohio, but

this league was as distant from the modern NFL as 19th century baseball is from today's major leagues. Twelve of the 90 games that counted in APFA standings in 1920 ended as 0–0 ties.

Throwing five passes in a game would constitute a major emphasis on passing at this time. Al Mahrt of the Dayton Triangles was the most successful passer in this first year of the NFL's heritage; he threw for 591 yards and 7 touchdowns for the season. The champions were the Akron Pros and their leading passer was fullback Rip King who threw 42 passes all year. Hall of Famer Fritz Pollard, who is sometimes called the first black quarterback, completed one of two passes for Akron, while leading the team in rushing with 205 yards and receiving with six catches. The most famous player of the time and the titular league president, Jim Thorpe, threw just 24 passes for no touchdowns and had six intercepted.

1920 Incomplete and Unofficial League Passing Statistics

Att	Comp	%	Yards	Y/Att	Y/Comp	TD	Int	Rating
425	168	39.5%	2753	6.5	16.4	18	60	36.5

1920 Leading Passers

Name	Team	Attempts	Comp	%	Yards	Y/Att	Y/Comp	TD	Int	Rating
Al Mahrt	XDAY	54	28	51.9	591	10.9	21.1	7	2	115.0
Rip King	XAKR	42	19	45.2	267	6.4	14.1	3	4	50.5
Ockie Anderson	XBUF	23	8	34.8	164	7.1	20.5	0	4	21.2
Jim Thorpe	XCAN	24	8	33.3	159	6.6	19.9	0	6	17.9
Jimmy Conzelman	CHI	20	8	40	138	6.9	17.3	2	1	76.7
Frank Nesser	XCOL	6	5	83.3	135	22.5	27.0	1	1	118.8
George Roudebush	XDAY	18	9	50	130	7.2	14.4	0	3	34.3
Arnie Wyman	XRII	30	9	30	123	4.1	13.7	2	5	26.8
Tommy Hughitt	XBUF	12	7	58.3	115	9.6	16.4	0	1	55.9

The leaders in the major passing categories for 1920 were:

Yards	Al Mahrt	591
TD	Al Mahrt	7
Interceptions	Jim Thorpe & Robert Specht	6

1921

The APFA made some administrative progress in its second year. Joe Carr was named commissioner, and the league expanded from 14 to 21 teams although several would play only one to four games. There was no set schedule, but only league games counted in the league standings in 1921. George Halas' Decatur Staleys moved to Chicago and won the league title although its leading passers Chic Harley and Ken Huffine threw a mere 22 passes in 11 games. Rip King of Akron and Al Mahrt of Dayton were again the most prolific passers in the league, but newcomer Curly Lambeau joined them. Benny Boynton and Elmer Oliphant led the league with seven touchdown passes each: Boynton on 21 attempts and Oliphant on 20.

1921 Incomplete and Unofficial League Passing Statistics

Att	Comp	%	Yards	Y/Att	Y/Comp	TD	Int	Rating
646	274	42.4%	4873	7.5	17.8	51	77	55.6

1921 Leading Passers

Name	Team	Attempts	Comp	%	Yards	Y/Att	Y/Comp	TD	Int	Rating
Rip King	XAKR	92	33	35.9	533	5.8	16.2	3	9	27.4

Name	Team	Attempts	Comp	%	Yards	Y/Att	Y/Comp	TD	Int	Rating
Al Mahrt	XDAY	63	29	46	452	7.2	15.6	2	7	41.3
Curly Lambeau	GBP	58	18	31	361	6.2	20.1	1	8	20
Benny Boynton	XROC/XWAS	21	13	61.9	326	15.5	25.1	7	5	105.8
Jimmy Conzelman	XRII	53	21	39.6	324	6.1	15.4	2	8	33.6
Paddy Driscoll	ARZ	40	14	35	220	5.5	15.7	1	4	22.9
Frank Nesser	XCOL	9	6	66.7	210	23.3	35.0	3	1	109.7
Ockie Anderson	XBUF	29	12	41.4	208	7.2	17.3	1	4	38.4

The leaders in the major passing categories for 1921 were:

Yards	Rip King	533
TD	Elmer Oliphant & Benny Boynton	7
Interceptions	Rip King	9

1922

The APFA became the National Football League and the Chicago Staleys became the Chicago Bears in 1922. In January, the Green Bay Packers were suspended from the league for using college players in 1921 whose classes had not graduated, but then the team was reinstated under Lambeau in June. The top passers in the league were Wisconsin-based. Both player-coaches Lambeau of Green Bay and Jimmy Conzelman of the Milwaukee Badgers exceeded 400 yards passing. The leading passer on the league champion Canton Bulldogs was Texan Lou "Hammer" Smyth. The leading newcomer was the Bears' Laurie Walquist from Illinois who helped lead the Bears to a league-leading 184 points in 12 games.

1922 Incomplete and Unofficial League Passing Statistics

Att	Comp	%	Yards	Y/Att	Y/Comp	TD	Int	Rating
743	308	41.5%	5221	7	17	32	112	40.7

1922 Leading Passers

Name	Team	Attempts	Comp	%	Yards	Y/Att	Y/Comp	TD	Int	Rating
Jimmy Conzelman	XRII/XMIL	80	35	43.8	474	5.9	13.5	3	9	36.1
Curly Lambeau	GBP	55	26	47.3	469	8.5	18.0	2	4	58.8
Lou Smyth	XCAN	40	15	37.5	317	7.9	21.1	1	9	35.1
Rip King	XAKR	31	14	45.2	288	9.3	20.6	2	2	73.1
Rat Watson	XTOL	40	17	42.5	278	7	16.4	2	11	43.5
Laurie Walquist	CHI	44	21	47.7	261	5.9	12.4	1	8	34.6

The leaders in the major passing categories for 1922 were:

Yards	Jimmy Conzelman	474
TD	Jimmy Conzelman	3
Interceptions	Rat Watson	11

1923

The NFL expanded to 20 teams in 1923, and the Canton Bulldogs repeated as champions under Coach Guy Chamberlin. Once again, the leading Canton passer was Lou Smyth, who was one of three passers to throw more than 100 passes and led the NFL with six touchdown passes. The Bulldogs were the top scoring team as well with 246 points in 12 games. Newcomer Johnny Armstrong of Rock Island tied Curly Lambeau for the most interceptions, 17.

1923 Incomplete and Unofficial League Passing Statistics

Att	Comp	%	Yards	Y/Att	Y/Comp	TD	Int	Rating
1359	542	39.9%	8230	6.1	15.2	50	192	33.2

1923 Leading Passers

Name	Team	Attempts	Comp	%	Yards	Y/Att	Y/Comp	TD	Int	Rating
Johnny Armstrong	XRII	171	75	43.9	778	4.6	10.4	3	17	23.9
Curly Lambeau	GBP	118	43	36.4	752	6.4	17.5	3	17	27.9
Jimmy Conzelman	XMIL	91	49	53.8	735	8.1	15.0	2	12	48.4
Sonny Winters	XCOL	57	32	56.1	595	10.4	18.6	5	5	85.1
Lou Smyth	XCAN	103	27	26.2	594	5.8	22.0	6	12	30.9
Shorty Barr	XRAC	86	35	40.7	496	5.8	14.2	5	9	39.8
Johnny Bryan	CHI	47	33	70.2	360	7.7	10.9	2	6	67.1
Eber Simpson	XSTL	51	20	39.2	301	5.9	15.1	1	12	26.3
Jim Thorpe	XOOR	43	20	46.5	283	6.6	14.2	1	6	36.4

The leaders in the major passing categories for 1923 were:

Yards	Johnny Armstrong	778
TD	Lou Smyth	6
Interceptions	Johnny Armstrong & Curly Lambeau	17

1924

There were 18 teams in the NFL in 1924, and the league established starting and ending dates to the season, although it still had no set schedule. The Canton Bulldogs were absorbed by the Cleveland Indians to become the Cleveland Bulldogs and won the championship again. Bulldog Hoge Workman threw nine touchdowns on just 26 passes. Once more, the passing leaders hailed from Wisconsin with Lambeau of the Packers becoming the first passer to exceed 1,000 yards in a season, while Red Dunn of Milwaukee combined for over 1,000 yards with teammate Jimmy Conzelman. Lambeau also set a new undesirable standard in pass interceptions with 29. The top scoring team was a new franchise, the Frankford Yellow Jackets, and was led by Tex Hamer to 326 points in 14 games, 23 points per game.

1924 Incomplete and Unofficial League Passing Statistics

Att	Comp	%	Yards	Y/Att	Y/Comp	TD	Int	Rating
970	489	50.4%	8685	9	17.8	69	149	65.5

1924 Leading Passers

Name	Team	Attempts	Comp	%	Yards	Y/Att	Y/Comp	TD	Int	Rating
Curly Lambeau	GBP	179	75	41.9	1094	6.1	14.6	8	29	37.8
Red Dunn	XMIL	97	51	52.6	874	9	17.1	6	11	64.5
Sonny Winters	XCOL	41	30	73.2	616	15	20.5	8	8	115.1
Hoge Workman	XCLE	26	17	65.4	462	17.8	27.2	9	7	108.7
Benny Boynton	XROC/XBUF	40	26	65	430	10.8	16.5	6	3	109.4
Tex Hamer	XFRA	45	22	48.9	423	9.4	19.2	4	12	72
Jimmy Conzelman	XMIL	33	18	54.5	312	9.5	17.3	3	6	77.7
Paddy Driscoll	ARZ	22	14	63.6	303	13.8	21.6	2	3	97.9

The leaders in the major passing categories for 1924 were:

Yards	Curly Lambeau	1,094
TD	Hoge Workman	9
Interceptions	Curly Lambeau	29

1925

The NFL rose back to 20 teams and for the first time topped 10,000 yards of passing offense in 1925. The big news was Red Grange signing with the Bears at the conclusion of his college career at Illinois. Grange led Chicago on a lucrative postseason barnstorming tour that helped put a new franchise, the New York Giants, in the black for the year, and gave a great deal of favorable publicity to the NFL and professional football. The championship was awarded to the Chicago Cardinals in a controversial decision by the league office. Commissioner Joe Carr sus-

pended the league-leading Pottsville Maroon team late in the season because they had played an unauthorized exhibition game against a Notre Dame All Star team in Frankford's home territory. Meanwhile, the Cardinals, led by Paddy Driscoll and Red Dunn, scheduled some extra games and recorded a higher winning percentage than Pottsville for the season. Pottsville scored 270 points in 12 games and were led by newcomer Jack Ernst who threw the most passes in the NFL. Another notable newcomer, Jack McBride, led the fledgling Giants team. Houston Stockton, the grandfather of basketball great John Stockton, threw for the most yards.

1925 Incomplete and Unofficial League Passing Statistics

Att	Comp	%	Yards	Y/Att	Y/Comp	TD	Int	Rating
1600	667	41.7%	10341	6.5	15.5	95	213	44

1925 Leading Passers

Name	Team	Attempts	Comp	%	Yards	Y/Att	Y/Comp	TD	Int	Rating
Hust Stockton	XFRA	93	44	47.3	886	9.5	20.1	7	14	66.7
Jack Ernst	XPOT	130	61	46.9	714	5.5	11.7	8	13	45
Curly Lambeau	GBP	121	47	38.8	711	5.9	15.1	5	7	48.6
Jack McBride	NYG	48	33	68.8	650	13.5	19.7	6	5	111.5
Al Michaels	XCLE	71	36	50.7	630	8.9	17.5	3	11	55.8
Dick Vick	XDET	42	25	59.5	502	11.9	20.1	7	7	101.5
Red Dunn	ARZ	68	31	45.6	462	6.8	14.9	9	8	68.4
Lou Smyth	XROC/XFRA	65	24	36.9	421	6.5	17.5	3	8	35.6

The leaders in the major passing categories for 1925 were:

Yards	Hust Stockton	886
TD	Red Dunn	9
Interceptions	Hust Stockton	14

1926

After the successful barnstorming tour, Red Grange and his agent C.C. Pyle tried to strongarm the NFL into a partnership and were rebuffed. Pyle and Grange then started their own American Football League with Grange's New York Yankees as the main draw. Between the NFL's 22 teams and the AFL's 8, there were 30 professional foot-

ball teams in 1926, but not nearly enough fan interest to support them. The NFL set a limit of 18 players per team, with a minimum of 15. Frankford, led again by Stockton and coached by Guy Chamberlin, won the league title and scored 236 points in 16 games. The second place Bears scored 216 in 14 games. Jack Ernst of the reinstated Pottsville Maroons sank to a touchdown to interception ratio of 1:21, while newcomer Ernie

Nevers threw for over 900 yards, three touchdowns and 20 interceptions. Curly Lambeau began to fade as a player and was supplemented on the Packers by baseball player Pid Purdy. Triple-threat Paddy Driscoll moved across town to the Bears and had his best season as a passer.

1926 Incomplete and Unofficial League Passing Statistics

Att	Comp	%	Yards	Y/Att	Y/Comp	TD	Int	Rating
1643	672	40.9%	10717	6.5	15.9	62	222	36.3

1926 Leading Passers

Name	Team	Attempts	Comp	%	Yards	Y/Att	Y/Comp	TD	Int	Rating
Ernie Nevers	XDUL	159	67	42.1	913	5.7	13.6	3	20	27.8
Hust Stockton	XFRA	79	36	45.6	819	10.4	22.8	5	14	64.8
Paddy Driscoll	CHI	57	30	52.6	815	14.3	27.2	6	7	93.5
Jack Ernst	XPOT	163	65	39.9	729	4.5	11.2	1	21	16.4
Jim Kendrick	XBUF	79	38	48.1	695	8.8	18.3	5	9	60.3
Curly Lambeau	GBP	80	30	37.5	504	6.3	16.8	3	5	46
Pid Purdy	GBP	67	21	31.3	383	5.7	18.2	1	12	17.4
Red Dunn	ARZ	46	22	47.8	346	7.5	15.7	2	8	48.2

The leaders in the major passing categories for 1926 were:

Yards	Ernie Nevers	913
TD	Paddy Driscoll & Eddie Scharer	6
Interceptions	Jack Ernst	21

1927

The AFL collapsed after one season, and Grange's Yankees were taken into the NFL which contracted to just 13 teams in 1927. Grange injured his knee during the season though and was never the same player again. Red Dunn moved on to Green Bay and supplanted Curly Lambeau as the team's leading passer. Both Ernie Nevers and newcomer Benny Friedman topped Lambeau's season record for passing yards. Friedman led the Cleveland Bulldogs to league-best 209 points in 13 games while leading the league in attempts, completions, yards and touchdowns; his 1,721 yards and 12 touchdowns set new records. Although he was also an outstanding runner, he was the first tailback who clearly had the skills of a modern T formation quarterback. However, the title was won by the defense-minded Giants behind steady tailback Jack McBride.

1927 Incomplete and Unofficial League Passing Statistics

Att	Comp	%	Yards	Y/Att	Y/Comp	TD	Int	Rating
1619	673	41.6%	10523	6.5	15.6	60	183	36.6

1927 Leading Passers

Name	Team	Attempts	Comp	%	Yards	Y/Att	Y/Comp	TD	Int	Rating
Benny Friedman	XCLE	205	96	46.8	1721	8.4	17.9	12	11	73.2
Ernie Nevers	XDUL	197	89	45.2	1362	6.9	15.3	5	17	41
Wildcat Wilson	XPRV	89	51	57.3	782	8.8	15.3	4	11	61.8
Ken Mercer	XFRA	125	53	42.4	762	6.1	14.4	4	16	33.9
Frank Kirkleski	XPOT	116	42	36.2	730	6.3	17.4	3	17	27.5

Name	Team	Attempts	Comp	%	Yards	Y/Att	Y/Comp	TD	Int	Rating
Jack McBride	NYG	60	34	56.7	610	10.2	17.9	7	6	91
Red Dunn	GBP	85	32	37.6	556	6.5	17.4	3	7	38.2
Curly Lambeau	GBP	54	26	48.1	417	7.7	16.0	1	4	49.7

The leaders in the major passing categories for 1927 were:

Yards	Benny Friedman	1,721
TD	Benny Friedman	12
Interceptions	Ernie Nevers & Frank Kirkleski	17

1928

The NFL consisted of 12 teams in 1928, but the Cleveland Bulldogs were not one of them. Many of the best Bulldogs, including star passer and Michigan alum Benny Friedman, were signed by the Detroit Wolverines. In Detroit, Friedman was once again the leading passer with 1,348 yards and 10 touchdowns and led the Wolverines to a league-best 19 points per game. The title, though, was won by the Providence Steam Roller behind triple-threat tailback Wildcat Wilson. Red Dunn was again among the league passing leaders, now teaming with Verne Lewellen in Green Bay. Hust Stockton had a remarkable 0:17 touchdown pass to interception ratio. Hall of Famers Jim Thorpe and George Halas both played their last games in 1928.

1928 Incomplete and Unofficial League Passing Statistics

Att	Comp	%	Yards	Y/Att	Y/Comp	TD	Int	Rating
1424	558	39.2%	8877	6.2	15.9	63	191	35.9

1928 Leading Passers

Name	Team	Attempts	Comp	%	Yards	Y/Att	Y/Comp	TD	Int	Rating
Benny Friedman	XDET	155	77	49.7	1348	8.7	17.5	10	15	61.6
Wildcat Wilson	XPRV	143	55	38.5	920	6.4	16.7	5	21	33
Wild Bill Kelly	XNYY	70	35	50	778	11.1	22.2	7	10	83.8
Red Dunn	GBP	123	45	36.6	700	5.7	15.6	4	12	27.5
Ken Mercer	XFRA	90	39	43.3	525	5.8	13.5	5	11	41.4
Jack Ernst	XPOT/XNYY	77	28	36.4	457	5.9	16.3	3	8	30.5
Verne Lewellen	GBP	87	29	33.3	402	4.6	13.9	1	10	13.4
Hust Stockton	XFRA	67	23	34.3	371	5.5	16.1	0	17	14.2
Hap Moran	XPOT/NYG	63	22	34.9	324	5.1	14.7	3	10	28.9

The leaders in the major passing categories for 1928 were:

Yards	Benny Friedman	1,348
TD	Benny Friedman	10
Interceptions	Wildcat Wilson	21

1929

Once again, Benny Friedman's team went under, and this time the New York Giants obtained the star passer and several of his teammates. Taking advantage of a ball that was slimmed down from 23 to 22 inches in circumference, Friedman set a new touchdown pass record with 20 in 1929. The Giants contended with the Packers for supremacy in a 13-team league that came down to a late November showdown between the two unbeaten teams that Green Bay won 20–6. The formidable Packer defense gave up 22 points all season and held in check the potent Giant offense that scored 312 points in 14 games. Hall of Fame tailbacks Curly Lambeau and Paddy Driscoll played their final games in this year.

1929 Incomplete and Unofficial League Passing Statistics

Att	Comp	%	Yards	Y/Att	Y/Comp	TD	Int	Rating
1452	561	38.6%	9444	6.5	16.8	75	194	39

1929 Leading Passers

Name	Team	Attempts	Comp	%	Yards	Y/Att	Y/Comp	TD	Int	Rating
Benny Friedman	NYG	156	84	53.8	1677	10.8	20.0	20	10	104.6
Wild Bill Kelly	XFRA	123	43	35	677	5.5	15.7	4	9	34.5
Ernie Nevers	ARZ	82	36	43.9	641	7.8	17.8	6	8	56
Verne Lewellen	GBP	56	21	37.5	504	9	24.0	1	5	39.6
Wildcat Wilson	XPRV	66	24	36.4	500	7.6	20.8	3	8	39.5
Ken Mercer	XFRA	112	35	31.3	479	4.3	13.7	3	19	15.3
Red Dunn	GBP	87	34	39.1	479	5.5	14.1	5	8	38.4
Hust Stockton	XPRV/XBST	33	12	36.4	330	10	27.5	2	4	54.7
Walter Holmer	CHI	44	13	29.5	314	7.1	24.2	5	15	55.1

The leaders in the major passing categories for 1929 were:

Yards	Benny Friedman	1,677
TD	Benny Friedman	20
Interceptions	Ken Mercer	19

1930

The 11-team NFL established new roster limits of not more than 20 and not fewer than 16 players in 1930. The Packers repeated as champions behind Red Dunn and Verne Lewellen and averaged 16.7 points per game. The best offense, though, was Benny Friedman's Giants who scored 308 points in 17 games for an 18 point per game average. Friedman again topped the league in all major categories. Green Bay's hometown hero Arnie Herber did not play much as a rookie in 1930, but would become the top passer in the NFL through most of the 1930s. George Halas took a break from coaching the Bears and brought in Ralph Jones to replace himself. Jones instituted the man-in-motion series to the stodgy T formation run by Chicago and opened up their offense considerably.

1930 Incomplete and Unofficial League Passing Statistics

Att	Comp	%	Yards	Y/Att	Y/Comp	TD	Int	Rating
1387	540	38.9%	8591	6.2	15.9	81	193	40.2

1930 Leading Passers

Name	Team	Attempts	Comp	%	Yards	Y/Att	Y/Comp	TD	Int	Rating
Benny Friedman	NYG	124	71	57.3	1246	10.1	17.5	13	9	96.4
Red Dunn	GBP	83	43	51.8	825	9.9	19.2	11	7	91.1
Doug Wycoff	XSIS	143	41	28.7	689	2.9	16.8	5	15	46.8
Verne Lewellen	GBP	71	28	39.4	497	7	17.8	3	8	38.6
Ernie Nevers	ARZ	55	25	45.5	447	8.1	17.9	5	9	64.5
Wild Bill Kelly	XBKN	41	20	48.8	358	8.7	17.9	7	6	79.1
Neil Rengel	XFRA	64	24	37.5	344	5.4	14.3	1	10	21.4
Jack McBride	XBKN	30	18	60	256	8.5	14.2	2	1	96

The leaders in the major passing categories for 1930 were:

Yards	Benny Friedman	1,246
TD	Benny Friedman	13
Interceptions	Doug Wycoff	15

1931

The NFL went down to 11 teams in 1931, while the original Dayton franchise became the Brooklyn Dodgers and the independent powerhouse Portsmouth Spartans joined the league. Portsmouth was led by two triple-threat backs in Glenn Presnell and Dutch Clark who were both among the year's passing leaders; however, Benny Friedman again topped the circuit in passing yards. The Packers won their third straight NFL championship behind the passing of Red Dunn and Bo Molenda and scored a league best 291 points, 21 per game.

1931 Incomplete and Unofficial League Passing Statistics

Att	Comp	%	Yards	Y/Att	Y/Comp	TD	Int	Rating
1137	448	39.4%	7017	6.2	15.7	59	156	38.3

1931 Leading Passers

Name	Team	Attempts	Comp	%	Yards	Y/Att	Y/Comp	TD	Int	Rating
Benny Friedman	NYG	68	42	61.8	729	10.7	17.4	3	4	88.4
Glenn Presnell	DET	90	37	41.1	651	7.2	17.6	5	9	45.4
Ernie Nevers	ARZ	80	40	50	649	8.1	16.2	6	7	66.1
Red Dunn	GBP	31	17	54.8	399	12.9	23.5	8	2	112.6
Deck Shelley	XPRV/DET	95	32	33.7	386	4.1	12.1	3	13	18
Bo Molenda	GBP	47	16	34	342	7.23	21.4	4	6	49.6
Jack McBride	XBKN	50	17	34	308	6.2	18.1	2	13	29.8
Dutch Clark	DET	53	21	39.6	231	4.4	11.0	1	8	20

The leaders in the major passing categories for 1931 were:

Yards	Benny Friedman	729
TD	Red Dunn	8
Interceptions	Deck Shelley & Jack McBride	13

1932

The Depression-affected NFL shrank to eight teams in 1932, but started collecting official passing statistics for the first time. Showman George P. Marshall bought into the league with the new Boston Braves franchise that five years later would become the Washington Redskins. The New York Giants could not afford to pay the aging Benny Friedman any longer so he moved on to the Brooklyn Dodgers. The league's top passer, judged by passing yards, was Arnie Herber who led the Packers to a 10–3–1 record that would have been a fourth straight title if ties had counted as ½ win and ½ loss as they do today. Instead, ties did not count at all in winning percentage at the time so the Bears at 6–1–6 and the Spartans at 6–1–4 were tied at the top of the standings. To determine the champion, the NFL's first playoff game was played on a shortened field indoors at the Chicago Stadium due to blizzard conditions outside. The Bears won the game on a jump pass close to the line from Bronko Nagurski to Red Grange. Because the rule at the time required passers to be at least five yards behind the line, the Spartans contested the call but to no avail. The excitement caused by this game would lead to several important changes in the league in a new era for passing and pro football beginning in 1933.

1932 League Passing Statistics

Games	Attempts	Comp	%	Yards	Y/ Att	Y/ Comp	Att/g	Y/g	TD	TD/g	Int	Rating	300-Yd Gms
58	1044	372	35.6%	5300	5.1	14.2	18.0	91.4	42	0.7	98	27.2	0

1932 Leading Passers

Name	Team	Attempts	Comp	%	Yards	Y/ Att	Y/ Comp	TD	Int	Rating	Relative Rating
Bronko Nagurski	CHI	26	11	42.3	150	5.8	13.6	3	2	67.8	275
Walt Holmer	ARZ	78	25	32.1	449	5.8	18	2	1	56	227
Arnie Herber	GBP	101	37	36.6	639	6.3	17.3	9	9	51.5	209
Jack McBride	NYG	74	36	48.6	363	4.9	10.1	6	9	50.5	205
Keith Molesworth	CHI	64	25	39.1	346	5.4	13.8	3	4	46.7	190
Benny Friedman	XBKN	74	23	31.1	319	4.3	13.9	5	10	28.9	117
Dutch Clark	DET	52	17	32.7	272	5.2	16	2	8	24.4	99

The leaders in the major passing categories for 1932 were:

Attempts	Arnie Herber	101	TD	Arnie Herber	9
Completions	Arnie Herber	37	TD%	Arnie Herber	8.9
Yards	Arnie Herber	639	Int %	Walt Holmer	1.3
Yards/Pass	Arnie Herber	6.33	Rating	Walt Holmer	56
Comp %	Jack McBride	48.6	Interceptions	Benny Friedman	10

8

1933–1945: The Emerging T

From the baseline numbers of 1932 when the NFL began to collect passing statistics, the second era of passing saw marked gains across the board. Completion percentage went from 35.6 percent to 40.7 percent; yards per attempted pass went from 5.1 to 5.9. Pass attempts per game increased from 18 per game to 36, while touchdown passes went from .7 to 1.7 per game. The first six 300-yard games were attained during this period. By 1945, with half the league running the T formation, completion percentage was up to 45.4 percent, yards per attempt to 6.8 and touchdown passes to 2.2 per game.

The NFL was still primarily a single wing league throughout the period, but a series of rules changes opened up the passing possibilities within the single wing. The league's first playoff game to determine the 1932 champion demonstrated a number of things for league owners. First, that a championship game was a good way to develop public interest in the game and so the teams were divided into Eastern and Western Divisions and an annual championship game was instituted. Second, the shortened field of the 1932 playoff necessitated that the goal post be moved back to the goal line and that hashmarks be drawn 10 yards from the sidelines for ball placement on sideline plays. Those hashmarks would be subsequently moved to 15 and then 20 feet from the sideline within this period, and that allowed offense to operate more wide open and freely. Third, the controversy over the "five yards behind the line to pass" rule led to it being abolished. Further changes during the period allowed for coaches to communicate with players on the field and for incomplete passes in the end zone to count as mere incompletions and not touchbacks. The NFL draft also began in 1936.

Several outstanding tailbacks who were primarily passers developed in this more open atmosphere including Arnie Herber and Cecil Isbell of the Packers, Harry Newman and Ed Danowski of the Giants, Parker Hall of the Rams, Ace Parker of the Dodgers and Frankie Filchock and Sammy Baugh of the Redskins. Baugh was the greatest of this group, but he met his match in Sid Luckman, the first modern T formation quarterback. Clark Shaughnessy, who coached at the University of Chicago but helped out with the Bears as well, made major renovations to the venerable T formation in 1939. In particular, he moved the quarterback directly behind the center rather than a yard back so he could take a direct snap and start the play quicker. In addition, he split the linemen about a yard apart rather than bunching them shoulder-to-shoulder which opened up holes in the defense for quick dive plays in the running game. Furthermore, he devised a new set of man-in-motion and counter plays to further confuse the defense.

The Bears had great success with this revised offense in 1939, but exploded with it in 1940 with second-year quarterback Sid Luckman directing the offense flawlessly. Their 73–0 crushing of the Redskins in the 1940 championship game sent shock waves throughout the game. The lowly Eagles jumped on board with the T the next year, while the Rams, Yanks and Lions experimented with a "modified" T in the next few seasons. The Redskins converted to the T in 1944 and the Rams and Cardinals in 1945. Newcomers Tommy Thompson, Bob Waterfield and Paul Christman became stars in the T, while Sammy Baugh converted mid-career to continue his stardom.

The game lost two star passers to early retirement in Cecil Isbell and Davey O'Brien, and several other careers were interrupted by World War II. Tommy Thompson, Ace Parker, Parker Hall and Frankie Filchock all left the NFL for the armed services during the War (see full list below). Arnie Herber, who had retired in 1940, returned to the game during its wartime manpower shortage in 1944–45 as teams disbanded or merged to survive. In a precursor to the future, free substitution was instituted during the War in recognition of the shortage of able bodies to play 60 minutes.

The aggregate league-wide passing data for the period from 1933 through 1945 in the NFL indicate that passing yardage began to exceed rushing yardage throughout the 1940s:

Games	Att	Comp	%	Yards	Y/ Att	Y/ Comp	Att/g	Y/g	TD	TD/g	Int	Rating	300-Yd Gm
694	25276	10275	40.7%	148845	5.9	14.5	36.4	214.5	1173	1.7	2815	36.4	6

Eighteen quarterbacks threw for at least 1,500 yards in this era, yet only Sid Luckman, Cecil Isbell and Bob Monnett of the Packers threw for more touchdowns than interceptions, and only Luckman, Isbell and Sammy Baugh completed more than half their passes. Baugh was the most prolific passer of the time and dominated the leader board in almost every category. Of this group, Tuffy Leemans, Dutch Clark and Frankie Sinkwich were better known as runners, Irv Comp, Roy Zimmerman and Bob Snyder were definite lesser lights and Tommy Thompson would have his greatest success in the years after the War. The top 18 ranked by passer rating:

Name	Attempts	Comp	%	Yards	Y/Att	Y/Comp	TD	Int	Rating
Sid Luckman	942	494	52.4%	8720	9.3	17.7	81	66	83.8
Cecil Isbell	818	411	50.2%	5945	7.3	14.5	61	52	72.6
Sammy Baugh	1557	889	57.1%	10897	7.0	12.3	95	105	71.1
Bob Monnett	336	158	47.0%	2227	6.6	14.1	28	26	64.4

Name	Attempts	Comp	%	Yards	Y/Att	Y/Comp	TD	Int	Rating
Ed Danowski	637	309	48.5%	3817	6.0	12.4	38	43	59.2
Bernie Masterson	409	156	38.1%	3366	8.2	21.6	36	38	58.8
Frank Filchock	505	254	50.3%	3658	7.2	14.4	35	54	57.7
Irv Comp	375	170	45.3%	2686	7.2	15.8	26	36	53.2
Tuffy Leemans	383	167	43.6%	2324	6.1	13.9	25	32	50.6
Arnie Herber	1074	444	41.3%	7402	6.9	16.7	70	97	49.3
Roy Zimmerman	384	155	40.4%	2688	7.0	17.3	26	40	47.9
Tommy Thompson	421	205	48.7%	2660	6.3	13.0	17	35	47.8
Ace Parker	603	273	45.3%	3938	6.5	14.4	22	47	46.7
Frankie Sinkwich	274	108	39.4%	1759	6.4	16.3	19	40	45.2
Bob Snyder	241	91	37.8%	1758	7.3	19.3	13	24	42.3
Davey O'Brien	478	223	46.7%	2614	5.5	11.7	11	34	41.8
Dutch Clark	250	114	45.6%	1507	6.0	13.2	10	26	39.0
Parker Hall	721	329	45.6%	4013	5.6	12.2	29	67	38.0

Overall, the quarterbacks who led the league the most times in passing categories over this era were:

Attempts	Sammy Baugh & Arnie Herber	2
Completions	Sammy Baugh	3
Yards	Arnie Herber & Sammy Baugh & Cecil Isbell & Sid Luckman	2
Yards/Pass	Sid Luckman	3
Comp %	Sammy Baugh	4
TD	Arnie Herber & Frank Filchock & Cecil Isbell & Sid Luckman	2
TD%	Arnie Herber	3
Int %	Sammy Baugh	3
Rating	Bob Monnett & Frank Filchock & Sammy Baugh & Sid Luckman	2
Comebacks	Arnie Herber	3
Interceptions	Sammy Baugh	2

And the complete list of leaders for 1933–1945 is as follows

Attempts	Sammy Baugh	1,557	TD%	Sid Luckman	8.6
Completions	Sammy Baugh	889	Int %	Cecil Isbell	6.36
Yards	Sammy Baugh	10,897	Rating	Sid Luckman	83.8
Yards/Pass	Sid Luckman	9.3	Wins (est)	Arnie Herber	81
Comp %	Sammy Baugh	57.1	Comebacks	Sammy Baugh	11
TD	Sammy Baugh	95	Interceptions	Sammy Baugh	105

1933

As noted above, 1933 was a year of change — Eastern and Western Divisions were established, the ball shrank from 22 to 21¼ inches in circumference, the goal posts were moved back to the goal line, hashmarks were instituted 10 yards in from the sideline, and passing was permitted from anywhere behind the line. In addition, new teams in Philadelphia, Pittsburgh and Cincinnati brought the NFL up to 10 teams. On a more disturbing note, 1933 also marked the last year before the unwritten color line excluding black players from the league was instituted. Tailback Joe Lillard of the Cardinals was the last black player till the post war era.

The big passing star of the league was rookie Harry Newman who followed Benny Friedman on the Giants just as he had previously followed Friedman at Michigan. Newman led the NFL in attempts, completions, yards, touchdowns and interceptions. His Giants led the league with 244 points in 14 games, 17.5 points per game, and met the Bears in one of the most exciting title games in history. Newman threw for 201 yards and led the Giants on a late drive to give them a 21–16 lead with minutes to play. Chicago responded with a hook and lateral pass from Bronko Nagurski to Bill Hewitt to trailing Bill Karr for the go-ahead touchdown. As time expired, Newman was driving the Giants through the air again, but ran out of time.

1933 League Passing Statistics

Games	Att	Comp	%	Yards	Y/ Att	Y/ Comp	Att/g	Y/g	TD	TD/g	Int	Rating	300-Yd Gms
57	1631	576	35.3%	8878	5.4	15.4	28.6	155.8	57	1.0	249	26.3	0

1933 Leading Passers

Name	Team	Attempts	Comp	%	Yards	Y/Att	Y/Comp	TD	Int	Rating	Relative Rating
Keith Molesworth	CHI	50	19	38	433	8.66	22.8	4	4	63.2	236
Benny Friedman	XBKN	80	42	52.5	594	7.43	14.1	5	7	61.1	229
Harry Newman	NYG	136	53	39	973	7.15	18.4	11	17	51.7	194
Bernie Holm	PIT	52	17	32.7	406	7.81	23.9	2	13	35.1	131
Glenn Presnell	DET	125	50	40	774	6.19	15.5	5	12	35	131
Chris Cagle	XBKN	74	31	41.9	457	6.18	14.7	2	10	32.2	120
Arnie Herber	GBP	124	50	40.3	656	5.29	13.1	4	12	28.9	108

The leaders in the major passing categories for 1933 were:

Attempts	Harry Newman	136	TD%	Harry Newman	8.1
Completions	Harry Newman	53	Int %	Keith Molesworth	8
Yards	Harry Newman	973	Rating	Keith Molesworth	63.2
Yards/Pass	Keith Molesworth	8.66	Comebacks	Keith Molesworth	3
Comp %	Benny Friedman	52.5	Interceptions	Harry Newman	17
TD	Harry Newman	11			

1934

The Cincinnati franchise failed during the year and was replaced for the tail end of the season by the independent St. Louis Gunners. A rule change permitted new players reporting to the huddle to be able to speak to their teammates immediately rather than having to wait for one play as the restrictions on coaching from the bench were eased. Arnie Herber resumed his spot at the top of the NFL's passers by leading the league in attempts, completions, yards and touchdowns, while Harry Newman had a rough second season that ended when he was injured in a late season tilt with Chicago. The undefeated Bears, who led the league with 286 points in 13 games, met the Giants again for the title. This was the famous "Sneaker Game" played on an icy field and won by the sneaker-clad Giants who were led by rookie tailback Ed Danowski. The Giants scored 27 of their 30 points in the fourth quarter and won 30–13

1934 League Passing Statistics

Games	Att	Comp	%	Yards	Y/ Att	Y/ Comp	Att/g	Y/g	TD	TD/g	Int	Rating	300-Yd Gms
60	1606	505	31.4%	7117	4.4	14.1	26.8	118.6	56	0.9	206	18.8	0

1934 Leading Passers

Name	Team	Attempts	Comp	%	Yards	Y/Att	Y/Comp	TD	Int	Rating	Relative Rating
Dutch Clark	DET	50	23	46	383	7.66	16.7	0	3	47.3	253
Arnie Herber	GBP	115	42	36.5	799	6.95	19.0	8	12	45.1	241
Keith Molesworth	CHI	39	13	33.3	249	6.38	19.2	3	4	42.5	227
Gene Ronzani	CHI	36	9	25	150	4.17	16.7	3	6	32.6	174

Name	Team	Attempts	Comp	%	Yards	Y/Att	Y/Comp	TD	Int	Rating	Relative Rating
Ed Matesic	PHL	60	20	33.3	278	4.63	13.9	2	5	25.6	136
Steve Hokuf	XBOS	51	13	25.5	203	3.98	15.6	3	10	23.7	126
Chris Cagle	XBKN	60	14	23.3	224	3.73	16.0	3	7	19.7	105
Harry Newman	NYG	93	35	37.6	391	4.2	11.2	1	12	15	80
Warren Heller	PIT	112	31	27.7	511	4.56	16.5	2	15	12.5	67

The leaders in the major passing categories for 1934 were:

Attempts	Arnie Herber	115	TD%	Arnie Herber	7
Completions	Arnie Herber	42	Int %	Dutch Clark	6
Yards	Arnie Herber	799	Rating	Dutch Clark	47.3
Yards/Pass	Dutch Clark	7.66	Comebacks	Arnie Herber & six others	1
Comp %	Dutch Clark	46	Interceptions	Warren Heller	1
TD	Arnie Herber	8			

1935

With the demise of the Cincinnati/St. Louis entry, the NFL was down to nine teams in 1935. Roster limits were increased to 24 players, hashmarks were moved in five yards further to 15 yards from the sidelines and the rule making an incomplete pass in the end zone a touchback was eliminated.

In his first season as a starter, Ed Danowski led the league in almost all passing categories, and the Giants returned to the title game where they lost to the dominating defense of the Detroit Lions who were led by triple-threats Glenn Presnell and Dutch Clark on offense. The big advance for the season was the bomb. Rookie receiver Don Hutson made an immediate impact on the NFL by making his first catch an 83-yard touchdown pass from the strong arm of Arnie Herber on the first play of the showdown against the Bears. Herber averaged 18.2 yards per completion with the fleet Hutson to target, but the Bears' Bernie Masterson averaged nearly 25 yards per completion on roughly half as many passes.

1935 League Passing Statistics

Games	Att	Comp	%	Yards	Y/Att	Y/Comp	Att/g	Y/g	TD	TD/g	Int	Rating	300-Yd Gms
53	1630	552	33.9%	8453	5.2	15.3	30.8	159.5	64	1.2	238	25.4	0

1935 Leading Passers

Name	Team	Attempts	Comp	%	Yards	Y/Att	Y/Comp	TD	Int	Rating	Relative Rating
Bernie Masterson	CHI	44	18	40.9	446	10.14	24.8	7	4	80.1	315
Ed Danowski	NYG	113	57	50.4	794	7.03	13.9	10	9	69.7	274
Ed Storm	PHL	44	15	34.1	372	8.45	24.8	3	10	48.9	192
Arnie Herber	GBP	109	40	36.7	729	6.69	18.2	8	14	45.4	179
Bob Monnett	GBP	65	31	47.7	354	5.45	11.4	2	5	42.7	168
Phil Sarboe	ARZ	67	31	46.3	368	5.49	11.9	0	10	23.9	94
John Gildea	PIT	105	28	26.7	529	5.04	18.9	3	20	18	71
Ed Matesic	PHL	64	15	23.4	284	4.44	18.9	2	13	16.4	65

The leaders in the major passing categories for 1935 were:

Attempts	Ed Danowski	113	TD%	Ed Danowski	8.8
Completions	Ed Danowski	57	Int %	Bob Monnett	7.7
Yards	Ed Danowski	794	Rating	Ed Danowski	69.7

Yards/Pass	Ed Danowski	7.03	Comebacks	Arnie Herber	2
Comp %	Ed Danowski	50.4	Interceptions	John Gildea	20
TD	Ed Danowski	10			

1936

The NFL draft was begun with nine teams in 1936. The first quarterback taken was Riley Smith by the Redskins, but he was primarily a single wing blocking back. The Giants took Tuffy Leemans who was primarily a runner, but was also fairly active as a passer in the Giants' A formation — another single wing variant.

Arnie Herber topped the league in most categories and had the first official season of over 1,000 yards passing. He led Green Bay to 248 points in 12 games, 21 points per game, and the Packers easily beat the Boston Redskins in the title game that was played in New York because owner George Marshall was set to move the team to Washington.

1936 League Passing Statistics

Games	Att	Comp	%	Yards	Y/Att	Y/Comp	Att/g	Y/g	TD	TD/g	Int	Rating	300-Yd Gms
54	1656	604	36.5%	8960	5.4	14.8	30.7	165.9	67	1.2	216	28.9	0

1936 Leading Passers

Name	Team	Attempts	Comp	%	Yards	Y/Att	Y/Comp	TD	Int	Rating	Relative Rating
Arnie Herber	GBP	173	77	44.5	1239	7.16	16.1	11	13	58.9	202
Dutch Clark	DET	71	38	53.5	467	6.58	12.3	4	6	57.7	198
Ed Danowski	NYG	104	47	45.2	515	4.95	11.0	6	10	40	137
Ed Matesic	PIT	138	64	46.4	850	6.16	13.3	4	16	36.5	125
Phil Sarboe	XBKN	52	22	42.3	282	5.42	12.8	2	5	33.2	114
Pug Vaughan	ARZ	79	30	38	546	6.91	18.2	2	10	31.4	108

The leaders in the major passing categories for 1936 were:

Attempts	Arnie Herber	173	TD%	Arnie Herber	6.4
Completions	Arnie Herber	77	Int %	Arnie Herber	7.5
Yards	Arnie Herber	1,239	Rating	Arnie Herber	58.9
Yards/Pass	Arnie Herber	7.16	Comebacks	Arnie Herber &	
Comp %	Dutch Clark	53.5		Dutch Clark & Dave Smukler	2
TD	Arnie Herber	11	Interceptions	Ed Matesic	16

1937

The Redskins moved to Washington and the Cleveland Rams joined the NFL to create a 10-team league in 1937. All players had to have a number on their uniform. Sammy Baugh became the first primary passer ever drafted when the Redskins selected him in the first round of the draft. Other rookie passers of note included the Dodgers Hall of Fame tailback Ace Parker and Pat Coffee who joined the Cardinals along with his receiving LSU teammate Gaynell Tinsley. Coffee teamed up with Tinsley on the longest pass reception in

NFL history with a 97-yard pass play in the midst of Coffee becoming the first passer to ever throw for 300 yards in a game on December 5th.

The Packers behind the arms of Arnie Herber and Bob Monnett were the top scorers with 220 points in 11 games. However, Baugh was the biggest star right from the start and directed the Redskins to a title showdown against the Bears, led by bomber Bernie Masterson who averaged 23.7 yards per completion. Washington won 28–21 in a shootout in which Baugh set a championship game record by passing for 358 yards and three touchdowns.

1937 League Passing Statistics

Games	Att	Comp	%	Yards	Y/ Att	Y/ Comp	Att/g	Y/g	TD	TD/g	Int	Rating	300-Yd Gms
55	1815	697	38.4%	10227	5.6	14.7	33.0	185.9	90	1.6	206	34.5	1

1937 Leading Passers

Name	Team	Attempts	Comp	%	Yards	Y/Att	Y/Comp	TD	Int	Rating	Relative Rating
Bob Monnett	GBP	73	37	50.7	580	7.95	15.7	8	8	74.4	216
Ed Danowski	NYG	134	66	49.3	814	6.07	12.3	8	5	72.8	211
Bernie Masterson	CHI	72	26	36.1	615	8.54	23.7	9	7	67.8	196
Sammy Baugh	WSH	171	81	47.4	1127	6.59	13.9	8	14	50.5	146
Arnie Herber	GBP	104	47	45.2	684	6.58	14.6	7	10	50	145
Ace Parker	XBKN	61	28	45.9	514	8.43	18.4	1	7	41.3	120
Pat Coffee	ARZ	119	52	43.7	824	6.92	15.8	4	11	40	116

The leaders in the major passing categories for 1937 were:

Attempts	Sammy Baugh	171	TD%	Bernie Masterson	12.5
Completions	Sammy Baugh	81	Int %	Ed Danowski	3.7
Yards	Sammy Baugh	1,127	Rating	Bob Monnett	74.4
Yards/Pass	Bernie Masterson	8.54	Comebacks	Reino Nori	2
Comp %	Bob Monnett	50.7	Interceptions	Sammy Baugh &Dave Smukler	14
TD	Bernie Masterson	9			

1938

Green Bay repeated as the top scoring team, again averaging 20 points per game, and met the Giants for the championship behind three top passing tailbacks, Arnie Herber, Bob Monnett and impressive rookie Cecil Isbell. Monnett was in his last year and led the league in touchdowns, completion percentage and yards per attempt. The Packers were upended by their own mistakes, though, in losing to the Giants for the title.

The roster limit was raised again to 30 players per team, and the league was enlivened by several top rookie tailbacks in addition to Isbell. Jack Robbins and Dwight "Paddlefoot" Sloan both joined the Cardinals from Arkansas, although the record setting 98-yard touchdown pass caught by the Cards' Gaynell Tinsley was the only pass completion by veteran Doug Russell in 1938. Newcomer Frankie Filchock showed great promise after being traded from Pittsburgh to Washington where Sammy Baugh was suffering with a shoulder injury. Pittsburgh's Whizzer White led the league in rushing as a rookie but also set the standard for interceptions thrown with 18. Hall of Fame tailback Dutch Clark retired.

1938 League Passing Statistics

Games	Att	Comp	%	Yards	Y/ Att	Y/ Comp	Att/g	Yds/g	TD	TD/g	Int	Rating	300-Yd Gms
55	2030	824	40.6%	11641	5.7	14.1	36.9	211.7	93	1.7	221	35.5	0

1938 Leading Passers

Name	Team	Attempts	Comp	%	Yards	Y/Att	Y/Comp	TD	Int	Rating	Relative Rating
Bob Monnett	GBP	57	31	54.4	465	8.16	15.0	9	4	91.7	258

Name	Team	Attempts	Comp	%	Yards	Y/Att	Y/Comp	TD	Int	Rating	Relative Rating
Ed Danowski	NYG	129	70	54.3	848	6.57	12.1	7	8	66.9	189
Bernie Masterson	CHI	112	46	41.1	848	7.57	18.4	7	9	55.2	156
Bob Snyder	STL	87	36	41.4	631	7.25	17.5	7	9	54	152
Ace Parker	XBKN	148	63	42.6	865	5.84	13.7	5	7	53.5	151
Cecil Isbell	GBP	91	37	40.7	659	7.24	17.8	7	10	52.2	147
Bill Hartman	WSH	77	38	49.4	558	7.25	14.7	4	10	51.1	144
Sammy Baugh	WSH	128	63	49.2	853	6.66	13.5	5	11	48.1	135
Dave Smukler	PHL	102	42	41.2	524	5.14	12.5	7	8	48	135
Jack Robbins	ARZ	97	52	53.6	577	5.95	11.1	2	9	39.8	112

The leaders in the major passing categories for 1938 were:

Attempts	Ace Parker	148	TD%	Bob Monnett	15.8
Completions	Ed Danowski	70	Int %	Ace Parker	4.7
Yards	Ace Parker	865	Rating	Bob Monnett	91.8
Yards/Pass	Bob Monnett	8.16	Comebacks	Ed Danowski	2
Comp %	Bob Monnett	54.4	Interceptions	Whizzer White	18
TD	Bob Monnett	9			

1939

Arnie Herber and Cecil Isbell made a great team at tailback for the Packers in 1939, combining for over 1,800 yards passing and 14 touchdowns. Each threw a touchdown pass in the Packers championship win over the Giants. Frankie Filchock, who teamed with Sammy Baugh in Washington, set new marks by completing 61.8 percent of his passes and recording a passer rating over 100. He also set an unbreakable record when he hit Andy Farkas for a 99-yard touchdown in October. Davey O'Brien with the Eagles and Parker Hall of the Rams each tossed over 200 passes in their rookie seasons and finished one and two in passing yards as well.

The biggest rookie passer, though, spent most of the season at halfback and threw just 51 passes, Sid Luckman of the Bears. This was the season that Chicago's T formation was remade by Clark Shaughnessy, and they led the NFL in scoring with 298 points in 11 games, an average of 27 per game. Bomber Bernie Masterson started at quarterback for most of the year while Luckman learned the intricacies of being a T quarterback.

1939 League Passing Statistics

Games	Att	Comp	%	Yards	Y/ Att	Y/ Comp	Att/g	Y/g	TD	TD/g	Int	Rating	300-Yd Gms
55	2238	952	42.5%	14168	6.3	14.9	40.7	257.6	99	1.8	209	39.7	0

1939 Leading Passers

Name	Team	Attempts	Comp	%	Yards	Y/Att	Y/Comp	TD	Int	Rating	Relative Rating
Frank Filchock	WSH	89	55	61.8	1094	12.29	19.9	11	7	111.6	281
Cecil Isbell	GBP	103	43	41.7	749	7.27	17.4	6	5	66.4	167
Arnie Herber	GBP	139	57	41	1107	7.96	19.4	8	9	61.6	155
Dwight Sloan	DET	102	45	44.1	658	6.45	14.6	2	3	60	151
Bernie Masterson	CHI	113	44	38.9	914	8.09	20.8	8	9	58.6	148
Parker Hall	STL	208	106	51	1227	5.9	11.6	9	13	57.5	145
Sammy Baugh	WSH	96	53	55.2	518	5.4	9.8	6	9	52.3	132
Davey O'Brien	PHL	201	99	49.3	1324	6.59	13.4	6	17	45.3	114
Ace Parker	XBKN	157	72	45.9	977	6.22	13.6	4	13	40.2	101

The leaders in the major passing categories for 1939 were:

Attempts	Parker Hall	208	TD%	Frank Filchock	12.4
Completions	Parker Hall	106	Int %	Dwight Sloan	2.9
Yards	Davey O'Brien	1,324	Rating	Frank Filchock	111.7
Yards/Pass	Frank Filchock	12.29	Comebacks	Sid Luckman	2
Comp %	Frank Filchock	61.8	Interceptions	Davey O'Brien	17
TD	Frank Filchock	11			

1940

Since the Bears finished second in the West in 1939, not much was made of their revolutionary new offense. Surprisingly, they scored fewer points in 1940, but still led the league with 22 points per game. The 1940 championship game changed that. Beating the sturdy Redskins 73–0 was a shocking development. Luckman and his backup Bob Snyder only threw 9 passes in the entire game as the Bears ran for almost 400 yards in the game. Washington passers Sammy Baugh, Frankie Filchock and Roy Zimmerman, by contrast, threw 51 desperate passes, completed 20 and had 8 intercepted. Baugh after all, had led the league in yards, touchdowns and set a new completion percentage high with 62.7 percent.

1939's rookie stars Davey O'Brien and Parker Hall each had major setbacks in 1940, although O'Brien set records with 277 passes in a season, 60 passes in a game and 316 yards in his final game. He, Arnie Herber and Bernie Masterson retired after the 1940 season. Rookies Tommy Thompson and Roy Zimmerman would have greater success later in the decade. On the downside, Hugh McCullough of the Cardinals set a new season record with 21 interceptions. Roster limits were adjusted to a minimum of 22 and maximum of 33 players.

1940 League Passing Statistics

Games	Att	Comp	%	Yards	Y/ Att	Y/ Comp	Att/g	Y/g	TD	TD/g	Int	Rating	300-Yd Gms
55	2254	968	42.9%	13788	6.1	14.2	41.0	250.7	100	1.8	223	38.6	1

1940 Leading Passers

Name	Team	Attempts	Comp	%	Yards	Y/ Att	Y/ Comp	TD	Int	Rating	Relative Rating
Sammy Baugh	WSH	177	111	62.7	1367	7.72	12.3	12	10	85.6	222
Ace Parker	XBKN	111	49	44.1	817	7.36	16.7	10	7	73.3	190
Cecil Isbell	GBP	150	68	45.3	1037	6.91	15.3	9	12	55.3	143
Sid Luckman	CHI	105	48	45.7	941	8.96	19.6	4	9	54.5	141
Arnie Herber	GBP	89	38	42.7	560	6.29	14.7	5	7	49.8	129
Cotton Price	DET	66	33	50	456	6.91	13.8	3	7	48.1	125
Eddie Miller	NYG	73	35	47.9	505	6.92	14.4	3	7	45	117
Davey O'Brien	PHL	277	124	44.8	1290	4.66	10.4	5	17	39.2	102
Parker Hall	STL	183	77	42.1	1108	6.05	14.4	6	16	36.9	96

The leaders in the major passing categories for 1940 were:

Attempts	Davey O'Brien	277	TD%	Ace Parker	9
Completions	Davey O'Brien	124	Int %	Foster Watkins	3.5
Yards	Sammy Baugh	1,367	Rating	Sammy Baugh	85.6
Yards/Pass	Sid Luckman	8.96	Comebacks	Frank Filchock	2
Comp %	Sammy Baugh	62.7	Interceptions	Hugh McCullough	21
TD	Sammy Baugh	12			

1941

With Sid Luckman now fully comfortable operating the T, the Bears put up 396 points in 11 games, an unheard of 36 points per game. They swept through the regular season and dismantled the outclassed Giants 37–9 in the title game. While Luckman had a fine season, averaging nearly 10 yards per pass, Cecil Isbell led the NFL in yards and touchdowns. The

last place Eagles became the first team to copy the Bears offense and made one-eyed Tommy Thompson the second T formation quarterback in the league. The Rams experimented with a "modified" T for some snaps, but their passer, Parker Hall, had a disastrous year, averaging just 4.5 yards per pass and tying Sammy Baugh for the lead in interceptions with 19. Giants passer Ed Danowski retired at the end of the season.

1941 League Passing Statistics

Games	Att	Comp	%	Yards	Y/ Att	Y/ Comp	Att/g	Y/g	TD	TD/g	Int	Rating	300-Yd Gms
55	2210	978	44.3%	13397	6.1	13.7	40.2	243.6	99	1.8	219	39.6	0

1941 Leading Passers

Name	Team	Attempts	Comp	%	Yards	Y/Att	Y/Comp	TD	Int	Rating	Relative Rating
Sid Luckman	CHI	119	68	57.1	1181	9.92	17.4	9	6	95.3	241
Cecil Isbell	GBP	206	117	56.8	1479	7.18	12.6	15	11	81.4	206
Ray Mallouf	ARZ	96	48	50	725	7.55	15.1	2	4	64.8	164
Tuffy Leemans	NYG	66	31	47	475	7.2	15.3	4	5	59.8	152
Sammy Baugh	WSH	193	106	54.9	1236	6.4	11.7	10	19	52.2	132
Tommy Thompson	PHL	162	86	53.1	959	5.92	11.2	8	14	51.4	130
Parker Hall	STL	190	84	44.2	863	4.54	10.3	7	19	30.5	77

The leaders in the major passing categories for 1941 were:

Attempts	Cecil Isbell	206	TD%	Sid Luckman	7.6
Completions	Cecil Isbell	117	Int %	Ray Mallouf	4.2
Yards	Cecil Isbell	1,479	Rating	Sid Luckman	95.3
Yards/Pass	Sid Luckman	9.92	Comebacks	Cecil Isbell	3
Comp %	Sid Luckman	57.1	Interceptions	Sammy Baugh & Parker Hall	19
TD	Cecil Isbell	15			

1942

1942 marks the beginning of the War years, and many fine football players went into the military for the duration. In the NFL, Cecil Isbell teamed with Don Hutson to put on a memorable show during the season. Hutson caught 17 touchdowns, mostly from Isbell who set new records with 24 touchdown passes and touchdown passes in 22 consecutive games. Isbell also became the first passer to top 2,000 yards passing officially in a season. Sammy Baugh threw for 16 touchdowns, while Sid Luckman shared the load in Chicago with rookie Charlie

O'Rourke who averaged an amazing 25.7 yards per completions and threw for 11 touchdowns to Sid's 10. Another rookie, Bud Schwenk of the Cardinals, set new marks for most attempts, 295, and interceptions, 27. In New York, runner Tuffy Leemans took over more passing responsibilities in light of the team's loss of passers to the armed services.

In the championship game, Sammy Baugh finally got the best of Sid Luckman as the Redskins edged the undefeated Bears 14–6 in a defensive battle. The Bears led the league in scoring with 376 points in 11 games, 34 points a game.

1942 League Passing Statistics

Games	Att	Comp	%	Yards	Y/Att	Y/Comp	Att/g	Y/g	TD	TD/g	Int	Rating	300-Yd Gms
55	2249	986	43.8%	13608	6.1	13.8	40.9	247.4	108	2.0	219	40.3	1

1942 Leading Passers

Name	Team	Attempts	Comp	%	Yards	Y/Att	Y/Comp	TD	Int	Rating	Relative Rating
Tuffy Leemans	NYG	69	35	50.7	555	8.04	15.9	7	4	87.5	217
Cecil Isbell	GBP	268	146	54.5	2021	7.54	13.8	24	14	87	216
Sammy Baugh	WSH	225	132	58.7	1524	6.77	11.5	16	11	82.5	205
Charley O'Rourke	CHI	88	37	42	951	10.81	25.7	11	16	82.1	204
Sid Luckman	CHI	105	57	54.3	1023	9.74	17.9	10	13	80.1	199
Tommy Thompson	PHL	203	95	46.8	1410	6.95	14.8	8	16	50.3	125
Bud Schwenk	ARZ	295	126	42.7	1360	4.61	10.8	6	27	25.5	63

The leaders in the major passing categories for 1942 were:

Attempts	Bud Schwenk	295	TD%	Charley O'Rourke	12.5
Completions	Cecil Isbell	146	Int %	Sammy Baugh	4.9
Yards	Cecil Isbell	2,021	Rating	Tuffy Leemans	87.5
Yards/Pass	Charley O'Rourke	10.81	Comebacks	Sammy Baugh	3
Comp %	Sammy Baugh	58.7	Interceptions	Bud Schwenk	27
TD	Cecil Isbell	24			

1943

In light of wartime restrictions, the NFL lowered the roster limit to 28 men per team and instituted free substitution in games. The Rams shut down operations for 1943, while the Eagles and Steelers combined to form the Steagles. One Steagle player who returned from retirement was bareheaded Bill Hewitt who was then forced to comply with the new league regulation that all players wear helmets. Several passers like Frankie Filchock, Ace Parker, Parker Hall and Tommy Thompson were off to war, but 28-year old star Cecil Isbell simply retired to start a coaching career. Among rookies, Ronnie Cahill and John Grigas both joined the Cardinals from Holy Cross and combined to throw three touchdowns and 25 interceptions. Irv Comp of the Packers had some success, but Frankie Sinkwich of the Lions struggled as a passer.

The top stars again were Sammy Baugh and Sid Luckman. Baugh threw 23 touchdowns and not only led the league in completion percentage with 55.6 percent, but punting and defensive interceptions as well. Luckman broke the records set the previous season by Cecil Isbell by throwing for 2,194 yards and 28 touchdowns. Seven of those touchdowns came in a 56–7 November battering of the Giants in which Sid set the standard for touchdowns in a game and also became the first passer to exceed 400 yards in a game with 433. The Bears scored 303 points in the 10-game season, and beat Washington 41–21 in the title match where Luckman threw for five touchdowns. Baugh suffered a concussion in that game when he tried to tackle Luckman returning a punt.

1943 League Passing Statistics

Games	Att	Comp	%	Yards	Y/Att	Y/Comp	Att/g	Y/g	TD	TD/g	Int	Rating	300-Yd Gms
40	1732	769	44.4%	11308	6.5	14.7	43.3	282.7	114	2.9	182	48.6	2

1943 Leading Passers

Name	Team	Attempts	Comp	%	Yards	Y/Att	Y/Comp	TD	Int	Rating	Relative Rating
Sid Luckman	CHI	202	110	54.5	2194	10.86	19.9	28	12	107.5	221
Irv Comp	GBP	92	46	50	662	7.2	14.4	7	4	81	166
Sammy Baugh	WSH	239	133	55.6	1754	7.34	13.2	23	19	78	160
Tony Canadeo	GBP	129	56	43.4	875	6.78	15.6	9	12	51	105
Tuffy Leemans	NYG	87	37	42.5	366	4.21	9.9	5	5	50.3	103
Roy Zimmerman	PHL/PIT	124	43	34.7	846	6.82	19.7	9	17	44	90
Frankie Sinkwich	DET	126	50	39.7	699	5.55	14.0	7	20	37.2	76
Ron Cahill	ARZ	109	50	45.9	608	5.58	12.2	3	21	33.1	68
Dean McAdams	XBKN	75	37	49.3	315	4.2	8.5	0	7	21.8	45

The leaders in the major passing categories for 1943 were:

Attempts	Sammy Baugh 239	TD%	Sid Luckman	13.9
Completions	Sammy Baugh 133	Int %	Irv Comp	4.3
Yards	Sid Luckman 2,194	Rating	Sid Luckman	107.6
Yards/Pass	Sid Luckman 10.86	Comebacks	Sid Luckman &	
Comp %	Sammy Baugh 55.6		Roy Zimmerman & Tuffy Leemans	1
TD	Sid Luckman 28	Interceptions	Ron Cahill	21

1944

Free substitution was extended for another year in 1944, but the Steagles were not. Philadelphia went on its own, while Pittsburgh teamed with the Cardinals to form the winless Card-Pitts. The Rams returned from a one-year absence, and the Boston Yanks were an expansion franchise that indicated a sense of optimism by the league. The final restriction on coaching from the bench was lifted as coaches were now permitted to talk with players on the field. While Detroit and Boston experimented with a version of the T, only the Redskins actually adopted it in 1944, and veteran Sammy Baugh struggled to master it. Frankie Filchock returned to the Redskins from the service, though, and was the league's best passer in the T. The Eagles led the league in scoring with 267 points in 10 games, but the championship game came down to the Packers and Giants. The Packers were led by the interception-prone Irv Comp while the Giants brought back former Packer Arnie Herber from four years of retirement. Green Bay won 14–6.

1944 League Passing Statistics

Games	Att	Comp	%	Yards	Y/Att	Y/Comp	Att/g	Y/g	TD	TD/g	Int	Rating	300-Yd Gms
50	2114	906	42.9%	12925	6.1	14.3	42.3	258.5	117	2.3	234	42.1	0

1944 Leading Passers

Name	Team	Attempts	Comp	%	Yards	Y/Att	Y/Comp	TD	Int	Rating	Relative Rating
Frank Filchock	WSH	147	84	57.1	1139	7.75	13.6	13	9	86	204
Gene Ronzani	CHI	56	26	46.4	448	8	17.2	9	5	76.5	182
Sid Luckman	CHI	143	71	49.7	1018	7.12	14.3	11	12	63.8	151
Sammy Baugh	WSH	146	82	56.2	849	5.82	10.4	4	8	59.4	141
Albie Reisz	STL	113	49	43.4	777	6.88	15.9	8	10	53.6	127
Arnie Herber	NYG	86	36	41.9	651	7.57	18.1	6	8	53	126
Frankie Sinkwich	DET	148	58	39.2	1060	7.16	18.3	12	20	52	123
Irv Comp	GBP	177	80	45.2	1159	6.55	14.5	12	21	50	119
George Cafego	XBOS	73	35	47.9	454	6.22	13.0	3	7	42.1	100

The leaders in the major passing categories for 1944 were:

Attempts	Irv Comp	177	TD%	Frank Filchock	8.8
Completions	Frank Filchock	84	Int %	Sammy Baugh	5.5
Yards	Irv Comp	1,159	Rating	Frank Filchock	86
Yards/Pass	Frank Filchock	7.75	Comebacks	Albie Riesz	2
Comp %	Frank Filchock	57.1	Interceptions	Irv Comp	21
TD	Frank Filchock	13			

1945

Free substitution was brought back for one more wartime season, and the Dodgers dropped out of the league. However, the NFL stayed at 10 teams because the Steelers and Cardinals separated again. The hashmarks were moved once more, this time to 20 feet in and fumbles began to be counted by the league. Once again, the Eagles displayed a mastery of the T formation by leading the league in scoring with 272 points in 10 games. Both the Cardinals and Rams fully adopted the T formation in 1945, the fourth and fifth teams to do so. While Cardinals rookie Paul Christman struggled in the new system, Rams rookie Bob Waterfield was named league MVP and led the Rams to a 15–14 title win over Sammy Baugh's Redskins. Baugh settled in with the T in his second year as a quarterback and completed 70.3 percent of his passes a record that would stand for 37 years. Hall of Famer Arnie Herber retired once more and for good.

1945 League Passing Statistics

Games	Att	Comp	%	Yards	Y/Att	Y/Comp	Att/g	Yds/g	TD	TD/g	Int	Rating	300-Yd Gms
50	2111	958	45.4%	14375	6.8	15.0	42.2	287.5	109	2.2	193	47.4	1

1945 Leading Passers

Name	Team	Attempts	Comp	%	Yards	Y/Att	Y/Comp	TD	Int	Rating	Relative Rating
Sammy Baugh	WSH	182	128	70.3	1669	9.17	13.0	11	4	109.9	232
Sid Luckman	CHI	217	117	53.9	1727	7.96	14.8	14	10	82.5	174
Roy Zimmerman	PHL	132	67	50.8	991	7.51	14.8	9	8	73.1	154
Bob Waterfield	STL	171	89	52	1609	9.41	18.1	14	17	72.4	153
Arnie Herber	NYG	80	35	43.8	641	8.01	18.3	9	8	69.8	147
Paul Christman	ARZ	219	89	40.6	1147	5.24	12.9	5	12	42.6	90

The leaders in the major passing categories for 1945 were:

Attempts	Paul Christman	219	TD%	Arnie Herber	11.3
Completions	Sammy Baugh	128	Int %	Sammy Baugh	2.2
Yards	Sid Luckman	1,727	Rating	Sammy Baugh	109.9
Yards/Pass	Bob Waterfield	9.41	Comebacks	Sammy Baugh &	
Comp %	Sammy Baugh	70.3		Bob Waterfield	2
TD	Bob Waterfield &		Interceptions	Bob Waterfield	17
	Sid Luckman	14	Fumbles	Paul Christman	12

The following quarterbacks and passing tailbacks served in the armed forces during World War II:

Frankie Albert	George Cafego	Ed Danowski	Frank Filchock	Jack Jacobs
Len Barnum	Paul Christman	Glenn Dobbs	Benny Friedman	Tom Landry
Angelo Bertelli	Johnny Clement	Bill Dudley	Jug Girard	Cliff Lewis
Ray Buivid	Tom Colella	Fred Enke	Parker Hall	Sid Luckman
Young Bussey	Charlie Conerly	Chuck Fenenbock	Harry Hopp	Bill Mackrides

Ray Mallouf	Perry Moss	Billy Patterson	Frankie Sinkwich	Norm Van Brocklin
Joe Margucci	Steve Nemeth	Cotton Price	Dwight Sloan	Bob Waterfield
Bernie Masterson	Ernie Nevers	Marion Pugh	Dave Smukler	Doster Watkins
Hugh McCullough	Emery Nix	Doug Russell	Hank Soar	Whizzer White
Coley McDonough	Charlie O'Rourke	Spec Sanders	Leo Stasica	Jim Youel
Eddie Miller	Ace Parker	Tony Sarausky	Tommy Thompson	
Tommy Mont	Frank Patrick	Bud Schwenk	Charlie Trippi	

9

1946–1949:
The All America Football Conference

The All America Football Conference was started by *Chicago Tribune* columnist Arch Ward, the same imaginative sportswriter who originated the baseball All Star Game and the College Football All Star Game. Ward envisioned the AAFC as a post war competitor to the NFL and hoped for a championship game between the two leagues. Ward brought together wealthy owners from NFL cities New York, Chicago, Cleveland and Brooklyn as well as untapped territory like Los Angeles, San Francisco, Buffalo, Miami and Baltimore. The AAFC claimed to respect NFL player contracts, but there was such a backlog of college players who had gone into the service and never played pro football that there were plenty of talented players to sign. Ironically, the one person who could be accused of jumping was owner Dan Topping who took his Brooklyn Dodgers football team from the NFL into the AAFC as the New York Yankees football team. Topping, of course, also owned the baseball Yankees at the time. The Brooklyn Dodgers of the AAFC were a wholly unrelated new franchise.

Paul Brown's Cleveland Browns were the class of the league right from the start. They lost only four games in the four years of the league and won all four titles. They were so far superior to the rest of the AAFC that the league suffered from a lack of competition. Brown was an innovative coach who took the modern T formation and created an explosive passing offense that relied on unstoppable timing passes in a wide mix of precision pass patterns. Brown's high-scoring offense was matched with the best defense in the league to form a team almost-literally unbeatable. The Browns key rivals in the AAFC were the New York Yankees and the San Francisco 49ers. The Yankees ran a single wing offense and were coached by former Redskin coach Ray Flaherty, whom Brown sarcastically referred to as "Ray Flattery." The 49ers were a power-running T formation squad coached by Buck Shaw. While the NFL steadily increased its number of pass attempts per game from 42 to 55 in this period, the AAFC fluctuated from 40 to 41 to 50 to 47. Furthermore, the AAFC was evenly divided between the T and the single wing throughout its existence; by 1949, only the Steelers still ran the single wing in the NFL.

After four years of expensive battling for players, the NFL and AAFC agreed to merge for the 1950 season. The Eastern and Western Conferences were initially renamed the American and National Conferences, but only three of the remaining seven AAFC franchises were invited to join the NFL. Los Angeles, New York and

Chicago were disbanded with most of their players joining the NFL teams in those cities. The fan-supported Buffalo Bills were shut out in the merger and curiously replaced by the floundering Colts franchise.

There is no question that the AAFC was a high quality league as the subsequent records of the Browns and 49ers attest, and it featured some great quarterbacks. Hall of Famers Otto Graham and Y.A. Tittle got started in the AAFC, and Hall of Famer Ace Parker finished up there. Frankie Albert, George Ratterman and Glenn Dobbs also first starred in the AAFC; Albert and Ratterman moved on to the NFL, while Dobbs went to Canada instead. AAFC numbers generally are not included in the statistical totals of players who played in both leagues, and that is unfair, since the two leagues merged. The AAFC was not like the World Football League or the USFL which simply went bankrupt; a closer parallel was the American Football League of the 1960s. The AAFC's legacy continues to live on today in Cleveland and San Francisco, and its players deserve to have their records counted.

The aggregate league-wide passing data for the period from 1946 through 1949 in the AAFC was:

Games	Att	Comp	%	Yards	Y/ Att	Y/ Comp	Att/g	Y/g	TD	TD/g	Int	Rating	300-Yd Gm
210	9324	4519	48.5%	65317	7.0	14.5	44.4	311.0	551	2.6	681	60.9	13

Eight passers threw for at least 2,500 yards in this four-year league. All of the five quarterbacks in the group completed at least half their passes, while none of the three tailbacks did. Otto Graham was tops in every passing category except for touchdown passes where 49er field general Frankie Albert bested Otto by two, 88 to 86. Graham, Albert and Tittle all threw more touchdowns than interceptions, and there is an odd connection among the trio. Tittle was drafted by the Browns, but then sent on to the Colts for the good of the league before he ever got to back up Graham. When the leagues merged in 1950, they were the starting quarterbacks on the three teams that were absorbed into the NFL. Once the original Colts failed, though, Tittle was drafted by the 49ers and spent a season backing up Albert before winning the starting job in San Francisco. The AAFC's top eight ranked by passer rating:

Name	Attempts	Comp	%	Yards	Y/Att	Y/Comp	TD	Int	Rating
Otto Graham	1061	592	55.8%	10085	9.5	17.0	86	41	99.1
Frankie Albert	963	515	53.5%	6948	7.2	13.5	88	55	83.4
Y.A. Tittle	578	309	53.5%	4731	8.2	15.3	30	27	78.6
George Ratterman	831	438	52.7%	6194	7.5	14.1	52	55	70.3
Charley O'Rourke	418	219	52.4%	3088	7.4	14.1	28	35	64.0
Glenn Dobbs	934	446	47.8%	5876	6.3	13.2	45	52	61.0
Spec Sanders	418	204	48.8%	2771	6.6	13.6	23	37	51.8
Bob Hoernschemeyer	688	308	44.8%	4109	6.0	13.3	32	51	48.9

Overall, the quarterbacks who led the league the most times in passing categories over this era were:

Attempts	Glenn Dobbs	2	TD	Frankie Albert & Otto Graham	2
Completions	Glenn Dobbs	2	TD%	Frankie Albert & Otto Graham	2
Yards	Otto Graham	3	Int %	Otto Graham	2
Yards/Pass	Otto Graham	3	Rating	Otto Graham	3
Comp %	Charley O'Rourke &		Wins	Otto Graham	4
	Otto Graham &		Comebacks	Charley O'Rourke	2
	Frankie Albert &		Interceptions	George Ratterman	2
	George Ratterman	1			

And the AAFC All-Time leaders were:

Attempts	Glenn Dobbs	1,061	TD%	Frankie Albert	9.14
Completions	Glenn Dobbs	592	Int%	Otto Graham	3.96
Yards	Otto Graham	10,085	Rating	Otto Graham	99.1

Yards/Pass	Otto Graham	9.5	Wins	Otto Graham	46
Comp %	Otto Graham	55.8%	Interceptions	Frankie Albert &	
TD	Frankie Albert	88		George Ratterman	55

1946

The Cleveland Browns drubbed the pathetic Miami Seahawks 44–0 in the very first game of the All America Conference and set the tone for the year. The Browns gave up the fewest points in the league and scored the most, 423 in 14 games. Otto Graham had an unreal rookie year with a passer rating of 112.1, twice the league average. Single wing tailback Glenn Dobbs of Brooklyn was voted the league MVP, though. He threw the most passes and was a skilled runner as well as the best punter in the league.

In the championship game, the Browns beat the Yankees, the best of the East, 14–9 on a touchdown pass from Otto Graham to Dante Lavelli with under five minutes to play. Then, two-way star Graham clinched the victory by intercepting Ace Parker in the closing minutes. The other two star T quarterbacks that year were both former draftees of the Chicago Bears, Frankie Albert and Charlie O'Rourke; O'Rourke even spent a season backing up Sid Luckman in Chicago before going into the service. Rookies Bob Hoernschemeyer and Spec Sanders also made their marks as talented single wing tailbacks. The biggest disappointment was Angelo Bertelli who had won the Heisman Trophy at Notre Dame. The Los Angeles Dons won a court fight with the NFL's Boston Yanks over Bertelli, but he had injury problems and was interception-prone.

1946 AAFC Passing Statistics

Games	Att	Comp	%	Yards	Y/ Att	Y/ Comp	Att/g	Y/g	TD	TD/g	Int	Rating	300-Yd Gms
56	2255	1091	48.4%	15073	6.7	13.8	40.3	269.2	133	2.4	187	55.4	0

1946 AAFC Leading Passers

Name	Team	Attempts	Comp	%	Yards	Y/Att	Y/Comp	TD	Int	Rating	Relative Rating
Otto Graham	CLE	174	95	54.6	1834	10.54	19.3	17	5	112.1	202
Ace Parker	ZNYY	115	62	53.9	763	6.63	12.3	8	3	87	157
Frankie Albert	SFF	197	104	52.8	1404	7.13	13.5	14	14	69.8	126
Charley O'Rourke	ZLAD	182	105	57.7	1250	6.87	11.9	12	14	68.7	124
Glenn Dobbs	ZBKN	269	135	50.2	1886	7.01	14.0	13	15	66	119
Bob Hoernschemeyer	ZCHI	193	95	49.2	1266	6.56	13.3	14	14	64.4	116
Angelo Bertelli	ZLAD	127	67	52.8	917	7.22	13.7	7	14	54.9	99

The leaders in the major passing categories for 1946 were:

Attempts	Glenn Dobbs	269	TD%	Otto Graham	9.8
Completions	Glenn Dobbs	135	Int %	Ace Parker	2.6
Yards	Glenn Dobbs	1886	Rating	Otto Graham	112.1
Yards/Pass	Otto Graham	10.54	Wins	Otto Graham	11
Comp %	Charley O'Rourke	57.7	Comebacks	Ace Parker & Charley O'Rourke	3
TD	Otto Graham	17	Interceptions	Glenn Dobbs	15

1947

The Miami Seahawks disbanded in 1946 and were replaced by the new Baltimore Colts franchise in 1947, but the Colts were terrible, too. Their quarterback, Bud Schwenk, led the AAFC in attempts, completions and interceptions, but showed he had learned little from backing up Otto Graham the previous season. Graham had another terrific year with his passer rating again over 100, his yards per pass again over 10 and his completion percentage was 60.6 percent. He also threw 25 touchdowns and was named league MVP.

The Browns again led the AAFC in fewest points allowed and most points scored (410), and again met the Yankees for the title. The Yankees were led by versatile tailback Spec Sanders who ran for a professional record 1,432 yards and passed for 1,442. In another defensive battle, Cleveland prevailed 14–3 for their second championship. The big news during the season was a three-way trade of passers. Reigning MVP Glenn

Dobbs was sent from Brooklyn to Los Angeles where he competed for time as a T quarterback with Charlie O'Rourke. The Dons sent disappointing Angelo Bertelli to Chicago where he was too injured to beat out unimpressive rookie Sam Vacanti in the dud Rockets' new T formation offense. Finally, Hunchy Hoernschemeyer went from inept Chicago to the struggling Brooklyn Dodgers and gained 702 yards on the ground. The top rookie was George Ratterman, who was Johnny Lujack's backup at Notre Dame before leaving school a year early to have an impressive season at quarterback for second place Buffalo.

1947 AAFC Passing Statistics

Games	Att	Comp	%	Yards	Y/Att	Y/Comp	Att/g	Y/g	TD	TD/g	Int	Rating	300-Yd Gms
56	2301	1128	49.0%	16551	7.2	14.7	41.1	295.6	147	2.6	164	64.5	1

1947 AAFC Leading Passers

Name	Team	Attempts	Comp	%	Yards	Y/Att	Y/Comp	TD	Int	Rating	Relative Rating
Otto Graham	CLE	269	163	60.6	2753	10.23	16.9	25	11	109.2	169
Frankie Albert	SFF	242	128	52.9	1692	6.99	13.2	18	15	74.3	115
George Ratterman	ZBUF	244	124	50.8	1840	7.54	14.8	22	20	71.8	111
Spec Sanders	ZNYY	171	93	54.4	1442	8.43	15.5	14	17	70.2	109
Bud Schwenk	ZBAL	327	168	51.4	2236	6.84	13.3	13	20	61.2	95
Sam Vacanti	ZCHI	225	96	42.7	1571	6.98	16.4	16	16	60.8	94

The leaders in the major passing categories for 1947 were:

Attempts	Bud Schwenk	327	Int %	Otto Graham	4.1
Completions	Bud Schwenk	168	Rating	Otto Graham	109.2
Yards	Otto Graham	2753	Wins	Otto Graham	12
Yards/Pass	Otto Graham	10.23	Comebacks	Frankie Albert &	
Comp %	Otto Graham	60.6		George Ratterman &	
TD	Otto Graham	25		Charley O'Rourke & Spec Sanders	2
TD%	Otto Graham	9.3	Interceptions	Bus Schwenk & George Ratterman	20

1948

Twice the San Francisco 49ers had finished second in the West to the Browns, and they geared up for a big push in 1948. The 49ers set a pro football record that still stands by rushing for 3,663 yards over the course of their 14-game season. Led by crafty Frankie Albert's 29 touchdown passes, San Francisco scored 495 points, a monstrous 35 per game, and finished 12–2. Of course, the Browns still had the best defense in the league to go with the second best offense and

finished 14–0. Otto Graham threw for 25 touchdowns again and shared the MVP with Albert. The 7–7 Buffalo Bills behind lanky George Ratterman had to beat the 7–7 Colts behind top rookie Y.A. Tittle just to get to the championship game. In the mismatch of a title game, the Browns dismantled the Bills 48–7. Ratterman set a new standard for interceptions with 22.

The Dons had a new coach in Jimmy Phelan, and he installed a single wing spread passing formation for Glenn Dobbs who once again led the league in attempts and completions in addition to rushing for 539 yards. The mediocre Dons, though won seven games for the third straight year, while Brooklyn lost at least 10 games for the third consecutive season. For the second straight ignoble season, Chicago finished 1–13.

1948 AAFC Passing Statistics

Games	Att	Comp	%	Yards	Y/ Att	Y/ Comp	Att/g	Y/g	TD	TD/g	Int	Rating	300-Yd Gms
56	2805	1370	48.8%	19772	7.0	14.4	50.1	353.1	167	3.0	187	64.2	7

1948 AAFC Leading Passers

Name	Team	Attempts	Comp	%	Yards	Y/Att	Y/Comp	TD	Int	Rating	Relative Rating
Frankie Albert	SFF	264	154	58.3	1990	7.54	12.9	29	10	102.9	160
Y.A. Tittle	ZBAL	289	161	55.7	2522	8.73	15.7	16	9	90.3	141
Otto Graham	CLE	333	173	52	2713	8.15	15.7	25	15	85.6	133
Jesse Freitas	ZCHI	167	84	50.3	1425	8.53	17.0	14	16	67.9	106
Glenn Dobbs	ZLAD	369	185	50.1	2403	6.51	13.0	21	20	67.4	105
George Ratterman	ZBUF	335	168	50.1	2577	7.69	15.3	16	22	64.5	100

The leaders in the major passing categories for 1948 were:

Attempts	Glenn Dobbs	369	TD%	Frankie Albert	11
Completions	Glenn Dobbs	185	Int %	Y.A. Tittle	3.1
Yards	Otto Graham	2713	Rating	Frankie Albert	102.9
Yards/Pass	Y.A. Tittle	8.73	Wins	Otto Graham	14
Comp %	Frankie Albert	58.3	Comebacks	Glenn Dobbs	3
TD	Frankie Albert	29	Interceptions	George Ratterman	22

1949

Brooklyn was merged into the Yankee franchise and the AAFC went with a one-division, seven-team, league for its last 12-game season. The 49ers repeated as the top offense, scoring 416 points, 35 a game. However, the Browns again had the second best offense and top defense to finish ahead of the 49ers. Cleveland then beat San Francisco 21–7 in the final AAFC title game. Frankie Albert threw 27 touchdowns to lead the league, while George Ratterman completed a league best 57.9 percent of his passes, but Otto Graham was the best overall quarterback and a champion once more.

Y.A. Tittle threw the most passes in the AAFC, but the Colts had a tough year, dropping to a last place 1–11 mark. Chicago brought in single wing guru Ray Flaherty as coach and improved to four wins behind Bob Hoernschemeyer and former Steeler tailback Johnny Clement. The top rookie passer was mediocre Dom Panciera of New York, while the Los Angeles Dons had rookie tailback George Taliaferro who shared time with slumping Glenn Dobbs. Taliaferro was the first black passing tailback in pro football since the Cardinals' Joe Lillard in 1933.

1949 AAFC Passing Statistics

Games	Att	Comp	%	Yards	Y/ Att	Y/ Comp	Att/g	Y/g	TD	TD/g	Int	Rating	300-Yd Gms
42	1963	930	47.4%	13921	7.1	15.0	46.7	331.5	104	2.5	143	58.4	5

1949 AAFC Leading Passers

Name	Team	Attempts	Comp	%	Yards	Y/Att	Y/Comp	TD	Int	Rating	Relative Rating
Otto Graham	CLE	285	161	56.5	2785	9.77	17.3	19	10	97.5	167
Frankie Albert	SFF	260	129	49.6	1862	7.16	14.4	27	16	82.2	141
George Ratterman	ZBUF	252	146	57.9	1777	7.05	12.2	14	13	76.8	131
Y.A. Tittle	ZBAL	289	148	51.2	2209	7.64	14.9	14	18	66.8	114
Johnny Clement	ZCHI	114	58	50.9	906	7.95	15.6	6	13	55.6	95
Bob Hoernschemeyer	ZCHI	167	69	41.3	1063	6.37	15.4	6	11	47.6	81

The leaders in the major passing categories for 1949 were:

Attempts	Y.A. Tittle	289	TD%	Frankie Albert	10.4
Completions	Otto Graham	161	Int %	Otto Graham	3.5
Yards	Otto Graham	2785	Rating	Otto Graham	97.5
Yards/Pass	Otto Graham	9.77	Wins	Otto Graham	9
Comp %	George Ratterman	57.9	Comebacks	Dom Panciera	3
TD	Frankie Albert	27	Interceptions	Y.A. Tittle	18

10

1946–59: Taking Flight

The immediate post–World War II era displayed a marked increase in passing offense league-wide. The average yards passing per game went from 214 during the previous era to 363 in this one. The average number of touchdown passes per game went from 1.7 to 2.7. The completion percentage went from 40.7 percent to 48.1 percent. The league passer rating in 1945 was 47.4; by 1959, it was 66.9. There had been six 300-yard passing games before 1946; there were 70 recorded in this era.

One of the main reasons for this jump in the passing game was the move to the T formation. In 1946, half of the 10 teams in the NFL were still using the Single Wing, but within three years, only the Pittsburgh Steelers were. The Steelers would hold out until 1952. Furthermore, the T itself evolved in this period to the Pro Set. Instead of sending one of the three running backs in motion on each play, the Rams in the late 1940s converted the second halfback to a flanker, i.e., a second wide receiver who lined up in the slot in the backfield or out on the flank. By the end of the 1950s, every team was using the Pro Set. The increase in speedy receivers opened up offenses even more with more reliance on the long pass, the bomb. On the other side of the ball, the 4–3 defense featuring a middle linebacker and a four man defensive backfield emerged during the 1950s to combat the pass-oriented offenses. Finally, free substitution was instituted for good in 1950 and ushered in two-platoon football where a team's passer no longer had to double as a defensive back.

Despite the move to two-platoon football, the game continued to be violent and brutal and several steps were taken to alleviate that. A ball carrier no longer had to be pinned to the ground before a play was blown dead. Plastic helmets replaced leather ones, and after much experimentation with different designs, facemasks were added as a safety feature — most prominently to Otto Graham's helmet after his jaw was broken in 1953. Ironically, the facemasks themselves brought about their own dangers in that it was fully legal at the time to tackle a ball carrier by grabbing the mask and dragging him down.

Paul Brown was the only coach regularly calling the plays on the field at this time, using a messenger guard system, but other coaches experimented with other systems. In 1953, Hampton Pool of the Rams tried alternating quarterbacks Norm Van Brocklin and Rudy Bukich on each play. Paul Brown later tried this with Milt Plum and Jim Ninowski. Then in a 1954 exhibition game, Pool tried sending backup quarterback Billy Wade into the huddle to give the play to Van Brocklin before racing back to the bench for the next play. This practice was outlawed by the league, so Paul Brown came up with radio helmets in the 1956. The Cardinals and Lions also tried this during the regular season before it too was outlawed.

Since the purely offensive position of quarterback was new, some coaches experimented with how to best utilize their personnel. Joe Stydahar had two future Hall of Fame quarterbacks

in Bob Waterfield and Norm Van Brocklin so he tried alternating them by quarter — Waterfield first and third and Van Brocklin second and fourth. In a similar fashion, the 1957 Lions used both Bobby Layne and Tobin Rote in each game until Layne was injured. Even stranger, the Giants started backup quarterback Don Heinrich for several seasons, allowing first stringer Charley Conerly to survey the defense from the sideline for a series or two before entering the game by the second quarter.

This era saw the end of the careers of Hall of Famers Sid Luckman and Sammy Baugh and the beginning of Hall of Fame careers for Johnny Unitas and Bart Starr. It featured the prime years of Bob Waterfield, Norm Van Brocklin, Otto Graham, Bobby Layne, Y.A. Tittle, Tommy Thompson and Charley Conerly. On the other side, Tobin Rote, George Blanda Jim Hardy and Lamar McHan could be looked on as underachievers. The biggest what if career belonged to the Bears' Johnny Lujack who proved himself a worthy Pro Bowl followup to aging Sid Luckman before injuring his shoulder playing defense and prematurely ending his quarterback career.

The aggregate league-wide passing data for the period from 1946 through 1959 in the NFL was:

Games	Att	Comp	%	Yards	Y/ Att	Y/ Comp	Att/g	Y/g	TD	TD/g	Int	Rating	300-Yd Gm
961	50541	24298	48.1%	348933	6.9	14.4	52.6	363.1	2641	2.7	3651	58.2	70

Twenty-two quarterbacks threw for at least 5,000 yards during this era. Their percentage of completed passes ranges from Tobin Rote's 44.2 percent to Automatic Otto Graham's 55.7 percent. According to yards per attempt and completion, the long bombers in the group were Graham, Ed Brown, John Lujack and Norm Van Brocklin, while Charley Conerly, Y.A. Tittle,

George Blanda, Jim Hardy and Jim Finks specialized more in short passes. Only John Unitas, Tommy Thompson and Charley Conerly threw more TD passes than interceptions during this time. Those most susceptible to the interception were Sid Luckman, Adrian Burk, Eddie LeBaron and Jim Hardy. The 22 5,000-yard passers ranked by passer rating:

Name	Attempts	Comp	%	Yards	Y/Att	Y/Comp	TD	Int	Rating
John Unitas	1129	611	54.1%	8954	7.9	14.7	84	48	87.3
Otto Graham	1565	872	55.7%	13499	8.6	15.5	88	94	78.2
Tommy Thompson	1003	527	52.5%	7725	7.7	14.7	74	68	74.3
Norm Van Brocklin	2611	1400	53.6%	21140	8.1	15.1	149	161	73.8
Sammy Baugh	1438	804	55.9%	10989	7.6	13.7	92	98	73.4
Bill Wade	934	497	53.2%	7278	7.8	14.6	44	57	69.2
Charley Conerly	2593	1308	50.4%	17900	6.9	13.7	158	152	68.8
Y.A. Tittle	2382	1318	55.3%	17206	7.2	13.1	112	150	67.7
Ed Brown	999	502	50.3%	7877	7.9	15.7	52	66	66.6
Johnny Lujack	808	404	50.0%	6295	7.8	15.6	41	54	65.3

Name	Attempts	Comp	%	Yards	Y/Att	Y/Comp	TD	Int	Rating
Sid Luckman	802	410	51.1%	5965	7.4	14.5	56	66	64.7
Bobby Layne	3109	1520	48.9%	22063	7.1	14.5	163	193	64.0
Bobby Thomason	1346	687	51.0%	9480	7.0	13.8	68	90	62.9
Bob Waterfield	1446	725	50.1%	10240	7.1	14.1	83	111	60.5
Eddie LeBaron	1104	539	48.8%	8068	7.3	15.0	59	88	57.8
Paul Christman	921	415	45.1%	6147	6.7	14.8	53	64	57.7
Jim Finks	1382	661	47.8%	8622	6.2	13.0	55	88	54.7
Tobin Rote	2450	1082	44.2%	15144	6.2	14.0	119	158	54.0
Jim Hardy	912	423	46.4%	5690	6.2	13.5	54	73	53.1
Adrian Burk	1079	500	46.3%	7001	6.5	14.0	61	89	52.2
George Blanda	988	445	45.0%	5936	6.0	13.3	48	70	51.3
Lamar McHan	1120	481	42.9%	7383	6.6	15.3	58	86	50.6

Overall, the quarterbacks who led the league the most times in passing categories over this era are:

Attempts	Sammy Baugh & Tobin Rote & Bobby Layne & John Unitas	2
Completions	Sammy Baugh & Tobin Rote & Y.A. Tittle	2
Yards	Sammy Baugh & Bobby Layne & Otto Graham & John Unitas	2
Yards/Pass	Norm Van Brocklin	3
Comp %	Sammy Baugh & Otto Graham	3
TD	John Unitas	3
TD%	Tommy Thompson	3
Int %	Charlie Conerly	3
Rating	Tommy Thompson & Otto Graham	2
Wins	Otto Graham	5
Comebacks	Charlie Conerly	4
Interceptions	Bobby Layne	2
Fumbles	Bobby Layne & Tobin Rote	3

And the complete list of 1946–1959 leaders is as follows:

Attempts	Bobby Layne	3,109	Int %	Johnny Unitas	4.3
Completions	Bobby Layne	1,520	Rating	Johnny Unitas	87.3
Yards	Bobby Layne	22,063	Wins	Norm Van Brocklin	75
Yards/Pass	Otto Graham	8.6	Comebacks	Y.A. Tittle	19
Comp %	Otto Graham	55.7	Interceptions	Bobby Layne	193
TD	Bobby Layne	163	Fumbles	Bobby Layne	68
TD%	Johnny Unitas	7.44			

1946

There were two rule changes of note in 1946 — substitutions were limited to no more than three at a time, and a pass that hit the goal post was to be ruled incomplete rather than a safety as it was in the 1945 championship game when Sammy Baugh's safety cost the Redskins the title to the Cleveland Rams (who then moved to Los Angeles).

Sid Luckman and Bob Waterfield topped the league in yards and touchdowns, while Frankie Filchock led the Giants to the title game despite throwing 25 interceptions. Filchock threw six more in the championship game and was later suspended from the NFL for not reporting a bribe attempt before the game. Luckman, who led the Bears to a league best 289 points, won his final title in that game on a 19-yard naked bootleg run for the deciding touchdown. Sammy Baugh was hurt and had one of his worst seasons. First round picks Boley Dancewicz of Boston and Jim Hardy of the Rams were both unimpressive in brief trials as rookie quarterbacks, but Paul Governali had a successful first year for Boston.

1946 League Passing Statistics

Games	Att	Comp	%	Yards	Y/ Att	Y/ Comp	Att/g	Y/g	TD	TD/g	Int	Rating	300-Yd Gms
55	2342	1050	44.8%	15836	6.8	15.1	42.6	287.9	126	2.3	211	48.0	1

1946 Leading Passers

Name	Team	Attempts	Comp	%	Yards	Y/Att	Y/Comp	TD	Int	Rating	Relative Rating
Sid Luckman	CHI	229	110	48	1826	7.97	16.6	17	16	71	149
Bob Waterfield	STL	251	127	50.6	1747	6.96	13.8	17	17	67.6	142
Paul Governali	XBOS	192	83	43.2	1293	6.73	15.6	13	10	67	141
Tommy Thompson	PHL	103	57	55.3	745	7.23	13.1	6	9	61.3	129
Frank Filchock	NYG	169	87	51.5	1262	7.47	14.5	12	25	60.2	127
Paul Christman	ARZ	229	100	43.7	1656	7.23	16.6	13	18	54.8	115
Sammy Baugh	WSH	161	87	54	1163	7.22	13.4	8	17	54.2	114
Roy Zimmerman	PHL	79	41	51.9	597	7.56	14.6	4	8	54.1	114

The leaders in the major passing categories for 1946 were:

Attempts	Bob Waterfield	257	Int %	Paul Governali	5.2
Completions	Bob Waterfield	127	Rating	Sid Luckman	71
Yards	Sid Luckman	1,826	Wins	Sid Luckman	8
Yards/Pass	Sid Luckman	7.97	Comebacks	Sammy Baugh &	
Comp %	Tommy Thompson	55.3		Bob Waterfield & Sid Luckman	
TD	Bob Waterfield	17		& Paul Christman	2
	& Sid Luckman		Interceptions	Frank Filchock	25
TD%	Sid Luckman	7.4	Fumbles	Paul Christman	15

1947

The Bears again led the league in scoring with 383 points, but the other team in Chicago won the title for a change. The Cardinals were powered by their "Dream Backfield" of quarterback Paul Christman, halfbacks Charley Trippi and Elmer Angsman and fullback Pat Harder and met the Eagles for the championship. Philadelphia first had to dispose of the single wing Steelers in a playoff to get to the title game. Comiskey Park was covered with ice for the championship, and the home team slid to a victory behind two 70-yard touchdown runs, a 75-yard punt return and a 44-yard touchdown run. Christman completed just three of 14 passes for 54 yards and two interceptions, while the Eagles' Tommy Thompson completed 27 of 44 for 297 yards in a losing effort. Sammy Baugh led the league in most passing categories, including 25 touchdown passes and nearly 3,000 yards passing. Sid Luckman threw for 24 scores, but also set a new record with 31 interceptions. Bob Waterfield also slipped a bit to eight touchdowns and 18 interceptions and had to share playing time with Jim Hardy.

Green Bay, Boston and Detroit installed the T formation in 1947. The Packers' first quarterback was Jack Jacobs who threw for 16 touchdowns. The Yanks had Paul Governali and Boley Dancewicz, but traded Governali to the Giants and went with Dancewicz who completed 39 percent of his passes and threw 11 touchdowns to 18 interceptions. The Lions relied on rookie Clyde LeForce who completed 53 percent of his passes but also threw 20 interceptions.

1947 League Passing Statistics

Games	Att	Comp	%	Yards	Y/ Att	Y/ Comp	Att/g	Y/g	TD	TD/g	Int	Rating	300-Yd Gms
60	2991	1407	47.0%	21670	7.2	15.4	49.9	361.2	188	3.1	250	57.6	8

1947 Leading Passers

Name	Team	Attempts	Comp	%	Yards	Y/Att	Y/Comp	TD	Int	Rating	Relative Rating
Sammy Baugh	WSH	354	210	59.3	2938	8.3	14.0	25	15	92	160
Tommy Thompson	PHL	201	106	52.7	1680	8.36	15.8	16	15	76.3	132
Sid Luckman	CHI	323	176	54.5	2712	8.4	15.4	24	31	67.7	117
Clyde LeForce	DET	175	94	53.7	1384	7.91	14.7	13	20	65	113
Jack Jacobs	GBP	242	108	44.6	1615	6.67	15.0	16	17	59.8	104
Paul Christman	ARZ	301	138	45.8	2191	7.28	15.9	17	22	59	102

The leaders in the major passing categories for 1947 were:

Attempts	Sammy Baugh	354	Int %	Sammy Baugh	4.2
Completions	Sammy Baugh	210	Rating	Sammy Baugh	92
Yards	Sammy Baugh	2,938	Wins	Paul Christman	9
Yards/Pass	Sid Luckman	8.4	Comebacks	Johnny Clement	3
Comp %	Sammy Baugh	59.3	Interceptions	Sid Luckman	31
TD	Sammy Baugh	25	Fumbles	Sammy Baugh	15
TD%	Tommy Thompson	8			

1948

The Cardinals opened 1948 the way they closed 1947, by beating the Eagles, but were struck by tragedy after the game when their star tackle Stan Mauldin died of a heart attack. The Cards led the league with 395 points despite starting quarterback Paul Christman missing time with injuries because backup Ray Mallouf played very well. In the title game, though, a blizzard shut down the passing game — Mallouf completed three of seven passes, while Tommy Thompson of the Eagles completed just two of 12 for seven yards. Philadelphia won 7–0, scoring the lone touchdown after a turnover. During the season, Thompson became just the third quarterback in history to throw at least 25 touchdown passes. In Los Angeles, Jim Hardy set a new mark by throwing 114 straight passes without an interception in his battle for playing time with Bob Waterfield.

Steeler coach Jock Sutherland died, but they continued as the only team to use the straight single wing with the Giants switching to the Wing T in 1948 with Paul Governali and rookie Charlie Conerly behind center. Conerly was spectacular in setting rookie records with 22 touchdowns and 2,175 yards. Washington originally held Conerly's draft rights, but traded him to New York to make room to draft Harry Gilmer from Alabama. Similarly, the Bears traded the rights to tailback Ray Evans to the Steelers for the rights to Bobby Layne. Conerly and Layne became stars, while Gilmer was never more than a backup and Evans was out of football after throwing five touchdowns and 17 interceptions in rookie season. Other rookies of note in 1948 included Johnny Lujack with the Bears, Fred Enke with the Lions and Y.A. Tittle in the AAFC. On the equipment front, plastic helmets were banned because they tended to shatter.

1948 League Passing Statistics

Games	Att	Comp	%	Yards	Y/Att	Y/Comp	Att/g	Y/g	TD	TD/g	Int	Rating	300-Yd Gms
60	3116	1498	48.1%	20871	6.7	13.9	51.9	347.9	196	3.3	232	60.0	2

1948 Leading Passers

Name	Team	Attempts	Comp	%	Yards	Y/Att	Y/Comp	TD	Int	Rating	Relative Rating
Tommy Thompson	PHL	246	141	57.3	1965	7.99	13.9	25	11	98.4	164
Ray Mallouf	ARZ	143	73	51	1160	8.11	15.9	13	6	91.2	152
Charley Conerly	NYG	299	162	54.2	2175	7.27	13.4	22	13	84	140
Jim Hardy	STL	211	112	53.1	1390	6.59	12.4	14	7	82.1	137
Sammy Baugh	WSH	315	185	58.7	2599	8.25	14.0	22	23	78.3	130
Sid Luckman	CHI	163	89	54.6	1047	6.42	11.8	13	14	65.1	109
Bob Waterfield	STL	180	87	48.3	1354	7.52	15.6	14	18	60	100

The leaders in the major passing categories for 1948 were:

Attempts	Sammy Baugh	315	Int %	Jim Hardy	3.3
Completions	Sammy Baugh	185	Rating	Tommy Thompson	98.4
Yards	Sammy Baugh	2,599	Wins	Sid Luckman	10
Yards/Pass	Clyde LeForce	9.03	Comebacks	Sammy Baugh & Bob Waterfield	
Comp %	Sammy Baugh	58.7		& Johnny Clement & Paul Christman	2
TD	Tommy Thompson	25	Interceptions	Sammy Baugh	23
TD%	Tommy Thompson	10.2	Fumbles	Ray Evans	9

1949

The top scoring Eagles (364 points) repeated as champions by defeating the high-powered Rams 14–0 in a driving rainstorm. That made back-to-back championship game shutouts for Philadelphia, and the third year in a row they played for the title in terrible weather conditions. Despite the success on the field, they were under new ownership since Lex Thompson had sold the team because the competition with the AAFC was too expensive. In a playoff game against the Bears, the Rams' Bob Waterfield threw for 280 yards, but was limited to just 43 in the rain against the Eagles. Rams coach Clark Shaughnessy created the modern Pro Set with two running backs and a flanker, but also was punished for success by being fired at the end of the season. In Chicago, Sid Luckman came down with a thyroid problem, and the Bears went with Johnny Lujack who threw for six touchdowns and 468 yards in one game against the Cardinals.

In New York, coach Steve Owen switched to the pure T formation with Charlie Conerly under center. Meanwhile, the Boston Yanks became the New York Bulldogs and obtained Bobby Layne as their quarterback. The Rams sent Jim Hardy to the Cardinals after drafting Norm Van Brocklin, who averaged 10 yards per pass, and Bobby Thomason. However, most rookies struggled: the Bears' George Blanda threw no touchdowns, but five interceptions; Frank Tripucka was waived by the Eagles and threw nine touchdowns and 14 interceptions for Detroit; Jim Finks was a quarterback misplaced on a single wing team in Pittsburgh; Stan Heath was drafted by Green Bay for the second year in a row and threw one touchdown and 14 interceptions while completing 24 percent of his passes. Heath combined with two other Packer quarterbacks for five touchdowns and 29 interceptions. Among rules changes, free substitution and plastic helmets were both reinstated. In addition, receivers were given permission to wear different colored helmets to stand out better for passers.

1949 League Passing Statistics

Games	Att	Comp	%	Yards	Y/Att	Y/Comp	Att/g	Y/g	TD	TD/g	Int	Rating	300-Yd Gms
60	3275	1527	46.6%	21436	6.5	14.0	54.6	357.3	168	2.8	247	53.9	8

1949 Leading Passers

Name	Team	Attempts	Comp	%	Yards	Y/Att	Y/Comp	TD	Int	Rating	Relative Rating
Tommy Thompson	PHL	214	116	54.2	1727	8.07	14.9	16	11	84.4	157
Sammy Baugh	WSH	255	145	56.9	1903	7.46	13.1	18	14	81.2	151
John Lujack	CHI	312	162	51.9	2658	8.52	16.4	23	22	76	141
Charley Conerly	NYG	305	152	49.8	2138	7.01	14.1	17	20	64.1	119
Fred Enke	DET	142	63	44.4	793	5.58	12.6	6	5	61.7	115
Bob Waterfield	STL	296	154	52	2168	7.32	14.1	17	24	61.3	114
Bobby Layne	XNYB	299	155	51.8	1796	6.01	11.6	9	18	55.3	103

The leaders in the major passing categories for 1949 were:

Attempts	Johnny Lujack	312	Int %	Fred Enke	3.5
Completions	Johnny Lujack	162	Rating	Tommy Thompson	84.4
Yards	Johnny Lujack	2,658	Wins	Tommy Thompson	11
Yards/Pass	Johnny Lujack	8.52	Comebacks	Charley Conerly & Frank Tripucka	2
Comp %	Sammy Baugh	56.9	Interceptions	Bob Waterfield	24
TD	Johnny Lujack	23	Fumbles	Bobby Layne	10
TD%	Tommy Thompson	7.5			

1950

The warring leagues merged for the 1950 season with the Cleveland Browns, San Francisco 49ers and Baltimore Colts joining the NFL, and the players from the other four disbanded AAFC teams being dispersed throughout the league. Players from the AAFC's New York Yankees were primarily distributed to the NFL's two New York teams, the Giants and the Bulldogs (who were renamed the Yanks.) The 13-team NFL played a 12-game schedule and also made free substitution permanent, solidifying the two-platoon game.

On the field, both the eastern and western divisions ended in ties that had to be resolved by playoff games. The Browns edged out the Giants 8–3, while the Rams beat the Bears 24–14. The Rams were a scoring machine that led the league with 466 points, 38.8 per game, behind two Hall of Fame quarterbacks. Norm Van Brocklin and Bob Waterfield alternated quarters for the Rams and combined for 3,600 yards and 28 touchdowns. The four-time AAFC champion Browns showed their mettle in the opening game of the season by creaming the two-time NFL champion

Eagles 35–10. In an exciting title game for the ages, Otto Graham led a last minute drive for the winning field goal to top the Rams 30–28.

Bobby Layne went from the Bulldogs to Detroit and was replaced by AAFC star George Ratterman. Johnny Lujack unfortunately severely damaged his shoulder playing defense and would never recover. This year marked the end for Sid Luckman, Paul Christman and Tommy Thompson, while Frank Filchock returned from his suspension to throw his last three NFL passes in Baltimore. The Colts' quarterbacking was handled by Y.A. Tittle and rookie Adrian Burk who combined for 14 touchdowns and 31 interceptions while winning just one game. Another rookie, Tobin Rote, accounted for seven touchdowns and 24 interceptions in Green Bay. The Packers brought in still another rookie, Tom O'Malley, for a one game trial when Rote was injured and he completed four of 15 passes with six interceptions; O'Malley earned a 0 passer rating for his one-game NFL career. Cardinal quarterback Jim Hardy topped that in one Sunday against the Eagles when he set the record for interceptions in a game with eight.

1950 League Passing Statistics

Games	Att	Comp	%	Yards	Y/Att	Y/Comp	Att/g	Y/g	TD	TD/g	Int	Rating	300-Yd Gms
78	4307	2008	46.6%	29050	6.7	14.5	55.2	372.4	220	2.8	343	52.9	6

1950 Leading Passers

Name	Team	Attempts	Comp	%	Yards	Y/Att	Y/Comp	TD	Int	Rating	Relative Rating
Norm Van Brocklin	STL	233	127	54.5	2061	8.85	16.2	18	14	85.1	161
Bob Waterfield	STL	213	122	57.3	1540	7.23	12.6	11	13	71.7	136
Sammy Baugh	WSH	166	90	54.2	1130	6.81	12.6	10	11	68.1	129
Charley Conerly	NYG	132	56	42.4	1000	7.58	17.9	8	7	67.1	127
Otto Graham	CLE	253	137	54.2	1943	7.68	14.2	14	20	64.7	122
George Ratterman	XNYY	294	140	47.6	2251	7.66	16.1	22	24	64.6	122
Bobby Layne	DET	336	152	45.2	2323	6.91	15.3	16	18	62.1	118
Y.A. Tittle	XBAL	315	161	51.1	1884	5.98	11.7	8	19	52.9	100
Jim Hardy	ARZ	257	117	45.5	1636	6.37	14.0	17	24	49.7	94

The leaders in the major passing categories for 1950 were:

Attempts	Bobby Layne	336	Int %	Charley Conerly	5.3
Completions	Y.A. Tittle	161	Rating	Norm Van Brocklin	85.1
Yards	Bobby Layne	2,323	Wins	Otto Graham	10
Yards/Pass	Norm Van Brocklin	8.85	Comebacks	Charley Conerly	4
Comp %	Bob Waterfield	57.3	Interceptions	George Ratterman &	
TD	George Ratterman	22		Tobin Rote & Jim Hardy	24
TD%	Norm Van Brocklin	7.7	Fumbles	Bobby Layne	13

1951

The Rams again led the league in scoring with 392 points this time as Waterfield and Van Brocklin combined for nearly 3,300 yards and 26 touchdowns. Again, they met the Browns for the title, but this time beat Cleveland 24–17 on Van Brocklin's fourth quarter 73-yard bomb to Tom Fears. Van Brocklin had a record-setting day at the outset of the season by throwing for 554 yards against the lowly Yanks who were on their last wobbly legs. The Colts had already folded, so the league was back to a more sensible 12 teams in 1951.

George Ratterman left the Yanks for Canada, but returned by midseason. Former Colts quarterbacks Adrian Burk and Y.A. Tittle ended up in Philadelphia and San Francisco respectively. Charlie Trippi switched from running back to quarterback for the Cardinals with predictably bad results. Green Bay obtained Bobby Thomason from Los Angeles, and he combined with a maturing Tobin Rote for 26 touchdowns and 29 interceptions; Rote also set a seasonal rushing record for quarterbacks with 523 yards. Johnny Lujack quit because of his bad shoulder, while Bob Celeri and Bob Williams were new quarterbacks who would not last long in the league.

1951 League Passing Statistics

Games	Att	Comp	%	Yards	Y/Att	Y/Comp	Att/g	Y/g	TD	TD/g	Int	Rating	300-Yd Gms
72	3881	1809	46.6%	26482	6.8	14.6	53.9	367.8	200	2.8	288	55.6	72

1951 Leading Passers

Name	Team	Attempts	Comp	%	Yards	Y/Att	Y/Comp	TD	Int	Rating	Relative Rating
Bob Waterfield	STL	176	88	50	1566	8.9	17.8	13	10	81.8	147
Norm Van Brocklin	STL	194	100	51.5	1725	8.89	17.3	13	11	80.8	145
Otto Graham	CLE	265	147	55.5	2205	8.32	15.0	17	16	79.2	142
Bobby Thomason	GBP	221	125	56.6	1306	5.91	10.4	11	9	73.5	132
John Lujack	CHI	176	85	48.3	1295	7.36	15.2	8	8	69.2	124

Name	Team	Attempts	Comp	%	Yards	Y/Att	Y/Comp	TD	Int	Rating	Relative Rating
Y.A. Tittle	SFF	114	63	55.3	808	7.09	12.8	8	9	68.2	123
Bobby Layne	DET	332	152	45.8	2403	7.24	15.8	26	23	67.6	122
Frankie Albert	SFF	166	90	54.2	1116	6.72	12.4	5	10	60.2	108
Bob Celeri	XNYY	238	102	42.9	1797	7.55	17.6	12	15	59.8	108
Tobin Rote	GBP	256	106	41.4	1540	6.02	14.5	15	20	48.6	87
Adrian Burk	PHL	218	92	42.2	1329	6.1	14.4	14	23	44.5	80

The leaders in the major passing categories for 1951 were:

Attempts	Bobby Layne	332	Int %	Bob Thomason	4.1
Completions	Bobby Layne	152	Rating	Bob Waterfield	81.8
Yards	Bobby Layne	2,403	Wins	Otto Graham	11
Yards/Pass	Bob Waterfield	8.9	Comebacks	Sammy Baugh & Y.A. Tittle	2
Comp %	Bob Thomason	56.6	Interceptions	Bobby Layne & Adrian Burk	23
TD	Bobby Layne	26	Fumbles	Bobby Layne	8
TD%	Bobby Layne	7.8			

1952

Los Angeles again led the NFL in scoring with 349 points, but lost a playoff game to Bobby Layne's Lions who went on to beat the Browns 17–7 in the title game with Layne completing seven of nine passes. The Yanks franchise was taken over by some Dallas investors, but their Dallas Texans went bankrupt before the end of 1952 and were taken over by the league. The Texans then operated out of Hershey, Pennsylvania until they folded at the end of the year. Dallas quarterbacks Frank Tripucka and Bob Celeri combined with black passing tailback George Taliaferro for eight touchdowns and 26 interceptions.

Pittsburgh became the last team to drop the single wing and finally made a quarterback out of Jim Finks who threw 20 touchdowns for the Steelers. Hall of Famers Sammy Baugh and Bob Waterfield finished their playing careers, as did Frankie Albert and Jim Hardy. The first three all would go on to have unsuccessful coaching careers in the pros. Rookies replacing them included 5'7" former Marine Eddie LeBaron, Vanderbilt's Bill Wade, Stanford's Gary Kerkorian and Kentucky's Babe Parilli. Babe completed 44 percent of his passes and combined with Tobin Rote in Green Bay for 26 touchdowns and 25 interceptions.

1952 League Passing Statistics

Games	Att	Comp	%	Yards	Y/Att	Y/Comp	Att/g	Y/g	TD	TD/g	Int	Rating	300-Yd Gms
72	4024	1863	46.3%	26781	6.7	14.4	55.9	372.0	218	3.0	287	56.7	3

1952 Leading Passers

Name	Team	Attempts	Comp	%	Yards	Y/Att	Y/Comp	TD	Int	Rating	Relative Rating
Tobin Rote	GBP	157	82	52.2	1268	8.08	15.5	13	8	85.6	154
Norm Van Brocklin	STL	205	113	55.1	1736	8.47	15.4	14	17	71.5	128
Charley Conerly	NYG	169	82	48.5	1090	6.45	13.3	13	10	70.4	126
Frankie Albert	SFF	129	71	55	964	7.47	13.6	8	10	67.5	121
Otto Graham	CLE	364	181	49.7	2816	7.74	15.6	20	24	66.6	120
Y.A. Tittle	SFF	208	106	51	1407	6.76	13.3	11	12	66.3	119
Jim Finks	PIT	336	158	47	2307	6.87	14.6	20	19	66.2	119
Eddie LeBaron	WSH	194	96	49.5	1420	7.32	14.8	14	15	65.7	118
Bobby Layne	DET	287	139	48.4	1999	6.97	14.4	19	20	64.5	116

The leaders in the major passing categories for 1952 were:

Attempts	Otto Graham	364	Int %	Bob Thomason	4.2
Completions	Otto Graham	181	Rating	Tobin Rote	85.6
Yards	Otto Graham	2,816	Wins	Bobby Layne	9
Yards/Pass	Norm Van Brocklin	8.47	Comebacks	Charley Conerly &	
Comp %	Norm Van Brocklin	55.1		Eddie LeBaron & Charlie Trippi	2
TD	Otto Graham & Jim Finks	20	Interceptions	Otto Graham	24
TD%	Tobin Rote	8.3	Fumbles	Tobin Rote	10

1953

Cleveland rolled through the regular season, winning their first 11 games as Otto Graham completed almost 65 percent of his passes and averaged 10½ yards per pass. In the title game, however, the Browns lost again to the Lions, this time 17–16 on Bobby Layne's 33-yard touchdown to backup end Jim Doran in the final minutes. The 49ers scored an NFL–best 372 points, but finished a game behind Detroit in the West. In Washington, Curly Lambeau coached the Redskins to an improbable 6–5–1 season even though his quarterbacks Jack Scarbath and Eddie LeBaron combined for 12 touchdowns and 29 interceptions. LeBaron actually set a new record with five fourth quarter game winning drives despite completing just 35 percent of his passes. In Green Bay, the quarterback pair of Tobin Rote and Babe Parilli was a disaster that combined for nine touchdowns and 34 interceptions.

Jim Root of the Cardinals, Ted Marchibroda of the Steelers, Rudy Bukich of the Rams, and Tommy O'Connell and Willie Thrower of the Bears made up an unimpressive rookie crop, although Thrower made history in October by becoming the first black quarterback to play in the NFL. A few weeks later, veteran tailback George Taliaferro of the reborn Baltimore Colts became the second black quarterback after a rash of injuries wiped out Fred Enke, Ed Mioduszewski and Jack Del Bello, the Colts lousy regular quarterbacks.

1953 League Passing Statistics

Games	Att	Comp	%	Yards	Y/ Att	Y/ Comp	Att/g	Y/g	TD	TD/g	Int	Rating	300-Yd Gms
72	4267	2020	47.3%	27925	6.5	13.8	59.3	387.8	189	2.6	306	53.7	12

1953 Leading Passers

Name	Team	Attempts	Comp	%	Yards	Y/Att	Y/Comp	TD	Int	Rating	Relative Rating
Otto Graham	CLE	258	167	64.7	2722	10.55	16.3	11	9	99.7	186
Norm Van Brocklin	STL	286	156	54.5	2393	8.37	15.3	19	14	84.1	157
Y.A. Tittle	SFF	259	149	57.5	2121	8.19	14.2	20	16	84.1	157
Bobby Thomason	PHL	304	162	53.3	2462	8.1	15.2	21	20	75.8	142
Bobby Layne	DET	273	125	45.8	2088	7.65	16.7	16	21	59.6	111
George Blanda	CHI	362	169	46.7	2164	5.98	12.8	14	23	52.3	98
Charley Conerly	NYG	303	143	47.2	1711	5.65	12.0	13	25	44.9	84

The leaders in the major passing categories for 1953 were:

Attempts	George Blanda	362	Int %	Otto Graham	3.5
Completions	George Blanda	169	Rating	Otto Graham	99.7
Yards	Otto Graham	2,722	Wins	Otto Graham	10
Yards/Pass	Otto Graham	10.56	Comebacks	Eddie LeBaron	5
Comp %	Otto Graham	64.7	Interceptions	Charley Conerly	25
TD	Bob Thomason	21	Fumbles	George Taliaferro	10
TD%	Y.A. Tittle	7.7			

1954

Two-time defending champion Detroit scored a league high 337 points, but were decimated in the title game by the Browns 56–10. In that game, Otto Graham threw for three touchdowns and ran for three more, while Bobby Layne threw six interceptions. Graham retired for the first time after the season. After 23 years in New York, Steve Owen was replaced by one of his former players, Jim Lee Howell; Howell showed how smart he was by hiring Vince Lombardi as his offensive coach and Tom Landry to be his player-coach on defense. Philadelphia's Adrian Burk had the best performance of 1954 when he threw for seven touchdowns in November against the Redskins. In fact 12 of Burk's league-high 23 touchdown passes came in his two games against Washington.

Eddie LeBaron jumped to Canada, so the Redskins were quarterbacked by rookie Al Dorow and returning Jack Scarbath; the two combined for 15 touchdowns and 30 interceptions. Lamar McHan was the top draft choice of the Cardinals and completed just 41 percent of his passes for six touchdowns and 22 interceptions. Chicago had two rookie quarterbacks in Ed Brown and Zeke Bratkowski who teamed with George Blanda as the Bears' three B's. Cotton Davidson and Bobby Clatterbuck were two touted rookies who would never become starters in the NFL.

1954 League Passing Statistics

Games	Att	Comp	%	Yards	Y/Att	Y/Comp	Att/g	Y/g	TD	TD/g	Int	Rating	300-Yd Gms
72	4232	2135	50.4%	30397	7.2	14.2	58.8	422.2	216	3.0	294	62.1	5

1954 Leading Passers

Name	Team	Attempts	Comp	%	Yards	Y/Att	Y/Comp	TD	Int	Rating	Relative Rating
Adrian Burk	PHL	231	123	53.2	1740	7.53	14.1	23	17	80.4	130
Tom Dublinski	DET	138	77	55.8	1073	7.78	13.9	8	7	79.2	128
Y.A. Tittle	SFF	295	170	57.6	2205	7.47	13.0	9	9	78.7	128
Bobby Layne	DET	246	135	54.9	1818	7.39	13.5	14	12	77.3	125
Otto Graham	CLE	240	142	59.2	2092	8.72	14.7	11	17	73.5	119
Norm Van Brocklin	STL	260	139	53.5	2637	10.14	19.0	13	21	71.9	116
Gary Kerkorian	IND	217	117	53.9	1515	6.98	12.9	9	12	66.9	108
Jim Finks	PIT	306	164	53.6	2003	6.55	12.2	14	19	63.4	103
George Blanda	CHI	281	131	46.6	1929	6.86	14.7	15	17	62.1	101
Tobin Rote	GBP	382	180	47.1	2311	6.05	12.8	14	18	59.1	96

The leaders in the major passing categories for 1954 were:

Attempts	Tobin Rote	382	Int %	Y.A. Tittle	3.1
Completions	Tobin Rote	180	Rating	Adrian Burk	80.4
Yards	Norm Van Brocklin	2,637	Wins	Otto Graham	9
Yards/Pass	Norm Van Brocklin	10.14	Comebacks	Bobby Layne & George Blanda	
Comp %	Otto Graham	59.2		& Jim Finks & Gary Kerkorian	2
TD	Adrian Burk	23	Interceptions	Lamar McHan	22
TD%	Adrian Burk	10	Fumbles	Adrian Burk	7

1955

Coach Paul Brown was unhappy with new starting quarterback George Ratterman in training camp so he coaxed Otto Graham out of retirement and voila! The Browns led the NFL in points with 349, won their 10th straight divisional crown and defeated Sid Gillman's Rams 38–14 for their second consecutive title. It was also the second consecutive title game that the Browns' defense picked off six passes from a Hall of Famer, in this case, Norm Van Brocklin. In

Graham's last game, he threw for two touchdowns and ran for two more. Meanwhile, Bobby Layne separated his shoulder in the off-season and was never right all year. The league tried to ease up on the violence inherent in pileups by amending the rules so that a ball carrier need not be pinned to the ground to be whistled down. As long as he was touched by a defender and had any part of his body except his hands or feet hit the ground, he was down and the play was dead.

Along with Graham, Jim Finks also retired

in 1955. The star rookie quarterback was the Colts' George Shaw who completed 50 percent of his passes, but threw 19 interceptions. The Redskins' Ralph Guglielmi did not play much as a rookie, and neither did the Packers' Choo Choo Charlie Brackins who became the third black NFL quarterback but only got to throw two passes before being cut. Another quarterback who was unfairly cut was Johnny Unitas whom the Steelers cut in order to keep the immortal Vic Eaton as their third stringer.

1955 League Passing Statistics

Games	Att	Comp	%	Yards	Y/Att	Y/Comp	Att/g	Y/g	TD	TD/g	Int	Rating	300-Yd Gms
72	3820	1829	47.9%	25285	6.6	13.8	53.1	351.2	180	2.5	258	57.1	5

1955 Leading Passers

Name	Team	Attempts	Comp	%	Yards	Y/Att	Y/Comp	TD	Int	Rating	Relative Rating
Otto Graham	CLE	185	98	53	1721	9.3	17.6	15	8	94	165
Bobby Thomason	PHL	171	88	51.5	1337	7.82	15.2	10	7	80	140
Ed Brown	CHI	164	85	51.8	1307	7.97	15.4	9	10	71.4	125
Charley Conerly	NYG	202	98	48.5	1310	6.49	13.4	13	13	64.2	112
Norm Van Brocklin	STL	272	144	52.9	1890	6.95	13.1	8	15	62	108
Bobby Layne	DET	270	143	53	1830	6.78	12.8	11	17	61.8	108
Tobin Rote	GBP	342	157	45.9	1977	5.78	12.6	17	19	57.8	101
Y.A. Tittle	SFF	287	147	51.2	2185	7.61	14.9	17	28	56.6	99
Jim Finks	PIT	344	165	48	2270	6.6	13.8	10	26	47.7	84

The leaders in the major passing categories for 1955 were:

Attempts	Jim Finks	349	Int %	Harry Gilmer	3.3
Completions	Jim Finks	165	Rating	Otto Graham	94
Yards	Jim Finks	2,270	Wins	Otto Graham	9
Yards/Pass	Otto Graham	9.3	Comebacks	Otto Graham &	
Comp %	Otto Graham	53		Norm Van Brocklin & Tobin Rote	3
TD	Y.A. Tittle & Tobin Rote	17	Interceptions	Y.A. Tittle	28
TD%	Otto Graham	8.1	Fumbles	Tobin Rote	10

1956

With Otto Graham retired in Cleveland, long-time backup George Ratterman assumed the starting role, but Paul Brown added a new wrinkle by putting a radio receiver in Ratterman's helmet to relay the plays. The Cardinals tried the same thing with Lamar McHan, and Detroit wired the helmet of middle linebacker Joe Schmidt. Before things got out of hand, though, radio transmissions were outlawed by the league. As it turned out, Ratterman blew out

his knee in the fourth game and retired, second stringer Babe Parilli hurt his shoulder, and the Browns settled on Tommy O'Connell as their new quarterback in a disappointing season. Other notable changes included Norm Van Brocklin being pushed aside by Bill Wade, Y.A. Tittle being pushed aside by rookie Earl Morrall and George Shaw hurting his knee to provide the opening that unknown rookie Johnny Unitas needed to prove he could play. Unitas completed 56 percent of his passes for nine touchdowns, while fellow newcomer Bart Starr completed 55 percent for two touchdowns. Veteran Adrian Burk retired in Philadelphia and would go on to become a referee.

The Bears led the league with 363 points with Ed Brown and George Blanda sharing the quarterback job, but were overwhelmed in the title game by the Giants 47–7. New York's Charlie Conerly was comfortable in Vince Lombardi's offense and completed seven of 10 passes for 195 yards in the championship. Chicago reached the

title game by beating the Lions in the final game of the season after defender Ed Meadows knocked Bobby Layne out of the game with a cheap shot to the head.

In other significant developments, CBS began broadcasting games nationally, and the NFL Players' Association was formed. Facemasks were just coming into popular usage so grabbing any player aside from the ball carrier by the facemask was outlawed.

1956 League Passing Statistics

Games	Att	Comp	%	Yards	Y/Att	Y/Comp	Att/g	Y/g	TD	TD/g	Int	Rating	300-Yd Gms
72	3282	1656	50.5%	23242	7.1	14.0	45.6	322.8	162	2.3	240	59.6	2

1956 Leading Passers

Name	Team	Attempts	Comp	%	Yards	Y/Att	Y/Comp	TD	Int	Rating	Relative Rating
Ed Brown	CHI	168	96	57.1	1667	9.92	17.4	11	12	83.1	139
Charley Conerly	NYG	174	90	51.7	1143	6.57	12.7	10	7	75	126
John Unitas	IND	198	110	55.6	1498	7.57	13.6	9	10	74	124
Lamar McHan	ARZ	152	72	47.4	1159	7.63	16.1	10	8	73.3	123
Tobin Rote	GBP	308	146	47.4	2203	7.15	15.1	18	15	70.6	118
Y.A. Tittle	SFF	218	124	56.9	1641	7.53	13.2	7	12	68.6	115
Bobby Layne	DET	244	129	52.9	1909	7.82	14.8	9	17	62	104
Norm Van Brocklin	STL	124	68	54.8	966	7.79	14.2	7	12	59.5	100
Earl Morrall	SFF	78	38	48.7	621	7.96	16.3	1	6	48.1	81

The leaders in the major passing categories for 1956 were:

Attempts	Tobin Rote	308	Int %	Charley Conerly	4
Completions	Tobin Rote	146	Rating	Ed Brown	83.1
Yards	Tobin Rote	2,203	Wins	Ed Brown	9
Yards/Pass	Ed Brown	9.92	Comebacks	John Unitas & Y.A. Tittle	
Comp %	Ed Brown	57.1		& Lamar McHan	3
TD	Tobin Rote	18	Interceptions	Bobby Thomason	21
TD%	Al Dorow	7.1	Fumbles	Tobin Rote	5

1957

Detroit coach Buddy Parker quit in the preseason, saying that his team could not win; however, the Lions roared to the title game under new coach George Wilson where they chewed up the Browns 59–14. With Bobby Layne out with a broken leg, former Packer Tobin Rote threw for 280 yards and four touchdowns in the championship game. Detroit had to stage a second half comeback to defeat the 49ers in a playoff game just to get to the title

game. Forty years before Randy Moss, Y.A. Tittle and receiver R.C. Owens of San Francisco came up with an exciting new play they dubbed the "Alley Oop" pass that was designed to have former basketball star Owens outleap defenders for the ball.

Norm Van Brocklin led the Rams to the most points in the league (307) in his last year in Los Angeles, while the three B's for the Bears combined for seven touchdowns and 28 interceptions. Bobby Thomason retired, but 1957's talented rookies included Hall of Famers Sonny

Jurgensen and Len Dawson as well as stars, John Brodie, Milt Plum and Jack Kemp. The drafting of Brodie made Earl Morrall expendable in San Francisco, and he was sent to Pittsburgh.

1957 League Passing Statistics

Games	Att	Comp	%	Yards	Y/Att	Y/Comp	Att/g	Y/g	TD	TD/g	Int	Rating	300-Yd Gms
72	3339	1685	50.5%	24745	7.4	14.7	46.4	343.7	170	2.4	231	63.2	2

1957 Leading Passers

Name	Team	Attempts	Comp	%	Yards	Y/Att	Y/Comp	TD	Int	Rating	Relative Rating
Tommy O'Connell	CLE	110	63	57.3	1229	11.17	19.5	9	8	93.3	148
John Unitas	IND	301	172	57.1	2550	8.47	14.8	24	17	88	139
Eddie LeBaron	WSH	167	99	59.3	1508	9.03	15.2	11	10	86.1	136
Y.A. Tittle	SFF	279	176	63.1	2157	7.73	12.3	13	15	80	127
Charley Conerly	NYG	232	128	55.2	1712	7.38	13.4	11	11	74.9	119
Norm Van Brocklin	STL	265	132	49.8	2105	7.94	15.9	20	21	68.8	109
Earl Morrall	PIT	289	139	48.1	1900	6.57	13.7	11	12	64.9	103

The leaders in the major passing categories for 1957 were:

Attempts	John Unitas	301	Int %	Earl Morrall	4.2
Completions	Y.A. Tittle	176	Rating	Tommy O'Connell	93.3
Yards	John Unitas	2,550	Wins	Tommy O'Connell	8
Yards/Pass	Tommy O'Connell	11.17	Comebacks	Y.A. Tittle	5
Comp %	Y.A. Tittle	63.1	Interceptions	Norm Van Brocklin	21
TD	John Unitas	24	Fumbles	Earl Morrall	12
TD%	Tommy O'Connell	8.2			

1958

Johnny Unitas had the Baltimore offense cranking to the tune of a league best 381 points despite missing a couple of games due to a broken rib and punctured lung. The Colts went on to win the championship over the Giants in what has been called the Greatest Game Ever Played. It wasn't that, but it was the first Sudden Death championship game and had a very exciting conclusion with Unitas leading a game-tying drive in the final seconds and then the game-winning drive in overtime. Unitas set a new record with 361 yards passing in this extra long game that seemed to jumpstart the public's interest in professional football. It was also Vince Lombardi's last game on the Giants' sideline.

Bobby Layne went from the Lions to the Steelers to reunite with Buddy Parker. Earl Morrall went to Detroit. Norm Van Brocklin went from the Rams to the lowly Eagles, and Hall of Famer Y.A. Tittle battled John Brodie for playing time in San Francisco where they combined for 15 touchdowns and 28 interceptions. The top rookies were Frank Ryan in Los Angeles, Jim Ninowski in Cleveland and King Hill with the Cardinals who were experimenting with a Double Wing T formation that was similar to the Spread and Shotgun formations.

1958 League Passing Statistics

Games	Att	Comp	%	Yards	Y/Att	Y/Comp	Att/g	Y/g	TD	TD/g	Int	Rating	300-Yd Gms
72	3951	1953	49.4%	28291	7.2	14.5	54.9	392.9	211	2.9	243	65.3	6

1958 Leading Passers

Name	Team	Attempts	Comp	%	Yards	Y/Att	Y/Comp	TD	Int	Rating	Relative Rating
John Unitas	IND	263	136	51.7	2007	7.63	14.8	19	7	90	138
Eddie LeBaron	WSH	145	79	54.5	1365	9.41	17.3	11	10	83.3	128
Bobby Layne	PIT	294	145	49.6	2510	8.73	17.3	14	12	80.4	123
Milt Plum	CLE	189	102	54	1619	8.57	15.9	11	11	77.9	119
Mack Reynolds	ARZ	195	105	53.8	1422	7.29	13.5	11	11	72.6	111
Bill Wade	STL	341	181	53.1	2875	8.43	15.9	18	22	72.2	111
Tobin Rote	DET	257	118	45.9	1678	6.53	14.2	14	10	69.5	106
Norm Van Brocklin	PHL	374	198	52.9	2409	6.44	12.2	15	20	64.1	98
Y.A. Tittle	SFF	208	120	57.7	1467	7.05	12.2	9	15	63.9	98
John Brodie	SFF	172	103	59.9	1224	7.12	11.9	6	13	61.8	95

The leaders in the major passing categories for 1958 were:

Attempts	Norm Van Brocklin	374	Int %	John Unitas	2.7
Completions	Norm Van Brocklin	198	Rating	John Unitas	90
Yards	Bill Wade	2,875	Wins	Charley Conerly	9
Yards/Pass	Eddie LeBaron	9.41	Comebacks	Charley Conerly	5
Comp %	John Brodie	59.9	Interceptions	Billy Wade	22
TD	John Unitas	19	Fumbles	Billy Wade	14
TD%	Eddie LeBaron	7.6			

1959

The Colts repeated as the league's top scores with 374 points and as champions by beating the Giants 31–16 with Johnny Unitas throwing for 265 yards and two touchdowns in another fourth quarter victory. Two stalwarts of the league passed away in 1959 — Giants founder Tim Mara in February; and Commissioner and Eagles founder Bert Bell who died at an October game between the Eagles and Steelers at Franklin Field where he once played for the University of Pennsylvania. A new league was on the horizon, Vince Lombardi was in Green Bay, and the 1960s were about to begin.

1959 League Passing Statistics

Games	Att	Comp	%	Yards	Y/Att	Y/Comp	Att/g	Y/g	TD	TD/g	Int	Rating	300-Yd Gms
72	3714	1858	50.0%	26922	7.2	14.5	51.6	373.9	197	2.7	221	66.9	5

1959 Leading Passers

Name	Team	Attempts	Comp	%	Yards	Y/Att	Y/Comp	TD	Int	Rating	Relative Rating
Charley Conerly	NYG	194	113	58.2	1706	8.79	15.1	14	4	102.7	154
John Unitas	IND	367	193	52.6	2899	7.9	15.0	32	14	92	138
Milt Plum	CLE	266	156	58.6	1992	7.49	12.8	14	8	87.2	130
Norm Van Brocklin	PHL	340	191	56.2	2617	7.7	13.7	16	14	79.5	119
Ed Brown	CHI	247	125	50.6	1881	7.62	15.0	13	10	76.7	115
Bill Wade	STL	261	153	58.6	2001	7.67	13.1	12	17	71.1	106
Bobby Layne	PIT	297	142	47.8	1986	6.69	14.0	20	21	62.8	94

The leaders in the major passing categories for 1959 were:

Attempts	John Unitas	367	Int %	Charley Conerly	2.1
Completions	John Unitas	193	Rating	Charley Conerly	102.7

Yards	John Unitas	2,899	Wins	John Unitas	9
Yards/Pass	Charley Conerly	8.79	Comebacks	John Unitas &	
Comp %	Milt Plum	58.6		Norm Van Brocklin	3
TD	John Unitas	32	Interceptions	Bobby Layne	21
TD%	John Unitas	8.7	Fumbles	King Hill	13

11

1960–1969:
The American Football League

The American Football League was an alternative league in a decade that thrived on change at all levels of society. The AFL was the wild, young upstart to the NFL's staid, parental figure, and the contrast mirrored the generation gap being exposed during the 1960s in America. Started by Lamar Hunt and Bud Adams, two rich young Texans who had tried unsuccessfully to buy the Chicago Cardinals franchise in the NFL, they were soon joined by six other men of varying finances to form the "Foolish Club" that would change the face of professional football, open up new markets for the game and create many more jobs for players.

By hiring mostly offensive-minded head coaches and instituting the two-point conversion, the AFL owners signaled that their league would be different from the NFL. There would not only be more passing, but more long passing as well. On average, the AFL threw seven more passes for an extra twenty yards a game and averaged a 300-yard passing performance every fifth game as opposed to every seventh by the NFL. While the NFL had a higher completion percentage (51.7 percent) and passer rating (69.8) than the AFL (47.7 percent and 61.4) throughout the decade, the AFL averaged more touchdown passes and interceptions; it was a more wide open league.

Sid Gillman developed the most far-reaching

offensive strategy with his downfield passing attack that was adapted in Oakland by his former assistant Al Davis. However, in Houston, the Oilers experimented with spread and shotgun formations, and Hank Stram in Kansas City utilized a moving, rollout pocket and an offense that featured lots of motion and misdirection. Above all, AFL teams relied on the bomb as a vital part of their attacks. There were defensive advances as well. Both Oakland and Kansas City experimented with 3–4 defenses, and Kansas City also used an offset defensive line and different variations of the Stack where linebackers were hidden directly behind defensive linemen. The AFL was also a man-to-man league for pass defense and developed and popularized bump-and-coverage to counter the relentless deep passing of the offenses.

As the war between the two leagues heated up, the competition to sign top draft picks became so intense that both leagues began hiring men to "babysit" (i.e., kidnap) their picks until they signed. When bold and belligerent Al Davis was named Commissioner in 1966, he opened up a cutthroat strategy to sign top NFL stars to contracts. John Brodie was signed by the Oilers, and Roman Gabriel was being courted by the Raiders. Within months a merger was announced, having been negotiated through back channels between Lamar Hunt of the Chiefs and Tex Schramm of the

Cowboys. The Super Bowl began at the end of the 1966 season with the NFL's Packers winning the first two, and Joe Namath's Jets winning III and Len Dawson's Chiefs taking IV. The two leagues were equals and became one in 1970.

The AFL had started out with older, NFL veterans as their quarterbacks, but outgrew such names as Frank Tripucka, Al Dorow and Cotton Davidson as time passed and began developing its own stars like Joe Namath, Daryle Lamonica, John Hadl and Bob Griese. The AFL saw the best years of Namath, Lamonica and Hadl as well as Len Dawson, Jack Kemp, Babe Parilli, George Blanda and Tom Flores. Those last four quarterbacks above, in addition to Jacky Lee, all lasted the en-

tire ten-year run of the league. Namath and Greg Cook of the Bengals were the most severely affected by injuries, and Bob Griese's career had the longest extension of any AFL quarterback, lasting until 1980. Wide receiver Charlie Joiner extended the AFL legacy the longest with a career that lasted through 1986. One other bequest of the AFL was the black quarterback. In 1968, the Raiders took Eldridge Dickey in the first round, and the Broncos made Marlin Briscoe their starter. The Bills drafted James Harris the following year, and he became the first black quarterback to lead a team to the playoffs in 1974 with the Rams.

The aggregate league-wide passing data for the American Football League was:

Games	Att	Comp	%	Yards	Att	Comp	Att/g	Y/g	Y/ TD	Y/ TD/g	Int	Rating	300-Yd Gm
602	37655	17961	47.7%	253384	6.7	14.1	62.5	420.9	1861	3.1	2252	61.4	116

Sixteen quarterbacks threw for at least 5,000 yards in the AFL. Their percentage of completed passes ranges from Steve Tensi's 42.3 percent to Len Dawson's 56.8 percent. Aside from Frank Tripucka and Bob Griese, they were all bombers. Only Len Dawson, Daryle Lamonica, Tom Flores and Steve Tensi threw more TD

passes than interceptions during this time. George Blanda threw the most interceptions in AFL history, and the worst touchdown to interception ratios belonged to Pete Beathard, Jack Kemp, Cotton Davidson and Tripucka. Blanda and Kemp were the most prolific passers. The AFL's top 16 ranked by passer rating:

Name	Attempts	Comp	%	Yards	Y/Att	Y/Comp	TD	Int	Rating
Len Dawson	2352	1335	56.8%	18899	8.0	14.2	182	117	87.9
Daryle Lamonica	1620	797	49.2%	12274	7.6	15.4	105	83	74.9
Joe Namath	2043	1026	50.2%	15487	7.6	15.1	97	104	70.1
John Hadl	2512	1239	49.3%	19026	7.6	15.4	143	145	69.7
Tom Flores	1715	838	48.9%	11959	7.0	14.3	93	92	67.6
Jacky Lee	836	430	51.4%	6124	7.3	14.2	46	55	66.4
Bob Griese	938	473	50.4%	6173	6.6	13.1	46	50	65.7
Babe Parilli	2679	1270	47.4%	18289	6.8	14.4	144	152	64.3
George Blanda	2884	1398	48.5%	20029	6.9	14.3	176	195	63.6
Steve Tensi	782	331	42.3%	5019	6.4	15.2	40	38	60.9
Jack Kemp	3055	1428	46.7%	21134	6.9	14.8	114	181	57.6
Cotton Davidson	1686	742	44.0%	11451	6.8	15.4	73	103	56.0
Al Dorow	909	428	47.1%	5732	6.3	13.4	47	63	56.0
Frank Tripucka	1277	662	51.8%	7676	6.0	11.6	51	85	55.9
Dick Wood	1193	522	43.8%	7151	6.0	13.7	51	70	53.3
Pete Beathard	1014	458	45.2%	6455	6.4	14.1	32	65	50.1

Overall, the quarterbacks who led the league the most times in passing categories over this era are:

Attempts	George Blanda	3	Int %	Butch Songin	2
Completions	George Blanda	3	Rating	Len Dawson	6
Yards	George Blanda & Frank Tripucka		Wins	Jack Kemp	4
	& Joe Namath & John Hadl	2	Comebacks	Joe Namath & John Hadl	3
Yards/Pass	Len Dawson	3	Interceptions	George Blanda	4
Comp %	Len Dawson	7	Fumbles	Jack Kemp	5
TD	Len Dawson	4	Sacked	Bob Griese	2
TD%	Len Dawson	5			

And the complete list of AFL All-Time Leaders is as follows:

Attempts	Jack Kemp	3,055	Int%	Steve Tensi	4.86
Completions	Jack Kemp	1,428	Rating	Len Dawson	87.9
Yards	Jack Kemp	21,134	Wins	Len Dawson	67
Yards/Pass	Len Dawson	8.0	Comebacks	John Hadl	11
Comp %	Len Dawson	56.8	Interceptions	George Blanda	195
TD	Len Dawson	182	Fumbles	Jack Kemp	77
TD%	Len Dawson	7.74			

1960

Right from the start, the AFL showed it was different from the NFL. Players had their names on the backs of their uniforms, there was the new two-point conversion, and AFL games averaged almost 15 more passes per game than NFL ones. What was familiar was who was lining up behind center. The eight quarterbacks who started their team's first games were: George Blanda, Al Dorow, Babe Parilli, Frank Tripucka, Jack Kemp, Cotton Davidson, Tommy O'Connell and Butch Songin. All but Songin had played in the NFL before; moreover, all but Blanda had played in the CFL. The eight averaged 30 years old, and only Davidson and Kemp were under that average.

The New York Titans behind Al Dorow throwing bombs to Don Maynard and Art Powell led the league in scoring with 382 points, but the 7–7 Titans also gave up 399. Only the Dallas Texans gave up fewer than 20 points per game. In the title game, the Houston Oilers prevailed over the Los Angeles Chargers 24–16 as George Blanda threw for 301 yards, including a fourth quarter swing pass that Billy Cannon took 88 yards for the winning touchdown. Frank Tripucka threw the AFL's first touchdown, a swing pass that Al Carmichael took 59 yards for the score, but also set a new pro record for interceptions with 34. Thirty-six-year old Butch Songin and Johnny Green were veteran rookies who had played in Canada, while rookies Tom Flores, Warren Rabb and Jacky Lee were untested youngsters.

1960 League Passing Statistics

Games	Att	Comp	%	Yards	Y/ Att	Y/ Comp	Att/g	Y/g	TD	TD/g	Int	Rating	300-Yd Gms
56	3699	1795	48.5%	24437	6.6	13.6	66.1	436.4	186	3.3	219	62.1	12

1960 Leading Passers

Name	Team	Attempts	Comp	%	Yards	Y/Att	Y/Comp	TD	Int	Rating	Relative Rating
Tom Flores	OAK	252	136	54	1738	6.9	12.8	12	12	71.8	116
Butch Songin	NEP	392	187	47.7	2476	6.32	13.2	22	15	70.9	114
Al Dorow	NYJ	396	201	50.8	2748	6.94	13.7	26	26	67.8	109
Jack Kemp	SDC	406	211	52	3018	7.43	14.3	20	25	67.1	108
George Blanda	TEN	363	169	46.6	2413	6.65	14.3	24	22	65.4	105
Cotton Davidson	KCC	379	179	47.2	2474	6.53	13.8	15	16	64.2	103
Frank Tripucka	DEN	478	248	51.9	3038	6.36	12.3	24	34	58.9	95

The leaders in the major passing categories for 1960 were:

Attempts	Frank Tripucka	478	Rating	Tom Flores	71.8
Completions	Frank Tripucka	248	Wins	Jack Kemp	9
Yards	Frank Tripucka	3,038	Comebacks	Jack Kemp	4
Yards/Pass	Jack Kemp	7.43	Interceptions	Frank Tripucka	34
Comp %	Tom Flores	54	Fumbles	Jack Kemp & Al Dorow	
TD	Al Dorow	26		& John Green	9
TD%	George Blanda	6.6	Sacked	Jack Kemp	36
Int %	Butch Songin	3.8			

1961

Lou Rymkus, coach of the defending champion Oilers, was fired after the team got off to a 1–3–1 start, but Houston then ran off nine straight wins under Wally Lemm to return to the title game against the Chargers who had moved south to San Diego. Along the way, George Blanda set a new pro record with 3,330 yards and 36 touchdown passes, including seven in one game, as the Oilers led the AFL in scoring with 513 points, almost 37 per game. In a defensive battle against the high-scoring Chargers, the Oilers won again, 10–3 this time. George Blanda threw five interceptions, but Jack Kemp threw four himself.

Several of the AFL's quarterbacks slipped a bit from 1960— Jack Kemp, Cotton Davidson and Al Dorow all were less effective in 1961. Babe Parilli was sent packing from Oakland to Boston where he teamed with Butch Songin to form a very venerable quarterback duo. In Denver, Frank Tripucka dropped to 4.9 yards per pass and threw 10 touchdowns to 21 interceptions, while his backup George Herring averaged 5.2 yards per pass and threw just five touchdowns to 22 interceptions. There were no rookies of note, but second year backup Jacky Lee threw for over 400 yards in one game for the Oilers and threw 12 touchdown passes.

1961 League Passing Statistics

Games	Att	Comp	%	Yards	Y/ Att	Y/ Comp	Att/g	Y/g	TD	TD/g	Int	Rating	300-Yd Gms
56	3630	1699	46.8%	24336	6.7	14.3	64.8	434.6	182	3.3	232	59.1	9

1961 Leading Passers

Name	Team	Attempts	Comp	%	Yards	Y/Att	Y/Comp	TD	Int	Rating	Relative Rating
George Blanda	TEN	362	187	51.7	3330	9.2	17.8	36	22	91.3	154
Babe Parilli	NEP	198	104	52.5	1314	6.64	12.6	13	9	76.5	129
Butch Songin	NEP	212	98	46.2	1429	6.74	14.6	14	9	73	124
Tom Flores	OAK	366	190	51.9	2176	5.95	11.5	15	19	62.1	105
Jack Kemp	SDC	364	165	45.3	2686	7.38	16.3	15	22	59.2	100
Cotton Davidson	KCC	330	151	45.8	2445	7.41	16.2	17	23	59.2	100
Al Dorow	NYJ	438	197	45	2651	6.05	13.5	19	30	50.7	86
Frank Tripucka	DEN	344	167	48.5	1690	4.91	10.1	10	21	47.3	80

The leaders in the major passing categories for 1961 were:

Attempts	Al Dorow	438	Int %	Butch Songin	4.2
Completions	Al Dorow	197	Rating	George Blanda	91.3
Yards	George Blanda	3,330	Wins	Jack Kemp	12
Yards/Pass	George Blanda	9.2	Comebacks	Al Dorow & John Green	2
Comp %	Babe Parilli	52.5	Interceptions	Al Dorow	30
TD	George Blanda	36	Fumbles	Jack Kemp & Al Dorow	10
TD%	George Blanda	9.9			

1962

In their final year in Dallas, the Texans scored a league best 389 points and won the AFL title in a thrilling 20–17 double overtime win over the Oilers. Len Dawson requested his release from the Browns and signed with the Texans where Hank Stram, his old college coach,

rescued his floundering career. Dawson led the AFL by completing 61 percent of his passes and throwing for 29 touchdowns. The Oilers' George Blanda set a dubious pro record this year by throwing 42 interceptions. He also threw 27 touchdowns and got Houston back to the championship game, but then threw five picks in the loss to Dallas.

Al Dorow finished his career, while John Hadl and Dick Wood were the top rookies. Hadl got to play quite a bit because Jack Kemp broke his hand, and then ended up in Buffalo in a waiver mistake. Cotton Davidson hurt his shoulder, lost his job and was traded to Oakland. Babe Parilli broke his collarbone, but still threw 18 touchdowns. The Broncos had their only .500 season in 1962 with Frank Tripucka throwing for 2,917 yards, 17 touchdowns and 25 interceptions; his backup George Shaw threw four touchdowns and 14 interceptions. The Raiders lost their 19th straight game over two seasons and finished 1–13, while the Titans were going bankrupt and couldn't meet their payroll. The AFL had another fan friendly innovation by having the official time kept on the scoreboard clock rather than just in the referee's pocket.

1962 League Passing Statistics

Games	Att	Comp	%	Yards	Y/Att	Y/Comp	Att/g	Y/g	TD	TD/g	Int	Rating	300-Yd Gms
56	3456	1644	47.6%	23515	6.8	14.3	61.7	419.9	176	3.1	242	57.9	6

1962 Leading Passers

Name	Team	Attempts	Comp	%	Yards	Y/Att	Y/Comp	TD	Int	Rating	Relative Rating
Len Dawson	KCC	310	189	61	2759	8.9	14.6	29	17	98.3	170
Babe Parilli	NEP	253	140	55.3	1988	7.86	14.2	18	8	91.5	158
Frank Tripucka	DEN	440	240	54.5	2917	6.63	12.2	17	25	64.4	111
John Green	NYJ	258	128	49.6	1741	6.75	13.6	10	18	55.4	96
George Blanda	TEN	418	197	47.1	2810	6.72	14.3	27	42	51.3	89
John Hadl	SDC	260	107	41.2	1632	6.28	15.3	15	24	43.3	75
Cotton Davidson	OAK	321	119	37.1	1977	6.16	16.6	7	23	36.1	62

The leaders in the major passing categories for 1962 were:

Attempts	Frank Tripucka	440	Rating	Len Dawson	98.3
Completions	Frank Tripucka	240	Wins	George Blanda &	
Yards	Frank Tripucka	2,917		Len Dawson	11
Yards/Pass	Len Dawson	8.9	Comebacks	George Blanda &	
Comp %	Len Dawson	61		Frank Tripucka	3
TD	Len Dawson	29	Interceptions	George Blanda	42
TD%	Len Dawson	9.4	Fumbles	Len Dawson	11
Int %	Babe Parilli	3.2			

1963

The AFL shored up its foundation in 1963 with three major franchise changes. The champion Dallas Texans moved to Kansas City to become the Chiefs. Although they slumped on the field, the Chiefs no longer had to compete for their fan base. The Titans were bought by a group led by promoter Sonny Werblin who rechristened them the Jets and hired respected Weeb Ewbank as their coach, while the Oakland Raiders brought in Al Davis from San Diego to run the franchise, and he took a squad that had gone 3–25 in the last two years and turned them into a 10–4 second place team. Tom Flores averaged 18.6 yards per completion and threw 20 touchdowns in Oakland, while his backup Cotton Davidson threw for 11 more scores.

Davis brought his version of Sid Gillman's offense to Oakland, but the Chargers had mastered the Lightning Bolt Offense in San Diego. Behind veteran quarterback Tobin Rote who completed 59 percent of his passes for 20 touchdowns, the Chargers led the league with 399 points and crushed the Patriots 51–10 in the title game. San Diego had both the top offense and defense in the league. Meanwhile, Frank Tripucka grew tired of the pounding in Denver and quit after two games; in his place, rookie Mickey Slaughter showed some promise with 12 touchdowns and 14 interceptions. Other rookies included Daryle Lamonica in Buffalo and Mike Taliaferro in New York.

1963 League Passing Statistics

Games	Att	Comp	%	Yards	Y/ Att	Y/ Comp	Att/g	Y/g	TD	TD/g	Int	Rating	300-Yd Gms
56	3539	1722	48.7%	22358	6.3	13.0	63.2	399.3	192	3.4	213	62.0	11

1963 Leading Passers

Name	Team	Attempts	Comp	%	Yards	Y/Att	Y/Comp	TD	Int	Rating	Relative Rating
Tobin Rote	SDC	286	170	59.4	2510	8.78	14.8	20	17	86.7	133
Tom Flores	OAK	247	113	45.7	2101	8.51	18.6	20	13	80.7	124
Len Dawson	KCC	352	190	54	2389	6.79	12.6	26	19	77.5	119
George Blanda	TEN	423	224	53	3003	7.1	13.4	24	25	70.1	108
Mickey Slaughter	DEN	223	112	50.2	1689	7.57	15.1	12	14	67.3	103
Jack Kemp	BUF	384	193	50.3	2914	7.59	15.1	13	20	65.2	100
Dick Wood	NYJ	351	160	45.6	2202	6.27	13.8	18	18	61.9	95
Babe Parilli	NEP	337	153	45.4	2345	6.96	15.3	13	24	52.1	80

The leaders in the major passing categories for 1963 were:

Attempts	George Blanda	423	Int %	Cotton Davidson	5.2
Completions	George Blanda	224	Rating	Tobin Rote	86.7
Yards	George Blanda	3,003	Wins	Tobin Rote	11
Yards/Pass	Tobin Rote	8.78	Comebacks	Cotton Davidson	2
Comp %	Tobin Rote	59.4	Interceptions	George Blanda	25
TD	Len Dawson	26	Fumbles	Jack Kemp	10
TD%	Tom Flores	8.1			

1964

Lou Saban got Buffalo to the top in 1964 with the help of Jack Kemp at the expense of Kemp's former team, the Chargers. Buffalo led the league in scoring with 400 points and gave up the fewest points as well. Cookie Gilchrist's pounding rushing attack softened defenses for Kemp's passing. Kemp threw just 13 touchdowns to 26 interceptions, but connected for 2,285 yards while his backup Daryle Lamonica threw for another six touchdowns and 1,137 yards. All three of the Bills' starting receivers averaged over 20 yards per catch. In San Diego, Tobin Rote slumped to 45 percent completions, nine touchdowns and 15 interceptions, but John Hadl threw for 18 touchdowns. However, the Bills mashed them 20–7 for the title.

Babe Parilli led the AFL with 3,467 yards and 31 touchdowns but also with 27 intercep-

tions. George Blanda threw 27 picks, too. The league pressured the Oilers to send one of their two good backup quarterbacks to the woeful Broncos, and Houston worked a deal where they lent Jacky Lee to Denver for two years in exchange for defensive tackle Bud McFaddin. Lee threw 11 touchdowns and 20 interceptions in Denver while averaging just 6.1 yards per pass; his backup Mickey Slaughter threw three touchdowns, 11 interceptions and averaged 4.9 yards per pass. Pete Beathard and Don Trull were rookies most noted for their scrambling, and neither would ever be very successful.

The AFL All Star Game became a civil rights focal point in January 1965. After several black players experienced discrimination at the New Orleans site of the game, they organized a boycott by both black and white players and the league moved the game to Houston.

1964 League Passing Statistics

Games	Att	Comp	%	Yards	Y/Att	Y/Comp	Att/g	Y/g	TD	TD/g	Int	Rating	300-Yd Gms
56	3750	1838	49.0%	26428	7.0	14.4	67.0	471.9	190	3.4	239	62.6	16

1964 Leading Passers

Name	Team	Attempts	Comp	%	Yards	Y/Att	Y/Comp	TD	Int	Rating	Relative Rating
Len Dawson	KCC	354	199	56.2	2879	8.13	14.5	30	18	89.9	144
John Hadl	SDC	274	147	53.6	2157	7.87	14.7	18	15	78.7	126
Cotton Davidson	OAK	320	155	48.4	2497	7.8	16.1	21	19	72.1	115
Babe Parilli	NEP	473	228	48.2	3465	7.33	15.2	31	27	70.8	113
George Blanda	TEN	505	262	51.9	3287	6.51	12.5	17	27	61.4	98
Dick Wood	NYJ	358	169	47.2	2298	6.42	13.6	17	25	54.9	88
Jacky Lee	DEN	265	133	50.2	1611	6.08	12.1	11	20	51.6	82
Mickey Slaughter	DEN	189	97	51.3	930	4.92	9.6	3	11	46.4	74

The leaders in the major passing categories for 1964 were:

Attempts	George Blanda	505	Int %	Len Dawson	5.1
Completions	George Blanda	262	Rating	Len Dawson	89.9
Yards	Babe Parilli	3,465	Wins	Jack Kemp	11
Yards/Pass	Jack Kemp	8.49	Comebacks	Daryle Lamonica	3
Comp %	Len Dawson	56.2	Interceptions	George Blanda	27
TD	Babe Parilli	31	Fumbles	Len Dawson	15
TD%	Len Dawson	8.5	Sacked	Babe Parilli	27

1965

The big news for the AFL was in New York where Sonny Werblin of the Jets signed not only Joe Namath to a $427,000 contract but also Notre Dame Heisman Trophy winner John Huarte for $225,000. In addition, Werblin was instrumental in negotiating a new TV contract with NBC that put all AFL teams on stable footing. Namath would prove to have charisma and star power as well as passing talent; he threw for 18 touchdowns as a rookie.

On the field, Cookie Gilchrist wore out his welcome in Buffalo and both starting wide receivers were injured; the effect on the offense was that Jack Kemp dropped from 8.5 yards per pass to 6.1. However, the Bills' defense was still the best in the league, and Buffalo defeated the top scoring Chargers (340 points) again for title in a 23–0 shutout. John Hadl of the Chargers averaged over eight yards per pass. Babe Parilli slumped to 18 touchdowns, 26 interceptions and a 40.6 completion percentage, while George Blanda dropped to 42.1 percent completions and led the AFL for the fourth and last time in interceptions with 30. At 38, Blanda still threw the most passes in the league.

1965 League Passing Statistics

Games	Att	Comp	%	Yards	Y/Att	Y/Comp	Att/g	Y/g	TD	TD/g	Int	Rating	300-Yd Gms
56	3652	1653	45.3%	23253	6.4	14.1	65.2	415.2	163	2.9	203	58.0	6

1965 Leading Passers

Name	Team	Attempts	Comp	%	Yards	Y/Att	Y/Comp	TD	Int	Rating	Relative Rating
Len Dawson	KCC	305	163	53.4	2262	7.42	13.9	21	14	81.3	140

Name	Team	Attempts	Comp	%	Yards	Y/Att	Y/Comp	TD	Int	Rating	Relative Rating
John Hadl	SDC	348	174	50	2798	8.04	16.1	20	21	71.3	123
Joe Namath	NYJ	340	164	48.2	2220	6.53	13.5	18	15	68.8	118
Dick Wood	OAK	157	69	43.9	1003	6.39	14.5	8	6	66.4	114
Tom Flores	OAK	269	122	45.4	1593	5.92	13.1	14	11	64.9	112
Jack Kemp	BUF	391	179	45.8	2368	6.06	13.2	10	18	54.8	94
Babe Parilli	NEP	426	173	40.6	2597	6.1	15.0	18	26	50	86
Mickey Slaughter	DEN	147	75	51	864	5.88	11.5	6	12	48.7	84
George Blanda	TEN	442	186	42.1	2542	5.75	13.7	20	30	47.9	83

The leaders in the major passing categories for 1965 were:

Attempts	George Blanda	442	Int %	Dick Wood	3.8
Completions	George Blanda	186	Rating	Len Dawson	81.3
Yards	John Hadl	2,798	Wins	Jack Kemp	10
Yards/Pass	John Hadl	8.04	Comebacks	John Hadl	
Comp %	Len Dawson	53.4		& George Blanda & Tom Flores	2
TD	Len Dawson	21	Interceptions	George Blanda	30
TD%	Len Dawson	6.9	Fumbles	Jack Kemp & John Hadl	9

1966

Kansas City led the AFL in scoring with 448 points and defeated the two-time champion Bills 31–7 for the AFL title and the right to represent the league in the first Super Bowl against the Packers. Len Dawson completed 56 percent of his passes and threw 26 touchdowns to just 10 interceptions, but it was a key interception by Green Bay's Willie Wood that led to the Chiefs' 35–10 loss in that momentous game. Jack Kemp completed just 43 percent of his passes in Buffalo, and his backup Daryle Lamonica just 39 percent. Sophomore Joe Namath led the league in yards with 3,379.

The Dolphins brought pro football back to Miami in 1966, but on the field weren't much more successful than the Seahawks from the All America Conference in 1946. Rookie Rick Norton completed 38 percent of his passes for three touchdowns and six interceptions, while Dick Wood completed 36 percent and threw 4 touchdowns to 14 interceptions and the coach's rookie son George Wilson Jr. completed 41 percent and threw five touchdowns to 10 interceptions. Add in John Stofa's four and two, and Dolphin quarterbacks threw 16 touchdowns and 32 interceptions. Another rookie, Max Choboian of the Broncos, threw four touchdowns to 12 interceptions and teamed with John McCormick's six touchdowns and 15 interceptions for a 10:27 ratio in Denver.

1966 League Passing Statistics

Games	Att	Comp	%	Yards	Y/ Att	Y/ Comp	Att/g	Y/g	TD	TD/g	Int	Rating	300-Yd Gms
63	3982	1842	46.3%	27128	6.8	14.7	63.2	430.6	199	3.2	217	63.0	13

1966 Leading Passers

Name	Team	Attempts	Comp	%	Yards	Y/Att	Y/Comp	TD	Int	Rating	Relative Rating
Len Dawson	KCC	284	159	56	2527	8.9	15.9	26	10	101.7	161
Tom Flores	OAK	306	151	49.3	2638	8.62	17.5	24	14	86.2	137
John Hadl	SDC	375	200	53.3	2846	7.59	14.2	23	14	83	132
Don Trull	TEN	172	84	48.8	1200	6.98	14.3	10	5	79.1	126
Babe Parilli	NEP	382	181	47.4	2721	7.12	15.0	20	20	66.9	106
Joe Namath	NYJ	471	232	49.3	3379	7.17	14.6	19	27	62.6	99
Max Choboian	DEN	163	82	50.3	1110	6.81	13.5	4	12	49.9	79

The leaders in the major passing categories for 1966 were:

Attempts	Joe Namath	471	Int %	Don Trull	2.9
Completions	Joe Namath	232	Rating	Len Dawson	101.7
Yards	Joe Namath	3,379	Wins	Len Dawson	11
Yards/Pass	Len Dawson	8.9	Comebacks	Joe Namath	2
Comp %	Len Dawson	56	Interceptions	Joe Namath	27
TD	Len Dawson	26	Fumbles	Babe Parilli	8
TD%	Len Dawson	9.2	Sacked	Dick Wood	20

1967

Two big trades sent backups Daryle Lamonica to Oakland and Pete Beathard to Houston, and the two new starters met in the AFL title game where the Raiders crushed the Oilers 40–7. Lamonica earned the moniker the "Mad Bomber," throwing for 3,228 yards and 30 touchdowns in leading Oakland to a league best 468 points, but came up short in the second Super Bowl when the Packers defeated the Raiders 31–13. The Raiders also signed George Blanda as their backup after Houston cut him. Beathard's Oilers had the league's best defense, but Beathard completed just 41 percent of his passes for nine touchdowns and 14 interceptions. Joe Namath became the first pro quarterback to pass for over 4,000 yards with 4,007, and he threw 26 touchdowns for the second place Jets.

Bob Griese was the top rookie throwing for 15 touchdowns and 18 interceptions while completing 50 percent of his passes in Miami. He beat out second-year-man Rick Norton who completed just 40 percent of his passes for one touchdown and nine interceptions. Buffalo declined drastically behind Jack Kemp's fourteen touchdowns and 26 interceptions and new backup Tom Flores's zero touchdowns and eight interceptions.

1967 League Passing Statistics

Games	Att	Comp	%	Yards	Y/Att	Y/Comp	Att/g	Y/g	TD	TD/g	Int	Rating	300-Yd Gms
63	3878	1846	47.6%	25969	6.7	14.1	61.6	412.2	190	3.0	227	61.6	14

1967 Leading Passers

Name	Team	Attempts	Comp	%	Yards	Y/Att	Y/Comp	TD	Int	Rating	Relative Rating
Len Dawson	KCC	357	206	57.7	2651	7.43	12.9	24	17	83.7	136
Daryle Lamonica	OAK	425	220	51.8	3228	7.6	14.7	30	20	80.8	131
John Hadl	SDC	427	217	50.8	3365	7.88	15.5	24	22	74.5	121
Joe Namath	NYJ	491	258	52.5	4007	8.16	15.5	26	28	73.8	120
Bob Griese	MIA	331	166	50.2	2005	6.06	12.1	15	18	61.6	100
Babe Parilli	NEP	344	161	46.8	2317	6.74	14.4	19	24	58.5	95
Jack Kemp	BUF	369	161	43.6	2503	6.78	15.5	14	26	50	81

The leaders in the major passing categories for 1967 were:

Attempts	Joe Namath	491	Int %	Daryle Lamonica	4.7
Completions	Joe Namath	258	Rating	Len Dawson	83.7
Yards	Joe Namath	4,007	Wins	Daryle Lamonica	13
Yards/Pass	Joe Namath	8.16	Comebacks	John Hadl	3
Comp %	Len Dawson	57.7	Interceptions	Joe Namath	28
TD	Daryle Lamonica	30	Fumbles	Jack Kemp	14
TD%	Daryle Lamonica	7.1	Sacked	Daryle Lamonica	37

1968

Joe Namath proved he was worth every dollar the Jets paid him, not only to the Jets, but to the AFL as well by backing up his guarantee and defeating the 18-point favorite Colts in Super Bowl III. The Jets earned their way to the Super Bowl by beating the top scoring Raiders (453 points) 27–23 for the AFL title in a game in which Daryle Lamonica threw for 401 yards. However, Joe Namath hit Don Maynard for a six yard score with seven minutes left, and Jet linebacker Ralph Baker recovered a missed lateral at the Jet 12 in the last two minutes to ice the win. A few weeks earlier, the Raiders had pulled out an equally thrilling win over the Jets in a contest still famous today as the "Heidi" game because NBC decided to switch from football to the little Swiss girl precisely at 7 P.M., enraging millions of football fans.

After the Broncos' Steve Tensi broke his collarbone, Marlin Briscoe made the greatest impact as a rookie. He became the first black regular starting quarterback in pro football history and threw for 14 touchdowns and 13 interceptions while rushing for 308 yards. That year, the Raiders had made Eldridge Dickey the first black quarterback selected in the first round of the draft, but then converted him to wide receiver. Veteran Raider Cotton Davidson hung up his cleats.

The Cincinnati Bengals became the 10th AFL team with legendary Paul Brown at the helm. They struggled, but not as much as the Bills who lost Jack Kemp, Tom Flores, Kay Stephenson and rookie Dan Darragh all to injuries during the season and ended up playing defensive back Ed Rutkowski at quarterback. Their quarterbacks totaled seven touchdowns and 28 interceptions and enabled Buffalo to earn the worst record in football and the right to draft O.J. Simpson.

1968 League Passing Statistics

Games	Att	Comp	%	Yards	Y/ Att	Y/ Comp	Att/g	Y/g	TD	TD/g	Int	Rating	300-Yd Gms
70	4037	1916	47.5%	27914	6.9	14.6	57.7	398.8	189	2.7	227	62.6	17

1968 Leading Passers

Name	Team	Attempts	Comp	%	Yards	Y/Att	Y/Comp	TD	Int	Rating	Relative Rating
Len Dawson	KCC	224	131	58.5	2109	9.42	16.1	17	9	98.6	157
Daryle Lamonica	OAK	416	206	49.5	3245	7.8	15.8	25	15	80.9	129
Bob Griese	MIA	355	186	52.4	2473	6.97	13.3	21	16	75.7	121
Joe Namath	NYJ	380	187	49.2	3147	8.28	16.8	15	17	72.1	115
John Hadl	SDC	440	208	47.3	3473	7.89	16.7	27	32	64.5	103
John Stofa	CIN	177	85	48	896	5.06	10.5	5	5	60.8	97

The leaders in the major passing categories for 1968 were:

Attempts	John Hadl	440	Rating	Len Dawson	98.6
Completions	John Hadl	208	Wins	Daryle Lamonica	12
Yards	John Hadl	3,473	Comebacks	Joe Namath & Bob Griese	
Yards/Pass	Len Dawson	9.42		& Len Dawson & John Sotfa	2
Comp %	Len Dawson	58.5	Interceptions	John Hadl	32
TD	John Hadl	27	Fumbles	Tom Sherman	8
TD%	Len Dawson	7.6	Sacked	Bob Griese	43
Int %	John Stofa	2.8			

1969

While the Jets proved an AFL team could beat an NFL one in Super Bowl III, the Chiefs proved it was no fluke in Super Bowl IV. Despite being 12-point underdogs to the Vikings, the Kansas City handily whipped Minnesota 26–7 and put the two leagues dead even. Actually, Len

Dawson had a subpar year in which he missed several games with a knee injury, while Oakland was scoring a league best 377 points behind Daryle Lamonica's 34 touchdowns. However, the Chiefs had the best defense in the league and beat the Raiders and Jets in the playoffs to reach the Super Bowl and avenge their loss to the Packers four years before. The Jets were distracted right from the start when Joe Namath retired in the spring rather than sell his interests in the bar Bachelors III that was said to be a gamblers' hangout. Namath recanted and returned, but the Jets did not repeat.

Babe Parilli, Jack Kemp, Tom Flores and Jacky Lee all were 10-year men in the AFL and would retire after the season. Fellow 10-year man George Blanda was still kicking, though, quite literally. The 10 starting quarterbacks at the end of the AFL's run were an average age of 28, and eight of them had never played in the NFL before; that would change in 1970. Greg Cook was a particularly promising rookie who averaged 9.4 yards per pass, completed 54 percent of his passes and threw 15 touchdowns to 11 interceptions, although he would hurt his shoulder and never get to truly show his stuff. The other rookie of note was Buffalo's James Harris who didn't get a full shot with the Bills, but would become the first black quarterback to lead a team to the playoffs five years later in Los Angeles.

1969 League Passing Statistics

Games	Att	Comp	%	Yards	Y/Att	Y/Comp	Att/g	Y/g	TD	TD/g	Int	Rating	300-Yd Gms
70	4032	2006	49.8%	28046	7.0	14.0	57.6	400.7	194	2.8	233	64.5	12

1969 Leading Passers

Name	Team	Attempts	Comp	%	Yards	Y/Att	Y/Comp	TD	Int	Rating	Relative Rating
Greg Cook	CIN	197	106	53.8	1854	9.41	17.5	15	11	88.3	137
Daryle Lamonica	OAK	426	221	51.9	3302	7.75	14.9	34	25	79.8	124
Joe Namath	NYJ	361	185	51.2	2734	7.57	14.8	19	17	74.3	115
Len Dawson	KCC	166	98	59	1323	7.97	13.5	9	13	69.9	108
Steve Tensi	DEN	286	131	45.8	1990	6.96	15.2	14	12	68.1	106
John Hadl	SDC	324	158	48.8	2253	6.95	14.3	10	11	67.8	105
Mike Livingston	KCC	161	84	52.2	1123	6.98	13.4	4	6	67.4	104
Mike Taliaferro	NEP	331	160	48.3	2160	6.53	13.5	19	18	66	102
Pete Beathard	TEN	370	180	48.6	2455	6.64	13.6	10	21	55.6	86

The leaders in the major passing categories for 1969 were:

Attempts	Daryle Lamonica	426	Rating	Greg Cook	88.3
Completions	Daryle Lamonica	221	Wins	Daryle Lamonica	12
Yards	Daryle Lamonica	3,302	Comebacks	Joe Namath &	
Yards/Pass	Greg Cook	9.41		Daryle Lamonica & John Hadl	3
Comp %	Len Dawson	59	Interceptions	Daryle Lamonica	25
TD	Daryle Lamonica	34	Fumbles	Greg Cook	10
TD%	Daryle Lamonica	8	Sacked	Bob Griese	33
Int %	John Hadl	3.4			

12

1960–1977: Ball Control

The average statistics of this period present a deceptive picture when compared to the averages from the 1946–59 period immediately before this one because the prior era was one of growth while this was one in retreat. Average yards per pass was 6.9 in both periods, but in 1958 and 1959 it was 7.2, while in 1976 and 1977 it was 6.6 and 6.5. Passing yards per game went up slightly from 363 to 367, but in 1959 it was 374, while in 1977 it was down to 324. Completion percentage did clearly rise from 48 percent in the prior era to 51.7 percent in this ball control time, but yards per completion went from an average of 14.4 to 13.3 with a low of 12.7 in 1977. On average, the overall passer rating seemed to improve from 58.2 to 66.6, but it was actually higher in 1959 at 64.2 than in 1977 at 61.2. From 1962 to 1965, though, the NFL passer rating was over 70 each year before the decline set in.

Vince Lombardi's Packers won five championships in seven years and created a model that other teams followed: a power running offense featuring option blocking teamed with a tough defense. Both the Miami Dolphins and the Pittsburgh Steelers followed this prescription to back-to-back Super Bowl titles in the 1970s. Tom Landry's Cowboys took a different approach to offense with more pre-snap shifting, more misdirection, more speed and more passing, and Sid Gillman in the AFL presented a more wide-open, deep passing attack, but the major innovations of the era ultimately were on defense.

Landry himself perfected the 4–3 defense where the defensive linemen occupied the blockers and left the linebackers free to make the stops. Don Shula's Colts and Dolphins relied mostly on zone coverage schemes to mask man-to-man coverage deficiencies, and Steeler defensive coach Bud Carson devised the Cover 2 wrinkle with two safeties shutting off any deep passes that still is used by so many teams today. Shula began experimenting with a 3–4 defense in the early 1970s and many teams adopted that as their base defense later in the decade. Other significant moves included overload packages, special blitzes and an offset line. Eagle defensive coach Jerry Williams introduced nickel and dime packages with five and six defensive backs on passing downs during the 1960 championship run. George Allen popularized these and many other special packages in his travels from Chicago to Los Angeles to Washington. The Cardinals unleashed fearless free safety Larry Wilson as a crazed safety blitzer in the early 1960s, and that inspired a series of new blitz looks. The Chiefs' Hank Stram added the offset line at the end of the 1960s by placing a bulky defensive tackle at an angle directly over the center to disrupt the blocking schemes of the offensive lines.

Defenses clamped down so strongly that the Cowboys won a playoff game over the Lions in 1970 by a 5–0 score that played like it was out of the 1920s. By 1977, the league had tried tinkering with the rules a number of times, but teams were down to a sickly average of 17 points a game. The NFL responded with major changes to open up the passing game, and the contemporary passing offense was the outcome. One other result was that the game evolved into more of a coach's game. In 1960, there were only two coaches who called the plays on the field; by the end of the decade, there were four coaches; by the end of the 1970s, half the coaches did so; by the end of the 1980s, every coach did so.

Off the field, the NFL battled the rival AFL throughout the 1960s before the two agreed to merge as equal partners for the 1970 season. They began to play a championship game starting in 1966, and since then the Super Bowl has grown to the status of unofficial national holiday as the sport has grown to be the most popular one in the country. While there were 12 NFL teams in 1959, by 1977 there were 28 —10 former AFL teams and six NFL expansion teams. As the league became a bigger and bigger business in this period, it continually faced pressure from Congress about its monopoly status. This was also the era in which the game was at last fully integrated and black quarterbacks began to gain a foothold.

Veteran stars concluding their careers in this era included Norm Van Brocklin, Charlie Conerly, Bobby Layne and Y.A. Tittle. Eight Hall of Famers enjoyed their prime seasons in this era: Johnny Unitas, Bart Starr, Fran Tarkenton, Sonny Jurgensen, Len Dawson, Bob Griese, Roger Staubach and Terry Bradshaw. Some other stars of note were John Brodie, Roman Gabriel,

Don Meredith, Frank Ryan, Ken Stabler, Ken Anderson and Bert Jones. Stars of the future who got their starts in this time included Steve Bartkowski, Steve Grogan, Danny White, Dan Fouts and Joe Theismann. Injuries robbed Bill Nelsen, Lynn Dickey, Dan Pastorini and Bert Jones of their full potential. The biggest disappointments were Norm Snead, Archie Manning, Mike Phipps and Steve Spurrier — all inconsistent and interception-prone.

The aggregate league-wide passing data for the period from 1960 through 1977 in the NFL was:

Games	Att	Comp	%	Yards	Y/ Att	Y/ Comp	Att/g	Y/g	TD	TD/g	Int	Rating	300-Yd Gm
2493	132613	68610	51.7%	915016	6.9	13.3	53.2	367.0	6071	2.4	7204	66.6	230

29 quarterbacks threw for at least 10,000 yards during this era. Their percentage of completed passes ranged from Jim Plunkett's 49.3 percent to Ken "Snake" Stabler's 59.9 percent. According to yards per attempt and completion, the long bombers in the group were Unitas, Tittle, Ryan, Morrall, Meredith, Nelsen, Morton, Starr and Charlie Johnson. Ken Anderson, Fran Tarkenton, Stabler, Munson and Livingston relied more on short passes. Fran Tarkenton, John

Unitas, Sonny Jurgensen, John Brodie and Roman Gabriel all threw at least 200 touchdown passes in this period, and about half the group threw more TD passes than interceptions. Norm Snead, Tarkenton, Unitas and Brodie all threw more than 200 interceptions. Meanwhile, Terry Bradshaw and Jim Plunkett still had their greatest triumphs ahead of them. The 29 10,000-yard quarterbacks ranked by passer rating:

Name	Attempts	Comp	%	Yards	Y/Att	Y/Comp	TD	Int	Rating
Bart Starr	2599	1519	58.4%	21057	8.1	13.9	133	106	84.6
Ken Stabler	1577	945	59.9%	12519	7.9	13.2	108	91	83.9
Y.A. Tittle	1435	800	55.7%	11133	7.8	13.9	100	71	83.5
Sonny Jurgensen	4165	2385	57.3%	31468	7.6	13.2	249	180	83.2
Bob Griese	1846	1068	57.9%	14178	7.7	13.3	115	91	82.5
Ken Anderson	2127	1208	56.8%	15471	7.3	12.8	99	69	81.7
Fran Tarkenton	5895	3341	56.7%	43535	7.4	13.0	317	234	81.5
Bert Jones	1458	820	56.2%	10422	7.1	12.7	71	52	80.1
Frank Ryan	2030	1043	51.4%	15299	7.5	14.7	146	104	78.9
Earl Morrall	2107	1112	52.8%	16723	7.9	15.0	139	115	78.4
John Unitas	4057	2219	54.7%	31285	7.7	14.1	206	205	75.7
Don Meredith	2308	1170	50.7%	17199	7.5	14.7	135	111	74.8
Roman Gabriel	4498	2366	52.6%	29444	6.5	12.4	201	149	74.3
Billy Wade	1589	873	54.9%	11252	7.1	12.9	80	77	74.0
John Brodie	4234	2325	54.9%	29810	7.0	12.8	204	201	73.5
Greg Landry	1670	909	54.4%	11999	7.2	13.2	79	80	73.2
Billy Kilmer	2938	1562	53.2%	20179	6.9	12.9	148	143	71.5
Bill Munson	1932	1043	54.0%	12537	6.5	12.0	80	78	71.1
Craig Morton	2446	1277	52.2%	17942	7.3	14.1	123	130	70.8
Bill Nelsen	1905	963	50.6%	14165	7.4	14.7	98	101	70.2
Milt Plum	1888	1007	53.3%	13335	7.1	13.2	95	103	70.0
Charley Johnson	3392	1737	51.2%	24410	7.2	14.1	170	181	69.2
Jim Hart	3424	1725	50.4%	23869	7.0	13.8	152	167	67.6
Norm Snead	4353	2276	52.3%	30797	7.1	13.5	196	257	65.5
John Hadl	2175	1124	51.7%	14477	6.7	12.9	101	123	64.8

Name	Attempts	Comp	%	Yards	Y/Att	Y/Comp	TD	Int	Rating
Mike Livingston	1590	828	52.1%	10172	6.4	12.3	52	77	62.9
Terry Bradshaw	2019	1008	49.9%	13279	6.6	13.2	93	118	62.1
Jim Plunkett	1994	983	49.3%	13217	6.6	13.4	84	117	60.4
Dan Pastorini	2076	1064	51.3%	12301	5.9	11.6	66	104	59.2

Overall, the quarterbacks who led the league the most times in passing categories over this era are:

Attempts	Sonny Jurgensen	3	Int %	Bart Starr	3
Completions	Sonny Jurgensen	4	Rating	Bart Starr	4
Yards	Sonny Jurgensen	5	Wins	Bart Starr	4
Yards/Pass	Bart Starr	3	Comebacks	Fran Tarkenton	3
Comp %	Bart Starr	4	Interceptions	Norm Snead	3
TD	Sonny Jurgensen & Y.A. Tittle &		Fumbles	Bill Nelsen	3
	Frank Ryan & Roman Gabriel &		Sacked	Fran Tarkenton &	
	John Brodie & Ken Stabler	2		Don Meredith	
TD%	Ken Stabler	2		& Archie Manning	3

And the complete list of leaders for 1960–1977 is as follows:

Attempts	Fran Tarkenton	5,895	Int%	Ken Anderson	3.24
Completions	Fran Tarkenton	3,341	Rating	Bart Starr	84.6
Yards	Fran Tarkenton	43,535	Wins	Fran Tarkenton	117
Yards/Pass	Bart Starr	8.1	Comebacks	Fran Tarkenton	35
Comp %	Ken Stabler	59.9	Interceptions	Norm Snead	257
TD	Fran Tarkenton	317	Fumbles	Fran Tarkenton	77*
TD%	Frank Ryan	7.19	Sacked	Fran Tarkenton	545

*Len Dawson had 81 fumbles in the NFL and AFL combined during this period.

1960

With a rival league starting up at the outset of this new decade, the NFL moved quickly to counter the fledgling American Football League by expanding. The NFL promised a team to the AFL's Minnesota investors to grab that territory and awarded a team to Dallas to compete directly with Lamar Hunt's Texans. Dallas coach Tom Landry picked up veteran quarterback Eddie LeBaron to lead his team, but LeBaron struggled with the misfit Cowboys who went 0–11–1 in their first season, although they did snag a quarterback of the future in rookie Don Meredith.

Paul Brown's Cleveland squad led the league in scoring with 362 points in 12 games behind Milt Plum, but they were edged out in the East by a mediocre Eagles team driven by veteran Norm Van Brocklin who pulled out half the team's 10 wins with last quarter heroics. In the title game, Van Brocklin came through again to defeat Vince Lombardi's young Packers 17–13 for the championship, and he retired from playing afterwards. It was the only postseason game that Lombardi or his quarterback Bart Starr would ever lose. The inexperienced Starr threw just four touchdown passes all year, but was efficient and gained confidence for the future.

Johnny Unitas' streak of 47 consecutive games throwing a touchdown pass ended, and the Colts started to slip, but the worst passing years were had by the Bears' Zeke Bratkowski who threw six touchdowns to 21 interceptions and the Lions' Jim Ninowski who threw just two touchdowns to 18 interceptions. The 49ers began to experiment with the new Shotgun Formation and would give that a full shot the following season.

1960 League Passing Statistics

Games	Att	Comp	%	Yards	Y/Att	Y/Comp	Att/g	Y/g	TD	TD/g	Int	Rating	300-Yd Gms
78	4114	2064	50.2%	29753	7.2	14.4	52.7	381.4	221	2.8	274	64.2	8

1960 Leading Passers

Name	Team	Attempts	Comp	%	Yards	Y/Att	Y/Comp	TD	Int	Rating	Relative Rating
Milt Plum	CLE	250	151	60.4	2297	9.19	15.2	21	5	110.4	172
Norm Van Brocklin	PHL	284	153	53.9	2471	8.7	16.2	24	17	86.5	135
Bill Wade	STL	182	106	58.2	1294	7.11	12.2	12	11	77	120
John Unitas	IND	378	190	50.3	3099	8.2	16.3	25	24	73.7	115
Bart Starr	GBP	172	98	57	1358	7.9	13.9	4	8	70.8	110
Bobby Layne	PIT	209	103	49.3	1814	8.68	17.6	13	17	66.2	103
John Roach	ARZ	188	87	46.3	1423	7.57	16.4	17	19	62.7	98
Ralph Guglielmi	WSH	223	125	56.1	1547	6.94	12.4	9	19	55.7	87
Eddie LeBaron	DAL	225	111	49.3	1736	7.72	15.6	12	25	53.5	83

The leaders in the major passing categories for 1960 were:

Attempts	John Unitas	378	Int %	Milt Plum	2
Completions	John Unitas	190	Rating	Milt Plum	110.4
Yards	John Unitas	3099	Wins	Norm Van Brocklin	10
Yards/Pass	Milt Plum	9.19	Comebacks	Norm Van Brocklin	5
Comp %	Milt Plum	60.4	Interceptions	Eddie Lebaron	25
TD	John Unitas	25	Fumbles	Milt Plum	9
TD%	John Roach	9	Sacked	Eddie Lebaron	26

1961

The Minnesota Vikings became the 14th NFL team in 1961 and developed a rookie who would signal a new breed of scrambling quarterbacks in Fran Tarkenton. Meanwhile, stationary Norm Snead in Washington managed to set rookie records for completions (172) and yards (2,337) when not flat on his back. The Cardinals had two rookie quarterbacks: Sam Etcheverry who had nine years experience in the CFL, and unheralded Charlie Johnson of New Mexico State who would have a much greater impact on the franchise. Rookie tailback Billy Kilmer fit right into coach Red Hickey's vision for the Shotgun Formation that he tried to use as an every down formation in San Francisco. Hickey traded away the aging Y.A. Tittle to make way for more mobile quarterbacks John Brodie, Bob Waters and Kilmer. After a big start, the Shotgun was muzzled, while Tittle had success in leading the Giants back to the top of the East.

Tittle took over from the ancient Charlie Conerly in his final year and beat out the Eagles that were led by former backup Sonny Jurgensen who set league records for yards (3,723) and touchdowns (32). In the championship game in Green Bay, the Packers smoked the Giants 37–0 behind Bart Starr's three touchdown passes. The Packers' power sweep led the team to a league best 391 points in 14 games. Another quarterback on the move was Billy Wade who came to the Bears from the Rams for Zeke Bratkowski and stabilized Chicago's quarterback situation. In Cleveland, Milt Plum punched his ticket out of town by criticizing Paul Brown's play calling.

1961 League Passing Statistics

Games	Att	Comp	%	Yards	Y/Att	Y/Comp	Att/g	Y/g	TD	TD/g	Int	Rating	300-Yd Gms
98	5292	2759	52.1%	39591	7.5	14.3	54.0	404.0	285	2.9	332	68.5	18

1961 Leading Passers

Name	Team	Attempts	Comp	%	Yards	Y/Att	Y/Comp	TD	Int	Rating	Relative Rating
Bill Wade	CHI	250	139	55.6	2258	9.03	16.2	22	13	93.7	137

Name	Team	Attempts	Comp	%	Yards	Y/Att	Y/Comp	TD	Int	Rating	Relative Rating
Milt Plum	CLE	302	177	58.6	2416	8	13.6	18	10	90.3	132
Sonny Jurgensen	PHL	416	235	56.5	3723	8.95	15.8	32	24	88.1	129
Y.A. Tittle	NYG	285	163	57.2	2272	7.97	13.9	17	12	85.3	125
John Brodie	SFF	283	155	54.8	2588	9.14	16.7	14	12	84.7	124
Bart Starr	GBP	295	172	58.3	2418	8.2	14.1	16	16	80.3	117
Fran Tarkenton	MIN	280	157	56.1	1997	7.13	12.7	18	17	74.7	109
Rudy Bukich	PIT	156	89	57.1	1253	8.03	14.1	11	16	67	98
John Unitas	IND	420	229	54.5	2990	7.12	13.1	16	24	66.1	96

The leaders in the major passing categories for 1961 were:

Attempts	John Unitas	420	Int %	Milt Plum	3.3
Completions	Sonny Jurgensen	235	Rating	Bill Wade	93.7
Yards	Sonny Jurgensen	3723	Wins	Bart Starr	11
Yards/Pass	John Brodie	9.14	Comebacks	John Unitas	4
Comp %	Milt Plum	58.6	Interceptions	John Unitas & Sonny Jurgensen	24
TD	Sonny Jurgensen	32	Fumbles	Sam Etcheverry	15
TD%	Bill Wade	8.8	Sacked	Fran Tarkenton	44

1962

Aside from a Thanksgiving Day spanking administered by the Detroit Lions, the Packers romped through their schedule 13–1 and again led the NFL in points with 415. Again they met the Giants in the title game, and again Green Bay prevailed, 16–7 this time. Tittle raised the NFL touchdown pass mark to 33, including seven in one game against the Redskins. The Redskins were greatly improved by the addition of converted flanker Bobby Mitchell from Cleveland, the first black player on the last lily-white pro football team. Eddie LeBaron and Don Meredith began alternating plays in Dallas and combined for 31 touchdowns and only 17 interceptions in leading the Cowboys to 398 points.

Milt Plum got what he wished for and was traded from the Browns to the Lions for Jim Ninowski. Without runners Jim Brown and Bobby Mitchell and Paul Brown's play calling, however, his statistics dropped drastically. The Browns also picked up Frank Ryan from the Rams and that would pay off in the future. The Rams meanwhile drafted the top rookie quarterback in Roman Gabriel. Battered Bobby Layne played in his final game and was the last quarterback to play without a facemask. Coincidentally, tackling by the facemask was outlawed that year.

1962 League Passing Statistics

Games	Att	Comp	%	Yards	Y/ Att	Y/ Comp	Att/g	Y/g	TD	TD/g	Int	Rating	300-Yd Gms
98	5356	2851	53.2%	42057	7.9	14.8	54.7	429.2	300	3.1	325	72.5	19

1962 Leading Passers

Name	Team	Attempts	Comp	%	Yards	Y/Att	Y/Comp	TD	Int	Rating	Relative Rating
Eddie LeBaron	DAL	166	95	57.2	1436	8.65	15.1	16	9	95.4	131
Bart Starr	GBP	285	178	62.5	2438	8.55	13.7	12	9	90.7	125
Y.A. Tittle	NYG	375	200	53.3	3224	8.6	16.1	33	20	89.5	123
Frank Ryan	CLE	194	112	57.7	1541	7.94	13.8	10	7	85.4	118
Don Meredith	DAL	212	105	49.5	1679	7.92	16.0	15	8	84.2	116
John Brodie	SFF	304	175	57.6	2272	7.47	13.0	18	16	79	109
John Unitas	IND	389	222	57.1	2967	7.63	13.4	23	23	76.5	105

Name	Team	Attempts	Comp	%	Yards	Y/Att	Y/Comp	TD	Int	Rating	Relative Rating
Norm Snead	WSH	354	184	52	2926	8.27	15.9	22	22	74.7	103
Sonny Jurgensen	PHL	366	196	53.6	3261	8.91	16.6	22	26	74.3	102
Bill Wade	CHI	412	225	54.6	3172	7.7	14.1	18	24	70	96

The leaders in the major passing categories for 1962 were:

Attempts	Bill Wade	412	Int %	Bart Starr	3.2
Completions	Bill Wade	225	Rating	Eddie LeBaron	95.4
Yards	Sonny Jurgensen	3261	Wins	Bart Starr	13
Yards/Pass	Sonny Jurgensen	8.91	Comebacks	Bill Wade & Bobby Layne	4
Comp %	Bart Starr	62.5	Interceptions	Sonny Jurgensen	26
TD	Y.A. Tittle	33	Fumbles	Don Meredith	10
TD%	Eddie LeBaron	9.6	Sacked	Fran Tarkenton	45

1963

Packers halfback Paul Hornung and Lions tackle Alex Karras were both suspended for gambling in 1963, and the Packers and Lions both slipped while the Bears took a step forward. Green Bay was also affected by Bart Starr's broken hand, and Milt Plum went down for Detroit and was replaced by Earl Morrall who was effective. Billy Wade, though, was a smart game manager who did just enough on offense while the great Bears defense under defensive coach George Allen set a new low for points allowed in a 14–game season. For the title, they beat the top scoring team in the NFL, the Giants, 14–10 on short drives of five and 14 yards set up by turnovers. Y.A. Tittle topped the Giants with a record 36 touchdowns. Frank Ryan, who threw 25 touchdowns under new Browns coach Blanton Collier, joined him at the top of the quarterback rankings. Veterans Eddie LeBaron and Lamar McHan (in for the injured John Brodie in San Francisco) played their last games, while the top rookies were Heisman Trophy winner Terry Baker who flopped with the Rams and injury-prone Bill Nelsen of the Steelers. Sonny Jurgensen and his backup King Hill made headlines during training camp when they staged a joint holdout for more money and won; that would be just about the last thing they won all year. Failed former first round pick George Izo had the highlight of his career when he hit Bobby Mitchell for a 99-yard score.

1963 League Passing Statistics

Games	Att	Comp	%	Yards	Y/Att	Y/Comp	Att/g	Y/g	TD	TD/g	Int	Rating	300-Yd Gms
98	5415	2791	51.5%	41746	7.7	15.0	55.3	426.0	302	3.1	302	72.5	21

1963 Leading Passers

Name	Team	Attempts	Comp	%	Yards	Y/Att	Y/Comp	TD	Int	Rating	Relative Rating
Y.A. Tittle	NYG	367	221	60.2	3145	8.57	14.2	36	14	104.8	146
Frank Ryan	CLE	256	135	52.7	2026	7.91	15.0	25	13	90.4	126
John Unitas	IND	410	237	57.8	3481	8.49	14.7	20	12	89.7	125
Earl Morrall	DET	328	174	53	2621	7.99	15.1	24	14	86.2	120
Bart Starr	GBP	244	132	54.1	1855	7.6	14.1	15	10	82.3	115
Charlie Johnson	ARZ	423	222	52.5	3280	7.75	14.8	28	21	79.5	111
Fran Tarkenton	MIN	297	170	57.2	2311	7.78	13.6	15	15	78	109
Bill Wade	CHI	356	192	53.9	2301	6.46	12.0	15	12	74	103
Ed Brown	PIT	362	168	46.4	2982	8.24	17.8	21	20	71.4	100
Norm Snead	WSH	363	175	48.2	3043	8.38	17.4	13	27	58.1	81

The leaders in the major passing categories for 1963 were:

Attempts	Charlie Johnson	423	Int %	John Unitas	2.9
Completions	John Unitas	237	Rating	Y.A. Tittle	104.8
Yards	John Unitas	3481	Wins	Bill Wade & Y.A. Tittle	11
Yards/Pass	Y.A. Tittle	8.57	Comebacks	Ed Brown	5
Comp %	Y.A. Tittle	60.2	Interceptions	Norm Snead	27
TD	Y.A. Tittle	36	Fumbles	John Unitas	13
TD%	Y.A. Tittle	9.8	Sacked	Roman Gabriel	44

1964

Johnny Unitas and the Colts were back on top in the West under second-year coach Don Shula in 1964, scoring a league best 428 points en route to a 12–2 record. In the title game, however, they were upset 27–0 by a solid Browns team led by Doctor of Mathematics Frank Ryan's 25 touchdowns. Sonny Jurgensen was traded by the Eagles to the Redskins for Norm Snead in one of the most lopsided deals in league history. John Brodie and Milt Plum were back from injuries, but both struggled. Don Meredith was bothered by an injured leg and threw just nine touchdowns to 16 interceptions in Dallas. Rudy Bukich began to edge past Billy Wade in Chicago, while rookie Bill Munson pushed Roman Gabriel for playing time in Los Angeles. Bart Starr was the NFL's top passer.

1964 League Passing Statistics

Games	Att	Comp	%	Yards	Y/ Att	Y/ Comp	Att/g	Y/g	TD	TD/g	Int	Rating	300-Yd Gms
98	5436	2794	51.4%	38914	7.2	13.9	55.5	397.1	278	2.8	276	70.6	11

1964 Leading Passers

Name	Team	Attempts	Comp	%	Yards	Y/Att	Y/Comp	TD	Int	Rating	Relative Rating
Bart Starr	GBP	272	163	59.9	2144	7.88	13.2	15	4	97.1	135
John Unitas	IND	305	158	51.8	2824	9.26	17.9	19	6	96.4	134
Fran Tarkenton	MIN	306	171	55.9	2506	8.19	14.7	22	11	91.8	128
Rudy Bukich	CHI	160	99	61.9	1099	6.87	11.1	12	7	89	124
Sonny Jurgensen	WSH	385	207	53.8	2934	7.62	14.2	24	13	85.4	119
Frank Ryan	CLE	334	174	52.1	2404	7.2	13.8	25	19	76.7	107
Charlie Johnson	ARZ	420	223	53.1	3045	7.25	13.7	21	24	69.4	97
Bill Wade	CHI	327	182	55.7	1944	5.94	10.7	13	14	68.6	96
John Brodie	SFF	392	193	49.2	2498	6.37	12.9	14	16	64.6	90

The leaders in the major passing categories for 1964 were:

Attempts	Charlie Johnson	420	Int %	Bart Starr	1.5
Completions	Charlie Johnson	223	Rating	Bart Starr	97.1
Yards	Charlie Johnson	3045	Wins	John Unitas	12
Yards/Pass	John Unitas	9.26	Comebacks	Fran Tarkenton	4
Comp %	Rudy Bukich	61.9	Interceptions	Charlie Johnson	24
TD	Frank Ryan	25	Fumbles	Don Meredith	16
TD%	Rudy Bukich	7.5	Sacked	Don Meredith	58

1965

Johnny Unitas and Bart Starr had typically excellent seasons, and their teams ended up tied for the lead in the West. However, both Unitas and his backup Gary Cuozzo went down to injuries late in the year so halfback Tom Matte, who had been a quarterback for run-oriented

Ohio State in college, quarterbacked the Colts for the division playoff. On the first play of the playoff, Starr was injured trying to make a tackle after a fumble and bruised his ribs. Backup Zeke Bratkowski led the Packers to an overtime victory, and Starr returned the following week to lead the team past Cleveland 23–12 on a muddy field for the title. It was Hall of Fame runner Jim Brown's final game.

The top scoring team, though, was the Chicago Bears who racked up 401 points behind rookie runner Gale Sayers and surprising veteran backup quarterback Rudy Bukich. John Brodie turned in the best quarterback performance, throwing for over 3,000 yards and 30 touchdowns for the mediocre 49ers. Earl Morrall was traded from the Lions to the Giants and had a good year, while Milt Plum continued to stink in Detroit, throwing 12 touchdowns and 19 interceptions. Ed Brown played his final game as an emergency pickup by the Colts, but was not eligible for the postseason. The Cowboys drafted Craig Morton and Jerry Rhome to go with last year's future pick of Roger Staubach as competition for Don Meredith who responded with a much better season in 1965.

1965 League Passing Statistics

Games	Att	Comp	%	Yards	Y/Att	Y/Comp	Att/g	Y/g	TD	TD/g	Int	Rating	300-Yd Gms
98	5407	2774	51.3%	40349	7.5	14.5	55.2	411.7	307	3.1	277	73.5	16

1965 Leading Passers

Name	Team	Attempts	Comp	%	Yards	Y/Att	Y/Comp	TD	Int	Rating	Relative Rating
John Unitas	IND	282	164	58.2	2530	8.97	15.4	23	12	97.4	132
John Brodie	SFF	391	242	61.9	3112	7.96	12.9	30	16	95.3	130
Rudy Bukich	CHI	312	176	56.4	2641	8.46	15.0	20	9	93.7	127
Bart Starr	GBP	251	140	55.8	2055	8.19	14.7	16	9	89	121
Earl Morrall	NYG	302	155	51.3	2446	8.1	15.8	22	12	86.3	117
Fran Tarkenton	MIN	329	171	52	2609	7.93	15.3	19	11	83.8	114
Don Meredith	DAL	305	141	46.2	2415	7.92	17.1	22	13	79.9	109
Bill Munson	STL	267	144	53.9	1701	6.37	11.8	10	14	64.2	87

The leaders in the major passing categories for 1965 were:

Attempts	John Brodie	391	Rating	John Unitas	97.4
Completions	John Brodie	242	Wins	Bart Starr & Frank Ryan	10
Yards	John Brodie	3112	Comebacks	Don Meredith & Frank Ryan	
Yards/Pass	John Unitas	8.97		& Milt Plum & Norm Snead	3
Comp %	John Brodie	61.9	Interceptions	Milt Plum	19
TD	John Brodie	30	Fumbles	Rudy Bukich	12
TD%	John Unitas	8.2	Sacked	Don Meredith	38
Int %	Rudy Bukich	2.9			

1966

The two leagues announced that they would merge in four years and would begin to meet in a World Championship game after the 1966 season. Green Bay lost only two games all year by a combined four points and met high scoring (445 points) Dallas for the NFL title where they held off the rallying Cowboys at the goal line in the closing minute. In the first Super Bowl, Bart Starr hit reserve end Max McGee seven times for two scores in leading the Packers over the Chiefs 35–10.

Frank Ryan threw for 29 more touchdowns in 1966, while Sonny Jurgensen tossed 28. Charlie Johnson and Bill Nelsen went down to knee injuries, and Earl Morrall broke his wrist. Inconsistent John Brodie had a big decline, and Milt Plum was injured while throwing four touchdowns and 13 interceptions.

Plum's backup, Karl Sweetan, matched Milt with four touchdowns and 14 interceptions. However, Sweetan did hit Pat Studstill for a 99-yard touchdown pass as well. The NFL welcomed the Atlanta Falcons as their 15th team, and the Falcons were led to three wins by rookie Randy Johnson who threw 12 touchdowns and 21 interceptions.

1966 League Passing Statistics

Games	Att	Comp	%	Yards	Y/ Att	Y/ Comp	Att/g	Y/g	TD	TD/g	Int	Rating	300-Yd Gms
105	6108	3149	51.6%	42225	6.9	13.4	58.2	402.1	280	2.7	318	67.4	13

1966 Leading Passers

Name	Team	Attempts	Comp	%	Yards	Y/Att	Y/Comp	TD	Int	Rating	Relative Rating
Bart Starr	GBP	251	156	62.2	2257	8.99	14.5	14	3	105	156
Frank Ryan	CLE	382	200	52.4	2974	7.79	14.9	29	14	88.2	131
Don Meredith	DAL	344	177	51.5	2805	8.15	15.8	24	12	87.7	130
Sonny Jurgensen	WSH	436	254	58.3	3209	7.36	12.6	28	19	84.5	125
John Unitas	IND	348	195	56	2748	7.9	14.1	22	24	74	110
Fran Tarkenton	MIN	358	192	53.6	2561	7.15	13.3	17	16	73.8	109
Roman Gabriel	STL	397	217	54.7	2540	6.4	11.7	10	16	65.9	98
John Brodie	SFF	427	232	54.3	2810	6.58	12.1	16	22	65.8	98
Milt Plum	DET	146	82	56.2	943	6.46	11.5	4	13	47.8	71

The leaders in the major passing categories for 1966 were:

Attempts	Sonny Jurgensen	436	Rating	Bart Starr	105
Completions	Sonny Jurgensen	254	Wins	Bart Starr	11
Yards	Sonny Jurgensen	3209	Comebacks	Charlie Johnson	4
Yards/Pass	Bart Starr	8.99	Interceptions	John Unitas	24
Comp %	Bart Starr	62.2	Fumbles	Randy Johnson	13
TD	Frank Ryan	29	Sacked	Fran Tarkenton	
TD%	Frank Ryan	7.6		& Don Meredith	37
Int %	Bart Starr	1.2			

1967

The NFL added its 16th team, the New Orleans Saints, in 1967 and went to a four-divisions arrangement with an expanded playoff structure. Second-year Rams coach George Allen dealt Bill Munson to Detroit and made Roman Gabriel his starter. Gabriel led the Rams to a league best 398 points and an 11–1–2 record. They were beaten in the playoffs by Vince Lombardi's more experienced Packers who then moved on to win the frigid Ice Bowl over the Cowboys on Bart Starr's game-winning drive in the final minutes. The Packers then defended their Super Bowl title by beating the Raiders and became the first team since the 1929–31 Packers to win three straight league titles. No team has duplicated the feat since then. Starr had fought off nagging injuries all year and was named Super Bowl MVP for the second straight season.

Fran Tarkenton was traded to the Giants where he threw for 29 touchdowns, tied with Norm Snead behind Sonny Jurgensen's league leading 31. Frank Ryan began to have arm problems, and Bill Nelsen went down to a knee injury for the third straight year. Charlie Johnson had a different problem — he was drafted — so the Cardinals installed unknown, inexperienced backup Jim Hart who threw for 19 touchdowns, but also 30 interceptions. Steve Spurrier, Don Horn and Kent Nix were an unimpressive rookie crop, and not much better was a fiery newcomer from the CFL, Joe Kapp on the Vikings.

1967 League Passing Statistics

Games	Att	Comp	%	Yards	Y/Att	Y/Comp	Att/g	Y/g	TD	TD/g	Int	Rating	300-Yd Gms
112	6451	3292	51.0%	44801	6.9	13.6	57.6	400.0	324	2.9	366	66.6	19

1967 Leading Passers

Name	Team	Attempts	Comp	%	Yards	Y/Att	Y/Comp	TD	Int	Rating	Relative Rating
Sonny Jurgensen	WSH	508	288	56.7	3747	7.38	13.0	31	16	87.3	131
Fran Tarkenton	NYG	377	204	54.1	3088	8.19	15.1	29	19	85.9	129
Roman Gabriel	STL	371	196	52.8	2779	7.49	14.2	25	13	85.2	128
John Unitas	IND	436	255	58.5	3428	7.86	13.4	20	16	83.6	125
Norm Snead	PHL	434	240	55.3	3399	7.83	14.2	29	24	80	120
Bart Starr	GBP	210	115	54.8	1823	8.68	15.9	9	17	64.4	97
Jim Hart	ARZ	397	192	48.4	3008	7.58	15.7	19	30	58.4	88

The leaders in the major passing categories for 1967 were:

Attempts	Sonny Jurgensen	508	Rating	Sonny Jurgensen	87.3
Completions	Sonny Jurgensen	288	Wins	John Unitas & Roman Gabriel	11
Yards	Sonny Jurgensen	3747	Comebacks	John Unitas & Bart Starr	
Yards/Pass	Bart Starr	8.68		& Fran Tarkenton	3
Comp %	John Unitas	58.5	Interceptions	Jim Hart	30
TD	Sonny Jurgensen	31	Fumbles	Bill Nelsen	7
TD%	Fran Tarkenton	7.7	Sacked	Norm Snead	48
Int %	Sonny Jurgensen	3.1			

1968

The Packer dynasty was done, and into the breach stepped the 13–1 Colts, but without Johnny Unitas. Unitas missed the season with arm woes, but veteran backup Earl Morrall won the league MVP trophy with 26 touchdown passes before being ridiculed by the Jets' Joe Namath as the equivalent of the sixth best quarterback in the AFL. Namath of course guaranteed a win in Super Bowl III and backed it up, aided by Morrall's abysmal performance. The Colts won the NFL title by beating Cleveland 34–0, and the Browns had also switched quarterbacks in 1968. They replaced sore-armed Frank Ryan with former Steeler Bill Nelsen who managed to stay upright and salvage his career despite his ravaged knees.

Bart Starr had arm problems as well, and Don Meredith decided that he had taken enough of a beating and quit at the end of the season despite leading the Cowboys to a league best 431 points. Sonny Jurgensen threw a 99-yard touchdown to running back Gerry Allen in an otherwise quiet season for the redhead. Greg Landry was the most promising rookie, but did not play much behind Bill Munson in Detroit.

1968 League Passing Statistics

Games	Att	Comp	%	Yards	Y/Att	Y/Comp	Att/g	Y/g	TD	TD/g	Int	Rating	300-Yd Gms
112	5997	3093	51.6%	42095	7.0	13.6	53.5	375.8	324	2.9	327	69.6	6

1968 Leading Passers

Name	Team	Attempts	Comp	%	Yards	Y/Att	Y/Comp	TD	Int	Rating	Relative Rating
Bart Starr	GBP	171	109	63.7	1617	9.46	14.8	15	8	104.3	152
Earl Morrall	IND	317	182	57.4	2909	9.18	16.0	26	17	93.2	136

Name	Team	Attempts	Comp	%	Yards	Y/Att	Y/Comp	TD	Int	Rating	Relative Rating
Don Meredith	DAL	309	171	55.3	2500	8.09	14.6	21	12	88.4	129
Bill Nelsen	CLE	293	152	51.9	2366	8.08	15.6	19	10	86.4	126
Fran Tarkenton	NYG	337	182	54	2555	7.58	14.0	21	12	84.6	123
Sonny Jurgensen	WSH	292	167	57.2	1980	6.78	11.9	17	11	81.7	119
John Brodie	SFF	404	234	57.9	3020	7.48	12.9	22	21	78	114

The leaders in the major passing categories for 1968 were:

Attempts	John Brodie	409	Rating	Bart Starr	104.3
Completions	John Brodie	234	Wins	Earl Morrall	13
Yards	John Brodie	3020	Comebacks	Roman Gabriel	
Yards/Pass	Bart Starr	9.46		& Virgil Carter	3
Comp %	Bart Starr	63.7	Interceptions	John Brodie	21
TD	Earl Morrall	26	Fumbles	Earl Morrall	7
TD%	Bart Starr	8.8	Sacked	Bob Berry	49
Int %	Bill Munson	2.4			

1969

Johnny Unitas returned in a diminished capacity in 1969, and Bart Starr had more shoulder problems. The 12–2 Vikings, who scored 379 points behind rough and ready Joe Kapp, took the top spot in the NFL. Kapp completed just 51 percent of his wobbly passes and threw 19 touchdowns and 13 interceptions. Seven of his TDs came in a September thrashing of the shell-shocked Colts. In confronting the AFL champion Chiefs in the Super Bowl, though, Kapp came up empty and lost 23–

7. Thus, the AFL came into the merger in 1970 as an equal, all even at 2–2 in four Super Bowls.

Milt Plum ended his mediocre career as a backup in Los Angeles. The top rookies were running quarterback Bobby Douglass who threw five touchdowns and 8 interceptions and Terry Hanratty who completed just 41 percent of his passes for eight touchdowns and 13 interceptions. Roger Staubach got out of the Navy and watched Craig Morton lead the Cowboy offense.

1969 League Passing Statistics

Games	Att	Comp	%	Yards	Y/Att	Y/Comp	Att/g	Y/g	TD	TD/g	Int	Rating	300-Yd Gms
112	6345	3340	52.6%	44324	7.0	13.3	56.7	395.8	323	2.9	311	71.6	12

1969 Leading Passers

Name	Team	Attempts	Comp	%	Yards	Y/Att	Y/Comp	TD	Int	Rating	Relative Rating
Bart Starr	GBP	148	92	62.2	1161	7.84	12.6	9	6	89.9	126
Fran Tarkenton	NYG	409	220	53.8	2918	7.13	13.3	23	8	87.2	122
Roman Gabriel	STL	399	217	54.4	2549	6.39	11.7	24	7	86.8	121
Sonny Jurgensen	WSH	442	274	62	3102	7.02	11.3	22	15	85.4	119
Craig Morton	DAL	302	162	53.6	2619	8.67	16.2	21	15	85.4	119
Bill Nelsen	CLE	352	190	54	2743	7.79	14.4	23	19	78.8	110
John Brodie	SFF	347	194	55.9	2405	6.93	12.4	16	15	74.9	105
Norm Snead	PHL	379	190	50.1	2768	7.3	14.6	19	23	65.7	92
John Unitas	IND	327	178	54.4	2342	7.16	13.2	12	20	64	89
Steve Spurrier	SFF	146	81	55.5	926	6.34	11.4	5	11	54.8	76

The leaders in the major passing categories for 1969 were:

Attempts	Sonny Jurgensen	442	Int %	Roman Gabriel	1.8
Completions	Sonny Jurgensen	274	Rating	Bart Starr	89.9
Yards	Sonny Jurgensen	3102	Wins	Joe Kapp	12
Yards/Pass	Don Horn	8.96	Comebacks	Fran Tarkenton	4
Comp %	Bart Starr	62.2	Interceptions	Norm Snead	23
TD	Roman Gabriel	24	Fumbles	Bill Nelsen	8
TD%	Joe Kapp	8	Sacked	Sonny Jurgensen	40

1970

The newly merged NFL consisted of 26 teams in six divisions in 1970. The NFL adopted the AFL convention of adding names to the backs of uniforms, but not the AFL's exciting two-point conversion. The Colts, Steelers and Browns all shifted to the American Football Conference for league balance, and the Colts won the first merged Super Bowl in a sloppy triumph of graybeards Johnny Unitas and Earl Morrall over inconsistent Craig Morton. The top scoring team in a league of declining offense was the 49ers who put up 352 points behind John Brodie, but lost to Dallas in the playoffs.

Don Shula moved on to coach the Dolphins where he developed young quarterback Bob Griese into a champion. In other changes, Charlie Johnson went to the Oilers and Joe Kapp played out his option and went to the Patriots.

Neither quarterback played very well in his new city; Kapp's three touchdowns and 17 interceptions combined with backup Mike Taliaferro's four and 11 for seven touchdowns and 28 interceptions.

Frank Ryan retired, and Bart Starr should have as he continued to have arm problems. Joe Namath broke his wrist, while 40-year old George Blanda was the MVP for his clutch kicking and relief pitching at quarterback. Top rookie Terry Bradshaw threw six touchdowns and 24 interceptions. He and fellow rookie Ken Stabler would develop, but other freshmen Mike Phipps and Dennis Shaw would not. Little noticed at the time was the short passing offense that Bengals assistant coach Bill Walsh developed in Cincinnati to make the best of quarterback Virgil Carter's weak arm. The nascent West Coast Offense would begin to make an impact in the next decade.

1970 League Passing Statistics

Games	Att	Comp	%	Yards	Y/ Att	Y/ Comp	Att/g	Y/g	TD	TD/g	Int	Rating	300-Yd Gms
182	9796	5008	51.1%	65904	6.7	13.2	53.8	362.1	427	2.3	510	65.6	13

1970 Leading Passers

Name	Team	Attempts	Comp	%	Yards	Y/Att	Y/Comp	TD	Int	Rating	Relative Rating
John Brodie	SFF	378	223	59	2941	7.78	13.2	24	10	93.8	143
Sonny Jurgensen	WSH	337	202	59.9	2354	6.99	11.7	23	10	91.5	140
Craig Morton	DAL	207	102	49.3	1819	8.79	17.8	15	7	89.8	137
Fran Tarkenton	NYG	389	219	56.3	2777	7.14	12.7	19	12	82.2	125
Bob Berry	ATL	269	156	58	1806	6.71	11.6	16	13	78.1	119
John Hadl	SDC	327	162	49.5	2388	7.3	14.7	22	15	77.1	118
Daryle Lamonica	OAK	356	179	50.3	2516	7.07	14.1	22	15	76.5	117
Roman Gabriel	STL	407	211	51.8	2552	6.27	12.1	16	12	72.2	110
Bob Griese	MIA	245	142	58	2019	8.24	14.2	12	17	72.1	110
Jim Hart	ARZ	373	171	45.8	2575	6.9	15.1	14	18	61.5	94
Billy Kilmer	NOS	237	135	57	1557	6.57	11.5	6	17	55.5	85

The leaders in the major passing categories for 1970 were:

Attempts	Roman Gabriel	407	Rating	John Brodie	93.8
Completions	John Brodie	223	Wins	John Unitas & John Brodie	
Yards	John Brodie	2941		& Bob Griese	10
Yards/Pass	Craig Morton	8.79	Comebacks	Fran Tarkenton	5
Comp %	Sonny Jurgensen	59.9	Interceptions	Terry Bradshaw	24
TD	John Brodie	24	Fumbles	Dennis Shaw	10
TD%	Craig Morton	7.2	Sacked	John Hadl	42
Int %	John Brodie	2.6			

1971

The NFL tried to liberalize the rules for pass blocking a bit as zone defenses continued to strangle offenses in 1971— John Hadl led the NFL with a measly 21 touchdown passes that year. Dallas led the league in scoring with 406 points behind mobile Roger Staubach who won an extended competition with stiff Craig Morton that even saw Tom Landry revert to alternating quarterbacks for each play in a game against the Bears. The Cowboys overwhelmed the inexperienced Dolphins in a 24–3 Super Bowl win.

This was finally the final year for the ailing Bart Starr. Other veterans had health problems as well. Sonny Jurgensen went down and was replaced by Billy Kilmer in Washington. Johnny Unitas was recovering from an Achilles injury and shared duties with Earl Morrall in Baltimore, and Joe Namath was hurt again in New York. A fabled quarterback draft began to bring in new blood, however. Jim Plunkett, Archie Manning and Dan Pastorini were drafted 1–2–3, and later in the draft came Lynn Dickey, Ken Anderson, Joe Theismann, Scott Hunter and Joe Reed.

1971 League Passing Statistics

Games	Att	Comp	%	Yards	Y/Att	Y/Comp	Att/g	Y/g	TD	TD/g	Int	Rating	300-Yd Gms
182	9412	4788	50.9%	63253	6.7	13.2	51.7	347.5	289	1.6	544	58.6	11

1971 Leading Passers

Name	Team	Attempts	Comp	%	Yards	Y/Att	Y/Comp	TD	Int	Rating	Relative Rating
Roger Staubach	DAL	211	126	59.7	1882	8.92	14.9	15	4	104.8	169
Bob Griese	MIA	263	145	55.1	2089	7.94	14.4	19	9	90.9	146
Virgil Carter	CIN	222	138	62.2	1624	7.32	11.8	10	7	86.2	139
Len Dawson	KCC	301	167	55.5	2504	8.32	15.0	15	13	81.6	131
Greg Landry	DET	261	136	52.1	2237	8.57	16.4	16	13	80.9	130
Bob Berry	ATL	226	136	60.2	2005	8.87	14.7	11	16	75.9	122
Roman Gabriel	STL	352	180	51.1	2238	6.36	12.4	17	10	75.4	121
John Hadl	SDC	431	233	54.1	3075	7.13	13.2	21	25	68.9	111
Jim Plunkett	NEP	328	158	48.2	2158	6.58	13.7	19	16	68.6	110
Fran Tarkenton	NYG	386	226	58.5	2567	6.65	11.4	11	21	65.4	105
John Brodie	SFF	387	208	53.7	2642	6.83	12.7	18	24	65	105
Bill Nelsen	CLE	325	174	53.5	2319	7.14	13.3	13	23	60.3	97

The leaders in the major passing categories for 1971 were:

Attempts	John Hadl	431	Rating	Roger Staubach	104.8
Completions	John Hadl	233	Wins	Roger Staubach & Bob Griese	10
Yards	John Hadl	3075	Comebacks	Len Dawson & John Hadl &	
Yards/Pass	Roger Staubach	8.92		Terry Bradshaw & Bill Nelsen	3
Comp %	Virgil Carter	62.2	Interceptions	Dennis Shaw	26

TD	John Hadl	21	Fumbles	Bill Nelsen	10
TD%	Bob Griese	7.2	Sacked	Archie Manning	40
Int %	Roger Staubach	1.9			

1972

The NFL tinkered with the hashmarks, moving them in to 23½ yards from the sidelines, in an attempt to open up the passing game, but the passing decline continued. Billy Kilmer and Joe Namath tied for the league lead in touchdown passes with an anemic 19. Kilmer led George Allen's Over the Hill Gang in Washington to the Super Bowl where they were bested 14–7 in a dull game in which Dolphins quarterback Bob Griese threw just 11 passes and completed eight, while kicker Garo Yepremian had his only pass intercepted for a touchdown. The undefeated Dolphins led the league with 385 points despite losing Greise for half the season to a broken leg. Don Shula brought back his old reliable Earl Morrall to hand off to Larry Csonka, Mercury Morris and Jim Kiick in Miami's relentless rushing attack. The most exciting moment in the playoffs was the fourth down Immaculate Reception from Terry Bradshaw to Franco Harris by way of Jack Tatum/ Frenchy Fuqua that beat the Raiders.

Like Griese, Roger Staubach also missed most of the season to injury before returning in the playoffs. Roman Gabriel had a sore arm, and Bill Nelsen's disabled career came to a close. Meanwhile, Fran Tarkenton was re-obtained by the Vikings and started the most productive portion of his long career. In his final year in Baltimore, Johnny Unitas had one last big game in September, matching up with Joe Namath for 892 yards passing, although the Jets won the game.

Chicago's Bobby Douglass encapsuled the league's overall direction when he set a new rushing record for quarterbacks with 968 yards; he averaged 6.8 yards per rush, while his 1,246 passing yards averaged just 6.3 yards per attempt. None of the rookies (John Reaves, Joe Gilliam, Jerry Tagge and Pat Sullivan) from this crop ever developed.

1972 League Passing Statistics

Games	Att	Comp	%	Yards	Y/ Att	Y/ Comp	Att/g	Y/g	TD	TD/g	Int	Rating	300-Yd Gms
182	9011	4659	51.7%	61425	6.8	13.2	49.5	337.5	404	2.2	480	66.3	8

1972 Leading Passers

Name	Team	Attempts	Comp	%	Yards	Y/Att	Y/Comp	TD	Int	Rating	Relative Rating
Earl Morrall	MIA	150	83	55.3	1360	9.07	16.4	11	7	91	137
Billy Kilmer	WSH	225	120	53.3	1648	7.32	13.7	19	11	84.8	128
Norm Snead	NYG	325	196	60.3	2307	7.1	11.8	17	12	84	127
Fran Tarkenton	MIN	378	215	56.9	2651	7.01	12.3	18	13	80.2	121
Daryle Lamonica	OAK	281	149	53	1998	7.11	13.4	18	12	79.5	120
Len Dawson	KCC	305	175	57.4	1835	6.02	10.5	13	12	72.8	110
Joe Namath	NYJ	324	162	50	2816	8.69	17.4	19	21	72.5	109
Bob Griese	MIA	97	53	54.6	638	6.58	12.0	4	4	71.6	108
John Unitas	IND	157	88	56.1	1111	7.08	12.6	4	6	70.8	107
Craig Morton	DAL	339	185	54.6	2396	7.07	13.0	15	21	65.9	99
Archie Manning	NOS	448	230	51.3	2781	6.21	12.1	18	21	64.6	97
John Hadl	SDC	370	190	51.4	2449	6.62	12.9	15	26	56.7	85

The leaders in the major passing categories for 1972 were:

Attempts	Archie Manning	448	Rating	Earl Morrall	91
Completions	Archie Manning	230	Wins	Terry Bradshaw	11

Yards	Joe Namath	2816	Comebacks	Mike Phipps	5
Yards/Pass	Earl Morrall	9.07	Interceptions	John Hadl	26
Comp %	Norm Snead	60.3	Fumbles	Bobby Douglass &	
TD	Billy Kilmer & Joe Namath	19		Archie Manning	9
TD%	Billy Kilmer	8.4	Sacked	Archie Manning	43
Int %	Ken Anderson	2.3			

1973

Miami triumphed again in the Super Bowl; this time beating the Vikings behind Bob Griese's six of seven passing and a ton of running. Oakland shifted from Mad Bomber Daryle Lamonica to the more ball-control oriented passer Kenny Stabler in another sign of the times. The Rams, behind newly obtained John Hadl, led the NFL with 388 points. To replace Hadl, the Chargers brought in Johnny Unitas, but he proved to have nothing left. Unitas, John Brodie and Greg Cook all called it quits at the end of the year.

With Hadl in hand, the Rams dealt Roman Gabriel to the Eagles where he had a resurgence. Roger Staubach also came back from injury, but Joe Namath came down with a shoulder problem. On a positive note, Don Coryell was hired by the Cardinals and brought a fresh offensive mind to the NFL. Kenny Anderson emerged as a top quarterback in Cincinnati, and four rookies would go on to have good-to-great careers: Dan Fouts, Bert Jones, Joe Ferguson and Don Strock.

1973 League Passing Statistics

Games	Att	Comp	%	Yards	Y/Att	Y/Comp	Att/g	Y/g	TD	TD/g	Int	Rating	300-Yd Gms
182	8845	4603	52.0%	58009	6.6	12.6	48.6	318.7	378	2.1	470	64.9	10

1973 Leading Passers

Name	Team	Attempts	Comp	%	Yards	Y/Att	Y/Comp	TD	Int	Rating	Relative Rating
Roger Staubach	DAL	286	179	62.6	2428	8.49	13.6	23	15	94.6	146
Fran Tarkenton	MIN	274	169	61.7	2113	7.71	12.5	15	7	93.2	144
John Hadl	STL	258	135	52.3	2008	7.78	14.9	22	11	88.8	137
Ken Stabler	OAK	260	163	62.7	1997	7.68	12.3	14	10	88.3	136
Roman Gabriel	PHL	460	270	58.7	3219	7	11.9	23	12	86	132
Bob Griese	MIA	218	116	53.2	1422	6.52	12.3	17	8	84.3	130
Ken Anderson	CIN	329	179	54.4	2428	7.38	13.6	18	12	81.2	125
Sonny Jurgensen	WSH	145	87	60	904	6.23	10.4	6	5	77.5	119
Charley Johnson	DEN	346	184	53.2	2465	7.12	13.4	20	17	74.9	115
Jim Plunkett	NEP	376	193	51.3	2550	6.78	13.2	13	17	65.8	101

The leaders in the major passing categories for 1973 were:

Attempts	Roman Gabriel	460	Int %	Fran Tarkenton	2.6
Completions	Roman Gabriel	270	Rating	Roger Staubach	94.6
Yards	Roman Gabriel	3219	Wins	Fran Tarkenton & John Hadl	12
Yards/Pass	Roger Staubach	8.49	Comebacks	Ken Stabler	3
Comp %	Ken Stabler	62.7	Interceptions	Norm Snead	22
TD	Roger Staubach &		Fumbles	Dan Pastorini	17
	Roman Gabriel	23	Sacked	Mike Phipps	44
TD%	John Hadl	8.5			

1974

The NFL instituted a host of changes in 1974 to try to boost offense and cut down on field goals. The goal posts were moved back to the end line; after a missed field goal, the ball was returned to the line of scrimmage, not the 20, in the change of possession; kickoffs were moved back to the 35 yard line; sudden death was instituted for regular season games; receivers were to be chucked just once past the first three yards from scrimmage; and when a runner went down, play was whistled dead as soon as a defender touched him. Fran Tarkenton began to manipulate this last rule as an excuse to slide and avoid being tackled hard although the actual "quarterback sliding" rule would not come for several more years. The result of all this change was still fewer points scored however. In this at-mosphere, a rival league, the World Football League, was established, but it was undercapitalized.

Oakland led the league in points with 355 behind Snake Stabler, but Pittsburgh won the Super Bowl behind their impregnable Steel Curtain defense and a solid rushing attack. After a stiff challenge from Joe Gilliam, one of two black starting quarterbacks in 1974, Terry Bradshaw finally took control of the Steeler offense for good. In Los Angeles, last year's hero John Hadl was replaced by James Harris, the other black starting quarterback, and the Rams went to the playoffs again. The Cardinals with quarterback Jim Hart became the initial Air Coryell and won their first division title. Joe Theismann saw his first action in Washington, primarily as a punt returner. He and fellow rookies Ron Jaworski and Brian Sipe would have greater success later.

1974 League Passing Statistics

Games	Att	Comp	%	Yards	Y/Att	Y/Comp	Att/g	Y/g	TD	TD/g	Int	Rating	300-Yd Gms
182	9609	5041	52.5%	62391	6.5	12.4	52.8	342.8	376	2.1	500	64.2	11

1974 Leading Passers

Name	Team	Attempts	Comp	%	Yards	Y/Att	Y/Comp	TD	Int	Rating	Relative Rating
Ken Anderson	CIN	328	213	64.9	2667	8.13	12.5	18	10	95.7	149
Ken Stabler	OAK	310	178	57.4	2469	7.96	13.9	26	12	94.9	148
Sonny Jurgensen	WSH	167	107	64.1	1185	7.1	11.1	11	5	94.5	147
James Harris	STL	198	106	53.5	1544	7.8	14.6	11	6	85.1	132
Charley Johnson	DEN	244	136	55.7	1969	8.07	14.5	13	9	84.5	132
Billy Kilmer	WSH	234	137	58.5	1632	6.97	11.9	10	6	83.5	130
Fran Tarkenton	MIN	351	199	56.7	2598	7.4	13.1	17	12	82.1	128
Bob Griese	MIA	253	152	60.1	1968	7.78	12.9	16	15	80.9	126
Jim Hart	ARZ	388	200	51.5	2411	6.21	12.1	20	8	79.5	124
Joe Namath	NYJ	361	191	52.9	2616	7.25	13.7	20	22	69.4	108
Roger Staubach	DAL	360	190	52.8	2552	7.09	13.4	11	15	68.4	107
Len Dawson	KCC	235	138	58.7	1573	6.69	11.4	7	13	65.8	102
Jim Plunkett	NEP	352	173	49.1	2457	6.98	14.2	19	22	64.1	100

The leaders in the major passing categories for 1974 were:

Attempts	Jim Hart	388	Rating	Ken Anderson	95.7
Completions	Ken Anderson	213	Wins	Ken Stabler	12
Yards	Ken Anderson	2667	Comebacks	Joe Ferguson & Bob Griese & Bill Munson	
Yards/Pass	Ken Anderson	8.13		& Roger Staubach & Joe Namath	3
Comp %	Ken Anderson	64.9	Interceptions	Joe Namath & Jim Plunkett	22
TD	Ken Stabler	26	Fumbles	Joe Ferguson & Gary Huff	14
TD%	Ken Stabler	8.4	Sacked	Roger Staubach	45
Int %	Jim Hart	2.1			

1975

Buffalo led the league in scoring behind O.J. Simpson's 1,817 yards rushing and Joe Ferguson's 25 touchdown passes. Fran Tarkenton tied Ferguson for the league lead in TDs and moved past Johnny Unitas on the all time list. The Steelers repeated as Super Bowl champions in the first thrilling Super Bowl in years by beating Roger Staubach's Cowboys 21–17. The winning points came on a 64-yard bomb from Terry Bradshaw to Lynn Swann on which Bradshaw was knocked out cold.

Dallas reintroduced the Shotgun Formation for some passing plays and soon most teams would add it to their offenses. Bob Griese had toe problems; Jim Plunkett had shoulder problems; and Mike Phipps, Archie Manning and Joe Namath just had problems. Phipps threw four touchdowns to 19 interceptions; Maning threw seven and 20, while Namath threw 15 and 28. Old pros George Blanda, Len Dawson and Charlie Johnson all hung up their cleats in 1975, as did the bankrupt WFL. Newcomers Steve Grogan and Steve Bartkowski showed promise for the future, and Bert Jones emerged as a new star in Baltimore.

1975 League Passing Statistics

Games	Att	Comp	%	Yards	Y/Att	Y/Comp	Att/g	Y/g	TD	TD/g	Int	Rating	300-Yd Gms
182	9973	5231	52.5%	66595	6.7	12.7	54.8	365.9	433	2.4	533	65.8	16

1975 Leading Passers

Name	Team	Attempts	Comp	%	Yards	Y/Att	Y/Comp	TD	Int	Rating	Relative Rating
Ken Anderson	CIN	377	228	60.5	3169	8.41	13.9	21	11	93.9	143
Fran Tarkenton	MIN	425	273	64.2	2994	7.04	11.0	25	13	91.8	140
Len Dawson	KCC	140	93	66.4	1095	7.82	11.8	5	4	90	137
Bert Jones	IND	344	203	59	2483	7.22	12.2	18	8	89.1	135
Terry Bradshaw	PIT	286	165	57.7	2055	7.19	12.5	18	9	88	134
Bob Griese	MIA	191	118	61.8	1693	8.86	14.3	14	13	86.6	132
Joe Ferguson	BUF	321	169	52.6	2426	7.56	14.4	25	17	81.3	124
Roger Staubach	DAL	348	198	56.9	2666	7.66	13.5	17	16	78.5	119
Billy Kilmer	WSH	346	178	51.4	2440	7.05	13.7	23	16	77.2	117
Jim Hart	ARZ	345	182	52.8	2507	7.27	13.8	19	19	71.7	109

The leaders in the major passing categories for 1975 were:

Attempts	Fran Tarkenton	425	Int %	Bert Jones	2.3
Completions	Fran Tarkenton	273	Rating	Ken Anderson	93.9
Yards	Ken Anderson	3169	Wins	Terry Bradshaw &	
Yards/Pass	Bob Griese	8.86		Fran Tarkenton	12
Comp %	Len Dawson	66.4	Comebacks	Jim Hart & Dan Pastorini	4
TD	Joe Ferguson &		Interceptions	Joe Namath	28
	Fran Tarkenton	25	Fumbles	Craig Morton	9
TD%	Joe Ferguson	7.8	Sacked	Archie Manning	49

1976

The defending champion Steelers had injury problems on offense and had to rely on their defense to win their last nine games by allowing just 28 points in that streak. They were ousted in the playoffs, however, by the Raiders who rode Snake Stabler's 27 touchdown passes and 66.7 completion percentage to a Super Bowl triumph over Fran Tarkenton's Vikings. Bert Jones

threw for over 3,000 yards in leading the Colts to a league best 417 points, and Dan Fouts and Steve Grogan began to emerge as stars.

Two expansion teams, the Seattle Seahawks and the Tampa Bay Buccaneers, began operations respectively directed by impressive rookie Jim Zorn and disappointing veteran Steve Spurrier. Spurrier, along with Earl Morrall, Norm Snead and Randy Johnson finished his career in 1976. Zorn set new rookie marks with

208 completions and 2,571 yards. Richard Todd was the big name in the draft, but several NFL rookies came out of the failed WFL including Danny White, Pat Haden and Gary Danielson. Former rookie phenom Jim Plunkett was traded to the 49ers, while Archie Manning missed the season with a shoulder injury. Joe Ferguson hurt his back and Lynn Dickey hurt his shoulder. Joe Namath threw four touchdowns and 16 interceptions. Technology offered a positive step as 30-second play clocks were installed in all stadiums.

1976 League Passing Statistics

Games	Att	Comp	%	Yards	Y/ Att	Y/ Comp	Att/g	Y/g	TD	TD/g	Int	Rating	300-Yd Gms
196	10260	5351	52.2%	67990	6.6	12.7	52.3	346.9	432	2.2	497	67.0	13

1976 Leading Passers

Name	Team	Attempts	Comp	%	Yards	Y/Att	Y/Comp	TD	Int	Rating	Relative Rating
Ken Stabler	OAK	291	194	66.7	2737	9.41	14.1	27	17	103.4	154
Bert Jones	IND	343	207	60.3	3104	9.05	15.0	24	9	102.5	153
Joe Ferguson	BUF	151	74	49	1086	7.19	14.7	9	1	90	134
Greg Landry	DET	291	168	57.7	2191	7.53	13.0	17	8	89.6	134
James Harris	STL	158	91	57.6	1460	9.24	16.0	8	6	89.6	134
Fran Tarkenton	MIN	412	255	61.9	2961	7.19	11.6	17	8	89.3	133
Jim Hart	ARZ	388	218	56.2	2946	7.59	13.5	18	13	82	122
Roger Staubach	DAL	369	208	56.4	2715	7.36	13.1	14	11	79.9	119
Bob Griese	MIA	272	162	59.6	2097	7.71	12.9	11	12	78.9	118
Dan Fouts	SDC	359	208	57.9	2535	7.06	12.2	14	15	75.4	112
Steve Grogan	NEP	302	145	48	1903	6.3	13.1	18	20	60.6	90

The leaders in the major passing categories for 1976 were:

Attempts	Jim Zorn	439	Rating	Ken Stabler	103.4
Completions	Fran Tarkenton	255	Wins	Bert Jones & Steve Grogan	
Yards	Bert Jones	3104		& Roger Staubach & Ken Stabler	11
Yards/Pass	Ken Stabler	9.41	Comebacks	Ken Stabler & Bill Kilmer & Jim Hart	4
Comp %	Ken Stabler	66.7	Interceptions	Jim Zorn	27
TD	Ken Stabler	27	Fumbles	Gary Marangi	12
TD%	Ken Stabler	9.3	Sacked	Greg Landry	55
Int %	Joe Ferguson	0.7			

1977

The NFL again tried to open up the passing lanes in 1977. The head slap was outlawed to slow down pass rushers, and pass defenders were only permitted to chuck receivers one time. Oakland led the league in points again with 351, but were beaten on a controversial touchdown in the AFC championship game in Denver. The Broncos were led by resurrected failure Craig Morton who faced the man who beat him out in Dallas, Roger Staubach, in the Super Bowl. Staubach went 17 for 25 with a touchdown while Morton went four for 15 with four interceptions as the Cowboys crushed Denver's Orange Crush 27–10.

Dan Fouts missed most of the year as a hold-out, and Archie Manning returned to New Orleans healthy. Mike Phipps was traded to the Bears after failing in Cleveland. Fran Tarkenton, Lynn Dickey and Bill Munson each broke a leg on the same weird Sunday in November, while Steve Bartkowski had knee problems and Brian Sipe had a bad shoulder. Far removed from their glory days, John Hadl's career ended in Houston, Joe Namath's in Los Angeles and Roman Gabriel's in Philadelphia. Tommy Kramer and Vince Ferragamo were the rookies with the most upside. The Bucs set a new standard for inept quarterback play with Gary Huff's 3 touchdowns and 13 interceptions, Randy Hedberg's 0 and 10 and Jeb Blount's 0 and seven, a combination of 3 touchdown passes to 30 interceptions.

1977 League Passing Statistics

Games	Att	Comp	%	Yards	Y/ Att	Y/ Comp	Att/g	Y/g	TD	TD/g	Int	Rating	300-Yd Gms
196	9786	5022	51.3%	63594	6.5	12.7	49.9	324.5	388	2.0	562	61.2	5

1977 Leading Passers

Name	Team	Attempts	Comp	%	Yards	Y/Att	Y/Comp	TD	Int	Rating	Relative Rating
Bob Griese	MIA	307	180	58.6	2252	7.34	12.5	22	13	87.8	143
Roger Staubach	DAL	361	210	58.2	2620	7.26	12.5	18	9	87	142
Pat Haden	STL	216	122	56.5	1551	7.18	12.7	11	6	84.5	138
Craig Morton	DEN	254	131	51.6	1929	7.59	14.7	14	8	82	134
Bert Jones	IND	393	224	57	2686	6.83	12.0	17	11	80.8	132
Ken Stabler	OAK	294	169	57.5	2176	7.4	12.9	20	20	75.2	123
Terry Bradshaw	PIT	314	162	51.6	2523	8.04	15.6	17	19	71.4	117
Fran Tarkenton	MIN	258	155	60.1	1734	6.72	11.2	9	14	69.2	113
Steve Grogan	NEP	305	160	52.5	2162	7.09	13.5	17	21	65.2	107
Jim Hart	ARZ	355	186	52.4	2542	7.16	13.7	13	20	64.3	105
Brian Sipe	CLE	195	112	57.4	1233	6.32	11.0	9	14	61.8	101
Ron Jaworski	PHL	346	166	48	2183	6.31	13.2	18	21	60.4	99
Joe Ferguson	BUF	457	221	48.4	2803	6.13	12.7	12	24	54.8	90

The leaders in the major passing categories for 1977 were:

Attempts	Joe Ferguson	457	Int %	Scott Hunter	2
Completions	Bert Jones	224	Rating	Bob Griese	87.8
Yards	Joe Ferguson	2803	Wins	Roger Staubach & Craig Morton	12
Yards/Pass	Terry Bradshaw	8.04	Comebacks	Craig Morton & Bob Avellini	4
Comp %	Fran Tarkenton	60.1	Interceptions	Joe Ferguson	24
TD	Bob Griese	22	Fumbles	Joe Ferguson	12
TD%	Bob Griese	7.2	Sacked	Ron Jaworski	47

13

1978–1993: Full Throttle

The year 1978 is the demarcation line for contemporary football. By 1977, defenses had clamped down so tightly in the NFL that team scoring was down to 17 points per game on average, the league passer rating was down to 61.5, and there were only five 300-yard passing games recorded all year. To usher in a new era of football, the NFL opened up the rules for the offense. Defensive contact of receivers was restricted to the first five yards from the line of scrimmage, pass blockers were permitted to extend their arms and open their hands, and quarterbacks were given additional protection by being ruled down when "in the grasp" of a defender.

League statistics inched up in 1978 to 18 points per game, a passer rating of 65 and 15 300-yard games, but made a leap forward in 1979 to 20 points per game, a passer rating of 70.4 and 44 300-yard games. Overall, the 1978–93 period compared very favorably to the ball control period immediately before it. Completion percentage increased from 51.7 percent to 56 percent. Passes per game went from 53 to 62, and the percentage of passes in comparison to running plays went from 44 percent to 50 percent. Touchdowns went up, interceptions went down and passer rating went from 66.6 to 74.5. There was a 300-yard passing performance every 4½ games rather than every 10 games in the earlier era.

The only decline was in yards per completion which went from 13.3 to 12.5 yards, and that was reflective of the increasing spread of 49ers coach Bill Walsh's offense of short, high percentage passes. Walsh's offense is also a factor in the continuing decline of interceptions. There were other approaches to passing offense during this time as well, and all had roots in the 1960s. Air Coryell in San Diego was the descendant of Sid Gillman's Lightning Bolt Attack from the AFL, and Don Coryell's assistant Joe Gibbs brought that approach to Washington and added more power running to the mix. Bill Parcells in New York tended more to a Smash Mouth offense that emphasized power running in a similar fashion to Vince Lombardi's Packers. The Run and Shoot was brought to the NFL by Jerry Glanville in Houston and was more reminiscent of the 49ers' failed Shotgun Formation offense from 1961. In this pass-happy era, the Run and Shoot had enough success that it has since been incorporated as a minor part into the offensive games of many teams.

Defenses countered with their own angles. In Chicago, Buddy Ryan devised the 46 Defense that utilized eight defenders close to the line and lots of varied blitz packages. Dick LeBeau in Cincinnati and Pittsburgh developed the Zone Blitz where a defensive lineman drops back into zone coverage to replace a blitzing linebacker or safety. The 3–4 defense peaked during this time and then receded as more teams found the venerable 4–3 more versatile to stop the newer passing attacks.

During this time, football continued to become more of a coaches' game. At the start of this period, about half the coaches called the plays either by sending in a wide receiver with the play or by having a coach or backup quarterback give hand signals from the sideline. By the end of the 1980s, only Jim Kelly of the Bills and Boomer Esiason of the Bengals sometimes called their own plays, and that was just when those teams were running their No Huddle offenses. The No Huddle itself was a response to defensive coaches sending in different squadrons of players for almost every play depending on the down and distance. Of course, offensive coaches did the same thing.

On the social front, black quarterbacks finally began to be accepted as legitimate starters because of the ongoing success had by Randall Cunningham and Warren Moon and the stunning Super bowl performance of Doug Williams in the 1980s. Hall of Famers Roger Staubach, Fran Tarkenton, Bob Griese and Terry Bradshaw finished their careers at the outset of this period, as did stars Billy Kilmer, Craig Morton, Bert Jones, Ken Stabler and Jim Hart. This period of the full throttle air attack saw the prime years of Joe Montana, Dan Fouts, Joe Theismann, Steve Bartkowski, Phil Simms, Dan Marino, John Elway, Jim Kelly, Dave Krieg, Boomer Esiason, Bernie Kosar, Randall Cunningham, Troy Aikman and Steve Young. Future stars Brett Favre and Drew Bledsoe opened their careers at the conclusion of this era. The biggest disappointments of the era included Richard Todd, Todd Blackledge, Tony Eason, Jay Schroeder and Vinny Testaverde.

The aggregate league-wide passing data for the period from 1978 through 1993 in the NFL was:

Games	Att	Comp	%	Yards	Y/Att	Y/Comp	Att/g	Y/g	TD	TD/g	Int	Rating	300-Yd Gm
3472	214139	119909	56.0	1499055	7.0	12.5	61.7	431.8	8815	2.5	8816	74.5	815

Twenty-five quarterbacks threw for at least 18,000 yards during this era. Their percentage of completed passes ranged from Jay Schroeder's 50.3 percent to Joe Montana's 63.5 percent.

Schroeder and Steve Grogan were the only quarterbacks to average at least 14 yards per completion, but other long bombers in the group included Dan Fouts, Lynn Dickey, Boomer

Esiason and Phil Simms. By contrast, Ken O'Brien, Bernie Kosar and Steve DeBerg were most noted for their short passing games. Only Grogan, DeBerg and Joe Ferguson threw more interceptions than TD passes during this time, while Joe Montana had a remarkable nearly 2:1 touchdown pass to interception ratio. Tops in bumps and bruises were Simms, Dave Krieg, John Elway and Randall Cunningham all found themselves sacked more than 400 times. Marino, with his quick release, was sacked the fewest times despite throwing the most passes. The 25 top passers of the Full Throttle era, ranked by passer rating:

Name	Attempts	Completions	%	Yards	Y/Att	Y/Comp	TD	Int	Sacked	Rating
Joe Montana	4898	3110	63.5%	37268	7.6	12.0	257	130	294	93.1
Dan Marino	5434	3219	59.2%	40720	7.5	12.6	298	168	160	88.1
Jim Kelly	3494	2112	60.4%	26413	7.6	12.5	179	126	226	86.0
Dan Fouts	4510	2712	60.1%	35382	7.8	13.0	220	185	219	84.1
Neil Lomax	3153	1817	57.6%	22771	7.2	12.5	136	90	362	82.7
Boomer Esiason	3851	2185	56.7%	29092	7.6	13.3	190	140	248	82.1
Dave Krieg	4178	2431	58.2%	30485	7.3	12.5	217	163	411	82.0
Danny White	2920	1744	59.7%	21711	7.4	12.4	153	129	238	81.9
Bernie Kosar	3213	1889	58.8%	22314	6.9	11.8	119	81	261	81.9
Ken O'Brien	3602	2110	58.6%	25094	7.0	11.9	128	98	353	80.4
Warren Moon	4546	2632	57.9%	33685	7.4	12.8	196	166	315	80.4
Randall Cunningham	2751	1540	56.0%	19043	6.9	12.4	131	87	366	80.3
Steve Bartkowski	2945	1696	57.6%	20989	7.1	12.4	136	107	290	80.0
Joe Theismann	3224	1862	57.8%	22832	7.1	12.3	143	116	284	79.5
Phil Simms	4647	2576	55.4%	33462	7.2	13.0	199	157	477	78.5
Lynn Dickey	2368	1364	57.6%	18558	7.8	13.6	121	123	219	78.1
Jim Everett	3277	1847	56.4%	23758	7.2	12.9	142	123	186	78.1
Brian Sipe	2736	1550	56.7%	19337	7.1	12.5	126	111	169	77.2
John Elway	4890	2723	55.7%	34246	7.0	12.6	183	167	370	75.9
Ron Jaworski	3647	1967	53.9%	25288	6.9	12.9	160	135	299	75.1
Steve DeBerg	4926	2821	57.3%	33686	6.8	11.9	192	200	287	74.4
Tommy Kramer	3594	1982	55.1%	24352	6.8	12.3	154	154	243	72.7
Steve Grogan	2712	1435	52.9%	20845	7.7	14.5	136	149	193	72.0
Jay Schroeder	2570	1293	50.3%	18553	7.2	14.3	110	101	197	72.0
Joe Ferguson	3194	1713	53.6%	20975	6.6	12.2	134	145	193	69.2

Overall, the quarterbacks who led the league the most times in passing categories over this era were:

Attempts	Dan Marino	4	Wins	Joe Montana	3
Completions	Dan Marino	5	Comebacks	Bernie Kosar & Boomer Esiason	
Yards	Dan Marino	5		& Joe Montana	2
Yards/Pass	Steve Young	3	Interceptions	Vinny Testaverde & Warren Moon	
Comp %	Joe Montana	5		& Dave Krieg & Brian Sipe	2
TD	Dan Marino	3	Fumbles	Danny White & Randall Cunningham	
TD%	Dan Marino	3		& Warren Moon & Eric Hipple	2
Int %	Ken O'Brien	3	Sacked	Randall Cunningham	5
Rating	Steve Young	3			

And the complete list of leaders for 1978–1993 is as follows:

Attempts	Dan Marino	5,434	Int %	Jeff Hostetler	2.09
Completions	Dan Marino	3,219	Rating	Joe Montana	93.1
Yards	Dan Marino	40,720	Wins	Joe Montana	108
Yards/Pass	Steve Young	8.1	Comebacks	John Elway & Dan Marino	28
Comp %	Joe Montana	63.5	Interceptions	Steve DeBerg	200
TD	Dan Marino	298	Fumbles	Dave Krieg	124
TD%	Terry Bradshaw	6.32	Sacked	Phil Simms	477

1978

This was a watershed year in NFL history. The schedule expanded to 16 games, a second wild card team was added to the playoffs and passing rules were greatly liberalized by restricting any contact with a receiver to the first five yards and by allowing pass blockers to extend their arms and open their hands. The league made these sweeping changes because teams were down to averaging just 17 points per game. The effect of the changes was a slight improvement in 1978, but once players and coaches got used to their new offensive freedom, passing offenses bloomed in 1979. Despite the changes, Marv Levy was even dusting off the old Wing T in Kansas City.

The Super Bowl was a rematch between the top scoring (384 points) Cowboys led by Roger Staubach and the Steelers led by blonde bomber Terry Bradshaw. Bradshaw threw four touchdowns to Staubach's three (although Jackie Smith dropped one for Roger) to win the exciting game 35–31. During the season, five quarterbacks threw for over 3,000 yards, and Dan Fouts, in his first great year under new coach Don Coryell, missed the mark by one and Pat Haden by just five. Steve Grogan ran for 539 yards.

Disaster befell Joe Pisarcik when he fumbled away a handoff against the Eagles in the closing seconds to hand them a victory since known in Philly as the "Miracle of the Meadowlands." Disaster also struck Jim Plunkett who was cut by the lowly 49ers. Fran Tarkenton in his last season averaged just 10 yards a completion and threw 32 interceptions. Billy Kilmer and Bobby Douglass also played their last games. Two rookies of note were Doug Williams who completed just 38 percent of his passes in Tampa and Steve DeBerg who completed 45 percent of his passes in San Francisco while throwing eight touchdowns and 22 interceptions.

1978 League Passing Statistics

Games	Att	Comp	%	Yards	Yl/Att	Yl/Comp	Att/g	Y/g	TD	TD/g	Int	Rating	300-Yd Gms
224	11829	6278	53.1	79557	6.7	12.7	52.8	355.2	468	2.1	639	65.0	15

1978 Leading Passers

Name	Team	Attempts	Comp	%	Yards	Y/Att	Y/Comp	TD	Int	Rating	Relative Rating
Roger Staubach	DAL	413	231	55.9	3190	7.72	13.8	25	16	84.9	131
Terry Bradshaw	PIT	368	207	56.3	2915	7.92	14.1	28	20	84.7	130
Dan Fouts	SDC	381	224	58.8	2999	7.87	13.4	24	20	83	128
Bob Griese	MIA	235	148	63	1791	7.62	12.1	11	11	82.4	127
Archie Manning	NOS	471	291	61.8	3416	7.25	11.7	17	16	81.7	126
Brian Sipe	CLE	399	222	55.6	2906	7.28	13.1	21	15	80.7	124
Jim Zorn	SEA	443	248	56	3283	7.41	13.2	15	20	72.1	111
Fran Tarkenton	MIN	572	345	60.3	3468	6.06	10.1	25	32	68.9	106
Jim Hart	ARZ	477	240	50.3	3121	6.54	13.0	16	18	66.7	103
Ken Stabler	OAK	406	237	58.4	2944	7.25	12.4	16	30	63.3	97

The leaders in the major passing categories for 1978 were:

Attempts	Fran Tarkenton	572	Rating	Roger Staubach	84.9
Completions	Fran Tarkenton	345	Wins	Terry Bradshaw	14
Yards	Fran Tarkenton	3,468	Comebacks	Dan Pastorini & Steve Bartkowski	
Yards/Pass	Terry Bradshaw	7.92		& Steve Grogan	6
Comp %	Bob Griese	63	Interceptions	Fran Tarkenton	32
TD	Terry Bradshaw	28	Fumbles	Brian Sipe	12
TD%	Terry Bradshaw	7.6	Sacked	Jim Zorn	44
Int %	Craig Morton	3			

1979

Pittsburgh topped the league with 416 points and repeated as Super Bowl champs by beating the underdog Rams 31–19 on the strength of another 300-yard Super Bowl performance by Terry Bradshaw. Dan Fouts piloted Air Coryell in San Diego to the tune of 4,082 yards, while Bill Walsh installed his offense in San Francisco for Steve DeBerg with rookie Joe Montana waiting in the wings. League-wide, teams averaged 20 points per game.

The NFL tried to protect quarterbacks more by having officials whistle a play dead when a quarterback was merely "in the grasp" of a defender; spearing was outlawed as well. However, Bert Jones hurt his shoulder for the second straight year, Dan Pastorini hurt his shoulder and his ribs, Pat Haden broke a finger and Gary Danielson tore up his knee. Pastorini's rib injury in the playoffs led to a new piece of quarterback equipment — the flak jacket. Roger Staubach had one concussion too many and retired on the strength of a 27-touchdown, 3,586-yard season. Veteran backup Bill Munson also retired. With Montana barely playing, the top rookie was Phil Simms in New York who threw for 13 touchdowns and 14 interceptions. Steve Fuller threw six touchdowns and 14 interceptions in Marv Levy's Wing T and Jeff Komlo threw for 2,238 yards in Detroit but with 23 interceptions.

1979 League Passing Statistics

Games	Att	Comp	%	Yards	Y/ Att	Y/ Comp	Att/g	Y/g	TD	TD/g	Int	Rating	300-Yd Gms
224	12979	7022	54.1	89170	6.9	12.7	57.9	398.1	538	2.4	597	70.4	44

1979 Leading Passers

Name	Team	Attempts	Comp	%	Yards	Y/Att	Y/Comp	TD	Int	Rating	Relative Rating
Roger Staubach	DAL	461	267	57.9	3586	7.78	13.4	27	11	92.3	131
Joe Theismann	WSH	395	233	59	2797	7.08	12.0	20	13	83.9	119
Dan Fouts	SDC	530	332	62.6	4082	7.7	12.3	24	24	82.6	117
Ken Stabler	OAK	498	304	61	3615	7.26	11.9	26	22	82.2	117
Ken Anderson	CIN	339	189	55.8	2340	6.9	12.4	16	10	80.7	115
Jim Zorn	SEA	505	285	56.4	3661	7.25	12.8	20	18	77.7	110
Steve Grogan	NEP	423	206	48.7	3286	7.77	16.0	28	20	77.4	110
Archie Manning	NOS	420	252	60	3169	7.55	12.6	15	20	75.6	107
Greg Landry	IND	457	270	59.1	2932	6.42	10.9	15	15	75.3	107
Brian Sipe	CLE	535	286	53.5	3793	7.09	13.3	28	26	73.4	104
Steve DeBerg	SFF	578	347	60	3652	6.32	10.5	17	21	73.1	104

The leaders in the major passing categories for 1979 were:

Attempts	Steve DeBerg	578	Int %	Roger Staubach	2.4
Completions	Steve DeBerg	347	Rating	Roger Staubach	92.3
Yards	Dan Fouts	4,082	Wins	Terry Bradshaw & Dan Fouts	12
Yards/Pass	Richard Todd	7.96	Comebacks	Brian Sipe	7
Comp %	Dan Fouts	62.6	Interceptions	Brian Sipe	26
TD	Brian Sipe	28	Fumbles	Dan Fouts	13
TD%	Steve Grogan	6.6	Sacked	Ken Anderson	46

1980

Under new quarterback Danny White, Dallas led the league in scoring with 454 points, but they were beaten in the playoffs by the gritty Eagles led by Ron Jaworski who was being tutored by pass master Sid Gillman. The Raiders traded long-time starter Ken Stabler for the stronger-armed Dan Pastorini, but Pastorini broke his leg. Into the breach stepped forgotten

Jim Plunkett, and he led the wild card Raiders to a Super Bowl win with three touchdowns against Philadelphia. Oakland had gotten by the Kardiac Kid Browns whose Brian Sipe had a career year with 30 touchdowns and 4,132 yards, but threw a critical interception in the playoff loss to the Raiders.

Dan Fouts improved to 4,715 yards and 30 touchdowns, while Steve Bartkowski in Atlanta and Vince Ferragamo in Los Angeles threw 31 and 30 touchdowns respectively. Joe Montana won the starting job by midseason in San Francisco and served notice that he had arrived by leading the 49ers back from a 35–0 deficit to beat the Saints in overtime in a December contest. Journeyman backup Tom Owen had the gall to hold out in New England, and Matt Robinson was traded to Denver where he threw two touchdowns to 12 interceptions. Richard Todd, who had beaten out Robinson with the Jets, threw for 17 touchdowns and 30 interceptions. Hall of Famer Bob Griese retired in Miami and was replaced by rookie scrambler David Woodley who tossed 14 touchdowns and 17 interceptions. Other rookies in 1980 included Dave Krieg, Scott Brunner, Eric Hipple, Mark Malone, Marc Wilson, Paul McDonald and Gary Hogeboom.

1980 League Passing Statistics

Games	Att	Comp	%	Yards	Y/Att	Y/Comp	Att/g	Y/g	TD	TD/g	Int	Rating	300-Yd Gms
224	12705	7699	60.6	95935	7.6	12.5	56.7	428.3	606	2.7	627	79.4	54

1980 Leading Passers

Name	Team	Attempts	Comp	%	Yards	Y/Att	Y/Comp	TD	Int	Rating	Relative Rating
Brian Sipe	CLE	554	337	60.8	4132	7.46	12.3	30	14	91.4	124
Ron Jaworski	PHL	451	257	57	3529	7.82	13.7	27	12	91	123
Vince Ferragamo	STL	404	240	59.4	3199	7.92	13.3	30	19	89.7	122
Steve Bartkowski	ATL	463	257	55.5	3544	7.65	13.8	31	16	88.2	120
Joe Montana	SFF	273	176	64.5	1795	6.58	10.2	15	9	87.8	119
Dan Fouts	SDC	589	348	59.1	4715	8.01	13.5	30	24	84.7	115
Archie Manning	NOS	509	309	60.7	3716	7.3	12.0	23	20	81.8	111
Danny White	DAL	436	260	59.6	3287	7.54	12.6	28	25	80.7	109
Craig Morton	DEN	301	183	60.8	2150	7.14	11.7	12	13	77.8	106
Tommy Kramer	MIN	522	299	57.3	3582	6.86	12.0	19	23	72.2	98
Ken Stabler	TEN	457	293	64.1	3202	7.01	10.9	13	28	68.7	93

The leaders in the major passing categories for 1980 were:

Attempts	Dan Fouts	589	Rating	Brian Sipe	91.4
Completions	Dan Fouts	348	Wins	Ron Jaworski & Danny White	
Yards	Dan Fouts	4,715		& Steve Bartkowski	12
Yards/Pass	Steve Grogan	8.09	Comebacks	Terry Bradshaw	5
Comp %	Joe Montana	64.5	Interceptions	Richard Todd	30
TD	Steve Bartkowski	31	Fumbles	Steve Fuller	16
TD%	Vince Ferragamo	7.4	Sacked	Steve Fuller	49
Int %	Brian Sipe	2.5			

1981

Paul Brown had passed over Bill Walsh as his successor in Cincinnati in 1976, and Walsh got his revenge by leading the 49ers past the Bengals 26–21 in Super Bowl XVI. Walsh had trained both starting quarterbacks in the game, and the 49ers' Joe Montana got the victory while Ken Anderson threw for 300 yards in defeat. Walsh had taken the 49ers from two wins to a championship in three years. San Diego led the league in points with 478 and prevailed 41–38 in a sweltering overtime thriller in Miami in the playoffs, but were shut down by the Bengals and a minus 59 wind chill in the AFC championship. Dan Fouts set a new mark with 4,802 yards passing and threw 33 touchdowns. Walsh had helped develop him as well.

Like Fouts, Steve Bartkowski had a second consecutive season with 30 touchdown passes. The combination of David Woodley and Don Strock became known as WoodStrock in Miami, while the combination of Pat Haden and Dan Pastorini in LA threw 11 touchdowns and 27 interceptions.

Brian Sipe led the league in picks with 25, but was glad to know that "stickum" was outlawed by the league, both for receivers and defensive backs. Phil Simms had shoulder troubles, Terry Bradshaw hurt his hand and Jim Zorn injured his ankle. Trailblazer James Harris appeared in his last game, while Neil Lomax, Dave Wilson, Wade Wilson and Rich Campbell each played in their first. Lomax threw for four touchdowns and 11 interceptions while Dave Wilson threw just one touchdown to 11 interceptions.

1981 League Passing Statistics

Games	Att	Comp	%	Yards	Y/Att	Y/Comp	Att/g	Y/g	TD	TD/g	Int	Rating	300-Yd Gms
224	14180	7745	54.6	99721	7.0	12.9	63.3	445.2	591	2.6	609	72.9	57

1981 Leading Passers

Name	Team	Attempts	Comp	%	Yards	Y/Att	Y/Comp	TD	Int	Rating	Relative Rating
Ken Anderson	CIN	479	300	62.6	3754	7.84	12.5	29	10	98.4	135
Dan Fouts	SDC	609	360	59.1	4802	7.89	13.3	33	17	90.6	124
Craig Morton	DEN	376	225	59.8	3195	8.5	14.2	21	14	90.5	124
Joe Montana	SFF	488	311	63.7	3565	7.31	11.5	19	12	88.4	121
Danny White	DAL	391	223	57	3098	7.92	13.9	22	13	87.5	120
Jim Zorn	SEA	397	236	59.4	2788	7.02	11.8	13	9	82.4	113
Richard Todd	NYJ	497	279	56.1	3231	6.5	11.6	25	13	81.8	112
Steve Bartkowski	ATL	533	297	55.7	3829	7.18	12.9	30	23	79.2	109
Joe Theismann	WSH	496	293	59.1	3568	7.19	12.2	19	20	77.3	106
Tommy Kramer	MIN	593	322	54.3	3912	6.6	12.1	26	24	72.6	100
Brian Sipe	CLE	567	313	55.2	3876	6.84	12.4	17	25	68.2	94

The leaders in the major passing categories for 1981 were:

Attempts	Dan Fouts	609	Int %	Ken Anderson	2.1
Completions	Dan Fouts	360	Rating	Ken Anderson	98.4
Yards	Dan Fouts	4,802	Wins	Joe Montana	13
Yards/Pass	Steve Grogan	8.61	Comebacks	Marc Wilson	4
Comp %	Joe Montana	63.7	Interceptions	Brian Sipe	25
TD	Dan Fouts	33	Fumbles	Eric Hipple & Danny White	14
TD%	Ken Anderson	6.1	Sacked	Craig Morton	54

1982

The NFL experienced its first regular season players' strike, and the 57-day work stoppage shortened the season to nine games and created a 16-team postseason tournament. Washington was the victor of the tournament, beating Miami 27–17 in the Super Bowl with Joe Theismann throwing to his "Fun Bunch" of receivers and handing off to thundering John Rig-

gins to run behind the celebrated Hogs line. San Diego led the league with 288 points in this abbreviated season, and Dan Fouts was on pace to top his yardage record.

The Raiders left Oakland for Los Angeles, and Vince Ferragamo returned to the LA Rams from an unsuccessful, one-year foray to Canada. Archie Manning was traded to the Oilers, Ken Stabler went to the Saints, Bert Jones to the Rams, and Steve DeBerg to Denver. None of these quarterbacks succeeded in their new residences. Jones actually played his last game in Los Angeles, and Craig Morton finished his career in Denver. Jim McMahon was an impertinent, impressive rookie, throwing nine touchdowns to seven interceptions and completing 57 percent of his passes. Art Schlichter, Mike Pagel, Mark Kofler and Bob Gagliano were not so impressive as rookies or over the rest of their careers.

1982 League Passing Statistics

Games	Att	Comp	%	Yards	Y/ Att	Y/ Comp	Att/g	Y/g	TD	TD/g	Int	Rating	300-Yd Gms
126	7933	4474	56.4	55657	7.0	12.4	63.0	441.7	320	2.5	349	73.4	35

1982 Leading Passers

Name	Team	Attempts	Comp	%	Yards	Y/Att	Y/Comp	TD	Int	Rating	Relative Rating
Ken Anderson	CIN	309	218	70.6	2495	8.07	11.4	12	9	95.3	130
Dan Fouts	SDC	330	204	61.8	2883	8.74	14.1	17	11	93.3	127
Joe Theismann	WSH	252	161	63.9	2033	8.07	12.6	13	9	91.3	124
Danny White	DAL	247	156	63.2	2079	8.42	13.3	16	12	91.1	124
Joe Montana	SFF	346	213	61.6	2613	7.55	12.3	17	11	88	120
Terry Bradshaw	PIT	240	127	52.9	1768	7.37	13.9	17	11	81.4	111
Steve Bartkowski	ATL	262	166	63.4	1905	7.27	11.5	8	11	77.9	106
Ron Jaworski	PHL	286	167	58.4	2076	7.26	12.4	12	12	77.5	106
Tommy Kramer	MIN	308	176	57.1	2037	6.61	11.6	15	12	77.3	105
Ken Stabler	NOS	189	117	61.9	1343	7.11	11.5	6	10	71.8	98

The leaders in the major passing categories for 1982 were:

Attempts	Joe Montana	346	Int %	Steve Fuller	2.2
Completions	Ken Anderson	218	Rating	Ken Anderson	95.3
Yards	Dan Fouts	2,883	Wins	Joe Theismann & Jim Plunkett	8
Yards/Pass	Dan Fouts	8.74	Comebacks	Jim Plunkett	5
Comp %	Ken Anderson	70.6	Interceptions	Joe Ferguson	16
TD	Joe Montana & Dan Fouts & Terry Bradshaw	17	Fumbles	Danny White	10
			Sacked	Ron Jaworski	31
TD%	Terry Bradshaw	7.1			

1983

The defending champion Redskins were the focal point of the NFL, scoring a league best 541 points and being nicked 48–47 by the Packers in a memorable Monday Night Football game that saw 785 yards passing by Joe Theismann and Lynn Dickey. However, they were upset in the Super Bowl by Jim Plunkett and the Raiders, 38–9. Green Bay's Dickey led the league with 4,458 yards, 32 touchdowns and 29 interceptions.

This was the year of the most fabled quarterback draft in history. Hall of Famers, John Elway, Dan Marino and Jim Kelly plus Ken O'Brien, Tony Eason and Todd Blackledge were all taken in the first round. Kelly signed with the new USFL spring football league. Elway refused to report to the Colts, and they were forced to trade his rights to Denver for Mark Herrmann and tackle Chris Hinton. Another Colt quarterback, Art Schlichter, was suspended for gambling, and at the end of the season, the entire Colt franchise snuck out of Baltimore for Indianapolis. Elway struggled as a rookie with seven touchdowns and 14 interceptions, but Marino threw 20 touchdowns to just six interceptions and completed 58 percent of his passes. Dave Krieg of Seattle defeated both of these icons in the playoffs before losing to Plunkett's Raiders in the AFC championship. Terry Bradshaw had elbow problems and was forced to retire. Dan Pastorini chose to retire as well rather than take any more punishment.

1983 League Passing Statistics

Games	Att	Comp	%	Yards	Y/ Att	Y/ Comp	Att/g	Y/g	TD	TD/g	Int	Rating	300-Yd Gms
224	14047	7993	56.9	100922	7.2	12.6	62.7	450.5	625	2.8	620	75.9	65

1983 Leading Passers

Name	Team	Attempts	Comp	%	Yards	Y/Att	Y/Comp	TD	Int	Rating	Relative Rating
Steve Bartkowski	ATL	432	274	63.4	3167	7.33	11.6	22	5	97.6	129
Joe Theismann	WSH	459	276	60.1	3714	8.09	13.5	29	11	97	128
Dan Marino	MIA	296	173	58.4	2210	7.47	12.8	20	6	96	126
Dave Krieg	SEA	243	147	60.5	2139	8.8	14.6	18	11	95	125
Joe Montana	SFF	515	332	64.5	3910	7.59	11.8	26	12	94.6	125
Dan Fouts	SDC	340	215	63.2	2975	8.75	13.8	20	15	92.5	122
Lynn Dickey	GBP	484	289	59.7	4458	9.21	15.4	32	29	87.3	115
Danny White	DAL	533	334	62.7	3980	7.47	11.9	29	23	85.6	113
Ken Anderson	CIN	297	198	66.7	2333	7.86	11.8	12	13	85.6	113
Bill Kenney	KCC	603	346	57.4	4348	7.21	12.6	24	18	80.8	106
Brian Sipe	CLE	496	291	58.7	3566	7.19	12.3	26	23	79.1	104

The leaders in the major passing categories for 1983 were:

Attempts	Bill Kenney	603	Int %	Steve Bartkowski	1.2
Completions	Bill Kenney	346	Rating	Steve Bartkowski	97.6
Yards	Lynn Dickey	4,458	Wins	Joe Theismann	14
Yards/Pass	Lynn Dickey	9.21	Comebacks	Lynn Dickey	5
Comp %	Ken Anderson	66.7	Interceptions	Lynn Dickey	29
TD	Lynn Dickey	32	Fumbles	Eric Hipple	12
TD%	Dave Krieg	7.4	Sacked	Ron Jaworski	53

1984

In Dan Marino's record-setting sophomore season, he threw for 5,084 yards and 48 touchdowns in leading the Dolphins to a league best 513 points. In the Super Bowl, however, it was the other quarterback with a passer rating over 100, Joe Montana, who emerged victorious as San Francisco topped Miami 38–16 with Montana throwing for 331 yards and three touchdowns. Behind Marino, the Cardinals' Neil Lomax threw for 4,614 yards, and the Giants' Phil Simms finally shook off the injuries that had plagued him the previous two seasons and threw for 4,044 yards.

The extensive injury list included Ron Jaworski's leg, Jim McMahon's kidney, Jim Plunkett's stomach muscle, Steve Bartkowski's knee, Ken Anderson's back and shoulder, Joe Ferguson's ankle and Steve Fuller's ankle. Because of his leg, Jaworski's record streak of 116 consecutive starts ended. Steve DeBerg was beaten out by John Elway and sent to Tampa. Another 1983 draftee, Ken O'Brien, saw his first action for the Jets and threw six touchdowns and seven interceptions. Warren Moon came down from Canada as a free agent and signed with the Oilers; he threw for over 3,000 yards and 12 touchdowns as a 27-year-old rookie. Other rookies of note included Boomer Esiason, Jeff Hostetler and Steve Pelluer. At the opposite end were veterans Jim Hart, Ken Stabler, Archie Manning and Greg Landry who all finished their long careers in 1984.

1984 League Passing Statistics

Games	Att	Comp	%	Yards	Y/ Att	Y/ Comp	Att/g	Y/g	TD	TD/g	Int	Rating	300-Yd Gms
224	14325	8076	56.4	102233	7.1	12.7	64.0	456.4	615	2.7	584	76.1	68

1984 Leading Passers

Name	Team	Attempts	Comp	%	Yards	Y/Att	Y/Comp	TD	Int	Rating	Relative Rating
Dan Marino	MIA	564	362	64.2	5084	9.01	14.0	48	17	108.9	143
Joe Montana	SFF	432	279	64.6	3630	8.4	13.0	28	10	102.9	135
Tony Eason	NEP	431	259	60.1	3228	7.49	12.5	23	8	93.4	123
Neil Lomax	ARZ	560	345	61.6	4614	8.24	13.4	28	16	92.5	122
Steve Bartkowski	ATL	269	181	67.3	2158	8.02	11.9	11	10	89.7	118
Lynn Dickey	GBP	401	237	59.1	3195	7.97	13.5	25	19	85.6	112
Dan Fouts	SDC	507	317	62.5	3740	7.38	11.8	19	17	83.4	110
Dave Krieg	SEA	480	276	57.5	3671	7.65	13.3	32	24	83.3	109
Ken Anderson	CIN	275	175	63.6	2107	7.66	12.0	10	12	81	106
Phil Simms	NYG	533	286	53.7	4044	7.59	14.1	22	18	78.1	103

The leaders in the major passing categories for 1984 were:

Attempts	Dan Marino	564	Int %	Joe Pisarcik	1.7
Completions	Dan Marino	362	Rating	Dan Marino	108.9
Yards	Dan Marino	5,014	Wins	Joe Montana	15
Yards/Pass	Dan Marino	9.01	Comebacks	Richard Todd & Tony Eason	4
Comp %	Steve Bartkowski	67.3	Interceptions	Dave Krieg	24
TD	Dan Marino	48	Fumbles	Warren Moon	17
TD%	Dan Marino	8.5	Sacked	Tony Eason	59

1985

This was the year of the Bears and their vaunted 46 defense, but Chicago also led the league with 456 points en route to demolishing every team in their path, including the Patriots 46–10 in the Super Bowl. Tony Eason got New England to the championship as a wild card team, but was removed from the Super Bowl after going zero for six passing and looking unmistakably terrified. The Bears' oft-injured Jim McMahon managed 15 touchdowns and 2,392 yards in 13 games. Dan Marino was the only quarterback to beat the Bears; he threw for 20 percent fewer yards and 35 percent fewer touchdowns than 1984, but still led the league in both as he came back down toward earth. John Elway and Ken O'Brien both had their first 3,000-yard seasons as passers, as did Boomer Esiason.

Among the remarkable performances in 1985 were Phil Simms's 513-yard game against Cincinnati, Ron Jaworski's 99-yard touchdown pass to Mike Quick for the winning score in overtime against the Falcons, and the conclusion of Dave Krieg's streak of 28 games throwing a touchdown pass. In contrast, Nebraska Cornhuskers Vince Ferragamo and Bruce Mathison in Buffalo combined for nine touchdowns and 31 interceptions.

The rules were changed so that a quarterback sliding at any point or taking a knee in the final two minutes of a half is considered down. Joe Theismann, however, was sacked violently by Lawrence Taylor during a Monday Night Football game and had his leg gruesomely snapped to end his career. Lynn Dickey, tired of the pounding, benched himself and then retired. Steve Bartkowski and Richard Todd also reached the end of the line. Bernie Kosar threw seven touchdowns and 1,578 yards as a rookie, but 34-year-old rookie Dieter Brock from Canada set a new mark with 2,658 yards in his one season in the NFL. Fellow newcomers Randall Cunningham, Jay Schroeder, Frank Reich, Steve Bono and USFL graduates Steve Young and Bobby Hebert would all have much longer careers.

1985 League Passing Statistics

Games	Att	Comp	%	Yards	Y/Att	Y/Comp	Att/g	Y/g	TD	TD/g	Int	Rating	300-Yd Gms
224	14423	7911	54.8	101518	7.0	12.8	64.4	453.2	598	2.7	602	73.5	66

1985 Leading Passers

Name	Team	Attempts	Comp	%	Yards	Y/Att	Y/Comp	TD	Int	Rating	Relative Rating
Ken O'Brien	NYJ	488	297	60.9	3888	7.97	13.1	25	8	96.2	131
Boomer Esiason	CIN	431	251	58.2	3443	7.99	13.7	27	12	93.2	127
Joe Montana	SFF	494	303	61.3	3653	7.39	12.1	27	13	91.3	124
Dan Fouts	SDC	430	254	59.1	3638	8.46	14.3	27	20	88.1	120
Dan Marino	MIA	567	336	59.3	4137	7.3	12.3	30	21	84.1	114
Dieter Brock	STL	365	218	59.7	2658	7.28	12.2	16	13	82	111
Danny White	DAL	450	267	59.3	3157	7.02	11.8	21	17	80.6	110
Phil Simms	NYG	495	275	55.6	3829	7.74	13.9	22	20	78.6	107
Dave Krieg	SEA	532	285	53.6	3602	6.77	12.6	27	20	76.2	104
John Elway	DEN	605	327	54	3891	6.43	11.9	22	23	70.2	95

The leaders in the major passing categories for 1985 were:

Attempts	John Elway	605	Int %	Ken O'Brien	1.6
Completions	Dan Marino	336	Rating	Ken O'Brien	96.2
Yards	Dan Marino	4,137	Wins	Dan Marino	12
Yards/Pass	Dan Fouts	8.46	Comebacks	John Elway	6
Comp %	Joe Montana	61.3	Interceptions	Tommy Kramer	26
TD	Dan Marino	30	Fumbles	Phil Simms	16
TD%	Dan Fouts	6.3	Sacked	Ken O'Brien	62

1986

Dan Marino cranked it back up with 44 touchdowns and 4,746 yards in leading Miami to a league best 430 points, but John Elway's Broncos represented the AFC in the Super Bowl where they lost to the Giants. New York's Phil Simms completed an astounding 22 of 25 passes for 268 yards in the 39–20 victory. Elway's highlight in 1986 was The Drive, a 98-yard drive in the closing minutes to force overtime in the AFC championship win over Bernie Kosar's Browns. The USFL folded, and former Houston Gambler Jim Kelly became the last of the 1983 draftees to join the NFL. Among them, Marino, Kelly, Elway, O'Brien and Tony Eason all surpassed 3,000 yards passing, while Todd Blackledge was stuck at 1,200. Washington's Jay Schroeder passed for 4,109 yards, second highest in the league, but completed just 51 percent of his passes and tossed 22 interceptions. Warren Moon led the league in picks with 26 against only 13 touchdowns. Randall Cunningham ran for 540 yards and was sacked 72 times in his first season as a starter.

While Jim Kelly is not considered a true rookie because of his USFL experience, he did throw for 3,593 yards in his first year. Doug Flutie also joined the NFL from the USFL, while Jim Everett, Jack Trudeau, Bubby Brister and Chuck Long all were new draftees. Joe Montana missed much of the year after back surgery, and Jim McMahon was brutalized by Packer defender Charles Martin who lifted up the Bear quarterback and threw him down on his bad shoulder. Jim Plunkett and Ken Anderson both retired after 16 years, and Steve Bartkowski and Vince Ferragamo also played their last games. Instant replay was instituted on an experimental basis.

1986 League Passing Statistics

Games	Att	Comp	%	Yards	Y/Att	Y/Comp	Att/g	Y/g	TD	TD/g	Int	Rating	300-Yd Gms
224	14469	8014	55.4	101128	7.0	12.6	64.6	451.5	586	2.6	581	74.1	60

1986 Leading Passers

Name	Team	Attempts	Comp	%	Yards	Y/Att	Y/Comp	TD	Int	Rating	Relative Rating
Tommy Kramer	MIN	372	208	55.9	3000	8.06	14.4	24	10	92.6	125
Dan Marino	MIA	623	378	60.7	4746	7.62	12.6	44	23	92.5	125
Dave Krieg	SEA	375	225	60	2921	7.79	13.0	21	11	91	123
Tony Eason	NEP	448	276	61.6	3328	7.43	12.1	19	10	89.2	120
Boomer Esiason	CIN	469	273	58.2	3959	8.44	14.5	24	17	87.7	118
Ken O'Brien	NYJ	482	300	62.2	3690	7.66	12.3	25	20	85.8	116
Bernie Kosar	CLE	531	310	58.4	3854	7.26	12.4	17	10	83.8	113
Jim Kelly	BUF	480	285	59.4	3593	7.49	12.6	22	17	83.3	112
Joe Montana	SFF	307	191	62.2	2236	7.28	11.7	8	9	80.7	109
Eric Hipple	DET	305	192	63	1919	6.29	10.0	9	11	75.6	102
Jay Schroeder	WSH	541	276	51	4109	7.6	14.9	22	22	72.9	98

The leaders in the major passing categories for 1986 were:

Attempts	Dan Marino	623	Int %	Bernie Kosar	1.9
Completions	Dan Marino	378	Rating	Tommy Kramer	92.6
Yards	Dan Marino	4,746	Wins	Phil Simms	14
Yards/Pass	Boomer Esiason	8.44	Comebacks	Bernie Kosar	6
Comp %	Eric Hipple	63	Interceptions	Warren Moon	26
TD	Dan Marino	44	Fumbles	Jack Trudeau	13
TD%	Dan Marino	7.1	Sacked	Randall Cunningham	72

1987

In spite of the travesty of the 1982 strike, NFL owners and players upped the ante in 1987 with a second regular season strike. However, this time scabs were recruited to replace the unionized players for three games that counted in the standings during a 15-game season. Joe Montana returned to lead the 49ers to a league best 459 points. Montana had 31 touchdowns and 13 interceptions, and his newly-acquired backup Steve Young had 10 and zero. However, they were upset by Washington in the playoffs. The Redskins went on to win the championship by running roughshod over the Broncos behind the first black quarterback to play in a Super Bowl, Doug Williams. Washington signed the veteran quarterback after the USFL folded, but he didn't become the starter till the very end of the season. In the Super Bowl, Williams threw for four touchdowns in a 35-point second quarter to clinch the win.

Jerry Glanville's Houston Oilers unveiled a new offense called the Run and Shoot that featured four wideouts and one back. Warren Moon had his first good season in the new offense throwing for 21 touchdowns. Dan Marino's streak of 30 consecutive games with a touchdown pass ended. Randall Cunningham ran for 505 yards. Dan Fouts and Jim Zorn finished their careers, while Vinny Testaverde, Don Majkowski, Chris Miller, Jim Harbaugh and Rich Gannon all started theirs. A new rule permitted throwing the ball into the ground immediately after taking the snap as a way to stop the clock without incurring an intentional grounding penalty. Replacement quarterbacks of note included Erik Kramer who would later surface in Detroit, Sean Payton who would go on to coach in the NFL and Rick Neuheisel who became a prominent college coach.

1987 League Passing Statistics

Games	Att	Comp	%	Yards	Y/Att	Y/Comp	Att/g	Y/g	TD	TD/g	Int	Rating	300-Yd Gms
210	13491	7396	54.8	93822	7.0	12.7	64.2	446.8	611	2.9	540	75.2	58

1987 Leading Passers

Name	Team	Attempts	Comp	%	Yards	Y/Att	Y/Comp	TD	Int	Rating	Relative Rating
Joe Montana	SFF	398	266	66.8	3054	7.67	11.5	31	13	102.1	136
Bernie Kosar	CLE	389	241	62	3033	7.8	12.6	22	9	95.4	127
Phil Simms	NYG	282	163	57.8	2230	7.91	13.7	17	9	90	120
Dan Marino	MIA	444	263	59.2	3245	7.31	12.3	26	13	89.2	119
Neil Lomax	ARZ	463	275	59.4	3387	7.32	12.3	24	12	88.5	118
Dave Krieg	SEA	294	178	60.5	2131	7.25	12.0	23	15	87.6	116
Jim McMahon	CHI	210	125	59.5	1639	7.8	13.1	12	8	87.4	116
Jim Kelly	BUF	419	250	59.7	2798	6.68	11.2	19	11	83.8	111
John Elway	DEN	410	224	54.6	3198	7.8	14.3	19	12	83.4	111
Randall Cunningham	PHL	406	223	54.9	2786	6.86	12.5	23	12	83	110
Ken O'Brien	NYJ	393	234	59.5	2696	6.86	11.5	13	8	82.8	110
Boomer Esiason	CIN	440	240	54.5	3321	7.55	13.8	16	19	73.1	97

The leaders in the major passing categories for 1987 were:

Attempts	Neil Lomax	463	Wins	Bobby Hebert	10
Completions	Neil Lomax	275	Comebacks	Boomer Esiason, Warren Moon,	
Yards	Neil Lomax	3,387		Danny White, Joe Montana,	
Yards/Pass	Wade Wilson	7.98		Jim McMahon, Mark Malone	
Comp %	Joe Montana	66.8		and Randall Cunningham	3
TD	Joe Montana	31	Interceptions	Chuck Long	20
TD%	Dave Krieg	7.8	Fumbles	Randall Cunningham	12
Int %	Ken O'Brien	2	Sacked	Randall Cunningham	54
Rating	Joe Montana	102.1			

1988

Joe Montana beat back Steve Young's challenge during the 1988 season in San Francisco and led the 49ers to a 20–16 victory over Cincinnati in the Super Bowl. Montana drove the Niners 92 yards in the final three minutes to beat the league's top scoring Bengals (448 points) in coach Bill Walsh's last game. Cincinnati and Buffalo both developed a No Huddle Offense to combat defensive personnel packages, and Detroit adopted the Run and Shoot as its offense. Dan Marino threw for 521 yards in an October game against the Jets, and Randall Cunningham had another big season, running for 624 yards and throwing for 3,808.

The Cardinals left St. Louis for Phoenix after 28 years. Steve DeBerg was off to Kansas City as Vinny Testaverde beat him out in Tampa. Vinny threw for 13 touchdowns and 35 interceptions in his second season. Jay Schroeder was traded to Oakland, and then Doug Williams had an appendectomy so Mark Rypien got his shot to start in Washington. Other newcomers included Steve Beuerlein, Chris Chandler and Kelly Stouffer. Neil Lomax was forced to quit because of an arthritic hip, and Gary Danielson retired with leg problems. Danny White and his coach Tom Landry both came to the end of the trail in Dallas. The circumference of the ball shrank a quarter of an inch, and the 30-second clock became the 45-second clock, although 30 seconds was still the time allotted for administrative stoppages of play.

1988 League Passing Statistics

Games	Att	Comp	%	Yards	Y/Att	Y/Comp	Att/g	Y/g	TD	TD/g	Int	Rating	300-Yd Gms
224	14131	7670	54.3	97635	6.9	12.7	63.1	435.9	556	2.5	553	72.9	52

1988 Leading Passers

Name	Team	Attempts	Comp	%	Yards	Y/Att	Y/Comp	TD	Int	Rating	Relative Rating
Boomer Esiason	CIN	388	223	57.5	3572	9.21	16.0	28	14	97.4	134
Dave Krieg	SEA	228	134	58.8	1741	7.64	13.0	18	8	94.6	130
Wade Wilson	MIN	332	204	61.4	2746	8.27	13.5	15	9	91.5	126
Jim Everett	STL	517	308	59.6	3964	7.67	12.9	31	18	89.2	122
Warren Moon	TEN	294	160	54.4	2327	7.91	14.5	17	8	88.4	121
Joe Montana	SFF	397	238	59.9	2981	7.51	12.5	18	10	87.9	121
Neil Lomax	ARZ	443	255	57.6	3395	7.66	13.3	20	11	86.7	119
Bernie Kosar	CLE	259	156	60.2	1890	7.3	12.1	10	7	84.3	116
Phil Simms	NYG	479	263	54.9	3359	7.01	12.8	21	11	82.1	113
Dan Marino	MIA	606	354	58.4	4434	7.32	12.5	28	23	80.8	111
Jim Kelly	BUF	452	269	59.5	3380	7.48	12.6	15	17	78.2	107
Randall Cunningham	PHL	560	301	53.8	3808	6.8	12.7	24	16	77.6	106

The leaders in the major passing categories for 1988 were:

Attempts	Dan Marino	606	Int %	Ken O'Brien	1.7
Completions	Dan Marino	354	Rating	Boomer Esiason	97.4
Yards	Dan Marino	4,434	Wins	Jim Kelly & Boomer Esiason	12
Yards/Pass	Boomer Esiason	9.21	Comebacks	Boomer Esiason & Bernie Kosar	4
Comp %	Wade Wilson	61.4	Interceptions	Vinny Testaverde	35
TD	Jim Everett	31	Fumbles	Randall Cunningham	12
TD%	Dave Krieg	7.9	Sacked	Randall Cunningham	57

1989

Defending champion San Francisco led the league with 442 points and roared through the playoffs under new coach George Seifert, outscoring their opponents 126–26 in three post-season games. Joe Montana threw for five touchdowns and won his third Super Bowl MVP trophy to go with his fourth championship ring. John Elway lost his third Super Bowl, completing just 10 of 26 passes.

Plan B Free Agency was ushered in, and the Packers signed several bit players who Don "Majik Man" Majkowski drove to a record-tying seven fourth quarter comeback wins. Majkowski led the league with 4,318 yards. Buffalo devel-oped its rapid-fire K-Gun offense and entrusted the play calling to Jim Kelly. Randall Cunningham had another big year on the ground with 621 yards rushing. Vinny Testaverde dropped from 35 interceptions to 22, but still led the league. Mike Ditka packed Jim McMahon off to San Diego, and Doug Williams and Ron Jaworski retired. Disappointing Todd Blackledge became the first of the class of 1983 to drop out of football. In Dallas, Troy Aikman and Steve Walsh were both first round picks, but Aikman won the starting job, throwing for nine touchdowns and 18 interceptions. Rodney Peete, Stan Humphries, Billy Joe Tolliver, Timm Rosenbach and Anthony Dilweg were rookies of lesser notice in 1989 as well.

1989 League Passing Statistics

Games	Att	Comp	%	Yards	Y/Att	Y/Comp	Att/g	Y/g	TD	TD/g	Int	Rating	300-Yd Gms
224	14338	8000	55.8	102456	7.1	12.8	64.0	457.4	582	2.6	559	75.6	66

1989 Leading Passers

Name	Team	Attempts	Comp	%	Yards	Y/Att	Y/Comp	TD	Int	Rating	Relative Rating
Joe Montana	SFF	386	271	70.2	3521	9.12	13.0	26	8	112.4	149

Name	Team	Attempts	Comp	%	Yards	Y/Att	Y/Comp	TD	Int	Rating	Relative Rating
Boomer Esiason	CIN	455	258	56.7	3525	7.75	13.7	28	11	92.1	122
Jim Everett	STL	518	304	58.7	4310	8.32	14.2	29	17	90.6	120
Warren Moon	TEN	464	280	60.3	3631	7.83	13.0	23	14	88.9	118
Mark Rypien	WSH	476	280	58.8	3768	7.92	13.5	22	13	88.1	116
Jim Kelly	BUF	391	228	58.3	3130	8.01	13.7	25	18	86.2	114
Bobby Hebert	NOS	353	222	62.9	2686	7.61	12.1	15	15	82.7	109
Don Majkowski	GBP	599	353	58.9	4318	7.21	12.2	27	20	82.3	109
Dan Marino	MIA	550	308	56	3997	7.27	13.0	24	22	76.9	102
Steve DeBerg	KCC	324	196	60.5	2529	7.81	12.9	11	16	75.8	100
Ken O'Brien	NYJ	477	288	60.4	3346	7.01	11.6	12	18	74.3	98

The leaders in the major passing categories for 1989 were:

Attempts	Don Majkowski	599	Rating	Joe Montana	112.4
Completions	Don Majkowski	353	Wins	Randall Cunningham & Jim Everett	
Yards	Don Majkowski	4,318		& Joe Montana & Phil Simms	11
Yards/Pass	Joe Montana	9.12	Comebacks	Don Majkowski	7
Comp %	Joe Montana	70.2	Interceptions	Vinny Testaverde & Dan Marino	22
TD	Jim Everett	29	Fumbles	Dave Krieg	18
TD%	Joe Montana	6.7	Sacked	Ken O'Brien	50
Int %	Chris Miller	1.9			

1990

San Francisco's drive for a three-peat was upended by the Giants in the NFC championship. With Phil Simms out with a foot injury, Jeff Hostetler took New York to the Super Bowl by outlasting the 49ers 15–13, and then slowed down Buffalo to win the title 20–19. Joe Montana was hurt in the conference title game and would not return for almost two years. The Bills were the top scoring team in the league with 428 points, and this was the first of their four straight Super Bowl appearances. They would never again come as close to winning as Scott Norwood's wide right 47-yard field goal try, though.

Warren Moon threw for 527 yards against the Chiefs in one game and led the league in yards and touchdowns in the Oilers' flashy Run and Shoot offense. Under former Oilers coach Jerry Glanville, the Atlanta Falcons adapted their version of the Run and Shoot, the Red Gun. Randall Cunningham was dubbed the "Ultimate Weapon" by *Sports Illustrated* and ran for 942 yards on top of his 3,466 yards passing. Steve DeBerg settled in with the Chiefs and threw 23 touchdowns to just four interceptions. Promising starters Bobby Hebert of New Orleans and Don Majkowski of Green Bay both held out of training camp. Majkowski then hurt his shoulder and was never the same. Troy Aikman hurt his shoulder, too, but his backup Steve Walsh was sent to New Orleans for draft picks. Joe Ferguson, Steve Grogan, Tony Eason and Tommy Kramer all ended their careers, while Jeff George, Andre Ware, Scott Mitchell, John Friesz, Peter Tom Willis and Tommy Hodson started theirs — clearly a net loss for the NFL.

1990 League Passing Statistics

Games	Att	Comp	%	Yards	Y/Att	Y/Comp	Att/g	Y/g	TD	TD/g	Int	Rating	300-Yd Gms
224	13516	7572	56.0	94700	7.0	12.5	60.3	422.8	575	2.6	480	77.3	42

1990 Leading Passers

Name	Team	Attempts	Comp	%	Yards	Y/Att	Y/Comp	TD	Int	Rating	Relative Rating
Jim Kelly	BUF	346	219	63.3	2829	8.18	12.9	24	9	101.2	131

Name	Team	Attempts	Comp	%	Yards	Y/Att	Y/Comp	TD	Int	Rating	Relative Rating
Warren Moon	TEN	584	362	62	4689	8.03	13.0	33	13	96.8	125
Steve DeBerg	KCC	444	258	58.1	3444	7.76	13.3	23	4	96.3	125
Phil Simms	NYG	311	184	59.2	2284	7.34	12.4	15	4	92.7	120
Randall Cunningham	PHL	465	271	58.3	3466	7.45	12.8	30	13	91.6	118
Joe Montana	SFF	520	321	61.7	3944	7.58	12.3	26	16	89	115
Dan Marino	MIA	531	306	57.6	3563	6.71	11.6	21	11	82.6	107
Jim Everett	STL	554	307	55.4	3989	7.2	13.0	23	17	79.3	103
John Elway	DEN	502	294	58.6	3526	7.02	12.0	15	14	78.5	101
Boomer Esiason	CIN	402	224	55.7	3031	7.54	13.5	24	22	77	100
Dave Krieg	SEA	448	265	59.2	3194	7.13	12.1	15	20	73.6	95

The leaders in the major passing categories for 1990 were:

Attempts	Warren Moon	584	Int%	Steve DeBerg	0.9
Completions	Warren Moon	362	Rating	Jim Kelly	101.2
Yards	Warren Moon	4,689	Wins	Joe Montana	14
Yards/Pass	Jay Schroeder	8.53	Comebacks	Troy Aikman	6
Comp %	Jim Kelly	63.3	Interceptions	Dave Krieg	20
TD	Warren Moon	33	Fumbles	Warren Moon	18
TD%	Jim Kelly	6.9	Sacked	Randall Cunningham	49

1991

The Redskins were the top scoring team in the league with 485 points, and it was their turn to beat Buffalo in the Super Bowl, which they did 37–24 behind Mark Rypien's 292 yards passing. Jim Kelly had the most touchdown passes in the NFL, while Warren Moon had the most yards and interceptions. Joe Montana was out all year with a bad elbow, and his replacement Steve Young sprained his knee to give way to Steve Bono. Young and Bono combined for 28 touchdowns and 12 interceptions in San Francisco as Young won the first of four straight passing crowns. Randall Cunningham blew out his knee in the very first game, and the Eagles re-

lied on backup Jim McMahon and their defense, but missed the playoffs just like the 49ers.

For the defending champion Giants, Jeff Hostetler beat out veteran Phil Simms as starter under new head coach Ray Handley, but he threw just five touchdown passes. Neil O'Donnell had the best rookie season with 11 touchdowns, seven interceptions and 1,963 yards, but Brett Favre, who had two interceptions in four pass attempts from the Falcons doghouse, had the brightest future. Other newcomers Todd Marinovich, Browning Nagle and Dan McGwire all flamed out within five years. League wide, 1991 was the first season since 1978 in which the average points per game dipped below 20.

1991 League Passing Statistics

Games	Att	Comp	%	Yards	Y/Att	Y/Comp	Att/g	Y/g	TD	TD/g	Int	Rating	300-Yd Gms
224	13951	8003	57.4	96100	6.9	12.0	62.3	429.0	511	2.3	488	76.2	53

1991 Leading Passers

Name	Team	Attempts	Comp	%	Yards	Y/Att	Y/Comp	TD	Int	Rating	Relative Rating
Steve Young	SFF	279	180	64.5	2517	9.02	14.0	17	8	101.8	134
Mark Rypien	WSH	421	249	59.1	3564	8.47	14.3	28	11	97.9	128
Jim Kelly	BUF	474	304	64.1	3844	8.11	12.6	33	17	97.6	128
Steve Bono	SFF	237	141	59.5	1617	6.82	11.5	11	4	88.5	116

Name	Team	Attempts	Comp	%	Yards	Y/Att	Y/Comp	TD	Int	Rating	Relative Rating
Bernie Kosar	CLE	494	307	62.1	3487	7.06	11.4	18	9	87.8	115
Troy Aikman	DAL	363	237	65.3	2754	7.59	11.6	11	10	86.7	114
Dan Marino	MIA	549	318	57.9	3970	7.23	12.5	25	13	85.8	113
Jeff Hostetler	NYG	285	179	62.8	2032	7.13	11.4	5	4	84.1	110
Dave Krieg	SEA	285	187	65.6	2080	7.3	11.1	11	12	82.5	108
Warren Moon	TEN	655	404	61.7	4690	7.16	11.6	23	21	81.7	107
Chris Miller	ATL	413	220	53.3	3103	7.51	14.1	26	18	80.6	106

The leaders in the major passing categories for 1991 were:

Attempts	Warren Moon	655	Int %	Jeff Hostetler	1.4
Completions	Warren Moon	404	Rating	Steve Young	101.8
Yards	Warren Moon	4,690	Wins	Mark Rypien	14
Yards/Pass	Steve Young	9.02	Comebacks	Hugh Millen	6
Comp %	Dave Krieg	65.6	Interceptions	Warren Moon	21
TD	Jim Kelly	33	Fumbles	John Elway & Jim Everett	12
TD%	Jim Kelly	7	Sacked	Jeff George	56

1992

San Francisco scored the most points in the league, 431, but they found a nasty nemesis in a new Dallas dynasty led by the maturing Troy Aikman. The Cowboys brushed past the 49ers and then crushed the Bills 52–17 in the Super Bowl. Buffalo's season highlight was the 32-point comeback engineered by backup quarterback Frank Reich over the Oilers in the playoffs. The Niners were led again by Steve Young, one of two quarterbacks to rush for over 500 yards in 1992, along with Eagles Comeback Player of the Year, Randall Cunningham. This was the first year of true free agency, and Dave Krieg was the most significant signing, moving from Seattle to Kansas City where he replaced Steve De-Berg. Brett Favre was traded to Green Bay and emerged as a star after he was forced to start due to an injury to Don Majkowski in the third game.

John Elway had a terrible year with 10 touchdowns and 17 interceptions and visibly chafed under his long-time coach Dan Reeves. When Elway was hurt, Reeves reverted to an old Tom Landry move and alternated his rookie quarterbacks Tommy Maddox and Shawn Moore on each play in one game. Other newcomers included David Klingler, Dave Brown, Kent Graham, Scott Zolak and Jeff Blake, so it is no surprise that average scoring dipped below 19 points per game in 1992.

1992 League Passing Statistics

Games	Att	Comp	%	Yards	Y/Att	Y/Comp	Att/g	Y/g	TD	TD/g	Int	Rating	300-Yd Gms
224	13408	7705	57.5	92011	6.9	11.9	59.9	410.8	516	2.3	519	75.3	43

1992 Leading Passers

Name	Team	Attempts	Comp	%	Yards	Y/Att	Y/Comp	TD	Int	Rating	Relative Rating
Steve Young	SFF	402	268	66.7	3465	8.62	12.9	25	7	107	142
Chris Miller	ATL	253	152	60.1	1739	6.87	11.4	15	6	90.7	120
Troy Aikman	DAL	473	302	63.8	3445	7.28	11.4	23	14	89.5	119
Warren Moon	TEN	346	224	64.7	2521	7.29	11.3	18	12	89.3	119
Randall Cunningham	PHL	384	233	60.7	2775	7.23	11.9	19	11	87.3	116
Brett Favre	GBP	471	302	64.1	3227	6.85	10.7	18	13	85.3	113
Dan Marino	MIA	554	330	59.6	4116	7.43	12.5	24	16	85.1	113

Name	Team	Attempts	Comp	%	Yards	Y/Att	Y/Comp	TD	Int	Rating	Relative Rating
Jim Kelly	BUF	462	269	58.2	3457	7.48	12.9	23	19	81.2	108
Cody Carlson	TEN	227	149	65.6	1710	7.53	11.5	9	11	81.2	108
Jim Everett	STL	475	281	59.2	3323	7	11.8	22	18	80.2	107
Stan Humphries	SDC	454	263	57.9	3356	7.39	12.8	16	18	76.4	101

The leaders in the major passing categories for 1992 were:

Attempts	Dan Marino	554	Int %	Steve Young	1.7
Completions	Dan Marino	330	Rating	Steve Young	107
Yards	Dan Marino	4,116	Wins	Steve Young	14
Yards/Pass	Steve Young	8.62	Comebacks	Dan Marino & Steve Young	5
Comp %	Steve Young	66.7	Interceptions	Jim Kelly	19
TD	Steve Young	25	Fumbles	Randall Cunningham	13
TD%	Steve Young	6.2	Sacked	Randall Cunningham	60

1993

Once again, the 49ers led the NFL in scoring with 473 points, Steve Young led the league in passing, and Dallas beat San Francisco in the NFC championship for the right to go to the Super Bowl and dispose of Buffalo. There were lots of changes in the league though. The 45-second clock became the 40-second clock. Joe Montana went to the Chiefs, Boomer Esiason went to the Jets, Rich Gannon went to the Redskins, Jim McMahon went to the Vikings, Bubby Brister went to the Eagles, Vinny Testaverde went to the Browns and Bernie Kosar was cut and signed as a backup in Dallas. Only Montana, McMahon and Kosar went to the playoffs, however.

John Elway reached 4,000 yards and 25 touchdowns for the first time under new head coach Wade Phillips. Vinny Testaverde settled down and had his first good year with 14 touchdowns and just nine interceptions while completing 56 percent of his passes. On the disabled list, Randall Cunningham broke his leg, Dan Marino tore his Achilles and Stan Humphries hurt his shoulder. Don Shula had to win his record 325th game with third stringer Doug Pederson beating the Eagles. In Houston, defensive coach Buddy Ryan got so angry with offensive coach Kevin Gilbride's play calling that Ryan slugged Gilbride on the sidelines during a game. Phil Simms won back the starting job in New York and had a terrific year, but was forced to retire at the end of the year due to the salary cap. Ken O'Brien also hung up his cleats. New quarterbacks Drew Bledsoe and Rick Mirer were drafted 1–2 and both showed promise. Bledsoe threw for 15 touchdowns and 2,493 yards, while Mirer threw 12 touchdowns, 17 interceptions and a rookie record 2,833 yards. Points per game dipped slightly once more as an era came to a close.

1993 League Passing Statistics

Games	Att	Comp	%	Yards	Y/Att	Y/Comp	Att/g	Y/g	TD	TD/g	Int	Rating	300-Yd Gms
224	14414	8351	57.9	96490	6.7	11.6	64.3	430.8	517	2.3	469	76.7	37

1993 Leading Passers

Name	Team	Attempts	Comp	%	Yards	Y/Att	Y/Comp	TD	Int	Rating	Relative Rating
Steve Young	SFF	462	314	68	4023	8.71	12.8	29	16	101.5	132
Troy Aikman	DAL	392	271	69.1	3100	7.91	11.4	15	6	99	129
John Elway	DEN	551	348	63.2	4030	7.31	11.6	25	10	92.8	121
Phil Simms	NYG	400	247	61.8	3038	7.6	12.3	15	9	88.3	115

Name	Team	Attempts	Comp	%	Yards	Y/Att	Y/Comp	TD	Int	Rating	*Relative* Rating
Joe Montana	KCC	298	181	60.7	2144	7.19	11.8	13	7	87.4	114
Boomer Esiason	NYJ	473	288	60.9	3421	7.23	11.9	16	11	84.5	110
Bobby Hebert	ATL	430	263	61.2	2978	6.93	11.3	24	17	84	110
Steve Beuerlein	ARZ	418	258	61.7	3164	7.57	12.3	18	17	82.5	108
Jim Kelly	BUF	470	288	61.3	3382	7.2	11.7	18	18	79.9	104
Warren Moon	TEN	520	303	58.3	3485	6.7	11.5	21	21	75.2	98
Craig Erickson	TBB	457	233	51	3054	6.68	13.1	18	21	66.4	87
Rodney Peete	DET	252	157	62.3	1670	6.63	10.6	6	14	66.4	87

The leaders in the major passing categories for 1993 were:

Attempts	John Elway	551	Int %	Neil O'Donnell	1.4
Completions	John Elway	348	Rating	Steve Young	101.5
Yards	John Elway	4,030	Wins	Jim Kelly	12
Yards/Pass	Steve Young	8.71	Comebacks	Jim Kelly & Dave Wilson	4
Comp %	Troy Aikman	69.1	Interceptions	Brett Favre	24
TD	Steve Young	29	Fumbles	Jim Harbaugh	15
TD%	Steve Young	6.3	Sacked	Rick Mirer	47

14

1994–2006: Air Time

One could argue that the current era is merely a continuation of the 1978–1993 period of pass-oriented offenses because the statistics of the quarterbacks from the previous era are fairly close to those of current quarterbacks. However, in the three-year run from 1991 through 1993, the league average for points per game sank below 20 and that led to rule changes to further protect the quarterback and devalue the kicking game. Those changes returned the per-game average back to 20 for this new era. Furthermore, if the two eras were combined into one, nine of the top 10 in passer rating for the extended period would come from the most recent years; only Joe Montana would have spent the bulk of his career in the previous era. There has been a continual uptick in passing efficiency.

Completion percentage went from 56 per-cent in the previous era to 58.3 percent in the current one — and from 57.9 percent in 1993 to 59.8 percent in 2006. Passer rating went from 74.5 to 78.8; passing yards per game from 431 to 441; touchdown passes from 2.5 to 2.7 per game. The rate of 300-yard games increased a bit as well. Meanwhile, yards per attempt declined from 7.0 to 6.7, yards per completion went from 12.5 to 11.5 and interception percentage shrank from 4.1 to 3.2.

Strategically, the influence of Bill Walsh's offense went beyond the 40–50 percent of teams actually running his offense at any one time because the emphasis on short, timed, high percentage passes was league-wide. While the Rams and Chiefs based their offense on longer passes on the whole, all offenses today are a mix. Everyone uses the Shotgun sometimes; everyone uses a spread formation at times; everyone lines up an H-back from time to time, and no one has much use for a throwback fullback.

On the field, the NFL is more of a coaches' game than ever before: personnel deployments changes with every play; defensive schemes and blitz packages adapt constantly; there is a 53-man roster to manipulate with new specialties such as long-snappers; radio contact was established with the quarterback to signal plays; instant replay is available to challenge officials; the two-point conversion is offered as an option. The game has become more specialized and less spontaneous. Off the field, the league has become more corporate than ever: five franchises moved to a new city; four expansion franchises were born; 19 franchises have new or completely rebuilt stadiums; the NFL Sunday Ticket satellite service is offered to fans on a subscription basis; more games are played at night and during the week; the league started its own cable network, the NFL Network. If there is money to be had, the NFL finds a way to tap into it.

Hall of Famers who ended their careers during this profitable time include Joe Montana, Jim Kelly, John Elway and Dan Marino. This period marked the prime seasons for Brett Favre, Rich Gannon, Steve McNair, Drew Bledsoe, Mark Brunell, Peyton Manning, Kurt Warner, Trent Green, Donovan McNabb and Tom Brady. New stars emerging at the present are Ben Roethlisberger, Carson Palmer and Philip Rivers, while Jake Plummer and Aaron Brooks have been major disappointments. Injuries had the strongest effect on the careers of Chris Chandler, Steve McNair, Daunte Culpepper and Donovan McNabb.

The aggregate league-wide passing data for the period from 1994 through 2006 in the NFL was:

Games	Att	Comp	%	Yards	Y/ Att	Y/ Comp	Att/g	Y/g	TD	TD/g	Int	Rating	300-Yd Gm
2952	194857	113442	58.2%	1311222	6.7	11.6	66.0	444.2	7906	2.7	6248	78.8	787

Twenty-one quarterbacks have thrown for at least 20,000 yards during this era. Their percentage of completed passes ranges from Kerry Collins' 55.5 percent to Kurt Warner's 65.6 percent. According to yards per attempt and completion, the long bombers in the group have been Warner, Trent Green, Peyton Manning and Daunte Culpepper, although Brett Favre and Donovan McNabb were noted for their arm strength and accuracy on deep balls. Brad Johnson, Jeff Garcia and Jon Kitna relied more on short passes. All of these quarterbacks threw more TD passes than interceptions except Jake

Plummer who threw an equal amount of each. Of prominent contemporary quarterbacks not on this list, Trent Dilfer, Kordell Stewart, David Carr and Joey Harrington all threw more interceptions than touchdowns. Brett Favre threw the most interceptions with 234, but he also had the most attempts, completions, yards, touchdowns and wins. Drew Bledsoe was the most immobile of this group and found himself sacked 451 times. Of the rest, only Mark Brunell, Favre and Collins were sacked as many as 300 times. The 22 20,000-yard passers ranked by passer rating:

Name	Games	Attempts	Comp	%	Yards	Y/Att	Y/Comp	TD	Int	Sacked	Rating
Peyton Manning	144	4890	3131	64.0%	37586	7.7	12.0	275	139	170	94.4
Kurt Warner	81	2508	1645	65.6%	20591	8.2	12.5	125	83	190	93.8
Daunte Culpepper	86	2741	1759	64.2%	21091	7.7	12.0	137	89	249	90.8
Rich Gannon	101	3078	1898	61.7%	21582	7	11.4	137	61	205	89.3
Tom Brady	96	3064	1896	61.9%	21564	7	11.4	147	78	182	88.4
Trent Green	112	3527	2143	60.8%	26963	7.6	12.6	157	101	246	87.5
Jeff Garcia	99	2973	1811	60.9%	20385	6.9	11.3	136	73	138	86.4
Brett Favre	208	7226	4401	60.9%	50970	7.1	11.6	377	234	359	86.1
Donovan McNabb	104	3259	1898	58.2%	22080	6.8	11.6	152	72	255	85.2
Mark Brunell	157	4594	2738	59.6%	31826	6.9	11.6	182	106	389	84.2
Chris Chandler	129	2939	1743	59.3%	21715	7.4	12.5	136	98	294	83.8
Steve McNair	155	4339	2600	59.9%	30191	7	11.6	172	115	243	83.2
Dan Marino	86	2924	1748	59.8%	20623	7.1	11.8	122	84	111	83.2
Brad Johnson	145	4237	2620	61.8%	28548	6.7	10.9	164	117	242	83.1

Name	Games	Attempts	Comp	%	Yards	Y/Att	Y/Comp	TD	Int	Sacked	Rating
Vinny Testaverde	140	4139	2437	58.9%	28664	6.9	11.8	179	140	195	80.3
Aaron Brooks	93	2963	1673	56.5%	20261	6.8	12.1	123	92	235	78.5
Jeff Blake	108	3232	1823	56.4%	21671	6.7	11.9	134	98	246	78.2
Drew Bledsoe	181	6288	3625	57.6%	42117	6.7	11.6	236	191	451	77.9
Jon Kitna	107	3433	2039	59.4%	22467	6.5	11.0	129	126	236	76.1
Jake Plummer	143	4350	2484	57.1%	29253	6.7	11.8	161	161	284	74.6
Kerry Collins	156	5173	2869	55.5%	34184	6.6	11.9	174	172	300	73.2

Overall, the quarterbacks who led the league the most times in passing categories over this era are:

Attempts	Drew Bledsoe	3	Int %	Jim Harbaugh & Brad Johnson	2
Completions	Drew Bledsoe	3	Rating	Steve Young	3
Yards	Brett Favre &		Wins	Brett Favre	3
	Peyton Manning	2	Comebacks	each	1
Yards/Pass	Kurt Warner	3	Interceptions	Jake Plummer & Kerry Collins	2
Comp %	Steve Young	4	Fumbles	Daunte Culpepper	2
TD	Brett Favre	4	Sacked	David Carr	3
TD%	Brett Favre	4			

And the complete list of leaders 1994–2006 is as follows:

Attempts	Brett Favre	7,226	Rating	Steve Young	100.2
Completions	Brett Favre	4,401	Wins	Brett Favre	130
Yards	Brett Favre	50,970	Comebacks	Peyton Manning &	
Yards/Pass	Kurt Warner	8.2		Jake Plummer	28
Comp %	Steve Young	66.3	Interceptions	Brett Favre	234
TD	Brett Favre	377	Fumbles	Kerry Collins	117
TD%	Steve Young	5.82	Sacked	Drew Bledsoe	451
Int %	Rich Gannon	1.98			

1994

After three consecutive years with points per game below 20, the NFL made some changes for its 75th anniversary season besides throwback jerseys. The two-point conversion was instituted, kickoffs were moved back to the 30, the ball was returned to the spot of the kick after a missed field goal and radio helmets for quarterbacks were approved. The league scoring average floated back above 20 and has remained there since. In 1994, San Francisco led the NFL with 505 points and overwhelmed San Diego in the Super Bowl 49–26 behind Steve Young's 325 yards and six touchdown passes. Young, Dan Marino and Brett Favre all topped 30 touchdown passes for the season, and

Drew Bledsoe set a record with 691 pass attempts in New England. Stan Humphries of the Chargers became the latest quarterback to throw a 99-yard touchdown by hitting Tony Martin in September.

The Cardinals moved from Phoenix to Tempe and became the Arizona Cardinals. Several quarterbacks were on the move as well. Warren Moon went to Minnesota, Jeff George to Atlanta, Scott Mitchell to Detroit, Jim Everett to New Orleans and Jim Harbaugh to Indianapolis. Joe Montana finished his Hall of Fame career in Kansas City, while Heath Shuler, Gus Frerotte, Trent Dilfer, Mark Brunell, Elvis Grbac, Brad Johnson and Glenn Foley all started their NFL careers.

1994 League Passing Statistics

Games	Att	Comp	%	Yards	Y/Att	Y/Comp	Att/g	Y/g	TD	TD/g	Int	Rating	300-Yd Gms
224	15056	8739	58.0%	101884	6.8	11.7	67.2	454.8	583	2.6	474	78.4	64

1994 Leading Passers

Name	Team	Attempts	Comp	%	Yards	Y/Att	Y/Comp	TD	Int	Rating	Relative Rating
Steve Young	SFF	461	324	70.3	3969	8.61	12.3	35	10	112.8	144
Brett Favre	GBP	582	363	62.4	3882	6.67	10.7	33	14	90.7	116
Dan Marino	MIA	615	385	62.6	4453	7.24	11.6	30	17	89.2	114
John Elway	DEN	494	307	62.1	3490	7.06	11.4	16	10	85.7	109
Troy Aikman	DAL	361	233	64.5	2676	7.41	11.5	13	12	84.9	108
Jim Everett	NOS	540	346	64.1	3855	7.14	11.1	22	18	84.9	108
Jim Kelly	BUF	448	285	63.6	3114	6.95	10.9	22	17	84.6	108
Jeff George	ATL	524	322	61.5	3734	7.13	11.6	23	18	83.3	106
Warren Moon	MIN	601	371	61.7	4264	7.09	11.5	18	19	79.9	102
Drew Bledsoe	NEP	691	400	57.9	4555	6.59	11.4	25	27	73.6	94

The leaders in the major passing categories for 1994 were:

Attempts	Drew Bledsoe	691	Int %	Joe Montana	1.8
Completions	Drew Bledsoe	400	Rating	Steve Young	112.8
Yards	Drew Bledsoe	4555	Wins	Steve Young	13
Yards/Pass	Steve Young	8.61	Comebacks	Warren Moon	5
Comp %	Steve Young	70.3	Interceptions	Drew Bledsoe	27
TD	Steve Young	35	Fumbles	Jeff George	12
TD%	Steve Young	7.6	Sacked	Randall Cunningham	43

1995

The defending champion 49ers again topped the NFL in points with 457, but were upended in the playoffs by the Packers behind MVP Brett Favre who led the league in yards and touchdown passes. Favre also completed a 99-yard touchdown to Robert Brooks during the season. In the playoffs though, Green Bay was stopped by the Cowboys who swept to a Super Bowl win over the Steelers by picking off some lame Neil O'Donnell passes. Dan Marino became the all time leader in attempts, completions, yards and touchdowns by passing Fran Tarkenton in all categories. Meanwhile, Trent Dilfer was struggling in Tampa with four touchdowns and 18 interceptions.

Los Angeles lost both the Raiders, who returned to Oakland after 13 seasons, and the Rams, who moved to St. Louis, but did not express concern. Carolina and Jacksonville became the best two expansion teams in history, Carolina going 7–9 and Jacksonville 4–12. Respectively, their quarterbacks were rookie Kerry Collins who threw 14 touchdowns and Mark Brunell who threw 15 touchdowns and ran for 480 yards. Other newcomers included Steve McNair, Kordell Stewart, Rob Johnson, Todd Collins, Jim Miller and Eric Zeier.

1995 League Passing Statistics

Games	Att	Comp	%	Yards	Y/Att	Y/Comp	Att/g	Y/g	TD	TD/g	Int	Rating	300-Yd Gms
240	16699	9717	58.2%	113069	6.8	11.6	69.6	471.1	663	2.8	512	79.2	79

1995 Leading Passers

Name	Team	Attempts	Comp	%	Yards	Y/Att	Y/Comp	TD	Int	Rating	Relative Rating
Jim Harbaugh	IND	314	200	63.7	2575	8.2	12.9	17	5	100.7	127
Brett Favre	GBP	570	359	63	4413	7.74	12.3	38	13	99.5	126
Troy Aikman	DAL	432	280	64.8	3304	7.65	11.8	16	7	93.6	118

Name	Team	Attempts	Comp	%	Yards	Y/Att	Y/Comp	TD	Int	Rating	*Relative* *Rating*
Erik Kramer	CHI	522	315	60.3	3838	7.35	12.2	29	10	93.5	118
Scott Mitchell	DET	583	346	59.3	4338	7.44	12.5	32	12	92.3	116
Steve Young	SFF	447	299	66.9	3200	7.16	10.7	20	11	92.3	116
Warren Moon	MIN	606	377	62.2	4228	6.98	11.2	33	14	91.5	115
Dan Marino	MIA	482	309	64.1	3668	7.61	11.9	24	15	90.8	115
Jeff George	ATL	557	336	60.3	4143	7.44	12.3	24	11	89.5	113
Chris Chandler	TEN	356	225	63.2	2460	6.91	10.9	17	10	87.8	111
Jim Everett	NOS	567	345	60.8	3970	7	11.5	26	14	87	110
John Elway	DEN	542	316	58.3	3970	7.32	12.6	26	14	86.4	109
Jeff Blake	CIN	567	326	57.5	3822	6.74	11.7	28	17	82.1	104

The leaders in the major passing categories for 1995 were:

Attempts	Drew Bledsoe	636	Rating	Jim Harbaugh	100.7
Completions	Drew Bledsoe	377	Wins	Steve Bono	13
Yards	Brett Favre	4,413	Comebacks	Jeff George, Neil O'Donnell,	
Yards/Pass	Jim Harbaugh	8.2		Dave Krieg, John Elway and	
Comp %	Steve Young	66.9		Rodney Peete	4
TD	Brett Favre	38	Interceptions	Dave Krieg	21
TD%	Brett Favre	6.7	Fumbles	Dave Krieg	16
Int %	Jim Harbaugh	1.6	Sacked	Dave Krieg	53

1996

Green Bay scored the most points (456) and gave up the fewest for the season and appropriately won the Super Bowl 35–21 over New England. Brett Favre threw 39 touchdowns, was MVP for the second straight season and threw two touchdowns in the Super Bowl where Drew Bledsoe faltered by throwing four interceptions. In the playoffs, the Packers and Patriots had to overcome Carolina and Jacksonville, both of which remarkably made it to the conference championships in their second years. Cardinal Boomer Esiason had the top day of the year by throwing for 522 yards against the Redskins.

The Browns abandoned their long suffering Cleveland fans to become the Baltimore Ravens, while long suffering Jet fans were given the questionable pleasure of having Neil O'Donnell sign with their team. Petulant Jeff George was suspended for the bulk of the season in Atlanta, but the worst seasons were had by Dave Brown of the Giants and Trent Dilfer of the Bucs who each threw for 12 touchdowns and averaged 6 yards per pass while throwing 20 and 19 interceptions respectively. Former commissioner Pete Rozelle died and Jim Kelly, Bernie Kosar and Jim McMahon all completed their playing careers. Tony Banks was the only notable rookie, and he threw for 15 touchdowns, but also set an NFL record with 21 fumbles. Helmet to helmet contact was outlawed, especially involving quarterbacks.

1996 League Passing Statistics

Games	Att	Comp	%	Yards	Y/ Att	Y/ Comp	Att/g	Y/g	TD	TD/g	Int	Rating	*300-Yd* *Gms*
240	15967	9199	57.6%	106691	6.7	11.6	66.5	444.5	726	3.0	540	79.0	50

1996 Leading Passers

Name	Team	Attempts	Comp	%	Yards	Y/Att	Y/Comp	TD	Int	Rating	*Relative* *Rating*
Steve Young	SFF	316	214	67.7	2410	7.63	11.3	14	6	97.2	126
Brett Favre	GBP	543	325	59.9	3899	7.18	12.0	39	13	95.8	125
Brad Johnson	MIN	311	195	62.7	2258	7.26	11.6	17	10	89.4	116

Name	Team	Attempts	Comp	%	Yards	Y/Att	Y/Comp	TD	Int	Rating	Relative Rating
John Elway	DEN	466	287	61.6	3328	7.14	11.6	26	14	89.2	116
Vinny Testaverde	BAL	549	325	59.2	4177	7.61	12.9	33	19	88.7	115
Mark Brunell	JAX	557	353	63.4	4367	7.84	12.4	19	20	84	109
Drew Bledsoe	NEP	623	373	59.9	4086	6.56	11.0	27	15	83.7	109
Jeff Blake	CIN	549	308	56.1	3624	6.6	11.8	24	14	80.3	104
Troy Aikman	DAL	465	296	63.7	3126	6.72	10.6	12	13	80.1	104

The leaders in the major passing categories for 1996 were:

Attempts	Drew Bledsoe	623	Int %	Steve Young	1.9
Completions	Drew Bledsoe	373	Rating	Steve Young	97.2
Yards	Mark Brunell	4,367	Wins	Brett Favre & John Elway	13
Yards/Pass	Mark Brunell	7.84	Comebacks	Jeff Blake	5
Comp %	Steve Young	67.7	Interceptions	Bobby Hebert	25
TD	Brett Favre	39	Fumbles	Tony Banks	21
TD%	Brett Favre	7.2	Sacked	Mark Brunell	50

1997

Brett Favre won his third consecutive MVP award, and the Packers returned to the Super Bowl as a two-touchdown favorite, but lost 31–24 to Broncos who led the NFL with 472 points. John Elway of the Broncos only threw for 123 yards, but showed how determined he was to win his first championship on the reckless "helicopter" play when he went spinning upside down for a crucial first down near the Packer goal. In Tampa, Trent Dilfer had his first good season with 21 touchdowns and only 11 interceptions, while Kordell Stewart emerged as the Steeler quarterback with 21 touchdowns and 476 yards rushing. Steve McNair rushed for 674 yards with the Oilers who moved from Houston to Tennessee.

Jeff George moved to Oakland, Chris Chandler to Atlanta, Warren Moon to Seattle, Boomer Esiason to Cincinnati and Heath Shuler to New Orleans. Shuler threw two touchdowns and 14 interceptions in his last NFL season and combined with four other Saint quarterbacks for a putrid 13 touchdowns and 37 interceptions. Esiason, Jim Everett and Jeff Hostetler played their last games while rookies Jake Plummer, Trent Green, Jim Druckenmiller, Danny Wuerffel and Craig Whelihan played their first ones.

1997 League Passing Statistics

Games	Att	Comp	%	Yards	Y/Att	Y/Comp	Att/g	Y/g	TD	TD/g	Int	Rating	300-Yd Gms
240	15729	8844	56.2%	105288	6.7	11.9	65.5	438.7	617	2.6	479	77.2	46

1997 Leading Passers

Name	Team	Attempts	Comp	%	Yards	Y/Att	Y/Comp	TD	Int	Rating	Relative Rating
Steve Young	SFF	356	241	67.7	3029	8.51	12.6	19	6	104.7	136
Chris Chandler	ATL	342	202	59.1	2692	7.87	13.3	20	7	95.1	123
Brett Favre	GBP	513	304	59.3	3867	7.54	12.7	35	16	92.6	120
Jeff George	OAK	521	290	55.7	3917	7.52	13.5	29	9	91.2	118
Mark Brunell	JAX	435	264	60.7	3281	7.54	12.4	18	7	91.2	118
Drew Bledsoe	NEP	522	314	60.2	3706	7.1	11.8	28	15	87.7	114
John Elway	DEN	502	280	55.8	3635	7.24	13.0	27	11	87.5	113
Jim Harbaugh	IND	309	189	61.2	2060	6.67	10.9	10	4	86.2	112
Brad Johnson	MIN	452	275	60.8	3036	6.72	11.0	20	12	84.5	109

Name	Team	Attempts	Comp	%	Yards	Y/Att	Y/Comp	TD	Int	Rating	Relative Rating
Warren Moon	SEA	528	313	59.3	3678	6.97	11.8	25	16	83.7	108
Dan Marino	MIA	548	319	58.2	3780	6.9	11.8	16	11	80.7	105

The leaders in the major passing categories for 1997 were:

Attempts	Dan Marino	548	Rating	Steve Young	104.7
Completions	Dan Marino	319	Wins	Brett Favre	13
Yards	Jeff George	3,917	Comebacks	Kordell Stewart	
Yards/Pass	Steve Young	8.51		and Todd Collins	5
Comp %	Steve Young	67.7	Interceptions	Kerry Collins	21
TD	Brett Favre	35	Fumbles	Steve McNair	16
TD%	Brett Favre	6.8	Sacked	Jeff George	58
Int %	Jim Harbaugh	1.3			

1998

The Vikings scored a record 556 points led by a reborn Randall Cunningham arching long, high bombs for rookie Randy Moss to snatch from the sky. In the NFC conference championship, though, Gary Anderson missed on a field goal for the first time all year and the 15-win Vikings were defeated in overtime by the 14-win Falcons. Atlanta then lost 34–19 to the Broncos in the Super Bowl; it was John Elway's final game, and he threw for 336 yards to leave the stage a winner. Doug Flutie returned to the NFL from Canada and threw for 20 touchdowns in Buffalo, while Steve McNair ran for 559 yards in Tennessee.

The Colts chose Peyton Manning over Ryan Leaf with the first draft pick and have celebrated ever since. Manning set rookie records with 3,739 yards and 26 touchdowns, while Leaf completed 45 percent of his passes for two touchdowns and 15 interceptions. Charlie Batch had a quiet rookie year in Detroit with 11 touchdowns and just six interceptions. Disaster befell Kordell Stewart, Kerry Collins and Bobby Hoying. Stewart threw 11 touchdowns and 18 interceptions and was reduced to tears on the Pittsburgh sideline; Collins had alcohol problems, asked to be benched and was waived by Carolina during the season; Hoying threw zero touchdowns and nine interceptions in Philadelphia.

1998 League Passing Statistics

Games	Att	Comp	%	Yards	Y/Att	Y/Comp	Att/g	Y/g	TD	TD/g	Int	Rating	300-Yd Gms
240	15489	8766	56.6%	106086	6.8	12.1	64.5	442.0	658	2.7	509	78.3	53

1998 Leading Passers

Name	Team	Attempts	Comp	%	Yards	Y/Att	Y/Comp	TD	Int	Rating	Relative Rating
Randall Cunningham	MIN	425	259	60.9	3704	8.72	14.3	34	10	106	135
Vinny Testaverde	NYJ	421	259	61.5	3256	7.73	12.6	29	7	101.6	130
Steve Young	SFF	517	322	62.3	4170	8.07	13.0	36	12	101.1	129
Chris Chandler	ATL	327	190	58.1	3154	9.65	16.6	25	12	100.9	129
John Elway	DEN	356	210	59	2806	7.88	13.4	22	10	93	119
Neil O'Donnell	CIN	343	212	61.8	2216	6.46	10.5	15	4	90.2	115
Steve Beuerlein	CAR	343	216	63	2613	7.62	12.1	17	12	88.2	113
Brett Favre	GBP	551	347	63	4212	7.64	12.1	31	23	87.8	112
Jake Plummer	ARZ	547	324	59.2	3737	6.83	11.5	17	20	75	96
Peyton Manning	IND	575	326	56.7	3739	6.5	11.5	26	28	71.2	91

The leaders in the major passing categories for 1998 were:

Attempts	Peyton Manning	575	Int %	Neil O'Donnell	1.2
Completions	Brett Favre	347	Rating	Randall Cunningham	106
Yards	Brett Favre	4,212	Wins	Chris Chandler & Randall Cunningham	13
Yards/Pass	Chris Chandler	9.65	Comebacks	Jake Plummer	7
Comp %	Brett Favre	63	Interceptions	Peyton Manning	28
TD	Steve Young	36	Fumbles	Trent Green	14
TD%	Randall Cunningham	8	Sacked	Jake Plummer & Trent Green	49

1999

Kurt Warner burst onto the scene from Arena Football when Trent Green went down to injury in St. Louis, and Warner led Mike Martz's "Greatest Show on Turf" offense to 526 points and a 23–17 Super Bowl win over Tennessee. Warner had 414 yards passing in the Super Bowl and won the game on a fourth quarter 73-yard touchdown toss to Isaac Bruce. Five quarterbacks exceeded 4,000 yards passing in 1999, with the Panthers' Steve Beuerlein the biggest surprise after Warner. Brian Griese found out it is difficult to follow a legend in Denver and led the league in fumbles with sixteen, but Jake Plummer had a worse time in Arizona, throwing just nine touchdowns to 24 interceptions.

Kerry Collins straightened out his life and moved to the Giants. Brad Johnson went to Washington, and Rich Gannon rejuvenated his career in Oakland under Jon Gruden. Dan Marino ended his career in a 62–7 playoff loss to the Jaguars, while Steve Young went down to one final concussion early in the year; Erik Kramer and Steve Bono also retired. Five quarterbacks — Tim Couch, Donovan McNabb, Akili Smith, Cade McNown and Daunte Culpepper — went in the first round of the draft, but low-round pick Shaun King took the Bucs to the NFC Conference game. Other newcomers included Jeff Garcia who came down from Canada, Jake Delhomme who was undrafted and Matt Hasselbeck who finally got to play a little in Green Bay.

1999 League Passing Statistics

Games	Att	Comp	%	Yards	Y/Att	Y/Comp	Att/g	Y/g	TD	TD/g	Int	Rating	300-Yd Gms
248	16760	9567	57.1%	113254	6.8	11.8	67.6	456.7	675	2.7	562	77.3	73

1999 Leading Passers

Name	Team	Attempts	Comp	%	Yards	Y/Att	Y/Comp	TD	Int	Rating	Relative Rating
Kurt Warner	STL	499	325	65.1	4353	8.72	13.4	41	13	109.2	142
Steve Beuerlein	CAR	571	343	60.1	4436	7.77	12.9	36	15	94.6	123
Jeff George	MIN	329	191	58.1	2816	8.56	14.7	23	12	94.2	122
Peyton Manning	IND	533	331	62.1	4135	7.76	12.5	26	15	90.7	118
Brad Johnson	WSH	519	316	60.9	4005	7.72	12.7	24	13	90	117
Rich Gannon	OAK	515	304	59	3840	7.46	12.6	24	14	86.5	112
Gus Frerotte	DET	288	175	60.8	2117	7.35	12.1	9	7	83.6	109
Shane MAtthews	CHI	275	167	60.7	1645	5.98	9.9	10	6	80.6	105
Brett Favre	GBP	595	341	57.3	4091	6.88	12.0	22	23	74.7	97

The leaders in the major passing categories for 1999 were:

Attempts	Brett Favre	595	Rating	Kurt Warner	109.2
Completions	Steve Beuerlein	343	Wins	Kurt Warner & Peyton Manning	
Yards	Steve Beuerlein	4,436		& Mark Brunell	13
Yards/Pass	Kurt Warner	8.72	Comebacks	Peyton Manning	7

Comp %	Kurt Warner	65.1	Interceptions	Jake Plummer	24
TD	Kurt Warner	41	Fumbles	Brian Griese	16
TD%	Kurt Warner	8.2	Sacked	Tim Couch	56
Int %	Mark Brunell	2			

2000

The Rams repeated as the top scoring team with 540 points but lost a wildcard game in the playoffs. The Ravens won the Super Bowl behind a defense that gave up 10 points a game with game manager Trent Dilfer at quarterback. Champion Dilfer had 12 touchdowns and 11 interceptions, while Kurt Warner and his backup Trent Green combined for 37 touchdowns and 5,482 yards in St. Louis. Brian Griese had a remarkable 19:4 touchdown pass to interception ratio, but went down to a shoulder injury. Two quarterbacks gained over 500 yards rushing — Donovan McNabb with 629 and Rich Gannon with 529, and Elvis Grbac threw for 504 yards for the Chiefs against the Raiders in November.

Charger Ryan Leaf returned from a shoulder injury and threw for 11 touchdowns and 18 interceptions, while second-year men Tim Couch, Akili Smith and Cade McNown all struggled as well. Aaron Brooks was the top rookie in leading the Saints to the playoffs, but Tom Brady and Chad Pennington also got their start in the new millennium. Warren Moon and Jim Harbaugh gave in to age and Troy Aikman to more concussions; all three retired.

2000 League Passing Statistics

Games	Att	Comp	%	Yards	Y/ Att	Y/ Comp	Att/g	Y/g	TD	TD/g	Int	Rating	300-Yd Gms
248	16372	9497	58.0%	110131	6.7	11.6	66.0	444.1	634	2.6	531	77.8	65

2000 Leading Passers

Name	Team	Attempts	Comp	%	Yards	Y/Att	Y/Comp	TD	Int	Rating	Relative Rating
Brian Griese	DEN	336	216	64.3	2688	8	12.4	19	4	102.9	132
Trent Green	STL	240	145	60.4	2063	8.6	14.2	16	5	101.8	130
Kurt Warner	STL	347	235	67.7	3429	9.88	14.6	21	18	98.3	126
Daunte Culpepper	MIN	474	297	62.7	3937	8.31	13.3	33	16	98	126
Jeff Garcia	SFF	561	355	63.3	4278	7.63	12.1	31	10	97.6	125
Peyton Manning	IND	571	357	62.5	4413	7.73	12.4	33	15	94.7	121
Rich Gannon	OAK	473	284	60	3430	7.25	12.1	28	11	92.4	118
Elvis Grbac	KCC	547	326	59.6	4169	7.62	12.8	28	14	89.9	115
Steve McNair	TEN	396	248	62.6	2847	7.19	11.5	15	13	83.2	107
Brett Favre	GBP	580	338	58.3	3812	6.57	11.3	20	16	78	100

The leaders in the major passing categories for 2000 were:

Attempts	Vinny Testaverde	590	Int %	Brian Griese	1.2
Completions	Peyton Manning	357	Rating	Brian Griese	102.9
Yards	Peyton Manning	4,413	Wins	Rich Gannon & Steve McNair	
Yards/Pass	Kurt Warner	9.88		& Kerry Collins	12
Comp %	Kurt Warner	67.7	Comebacks	Charlie Batch	5
TD	Daunte Culpepper &		Interceptions	Jake Plummer	21
	Peyton Manning	33	Fumbles	Jon Kitna	17
TD%	Daunte Culpepper	7	Sacked	Steve Beuerlein	62

2001

In light of the 9/11 terrorist attack, the NFL schedule was interrupted for a week, but the delayed season came to the appropriate conclusion of having the Patriots win the Super Bowl 20–17. New England rode the arm of unheralded Tom Brady who replaced injured Drew Bledsoe early in the year and began to build his legend. The Rams led the NFL again with 503 points behind Kurt Warner's 4,830 yards and 36 touchdowns, but were bested by Brady's game-winning drive in the Super Bowl. Kordell Stewart ran for 537 yards and threw for over 3,000 in Pittsburgh who lost to the Patriots in the conference final.

Kerry Collins set a rather dubious record by fumbling 23 times.

Trent Green went to Kansas City, Brad Johnson to Tampa, Doug Flutie to San Diego, Matt Hasselbeck to Seattle and Ray Lucas to Miami. The defending champion Ravens released Trent Dilfer to sign Elvis Grbac, but Elvis threw 15 touchdowns to 18 interceptions and left the building, or football at least, at the end of the season. Randall Cunningham and Jeff George also retired, and flops Ryan Leaf and Cade McNown dropped out of the game as well. Newcomers included Michael Vick, Drew Brees, Quincy Carter and 29-year-old Chris Weinke who threw 19 interceptions and lost 15 games in a row in Carolina.

2001 League Passing Statistics

Games	Att	Comp	%	Yards	Y/ Att	Y/ Comp	Att/g	Y/g	TD	TD/g	Int	Rating	300-Yd Gms
248	16181	9542	59.0%	109639	6.8	11.5	65.2	442.1	635	2.6	545	78.5	71

2001 Leading Passers

Name	Team	Attempts	Comp	%	Yards	Y/Att	Y/Comp	TD	Int	Rating	Relative Rating
Kurt Warner	STL	546	375	68.7	4830	8.85	12.9	36	22	101.4	129
Rich Gannon	OAK	549	361	65.8	3828	6.97	10.6	27	9	95.5	122
Jeff Garcia	SFF	504	316	62.7	3538	7.02	11.2	32	12	94.8	121
Brett Favre	GBP	510	314	61.6	3921	7.69	12.5	32	15	94.1	120
Steve McNair	TEN	431	264	61.3	3350	7.77	12.7	21	12	90.2	115
Tom Brady	NEP	413	264	63.9	2843	6.88	10.8	18	12	86.5	110
Peyton Manning	IND	547	343	62.7	4131	7.55	12.0	26	23	84.1	107
Daunte Culpepper	MIN	366	235	64.2	2612	7.14	11.1	14	13	83.3	106
Aaron Brooks	NOS	558	312	55.9	3832	6.87	12.3	26	22	76.4	97

The leaders in the major passing categories for 2001 were:

Attempts	Jon Kitna	581	Int %	Rich Gannon	1.6
Completions	Kurt Warner	375	Rating	Kurt Warner	101.4
Yards	Kurt Warner	4,830	Wins	Kurt Warner	14
Yards/Pass	Kurt Warner	8.85	Comebacks	Brad Johnson	6
Comp %	Kurt Warner	68.7	Interceptions	Trent Green	24
TD	Kurt Warner	36	Fumbles	Kerry Collins	23
TD%	Kurt Warner	6.6	Sacked	Mark Brunell	57

2002

The Bucs traded top draft choices for Raider coach Jon Gruden, and it paid off with a 48–21 Super Bowl win over Oakland in which Rich Gannon threw five interceptions for the Raiders. The Chiefs led the NFL with 467 points behind

Trent Green who also threw a 99-yard score to Marc Boerigter. Receiver Marvin Harrison set a new record by catching 143 of Peyton Manning's passes for the Colts. Daunte Culpepper ran for 609 yards, but was a turnover machine throwing 23 interceptions and fumbling 23 times to lead the league in both categories. Michael Vick accumulated 777 yards rushing, and helped the Falcons become the first visiting team to ever win a playoff game in Green Bay.

Drew Bledsoe was traded to Buffalo, and Marc Bulger pushed past the injured Kurt Warner in St. Louis. XFL refugee Tommy Maddox beat out Kordell Stewart in Pittsburgh, while draft flop Akili Smith dropped out of football. David Carr and Joey Harrington were the top rookies, but neither was consistent or effective. Other newcomers included backups Patrick Ramsey, Chad Hutchinson, Josh McCown and David Garrard. Quarterback icon Johnny Unitas died and was mourned throughout football.

2002 League Passing Statistics

Games	Att	Comp	%	Yards	Y/ Att	Y/ Comp	Att/g	Y/g	TD	TD/g	Int	Rating	300-Yd Gms
256	17292	10314	59.6%	116201	6.7	11.3	67.5	453.9	694	2.7	528	80.4	79

2002 Leading Passers

Name	Team	Attempts	Comp	%	Yards	Y/Att	Y/Comp	TD	Int	Rating	Relative Rating
Chad Pennington	NYJ	399	275	68.9	3120	7.82	11.3	22	6	104.2	130
Rich Gannon	OAK	618	418	67.6	4689	7.59	11.2	26	10	97.3	121
Peyton Manning	IND	591	392	66.3	4200	7.11	10.7	27	19	93.7	117
Brad Johnson	TBB	451	281	62.3	3049	6.76	10.9	22	6	92.9	115
Trent Green	KCC	470	287	61.1	3690	7.85	12.9	26	13	92.6	115
MAtt Hasselbeck	SEA	419	267	63.7	3075	7.34	11.5	15	10	87.8	109
Drew Bledsoe	BUF	610	375	61.5	4359	7.15	11.6	24	15	86	107
Tom Brady	NEP	601	373	62.1	3764	6.26	10.1	28	14	85.7	107
Brett Favre	GBP	551	341	61.9	3658	6.64	10.7	27	16	85.6	106
Brian Griese	DEN	436	291	66.7	3214	7.37	11.0	15	15	85.6	106
Kerry Collins	NYG	545	335	61.5	4073	7.47	12.2	19	14	85.4	106
Aaron Brooks	NOS	528	283	53.6	3572	6.77	12.6	27	15	80.1	100
Daunte Culpepper	MIN	549	333	60.7	3853	7.02	11.6	18	23	75.3	94

The leaders in the major passing categories for 2002 were:

Attempts	Rich Gannon	618	Rating	Chad Pennington	104.2
Completions	Rich Gannon	418	Wins	Brett Favre	12
Yards	Rich Gannon	4,689	Comebacks	Peyton Manning	
Yards/Pass	Trent Green	7.85		and Kerry Collins	5
Comp %	Chad Pennington	68.9	Interceptions	Daunte Culpepper	23
TD	Tom Brady	28	Fumbles	Daunte Culpepper	23
TD%	Trent Green	5.5	Sacked	David Carr	76
Int %	Brad Johnson	1.3			

2003

Kansas City got off to a 9–0 start and led the NFL with 484 points, but again folded in the playoffs. The Patriots retooled, and Tom Brady began his mastery over rival Peyton Manning in the playoffs. In a 32–29 Super Bowl win over the Panthers, Brady threw for 354 yards, three touchdowns and led the team to a game-winning field goal as time expired. Carolina's fiery Jake Delhomme threw for 323 yards and three touchdowns in the loss. The most remarkable play in the playoffs, though, was Donovan McNabb completing a fourth and 26 pass to lead the Eagles to a game-tying field goal on the way to beating the Packers in overtime.

Jake Plummer was rejuvenated in Denver, but Chad Pennington and Rich Gannon went down to injuries. Rookies Byron Leftwich, Rex Grossman and Kyle Boller have each struggled with inconsistency, injuries or both. Veterans Neil O'Donnell and Steve Beuerlein retired, while Tim Couch flopped in Cleveland and dropped out of football. For the second straight year an All Timer died when former Brown Otto Graham passed away.

2003 League Passing Statistics

Games	Att	Comp	%	Yards	Y/Att	Y/Comp	Att/g	Y/g	TD	TD/g	Int	Rating	300-Yd Gms
256	16493	9695	58.8%	109467	6.6	11.3	64.4	427.6	654	2.6	538	78.3	59

2003 Leading Passers

Name	Team	Attempts	Comp	%	Yards	Y/Att	Y/Comp	TD	Int	Rating	Relative Rating
Steve McNair	TEN	400	250	62.5	3215	8.04	12.9	24	7	100.4	127
Peyton Manning	IND	566	379	67	4267	7.54	11.3	29	10	99	125
Daunte Culpepper	MIN	454	295	65	3479	7.66	11.8	25	11	96.4	122
Trent Green	KCC	523	330	63.1	4039	7.72	12.2	24	12	92.6	117
Brett Favre	GBP	471	308	65.4	3361	7.14	10.9	32	21	90.4	114
Matt Hasselbeck	SEA	513	313	61	3841	7.49	12.3	26	15	88.8	112
Jon Kitna	CIN	520	324	62.3	3591	6.91	11.1	26	15	87.4	111
Chad Pennington	NYJ	297	189	63.6	2139	7.2	11.3	13	12	82.9	105
Brad Johnson	TBB	570	354	62.1	3811	6.69	10.8	26	21	81.5	103
Marc Bulger	STL	532	336	63.2	3845	7.23	11.4	22	22	81.4	103
Kelly Holcomb	CLE	302	193	63.9	1797	5.95	9.3	10	12	74.6	94

The leaders in the major passing categories for 2003 were:

Attempts	Brad Johnson	570	Int %	Aaron Brooks	1.5
Completions	Peyton Manning	379	Rating	Steve McNair	100.4
Yards	Peyton Manning	4,267	Wins	Tom Brady	14
Yards/Pass	Steve McNair	8.04	Comebacks	Jake Delhomme	7
Comp %	Peyton Manning	67	Interceptions	Joey Harrington & Marc Bulger	22
TD	Brett Favre	32	Fumbles	Daunte Culpepper	16
TD%	Brett Favre	6.8	Sacked	Drew Bledsoe	49

2004

Peyton Manning led the Colts to a league best 522 points in setting a new record for touchdown passes in a season with 49. In the playoffs, however, Manning again met Tom Brady and the Patriots and left a loser. Brady led the defending champions to another Super Bowl win, 24–21 over Philadelphia this time. The Eagles were driven by the short-lived passing combination of Donovan McNabb to Terrell Owens and finally got past the NFC championship game where they had lost three straight years. Brett Favre's streak of 36 games throwing a touchdown pass ended, still 11 games shy of Johnny Unitas' record. Michael Vick ran for 902 yards in Atlanta.

Although Eli Manning was more anticipated, Steeler Ben Roethlisberger was a rookie sensation, completing 66% of his passes for 17 touchdowns, and Carson Palmer threw for 18 scores in Cincinnati. Philip Rivers, Tony Romo, J.P. Losman and Chris Simms remained mostly under wraps as freshmen. Jeff Garcia went to Cleveland and completed a 99-yard touchdown to Andre Davis, but that was his only highlight of the year. Kurt Warner moved to New York, Kerry Collins to Oakland, A.J. Feeley to Miami and Vinny Testaverde to Dallas, but none had much success. Dented and damaged Chris Chandler and Rich Gannon both retired; Reggie White died from a heart attack, and Pat Tillman was killed in Afghanistan.

2004 League Passing Statistics

Games	Att	Comp	%	Yards	Y/ Att	Y/ Comp	Att/g	Y/g	TD	TD/g	Int	Rating	300-Yd Gms
256	16354	9772	59.8%	115338	7.1	11.8	63.9	450.5	722	2.8	524	82.6	80

2004 Leading Passers

Name	Team	Attempts	Comp	%	Yards	Y/Att	Y/Comp	TD	Int	Rating	Relative Rating
Peyton Manning	IND	497	336	67.6	4557	9.17	13.6	49	10	121.1	146
Daunte Culpepper	MIN	548	379	69.2	4717	8.61	12.4	39	11	110.9	134
Drew Brees	SDG	400	262	65.5	3159	7.9	12.1	27	7	104.8	126
Donovan McNabb	PHL	469	300	64	3875	8.26	12.9	31	8	104.7	126
Ben Roethlisberger	PIT	295	196	66.4	2621	8.88	13.4	17	11	98.1	118
Brian Griese	TBB	336	233	69.3	2632	7.83	11.3	20	12	97.5	118
Trent Green	KCC	556	369	66.4	4591	8.26	12.4	27	17	95.2	115
Brett Favre	GBP	540	346	64.1	4088	7.57	11.8	30	17	92.4	112
Jake Delhomme	CAR	533	310	58.2	3886	7.29	12.5	29	15	87.3	105
Jake Plummer	DEN	521	303	58.2	4089	7.85	13.5	27	20	84.5	102

The leaders in the major passing categories for 2004 were:

Attempts	Trent Green	556	Rating	Peyton Manning	121.1
Completions	Daunte Culpepper	379	Wins	Tom Brady	14
Yards	Daunte Culpepper	4,717	Comebacks	Ben Roethlisberger	
Yards/Pass	Peyton Manning	9.17		and Aaron Brooks	5
Comp %	Brian Griese	69.3	Interceptions	Vinny Testaverde &	
TD	Peyton Manning	49		Kerry Collins	20
TD%	Peyton Manning	9.9	Fumbles	Michael Vick	16
Int %	Kurt Warner	1.4	Sacked	David Carr	49

2005

Ben Roethlisberger led the Steelers to a 21–10 Super Bowl win over the Seahawks in his second year, but threw for just 123 yards and two interceptions in the game. Seattle's Matt Hasselbeck, who led the team to a league best 452 points, threw for 273 yards in the loss. The Colts started out 13–0, but lost to Pittsburgh in the playoffs. Aging Brett Favre threw 29 interceptions, the most since Vinny Testaverde threw 35 in 1988. Michael Vick ran for 597 yards.

Kurt Warner moved on to Arizona, Drew Bledsoe to Dallas, Brian Griese to Tampa and Trent Dilfer to Cleveland. While Harvard rookie Ryan Fitzpatrick threw for over 300 yards in his debut, he finished with four touchdowns and eight interceptions. Fellow rookies Alex Smith, Kyle Orton, Charlie Frye and Aaron Rodgers were not impressive either. Smith threw just one touchdown to 11 interceptions, and Orton threw 13 interceptions; both averaged just five yards per pass. Jeff Blake and Kordell Stewart probably played their last games, and Doug Flutie retired in New England after converting the first dropkick in the league in 64 seasons.

2005 League Passing Statistics

Games	Att	Comp	%	Yards	Y/ Att	Y/ Comp	Att/g	Y/g	TD	TD/g	Int	Rating	300-Yd Gms
256	16465	9790	59.5%	104174	6.3	10.6	64.3	406.9	645	2.5	506	78.2	68

2005 Leading Passers

Name	Team	Attempts	Comp	%	Yards	Y/Att	Y/Comp	TD	Int	Rating	Relative Rating
Peyton Manning	IND	453	305	67.3	3747	8.27	12.3	28	10	104.1	130
Carson Palmer	CIN	509	345	67.8	3836	7.54	11.1	32	12	101.1	126
Ben Roethlisberger	PIT	268	168	62.7	2385	8.9	14.2	17	9	98.6	123
Matt Hasselbeck	SEA	449	294	65.5	3459	7.7	11.8	24	9	98.2	123
Marc Bulger	STL	287	192	66.9	2297	8	12.0	14	9	94.4	118
Tom Brady	NEP	530	334	63	4110	7.75	12.3	26	14	92.3	115
Trent Green	KCC	507	317	62.5	4014	7.92	12.7	17	10	90.1	112
Drew Brees	SDG	500	323	64.6	3576	7.15	11.1	24	15	89.2	111
Jake Delhomme	CAR	435	262	60.2	3421	7.86	13.1	24	16	88.1	110
Kelly Holcomb	BUF	230	155	67.4	1509	6.56	9.7	10	8	85.6	107
Eli Manning	NYG	557	294	52.8	3762	6.75	12.8	24	17	75.9	95
Brett Favre	GBP	607	372	61.3	3881	6.39	10.4	20	29	70.9	88

The leaders in the major passing categories for 2005 were:

Attempts	Brett Favre	607	TD%	Ben Roethlisberger	6.3
Completions	Brett Favre	372	Int %	Brad Johnson	1.4
Yards	Tom Brady	4,110	Rating	Peyton Manning	104.1
Yards/Pass	Ben Roethlisberger	8.9	Wins	Peyton Manning	14
Comp %	Carson Palmer	67.8	Comebacks	Drew Bledsoe	5
TD	Carson Palmer	32			

2006

Although San Diego had the best record and led the league with 492 points, they were upended in the playoffs by the Patriots and that set up another duel between Tom Brady and Peyton Manning. For the first time in the post-season, Manning outdueled Brady and beat New England before steamrolling the Bears 29–17 in the Super Bowl to win his first title. The most memorable play in the playoffs was Tony Romo botching the hold for a game winning field goal against Seattle. Romo emerged as a star with 19 touchdowns in Dallas, as did Philip Rivers with 22 scores in San Diego. Drew Brees relocated to New Orleans and had a monster year including a 510-yard game against the Bengals. Michael Vick set a new rushing mark for quarterbacks with 1,039 yards but completed just 52 percent of his passes, while rookie Vince Young was magnificent with 552 yards rushing and a league best five game winning comebacks.

Because Carson Palmer went down to a low blow in the playoffs and Ben Roethlisberger and Brian Griese also were injured on low tackles, hits below the knee on the quarterback were banned. Quarterbacks continued to get hurt, however, including Donovan McNabb, Matt Hasselbeck, Trent Green, Byron Leftwich and Jake Delhomme. In addition to Vince Young, rookies Matt Leinart, Jay Cutler, Jason Campbell, Bruce Gradkowski and Andrew Walter all played their first games in 2006. Chris Weinke started for the first time since his rookie year five years before and ran his losing streak to 17 games before winning his final start.

2006 League Passing Statistics

Games	Att	Comp	%	Yards	Y/Att	Y/Comp	Att/g	Y/g	TD	TD/g	Int	Rating	300-Yd Gms
60	2991	1407	47.0%	21670	7.2	15.4	49.9	361.2	188	3.1	250	57.6	8

2006 Leading Passers

Name	Team	Attempts	Comp	%	Yards	Y/Att	Y/Comp	TD	Int	Rating	Relative Rating
Manning, Peyton	IND	557	362	65.0%	4397	7.9	12.1	31	9	101	128.7%
Huard, Damon	KCC	244	148	60.7%	1878	7.7	12.7	11	1	98	124.8%
Brees, Drew	NOS	554	356	64.3%	4418	8.0	12.4	26	11	96.2	122.5%
McNabb, Donovan	PHL	316	180	57.0%	2647	8.4	14.7	18	6	95.5	121.7%
Romo, Tony	DAL	337	220	65.3%	2903	8.6	13.2	19	13	95.1	121.1%
Palmer, Carson	CIN	520	324	62.3%	4035	7.8	12.5	28	13	93.9	119.6%
Bulger, Marc	STL	588	370	62.9%	4301	7.3	11.6	24	8	92.9	118.3%
Brady, Tom	NEP	516	319	61.8%	3529	6.8	11.1	24	12	87.9	112%
Pennington, Chad	NYJ	485	313	64.5%	3352	6.9	10.7	17	16	82.6	105.2%
Carr, David	HOU	442	302	68.3%	2767	6.3	9.2	11	12	82.1	104.6%
Kitna, Jon	DET	596	372	62.4%	4208	7.1	11.3	21	22	79.9	101.8%
Manning, Eli	NYG	522	301	57.7%	3244	6.2	10.8	24	18	77	98.1%

The leaders in the major passing categories for 2006 were:

Attempts	Brett Favre	613	Wins	Phillip Rivers	14
Completions	Jon Kitna	372	Comebacks	Vince Young	5
Yards	Drew Brees	4,418	Interceptions	Ben Roethlisberger	23
Yards/Pass	Tony Romo	8.6	Fumbles	David Carr	16
Comp %	David Carr	68.3	Sacked	Jon Kitna	63
TD	Peyton Manning	31	Interceptions	Brett Favre	29
TD%	Donovan McNabb	5.7	Fumbles	David Carr & Drew Bledsoe	17
Int %	Marc Bulger	1.4	Sacked	David Carr	68
Rating	Peyton Manning	101			

15

Arizona Cardinals

Leading Passers, by Yards

Quarterback	Years	G	Att	Comp	Pct	Yds	Y/A	Y/Cp	TD	Int	Int %	Rating
Jim Hart	1966–83	199	5,069	2,590	51.1	34,639	6.8	13.4	209	247	4.87%	66.6
Neil Lomax	1981–88	108	3,153	1,817	57.6	22,771	7.2	12.5	136	90	2.85%	82.7
Jake Plummer	1997–02	85	2,755	1,542	56	17,629	6.4	11.4	90	114	4.14%	69.0
Charley Johnson	1961–69	87	2,047	1,030	50.3	14,928	7.3	14.5	108	110	5.37%	69.6
Paul Christman	1945–49	50	1,014	453	44.7	6,749	6.7	14.9	51	69	6.80%	55.5
Lamar McHan	1954–58	60	1,012	433	42.8	6,578	6.5	15.2	50	77	7.61%	49.6
Josh McCown	2002–05	35	828	482	58.2	5,266	6.4	10.9	24	27	3.26%	73.2
Steve Beuerlein	1993–94	25	673	388	57.7	4,709	7.0	12.1	23	26	3.86%	74.6
Kurt Warner	2005–06	17	543	350	64.5	4,090	7.5	11.7	17	14	2.58%	86.9
Timm Rosenbach	1989–92	26	551	295	53.5	3,676	6.7	12.5	16	24	4.36%	66.0
Chris Chandler	1991–93	22	566	322	56.9	3,592	6.3	11.2	19	19	3.36%	73.1
Dave Krieg	1995	16	521	304	58.3	3,554	6.8	11.7	16	21	4.03%	72.6
Jim Hardy	1949–51	30	521	236	45.3	3,193	6.1	13.5	30	47	9.02%	47.0
Tom Tupa	1988–91	27	455	234	51.4	3,075	6.8	13.1	9	22	4.84%	59.5
Kent Graham	1996–97	18	524	276	52.7	3,032	5.8	11.0	16	12	2.29%	70.7

Quarterback	Rush Att	Rush Yds	Rush Avg	TD
Jim Hart	156	213	1.4	16
Neil Lomax	222	969	4.4	10
Jake Plummer	145	1183	8.2	10
Charley Johnson	165	520	3.2	10
Paul Christman	78	-44	-0.6	7
Lamar McHan	190	654	3.4	11
Josh McCown	94	429	4.6	3
Steve Beuerlein	44	84	1.9	1
Kurt Warner	26	31	1.2	0
Timm Rosenbach	101	507	5.0	3
Chris Chandler	47	183	3.9	1
Dave Krieg	19	29	1.5	0
Jim Hardy	29	58	2.0	2
Tom Tupa	44	172	3.9	1
Kent Graham	34	110	3.2	2

Record Holders

Passing Yards, Career: 34,639 Jim Hart
Passing Yards, Season: 4,614 Neil Lomax 1984
Completion Percentage, Career: 64.5 percent Kurt
    Warner
Completion Percentage, Season: 64.5 percent Kurt
    Warner 2005
Touchdown Passes, Career: 209 Jim Hart
Touchdown Passes, Season: 28 Charley Johnson
    1963 and Neil Lomax 1984
Interceptions, Career: 247 Jim Hart
Interceptions, Season: 30 Jim Hart 1967
Rating, Career: 82.7 Neil Lomax
Rating, Season: 92.5 Neil Lomax 1984
Rush Yards, Career: 1,183 Jake Plummer
Rush Yards, Season: 470 Timm Rosenbach 1990

Passers by Categories

Five best starters: Jim Hart was an un-drafted free agent who spent 18 years with the Cardinals, 15 as their starter, and thus holds all their career passing marks. However, Neil Lomax was the team's best quarterback, but his career was shortened by injury. Charley Johnson was an exciting quarterback in the 1960s who specialized in comebacks before the mistake-prone Jake Plummer came along. Pitchin' Paul Christman piloted the team to its only modern championship. Two Hall of Fame single-wing backs who deserve mention are Ernie Nevers who was a very skilled passer in his time and Paddy Driscoll who was not much of a passer but could do everything else.

Worst starters, career: In addition to all the one- and two-year passers listed below under worst seasonal performance, the worst extended-stay regular was Lamar McHan who quarter-backed the team from 1954 through 1958, never completing half his passes and only once throw-ing more touchdowns than interceptions. The owner suspended him briefly in 1956 for lack of effort. He would later play with the Packers, the Colts and 49ers.

Best stat line, season: In the same year, 1984, that Dan Marino set a new yards passing record with over 5,000, Neil Lomax completed 61.6 percent of his passes for 4,614 yards for 28 touchdowns and 16 interceptions. As usual, the Cardinals missed the playoffs.

Worst stat line, season: The Cardinals have had a lot of mediocre-to-bad passing in their long, dispiriting history, but in the years 1935–43, their main passers were abysmal even by the low standards of the time:

		Comp	TD	Int	Rating
1935	Phil Sarboe	46.3%	0	10	23.9
1936	Phil Sarboe	40.3%	1	8	28.2
1936	Pug Vaughan	38.0%	2	10	31.4
1937	Pat Coffee	43.7%	4	11	40.0
1938	Jack Robbins	53.6%	2	9	39.8
1938	Dwight Sloan	46.8%	1	7	26.0
1939	Jack Robbins	42.4%	4	10	37.9
1939	Frank Patrick	27.8%	1	13	7.1
1940	Hugh McCullough	37.1%	4	21	23.9
1942	Bud Schwenk	42.7%	6	27	25.5
1943	Ronnie Cahill	45.9%	3	21	33.1

The one exception was 1941 when Johnny Clement and Ray Mallouf were merely inade-quate. The only T-formation quarterback to ap-proach this wretchedness for the Cardinals was Lamar McHan as a rookie in 1954 when he com-pleted 41 percent of his passes for 6 touchdowns and 22 interceptions. Also to be noted are Jim Hart's 30 interceptions in 1967 and Jim Hardy's NFL record 8 interceptions in one game against the Eagles on September 25, 1950. Strangely, Hardy set the Cardinal team record for touch-downs with 6 the following week against the Colts.

Best stat line, playoffs: Neil Lomax in a losing cause against the Packers in a 1982 Wild-card game went 32–51, 385, 2–2.

Worst stat line, playoffs: In the 1947 championship, the Cardinals beat the Eagles on four long runs by Charlie Trippi and Elmer Angsman. Quarterback Paul Christman went 3–14, 54, 0–2.

Big Days: The first passer to exceed 300 yards passing in a game was Pat Coffee with 306 yards on December 5, 1937. The first to reach 400 yards was Charley Johnson with 428 on October 13, 1963. Neil Lomax had the biggest day in franchise history by throwing for 468 yards on December 16, 1984; he also had the most 300-yard days with 16.

Running QBs: Jake "the Snake" Plummer ran for more yards than any Cardinal quarterback and averaged 8.2 yards doing so. Neil Lomax and Timm Rosenbach were both very mobile before injuries ended their careers. Tailback John Grigas twice gained over 100 yards rushing in a game for the 1944 Cardinals/Steelers merged team.

Bomber: Charley Johnson was terrific at going long to Sonny Randle, Bobby Joe Conrad and Jackie Smith in the 1960s. Paul Christman and Jim Hart also liked to throw the bomb.

Most accurate: Neil Lomax.

Leader: Paul Christman had the respect of his teammates.

Comeback King: Jim Hart had 21 4th quarter comebacks in his 17-year Cardinal career, but Jake Plummer had 20 in just six years.

Highest Football IQ: Charlie Johnson was a smart guy on and off the field.

Toughest: Hart lasted 18 years in the league and achieved the longest streak of consecutive starts by a Cardinal quarterback with 63.

First signal caller/T-Formation QB: Hall of Famer Paddy Driscoll was the first signal caller in 1920. Paul Christman was the first T-quarterback in 1945.

First TD pass: On October 21, 1921, Paddy Driscoll hit Rube Marquadt for a 33-yard score in a 20–0 blanking of the Minneapolis Marines. There were no scoring tosses in the Cardinals' first season.

Black QBs: Before the color ban, the Cardinals star tailback in 1932–33 was Joe Lillard from Oregon. The first black quarterback on the roster was Greg Tipton in 1987, but he never appeared in a game. The first black quarterback to play for the team was journeyman Jeff Blake in 2003, followed by Shaun King in 2004.

Tallest QB: Six Cardinal quarterbacks have been 6'5": Scott Brunner, Kent Graham, Dave Brown, Tony Sacca, Boomer Esiason and Matt Leinart. The first three of them came from the Giants.

Smallest QB: Three at 5'8": Ronnie Cahill, Reino Nori and John McCarthy. Four at 5'10": Phil Sarboe, Walt Masters, Dwight Sloan and Ted Marchibroda. Paul Larson was 5'11". All are pre–1960.

Oldest QB: Jim Hart was a 37-year-old starter in 1981. He was a 39-year-old backup in 1983. Dave Krieg also started at 37 in 1995.

Rookie sensation: No Cardinal quarterback has made much of an impression as a rookie, but Charley Johnson in 1962, Jim Hart in 1967 and Timm Rosenbach in 1990 all had promising sophomore seasons after throwing fewer than 25 passes as rookies. Hart and Rosenbach threw for over 3,000 yards each, and Johnson exceeded 2,400.

Late bloomers: Steve Beuerlein and Chris Chandler both had their first big seasons after coming to Arizona — Chandler in his sixth season in 1992 and Beurlein in his fifth season in 1993. Both had injuries and left town soon after.

1st round picks: Let's start with those who never played for the Cardinals: George Cafego, the top pick in 1940, was traded to Brooklyn for linemen; Glenn Dobbs, the 3rd choice in 1943, eventually signed with Brooklyn of the All America Conference; Joe Namath, the 12th pick in 1965, of course signed with the Jets; Kelly Stoufer, 6th in 1987, refused to sign and was traded to Seattle a year later. King Hill was the top pick in 1958, but proved to be a better punter than passer. Lamar McHan and George Izo were the 2nd picks in 1954 and 1960 respectively, but neither achieved any success in the NFL. Steve Pisarkiewicz broke Paul Christman's records at Missouri, but the 19th pick of the 1977 draft flopped for the Cardinals. Timm Rosenbach, picked in the supplemental draft in 1989, was the only one of the first nine top Cardinal picks who had even fleeting success. Matt Leinart, 10th in 2006, is trying to run counter to Cardinals history.

Out of position: Hall of Fame tailback Charley Trippi spent two seasons as a quarterback late in his Cardinal career and was a fish out of water throwing the ball. Tom Tupa was drafted as a quarterback by the Cards, but had a long NFL career as a punter.

Long-time subs: Ray Mallouf was a very effective sub for Johnny Clement and Paul Christman for four years in the 1940s.

QB controversy: When Charley Johnson

was drafted in 1967, it created an opening for Jim Hart. For the next three years, the two battled before Johnson was traded to the Oilers in 1970 and Hart won the starter's job outright.

College affiliation: Five mediocre Cardinal quarterbacks went to Notre Dame: Frank Tripucka, George Izo, Ralph Guglielmi, Rusty Lisch and Steve Beuerlein.

Ones who got away: Red Dunn would lead the Packers to three consecutive titles from 1929 to 1931. Chris Chandler always had injury problems, but he also had several good seasons after he left Arizona. Jake Plummer had greater success in Denver than in the desert.

Has beens: The Cardinals have long made a habit of picking up elder veterans for a year or two. These include: Pete Beathard, Gary Cuozzo, Cliff Stoudt, Gary Hogeboom, Jim McMahon, Jay Schroeder, Dave Krieg, Boomer Esiason, Kent Graham, Dave Brown, Jeff Blake and Kurt Warner.

Ruinous injuries: Although he had not played well in the 1947 championship, Paul Christman was forced to miss the 1948 title match due to injury. Neil Lomax's career was shortened by an arthritic hip, and Timm Rosenbach's was abbreviated by knee and shoulder injuries. Chris Chandler got hurt so frequently he was known as "Crystal Chandelier."

Best trade: The Cardinals received a number one pick (Irv Goode) from Philadelphia for flop King Hill in 1961. That same year they traded one Notre Dame flop (George Izo) to Washington for another (Ralph Guglielmi).

Worst trade: Selling Paddy Driscoll to the cross-town Bears ripped the heart out of the team for decades. Giving up receiver John Gilliam and a number two pick to Minnesota for oft-traveled Gary Cuozzo was a mistake.

Title winners: Paddy Driscoll and Red Dunn in 1925; Paul Christman in 1947.

Hall of Famers: Paddy Driscoll, Ernie Nevers and Charlie Trippi, all tailbacks.

All Pro/Pro Bowl seasons: Paddy Driscoll, 5; Jim Hart, 5; Ernie Nevers, 3; Neil Lomax, 2; Charley Johnson, 2; Jim Hardy, 1.

QBs as coaches: Paddy Driscoll went 28–17–4 with the Cardinals and Bears; Ernie Nevers went 12–26–2 with the Cardinals and Duluth; Ted Marchibroda went 87–98–1 with the Colts and Ravens; Sam Wyche went 84–107 with the Bengals and Bucs.

Underrated: Both Charley Johnson and Neil Lomax could move a team and score points, but neither ever got the chance to play for a great team.

Overrated: Jake Plummer was noted for his fourth quarter comebacks, but made a lot of mistakes and lost a lot of games before the last quarter.

Best Nicknames: Pitchin' Paul Christman, Ray "the Slingin' Syrian" Mallouf, and Jake "the Snake" Plummer.

Time Capsule: Jim Hardy's eight interception day against the Eagles in 1950 is a record that will probably never be broken.

What If: Would the Cardinals have reached the playoffs in the 1960s if Charley Johnson had not been drafted by the Army? What kind of career numbers would Neil Lomax have amassed if he had not been forced to retire early due to injury?

Off the field: Charley Johnson earned a PhD in Chemical Engineering. Paul Christman was one of the broadcasters for the first Super Bowl game; he also appeared in the 1948 movie *Triple Threat* along with teammate Charlie Trippi. Jim Hardy appeared in both *Yes Sir That's My Baby* and *All American*. Ernie Nevers starred in *The Lost Special*, *Saturday's Millions* and *The Spirit of Stanford*.

Quarterback Bibliography

Ernie Nevers
Scott, Jim. *Ernie Nevers, Football Hero*. Minneapolis; Denison, 1969.

Neil Lomax
Lomax, Neil, and J. David Miller. *Third and Long*. Old Tappan, NJ: Revell, 1986.

Jim McMahon *see* Chicago Bears

Kurt Warner *see* St. Louis Rams

16

Atlanta Falcons

Leading Passers, by Yards

Quarterback	Years	G	Att	Comp	Pct	Yds	Y/A	Y/Cp	TD	Int	Int %	Rating
Steve Bartkowski	1975–85	123	3,330	1,871	56.2	23,470	7.0	12.5	154	141	4.23%	76.0
Chris Miller	1987–93	69	2,089	1,129	54	14,066	6.7	12.5	87	72	3.45%	74.7
Chris Chandler	1997–01	68	1,672	981	58.7	13,268	7.9	13.5	87	56	3.35%	87.4
Michael Vick	2001–06	68	1,730	930	53.8	11,505	6.7	12.4	71	52	3.01%	75.7
Jeff George	1994–96	35	1,180	714	60.5	8,575	7.3	12.0	50	32	2.71%	85.6
Bob Berry	1968–72	54	1,049	598	57	8,489	8.1	14.2	57	56	5.34%	79.2
Bobby Hebert	1993–96	40	1,066	637	59.8	7,053	6.6	11.1	50	49	4.60%	75.9
Randy Johnson	1966–70	46	904	435	48.1	5,538	6.1	12.7	34	65	7.19%	50.3
David Archer	1984–87	38	647	331	51.2	4,275	6.6	12.9	18	29	4.48%	62.8
Bob Lee	1973–74	21	402	198	49.3	2,638	6.6	13.3	13	22	5.47%	58.4

Quarterback	Rush Att	Rush Yds	Rush Avg	TD
Steve Bartkowski	172	236	1.4	11
Chris Miller	128	607	4.7	2
Chris Chandler	141	480	3.4	3
Michael Vick	529	3859	7.3	21
Jeff George	62	93	1.5	0
Bob Berry	105	396	3.8	4
Bobby Hebert	53	150	2.8	1
Randy Johnson	88	459	5.2	7
David Archer	130	692	5.3	2
Bob Lee	48	166	3.5	1

Record Holders

Passing Yards, Career: 23,470 Steve Bartkowski
Passing Yards, Season: 4,143 Jeff George 1995
Completion %, Career: 60.5% Jeff George
Completion %, Season: 68.1% Wade Wilson 1992
Touchdown Passes, Career: 154 Steve Bartkowski
Touchdown Passes, Season: 31 Steve Bartkowski 1980
Interceptions, Career: 141 Steve Bartkowski
Interceptions, Season: 25 Bobby Hebert 1996
Rating, Career: 87.4 Chris Chandler
Rating, Season: 110.2 Wade Wilson 1992
Rush Yards, Career: 3,859 Michael Vick
Rush Yards, Season: 1,139 Michael Vick 2006

Passers by Categories

Five best starters: Steve Bartkowski is one of only six NFL quarterbacks to throw over 30 touchdowns in consecutive seasons. Chris Chandler led the Falcons to their only Super Bowl appearance. Chris Miller showed a great deal of promise before being done in by concussions. Bob Berry was a surprisingly effective journeyman. Michael Vick is an exciting performer.

Worst starters, career: Randy Johnson was the team's second number one draft choice in 1966, but never panned out, throwing nearly twice as many interceptions as touchdowns. Pat Sullivan won the Heisman Trophy, but holds a lifetime quarterback rating of 36.5 with 5 touchdowns and

16 interceptions. David Archer threw 18 touchdowns to 29 interceptions, while Kim McQuilken threw just 4 touchdowns to 28 interceptions and completed just 39 percent of his passes.

Best stat line, season: Wade Wilson had the highest rating in 1992, but in a part-time role, while Jeff George threw for over 4,000 yards in 1995. Better still were these two seasons of Steve Bartkowski: 1980— 55.5 percent, 3,544 yards, 31 touchdowns and 16 interceptions and 1983 — 63.4 percent 3,167 yards, 22 touchdowns and 5 interceptions. Best of all was Chris Chandler's 1998 rating of 100.9 from completing 58.1 percent of his passes for 3,154 yards (9.65 per pass), 25 touchdowns and 12 interceptions.

Worst stat line, season: Kim McQuilken earned a 21.7 rating in 1976 completing 39.7 percent of his passes for 3.7 yards per pass, 2 touchdowns and 10 interceptions. This was slightly worse than Bob Lee's 1974 rating of 32.4 from completing 45.3 percent of his passes for 4.95 yards per pass, 3 touchdowns and 14 interceptions. In Steve Bartkowski's second and third seasons, 1976–1977, he had passer ratings of 39.5 and 38.4 by completing just 47 percent of his passes for a combined 7 touchdowns and 22 interceptions.

Best stat line, playoffs: Chris Chandler had a great conference championship beating the Vikings in 1998: 27–43, 340, 3–0. Honorable mention to Steve Bartkowski in 1980 losing to Dallas in a Divisional game: 18–33, 320, 2–1. A special multitalented award should go to Michael Vick against the Rams in a 2004 Divisional win: 12–16, 82, 2–0 + 8 carries for 119 yards rushing.

Worst stat line, playoffs: Steve Bartkowski had an awful Divisional loss to the Cowboys in 1978: 8–23, 95, 1–3. Chris Miller had a worse one in a 1991 Divisional loss to Washington: 17–32, 178, 0–4.

Big Days: The first passer to exceed 300 yards passing in a game was Bob Berry with 302 yards on September 27, 1970. The first to reach 400 yards was Steve Bartkowski with 416 on November 15, 1981, and Steve had the most, 12, 300 yard games in team history. Chris Chandler had the biggest day in franchise history by throwing for 431 yards on December 23, 2001.

Running QBs: While David Archer, Chris Miller, Randy Johnson and Chris Chandler were all mobile, Michael Vick is in a class by himself as a runner. He is faster and more elusive than any other quarterback in history and has gained over 100 yards rushing in a game a league-record eight times. Vick holds the quarterback rushing records for a game (173 yards) and season (1,039).

Bomber: Steve Bartkowski had a big arm most famous for "Big Ben" Hail Mary throws.

Most accurate: Jeff George could throw; he just couldn't lead.

Leader: Steve Bartkowski was the Falcons' unquestioned leader. Bob Berry was short and with average arm strength, but was a fiery leader.

Comeback King: Bartkowski had 22 4th quarter comebacks, plus one in the postseason.

Highest Football IQ: Bartkowski was cool and clever on the field.

Toughest: Randy Johnson wasn't very good, but he had to stand up to a lot of punishment as the first quarterback on a badly assembled expansion team.

First signal caller/T-Formation QB: Rookie Randy Johnson in 1966.

First TD pass: On September 11, 1966, Randy Johnson hit Gary Barnes for a 53-yard score in a 19–14 loss to the Rams.

Black QBs: Michael Vick is the first for the Falcons. D.J. Shockley joined the team in 2006.

Tallest QB: Hugh Millen was 6'5".

Smallest QB: Bob Berry was 5'11". Pat Sullivan was listed at 6', but that was dubious. Michael Vick is 6'1" and slight of build.

Oldest QB: Chris Chandler was still a starter at 36 in 2001. Three years prior, Steve DeBerg was his backup at age 44.

Rookie sensation: None. Randy Johnson threw for 1,795 yards in 1966 and Steve Bartkowski threw for 1,662 in 1975, but neither completed more than 45 percent of his passes and both threw more interceptions than touchdowns. Michael Vick only completed 44 percent of his passes in 2001 but ran for 289 yards.

Late bloomer: Bob Berry came from Minnesota and didn't get his chance till he was 26. Chris Chandler had his greatest and healthiest years in Atlanta in his thirties.

1st round picks: Three of the four quarterbacks the Falcons drafted in the first round worked out pretty well (Bartkowski, Miller and Vick). However, the first was Randy Johnson, and he flopped badly although his arm and potential kept him in the league for a decade.

Out of position: Bob Lee was more of a punter than quarterback; Michael Vick is more a tailback than quarterback. Running back Perry Lee Dunn was a quarterback in college.

Long-time subs: Mike Moroski was a backup for most of his six years in Atlanta.

QB controversy: Bob Berry had to wrest the starting job away from Randy Johnson in 1968. Some people wanted to see Matt Schaub start instead of Vick.

College affiliation: Three Oregon Ducks: Bob Berry, Chris Miller and Tony Graziani.

Ones who got away: Brett Favre was 0 for 4 with two interceptions in his only year in Atlanta. The Falcons had Erik Kramer as a replacement player in 1987, but did not hold onto him.

Has beens: Terry Nofsinger, Dick Shiner, Bob Holly, Hugh Millen, Steve Dils, Billy Joe Tolliver, Browning Nagle, Bobby Hebert, Scott Hunter and Steve DeBerg all passed through town.

Ruinous injuries: Steve Bartkowski had six knee operations that shortened his career. Chris Miller's propensity for concussions ended his career. Michael Vick takes a regular beating and has already missed a season's worth of games.

Best trade: Picking up Chris Chandler from the Titans for number 4 and number 6 draft picks was a steal. Another good deal was getting Andre Rison and Chris Hinton from the Colts for the draft rights to Jeff George.

Worst trade: Unfortunately, Atlanta could not leave well enough alone and four years later gave up two number 1 picks to the Colts to obtain George. Another bad deal was trading Bob Berry and a number 1 (Fred McNeil) to the Vikings for Bob Lee and a washed up Lonnie Warwick. The worst deal, however was giving Brett Favre to Green Bay for a number one pick.

Title winners: None.

Hall of Famers: None.

All Pro/Pro Bowl seasons: Michael Vick, 3; Steve Bartkowski, 2; Chris Miller, 1; Bob Berry, 1.

QBs as coaches: June Jones compiled a 22–36 record in Atlanta and San Diego.

Underrated: Steve Bartkowski was a terrific quarterback who is not remembered much today.

Overrated: Jeff George had a million dollar arm and a dime brain. Although he is an electrifying runner, Michael Vick has yet to prove he will be a top quarterback in the NFL and his career has gone to the dogs.

Best Nicknames: Chris "Crystal Chandelier" Chandler and Steve "Peachtree Bart" Bartkowski.

Time Capsule: Big Ben Right — Bartkowski's 57-yard Hail Mary touchdown pass that was deflected by receiver Wallace Francis to receiver Alfred Jackson with 19 seconds left in a win over the Saints. On the defensive side, the Falcons' 1970s Grits Blitz in which they would sometimes send everyone after the quarterback threatened the lives of quarterbacks around the league.

What If: How many more games would the Falcons have won if Jerry Glanville had coached Brett Favre rather than sticking him in the doghouse and trading him?

Off the field: Brett Favre partied himself out of Atlanta and Michael Vick was chased out of town.

Quarterback Bibliography

Steve Bartkowski
DeHaan, Dan. *Steve Bartkowski Intercepted: A Game Plan for Spiritual Growth.* Old Tappan, NJ: Revell, 1980.

17

Baltimore Ravens

Leading Passers, by Yards

Quarterback	Years	G	Att	Comp	Pct	Yds	Y/A	Y/Cp	TD	Int	Int %	Rating
Vinny Testaverde	1996–97	29	1,019	596	58.5	7,148	7.0	12.0	51	34	3.34%	82.8
Kyle Boller	2003–06	41	1,036	578	55.8	6,103	5.9	10.6	36	34	3.28%	71.0
Tony Banks	1999–00	23	594	319	53.7	3,714	6.3	11.6	25	16	2.69%	75.7
Steve McNair	2006	16	468	295	63.0	3,050	6.5	10.3	16	12	2.56%	82.5
Elvis Grbac	2001	14	467	265	56.7	3,033	6.5	11.4	15	18	3.85%	71.1
Anthony Wright	2003–05	16	444	258	58.1	2,781	6.3	10.8	15	17	3.83%	71.9
Eric Zeier	1996–98	16	318	184	57.9	2,367	7.4	12.9	12	5	1.57%	87.3
Jeff Blake	2002	11	295	165	55.9	2,084	7.1	12.6	13	11	3.73%	77.3
Jim Harbaugh	1998	14	293	164	56	1,839	6.3	11.2	12	11	3.75%	72.9
Trent Dilfer	2000	11	225	133	59.1	1,502	6.7	11.3	12	11	4.89%	76.6
Chris Redman	2000–03	9	198	106	53.5	1,111	5.6	10.5	7	5	2.53%	71.3

Quarterback	Rush Att	Rush Yds	Rush Avg	TD
Vinny Testaverde	68	326	4.8	2
Kyle Boller	128	351	2.7	2
Tony Banks	43	150	3.5	2
Steve McNair	45	119	2.6	1
Elvis Grbac	21	18	0.9	1
Anthony Wright	46	141	3.1	0
Eric Zeier	23	42	1.8	0
Jeff Blake	39	106	2.7	1
Jim Harbaugh	39	172	4.4	0
Trent Dilfer	20	75	3.8	0
Chris Redman	13	12	0.9	0

Record Holders

Passing Yards, Career: 7,148 Vinny Testaverde
Passing Yards, Season: 4,177 Vinny Testaverde 1996
Completion %, Career: 63% Steve McNair
Completion %, Season: 63% Steve McNair 2006
Touchdown Passes, Career: 51 Vinny Testaverde
Touchdown Passes, Season: 33 Vinny Testaverde 1996
Interceptions, Career: 34 Vinny Testaverde
Interceptions, Season: 19 Vinny Testaverde 1996
Rating, Career: 82.8 Vinny Testaverde
Rating, Season: 88.7 Vinny Testaverde 1996

Rush Yards, Career: 326 Vinny Testaverde
Rush Yards, Season: 189 Kyle Boller 2004

Passers by Categories

Best starters: No one has held the job for very long on the Ravens, who have averaged more than one starter per year of existence. The best was the first, Vinny Testaverde, although he only stayed two years. Trent Dilfer did his best not to screw things up in the championship season of 2000, and then was gone the next year. Steve McNair was a shadow of his days as a

Titan, but still was better than what had come before.

Worst starters, career: Of the series of journeymen the Ravens have hired as quarterbacks, Tony Banks was ineffective, Anthony Wright was very limited, and Elvis Grbac dropped out of football after one frustrating year in Baltimore.

Best stat line, season: No one has approached Vinny Testaverde's first year in town: 325–549, 59.2 percent, 4177 yards, 33 touchdowns and 19 interceptions.

Worst stat line, season: Stony Case earned a 50.3 rating for his 1999 numbers: 77–170, 45.3 percent, 988 yards, 3 touchdowns and 8 interceptions.

Best stat line, playoffs: In the 2000 AFC Championship against the Raiders, Trent Dilfer went 9–18, 190 yards, 1–1.

Worst stat line, playoffs: In a 2001 Divisional game against the Steelers, Elvis Grbac imploded: 18–37, 153 yards, 0–3. Steve McNair wasn't much better in a 2006 Divisional loss to the Colts: 18–29, 173, 0–2.

Big Days: The first passer to exceed 300 yards passing in a game was Vinny Testaverde with 353 yards on October 6, 1996. The first to reach 400 yards was Testaverde with 429 on October 27, 1996; that is still the highest total in team history. Testaverde had a team record eight 300-yard games in Baltimore.

Running QBs: Some of the top running quarterbacks in league history have passed through Baltimore, including Randall Cunningham, Steve McNair, Jim Harbaugh, Kordell Stewart and Jeff Blake. All were on the downside of their careers as both passers and runners.

Bomber: Testaverde was a big man with a big arm.

Most accurate: This has not a strong point for Raven quarterbacks. Steve McNair set new team records in 2006.

Leader: Trent Dilfer led the Ravens to a championship. Who would have guessed that would happen?

Comeback King: Jim Harbaugh was noted for this ability but only spent a year in Baltimore at the end of his career. Kyle Boller is the team leader with five 4th quarter comebacks.

Highest Football IQ: Jim Harbaugh or Steve McNair.

Toughest: Vinny Testaverde and Dilfer were tough to knock out.

First signal caller/T-Formation QB: Vinny Testaverde in 1996.

First TD pass: On September 8, 1996, Testaverde hit Charles Alexander for 17 yards in a 31–17 loss to the Steelers.

Black QBs: The Ravens have used more black quarterbacks than any other team. Wally Richardson in 1998, Tony Banks in 1999–2000, Randall Cunningham in 2001, Jeff Blake in 2002, Anthony Wright from 2003–2005. Kordell Stewart served as third quarterback in 2005. And Steve McNair was hired in 2006.

Tallest QB: Vinny Testaverde and Elvis Grbac were both 6'5".

Smallest QB: Jeff Blake was 6'. Anthony Wright, Kordell Stewart and Eric Zeier were all 6'1".

Oldest QB: Randall Cunningham was 38 in 2001. Jim Harbaugh was the oldest starter at 34 in 1998.

Rookie sensation: The only rookie starter was Kyle Boller in 2003, and he was no sensation, completing 51.8 percent of his passes for 1,260 yards, 7 touchdowns and 9 interceptions.

Late bloomer: At the outset of their careers, Vinny Testaverde and Trent Dilfer both suffered for several seasons in Tampa before displaying some talent in Baltimore.

1st round picks: Kyle Boller has been the Ravens only first round pick at number 19, and he has not been able to hold onto the starting job.

Out of position: Kordell Stewart was more of an emergency punter than quarterback for the Ravens in 2005.

Long-time subs: Chris Redman served four years as a backup.

QB controversy: Ineffective incumbent Tony Banks was beaten out as starter by Trent Dilfer during the 2000 championship season. When the Ravens signed Elvis Grbac instead of resigning Dilfer the following year, it was a controversial move that did not work out.

College affiliation: Both Jim Harbaugh and Elvis Grbac attended Michigan.

Ones who got away: As noted above, Dilfer.

Has beens: Stoney Case, Scott Mitchell, Randall Cunningham, Elvis Grbac and Kordell Stewart.

Ruinous injuries: Kyle Boller's progress was thwarted by injury in 2005.

Best trade: Nothing scintillating. The

Ravens got Jim Harbaugh from the Colts for a number 3 draft pick and gave a number 4 to the Titans for Steve McNair.

Worst trade: Giving up a number 3 to the Lions for Scott Mitchell.

Title winners: Trent Dilfer, 1.

Hall of Famers: Hah.

All Pro/Pro Bowl seasons: Testaverde, 1.

QBs as coaches: None.

Underrated: Trent Dilfer was the modern day Billy Wade. Like Dilfer, Wade was a highly drafted disappointment for his original team. He came to the Bears, who in 1963 featured a devastating defense of historic proportions, and guided a simple offense that avoided mistakes and relied on passes to his Hall of Fame tight end (Mike Ditka for Wade; Dilfer had Shannon Sharpe.) Dilfer also had a much better running game in 2000, but both maligned quarterbacks won a title.

Overrated: Prize free agent Elvis Grbac passed for over 3,000 yards in his one season in town, but he was prone to mistakes and a disaster as a leader.

Best Nicknames: Jim "Captain Comeback" Harbaugh.

Time Capsule: Trent Dilfer's 96-yard touchdown pass to Shannon Sharpe in the AFC Championship game for the 2000 season was a memorable play.

What If: How would the Ravens have done in 2001 if they had kept Trent Dilfer rather than releasing him to sign Elvis Grbac?

Off the field: Kyle Boller dated ditzy actress Tara Reid for a time and even brought her home to meet mom and dad.

Quarterback Bibliography

Randall Cunningham *see* Philadelphia Eagles

18

Buffalo Bills

Leading Passers, by Yards

Quarterback	Years	G	Att	Comp	Pct	Yds	Y/A	Y/Cp	TD	Int	Int %	Rating
Jim Kelly	1986–96	160	4,779	2,874	60.1	35,467	7.4	12.3	237	175	3.66%	84.4
Joe Ferguson	1973–84	164	4,166	2,188	52.5	27,590	6.6	12.6	181	190	4.56%	68.9
Jack Kemp	1962–69	88	2,240	1,039	46.4	15,134	6.8	14.6	77	132	5.89%	55.8
Drew Bledsoe	2002–04	48	1,530	905	59.2	10,151	6.6	11.2	55	43	2.81%	79.3
Doug Flutie	1998–00	11	1,063	598	56.3	7,582	7.1	12.7	47	30	2.82%	81.7
Dennis Shaw	1970–73	45	916	485	52.9	6,286	6.9	13.0	35	67	7.31%	57.1
Rob Johnson	1998–01	30	664	401	60.4	4,798	7.2	12.0	27	17	2.56%	85.4
J.P. Losman	2004–06	29	662	384	58.0	4,423	6.7	11.5	27	23	3.47%	77.4
Todd Collins	1995–97	28	519	284	54.7	3,218	6.2	11.3	16	19	3.66%	68.5
Alex Van Pelt	1995–03	30	477	262	54.9	2,985	6.3	11.4	16	24	5.03%	64.1
Frank Reich	1985–94	90	377	222	58.9	2,540	6.7	11.4	18	12	3.18%	81.9
Daryle Lamonica	1963–66	56	353	150	42.5	2,499	7.1	16.7	16	23	6.52%	55.0
Johnny Green	1960–61	18	354	145	41	2,170	6.1	15.0	16	15	4.24%	59.2
Warren Rabb	1961–62	23	251	101	40.2	1,782	7.1	17.6	15	16	6.37%	58.6

Quarterback	Rush Att	Rush Yds	Rush Avg	TD
Jim Kelly	304	1049	3.5	7
Joe Ferguson	339	1174	3.5	19
Jack Kemp	256	807	3.2	26
Drew Bledsoe	73	133	1.8	4
Doug Flutie	172	876	5.1	3
Dennis Shaw	92	408	4.4	0
Rob Johnson	110	746	6.8	3
J.P. Losman	71	309	4.4	1
Todd Collins	60	143	2.4	0
Alex Van Pelt	32	53	1.7	1
Frank Reich	62	45	0.7	0
Daryle Lamonica	83	333	4.0	8
Johnny Green	35	44	1.3	3
Warren Rabb	50	124	2.5	3

Record Holders

Passing Yards, Career: 35,467 Jim Kelly
Passing Yards, Season: 4,359 Drew Bledsoe 2002
Completion %, Career: 60.1% Jim Kelly
Completion %, Season: 64.1% Jim Kelly 1991
Touchdown Passes, Career: 237 Jim Kelly
Touchdown Passes, Season: 33 Jim Kelly 1991
Interceptions, Career: 190 Joe Ferguson
Interceptions, Season: 26 Jack Kemp 1964, 1967,
 Dennis Shaw 1971
Rating, Career: 85.4 Rob Johnson
Rating, Season: 101.2 Jim Kelly 1990
Rush Yards, Career: 1,174 Joe Ferguson
Rush Yards, Season: 476 Doug Flutie 1999

Passers by Categories

Five best starters: Jim Kelly was a strong-armed, tough leader who took the Bills to four straight Super Bowls. Fiery Jack Kemp won back-to-back AFL championships. Joe Ferguson progressed from being the guy who handed the ball off to O.J. Simpson to becoming a durable, solid starter for over a decade. Doug Flutie was an exciting winner and Drew Bledsoe was talented but immobile and inconsistent.

Worst starters, career: Dennis Shaw threw 35 touchdowns against 67 interceptions and never lived up to his potential. Todd Collins was a flop following Kelly, but has made a career of being a backup under Al Saunders in Kansas City and Washington. Dan Darragh completed 42.9 percent of his passes for 4 touchdowns and 22 interceptions. Gary Marangi completed just 36.7 percent of his passes 12 touchdowns and 21 interceptions. Nebraska Cornhuskers Bruce Mathison and Vince Ferragamo combined in 1985 for 9 touchdowns and 31 interceptions, and both were gone in 1986.

Best stat line, season: Jim Kelly completed 63.3 percent of his passes for 2,829 yards, 24 touchdowns and 9 interceptions in 1990 and 64.1 percent of his passes for 3,844 yards, 33 touchdowns and 17 interceptions in 1991. Drew Bledsoe completed 61.5 percent of his passes for 4,359 yards, 24 touchdowns and 15 interceptions in 2002.

Worst stat line, season: The 1985 season of Ferragamo and Mathison is noted above. In 1968, rookie Dan Darragh and halfback/end Ed Rutkowski combined to complete less than 42 percent of their passes for 3 touchdowns and 20 interceptions, averaging roughly 4 yards per attempt. Rutkowski had a passer rating of 27.1 while Darragh reached 33. M.C. Reynolds achieved a 37.2 passer rating in 1961 on a 45.9 completion percentage, 2 touchdowns and 13 interceptions.

Best stat line, playoffs: Jim Kelly had a great Divisional win over Miami in 1990: 19–29, 339, 3–1. He followed that in the Conference title game against Oakland with 17–23, 300, 2–1. Of course the most memorable is Frank Reich's miracle comeback from 32 points down against the Oilers in the 1992 Wildcard matchup: 21–34, 289, 4–1.

Worst stat line, playoffs: Jim Kelly's Super Bowl against the Redskins was embarrassing: 28–58, 275, 2–4.

Big Days: The first passer to exceed 300

yards passing in a game was Johnny Green with 334 yards on October 30, 1960. The first to reach 400 yards was Joe Ferguson with 419 on October 9, 1983. Drew Bledsoe had the biggest day in franchise history by throwing for 463 yards on September 15, 2002. Jim Kelly had the most 300-yard games with 26.

Running QBs: Doug Flutie and Rob Johnson both averaged over five yards per carry when they took off with the ball. Jack Kemp scored 25 touchdowns in his six years as quarterback.

Bomber: Both Jack Kemp and Daryle Lamonica liked to go deep for mid–60's championship Bills. Jim Kelly could throw the bomb as well as anyone. Drew Bledsoe always had a great arm as long as he had time to throw.

Most accurate: Jim Kelly.

Leader: Jim Kelly and Jack Kemp both inspired their teammates.

Comeback King: Kelly had 29 4th quarter comebacks and another in the postseason.

Highest Football IQ: Jack Kemp would find a way to win.

Toughest: Jim Kelly was built and played like a linebacker, but it was Joe Ferguson who had the longest streak of consecutive starts with 107.

First signal caller/T-Formation QB: Ex-Bear and Brown Tommy O'Connell was briefly the starting quarterback at the very beginning of the Bills' existence.

First TD pass: Tommy O'Connell 53 yards to Elbert "Golden Wheels" Dubenion in a 27–21 loss to Denver on September 18, 1960.

Black QBs: In 1969, the Bills drafted James Harris from Grambling and picked up Marlin Briscoe from Denver. Briscoe was converted to wide receiver, and Harris did not get many chances to play. Dave Mays played very little in 1978, and Willie Totten was a replacement player in 1987.

Tallest QB: Replacement player Brian McClure was 6'6" in 1987. Drew Bledsoe was 6'5".

Smallest QB: Doug Flutie was 5'9".

Oldest QB: Flutie was still starting at age 38 in 2000. Bill Munson was 38 as a backup in 1979.

Rookie sensation: Jim Kelly had the advantage of starting in the USFL, so he was 26 as a rookie but still completed 59.4 percent of his passes for 3,593 yards, 22 touchdowns and 17 interceptions in 1986.

Late bloomer: Doug Flutie didn't get a fair chance till he was turning 36 in 1998 and returned from Canada a success.

1st round picks: The Bills have only drafted a quarterback in the first round twice: Jim Kelly with the 14th pick in 1983 and J.P. Losman with the 22nd pick in 2004. Losman is still iffy.

Out of position: Marlin Briscoe was converted to wide receiver. All-around back and receiver Ed Rutkowski was forced to start several games for the Bills at quarterback in the disastrous 1968 season. Richie Lucas was a defensive back and backup quarterback in 1960–61.

Long-time subs: Frank Reich ably backed up Jim Kelly for 10 years, most memorably in the 32-point comeback against the Oilers in the playoffs.

QB controversy: Daryle Lamonica lost out to Jack Kemp and was traded to Oakland after four years as a relief man. Doug Flutie and Rob Johnson battled somewhat inconclusively from 1998–2000.

College affiliation: Three Nebraska quarterbacks have played in Buffalo: Bruce Mathison, Vince Ferragamo and David Humm. None distinguished themselves in a positive way.

Ones who got away: Daryle Lamonica became an All Pro in Oakland. James Harris went to the Pro Bowl with the Rams.

Has beens: Tommy O'Connell, M.C. Reynolds, Al Dorow, Mike Taliaferro, Tom Flores, Bill Munson, Matt Robinson and Vince Ferragamo.

Ruinous injuries: Jack Kemp missed the entire 1968 season and the Bills tanked, but did end up with O.J. Simpson as a result.

Best trade: Obtaining Jack Kemp on a waiver mistake by Sid Gillman's Chargers in 1962.

Worst trade: Giving up Daryle Lamonica and Glenn Bass to the Raiders for washed up Tom Flores and Art Powell as well as number 2 and 6 draft picks was a disaster. Giving up number 1 and 4 picks to the Jaguars for Rob Johnson and giving up a number 1 pick to the Patriots for Drew Bledsoe ultimately didn't work out either.

Title winners: Jack Kemp won AFL titles in 1964 and 1965. He lost the 1966 AFL title game that led to the first Super Bowl. Jim Kelly lost four Super Bowls in a row.

Hall of Famers: Jim Kelly.

All Pro/Pro Bowl seasons: Jack Kemp, 6; Jim Kelly, 5; Doug Flutie, 1; Drew Bledsoe, 1.

QBs as coaches: Tom Flores went 97–87 with Oakland and Seattle. Kay Stephenson went 10–26 with Buffalo.

Underrated: The Bills did not realize exactly what they had in Daryle Lamonica.

Overrated: Jack Kemp was very inconsistent, but played with the best defense in the AFL. Kemp threw 77 touchdowns and 132 interceptions while completing only 46.4 percent of his passes in Buffalo.

Best Nicknames: Joe "Stoney" Ferguson and Jim "Machine Gun" Kelly.

Time Capsule: Frank Reich's record-setting playoff comeback from being down 35–3 to the Oilers to winning 41–38. The hurry-up no-huddle K-Gun Offense in which Jim Kelly called the plays at the line of scrimmage.

What If: What if the Bills didn't get Jack Kemp by accident in 1962 and went with rookie Daryle Lamonica in 1963? Would the Bills still have gone to three straight AFL title games from 1964–66? Would they have kept Lamonica and altered Raiders history as well?

Off the field: Jack Kemp served Buffalo in the U.S. Congress from 1971–89 before serving in the Reagan cabinet and running as Bob Dole's vice-presidential candidate in 1996. Doug Flutie appeared in *Second String.* Jim Kelly appeared in *Necessary Roughness* and an episode of *General Hospital.* Drew Bledsoe appeared in *Jerry Maguire.*

Quarterback Bibliography

Jack Kemp: Kemp, Jack. *Advancing the American Idea into the 90s.* ?: Campaign for a New Majority, 1988.

Tom Flores *see* Oakland Raiders

Jim Kelly: Kelly, Jim, and Vic Carucci. *Armed and Dangerous.* New York: Doubleday, 1992.

Doug Flutie
Flutie, Doug, and Perry Lefko. *Flutie.* Toronto: Warwick, 1998.
Flutie, Doug, Greg Brown, and Doug Keith. *Never Say Never.* Dallas, TX: Taylor Trade, 2000.

19

Carolina Panthers

Leading Passers, by Yards

Quarterback	Years	G	Att	Comp	Pct	Yds	Y/A	Y/Cp	TD	Int	Int %	Rating
Jake Delhomme	2003–06	61	1,848	1,101	59.6	13,331	7.2	12.1	89	58	3.14%	84.8
Steve Beuerlein	1996–00	59	1,723	1,041	60.4	12,690	7.4	12.2	86	50	2.90%	87.7
Kerry Collins	1995–98	41	1,339	694	51.8	8,306	6.2	12.0	47	54	4.03%	66.0
Chris Weinke	2001–06	27	687	373	54.3	3,800	5.5	10.2	14	26	3.78%	61.4
Rodney Peete	2002–04	18	392	228	58.2	2,652	6.8	11.6	15	14	3.57%	76.6

Quarterback	Rush Att	Rush Yds	Rush Avg	TD
Jake Delhomme	108	153	1.4	3
Steve Beuerlein	109	305	2.8	3
Kerry Collins	107	217	2.0	4
Chris Weinke	54	148	2.7	6
Rodney Peete	24	14	0.6	0

Record Holders

Passing Yards, Career: 12,690 Steve Beuerlein
Passing Yards, Season: 4,436 Steve Beuerlein 1999
Completion %, Career: 60.4% Steve Beuerlein
Completion %, Season: 63% Steve Beuerlein 1998
Touchdown Passes, Career: Jake Delhomme 89
Touchdown Passes, Season: 36 Steve Beuerlein 1999
Interceptions, Career: 58 Jake Delhomme
Interceptions, Season: 21 Kerry Collins 1997
Rating, Career: 87.7 Steve Beuerlein
Rating, Season: 94.6 Steve Beuerlein 1999
Rush Yards, Career: 305 Steve Beuerlein
Rush Yards, Season: 128 Chris Weinke 2001

Passers by Categories

Best starters: Steve Beuerlein, a career backup, was the best thing the Panthers had in the late 1990s. Jake Delhomme took Carolina to the Super Bowl in 2003 where he had them ahead until Tom Brady's last minute heroics.

Worst starters, career: An immature Kerry Collins was an immense disappointment. Chris Weinke quickly proved he was a second stringer in the NFL. Weinke emphasized the point in 2006 when he made three more dreadful starts.

Best stat line, season: All the team seasonal records above were set in Steve Beuerlein's monster 1999 season when he drove a lousy team to an 8–8 finish.

Worst stat line, season: Kerry Collins threw a team record 21 interceptions and averaged only 5.6 yards per attempt in 1997. Chris Weinke's 2001 rookie year resulted in 11 touchdowns, 19 interceptions and a lowly 5.4 yards per attempt.

Best stat line, playoffs: In the Super Bowl, Jake Delhomme went 16–33, 323, 3–0 while in the Divisional match against Chicago in the 2005 postseason, he went 24–33, 319, 3–1.

Worst stat line, playoffs: The week after Chicago, though, Jake shot blanks in the Conference title against Seattle: 15–35, 196, 1–3.

Big Days: The first passer to exceed 300 yards passing in a game was Frank Reich with 329 yards on September 3, 1995. Steve Beuerlein had the biggest day in franchise history by throwing for 373 yards on December 12, 1999.

Beuerlein had nine 300-yard games and Jake Delhomme has had eight.

Running QBs: The closest Carolina has come is Randy Fasani who was an ineffective backup in 2002, but was mobile.

Bomber: Kerry Collins had a big, scattershot arm.

Most accurate: Steve Beuerlein.

Leader: Jake Delhomme is an animated leader on the field.

Comeback King: Delhomme has led 14 4th quarter comebacks and one in the postseason.

Highest Football IQ: Steve Beuerlein was not very mobile, but was a smart player.

Toughest: Kerry Collins was built like a block of stone and sometimes thought like one. Jake Delhomme had the longest starting streak in team history with 59.

First signal caller/T-Formation QB: Frank Reich had a three-game reign as a starter in Carolina after 10 years as a backup in Buffalo.

First TD pass: On September 3, 1995, Frank Reich hit tight end Pete Metzelaars for 8 yards against Pittsburgh.

Black QBs: Dameyune Craig in 2001 and Rodney Peete from 2002 to 2004.

Tallest QB: Kerry Collins was 6'5".

Smallest QB: Dameyune Craig was 6'1".

Oldest QB: Rodney Peete was 38 in 2004. He started his last game at 37 the year before.

Rookie sensation: Kerry Collins threw for 2,717 yards in his and the Panthers' first seasons, 1995.

Late bloomer: Steve Beuerlein had his greatest year by far at age 34 in 1999 with 36 touchdowns and over 4,000 yards. Jake Delhomme kicked around New Orleans for several seasons before getting a chance in Carolina at age 28.

1st round picks: After showing great promise in his first two seasons, Kerry Collins imploded and was driven from town for his play, his drinking and his racially incendiary remarks.

Out of position: None.

Long-time subs: Chris Weinke has been mostly a backup in his six seasons in Carolina.

QB controversy: Steve Beuerlein was brought in when things were going well with Kerry Collins and was perfectly placed to replace him when things blew up a year later.

College affiliation: None.

Ones who got away: Kerry Collins settled

down in New York and got to a Super Bowl, but has always been inconsistent.

Has beens: Frank Reich, Steve Bono and Rodney Peete.

Ruinous injuries: None.

Best trade: None, but the Panthers have made a couple of excellent free agent signings with Steve Beuerlein and Jake Delhomme.

Worst trade: Having to waive former first round pick Collins. Obtaining Jeff Lewis from Denver for a number 3 and number 4 pick. One pick would have been sufficient.

Title winners: None.

Hall of Famers: None.

All Pro/Pro Bowl seasons: Jake Delhomme, 1; Steve Beuerlein, 1.

QBs as coaches: None.

Underrated: Jake Delhomme does not al-ways get recognition for what a solid quarterback and leader he is.

Overrated: Kerry Collins.

Best Nicknames: None.

Time Capsule: None.

What If: If Kerry Collins didn't implode, would he have done any better with the Panthers than his followers?

Off the field: Kerry Collins had a very public drinking problem. He also appeared in *Jerry Maguire*. Rodney Peete appeared in an episode of *Half and Half* and is married to actress Holly Robinson Peete.

Quarterback Bibliography

Rodney Peete *see* Philadelphia Eagles

20

Chicago Bears

Leading Passers, by Yards

Quarterback	Years	G	Att	Comp	Pct	Yds	Y/A	Y/Cp	TD	Int	Int %	Rating
Sid Luckman	1939–50	128	1,744	904	51.8	14,686	8.4	16.2	137	132	7.57%	75.0
Jim Harbaugh	1987–93	89	1,759	1,023	58.2	11,567	6.6	11.3	50	56	3.18%	74.2
Jim McMahon	1982–88	66	1,513	874	57.8	11,203	7.4	12.8	67	56	3.70%	80.4
Erik Kramer	1994–98	26	1,557	913	58.6	10,582	6.8	11.6	63	45	2.89%	80.7
Billy Wade	1961–66	59	1,407	767	54.5	9,958	7.1	13.0	68	66	4.69%	73.6
Ed Brown	1954–61	98	1,246	607	48.7	9,698	7.8	16.0	63	88	7.06%	62.5
Bob Avellini	1975–84	71	1,110	560	50.5	7,111	6.4	12.7	33	69	6.22%	54.8
Johnny Lujack	1948–51	45	808	404	50	6,295	7.8	15.6	41	54	6.68%	65.3
Rudy Bukich	1958–59											
	1962–68	54	878	474	54	6,254	7.1	13.2	46	45	5.13%	72.9
Mike Tomczak	1985–90	77	915	454	49.6	6,247	6.8	13.8	33	47	5.14%	62.5
Vince Evans	1978–83	49	953	464	48.7	6,172	6.5	13.3	31	53	5.56%	57.3
George Blanda	1949–58	103	988	445	45	5,936	6.0	13.3	48	70	7.09%	51.3
Jim Miller	1999–02	32	965	565	58.5	5,867	6.1	10.4	34	26	2.69%	76.7
Jack Concannon	1967–71	51	951	486	51.1	5,222	5.5	10.7	31	52	5.47%	55.6
Bobby Douglass	1969–75	61	895	376	42	4,932	5.5	13.1	30	51	5.70%	47.5
Rex Grossman	2003–06	24	675	367	54.4	4,496	6.7	12.3	27	26	3.85%	72.4

Quarterback	Years	G	Att	Comp	Pct	Yds	Y/A	Y/Cp	TD	Int	Int %	Rating
Zeke Bratkowski	1954–60	59	537	263	49	3,639	6.8	13.8	24	58	10.80%	46.4
Shane Matthews	1996–01	9	599	366	61.1	3,461	5.8	9.5	19	18	3.01%	75.1
Bernie Masterson	1934–40	72	409	156	38.1	3,366	8.2	21.6	34	38	9.29%	57.2
Gary Huff	1973–75	35	614	310	50.5	3,271	5.3	10.6	12	34	5.54%	49.8
Cade McNown	1999–00	10	515	281	54.6	3,111	6.0	11.1	16	19	3.69%	67.7

Quarterback	Rush Att	Rush Yds	Rush Avg	TD
Sid Luckman	204	-239	-1.2	4
Jim Harbaugh	296	1609	5.4	15
Jim McMahon	235	1284	5.5	15
Erik Kramer	89	141	1.6	4
Billy Wade	159	647	4.1	14
Ed Brown	220	841	3.8	10
Bob Avellini	104	225	2.2	5
Johnny Lujack	133	742	5.6	21
Rudy Bukich	71	56	0.8	6
Mike Tomczak	92	326	3.5	8
Vince Evans	146	761	5.2	13
George Blanda	91	312	3.4	5
Jim Miller	52	6	0.1	0
Jack Concannon	164	586	3.6	8
Bobby Douglass	373	2470	6.6	20
Rex Grossman	38	49	1.3	1
Zeke Bratkowski	45	224	5.0	1
Shane Matthews	29	73	2.5	1
Bernie Masterson	108	-69	-0.6	7
Gary Huff	39	66	1.7	2
Cade McNown	81	486	6.0	3

Record Holders

Passing Yards, Career: 14,686 Sid Luckman
Passing Yards, Season: 3,838 Erik Kramer 1995
Completion %, Career: 61.1% Shane Matthews
Completion %, Season: 62.7% Erik Kramer 1994;
   65.1% Shane Matthews 2001 (129 att.)
Touchdown Passes, Career: 137 Sid Luckman
Touchdown Passes, Season: 29 Erik Kramer 1995
Interceptions, Career: 131 Sid Luckman
Interceptions, Season: 31 Sid Luckman 1947
Rating, Career: 80.7 Erik Kramer
Rating, Season: 107.5 Sid Luckman 1943
Rush Yards, Career: 2,470 Bobby Douglass
Rush Yards, Season: 968 Bobby Douglass 1972

Passers by Categories

Five best starters: Sid Luckman literally defined the quarterback position for modern professional football and won four NFL titles for the Bears. Injury-prone Jim McMahon was a punky leader who headed the 1985 championship Bears. Billy Wade was an effective game manager for the 1963 championship team. To fill our the five, pick two more from the unfulfilled promise of Johnny Lujack or Erik Kramer, Ed Brown and Jim Harbaugh who all had a couple of good years in Chicago.

Worst starters, career: Bob Avellini, Vince Evans, Mike Tomczak, Zeke Bratkowski, Gary Huff and Bobby Douglass all come to mind as quarterbacks who got extended tryouts to prove they were not starters. Their touchdown to interception ratios were: Avellini 33–69, Evans 31–53, Tomczak 33–47, Bratkowski 24–58, Huff 12–34 and Douglass 30–51.

Best stat line, season: Sid Luckman in 1943 threw for 2,194 yards and averaged almost 11 yards per attempt in a 10-game season. He also set a new league record with 28 touchdowns yet only threw 12 interceptions to finish with a 107.5 quarterback rating. Erik Kramer set team records in 1995 with 3,838 yards and 29 touchdowns while achieving a 93.5 rating.

Worst stat line, season: Johnny Lujack's

injured shoulder in 1950 led him to throw only 4 touchdowns to 21 interceptions. Three years before, Sid Luckman threw 31 interceptions to set the team record. Bobby Douglass in 1971 completed just 40 percent of his passes, averaged 5.15 yards per attempt and threw only five touchdowns to 15 interceptions. In 1960, his last year in Chicago, Zeke Bratkowski threw 6 touchdowns to 21 interceptions. In 1981, Vince Evans completed 44 percent of his passes for 11 touchdowns and 20 interceptions and averaged just 5.4 yards per attempt.

Best stat line, playoffs: In the 1943 title game against Washington, Sid Luckman went 15–26, 276, 5–0.

Worst stat line, playoffs: Surprisingly, even Sid Luckman could have a bad day in a title game—1942 against Washington 4–11, 9, 0–2. Other bad performances include: Johnny Lujack in a 1950 playoff against the Rams: 15–29, 193, 0–3; Bob Avellini in a 1977 Divisional loss to Dallas: 15–25, 177, 1–4; Mike Phipps in a 1979 Wildcard loss to Philadelphia: 13–30, 142, 0–2; Doug Flutie in a 1986 Divisional loss to Washington 11–31, 134, 1–2; and Rex Grossman in a 2005 Divisional loss to Seattle: 17–41, 192, 1–1.

Big Days: The first passer to exceed 300 yards passing in a game was Sid Luckman with 433 yards on November 14, 1943. Johnny Lujack had the biggest day in franchise history by throwing for 468 yards on December 11, 1949. Billy Wade had the most 300-yard games with nine.

Running QBs: Bobby Douglass set a seasonal rushing record for a quarterback that lasted 34 years in 1972 when he gained 968 yards on the ground. Three times in his career, he gained over 100 yards rushing in a game. Unfortunately, he could not pass the ball accurately at all. Jack Concannon and Cade McNown were two other Bear running quarterbacks who never measured up. Jim Harbaugh had a better mix of skills, and Johnny Lujack may have been great if he hadn't been injured; he scored 21 touchdowns in four seasons.

Bomber: Sid Luckman was the best deep thrower of his time. He and Ed Brown both averaged an amazing 16 yards per completion in Chicago. Rudy Bukich was able to throw the ball nearly the entire length of the football field. Rex Grossman throws a nice deep ball, on occasion.

Most accurate: Jim McMahon and Erik Kramer could hit their targets.

Leader: The Bears were Sid Luckman's team. Jim McMahon had great rapport with his linemen and the Bears' defense in addition to the skill players on offense.

Comeback King: Sid Luckman had 10 4th quarter comebacks plus one in the postseason, while Jim McMahon had nine.

Highest Football IQ: Sid Luckman was the master of the T-formation.

Toughest: Bobby Douglass was big and strong and tough to bring down.

First signal caller/T-Formation QB: Jimmy Conzelman and Dutch Sternaman were the signal callers on the 1920 Decatur Staleys. Sid Luckman was the first quarterback of the modern T-Formation in league history in 1940.

First TD pass: Jimmy Conzelman hit owner George Halas for 15 yards on November 21, 1920 in a 28–7 win over the Hammond Pros.

Black QBs: The Bears employed the first black quarterback in the post–War era: Willie Thrower of Michigan State in 1953. However, he only got to throw eight passes. Since then, there has been Vince Evans from 1978–83, Henry Burris in 2002, Kordell Stewart in 2003 and Jeff Blake in 2005.

Tallest QB: Jonathan Quinn was 6'6" and Chad Hutchinson was 6'5". Bernie Masterson was the tallest quarterback of his day in the 1930s at 6'3".

Smallest QB: Signal callers include 5'7" Johnny Bryan and 5'8" Paddy Driscoll and Laurie Walquist. Quarterbacks start at 5'9": Keith Molesworth, Billy Patterson, Young Bussey and Doug Flutie. Also of note was 5'10" Carl Brumbaugh.

Oldest QB: Both Dave Krieg in 1996 and Chris Chandler in 2003 were 38.

Rookie sensation: Neither Sid Luckman nor Johnny Lujack played much in their rookie years, but both had quarterback ratings over 90: Luckman's 91.6 in 1939 on 51 passes and Lujack's 97.5 in 1948 on 66 passes. Jim McMahon completed 57 percent of his passes for over 1,500 yards in 1982, and Cade McNown's rookie numbers were very similar to McMahon's.

Late bloomer: Billy Wade was 33 when he finally won a title with the Bears in 1963. Rudy Bukich won the passing title in 1965 at 33. Erik

Kramer got a chance to be a full-time starter at 31 and set a team record for touchdown passes in 1995.

1st round picks: The Bears have used a number one pick for a quarterback nine times. Sid Luckman, the second pick acquired from Pittsburgh in 1939, went to the Hall of Fame. Frankie Albert, 10th in 1942, signed with the All America Conference. Johnny Lujack (4th in 1946), Bobby Layne (3rd in 1948), Jim McMahon (5th in 1982) all became stars although Layne was traded away. Jim Harbaugh, 26th in 1987, was a quality starter. Rex Grossman (22nd in 2003) is an inconsistent starter, but Bob Williams (2nd in 1951) and Cade McNown (12th in 1999) were flops. In addition, the Bears lost coin flips for the number one pick in 1944 and 1969 and thus lost out on drafting Otto Graham and Terry Bradshaw.

Out of position: Johnny Lujack and Sid Luckman played defensive back as well, and George Blanda played linebacker at one point. Bobby Douglass should have been a running back.

Long-time subs: George Blanda was a backup for most of his 10 years in Chicago. Mike Tomczak and Vince Evans were mostly backups for six years. Rudy Bukich and Zeke Bratkowski were mostly backups for five years.

QB controversy: In 1948, the Bears had three 'L's': Luckman, Lujack and Layne. Layne was traded, Luckman retired and Lujack got hurt. Throughout the 1950's, George Blanda, Zeke Bratkowski and Ed Brown battled for the number one slot, but none of the three was good enough to keep it.

College affiliation: Four signal callers have come from George Halas' alma mater of Illinois: Dutch and Joey Sternaman, Laurie Walquist and Tommy O'Connell. Notre Dame produced four Bear quarterbacks: Johnny Lujack, Bob Williams, Rusty Lisch and Rick Mirer. Four Bear quarterbacks have hailed from Boston College, too: Charley O'Rourke, Jack Concannon, Mark Hartsell and Doug Flutie.

Ones who got away: Bobby Layne went on to the Hall of Fame and won three championships. George Blanda also went to the Hall of Fame, but that was for his kicking and longevity as much as his quarterbacking. On a lower scale, Jim Harbaugh and Doug Flutie had their best years elsewhere.

Has beens: An unending string: John Huarte, Kent Nix, Jack Concannon, Greg Landry, Mike Phipps, Steve Stenstrom, Steve Fuller, Steve Walsh, Rick Mirer, Dave Krieg, Chris Chandler, Kordell Stewart, Jim Miller, Shane Matthews, Henry Burris, Chad Hutchinson, Jeff Blake and Brian Griese.

Ruinous injuries: Johnny Lujack ruined his shoulder playing defensive back after leading the NFL in attempts, completions, yards and touchdowns in 1950. Jim McMahon had an unbroken string of injuries that took him off the field.

Best trade: Buying Paddy Driscoll from the Cardinals. Obtaining the rights from the Steelers to Sid Luckman for Eggs Manske and the rights to Bobby Layne for Ray Evans. Getting George Blanda back for cash one week after including him in a multiplayer deal with Baltimore for lineman Dick Barwegan. Essentially loaning Rudy Bukich to the Steelers for a couple of seasons. Getting Billy Wade from the Rams for Zeke Bratkowski and Erich Barnes. Getting a number one pick from the Steelers for Ed Brown.

Worst trade: Giving up Bobby Layne to the New York Bulldogs for a number 1 (Chuck Hunsinger). Trading Mike Ditka to the Eagles for Jack Concannon. Giving up a number 1 (Ozzie Newsome) and a number 4 to the Browns for Mike Phipps. Trading Jim McMahon to the Chargers for a number 2. Giving up a number 1 to Seattle for Rick Mirer.

Title winners: Sid Luckman, 4; Billy Wade, 1; Jim McMahon, 1; Keith Molesworth, 2; Carl Brumbaugh, 1; Dutch Sternaman, 1.

Hall of Famers: Sid Luckman, Paddy Driscoll and George Blanda.

All Pro/Pro Bowl seasons: Sid Luckman, 8; Paddy Driscoll, 3; Johnny Lujack, 3; Carl Brumbaugh, 2; Billy Wade, 2; Bernie Masterson, 1; Rudy Bukich, 1; Jim McMahon, 1.

QBs as coaches: Johnny Bryan went 2–13 with Milwaukee; Joey Sternaman went 4–3 with Duluth; Paddy Driscoll went 28–17–4 with the Cardinals and Bears; Jimmy Conzelman went 87–63–18 with Milwaukee, Rock Island, Providence, the Detroit Panthers and the Cardinals; Keith Molesworth went 3–9 with the Colts; Gene Ronzani went 14–31–1 with Green Bay; Bob Snyder went 6–6 with the Rams. Sean Payton is 10–6 with the Saints.

Underrated: Jim Harbaugh was a very mobile and effective quarterback.

Overrated: Jim McMahon couldn't stay healthy enough to stay on the field.

Best Nicknames: Bernie "Bat" Masterson, Rudy "the Rifle" Bukich and Doug "Bambi" Flutie.

Time Capsule: The emergence of the modern, split–T formation in 1940. Sid Luckman becoming the first quarterback to throw seven touchdown passes in a game in 1943. Luckman's surprise bootleg touchdown in the 1946 championship game against the Giants. Willie Thrower's benchmark appearance in 1953. Jim McMahon's headbands in the 1985 playoff run.

What If: If the Bears had kept Bobby Layne in the 1950s, would they have won more than one championship in the decade?

Off the field: Brian Griese's father was Bob Griese. Jim McMahon became the first quarterback ever to be suspended for steroid use in 1999. Cade McNown liked to party more than play football and he washed out quickly. He also appeared in *Outta Time* in 2002. Jim McMahon also liked to party and got into frequent scrapes

with his coaches and league officials, but he also loved to play the game. He appeared in *Johnny Be Good* in 1987 as well as episodes of *Grounded for Life* and *Sons of Thunder*. Jack Concannon appeared in *M*A*S*H* and the TV movie *Brian's Song*. Rudy Bukich appeared in *Spartacus* and an episode of *The Big Valley*. Sid Luckman appeared in *Triple Threat* in 1948.

Quarterback Bibliography

Sid Luckman
Luckman, Sid. *Luckman at Quarterback: Football as a Sport and a Career.* Chicago: Ziff-Davis, 1949.

Jim McMahon
McMahon, Jim, and Bob Verdi. *McMahon.* New York: Warner Books, 1986.

Bobby Layne *see* Detroit Lions

George Blanda *see* Oakland Raiders

Doug Flutie *see* Buffalo Bills

Brian Griese *see* Denver Broncos

21

Cincinnati Bengals

Leading Passers, by Yards

Quarterback	Years	G	Att	Comp	Pct	Yds	Y/A	Y/Cp	TD	Int	Int %	Rating
Ken Anderson	1971–86	192	4,475	2,654	59.3	32,838	7.3	12.4	197	160	3.58%	81.9
Boomer Esiason	1984–92, 1997	127	3,564	2,015	56.5	27,149	7.6	13.5	187	131	3.68%	83.1
Jeff Blake	1994–99	75	2,221	1,240	55.8	15,134	6.8	12.2	93	62	2.79%	79.3
Carson Palmer	2004–06	45	1461	932	63.8	10,768	7.4	11.6	78	43	2.94%	91.5
Jon Kitna	2001–05	52	1,708	1,010	59.1	10,721	6.3	10.6	59	59	3.45%	74.6
David Klingler	1992–95	31	687	375	54.6	3,880	5.6	10.3	16	21	3.06%	66.1
Virgil Carter	1970–72	33	582	328	56.4	3,850	6.6	11.7	22	20	3.44%	74.9
Turk Schonert	1981–85, 1987–89	53	350	216	61.7	2,756	7.9	12.8	7	12	3.43%	78.7
Neil O'Donnell	1998	13	343	212	61.8	2,216	6.5	10.5	15	4	1.17%	90.2
Akili Smith	1999–02	12	461	215	46.6	2,212	4.8	10.3	5	13	2.82%	52.8
Jack Thompson	1979–81	31	370	175	47.3	2,072	5.6	11.8	13	19	5.14%	55.1
Greg Cook	1969–73	12	200	107	53.5	1,865	9.3	17.4	15	11	5.50%	87.6

Quarterback	Rush Att	Rush Yds	Rush Avg	TD
Ken Anderson	397	2220	5.6	20
Boomer Esiason	340	1355	4.0	5
Jeff Blake	285	1499	5.3	10
Carson Palmer	78	125	1.6	2
Jon Kitna	101	299	3.0	5
David Klingler	69	430	6.2	0
Virgil Carter	54	345	6.4	4
Turk Schonert	62	276	4.5	3
Neil O'Donnell	13	34	2.6	0
Akili Smith	71	358	5.0	1
Jack Thompson	39	200	5.1	6
Greg Cook	25	148	5.9	1

Record Holders

Passing Yards, Career: 32,838 Ken Anderson

Passing Yards, Season: 4,035 Carson Palmer 2006

Completion %, Career: 63.8% Carson Palmer

Completion %, Season: 70.6% Ken Anderson 1982

Touchdown Passes, Career: 197 Ken Anderson

Touchdown Passes, Season: 32 Carson Palmer 2005

Interceptions, Career: 160 Ken Anderson

Interceptions, Season: 22 Ken Anderson 1978; Boomer Esiason 1990; Jon Kitna 2001

Rating, Career: 91.5 Carson Palmer

Rating, Season: 101.1 Carson Palmer 2005

Rush Yards, Career: 2,220 Ken Anderson

Rush Yards, Season: 332 Jeff Blake 1999

Passers by Categories

Five best starters: Ken Anderson was a smart and talented quarterback for 16 years in Cincinnati and took the Bengals to the Super Bowl. Boomer Esiason was a fiery left-handed leader who also took the Bengals to the Super Bowl. Carson Palmer has established himself as a top quarterback in the league in his first few years. Jeff Blake was an exciting performer on some lousy Bengal teams in the 1990s. Greg Cook showed as much promise in his rookie year as any quarterback ever has.

Worst starters, career: David Klingler couldn't make the transition from the Run-and-Shoot in college to the pro game. Akili Smith looked lost, and both he and Jack Thompson completed less than 50 percent of their passes

and threw more interceptions than touchdowns in their brief Bengal careers.

Best stat line, season: Carson Palmer set team seasonal records for touchdowns and passer rating in 2005 with 32 and 101.1 respectively. In 1988, Boomer Esiason threw for 3,572 yards, 28 touchdowns and averaged 9.21 yards per attempt for a 97.4 rating. Ken Anderson had four seasons in which his passer rating was in the 90s: 1974, 1975, 1981 and 1982. In the Super Bowl season of 1981, he threw for 3,754 yards and 29 touchdowns.

Worst stat line, season: Ken Anderson had an off season in 1978 when he threw only 10 touchdowns to 22 interceptions. In 1993 and 1994, David Klingler had very similar stats, throwing 6 touchdowns and 9 interceptions in both seasons and averaging fewer than 5.8 yards per attempt. In 2000, Akili Smith completed 44 percent of his passes and averaged only 4.7 yards per attempt. Also in 2000, Scott Mitchell completed 47 percent of his passes, averaged 5.2 yards per attempt and threw 3 touchdowns to 8 interceptions. In 2001, Jon Kitna averaged only 5.5 yards per attempt and threw 12 touchdowns to 22 interceptions.

Best stat line, playoffs: Ken Anderson in the Super Bowl against San Francisco went 25–34, 300, 2–2.

Worst stat line, playoffs: In the Super Bowl against the 49ers, Boomer Esiason was 11–25, 144, 0–1. In a 2005 Wildcard loss to Pittsburgh, Jon Kitna went 24–40, 197, 1–2. In the 1970 Divisional loss to the Colts, Virgil Carter went 7–20, 64, 0–1.

Big Days: The first passer to exceed 300 yards passing in a game was Greg Cook with 327 yards on September 21, 1969. The first to reach

400 yards was Ken Anderson with 447 on November 17, 1975. Boomer Esiason had the biggest day in franchise history by throwing for 490 yards on October 7, 1990. Esiason had 23 300-yard games to Anderson's 19.

Running QBs: Ken Anderson and Jeff Blake both were talented at escaping from the rush. Anderson scored 20 touchdowns on the ground.

Bomber: Carson Palmer can go deep with anyone. Jeff Blake made his career throwing long to Carl Pickens.

Most accurate: Ken Anderson broke Sammy Baugh's NFL season record for completion percentage in 1982 with 70.6 percent.

Leader: Ken Anderson was quiet and efficient and led by example.

Comeback King: Boomer Esiason had 21 4th quarter comebacks to Anderson's 16.

Highest Football IQ: Ken Anderson understood what was happening on the field like a coach and then became one.

Toughest: Anderson played 192 games in 16 years in Cincinnati.

First signal caller/T-Formation QB: Although John Stofa was the first Bengal signed by Paul Brown, Dewey Warren from Tennessee started in the first game and completed the first pass — a 2-yard dink to Tom Smiley.

First TD pass: John Stofa hit Bob Trumpy for 58 yards on September 15, 1968 in a 24–10 win over Denver.

Black QBs: Punter Dave Lewis from 1970–73, Jeff Blake from 1994–99, Akili Smith from 1999–2002 and Anthony Wright in 2006.

Tallest QB: Scott Mitchell was 6'6". Carson Palmer, Boomer Esiason and Mike Wells were all 6'5".

Smallest QB: Dewey Warren and Jeff Blake were both 6' and Virgil Carter claimed to be 6'1".

Oldest QB: Ken Anderson was 37 in his final year of 1986. Boomer Esiason was the oldest starter at 36 in 1997.

Rookie sensation: The legendary Greg Cook in 1969 before his shoulder problems had a yards per attempt figure of 9.4 and threw 15 touchdowns to only 11 interceptions for a 88.3 passer rating. Carson Palmer's rookie year was actually his second year since he did not appear in any games in 2003. He threw for 2,897 yards and 18 touchdowns in 2004.

Late bloomer: After Cook went down, Bill

Walsh devised his short passing offense expressly for 25-year-old weak-armed Virgil Carter in 1970, and he held the job till Ken Anderson showed up.

1st round picks: The Bengals have selected five quarterbacks in the first round. Two were successful — Carson Palmer 1st in 2003 and Greg Cook 5th in 1969. The other three flopped — Jack Thompson 3rd in 1979, David Klingler 6th in 1992 and Akili Smith 3rd in 1999.

Out of position: Dave Lewis was a punter and emergency quarterback.

Long-time subs: Turk Schonert was mostly a reserve for eight years over two terms in Cincinnati. Erik Wilhelm was a distant backup for six years.

QB controversy: There was debate over whether Ken Anderson should lose his job to Jack Thompson and then Boomer Esiason. There were the questions of whether Boomer Esiason should regain his job from Jeff Blake, and the wisdom of simply handing the starting job to Carson Palmer in his second year.

College affiliation: Boomer Esiason and Neil O'Donnell both were Maryland Terrapins. Turk Schonert and Dave Lewis were both from Stanford.

Ones who got away: None.

Has beens: John Reaves, Paul Justin, Todd Philcox, Jay Schroeder, Scott Mitchell, Gus Frerotte and Anthony Wright.

Ruinous injuries: As a rookie, Greg Cook looked like a future Hall of Famer until he tore up his shoulder. He tried to come back from several operations over four years, but his arm was ruined, and he finally retired after 1973.

Best trade: Cincinnati got a number 1 and a number 6 from the Eagles for Mike Boryla. After Jack Thompson flopped in Cincinnati, the Bengals were still able to get a number 1 pick for him from Tampa.

Worst trade: Giving up a number 1 and a number 2 to the Dolphins for John Stofa. Trading Pro Bowl tackle Stan Walters and Wayne Clark to the Eagles for John Reaves and a number 2.

Title winners: None.

Hall of Famers: None.

All Pro/Pro Bowl seasons: Ken Anderson, 5; Boomer Esison, 4; Carson Palmer, 2; Jeff Blake, 1.

QBs as coaches: Sam Wyche 84–107 in Cincinnati and Tampa.

Underrated: Ken Anderson was mobile, accurate and reliable over a long career in Cincinnati.

Overrated: Greg Cook looked like a Hall of Famer in his rookie year, but who knows what he actually would have done if he hadn't gotten hurt.

Best Nicknames: Jack "the Throwin' Samoan" Thompson, Dewey "Swamp Rat" Warren and David "Slinger" Klinger.

Time Capsule: Bill Walsh devising the West Coast Offense for Virgil Carter in 1970.

What If: Would Greg Cook have lived up to his potential if he had been healthy? Would he have been any better than the underappreciated Ken Anderson?

Off the field: John Reaves had some unfortunate drug problems in the 1970s. Boomer Esiason appeared in episodes of *Spin City* and *Brother's Keeper.*

Quarterback Bibliography

None.

22

Cleveland Browns

Leading Passers, by Yards

Quarterback	Years	G	Att	Comp	Pct	Yds	Y/A	Y/Cp	TD	Int	Int %	Rating
Brian Sipe	1974–83	125	3,439	1,944	56.5	23,713	6.9	12.2	154	149	4.33%	74.8
Otto Graham	1946–56	125	2,626	1,464	55.8	23,584	9.0	16.1	174	135	5.14%	86.6
Bernie Kosar	1985–93	108	3,150	1,853	58.8	21,904	7.0	11.8	116	81	2.57%	81.6
Otto Graham (NFL only)	1950–55	72	1,565	872	55.7	13,499	8.6	15.5	88	94	6.01%	78.2
Frank Ryan	1962–68	84	1,755	907	51.7	13,361	7.6	14.7	134	88	5.01%	81.4
Tim Couch	1999–03	31	1,715	1,026	59.8	11,144	6.5	10.9	64	67	3.91%	75.2
Bill Nelsen	1968–72	58	1,314	689	52.4	9,725	7.4	14.1	71	71	5.40%	72.1
Milt Plum	1957–61	59	1,083	627	57.9	8,914	8.2	14.2	66	39	3.60%	89.9
Mike Phipps	1970–76	88	1,317	633	48.1	7,700	5.8	12.2	40	81	6.15%	51.0
Vinny Testaverde	1993–95	37	998	578	57.9	7,255	7.3	12.6	47	37	3.71%	80.9
Paul McDonald	1981–84	53	767	411	53.6	5,269	6.9	12.8	24	37	4.82%	65.7
Charlie Frye	2005–06	21	556	350	62.9	3456	6.2	9.9	14	22	3.96%	72.3
Kelly Holcomb	2001–04	22	507	323	63.7	3,438	6.8	10.6	26	21	4.14%	83.3
Jim Ninowski	1958–59, 1962–66	40	371	184	49.6	2,630	7.1	14.3	20	22	5.93%	66.2

Quarterback	Rush Att	Rush Yds	Rush Avg	TD
Brian Sipe	223	762	3.4	11
Otto Graham	405	882	2.1	11
Bernie Kosar	162	216	1.3	4
Otto Graham	306	682	2.2	33

Quarterback	Rush Att	Rush Yds	Rush Avg	TD
Frank Ryan	229	1032	4.5	4
Tim Couch	123	567	4.6	2
Bill Nelsen	39	-5	-0.1	1
Milt Plum	128	204	1.6	8
Mike Phipps	198	1155	5.8	11
Vinny Testaverde	57	173	3.0	4
Paul McDonald	37	6	0.2	1
Charlie Frye	65	275	4.2	4
Kelly Holcomb	20	14	0.7	0
Jim Ninowski	25	35	1.4	0

Record Holders

Passing Yards, Career: 23,713 Brian Sipe
Passing Yards, Season: 4,132 Brian Sipe 1980
Completion %, Career: 63.7% Kelly Holcomb
(507 att.); 59.8% Tim Couch
Completion %, Season: 64.7% Otto Graham 1953
Touchdown Passes, Career: 154 Brian Sipe; 174
Otto Graham (Including AAFC)
Touchdown Passes, Season: 30 Brian Sipe 1980
Interceptions, Career: 149 Brian Sipe
Interceptions, Season: 26 Brian Sipe 1979
Rating, Career: 89.9 Milt Plum
Rating, Season: 110.4 Milt Plum 1960; 112.1 Otto
Graham 1946 (AAFC)
Rush Yards, Career: 1,155 Mike Phipps
Rush Yards, Season: 395 Mike Phipps 1973

Passers by Categories

Five best starters: Otto Graham has a legitimate claim on being the best quarterback in pro football history with 10 title games in 10 years. Frank Ryan showed what Blanton Collier's skillful coaching could do and led the team to its last championship. Bernie Kosar three times took the Browns to the brink of the Super Bowl only to be bested by John Elway. Brian Sipe, the leader of the Kardiac Kids, came within one bad pass against the Raiders of taking the Browns to the Super Bowl in 1980. Gimpy-kneed Bill Nelsen was another tribute to Blanton Collier's coaching.

Worst starters, career: Jim Ninowski and Doug Pederson were career backups who were given brief disastrous trials as starters. Mike Phipps was an ineffective dink-and-dunk flop. Paul McDonald was a left-handed broken bridge from Sipe to Kosar. Tim Couch had the skill to be an NFL quarterback, but the combination of thin skin, bad coaching and weak teams destroyed his career.

Best stat line, season: Otto Graham in 1953 completed 64.7 percent of his passes and averaged 10.6 yards per attempt. Milt Plum achieved an astronomical 110.4 passer rating by completing 60.4 percent of his passes for 21 touchdowns and only 5 interceptions and averaging 9.2 yards per attempt in 1960; throwing to Jim Brown and Bobby Mitchell out of the backfield helped. In 1966, Frank Ryan threw for nearly 3,000 yards and 29 touchdowns. In 1980, Brian Sipe set team seasonal records for yards with 4,132 and touchdowns with 30. Bernie Kosar threw for a career high 22 touchdowns and 95.4 passer rating in 1987.

Worst stat line, season: Tommy O'Connell tried to replace Otto Graham in 1956 by completing 43.8 percent of his passes and averaging 5.7 yards per attempt. Doug Pederson was even worse in 2000, throwing 2 touchdowns to 8 interceptions and averaging 4.99 yards per attempt. However, the bottom was Mike Phipps who earned passer ratings of 49.4, 46.7 and 47.5 for: 1973 — 49.5 percent completions, yards per attempt of 5.7, 9 touchdowns and 20 interceptions; 1974 — 45.7 percent completions, yards per attempt of 5.4, 9 touchdowns and 17 interceptions; 1975 — 51.8 percent completions, yards per attempt of 5.6, 4 touchdowns and 19 interceptions.

Best stat line, playoffs: In the 1950 championship against the Rams, Otto Graham went 22-33, 298, 4–1. In the 1964 title game against the Colts, Frank Ryan went 11-18, 208, 3–1. Bernie Kosar threw for 483 in beating the Jets in a 1986 Divisional game, but his greatest game was the 1987 AFC championship loss to Denver: 26-41, 336, 3–1.

Worst stat line, playoffs: In the 1953 title game against the Lions, Otto Graham was 2–15, 20, 0–2. Four years later against Detroit again, Milt Plum went 5–13, 51, 0–2. In the 1969 NFL title against the Colts, Bill Nelsen went 9–21, 104, 0–3. In a 1972 Divisional loss to Miami, Mike Phipps went 9–23, 131, 1–5. Finally, in the gut wrenching AFC title loss to Oakland in 1980, Brian Sipe was 13–40, 183, 0–3 including that last second end zone interception.

Big Days: The first passer to exceed 300 yards passing in a game was Otto Graham with 325 yards on November 23, 1947. After the Browns joined the NFL, Graham threw for 346 in their first game on September 15, 1950. After the Browns were reborn in 1999, Tim Couch threw for 316 on September 17, 2000. The first to reach 400 yards was Graham with 401 on October 4, 1952. The first for the reborn Browns was Kelly Holcomb with 413 on November 28, 2004. Brian Sipe had the biggest day in franchise history by throwing for 444 yards on October 25, 1981, and he leads the team with 18 300-yard games total.

Running QBs: Mike Phipps could run, but he could not pass. Otto Graham rushed for 44 touchdowns in his 10 seasons, more than any other quarterback in history.

Bomber: Otto Graham and Frank Ryan could go deep. Immobile Bill Nelsen loved to throw the bomb.

Most accurate: Otto Graham.

Leader: Otto Graham was the unquestioned leader of a team that won its division 10 years in a row.

Comeback King: Kardiac Kid Brian Sipe brought the Browns back 23 times in the 4th quarter.

Highest Football IQ: Otto Graham thought analytically like a coach.

Toughest: Graham never missed a game for the Browns and started 99 straight.

First signal caller/T-Formation QB: Cliff Lewis actually started the Browns first game in 1946. Graham suggested that since Lewis was from Cleveland, it would be nice for the hometown hero to start the team's first game in Cleveland.

First TD pass: On September 6, 1946, Cliff Lewis hit Mac Speedie for 19 yards in a 44–0 thrashing of the Miami Seahawks in the very first game of the All America Conference. On September 16, 1950, Otto Graham hit Dub Jones for 59 yards in a 35–10 dismantling of the NFL champion Eagles in Cleveland's first NFL game.

Black QBs: Dave Mays in 1976–77 and Spergon Wynn in 2000.

Tallest QB: Derek Anderson is 6'6" Bernie Kosar, Vinny Testaverde, Kevin Thompson and Don Strock were all 6'5".

Smallest QB: In the AAFC, George Terlep was 5'10". In the NFL, John Borton, Rick Trocano, Ty Detmer and Jerry Rhome all claimed to be 6'.

Oldest QB: Don Strock was 37 in 1988. Jeff Garcia was 34 as a starter in 2004, and Otto Graham turned 34 in his final year of 1955.

Rookie sensation: Otto Graham was terrific right from the start averaging 10.5 yards per attempt and compiling a passer rating of 112.1 in 1946. Bernie Kosar showed more promise than most rookies, throwing 8 touchdowns to 7 interceptions for over 1,500 yards.

Late bloomer: Frank Ryan and Bill Nelsen didn't get a chance to play for a good team like the Browns until they were 26 and 27 respectively. Brian Sipe was 27 when he finally got a chance to start. Vinny Testaverde had his career turned around in Cleveland at the age of 30.

1st round picks: Of the five Brown quarterbacks selected in the first round, only Bernie Kosar from 1985 was a success. Harry Agganis, 12th in 1952, played baseball instead and died while in his twenties. Bobby Garrett, 1st in 1954, had a stuttering problem and never developed. He and Babe Parilli were traded for each other twice. Mike Phipps, 3rd in 1970, was ineffective but lasted a decade in the league. Tim Couch, 1st in 1999 was out of football in five years.

Out of position: Cliff Lewis was more of a defensive back than quarterback. Johnny Evans was a punter and emergency quarterback. Receiver Frisman Jackson was a quarterback in college.

Long-time subs: George Ratterman was a reserve for five years. Jim Ninowski was a Browns backup for seven years over two terms in Cleveland.

QB controversy: There was some controversy about Ninowski and first Milt Plum and later Frank Ryan. The big stink in public was when local favorite Bernie Kosar was cut to make room for Vinny Testaverde who at the time appeared to be a complete failure.

College affiliation: Len Dawson, Mike Phipps and Gary Danielson all attended Purdue.

Ones who got away: Paul Brown could not see he had a Hall of Famer in Len Dawson.

Has beens: Babe Parilli, Dick Shiner, Jerry Rhome, Mike Pagel, Don Strock, Mike Tomczak, Doug Pederson, Ty Detmer, Mark Rypien, Jeff Garcia, Trent Dilfer and Ken Dorsey.

Ruinous injuries: Bill Nelsen's bad knees shortened his career. Bernie Kosar had a host of arm woes.

Best trade: Many to choose from: getting George Ratterman from the Yankees for Stan Williams and Hersch Forester; getting Frank Ryan from the Rams along with Tom Wilson for Larry Stephens, a number 3 and a number 6; getting Bill Nelsen from the Steelers for Dick Shiner, Frank Parker and a number 2; getting rid of Mike Phipps to the Bears for a number 1 (Ozzie Newsome) and a number 4; getting the rights to draft Bernie Kosar from the Bills for a number 1, a number 3 and a number 5.

Worst trade: Giving up Hall of Fame receiver Paul Warfield to the Dolphins for the rights to Mike Phipps.

Title winners: Otto Graham, 7 (4 in the AAFC and 3 in the NFL); Frank Ryan, 1.

Hall of Famers: Otto Graham and Len Dawson.

All Pro/Pro Bowl seasons: Otto Graham, 10; Frank Ryan, 3; Brian Sipe, 2; Bill Nelsen, 2; Bernie Kosar, 1; Vinny Testaverde, 1.

QBs as coaches: Otto Graham was 17–22–3 in Washington.

Underrated: Frank Ryan proved himself to be a very good quarterback who twice took Cleveland to the title game.

Overrated: Milt Plum had terrific, but empty stats year after year, but the team did not win. Bernie Kosar was very good, but is remembered as being better than he was.

Best Nicknames: Automatic Otto Graham.

Time Capsule: Otto Graham's great clutch performances in the 1950 opener against the defending champion Eagles and the 1950 title game against the Rams. Paul Brown's messenger guards and 1956 radio helmet. Brian Sipe's disastrous interception against the Raiders in the AFC championship.

What If: If Paul Brown had brought in Johnny Unitas in 1955, rather than telling the released Steeler to try again next year, would the two have been able to coexist? After all, Unitas was a great play caller who said you weren't a real quarterback until you could tell your coach to go to hell. If the reborn Browns had gone with Donovan McNabb rather than Tim Couch with their first pick, would the team have been less of a basket case?

Off the field: Despite Terrell Owens implying that his former quarterback was gay, Jeff Garcia at the time was dating the *Playboy* Playmate of the Year who was from Ohio. Tim Couch dated Playmate of the Year Heather Kozar. Frank Ryan got his PhD in Mathematics. Bernie Kosar appeared in an episode of *Drew Carey*.

Quarterback Bibliography

Otto Graham

Graham, Otto. *Otto Graham: T Quarterback.* Englewood Cliffs, NJ: Prentice Hall, 1953.

Graham, Duey. *Ottomatic: The Remarkable Story of Otto Graham.* Wayne, MI: Immortal Investments Publishing, 2004.

George Rutterman

Rutterman, George, and Robert G. Deindorfer. *Confessions of a Gypsy Quarterback: Inside the Wacky World of Pro Football.* New York: Coward-McCann, 1962.

Tim Couch

McGill, John, and Dave Baker. *Tim Couch: A Passion for the Game.* Champaign, IL: Sports Publishing, 1999.

23

Dallas Cowboys

Leading Passers, by Yards

Quarterback	Years	G	Att	Comp	Pct	Yds	Y/A	Y/Cp	TD	Int	Int %	Rating
Troy Aikman	1989–00	165	4,715	2,898	61.5	32,942	7.0	11.4	165	141	2.99%	81.6
Roger Staubach	1969–79	131	2,958	1,685	57	22,700	7.7	13.5	153	109	3.68%	83.4
Danny White	1976–88	166	2,950	1,761	59.7	21,959	7.4	12.5	155	132	4.47%	81.7
Don Meredith	1960–68	104	2,308	1,170	50.7	17,199	7.5	14.7	135	111	4.81%	74.8
Craig Morton	1965–74	97	1,308	685	52.4	10,279	7.9	15.0	80	73	5.58%	75.6
Steve Pelluer	1985–88	46	922	520	56.4	6,555	7.1	12.6	28	38	4.12%	71.7
Quincy Carter	2001–03	23	903	507	56.1	5,839	6.5	11.5	29	36	3.99%	69.9
Eddie LeBaron	1960–63	52	692	359	51.9	5,331	7.7	14.8	45	53	7.66%	67.2
Drew Bledsoe	2005–06	22	668	390	58.4	4,803	7.2	12.3	30	15	2.25%	86.3
Gary Hogeboom	1982–85	42	518	279	53.9	3,550	6.9	12.7	13	23	4.44%	65.4
Vinny Testaverde	2004	16	495	297	60	3,532	7.1	11.9	17	20	4.04%	76.4
Tony Romo	2005–06	32	337	220	65.3	2,903	8.6	13.2	19	13	3.86%	95.1
Jason Garrett	1993–99	23	294	165	56.1	2,042	6.9	12.4	11	5	1.70%	83.2

Quarterback	Rush Att	Rush Yds	Rush Avg	TD
Troy Aikman	327	1016	3.1	9
Roger Staubach	410	2264	5.5	20
Danny White	159	482	3.0	8
Don Meredith	242	1216	5.0	15
Craig Morton	74	246	3.3	6
Steve Pelluer	120	701	5.8	4
Quincy Carter	140	498	3.6	3
Eddie LeBaron	45	170	3.8	1
Drew Bledsoe	42	78	1.9	4
Gary Hogeboom	32	57	1.8	1
Vinny Testaverde	21	38	1.8	1
Tony Romo	34	102	3.0	0
Jason Garrett	29	15	0.5	0

Record Holders

Passing Yards, Career: 32,942 Troy Aikman
Passing Yards, Season: 3,980 Danny White 1980
Completion %, Career: 61.5% Troy Aikman
Completion %, Season: 69.1% Troy Aikman 1993
Touchdown Passes, Career: 165 Troy Aikman
Touchdown Passes, Season: 29 Danny White 1983
Interceptions, Career: 141 Troy Aikman
Interceptions, Season: 25 Eddie LeBaron 1960 and
   Danny White 1980

Rating, Career: 83.4 Roger Staubach
Rating, Season: 104.8 Roger Staubach 1971
Rush Yards, Career: 2,264 Roger Staubach
Rush Yards, Season: 343 Roger Staubach 1971

Passers by Categories

Five best starters: Troy Aikman and Roger
Staubach were all-time greats — the former tall
and stoic in the pocket and the latter scrambling

to make a play on the run. Don Meredith led the Cowboys to the playoffs the first three times in franchise history. Danny White could not measure up to Roger Staubach, his predecessor, but was a good, solid winning quarterback. Eddie LeBaron was a professional quarterback for the earliest weak rosters of the expansion Cowboys.

Worst starters, career: Gary Hogeboom and Steve Pelluer both unsuccessfully tried to replace Danny White and ended the Cowboys 25-year unbroken string of quality starting quarterbacks from LeBaron to White. Quincy Carter was inconsistent and had some problems with drugs that cost him his job.

Best stat line, season: As a part-time starter in 1962, Eddie LeBaron had a passer rating of 95.4 by completing 57.4 percent of his passes and averaging 8.7 yards per attempt. In 1966, Don Meredith threw for 24 touchdowns and averaged 8.2 yards per attempt. Roger Staubach's greatest two seasons were in 1973 when he 62.6 percent of his passes, averaged 8.5 yards per attempt and threw 23 touchdowns for a 94.6 rating and 1979 when he completed 57.9 percent of his passes, averaged 7.8 yards per attempt and threw 27 touchdowns for a 92.3 rating. Troy Aikman had a rating of 99 in 1993 when he completed 69.1 percent of his passes for 15 touchdowns and only 6 interceptions, and he had a rating of 93.6 in 1995 when he completed 64.8 percent of his passes for 16 touchdowns and only 7 interceptions. Tony Romo had a great first full season in 2006 throwing for 2,903 yards, averaging 8.6 yards per pass and completing 65 percent of his passes.

Worst stat line, season: In Troy Aikman's rookie year of 1989, he threw 9 touchdowns and 18 interceptions while completing just 52.9 percent of his passes. Steve Pelluer threw 8 touchdowns against 17 interceptions in 1986. In 1990, Babe Laufenberg completed 35.8 percent of his passes, averaged 4.2 yards per attempt and threw 1 touchdown against 6 interceptions for a 16.9 rating. Ryan Leaf completed just over half his passes in 2001 for 1 touchdown and 3 interceptions while averaging just 5.6 yards per attempt in the last gasp of his disappointing career.

Best stat line, playoffs: Roger Staubach had many great days in the playoffs. In the 1972 comeback win over the 49ers in a Divisional game, Roger went 12–20, 174, 2–0; in the 1975 NFC title game against the Rams, he went 16–26, 220, 4–1; and in the second Super Bowl loss to the Steelers, he went 17–30, 228, 3–1. Troy Aikman excelled in his first Super Bowl against the Bills by going 22–30, 273, 4–0 and in the 1994 NFC title loss to the 49ers, he threw for 380 yards. Danny White had a great Divisional win over the Falcons in 1980: 25–39, 322, 3–1.

Worst stat line, playoffs: In the Ice Bowl in the 1967 NFL title in Green Bay, Don Meredith went 10–25, 59, 0–1 and the following year went 3–9, 42, 0–3 in a Divisional loss to Cleveland, his sad final game as a Cowboy. In three playoff games in 1970, Craig Morton went a combined 23–66, 266, 2–4. Roger Staubach in the 1973 NFC title loss to the Vikings went 10–21, 89, 0–4. In a 1998 Wildcard loss to Arizona, Troy Aikman went 22–49, 191, 1–3.

Big Days: The first passer to exceed 300 yards passing in a game was Eddie LeBaron with 345 yards on September 24, 1960, the Cowboys first-ever game. The first to reach 400 yards was Don Meredith with 460 on November 10, 1963. That is still the team record for most yards. Troy Aikman had the most 300-yard games with 13.

Running QBs: Roger "the Dodger" Staubach was known for his scrambling which drove Tom Landry crazy, but he scored 20 touchdowns running. Don Meredith and Danny White were mobile and skilled passers. Steve Pelluer and Quincy Carter were mobile only.

Bomber: Troy Aikman and Don Meredith were the best at getting the ball downfield. Craig Morton had a big arm as well early in his career.

Most accurate: In the practices before one Super Bowl, it was said that almost no Aikman passes hit the ground. It wasn't much different at game time. Roger Staubach was accurate as well.

Leader: Roger Staubach was an inspirational leader.

Comeback King: Roger Staubach had 21 4th quarter comebacks and two more in the postseason.

Highest Football IQ: Troy Aikman thoroughly understood his team's offense.

Toughest: Don Meredith took a regular beating in the 1960s, but kept going.

First signal caller/T-Formation QB: Veteran Eddie LeBaron who came over from Washington.

First TD pass: Eddie LeBaron to Jim Doran for 75 yards in a 35–28 loss to Pittsburgh on September 24, 1960.

Black QBs: Reggie Collier was the first in 1986. Randall Cunningham and Anthony Wright came in 2000. Quincy Carter was the first regular starter in 2002.

Tallest QB: 6'7" Sonny Gibbs in 1963. Bernie Kosar, Vinny Testaverde, Drew Bledsoe, Ryan Leaf and Chad Hutchinson were all 6'5".

Smallest QB: Eddie LeBaron was 5'9" on his tippy-toes. Some reported him at 5'7". Jerry Rhome was 6' in his dreams and in the Media Guide.

Oldest QB: Vinny Testaverde started at age 40 in 2004.

Rookie sensation: None. Both Troy Aikman and Don Meredith saw action as rookies, but did not play well. Tony Romo had appeared in 22 games, but had never thrown a pass before his breakout 2006 season.

Late bloomer: Not only did Roger Staubach have to fulfill his Navy responsibilities, he didn't win the starting job till his third year, 1971, at age 29. Danny White was 28 before Staubach finally retired.

1st round picks: The Cowboys have selected three quarterbacks in the first round. Troy Aikman, 1st in 1989, was a success. Craig Morton, 5th in 1965, was mediocre. Steve Walsh, a supplemental pick in 1989, was a flop but brought three draft picks in trade.

Out of position: Dan Reeves, Perry Lee Dunn and Drew Pearson were college quarterbacks who were converted to runners and receivers by Dallas. Danny White was also the team's punter.

Long-time subs: Jason Garrett backed up Troy Aikman for seven years.

QB controversy: Don Meredith was continually dogged by fans who favored Craig Morton or Jerry Rhome. Craig Morton and Roger Staubach staged a three-year battle for the position, even alternating on each play at one point. There was some controversy between Troy Aikman and Steve Walsh until Aikman began to establish his dominance.

College affiliation: Three quarterbacks were former Miami Hurricanes: Steve Walsh, Bernie Kosar and Vinny Testaverde.

Ones who got away: Craig Morton had some success in New York and Denver, but not as much Roger Staubach.

Has beens: Don Heinrich, John Roach, Wade Wilson, Babe Laufenberg, Steve Beuerlein, Rodney Peete, Bernie Kosar, Randall Cunningham, Ryan Leaf, Vinny Testaverde and Drew Bledsoe.

Ruinous injuries: Don Meredith and Craig Morton each took a terrible beating at times. Roger Staubach and Troy Aikman both had their careers shortened by concussions.

Best trade: Craig Morton was traded to the Giants for a number 1 (Randy White). Combative backup Clint Longley was sent to San Diego for a number 1 and 2, and these were used in the trade package for Tony Dorsett. Steve Walsh was sent to New Orleans for a 1, 2 and 3.

Worst trade: The worst was giving up a number 3 to the Texans for Drew Henson.

Title winners: Troy Aikman, 3; Roger Staubach, 2.

Hall of Famers: Roger Staubach and Troy Aikman.

All Pro/Pro Bowl seasons: Roger Staubach, 5; Troy Aikman, 5; Don Meredith, 3; Danny White, 2; and Tony Romo, 1.

QBs as coaches: None.

Underrated: Don Meredith was extremely underappreciated in the 1960s. Danny White had the unenviable task of replacing legendary Roger Staubach.

Overrated: Craig Morton had a world of talent and had his fan base, but never could win the job fully.

Best Nicknames: Dandy Don Meredith and Roger "the Dodger" Staubach.

Time Capsule: Tom Landry using messenger quarterbacks with LeBaron and Meredith. Landry's complex multiple-shift offense. The desperation pass to Drew Pearson for a 46-yard winning last-minute touchdown against the Vikings in the 1975 Divisional playoff round that Roger Staubach later called the Hail Mary. Tony Romo's dropping the ball when trying to hold for the game-winning field goal attempt in the playoffs in Seattle in 2006.

What If: If Troy Aikman had thrown

more, what kind of numbers would he have racked up? Would the Cowboys have won as many championships?

Off the field: Don Meredith and Craig Morton were known as night owls. Troy Aikman was a very eligible bachelor who dated country music singers. Tony Romo is already dating every pop singer he can, Jessica Simpson, Carrie Underwood ... Don Meredith appeared in episodes of *McCloud, Midnight Caller, Supertrain, Police Woman* and *Police Story* as well as a dozen TV movies including *Banjo Hackett* and *The Night the City Screamed*. He also starred in *3 Days of Rain* which was written and directed by his son Michael in 2004 and was based on six Chekhov short stories. Troy Aikman and Drew Bledsoe were in *Jerry Maguire*, and Aikman also appeared in episodes of *The Simpsons, King of the Hill* and *Kablam*. Gary Hogeboom was a contestant on *Survivor*.

Quarterback Bibliography

Roger Staubach

Staubach, Roger, Sam Blair, and Bob St. John. *Staubach: First Down, Lifetime to Go*. Waco, TX: Word Books, 1974.

Staubach, Roger, and Frank Luksa. *Time Enough to Win*. Waco, TX: World Books, 1980.

Sullivan, George. *Roger Staubach: A Special Kind of Quarterback*. New York: Putnam, 1974.

Towle, Mike. *Roger Staubach: Captain America*. Nashville, TN: Cumberland House, 2002.

Troy Aikman

Aikman, Troy, Roger Staubach, and Jeanne T. Warren. *Reaching for the Stars*. Dallas, TX: Taylor, 1993.

Aikman, Troy, and Marc Serota. *Aikman: Mind Body & Soul*. Hollywood, FL: EGI Productions, 1998.

Don Meredith

Gent, Pete. *North Dallas Forty*. New York: Morrow, 1973. (Fictional representation of Gent's old teammate Meredith.)

Randall Cunningham *see* Philadelphia Eagles

24

Denver Broncos

Leading Passers, by Yards

Player	Years	G	Att	Comp	Pct	Yds	Y/A	Y/Cp	TD	Int	Int %	Rate
John Elway	1983–98	205	7,250	4,123	56.9	51,475	7.1	12.5	300	226	3.12%	79.9
Craig Morton	1977–82	72	1,594	907	56.9	11,895	7.5	13.1	74	65	4.08%	79.1
Jake Plummer	2003–06	59	1,519	944	62.2	11,632	7.7	12.3	71	47	3.09%	88.5
Brian Griese	1998–02	23	1,628	1,014	62.3	11,387	7.0	11.2	69	53	3.26%	83.7
Frank Tripucka	1960–63	44	1,277	662	51.8	7,676	6.0	11.6	51	85	6.66%	55.9
Charley Johnson	1972–75	54	970	517	53.3	7,238	7.5	14.0	52	52	5.36%	73.1
Steve Ramsey	1971–76	53	919	456	49.6	6,437	7.0	14.1	35	58	6.31%	59.0
Steve Tensi	1967–70	41	810	348	43	5,153	6.4	14.8	38	45	5.56%	56.9
Steve DeBerg	1981–83	33	546	314	57.5	3,819	7.0	12.2	22	24	4.40%	74.3
Mickey Slaughter	1963–66	40	584	291	49.8	3,607	6.2	12.4	23	38	6.51%	55.4
John McCormick	1963–68	38	537	207	38.5	2,791	5.2	13.5	17	33	6.15%	40.8
Jacky Lee	1964–65	18	345	177	51.3	2,303	6.7	13.0	16	23	6.67%	60.3
Pete Liske	1969–70	18	353	173	49	2,185	6.2	12.6	16	22	6.23%	57.9
Gus Frerotte	2000–01	14	280	168	60	2,084	7.4	12.4	12	8	2.86%	85.5
Gary Kubiak	1983–91	119	298	173	58.1	1,920	6.4	11.1	14	16	5.37%	70.6
Norris Weese	1976–79	57	251	143	57	1,887	7.5	13.2	7	14	5.58%	66.9

Quarterback	Rush Att	Rush Yds	Rush Avg	TD
John Elway	774	3407	4.4	33
Craig Morton	100	256	2.6	5
Jake Plummer	181	669	3.7	7
Brian Griese	166	516	3.1	5
Frank Tripucka	16	-9	-0.6	1
Charley Johnson	24	16	0.7	0
Steve Ramsey	33	108	3.3	2
Steve Tensi	46	81	1.8	0
Steve DeBerg	30	95	3.2	2
Mickey Slaughter	73	263	3.6	1
John McCormick	8	-5	-0.6	0
Jacky Lee	44	164	3.7	3
Pete Liske	17	92	5.4	1
Gus Frerotte	32	73	2.3	2
Gary Kubiak	65	238	3.7	2
Norris Weese	69	362	5.2	5

Record Holders

Passing Yards, Career: 51,475 John Elway
Passing Yards, Season: 4,089 Jake Plummer 2004
Completion %, Career: 62.3% Brian Griese
Completion %, Season: 66.7% Brian Griese 2002
Touchdown Passes, Career: 300 John Elway
Touchdown Passes, Season: 27 John Elway 1997
   and Jake Plummer 2004
Interceptions, Career: 226 John Elway
Interceptions, Season: 34 Frank Tripucka 1960
Rating, Career: 88.5 Jake Plummer
Rating, Season: 102.9 Brian Griese 2000
Rush Yards, Career: 3,407 John Elway
Rush Yards, Season: 304 John Elway 1987

Passers by Categories

Five best starters: John Elway was not only the team's greatest quarterback who led the team to five Super Bowls and won two, but had such a lengthy career that no one is close to him in any statistical category. Craig Morton also led the Broncos to a Super Bowl, and Charley Johnson was the first truly professional quarterback the team ever had. Since Elway retired, Brian Griese and Jake Plummer have shown talent but have been inconsistent.

Worst starters, career: Until Charlie Johnson arrived in 1972, Denver's starting quarterbacks were as bad as could be. Half of those seasons, none of the main starting quarterbacks could score a passer rating higher than the mid-

fifties. In 1961, Frank Tripucka and George Herring combined for 15 touchdowns and 43 interceptions; in 1964, Mickey Slaughter and Jacky Lee combined for 14 touchdowns and 31 interceptions; in 1965, Mickey Slaughter, John McCormick and Jacky Lee combined for 18 touchdowns and 29 interceptions; in 1970, Steve Tensi, Pete Liske and Chuck Pastrana combined for 11 touchdowns and 28 interceptions; in 1971, Don Horn and Steve Ramsey combined for 8 touchdowns and 27 interceptions.

Best stat line, season: John Elway's greatest year statistically was 1993 when he completed 63.2 percent of his passes for 4,030 yards, averaging 7.3 yards per attempt with 25 touchdowns and only 10 interceptions for a passer rating of 92.8. In 2000, Brian Griese completed 64.3 percent of his passes for 2,688 yards, averaging 8 yards per attempt with 19 touchdowns and only 4 interceptions for a passer rating of 102.9. In 2005, Jake Plummer had his best year by completing 60.7 percent of his passes for 3,366 yards, an average of 7.4 yards per attempt with 18 touchdowns and only 7 interceptions for a passer rating of 90.2.

Worst stat line, season: In 1961, George Herring's second and final season of 1961, he completed 93 of 211 passes, 44.1 percent for 1,160 yards, an average of 5.5 yards per attempt for 5 touchdowns and 22 interceptions. His passer rating was 30. John McCormick was comparable in 1966 by completing 68 of 193 passes, 35.2 percent for 993 yards, an average of 5.2 yards per attempt with 6 touchdowns and 15 interceptions. His passer rating was 30.9.

Best stat line, playoffs: In the third AFC

Championship victory over Cleveland in 1989, John Elway went 20–35, 385, 3–0. Nine years later in his final game in Super Bowl XXXIII against Atlanta, Elway was the MVP going 18–29, 336, 1–1.

Worst stat line, playoffs: John Elway played well for the first half against the Giants in his first Super Bowl. In his second Super Bowl against the Redskins, he played well for only a quarter and ended up 14–38, 257, 1–3. In his third Super Bowl against the 49ers, he never got started going 10–26, 108, 0–2. Still, the worst post-season line belongs to Craig Morton in the Broncos' first Super Bowl against the Cowboys when he went 4–15, 39, 0–4.

Big Days: The first passer to exceed 300 yards passing in a game was Frank Tripucka with 375 yards on November 6, 1960. The first to reach 400 yards was Tripucka with 417 on September 15, 1962. Jake Plummer had the biggest day in franchise history by throwing for 499 yards on October 31, 2004. John Elway had the most 300-yard games with 36.

Running QBs: One of the things that made Elway great was his ability to elude the rush and get away. He even scored 33 touchdowns rushing in his career. Jake "the Snake" Plummer is second on the Broncos in quarterback rushing yards after just four seasons. Norris Weese was more of an option runner than a drop-back quarterback, and he ran for 120 yards in a December 1976 game.

Bomber: No one had a stronger arm than John Elway. One of the few things that Steve Tensi could do well was throw the ball deep.

Most accurate: When he wasn't making stupid decisions, Jake Plummer could be very accurate. Elway got more accurate as his career went on.

Leader: John Elway, no doubt.

Comeback King: John Elway led an NFL record 42 4th quarter comebacks, plus six more in the postseason.

Highest Football IQ: Elway knew how to pull out a win under all situations.

Toughest: Big, strong John Elway took a lot of hits and won a lot of games.

First signal caller/T-Formation QB: The Broncos first coach Frank Filchock came from the CFL and brought his veteran quarterback Frank Tripucka with him. Tripucka was from Notre Dame and had washed out of the NFL way back in 1952.

First TD pass: In the AFL's first game in Boston on September 9, 1960, Frank Tripucka threw a swing pass to halfback Al Carmichael, and he took it 59 yards for a touchdown.

Black QBs: The Broncos employed the first African American starting quarterback in the NFL in 1968 when rookie Marlin "the Magician" Briscoe started 5 of the 11 games in which he appeared. By 1969, Briscoe was a receiver in Buffalo. Since then, Shawn Moore in 1992 and Jarious Jackson from 2001–03 have had brief shots in Denver.

Tallest QB: Steve Tensi from 1967–70, Dean May in 1987 and Hugh Millen from 1994–95 were both 6'5".

Smallest QB: Marlin Briscoe was only 5'10" and 178 pounds, and his size was a second factor against him staying a quarterback in the NFL. Backup quarterbacks George Shaw and Gary Kubiak were both 6 foot and slight of build.

Oldest QB: Craig Morton was 39 in 1982. Denver has had four 38 year old quarterbacks: Tobin Rote in 1966, Craig Morton in 1981, John Elway in 1998 and Steve Beuerlein in 2003. Elway and Morton were 38-year old starters.

Rookie sensation: Both Marlin Briscoe in 1968 (93–224, 41.5 percent, 1,589 yards, 7.1 per attempt for 14 touchdowns and 13 interceptions, a rating of 62.9) and Mickey Slaughter in 1963 (112–223, 50.2 percent, 1,689 yards, 7.6 per attempt for 13 touchdowns and 15 interceptions, a rating of 66.9) had better rookie seasons than John Elway, but neither fulfilled that promise. Jay Cutler had a passer rating of 88.5 in 2006 by completing 59.1 percent of his passes and averaging 7.3 yards per pass.

Late bloomer: Both Frank Tripucka and Craig Morton had their best seasons after arriving in the Mile High City at the end of their careers. Tripucka was 32 and Morton was 34.

1st round picks: The Broncos have traditionally tried to fill their quarterback slot through trades. Even Elway came in a trade. Jay Cutler, 11th in 2006, is only the second quarterback Denver has drafted in the first round. Tommy Maddox, 25th in 1992, was first, and he flopped badly.

Out of position: Marlin Briscoe went on to play eight years as a receiver with the Bills, Dolphins, Chargers, Lions and Patriots, catching 224 passes for 30 touchdowns.

Long-time subs: Gary Kubiak was an eighth round pick in 1983 and spent nine years backing up John Elway before moving into the coaching booth in 1992.

QB controversy: It took Elway half a year to push Steve DeBerg aside. Steve Ramsey backed up Charlie Johnson for three years before becoming a starter in 1975. By 1977, Ramsey was gone.

College affiliation: Four Bronco quarterbacks were once Oregon Ducks: George Shaw, Max Choboian, Bill Musgrave and Chris Miller.

Ones who got away: Brian Griese is not a terrible quarterback, but following Elway was too tough an assignment.

Has beens: George Shaw, John McCormick, Jacky Lee, Pete Liske, Don Horn, Matt Robinson and Steve DeBerg were given shots as starters; Shaw's only moment in Denver was his record 97-yard touchdown toss to Jerry Tarr. Tobin Rote, Don Breaux, Hunter Enis, Chris Miller, Danny Kanell, Bubby Brister, Gus Frerotte and Steve Beurelein were brought in as backups.

Ruinous injuries: A shoulder injury helped derail Brian Griese in Denver. Steve Tensi's broken collarbone gave Marlin Briscoe a chance. Craig Morton had bad knees and assorted other nagging injuries that combined with his age to make him largely immobile.

Best trade: Obviously, obtaining John Elway from the Colts for a good tackle (Chris Hinton) and a backup quarterback (Mark Herrmann) is the greatest trade in team history. However, getting Craig Morton from the Giants for Steve Ramsey and a number 5 and nabbing Charley Johnson for a number 3 were both excellent deals.

Worst trade: The oddest trade was obtaining Jacky Lee on two-year loan from the Oilers for Bud McFaddin and a number 2. After two years, the Broncos had nothing to show for the deal. Mediocre Steve Tensi cost two number 1's (Russ Washington and Marty Domres) for San Diego. Matt Robinson came from the Jets for a number 1, a number 2 and Craig Penrose. As it turned out, a fairer trade would have been Robinson for Penrose straight up because both stunk.

Title winners: John Elway, 2.

Hall of Famers: John Elway.

All Pro/Pro Bowl seasons: John Elway, 9; Frank Tripucka, 1; Craig Morton, 1; Brian Griese, 1; and Jake Plummer, 1.

QBs as coaches: Gary Kubiak went 6–10 in Houston.

Underrated: Charley Johnson is largely forgotten today, but he was the first good quarterback the franchise ever had and led the team to its first two winning seasons ever.

Overrated: Frank Tripucka's number 18 was retired by the Broncos in the 1960s despite the fact that in his 3+ years as Denver's quarterback, he threw just 51 touchdowns to 85 interceptions, and the team went 16–38–2. Moreover, he averaged just 6 yards per attempt and attained a miserable passer rating of 55.9.

Best Nicknames: Teammates called Elway "Wood," short for Elwood.

Time Capsule: The Drive, 98 yards against Cleveland in the AFC championship. Elway being flipped over in the "helicopter" play as he dove for a first down in the Super Bowl win over Green Bay. Jake Plummer's bone-headed left-handed interception toss in 2004.

What If: If Elway had played for the Colts, do the Broncos ever return to the Super Bowl?

Off the field: Craig Morton, Brian Griese and Jake Plummer have all been known to absorb some nightlife. John Elway once played himself on an episode of the TV show *Home Improvement.*

Quarterback Bibliography

Marlin Briscoe
Briscoe, Marlin, and Bob Schaller. *The First Black Quarterback: Marlin Briscoe's Journey to Break the Color Barrier and Start in the NFL.* Grand Island, NE: Cross Training Publications, 2002.

John Elway
Elway, John, Marc Serota, and Elise Glading. *Elway.* Hollywood, FL: EGI Productions, 1998.
Green, Jerry. *Mile High Miracle: Elway and the Broncos, Super Bowl Champions at Last.* Indianapolis: Masters Press, 1998.
Latimer, Clay. *John Elway: Armed and Dangerous.* Lenexa, KS: Addax, 1998.
Repeat! MVP John Elway Leads the Broncos to NFL Domination. Bannockburn, IL: H&S Media, 1999.
Rosato, Bob, and Clay Latimer. *John Elway.* Dallas, TX: Beckett Publications, 1999.
Silver, Michael. *John Elway: The Drive of a Champion: Stories Excerpted from the Pages of Sports Illustrated.* New York: Simon & Schuster, 1998.

Brian Griese
Griese, Bob, Brian Griese, and James D. Denney. *Undefeated: How Father and Son Triumphed Over Unbelievable Odds Both On and Off the Field.* Nashville, TN: Nelson, 2000.

25

Detroit Lions

Leading Passers, by Yards

Quarterback	Years	G	Att	Comp	Pct	Yds	Y/A	Y/Cp	TD	Int	Int %	Rating
Bobby Layne	1950–58	97	2,193	1,074	49	15,710	7.2	14.6	118	142	6.48%	63.7
Scott Mitchell	1994–98	41	1,850	1,049	56.7	12,647	6.8	12.1	79	57	3.08%	79.2
Greg Landry	1968–78	102	1,747	957	54.8	12,451	7.1	13.0	80	81	4.64%	73.4
Gary Danielson	1977–84	84	1,684	952	56.5	11,885	7.1	12.5	69	71	4.22%	74.7
Eric Hipple	1981–89	87	1,546	830	53.7	10,711	6.9	12.9	55	70	4.53%	68.7
Joey Harrington	2002–05	59	1,804	987	54.7	10,242	5.7	10.4	60	62	3.44%	68.1
Charlie Batch	1998–01	15	1,326	743	56	9,016	6.8	12.1	49	40	3.02%	76.9
Milt Plum	1962–67	65	1,315	671	51	8,536	6.5	12.7	55	87	6.62%	58.0
Bill Munson	1968–75	60	1,314	716	54.5	8,461	6.4	11.8	56	42	3.20%	75.2
Rodney Peete	1989–93	47	1,125	641	57	8,164	7.3	12.7	38	49	4.36%	72.9
Earl Morrall	1958–64	80	839	431	51.4	6,280	7.5	14.6	52	41	4.89%	76.4
Jon Kitna	2006	16	596	372	62.4	4,208	7.1	11.3	21	22	3.69%	79.9
Chuck Long	1986–89	23	602	330	54.8	3,743	6.2	11.3	19	28	4.65%	64.8
Tobin Rote	1957–59	34	596	256	43	3,609	6.1	14.1	30	39	6.54%	52.6
Jim Ninowski	1960–61	24	530	251	47.4	3,520	6.6	14.0	9	36	6.79%	46.6
Erik Kramer	1991–93	25	509	281	55.2	3,408	6.7	12.1	23	19	3.73%	75.5

Quarterback	Rush Att	Rush Yds	Rush Avg	TD
Bobby Layne	432	1793	4.2	13
Scott Mitchell	132	324	2.5	10
Greg Landry	389	2502	6.4	20
Gary Danielson	156	728	4.7	7
Eric Hipple	145	550	3.8	13
Joey Harrington	109	345	3.2	0
Charlie Batch	125	560	4.5	5
Milt Plum	89	155	1.7	5
Bill Munson	77	252	3.3	2
Rodney Peete	166	884	5.3	13
Earl Morrall	116	516	4.4	3
Jon Kitna	34	156	4.6	2
Chuck Long	34	88	2.6	0
Tobin Rote	182	873	4.8	6
Jim Ninowski	65	319	4.9	10
Erik Kramer	57	65	1.1	1

Record Holders

Passing Yards, Career: 15,710 Bobby Layne
Passing Yards, Season: 4,338 Scott Mitchell 1995
Completion %, Career: 57.9% Rodney Peete
Completion %, Season: 62.9% Eric Hipple 1986
Touchdown Passes, Career: 118 Bobby Layne

Touchdown Passes, Season: 32 Scott Mitchell 1995
Interceptions, Career: 142 Bobby Layne
Interceptions, Season: 23 Bobby Layne 1951; Jeff Komlo 1979
Rating, Career: 79.9 Jon Kitna (596 att.); 79.2 Scott Mitchell
Rating, Season: 101.7 Dave Krieg

Rush Yards, Career: 2,502 Greg Landry
Rush Yards, Season: 530 Greg Landry 1971

Passers by Categories

Five best starters: Bobby Layne was a Hall of Famer who won two titles in Detroit with personality and leadership skills that captured a city. There really has not been a valid quarterback in Detroit since. Dutch Clark was a single-wing tailback, but he did call signals, throw passes and lead the team to its first title. Tobin Rote only had one decent year in Detroit, but won a championship. Greg Landry was not a great passer, but won more than he lost. As for number five, the choice is from a number of mediocrities: Earl Morrall, Gary Danielson, Bill Munson, Scott Mitchell ... it doesn't matter.

Worst starters, career: Jim Ninowski threw 9 touchdowns against 36 interceptions in two seasons and was traded for Milt Plum. Plum, whom the Lions sent to the Dale Carnegie Institute to build his confidence as a leader, threw 55 touchdowns to 87 interceptions. Joey Harrington was better on the piano and averaged only 5.7 yards per attempt in Detroit. Mike McMahon's completion percentage of 43.8 percent was lower than that of Dutch Clark who played 70 years before him in the NFL's dinosaur age. Rusty Hilger was even lower at 41.2 percent.

Best stat line, season: On stats alone, Scott Mitchell had the greatest year in 1995 with 32 touchdowns, only 12 interceptions and over 4,300 yards, but he imploded whenever he faced a good defense like in the playoffs that year against the Eagles (see below). Earl Morrall got a chance to start in 1963, threw for over 2,600 yards, 8 yards per attempt and 24 touchdowns, and was back on the bench the next year. In Bobby Layne's first two years in Detroit, he led the league in passing yards and in 1951 also threw 26 touchdowns.

Worst stat line, season: Bobby Layne threw just 6 touchdowns to 12 interceptions and averaged only 6.5 yards per attempt in 1957. Tobin Rote was worse in 1959, completing just 38 percent of his passes, averaging only 5.3 yards per attempt and throwing 19 interceptions to 5 touchdowns; he left for Canada the next season. Milt Plum threw 2 touchdowns to 12 intercep-

tions in 1964 and 4 touchdowns to 13 interceptions in 1966. Jeff Komlo was an overmatched rookie in 1979, completing less than half his passes, averaging 6.1 yards per attempt and throwing 23 interceptions to just 11 touchdowns. Chuck Long's sophomore season was very similar in that he averaged 6.3 yards per attempt and threw 20 interceptions to 11 touchdowns. Jim Ninowski hit bottom in 1960, completing 47 percent of his passes, averaging 5.7 yards per attempt and throwing 18 interceptions to just 2 touchdowns.

Best stat line, playoffs: In the 1957 title game against the Browns, Tobin Rote was 12–19, 280, 4–0. In a Divisional win over the Cowboys in 1991, Erik Kramer went 29–38, 341, 3–0.

Worst stat line, playoffs: In the 1954 title loss to the Browns, Bobby Layne went 18–42, 177, 0–6. In a 1983 Divisional loss to the 49ers, Gary Danielson went 24–38, 236, 0–5. In a 1995 Wildcard loss to Philadelphia, Scott Mitchell went 13–29, 155, 1–4.

Big Days: The first passer to exceed 300 yards passing in a game was Bobby Layne with 374 yards on November 5, 1950. The first to reach 400 yards was Scott Mitchell with 410 on November 23, 1005. Charlie Batch had the biggest day in franchise history by throwing for 436 yards on November 18, 2001. Scott Mitchell had eight 300-yard games, the most in Lions history.

Running QBs: Greg Landry accumulated the most yards and scored 20 rushing touchdowns, but Bobby Layne and Tobin Rote were both former single-wing tailbacks that could run the ball. Speaking of single-wing tailbacks, Dutch Clark was more of a runner than a passer in the 1930s and gained over 100 yards rushing in a game in 1936. Tailbacks Bill Shepherd and Frankie Sinkwich both duplicated that feat twice in the 1930s and 1940s. Gary Danielson, Charlie Batch and Rodney Peete were all mobile pocket quarterbacks when they were young.

Bomber: Bobby Layne liked to go deep although he did not always throw the prettiest passes. He won a championship on a 4th quarter 33-yard touchdown pass.

Most accurate: The Lions have never really had a passer known for his accuracy. Weak-armed Rodney Peete, tellingly, has the highest lifetime completion percentage in team history.

Leader: Where Bobby Layne walked, the Lions followed.

Comeback King: Bobby Layne had 11 4th quarter comebacks and one in the postseason.

Highest Football IQ: Bobby Layne knew how to win on the best of days and the worst of days.

Toughest: Bobby Layne held the original NFL record for consecutive quarterback starts with 54.

First signal caller/T-Formation QB: This is a complicated answer. Bill Glassgow and Father Lumpkin called signals for the 1930 Portsmouth Spartans. When the team relocated to Detroit in 1934, Dutch Clark was the primary signal caller. When the Lions experimented with the T in 1944, tailback Frankie Sinkwich played some quarterback. When Detroit finally switched to the T full-time, its quarterbacks were Roy Zimmerman and Clyde LeForce.

First TD pass: Bill Glassgow hit Chuck Bennett for 11 yards in a 13–6 win over Newark in the Portsmouth Spartans first NFL game on September 14, 1930. For Detroit, Ernie Caddell found Harry Ebding for a 37-yard score in a 40–7 win over Pittsburgh on November 4, 1934.

Black QBs: Rodney Peete was the first in 1989, and he was joined the following year by top draft pick Andre Ware. Charlie Batch came along in 1998.

Tallest QB: Sonny Gibbs was 6'7", Scott Mitchell and Matt Blundin were 6'6", and Dan Orlovsky was 6'5".

Smallest QB: Bob Westfall was 5'8"; Chuck Fenenbock and Bill Shepherd were 5'9"; Dave Ryan and Dwight Sloan were 5'10". All were tailbacks. Clyde LeForce was the shortest quarterback at 5'11".

Oldest QB: Joe Ferguson and Frank Reich were 36-year old backups in 1986 and 1998 respectively. Dave Krieg was a 36-year old starter in 1994.

Rookie sensation: With so little good quarterbacking over the years, it is no surprise that there have been no phenoms in Detroit. Charlie Batch showed real promise in 1998, though, by completing 57 percent of his passes for 2,178 yards, 11 touchdowns and only 6 interceptions.

Late bloomer: Both Erik Kramer and Gary Danielson were 26 when they finally got a chance to start in Detroit.

1st round picks: The Lions drafted Otto Graham with the 4th pick in 1944 and Y.A. Tittle with the 6th pick in 1948, but both signed with the All America Conference. They drafted John Hadl with the 10th pick in 1962 and Pete Beathard with the 5th pick in 1964, but both signed with the AFL. Of the five quarterbacks the Lions drafted in the first round and signed, only Greg Landry, 11th in 1968, was any good. John Rauch, 2nd in 1949, Chuck Long, 12th in 1986, Andre Ware 9th in 1990 and Joey Harrington 3rd in 2002 all flopped badly.

Out of position: The first Lion to play T-quarterback was Frankie Sinkwich who was more of a tailback. Bobby Layne was also a placekicker. Jerry Reichow was a third-string quarterback and a wide receiver. He later caught 50 passes one year in Minnesota.

Long-time subs: Earl Morrall was the backup for six of his seven years in Detroit.

QB controversy: When the Lions traded for Tobin Rote in 1957, Bobby Layne must have seen the writing on the wall. Earl Morrall battled Jim Ninowski and Milt Plum unsuccessfully for the starting job for several seasons. Greg Landry and Bill Munson fought it out for eight years. Indecisive coach Wayne Fontes never stuck too long with any quarterback among Eric Hipple, Rodney Peete, Andre Ware and Erik Kramer.

College affiliation: Detroit has used three quarterbacks from Tulsa (Clyde LeForce, Greg Barton and Gus Frerotte) and three from Utah State (Bill Munson, Bob Gagliano and Eric Hipple). If you add in Tom Dublinski and Scott Mitchell from Utah and Ty Detmer from BYU, that's six quarterbacks who went to school in Utah.

Ones who got away: Besides the drafted but unsigned Otto Graham, Y.A. Tittle and John Hadl, Erik Kramer and Earl Morrall had more success after they left the Motor City.

Has beens: Roy Zimmerman, Harry Gilmer, Jim Ninowski, Jim Hardy, George Izo, Sonny Gibbs, Jack Concannon, Joe Ferguson, Scott Hunter, Joe Reed, Sam Wyche, Stoney Case, Rusty Hilger, Gus Frerotte, Dave Krieg, Frank Reich, Don Majkowski, Ty Detmer and Jeff Garcia.

Ruinous injuries: Bobby Layne had injury problems in 1955 and 1956, which influenced the team to obtain Tobin Rote who won the title after Layne broke his leg in 1957. Earl Morrall lost a big toe to a lawn mower in 1962.

Best trade: Getting Hall of Famer Bobby Layne from the New York Bulldogs for disgruntled receiver Bob Mann. Mann was a replacement for Camp Wilson who was originally in the deal. The Lions also traded Greg Barton who had thrown one pass in his career to the Eagles for two number 2's and a number 3. Barton went to Canada instead, but Detroit kept the draft choices.

Worst trade: Trading Bobby Layne to the Steelers for Earl Morrall and a number 2 pick. The year before, the Lions traded rookie Jack Kemp to Pittsburgh for number 8 and 9 picks.

Title winners: Bobby Layne, 2, Dutch Clark, 1 and Tobin Rote, 1.

Hall of Famers: Bobby Layne and Dutch Clark.

All Pro/Pro Bowl seasons: Dutch Clark, 6; Bobby Layne, 4; Greg Landry, 1; Dave Krieg, 1; Bill Shepherd, 1 and Bob Westfall, 1. Glenn Presnell was more of a runner than passer in the single-wing and was All Pro four times.

QBs as coaches: Dutch Clark was 30–34–2 with Detroit and the Rams. Harry Gilmer was 10–16–2 with Detroit. Sam Wyche was 84–107 with Cincinnati and Tampa.

Underrated: Earl Morrall and Rodney Peete were not great, but were better than their Lion competitors; they just never got the opportunity to play for any long stretch of time. Greg Landry was a better runner than passer, but he was still a pretty effective quarterback.

Overrated: Scott Mitchell was paid a high salary and he could throw the ball, but was so mistake-prone that he was not a winner.

Best Nicknames: Dwight "Paddlefoot" Sloan, Bobby "the Blond Bomber" Layne and Greg "Gomer" Landry.

Time Capsule: The late touchdown pass from Layne to Doran to beat the Browns for the title in 1953. Milt Plum throwing a stupid, needless interception to Herb Adderley in a critical early 1962 loss to the rival Packers that left the Lions' defense ready to kill Plum. Greg Landry's 76-yard quarterback sneak against the Packers on opening day 1970.

What If: Would the Lions have disrupted the Packer dynasty in the 1960s if they had better quarterback play? Would the Lions have been a factor in the playoffs in the 1980s if Wayne Fontes had picked a quarterback and stuck with him?

Off the field: Nobody ever partied heartier than Bobby Layne who also insisted that his teammates join him. Rodney Peete is married to actress Holly Robinson Peete. Eric Hipple appeared in *The Bear* and an episode of *Home Improvement.* Bill Munson appeared in an episode of *Perry Mason.* Scott Mitchell appeared in *Ace Ventura: Pet Detective.*

Quarterback Bibliography

Bobby Layne
St. John, Bob. *Heart of a Lion: The Wild and Woolly Life of Bobby Layne.* Dallas, TX: Taylor, 1991.

Earl Morrall
Morrall, Earl, and George Sullivan. *In the Pocket: My Life as a Quarterback.* New York: Grossett & Dunlap, 1969.
Morrall, Earl, and George Sullivan. *Comeback Quarterback: The Earl Morrall Story.* New York: Grossett & Dunlap, 1971.

Rodney Peete
Peete, Holly Robinson, and Daniel Paisner. *Get Your Own Damn Beer I'm Watching the Game: A Woman's Guide to Loving Pro Football.* Emmaus, PA: Rodale Books, 2005.

26

Green Bay Packers

Leading Passers, by Yards

Player	Years	G	Att	Comp	Pct	Yds	Y/A	Y/Cp	TD	Int	Int %	Rating
Brett Favre	1992–06	239	8,219	5,021	61.1	57,500	7.0	11.5	414	271	3.3%	85.2
Bart Starr	1956–71	196	3,149	1,808	57.4	24,718	7.8	13.7	152	138	4.4%	80.5
Lynn Dickey	1976–85	105	2,831	1,592	56.2	21,369	7.5	13.4	133	151	5.3%	73.8
Tobin Rote	1950–56	84	1,854	826	44.6	11,535	6.2	14.0	89	119	6.4%	54.4
Don Majkowski	1987–92	68	1,607	889	55.3	10,870	6.8	12.2	56	56	3.5%	73.5
Randy Wright	1984–88	46	1,119	602	53.8	7,106	6.4	11.8	31	57	5.1%	61.4
Arnie Herber	1930–40	109	1,050	425	40.5	7,032	6.7	16.5	66	93	8.9%	47.8
David Whitehurst	1977–83	54	980	504	51.4	6,205	6.3	12.3	28	51	5.2%	59.2
Cecil Isbell	1938–42	54	818	411	50.2	5,945	7.3	14.5	61	52	6.4%	72.6
Curly Lambeau	1921–29	77	700	278	39.7	4,493	6.4	16.2	24	78	11.1%	33.8
Babe Parilli	1952–53, 1957–58	48	602	258	42.9	3,983	6.6	15.4	31	61	10.1%	42.9
Irv Comp	1943–48	62	519	213	41	3,354	6.5	15.7	28	52	10.0%	41.6
John Hadl	1974–75	22	537	280	52.1	3,167	5.9	11.3	9	29	5.4%	53.2
Zeke Bratkowski	1963–68, 1971	43	416	220	52.9	3,093	7.4	14.1	21	29	7.0%	64.9
Red Dunn	1927–31	58	409	171	41.8	2,959	7.2	17.3	31	36	8.8%	55.7

Player	Rush Att	Rush Yds	Rush Avg	TD
Brett Favre	526	1774	3.4	13
Bart Starr	247	1308	5.3	15
Lynn Dickey	129	98	0.8	9
Tobin Rote	385	2155	5.6	29
Don Majkowski	199	1037	5.2	9
Randy Wright	55	173	3.1	3
Arnie Herber	237	201	0.8	3
David Whitehurst	77	242	3.1	7
Cecil Isbell	422	1522	3.6	10
Curly Lambeau	549	1762	3.2	8
Babe Parilli	106	375	3.5	7
Irv Comp	255	502	2.0	7
John Hadl	28	44	1.6	0
Zeke Bratkowski	25	35	1.4	1
Red Dunn	117	347	3.0	0

Record Holders

Passing Yards, Career: 5,7500 Brett Favre
Passing Yards, Season: 4,458 Lynn Dickey 1983
Completion %, Career: 61.1% Brett Favre
Completion %, Season: 65.4% Brett Favre 2003

Touchdown Passes, Career: 414 Brett Favre
Touchdown Passes, Season: 39 Brett Favre 1996
Interceptions, Career: 271 Brett Favre
Interceptions, Season: 29 Lynn Dickey 1983 and Brett Favre 2005
Rating, Career: 85.2 Brett Favre

Rating, Season: 105 Bart Starr 1966
Rush Yards, Career: 2,155 Tobin Rote
Rush Yards, Season: 523 Tobin Rote 1951

Passers by Categories

Five best starters: Brett Favre holds all the team's passing records. Bart Starr held them before Favre and won five championships. Arnie Herber was a Hall of Fame tailback known for his long passing on four championship teams. Cecil Isbell's stats for his brief five-year career are comparable to his contemporaries, Sammy Baugh and Sid Luckman. Lynn Dickey was a talented deep passer for some mediocre Packer teams in the 1970s and 1980s and three times threw for more than 3,000 yards.

Worst starters, career: Randy Wright threw 31 touchdowns against 57 interceptions while winning only seven of 32 games he started, although he did surpass 3,000 yards in 1986. David Whitehurst completed just barely half his passes and threw 28 touchdowns to 51 interceptions. Babe Parilli completed just 43 percent of his passes and threw 31 touchdowns to 61 interceptions.

Best stat line, season: In Brett Favre's first MVP season of 1995, he completed 359 of 570 passes, 63 percent, for 4,413 yards, an average of 7.7 yards per pass, for 38 touchdowns and only 13 interceptions. His passer rating was 99.5. Although he threw less than half as many passes as Favre, Bart Starr's 1966 season was perhaps even better. He completed 156 of 251 passes, 62.2 percent, for 2,257 yards, an average of 8.99 yards per pass, for 14 touchdowns and only 3 interceptions. His passer rating was 105.

Worst stat line, season: Stan Heath was the Packers' top draft pick in 1949. In his only season in the NFL he completed 26 of 106 passes, 24.5 percent, for 355 yards, and average of 3.3 yards per pass, for 1 touchdown and 14 interceptions. His passer rating was 4.6. And don't forget Tom O'Malley who had a one-game NFL career for the Packers. In an opening day 45–7 loss to Detroit in 1950, O'Malley completed just 4 of 15 passes with six interceptions and no touchdowns for a 0 passer rating. He was cut the next day and never played in the NFL again. Among stars, Tobin Rote had a 26.7 rating as a rookie in 1950, completing 37.1 percent of his passes for 7 touchdowns and 24 interceptions and followed that in 1953 with a 32.4

rating on a 38.9 percent completion percentage, 5 touchdowns and 15 interceptions.

Best stat line, playoffs: Bart Starr in the 1966 NFL Championship victory over Dallas went 19–28, 304, 4–0; Lynn Dickey in a 1982 Wildcard win over the Cardinals went 17–23, 260, 4–0; Brett Favre in a 1995 Divisional win over San Francisco went 21–28, 299, 2–0.

Worst stat line, playoffs: Brett Favre in a 2001 Divisional loss to the Rams went 26–44, 281, 2–6.

Big Days: The first passer to exceed 300 yards passing in a game was Cecil Isbell with 333 yards on November 1, 1942. The first to reach 400 yards was Don Horn with 410 on November 21, 1969. Lynn Dickey had the biggest day in franchise history by throwing for 418 yards on October 12, 1980. Brett Favre has had 48 300-yard games.

Running QBs: Tobin Rote was inconsistent as a passer but was a rugged runner who led the Packers in rushing three times. Sometimes, he even lined up as a tailback rather than a T-formation quarterback. Three times he ran for over 100 yards in a game, including 150 once in 1951. Tailback Cecil Isbell also surpassed 100 yards rushing in a game once. Both Bart Starr and Don Majkowski were mobile quarterbacks who averaged better than 5 yards per carry.

Bomber: Injury-prone Lynn Dickey was famous for his bombs to James Lofton; Arnie Herber, who cupped the ball in his hand rather than gripping it, was famous for his bombs to Don Hutson.

Most accurate: While Brett Favre's completion percentage is higher, Bart Starr played in a different era and different offense that focused more on getting the ball downfield. Starr was the most accurate passer of his day.

Leader: Bart Starr was the consummate quiet leader who was respected by every player on the team.

Comeback King: Brett Favre has had 33 4th quarter comebacks, plus two in the postseason.

Highest Football IQ: No one understood football better than Bart Starr.

Toughest: Brett Favre has started 237 straight games, the NFL record.

First signal caller/T-Formation QB: Curly Lambeau was the first signal caller in 1921, but Indian Jack Jacobs was the first T-formation quarterback in 1947.

First TD pass: On November 13, 1921, Curly

Lambeau threw a 60-yard touchdown pass to Billy DuMoe in a 14–7 win over the Hammond Pros.

Black QBs: The Packers' record in this has been abysmal. They briefly employed Choo Choo Charlie Brackins in 1955. Since then, only Willie Gillus has played for Green Bay and that was in a 1987 replacement game. In recent years, Aaron Brooks and Henry Burris have been on the practice squad but never appeared in a game.

Tallest QB: Frank Patrick was a 6'7" tight end at Nebraska and was converted to quarterback unsuccessfully in Green Bay. The tallest Packer starter was Lynn Dickey at 6'4".

Smallest QB: Charlie Mathys was a 5'7" 165-pound quarterback in the 1920s. More recently, Ty Detmer sure didn't look to be 6' 190 pounds as he claimed.

Oldest QB: Zeke Bratkowski was 40 when he appeared in six games in 1971. Starr was 37 when he finished his career; Favre was 37 in 2006.

Rookie sensation: No one was a real sensation, but Cecil Isbell threw seven touchdown passes and ran for over 400 yards as a rookie.

Late bloomer: Bart Starr didn't become a star until his sixth season in the league, 1961, when he was 27.

1st round picks: Eleven times the Packers have taken a passer with their top pick, and it only worked out the first time, 1938, when they picked Cecil Isbell with the seventh pick in the draft. In the 1940s, they picked a quarterback first three years in a row — Ernie Case in 1947, Jug Girard in 1948 and Stan Heath in 1949. Case didn't sign, Heath lasted one year and Girard converted to halfback. Twice, the Packers used the top pick in the draft for a quarterback — Paul Hornung in 1957 who became a Hall of Fame runner and Randy Duncan in 1959 who went to Canada. Rounding out the group are: Babe Parilli, the 4th pick in 1952, Don Horn, the 25th in 1967, Green Bay native Jerry Tagge, the 11th in 1971, Rich Campbell, the 6th in 1981 and Aaron Rodgers, the 24th in 2004.

Out of position: First round picks Paul Hornung and Jug Girard were both tried at quarterback and found wanting. Frank Patrick was a former tight end. Willie Wood was a running quarterback at USC.

Long-time subs: Zeke Bratkowski failed as a starter in Chicago and Los Angeles, but was a reliable backup to Bart Starr for seven years in the 1960s. Doug Pederson backed up Brett Favre for seven years and got to throw all of 97 passes.

QB controversy: Arnie Herber and Cecil Isbell shared the tailback duties for two years before Herber was cut. Tobin Rote and Babe Parilli were two struggling young passers in the early 1950s. They combined for 26 touchdowns and 25 interceptions in 1952 but sunk to 9 touchdowns and 34 picks the following year. After that, Parilli went into the service and was traded to the Browns. He returned in 1957 after Rote was traded and had a second lackluster tour in Green Bay. Bart Starr had to wrest the starting job away from Lamar McHan at the beginning of the Lombardi era.

College affiliation: The Packers have had four Nebraska quarterbacks — Dennis Claridge, Frank Patrick, Jerry Tagge and Vince Ferragamo — to no good effect.

Ones who got away: Brett Favre has forced Green Bay to part with Mark Brunell and Matt Hasselbeck who went to Jacksonville and Seattle respectively and did very well.

Has beens: Some of the retreads the Packers have tried at starting quarterback include Paul Christman, Paul Held, John Roach, Bobby Thomason, Bobby Garrett, Lamar McHan, John Hadl, Jack Concannon, Jim Del Gaizo, Bobby Douglass, Randy Johnson, Rick Norton, Bill Troup, Chuck Fusina, Brian Dowling, Steve Pisarkiewicz, Vince Ferragamo, Jim Zorn, Mike Tomczak, Jim McMahon, T.J. Rubley, Steve Bono and Doug Pederson.

Ruinous injuries: By the start of the 1980 season, Lynn Dickey had missed 30 of 60 games due to injury in his four years in Green Bay and 53 games altogether in his nine-year career to that point. Don Majkowski, the Majik Man, lost his arm strength when he ruined his shoulder in 1990. He lost his job to Favre after an ankle injury in 1992.

Best trade: The Packers picked up a second number one pick in the 1992 draft in a slot switch with Philadelphia and traded that extra pick to Atlanta for Brett Favre who spent his rookie season in the Falcon doghouse. Green Bay received 15 great years for that extra pick.

Worst trade: The deal Dan Devine made for John Hadl is known as the Lawrence Welk trade ("a one and a two and a three"); it decimated the franchise's future. The Packers gave the Rams #1s in 1975 (Mike Fanning) and 1976 (Dennis Lick), #2s in 1975 (Monte Jackson) and 1976 (Pat Thomas) and a #3 in 1975 (Geoff Reese) for a washed up John Hadl. Fanning, Jackson, and Thomas all had fine careers for the Rams. Hadl was traded to Houston two years later in the Lynn Dickey deal.

Title winners: Bart Starr, 5; Arnie Herber, 4, Red Dunn, 3; Cecil Isbell, 1; Irv Comp, 1, Brett Favre, 1.

Hall of Famers: Signal caller Curly Lambeau; tailback Arnie Herber and quarterback Bart Starr.

All Pro/Pro Bowl seasons: Brett Favre, 8; Bart Starr, 5; Cecil Isbell, 5; Arnie Herber, 3; Curly Lambeau, 3; Tobin Rote, 2; Lynn Dickey, 1; Don Majkowski, 1.

QBs as coaches: Curly Lambeau went 226–132–22 with the Packers, Cardinals and Redskins; Cecil Isbell went 10–23 in the All America Conference and with the Cardinals; Bart Starr went 52–76–3 with Green Bay.

Underrated: Despite being in the Hall of Fame, Bart Starr does not get the recognition he deserves for winning more NFL titles than any other quarterback in history. Cecil Isbell quit after only five seasons so he didn't amass the career numbers that would keep him in memory today, but he was among the very best passers of his time.

Overrated: Brett Favre in his last few seasons reverted to the impatience of his youth and cost the team playoff wins in the process.

Best Nicknames: Arnie "Flash" Herber, Indian Jack Jacobs, Don "Majik Man" Majkowski and Brett "Country" Favre.

Time Capsule: Curly Lambeau's early devotion to the pass gave the Packers an identity. The 83-yard touchdown pass from Arnie Herber to Don Hutson on Hutson's first professional reception set the tone for the Packer offense of the 1930s. Bart Starr's drive and quarterback sneak in the Ice Bowl. Bart Starr's patented 3rd and short or 4th and short touchdown bombs. The relentless passing in the Packers 1983 48–47 win over the Redskins on Monday Night Football. Brett Favre running to the wrong sideline after throwing his first Super Bowl touchdown pass against the Patriots.

What If: If Tom Landry had taken up Vince Lombardi's offer of Starr and any other player for Don Meredith in 1960, would the Packers have been as successful in that decade? If Green Bay had not obtained Brett Favre, would Mark Brunell or even Kurt Warner have emerged to lead the Packers to a Super Bowl?

Off the field: Curly Lambeau liked to date actresses in Hollywood. Don Majkowski was a stylish bachelor. Brett Favre was a good-old-drinking-boy in his younger days. He also played Cameron Diaz's boyfriend in the 1998 hit movie *There's Something About Mary.*

Carlos Brown acted under that name and under Alan Autry. He appeared in 10 movies, 14 TV movies and 14 episodes of TV series as well as starring in "In the Heat of the Night" and "Grace Under Fire." He later was elected mayor of Fresno, California. Paul Christman and Indian Jack Jacobs appeared in *Triple Threat.* Vince Ferragamo appeared in the TV movie *Policewoman Centerfold* and an episode of *Dynasty.* Jack Concannon appeared in *M*A*S*H* and the TV movie *Brian's Song.* David Whitehurst's son Charlie is with the Chargers. Ty Detmer's brother Koy was with Philadelphia. Matt Hasselbeck's brother Tim and father Don also played in the NFL. Tobin Rote's cousin Kyle played with the Giants. Brian Dowling was the inspiration for the B.D. character in "Doonesbury."

Quarterback Bibliography

Curly Lambeau
Zimmerman, David. *Lambeau: The Man Behind the Mystique.* Hales Corner, WI: Eagle Books, 2003.

Bart Starr
Claerbaut, David. *Bart Starr: When Leadership Mattered.* Dallas: Taylor, 2004.
Devaney, John. *Bart Starr.* NY: Scholastic Book Services, 1967.
Maule, Tex. *Bart Starr: Professional Quarterback.* NY: Franklin Watts, 1973.
Schoor, Gene. *Bart Starr: A Biography.* Garden City, NY: Doubleday, 1977.
Starr, Bart, and John Wiebusch. *A Perspective on Victory.* Chicago, IL, Follett, 1972.
Starr, Bart, and Murray Olderman. *Starr: My Life in Football.* New York: Morrow, 1987.
Sullivan, George. *Bart Starr: The Cool Quarterback.* New York: Putnam, 1970.

Brett Favre
Brett Favre. Dallas, TX: Beckett Publications, 1997.
Cameron, Steve. *Brett Favre: Huck Finn Grows Up.* Indianapolis, IN: Masters Press, 1996.
Favre, Brett, with Chris Havel. *Favre: For the Record.* New York: Doubleday, 1997.
Favre, Brett, and Marc Serota. *Favre: Most Valuable Player.* Hallendale, FL: EGI Productions, 1999.
Favre, Brett, and Bonita Favre with Chris Havel. *Favre.* New York: Rugged Land, 2004.
Kertscher, Tom. *Brett Favre: A Packers Fan's Tribute.* Nashville, TN: Cumberland House, 2006

Jim McMahon *see* Chicago Bears

27

Houston Texans

Leading Passers, by Yards

Quarterback	Years	G	Att	Comp	Pct	Yds	Y/A	Y/Cp	TD	Int	Int %	Rating
David Carr	2002–06	76	2,070	1,243	60	13,391	6.5	10.8	59	65	3.14%	75.5
Tony Banks	2003–05	15	129	76	58.9	882	6.8	11.6	6	5	3.88%	79.0
Sage Rosenfels	2006	4	39	27	69.2	265	6.8	9.8	3	1	2.56%	103.0
Dave Ragone	2003	2	40	20	50	135	3.4	6.8	0	1	2.50%	47.4

Quarterback	Rush Att	Rush Yds	Rush Avg	TD
David Carr	268	1,233	4.6	8
Tony Banks	8	25	3.1	0
Sage Rosenfels	4	5		0
Dave Ragone	6	51	8.5	0

Record Holders

Passing Yards, Career: 13,391 David Carr
Passing Yards, Season: 3,531 David Carr 2004
Completion %, Career: 60% David Carr
Completion %, Season: 68.3% David Carr 2006
Touchdown Passes, Career: 59 David Carr
Touchdown Passes, Season: 16 David Carr 2004
Interceptions, Career: 65 David Carr
Interceptions, Season: 15 David Carr 2002
Rating, Career: 75.5 David Carr
Rating, Season: 83.5 David Carr 2004
Rush Yards, Career: 1,233 David Carr
Rush Yards, Season: 299 David Carr 2004

Passers by Categories

Best/Worst starter: David Carr has been it so far, and did not measure up.

Best stat line, season: In 2004, Carr had his best season completing 61 percent of his passes, averaging 7.6 yards per attempt, throwing 16 touchdowns to 14 interceptions and surpassing 3,500 yards.

Worst stat line, season: As a rookie in 2002, Carr averaged only 5.8 yards per attempt and threw 15 interceptions to just 9 touchdowns.

Best stat line, playoffs: None.

Worst stat line, playoffs: None.

Big Days: The first passer to exceed 300 yards passing in a game was David Carr with 371 yards on October 12, 2003. Carr had the biggest day in franchise history by throwing for 372 yards on October 10, 2004. He also threw for over 300 yards on two other occasion.

Running QBs: If Carr weren't mobile, he would be dead by now. Behind a terrible line he's been sacked 249 times in his first five years.

Bomber: Carr has not been much of a deep thrower.

Most accurate: Carr has gained in accuracy.

Leader: By default, Carr.

Comeback King: Carr has 10 4th quarter comebacks.

Highest Football IQ: By default, David Carr.

Toughest: Carr does take a beating with the Texans' perennially poor line.

First signal caller/T-Formation QB: David Carr.

First TD pass: Carr to Billy Miller for 19

yards in a 19–10 win over Dallas on September 16, 2002.

Black QBs: Tony Banks backed up Carr from 2003–05.

Tallest QB: Quinton Porter was 6'5".

Smallest QB: Carr and Dave Ragone are both 6'3".

Oldest QB: Tony Banks was 32 in 2005.

Rookie sensation: Carr was no sensation.

Late bloomer: None.

1st round picks: Carr was the first pick in 2002. He has yet to live up to that billing.

Out of position: None.

Long-time subs: Tony Banks for three years.

QB controversy: The only controversy was whether the Texans should junk Carr and draft hometown hero Vince Young of Texas in the 2006 draft.

College affiliation: None.

Ones who got away: None.

Has beens: Tony Banks and Sage Rosenfels.

Ruinous injuries: None.

Best trade: Getting a number 3 from Dallas for Drew Henson.

Worst trade: None.

Title winners: None.

Hall of Famers: None.

All Pro/Pro Bowl seasons: None.

QBs as coaches: None.

Underrated/Overrated: David Carr is probably neither.

Best Nicknames: None.

Time Capsule: None.

What If: If the Texans had selected hometown hero Vince Young, could he lead them to victory?

Off the field: NA

Quarterback Bibliography

None.

28

Indianapolis Colts

Leading Passers, by Yards

Quarterback	Years	G	Att	Comp	Pct	Yds	Y/A	Y/Cp	TD	Int	Int %	Rating
Johnny Unitas	1956–72	206	5,110	2,796	54.7	39,768	7.8	14.2	287	246	4.81%	78.8
Peyton Manning	1998–06	144	4,890	3,131	64	37,586	7.7	12.0	275	139	2.84%	94.4
Bert Jones	1973–81	98	2,464	1,382	56.1	17,663	7.2	12.8	122	97	3.94%	78.8
Jack Trudeau	1986–93	61	1,536	812	52.9	9,647	6.3	11.9	41	62	4.04%	64.4
Jeff George	1990–93	52	1,532	874	57	9,551	6.2	10.9	41	46	3.00%	72.0
Jim Harbaugh	1994–97	53	1,230	746	60.7	8,705	7.1	11.7	49	26	2.11%	86.6
Mike Pagel	1982–85	51	1,154	587	50.9	7,474	6.5	12.7	39	47	4.07%	65.8
Earl Morrall	1968–71	51	676	363	53.7	5,666	8.4	15.6	47	40	5.92%	80.3
Marty Domres	1972–75	51	576	293	50.9	3,471	6.0	11.8	21	31	5.38%	59.3
Greg Landry	1979–81	43	533	308	57.8	3,402	6.4	11.0	17	19	3.56%	72.6
Gary Hogeboom	1986–88	20	443	260	58.7	3,295	7.4	12.7	22	18	4.06%	81.6
George Shaw	1955–58	36	410	210	51.2	2,820	6.9	13.4	21	31	7.56%	59.0
Chris Chandler	1988–89	18	313	168	53.7	2,156	6.9	12.8	10	15	4.79%	66.2

Quarterback	Rush Att	Rush Yds	Rush Avg	TD
Johnny Unitas	450	1,777	3.9	13
Peyton Manning	269	701	2.6	13
Bert Jones	236	1,356	5.7	14
Jack Trudeau	91	156	1.7	3
Jeff George	54	103	1.9	2
Jim Harbaugh	175	856	4.9	3
Mike Pagel	124	830	6.7	4
Earl Morrall	19	37	1.9	1
Marty Domres	88	454	5.2	6
Greg Landry	39	152	3.9	1
Gary Hogeboom	24	15	0.6	2
George Shaw	98	391	4.0	5
Chris Chandler	53	196	3.7	4

Record Holders

Passing Yards, Career: 39,768 Johnny Unitas
Passing Yards, Season: 4,557 Peyton Manning 2004
Completion %, Career: 64% Peyton Manning
Completion %, Season: 67.6% Peyton Manning 2004
Touchdown Passes, Career: 287 Johnny Unitas
Touchdown Passes, Season: 49 Peyton Manning 2004
Interceptions, Career: 246 Johnny Unitas
Interceptions, Season: 28 Peyton Manning 1998
Rating, Career: 94.4 Peyton Manning
Rating, Season: 121.1 Peyton Manning 2004
Rush Yards, Career: 1,777 Johnny Unitas
Rush Yards, Season: 441 Mike Pagel 1981

Passers by Categories

Five best starters: We begin with arguably the greatest quarterback in history, Johnny Unitas. Next comes Peyton Manning, perhaps the greatest contemporary quarterback, who is setting new statistical standards each year. Follow them with Bert Jones, one of the top quarterbacks of the 1970s. Finish up with Jim Harbaugh who was pretty good and Earl Morrall who is among the best backup quarterbacks ever.

Worst starters, career: Jack Trudeau was a weak-armed second round draft pick who started too many games for the Colts in the 1980s and 1990s and threw 41 touchdowns to 62 interceptions. Jeff George had a world of talent, but was a clubhouse lawyer who was neither a leader nor a winner and averaged only 6.2 yards per pass. Art Schlichter was even worse — an ineffective passer who was suspended from the NFL for gambling; he ended up serving multiple sentences in prison. Mark Herrmann was the quarterback the Colts got in the Elway deal; he threw 2 touchdowns and 13 interceptions in two years as a Colt. Marty Domres was supposed to replace Unitas, but threw 21 touchdowns to 31 interceptions while averaging 6 yards per pass.

Best stat line, season: It would be hard to top Peyton Manning's 2004 that earned an astronomical passer rating of 121.4: 67.6 percent completions, over 4,500 yards, 9.2 yards per attempt, 49 touchdowns and only 10 interceptions. In 12-game seasons, Johnny Unitas put up these numbers in 1957 and 1959: 1957 — 57.1 percent, 2,550 yards, 8.5 yards per attempt, 24 touchdowns and 17 interceptions; 1959 — 52.6 percent, 2,899 yards, 7.9 yards per attempt, 32 touchdowns and 14 interceptions. In a 14-game season in 1965, Unitas went 58.2 percent, 2,530 yards, 9.0 yards per attempt, 23 touchdowns and 12 interceptions. Earl Morrall won an MVP award in 1968 by completing 57.4 percent of his passes for 2,909 yards (an average of 9.2 yards per attempt), 26 touchdowns and 17 interceptions. Bert Jones completed 60.3 percent of his passes in 1976 for 3,104 yards (averaging 9.1 per attempt), 24 touchdowns and 9 interceptions.

Worst stat line, season: The mixed rookie seasons of Peyton Manning and George Shaw are noted below, but Bert Jones's rookie year was just bad: 39.8 percent completions, 5.0 yards per attempt, 4 touchdowns and 12 interceptions. Jack Trudeau's rookie year of 1986 produced 8 touchdowns, 18 interceptions and 5.3 yards per attempt. In his only season in the NFL, Mike Kirkland threw only 41 passes, but 8 of them ended up in the hands of the opponents. Johnny Unitas hit the wall in 1971 averaging only 5.4 yards per attempt and throwing 3 touchdowns to 9 interceptions. When Art Schlichter returned from suspension in 1984, he completed 44 percent of his passes and averaged 5 yards per attempt.

Best stat line, playoffs: In the 1958 sudden death title game against the Giants, Unitas went 26–40, 361, 1–1. In a 2003 Wildcard win over Denver, Manning went 22–26, 377, 5–0; the following season, Manning repeated the performance against the Broncos with 27–33, 457, 4–1.

Worst stat line, playoffs: In the 1964 title loss to the Browns, Unitas went 12–20, 95, 0–2. Tom Matte proved he could not impersonate a quarterback in the 1965 playoff loss to Green Bay by going 5–12, 40, 0–0. Earl Morrall flopped in Super Bowl III against the Jets: 6–17, 71, 0–3. In the 2003 AFC Conference loss to the Patriots, Manning went 23–47, 237, 1–4.

Big Days: The first passer to exceed 300 yards passing in a game was Johnny Unitas with 314 yards on November 18, 1956. Jack Trudeau was the first in Indianapolis with 315 yards on October 12, 1986. The first to reach 400 yards was Unitas with 401 on September 17, 1967. Peyton Manning had the biggest day in franchise history by throwing for 472 yards on October 31, 2004. Manning has had 39 300-yard games while Unitas had 26. Manning has had seven 400-yard games.

Running QBs: Bert Jones, Jim Harbaugh, George Shaw and Mike Pagel were all good at running. Jones was an all-around quarterback.

Bomber: I would take Unitas over Manning for the deep pass.

Most accurate: Manning might have a slight edge here, but it is close. Unitas completed almost 55 percent of his passes in an era of pro football with more down-the-field passing, fewer dinks to backs and less deference shown to wide receivers by defenders.

Leader: Johnny Unitas was God in the huddle.

Comeback King: Unitas had 37 4th quar-

ter comebacks, plus two in the postseason. Manning has had 28 plus one in the playoffs.

Highest Football IQ: Unitas called all his own plays with next to no help/interference from the sideline. Manning is close, but has a bit more help.

Toughest: Manning has started 144 straight games. Unitas held the league record at one time with 92.

First signal caller/T-Formation QB: Journeyman Fred Enke was the expansion Colts first quarterback in 1953.

First TD pass: Enke hit Tommy Kalmanir for a 22-yard score in a 27–17 loss to Detroit on October 3, 1953.

Black QBs: George Taliaferro was one of the first blacks to take some NFL snaps as a quarterback in 1953. Karl Douglass was on the practice squad in 1971.

Tallest QB: Peyton Manning and Jim Sorgi are 6'5" as were Sean Salisbury, Bill Troup and Dick Wood.

Smallest QB: Gary Kerkorian and George Taliaferro were 5'11", Cotton Davidson, Dick Flowers and Ricky Turner were 6' while George Shaw was 6'1". All were slightly built.

Oldest QB: Joe Ferguson was 40 in 1990. Mark Rypien was 39 in 2001, and Johnny Unitas was a 39-year old starter in 1972.

Rookie sensation: George Shaw struggled a bit as a rookie starter in 1955, throwing 19 interceptions to 10 touchdowns. He was replaced in 1956 by Johnny Unitas who tossed 9 touchdowns against 10 interceptions and averaged 7.57 yards per attempt as a rookie. Jeff George showed his potential in 1990 by surpassing 2,000 yards and throwing 16 touchdowns to 13 interceptions. Peyton Manning threw for over 3,700 yards and 26 touchdowns in 1998, but his rookie status was evinced by his team-record 28 interceptions.

Late bloomer: Earl Morrall became the NFL MVP at 34 replacing Johnny Unitas in 1968. Jim Harbaugh had his best years after coming to Indianapolis at 30.

1st round picks: Bert Jones, 2nd in 1973, and Peyton Manning, 1st in 1998, were unqualified successes. Cotton Davidson was the 5th pick in 1954, but played more in Canada and the AFL. George Shaw, the 1st pick in 1955, was an able backup, but never lived up to his billing in four cities. Art Schlichter, 4th in 1982, became more known as a compulsive gambler and convicted felon than professional quarterback. John Elway, 1st in 1983, refused to sign with the Irsays and forced a terrible trade to Denver. Jeff George, 1st in 1990, had great ability, but was never able to translate that to team wins.

Out of position: Most notable was Tom Matte, a former Ohio State quarterback forced to lead the 1965 Colts into the postseason after injuries to Unitas and backup Gary Cuozzo. Bob Boyd, Jack Mildren and Sam Havrilak were also former college quarterbacks who served the Colts as defensive and running backs. Finally, George Taliaferro, the team's only black quarterback, played more as a running back, return man and punter.

Long-time subs: Gary Cuozzo backed up Unitas for four years. George Shaw, Lamar McHan and Earl Morrall all served in the same capacity for three years a piece.

QB controversy: Whether Don Shula should have lifted Earl Morrall at halftime of Super Bowl III for the recovering Johnny Unitas will never go away as a controversy. The choice between Manning or Ryan Leaf as the top draft choice only seems like a no-brainer in retrospect.

College affiliation: Steve Walsh, Craig Erickson and Jack DelBello all hailed from Miami; Lamar McHan, Mike Kirkland and Joe Ferguson were all former Arkansas Razorbacks.

Ones who got away: Hall of Famer John Elway.

Has beens: Fred Enke, Lamar McHan, Ed Brown, Marty Domres, Greg Landry, Gary Hogeboom, Tom Ramsey, David Humm, Joe Ferguson, Browning Nagle, Craig Erickson, Don Majkowski, Mark Rypien and Steve Walsh.

Ruinous injuries: Unitas lost some time to arm injuries, but that is to be expected for a 17-year career. Bert Jones, however, lost two years out of his prime and had his career ended by back and shoulder problems.

Best trade: The Colts traded perennial backup Gary Cuozzo and Butch Allison to the Saints for the number 1 pick in the 1967 draft (Bubba Smith) along with Bill Curry and a number 3. The next year they picked up Earl Morrall from the Giants for Butch Wilson. They traded a banged-up Bert Jones to the Rams for number 1 and 2 draft picks. They traded malcon-

tent Jeff George to Atlanta for two number 1's and a number 3. One of those picks turned out to be Marvin Harrison.

Worst trade: Selling Unitas to the Chargers was heartless. Trading the rights for Elway to the Broncos for Mark Herrmann, Chris Hinton and a number 1 was not nearly equitable. Giving up Andre Rison and Chris Hinton to Atlanta for the rights to Jeff George was not worth it in the long run. Giving up a number 1 to Tampa for Craig Erickson was ridiculous.

Title winners: Johnny Unitas, 2; Peyton Manning, 1; Earl Morrall, 1.

Hall of Famers: Unitas.

All Pro/Pro Bowl seasons: Johnny Unitas, 11; Peyton Manning, 7; Bert Jones, 2; Earl Morrall, 1; Jim Harbaugh, 1.

QBs as coaches: None.

Underrated: Bert Jones had an injury-shortened career and lost all three playoff games he was in, but he led the rebuilt Colts to three straight division championships in the 1970s.

Overrated: Does anyone still think Peyton Manning is overrated?

Best Nicknames: George "Scoop" Taliaferro, Johnny U, Jeff "Boy" George.

Time Capsule: Johnny Unitas in the first Sudden Death championship game in 1958. Johnny Unitas' slope-shoulders and high-topped shoes. Earl Morrall not seeing Jimmy Orr in Super Bowl III. Peyton Manning's "chicken dance" as he audibles on almost every play.

What If: If Elway had signed with the Colts, would they have stayed in Baltimore? Would they have had a nearly unbroken string of Unitas-Bert Jones-Elway-Manning?

Off the field: Marty Domres fancied himself as a ladies' man; Art Schlichter fancied himself as a betting man. Gary Hogeboom was on a season of *Survivor.* Johnny Unitas appeared in *M*A*S*H, Gus* and *Any Given Sunday* as well as episodes of *The Simpsons, Coach* and the *Adventures of Pete and Pete.* Peyton Manning appeared in an episode of *The Girls Next Door.*

Quarterback Bibliography

Johnny Unitas
Fitzgerald, Ed. *Johnny Unitas: The Amazing Success Story of Mr. Quarterback.* New York: Bartholomew House, 1960.

Greene, Lee. *The Johnny Unitas Story*. New York: Putnam, 1962.

Unitas, Johnny, and Ed Fitzgerald. *Pro Quarterback: My Own Story*. New York: Simon and Shuster, 1965.

Lazenby, Roland. *Johnny Unitas: The Best There Ever Was*. Chicago: Triumph Books, 2002.

Towle, Mike. *Johnny Unitas: Mister Quarterback*. Nashville, TN: Cumberland House, 2003.

Sahadi, Lou. *Johnny Unitas: America's Quarterback*. Chicago: Triumph Books, 2004.

Callahan, Tom. *Johnny U: The Life and Times of John Unitas*. New York: Crown, 2006.

Earl Morrall *see* Detroit Lions

Marty Domres *see* San Diego Chargers

Bert Jones

Fox, Larry. *Bert Jones and the Baltimore Colts*. New York: Dodd Mead, 1977.

Art Schlichter

Collett, Ritter. *Straight Arrow: The Art Schlichter Story*. Dayton, OH: Landfall Press, 1981. (This is beyond irony.)

Peyton Manning

Manning, Archie, and John Underwood. *Manning: A Father His Sons and a Football Legacy*. New York: Harper Entertainment, 2000.

29

Jacksonville Jaguars

Leading Passers, by Yards

Quarterback	Years	G	Att	Comp	Pct	Yds	Y/A	Y/Cp	TD	Int	Int %	Rating
Mark Brunell	1995–03	120	3,616	2,184	60.4	25,698	7.1	11.8	144	86	2.38%	85.4
Byron Leftwich	2003–06	46	1,344	789	58.7	9,042	6.7	11.5	51	36	2.68%	80.5
David Garrard	2002–06	28	539	313	58.1	3,543	6.6	11.3	18	13	2.41%	78.9
Steve Beuerlein	1995	7	142	71	50	952	6.7	13.4	4	7	4.93%	60.5
Jonathan Quinn	1998–01	10	125	66	52.8	748	6.0	11.3	3	4	3.20%	65.7

Quarterback	Rush Att	Rush Yds	Rush Avg	TD
Mark Brunell	429	2,219	5.2	14
Byron Leftwich	120	364	3.0	8
David Garrard	115	637	5.5	6
Steve Beuerlein	5	32	6.4	0
Jonathan Quinn	19	119	6.3	0

Record Holders

Passing Yards, Career: 25,698 Mark Brunell

Passing Yards, Season: 4,367 Mark Brunell 1995

Completion %, Career: 60.4% Mark Brunell

Completion %, Season: 63.4% Mark Brunell 1996

Touchdown Passes, Career: 144 Mark Brunell

Touchdown Passes, Season: 20 Mark Brunell 1998 and 2000

Interceptions, Career: 86 Mark Brunell

Interceptions, Season: 20 Mark Brunell 1996

Rating, Career: 85.4 Mark Brunell

Rating, Season: 91.2 Mark Brunell 1997

Rush Yards, Career: 2,219 Mark Brunell

Rush Yards, Season: 480 Mark Brunell 1995

Passers by Categories

Five best starters: Mark Brunell gave the

Jags a quality starting quarterback right from the start. Byron Leftwich has shown talent and leadership whenever he is healthy enough to play.

Worst starters, career: Steve Beuerlein could not hold off Brunell for more than a few games in 1995.

Best stat line, season: In 1996, Mark Brunell led the league in yards and yards per attempt, but had some interception problems. His two best years were 1997 when he completed 60.7 percent of his passes for over 3,000 yards 18 touchdowns and only 7 interceptions and 1998 when he threw 20 touchdowns to only 9 interceptions.

Worst stat line, season: Beuerlein only managed four touchdowns against seven interceptions in 1995.

Best stat line, playoffs: In the shocking 1996 Divisional upset of the Broncos, Mark Brunell was 18–29, 245, 2–0.

Worst stat line, playoffs: In a 1998 Divisional loss to the Jets, Mark Brunell went 12–31, 156, 3–3.

Big Days: The first passer to exceed 300 yards passing in a game was Mark Brunell with 302 yards on October 15, 1995. The first to reach 400 yards was Brunell with 432 on September 22, 1996, the most yards ever by a Jags quarterback. Brunell had 22 300-yard games.

Running QBs: Mark Brunell was similar to Steve Young — a left-handed accurate passer and dangerous runner. David Garrard is a bull when he puts the ball under his arm to run.

Bomber: Byron Leftwich has a strong arm but no one to throw to deep.

Most accurate: Brunell.

Leader: Byron Leftwich seemed to inspire his teammates.

Comeback King: Mark Brunell had 19 4th quarter comebacks, plus one in the postseason.

Highest Football IQ: Brunell had a good feel for the game.

Toughest: Leftwich once played a game in college on a leg so badly injured that his linemen had to carry him upfield after a completion.

First signal caller/T-Formation QB: Steve Beuerlein was the team's starter for its first few games until Brunell took over.

First TD pass: Beuerlein hit Randy Jordan for 71 yards in a 21–17 loss to the Bengals on September 10, 1995.

Black QBs: With third stringer Quinn Gray, the Jaguars had three black quarterbacks in 2005 and 2006. Garrard joined the team in 2002 and Leftwich in 2003.

Tallest QB: Jonathan Quinn was 6'6". Leftwich is 6'5".

Smallest QB: Jay Fiedler was only 6'1".

Oldest QB: Brunell was 33 in 2003.

Rookie sensation: Leftwich threw for over 2,800 yards and 14 touchdowns in 2003.

Late bloomer: Mark Brunell was stuck behind Brett Favre for a couple of years in Green Bay before getting his shot in Jacksonville at age 25.

1st round picks: None. Leftwich has been the only quarterback taken in the first round (7th pick) by the Jaguars.

Out of position: Matt Jones was a quarterback in college before being switched to receiver in Jacksonville. Some advocated moving David Garrard to running back.

Long-time subs: Jonathan Quinn backed up Brunell for four years.

QB controversy: Replacing Brunell with Leftwich was a source of debate.

College affiliation: None.

Ones who got away: Jay Fiedler was the backup quarterback who had the most success after he left the Jaguars.

Has beens: Steve Beuerlein.

Ruinous injuries: Leftwich is so entrenched in the pocket that he has injury problems every year.

Best trade: Getting Mark Brunell from the Packers for a number 3 and a number 5. Unloading Rob Johnson on the Bills for a number 1 who turned out to be Donovan Darrius.

Worst trade: None.

Title winners: None.

Hall of Famers: None.

All Pro/Pro Bowl seasons: Mark Brunell 3.

QBs as coaches: None.

Underrated: Brunell achieved quite a lot with an expansion team.

Overrated: Rob Johnson proved he was nothing special in Buffalo.

Best Nicknames: None.

Time Capsule: Brunell's scrambling to lead the Jags to a shocking postseason upset of the Broncos in Denver in the Jags second year.

What If: If the Eagles had agreed to Mark Brunell's contract demands and he were traded to

Philadelphia rather than Jacksonville, how much early success would Tom Coughlin's Jags have had?

Off the field: Jay Fiedler's cousin twice removed was Boston Pops conductor Arthur Fiedler.

Quarterback Bibliography

None.

30

Kansas City Chiefs

Leading Passers, by Yards

Quarterback	Years	G	Att	Comp	Pct	Yds	Y/A	Y/Cp	TD	Int	Int %	Rating
Len Dawson	1962–75	183	3,696	2,115	57.2	28,507	7.7	13.5	230	185	5.01%	81.8
Trent Green	2001–06	88	2,777	1,720	61.9	21,457	7.7	12.5	118	85	3.06%	87.3
Bill Kenney	1980–88	106	2,430	1,330	54.7	17,277	7.1	13.0	105	86	3.54%	77.0
Steve DeBerg	1988–91	57	1,616	934	57.8	11,873	7.3	12.7	67	50	3.09%	81.8
Mike Livingston	1969–79	90	1,751	912	52.1	11,295	6.5	12.4	56	83	4.74%	63.3
Elvis Grbac	1997–00	49	1,548	897	57.9	10,638	6.9	11.9	66	47	3.04%	80.6
Steve Bono	1994–96	36	1,075	594	55.3	6,489	6.0	10.9	37	27	2.51%	74.3
Joe Montana	1993–94	25	791	480	60.7	5,427	6.9	11.3	29	16	2.02%	85.0
Steve Fuller	1979–82	52	817	465	56.9	5,333	6.5	11.5	22	32	3.92%	69.4
Cotton Davidson	1960–61	28	709	330	46.5	4,919	6.9	14.9	32	39	5.50%	61.9
Todd Blackledge	1983–87	40	742	364	49.1	4,510	6.1	12.4	26	32	4.31%	62.0
Dave Krieg	1992–93	28	602	335	55.6	4,353	7.2	13.0	22	15	2.49%	80.4
Rich Gannon	1995–98	27	630	365	57.9	3,997	6.3	11.0	23	11	1.75%	81.7
Tony Adams	1975–78	50	319	163	51.1	2,126	6.7	13.0	9	22	6.90%	53.1
Damon Huard	2006	10	244	148	60.7	1,878	7.7	12.7	11	1	0.41%	98.0
Pete Beathard	1964–67, 1973	52	254	110	43.3	1,649	6.5	15.0	8	13	5.12%	54.4

Quarterback	Rush Att	Rush Yds	Rush Avg	TD
Len Dawson	283	1,253	4.4	9
Trent Green	171	692	4.0	3
Bill Kenney	123	191	1.6	5
Steve DeBerg	74	2	0.0	1
Mike Livingston	156	682	4.4	7
Elvis Grbac	86	316	3.7	2
Steve Bono	58	139	2.4	5
Joe Montana	43	81	1.9	0
Steve Fuller	139	712	5.1	5
Cotton Davidson	35	159	4.5	2
Todd Blackledge	64	280	4.4	1
Dave Krieg	58	98	1.7	2
Rich Gannon	96	388	4.0	6

Quarterback	Rush Att	Rush Yds	Rush Avg	TD
Tony Adams	27	124	4.6	0
Damon Huard	9	9	1.0	0
Pete Beathard	49	333	6.8	5

Record Holders

Passing Yards, Career: 28,507 Len Dawson
Passing Yards, Season: 4,591 Trent Green 2004
Completion %, Career: 61.9% Trent Green
Completion %, Season: 66.43% Len Dawson 1975 (140 att.); 66.37% Trent Green 2004 (556 att.)
Touchdown Passes, Career: 230 Len Dawson
Touchdown Passes, Season: 30 Len Dawson 1964
Interceptions, Career: 185 Len Dawson
Interceptions, Season: 24 Trent Green 2001
Rating, Career: 87.3 Trent Green
Rating, Season: 101.9 Len Dawson 1966
Rush Yards, Career: 1,253 Len Dawson
Rush Yards, Season: 274 Steve Fuller 1980

Passers by Categories

Five best starters: Len Dawson is the Hall of Famer who held all the Chief passing records until Trent Green came along in the new century. Joe Montana did not play up to his Olympian level in his two years in Kansas City, but he was still a top quarterback getting by mostly on guile and intelligence. Steve DeBerg had the best years of his long and mostly mediocre career in KC. Rich Gannon never gained the confidence of the coaches, but he was better than the 49er retreads, Steve Bono and Elvis Grbac, that he backed up for the Chiefs.

Worst starters, career: It was all or nothing with Cotton Davidson who completed 46 percent of his passes for 32 touchdowns and 39 interceptions in two seasons. Todd Blackledge was the one quarterback flop of the legendary 1983 draft. Steve Fuller threw 32 interceptions and only 22 touchdowns as a Chief while Mike Livingston was worse with 56 touchdowns and 83 interceptions.

Best stat line, season: In Len Dawson's first season of 1962, he led the AFL in yards per attempt with 8.9, completion percentage with 61 percent and touchdowns with 29. Four years later, he led the Chiefs to the first Super Bowl by again leading the league in yards per attempt with 8.9 and touchdowns with 26 against only 10 interceptions. In 1990, Steve DeBerg threw 23 touchdowns to just 4 interceptions and surpassed 3,000 yards for the third time in his career. In 2004, Trent Green completed 66.4 percent of his passes, threw for 4,591 yards and tossed 27 touchdowns.

Worst stat line, season: In the Chiefs' second Super Bowl season of 1969, Len Dawson was banged up and threw just 9 touchdowns to 13 interceptions. In 1977, Tony Adams threw 11 interceptions on just 92 passes, while Mike Livingston threw 9 touchdowns and 15 interceptions. Livingston followed that in 1978 by averaging just 5.4 yards per attempt and throwing 5 touchdowns to 13 interceptions. Todd Blackledge averaged just 5.8 yards per attempt in 1984 and threw 6 touchdowns against 11 interceptions. He followed that in 1985 by throwing 14 interceptions despite throwing 120 fewer passes.

Best stat line, playoffs: In the 1966 AFL title game against Buffalo, Len Dawson went 16–24, 227, 2–1. In a 1993 comeback Divisional win over Houston, Joe Montana went 22–38, 299, 3–1.

Worst stat line, playoffs: In a 1968 Divisional loss to Oakland, Len Dawson went 17–36, 253, 0–4. In a 1985 Wildcard loss to the Jets, Todd Blackledge went 12–21, 80, 0–2. In a 1995 Divisional loss to the Colts, Steve Bono went 11–25, 122, 1–3. In a 2006 Wildcard loss to the Colts, Trent Green went 14–24, 107, 1–2.

Big Days: The first Dallas Texan passer to exceed 300 yards passing in a game was Cotton Davidson with 333 yards on October 2, 1960; the first to do so in Kansas City was Len Dawson with 320 on October 4, 1964. The first to reach 400 yards was Dawson with 435 on November 1, 1964. Elvis Grbac had the biggest day in franchise history by throwing for 504 yards on November 5, 2000. Trent Green has had 26 300-yard games.

Running QBs: Steve Fuller was a better runner than passer. Pete Beathard was best at scrambling, averaging 6.8 yards per carry while averaging just 6.5 yards per pass. Len Dawson and Mike Livingston were mobile in the pocket.

Bomber: Throwing the bomb was the one thing that Cotton Davidson could do. Trent Green is effective with the deep pass.

Most accurate: Len Dawson was known for his accuracy.

Leader: Joe Montana was still the greatest leader in football when he wrapped up his career in Kansas City.

Comeback King: Len Dawson had 17 4th quarter comebacks, plus two in the postseason.

Highest Football IQ: Len Dawson was a very smart play caller.

Toughest: Trent Green started 82 games in a row for the Chiefs.

First signal caller/T-Formation QB: NFL and CFL reject Cotton Davidson.

First TD pass: Cotton Davidson hit Chris Burford for 12 yards on September 10, 1960 in a 21–20 loss to the Chargers.

Black QBs: Warren Moon in 1999. Also on the roster in 1999 was Ted White from Howard University, but he never appeared in an NFL game. Rookie Casey Printers was on the roster in 2006.

Tallest QB: Jonathan Quinn and Matt Blundin were both 6'6" while Elvis Grbac and Sandy Osiecki were both 6'5".

Smallest QB: Tom Clements was 5'10". 6' Chief quarterbacks include Randy Duncan, Eddie Wilson, John Huarte, Tony Adams and Matt Stevens.

Oldest QB: Warren Moon was 43 in 2000 and 42 in 1999 as a backup. Len Dawson was a 40-year old starter in 1975.

Rookie sensation: None. Len Dawson was an AFL rookie sensation in 1962, but he had already spent five years in the NFL.

Late bloomer: Len Dawson was 27 when the Dallas Texans gave him his chance in 1962. Trent Green was 31 when he came to Kansas City in 2001.

1st round picks: Pete Beathard was the first round selection of both the Detroit Lions and the Chiefs in 1964, but was a scatter-armed scrambler. Steve Fuller, 23rd in 1979, flopped as a passer in both Kansas City and Chicago — two teams desperate for a quarterback. Todd Blackledge was the only flop of the six quarterbacks taken in the first round of the 1983 draft. While

John Elway was already taken, The Chiefs could have taken Dan Marino, Jim Kelly, Ken O'Brien or even Tony Eason rather than Blackledge with the 7th pick.

Out of position: Cotton Davidson was a better punter than passer. Versatile running back Ed Podolak was a quarterback in college. Mike Nott could also punt.

Long-time subs: Mike Livingston backed up Len Dawson for eight years before finally getting his chance and proving himself as nothing more than a backup.

QB controversy: Both Bill Kenney and Steve Fuller were mediocre at best so it was hard to choose between them. Steve Bono and Rich Gannon seemed to offer a similar choice, but Gannon developed into a star in Oakland when finally given a real shot.

College affiliation: Notre Dame has given Kansas City three quarterbacks: John Huarte, who almost won a national championship for the Irish, and Tom Clements and Joe Montana who did.

Ones who got away: Rich Gannon took Oakland to a Super Bowl.

Has beens: Cotton Davidson, Randy Duncan, Jacky Lee, Tom Flores, John Huarte, Steve Pelluer, Ron Jaworski, Dave Krieg, Steve Bono, Elvis Grbac and Warren Moon.

Ruinous injuries: Len Dawson was not a sturdy player and took a beating. He missed several games during the 1969 championship season. Aging Joe Montana went down to injury in his final game, a playoff loss to Buffalo in 1994. Trent Green missed half of 2006 after a massive concussion and never seemed right even after returning.

Best trade: Trading Cotton Davidson to the Raiders for a number 1 (Buck Buchanan). Trading backup Eddie Wilson to the Patriots for a number 2 (Jim Lynch). Trading Pete Beathard to the Oilers for Ernie Ladd, Jacky Lee and a number 1 (George Daney). Getting Trent Green from the Rams for a number 1.

Worst trade: None.

Title winners: Len Dawson, 1.

Hall of Famers: Len Dawson, Joe Montana.

All Pro/Pro Bowl seasons: Len Dawson, 6; Trent Green, 2; Dave Krieg, 2; Cotton Davidson, 1; Mike Livingston, 1; Bill Kenney, 1; Steve Bono, 1; Elvis Grbac, 2.

QBs as coaches: Tom Flores was 97–87 in Oakland and Seattle.

Underrated: Len Dawson is not remembered as much as he should be; he was the greatest AFL quarterback and a Super Bowl winner. Steve DeBerg had his best years in Kansas City.

Overrated: Elvis Grbac was an inconsistent stiff.

Best Nicknames: Lenny "the Cool" Dawson and Elvis "the King" Grbac.

Time Capsule: The moving pocket Offense of the Seventies. Lenny Dawson's cool, surgical performance in Super Bowl IV. Joe Montana besting rivals Steve Young and John Elway in the 1993 regular season.

What If: If the Chiefs had committed to Rich Gannon in 1997 or 1998, would they have not only helped themselves, but destroyed the rival Raiders as well?

Off the field: Len Dawson appeared in *The Love Butcher* and *Personal Best*. Steve DeBerg appeared in an episode of *Arli$$*. Warren Moon appeared in *Any Given Sunday*, *Warriors of Virtue*, *Air Bud: Golden Receiver* and *Jerry Maguire* as well as an episode of *Arli$$*.

Quarterback Bibliography

Len Dawson
Dawson, Len, and Lou Sahadi. *Len Dawson: Pressure Quarterback*. New York: Cowles Book Co., 1970.
Bortstein, Larry. *Len Dawson: Super Bowl Quarterback*. New York: Grossett & Dunlap, 1970.

Tom Flores *see* Oakland Raiders

Joe Montana *see* San Francisco 49ers

31

Miami Dolphins

Leading Passers, by Yards

Quarterback	Years	G	Att	Comp	Pct	Yds	Y/A	Y/Cp	TD	Int	Int %	Rating
Dan Marino	1983–99	242	8,358	4,967	59.4	61,361	7.3	12.4	420	252	3.02%	86.4
Bob Griese	1967–80	161	3,429	1,926	56.2	25,092	7.3	13.0	192	172	5.02%	77.1
Jay Fiedler	2000–04	32	1,603	936	58.4	11,042	6.9	11.8	66	63	3.93%	76.8
David Woodley	1980–83	42	961	508	52.9	5,928	6.2	11.7	34	42	4.37%	65.4
Don Strock	1975–87	162	688	388	56.4	4,613	6.7	11.9	39	37	5.38%	73.5
Gus Frerotte	2005	16	494	257	52	2,996	6.1	11.7	18	13	2.63%	71.9
Earl Morrall	1972–76	69	284	153	53.9	2,335	8.2	15.3	17	17	5.99%	76.2
Joey Harrington	2006	11	388	223	57.5	2,236	5.8	10.0	12	15	3.87%	68.2
A.J. Feeley	2004	11	356	191	53.7	1,893	5.3	9.9	11	15	4.21%	61.7
Scott Mitchell	1992–93	29	241	135	56	1,805	7.5	13.4	12	9	3.73%	81.0
Rick Norton	1966–69	31	377	156	41.4	1,751	4.6	11.2	6	30	7.96%	28.1
Damon Huard	1998–00	34	288	170	59	1,691	5.9	9.9	9	8	2.78%	74.6
Steve DeBerg	1993	5	188	113	60.1	1,521	8.1	13.5	6	7	3.72%	81.0
Ray Lucas	2001–02	17	163	94	57.7	1,090	6.7	11.6	4	6	3.68%	70.8

Quarterback	Rush Att	Rush Yds	Rush Avg	TD
Dan Marino	301	87	0.3	9
Bob Griese	261	994	3.8	7

Quarterback	Rush Att	Rush Yds	Rush Avg	TD
Jay Fiedler	201	834	4.1	11
David Woodley	173	771	4.5	9
Don Strock	51	20	0.4	2
Gus Frerotte	27	61	2.3	0
Earl Morrall	23	120	5.2	1
Joey Harrington	19	24	1.3	0
A.J. Feeley	14	13	0.9	1
Scott Mitchell	29	99	3.4	0
Rick Norton	19	41	2.2	0
Damon Huard	28	124	4.4	0
Steve DeBerg	4	−4	−1.0	0
Ray Lucas	44	132	3.0	3

Record Holders

Passing Yards, Career: 61,361 Dan Marino
Passing Yards, Season: 5,084 Dan Marino 1984
Completion %, Career: 59.4% Dan Marino
Completion %, Season: 64.2% Dan Marino 1984
Touchdown Passes, Career: 420 Dan Marino
Touchdown Passes, Season: 48 Dan Marino 1984
Interceptions, Career: 252 Dan Marino
Interceptions, Season: 23 Dan Marino 1986, 1988
Rating, Career: 86.4 Dan Marino
Rating, Season: 108.9 Dan Marino 1984
Rush Yards, Career: 994 Bob Griese
Rush Yards, Season: 321 Jay Fiedler 2001

Passers by Categories

Five best starters: Dan Marino passed for more yards and touchdowns than anyone in NFL history. Bob Griese led the Dolphins to back-to-back Super Bowl titles with a very efficient passing attack. Earl Morrall was a super sub who maintained Miami's perfect record during its undefeated season. Jay Fiedler was barely competent, and Don Strock started few games, but was an able backup for over a decade in South Florida.

Worst starters, career: Rick Norton only won one game as a starter and threw 30 interceptions to 6 touchdowns while averaging just 4.6 yards per attempt. Dick Wood was so bad that he couldn't beat out Norton, throwing 14 interceptions to just 4 touchdowns. In the franchise's first season, George Wilson, Jr. ended up as the starter and completed just 41 percent of his passes. David Woodley won more games than

he lost, but threw 34 touchdowns to 42 interceptions. Daunte Culpepper, Ray Lucas and A.J. Feeley were all major disappointments after being brought in and handed the starting position.

Best stat line, season: Dan Marino had one of the top two or three passing seasons in NFL history in 1984, throwing for 48 touchdowns and over 5,000 yards while averaging 9 yards per attempt in leading the Dolphins to the Super Bowl. He would have many more great seasons. Bob Griese's greatest year was in 1971 when he completed 55 percent of his passes, averaged 7.9 yards per attempt and threw 19 touchdowns to only 9 interceptions leading Miami to its first Super Bowl appearance.

Worst stat line, season: In 1966, Dick Wood completed 36 percent of his passes for 4 touchdowns and 14 interceptions. The following season, Rick Norton completed 39 percent of his passes for 1 touchdown and 9 interceptions while averaging 4.5 yards per pass. He built on that success in 1969 to complete 44 percent of his passes for 2 touchdowns and 11 interceptions while averaging 4.8 yards per pass. That same season, Bob Griese had his worst year, completing just 48 percent of his passes for 10 touchdowns and 16 interceptions. David Woodley averaged just 5.7 yards per pass in 1980 while A.J. Feeley lowered that to 5.3 in 2004. Dan Marino's last season of 1999 was the first in which he had more interceptions (17) than touchdowns (12).

Best stat line, playoffs: With a light load, Bob Griese was at his efficient best in the Super Bowl win over Minnesota when he went 6–7, 73, 0–0. Don Strock led Miami on a remarkable comeback from 24 points down against the Chargers in a 1981 Divisional game the Dolphins lost in overtime. Strock went 28–42, 397, 4–1. Dan Marino's best game was against the Steelers in the 1984 AFC Conference title when he went 21–32, 421, 4–1.

Worst stat line, playoffs: In a 1978 Wild-card loss to the Oilers, Bob Griese went 11–28, 114, 1–2. In beating the Jets in the muddy 1982 AFC Conference title, David Woodley was 9–21, 87, 0–3; luckily Richard Todd was even worse for New York. In 1995, Dan Marino went 33–64, 422, 2–3 in a Wildcard loss to the Bills. In Marino's last game, a 62–7 shellacking by the Jaguars in a 1999 Divisional match, Marino went 11–25, 95, 1–2 while Damon Huard relieved him and went 5–16, 46, 0–0.

Big Days: The first passer to exceed 300 yards passing in a game was John Stofa with 307 yards on December 18, 1966. The first to reach 400 yards was David Woodley with 408 on October 25, 1981. Dan Marino had the biggest day in franchise history by throwing for 521 yards on October 23, 1988, and he threw for an NFL record 63 300-yard games and 13 400-yard games.

Running QBs: Bob Griese started out as a scrambler and ran for a career high 230 yards in his second season of 1968. David Woodley was a better runner than passer. Jay Fiedler ran for more yards in a season than any other Dolphin quarterback.

Bomber: Dan Marino could hit a moving target at any spot on the field. Bob Griese did not have a big arm, but was very good at finding Paul Warfield deep whenever necessary.

Most accurate: Marino and Griese were both among the most accurate passers of their days.

Leader: Dan Marino took charge of the Dolphin offense.

Comeback King: Marino led 42 4th quarter comebacks, plus four more in the postseason.

Highest Football IQ: Bob Griese was very analytical.

Toughest: Marino once had a streak of 95 straight starts.

First signal caller/T-Formation QB: Dick Wood was intercepted four times in the first half of the Dolphins first game against the Raiders. Rookie Rick Norton took over in the second half.

First TD pass: Rick Norton found Rick Casares for a two-yard score in a 23–14 loss to Oakland on September 2, 1966.

Black QBs: Ray Lucas was the first in 2002. Cleo Lemon was on the roster in 2005 and played in 2006. Marcus Vick was on the practice squad in a "Slash" Stewart type of role in 2006.

Tallest QB: Dan McGwire was 6'8". Scott Mitchell was 6'6". Dick Wood, Don Strock, Scott Zolak and Bernie Kosar were all 6'5".

Smallest QB: George Mira was 5'11". Bob Griese was just barely 6'.

Oldest QB: Earl Morrall was 42 in 1976, 41 in 1975, 40 in 1974, 39 in 1973 and started at age 38 in 1972. Dan Marino was the regular starter at 38 in 1998. Steve DeBerg started some games at 39 in 1993.

Rookie sensation: Bob Griese showed great promise in 1967, throwing for 2,005 yards and 15 touchdowns for a second-year expansion team. Dan Marino was a star right from the start, throwing for 2,210 yards, 20 touchdowns and only 6 interceptions in 1983.

Late bloomer: Jay Fiedler was 28 when he earned the starting job with the Dolphins in 2000.

1st round picks: Rick Norton was the Dolphins' first ever draft choice, but was pushed aside one year later by Bob Griese, the 4th pick in round one in 1967. The third time the Dolphins picked a quarterback in the 1st round was in 1983, when they got the last of six quarterbacks taken in round one, Dan Marino.

Out of position: Former college quarterbacks transformed to pro receivers include Marlin Briscoe, Nat Moore, Freddie Solomon, Todd Doxon, Jim Jensen and Bruce Hardy. George Wilson Jr. doubled as a punter.

Long-time subs: Earl Morrall spent five years backing up Bob Griese. Don Strock spent a record 14 years backing up Griese, David Woodley and Dan Marino.

QB controversy: After Bob Griese was healthy again in the perfect season of 1972, it was debated when he would and should replace Earl Morrall who had gone 8–0. Once Griese retired, Strock was overtaken by rookie David Woodley, and the two-headed WoodStrock monster lasted for a couple of years until Marino. The controversy over Marino came at the end of his career when it was time for him to move on, but no one wanted to tell him.

College affiliation: George Mira, Bernie Kosar and Craig Erickson all played at the nearby University of Miami.

Ones who got away: None.

Has beens: Dick Wood, John Stofa, George Mira, Guy Benjamin, Ron Jaworski, Steve De-Berg, Craig Erickson, Bernie Kosar, Ray Lucas, Brian Griese, Gus Frerotte and Joey Harrington.

Ruinous injuries: Bob Griese missed most of 1972, but the team went undefeated anyway behind Earl Morrall. Dan Marino tore his Achilles in 1993.

Best trade: Getting Hall of Famer Nick Buoniconti from the Patriots for Kim Hammond and John Bramlett. Getting Hall of Famer Paul Warfield from the Browns for the rights to Mike Phipps. Getting a number 1 and a number 2 from the Bengals for John Stofa. Getting two number 2's from the Packers for the immortal Jim Del Gaizo.

Worst trade: Giving up a number 2 to the Eagles for A.J. Feeley.

Title winners: Bob Griese, 2.

Hall of Famers: Bob Griese and Dan Marino.

All Pro/Pro Bowl seasons: Dan Marino, 10; Bob Griese, 7, Earl Morrall, 1.

QBs as coaches: None.

Underrated: Bob Griese could have achieved higher passing numbers, but subordinated his personal statistics to the relentless rushing attack that brought two Super Bowl wins to Miami.

Overrated: Some would say Marino since he never won a title. I would not agree.

Best Nicknames: WoodStrock — the quarterback combination of David Woodley and Don Strock.

Time Capsule: Bob Griese wearing eyeglasses on the field. Don Strock's hook-and-lateral keyed a comeback against San Diego after being down 24–0. Dan Marino's 48-touchdown season in 1984. Dan Marino's fake grounding against the Jets.

What If: If Don Shula had built a defense and/or running game to accompany Marino at some point in his long career, would he have won a Super Bowl?

Off the field: A.J. Feeley has dated attractive Olympic soccer star Heather Mitts. Jay Fiedler is the twice-removed cousin of Boston Pops conductor Arthur Fiedler. Bob and Brian Griese are the only father-son quarterback duo to play for the same team. George Wilson Jr.'s father George Sr. was the first coach of the Dolphins and once played for the Bears. Kyle Mackey's father Dee played end for the 49ers, Colts and Jets. Both Dan Marino and Scott Mitchell appeared in *Ace Ventura: Pet Detective.* Marino also appeared in *Bad Boys II, Little Nicky, Holy Man* and an episode of *The Simpsons.*

Quarterback Bibliography

Bob Griese

Griese, Bob, Brian Griese, and James D. Denney. *Undefeated: How Father and Son Triumphed Over Unbelievable Odds Both On and Off the Field.* Nashville, TN: Nelson, 2000.

Earl Morrall *see* Detroit Lions

Dan Marino

Marino, Dan, and Steve Delsohn. *Marino!* Chicago: Contemporary Books, 1986.

Marino, Dan, and Marc Serota. *Marino: On the Record.* San Francisco, CA: Collins, 1996.

Dan Marino: The Making of a Legend. Dallas, TX: Beckett Publications, 1999.

Keidel, Ken. *Dan Marino: A Look Back at a Legend.* Miami, FL: Dolphin/Curtis Publications, 2000.

Marino, Dan, and Marc Serota. *My Life in Football.* Chicago: Triumph Books, 2005.

Funk, Joe. *Marino: Stories from a Hall of Fame Career.* Miami, FL: Miami Herald, 2005.

Brian Griese *see* above

32

Minnesota Vikings

Leading Passers, by Yards

Quarterback	Years	G	Att	Comp	Pct	Yds	Y/A	Y/Cp	TD	Int	Int %	Rating
Fran Tarkenton	1961–66, 1972–78	177	4,569	2,635	57.7	33,098	7.2	12.6	239	194	4.25%	80.1
Tommy Kramer	1977–89	128	3,648	2,011	55.1	24,775	6.8	12.3	159	157	4.30%	72.9
Daunte Culpepper	2000–05	54	2,576	1,656	64.3	19,918	7.7	12.0	134	84	3.26%	91.6
Wade Wilson	1981–91	83	1,665	929	55.8	12,135	7.3	13.1	66	75	4.50%	73.4
Brad Johnson	1994–98, 2005–06	68	1,669	1,035	62	11,098	6.6	10.7	65	48	2.88%	82.5
Warren Moon	1994–96	39	1,454	882	60.7	10,102	6.9	11.5	58	42	2.89%	82.8
Rich Gannon	1987–92	48	1,003	561	55.9	6,457	6.4	11.5	40	36	3.59%	73.9
Randall Cunningham	1997–99	27	713	427	59.9	5,680	8.0	13.3	48	23	3.23%	94.2
Joe Kapp	1967–69	40	699	351	50.2	4,807	6.9	13.7	37	47	6.72%	62.2
Steve Dils	1980–83	43	623	336	53.9	3,867	6.2	11.5	15	18	2.89%	68.9
Gary Cuozzo	1968–71	33	556	276	49.6	3,552	6.4	12.9	18	23	4.14%	63.6
Jeff George	1999	12	329	191	58.1	2,816	8.6	14.7	23	12	3.65%	94.2
Sean Salisbury	1992–94	22	404	228	56.4	2,772	6.9	12.2	14	9	2.23%	80.0
Bob Lee	1969–72, 1975–78	52	306	159	52	2,153	7.0	13.5	15	17	5.56%	67.9
Jim McMahon	1993	12	331	200	60.4	1,968	5.9	9.8	9	8	2.42%	76.2

Quarterback	Rush Att	Rush Yds	Rush Avg	TD
Fran Tarkenton	464	2548	5.5	22
Tommy Kramer	214	531	2.5	8
Daunte Culpepper	453	2571	5.7	29
Wade Wilson	159	679	4.3	9
Brad Johnson	139	268	1.9	2
Warren Moon	69	143	2.1	0
Rich Gannon	144	720	5.0	3
Randall Cunningham	61	317	5.2	1
Joe Kapp	99	540	5.5	5
Steve Dils	24	73	3.0	0
Gary Cuozzo	36	85	2.4	0
Jeff George	16	41	2.6	0
Sean Salisbury	24	1	0.0	0
Bob Lee	39	37	0.9	2
Jim McMahon	33	96	2.9	0

Record Holders

Passing Yards, Career: 33,098 Fran Tarkenton
Passing Yards, Season: 4,717 Daunte Culpepper 2004

Completion %, Career: 64.3% Daunte Culpepper
Completion %, Season: 69.2% Daunte Culpepper 2004
Touchdown Passes, Career: 239 Fran Tarkenton

Touchdown Passes, Season: 39 Daunte Culpepper 2004

Interceptions, Career: 194 Fran Tarkenton

Interceptions, Season: 32 Fran Tarkenton 1978

Rating, Career: 94.2 Randall Cunningham and Jeff George; for more than 750 attempts, 91.6 Daunte Culpepper

Rating, Season: 110.9 Daunte Culpepper 2004

Rush Yards, Career: 2,571 Daunte Culpepper

Rush Yards, Season: 603 Daunte Culpepper 2002

Passers by Categories

Five best starters: Fran Tarkenton scrambled the Vikings to three Super Bowls and himself to the Hall of Fame. Daunte Culpepper was a major talent who had some great seasons before his Loveboat and knee problems. Tommy Kramer followed Tarkenton and had reasonable success as an exciting, fiery leader. Brad Johnson proved himself a winner in both his terms in Minnesota. Randall Cunningham won his third league MVP award as a Viking.

Worst starters, career: Ron Vanderkelen had his shot to succeed Tarkenton in 1967, but could not hold off Joe Kapp. Gary Cuozzo cost the Vikings two number one picks, but could never really win the job outright because he completed less than half his passes and threw more interceptions than touchdowns. Norm Snead was given his first opportunity to play with a winning team in Minnesota after a decade with losers in Washington and Philadelphia and failed miserably. Steve Dils and Sean Salisbury were mediocrities at best.

Best stat line, season: Culpepper's 2000 and 2004 seasons were both great years, but his yardage, completion percentage and touchdowns all set team records in 2004 which earned him a 110.9 rating. Randall Cunningham posted a 106 rating in 1998 by completing 60 percent of his passes for 3,704 yards, averaging 8.7 yards per pass and throwing 34 touchdowns. In 1964, Fran Tarkenton averaged 8.2 yards per pass and threw 22 touchdowns, while in 1975 he threw for 2,994 yards and 25 touchdowns. Warren Moon was the first Viking quarterback to reach 30 touchdowns with 33 in 1995. Tommy Kramer led the league in passer rating with 92.6 on 3,000 yards, an 8.1 average and 24 touchdowns in 1986.

Worst stat line, season: Sadly, Daunte Culpepper 2005 crash of just 6 touchdowns and 12 interceptions in half a season is far from the bottom. Tommy Kramer threw 26 interceptions in 1985. Wade Wilson threw just 3 touchdowns to 10 picks in 1991. Fran Tarkenton ended his career by setting a team record with 32 interceptions in 1978. Joe Kapp completed only 47 percent of his passes in 1967 while throwing 8 touchdowns to 17 interceptions. Gary Cuozzo ended his tour in Minnesota in 1971 by completing 44 percent of his passes for an average of 5 yards per pass.

Best stat line, playoffs: In a 1987 Divisional win over the 49ers, Wade Wilson was 20–34, 298, 2–1. In a 1999 Divisional loss to the Rams, Jeff George was 29–50, 424, 4–1. In a 2004 Wildcard win over Green Bay, Daunte Culpepper was 19–29, 284, 4–0.

Worst stat line, playoffs: In a 1970 Divisional loss to San Francisco, Gary Cuozzo was 9–27, 146, 0–2. In the Super Bowl loss to Pittsburgh, Tarkenton was 11–26, 102, 0–3. In the 1976 NFC title win over the Rams, Tarkenton was 12–27, 143, 0–1. In a 1980 Divisional loss to Philadelphia, Tommy Kramer was 19–39, 209, 1–5. In the 2000 NFC title loss to the Giants, Culpepper was 13–28, 78, 0–3.

Big Days: The first passer to exceed 300 yards passing in a game was Fran Tarkenton with 311 yards on September 20, 1964. The first to reach 400 yards was Tarkenton with 407 on October 24, 1965. Tommy Kramer had the biggest day in franchise history by throwing for 490 yards on November 2, 1986. Both Kramer and Culpepper had 19 300-yard games.

Running QBs: Culpepper surpassed the Scrambler, Fran Tarkenton, by 23 yards and 7 touchdowns. Culpepper was much bigger and more powerful, while the smallish Tarkenton was more elusive. Randall Cunningham is the all-time leader in yards rushing by a quarterback, but didn't run much in Minnesota at the tail end of his career. Rich Gannon didn't get to play much; however, like all the other noted runners here, he averaged 5 yards per carry. Joe Kapp was not as big as Culpepper but was a bullish runner like him.

Bomber: Anyone with Randy Moss at wideout — especially Randall Cunningham and Jeff George. Kapp liked to go deep but was a lousy passer.

Most accurate: Culpepper, Tarkenton and Brad Johnson.

Leader: Fran Tarkenton would try anything to win.

Comeback King: Tarkenton had 21 4th quarter comebacks, plus one in the postseason. Tommy Kramer had 19 and one in the playoffs.

Highest Football IQ: Tarkenton used his brains and feet to make more with less.

Toughest: Culpepper was enormously stout, but Tarkenton had a streak of 73 straight starts and didn't miss a game due to injury until he broke his leg in his 17th season.

First signal caller/T-Formation QB: George Shaw started the Vikings' first ever game but was relieved by rookie Fran Tarkenton who led the team to victory.

First TD pass: Tarkenton to tight end Bob Schnelker for 14 yards in a 37–13 win over the Bears on September 17, 1961.

Black QBs: Larry Miller was a replacement player in 1987. He was followed by Warren Moon in 1994, Jay Walker in 1996, Randall Cunningham in 1997, Daunte Culpepper in 1999, Spergeon Wynn in 2001 and Tarvaris Jackson in 2006.

Tallest QB: Both Sean Salisbury and Brad Johnson were 6'5", as was Mike Wells who never actually played for the Vikings.

Smallest QB: Bob Berry was only 5'11". It's questionable whether he actually had to look up to the supposedly 6' Tarkenton.

Oldest QB: Warren Moon was still starting at 39 in 1996. His backup that year was Brad Johnson who was starting at 39 in 2006. Fran Tarkenton was still starting at 38 in 1978.

Rookie sensation: Fran Tarkenton as a 21-year-old rookie with an expansion team in 1961 completed 56 percent of his passes for 18 touchdowns and 17 interceptions. Daunte Culpepper was a second-year rookie in 2000—he appeared in only one game and threw no passes in 1999. At the age of 23, Culpepper completed 62 percent of his passes for 3,937 yards, 33 touchdowns and 16 interceptions.

Late bloomer: Wade Wilson was 27 before he became a full-time starter. Brad Johnson was 28, as was Joe Kapp who was returning from Canada.

1st round picks: The Vikings have only drafted two quarterbacks in the first round— Tommy Kramer with the 27th pick in 1977 and Culpepper with the 11th pick in 1999—and both were successful.

Out of position: Jerry Reichow was a former quarterback who was the first star receiver for the Vikings. Bob Lee was the team's punter.

Long-time subs: Bob Lee spent eight seasons as a backup over two terms in Minnesota. Bob Berry spent six seasons as a backup over two terms. Ron Vanderkelen spent five seasons in one term, as did Brad Johnson if you count his two years on the practice squad.

QB controversy: Tommy Kramer was involved in controversies at both ends of his career. At the beginning, he competed against the aging Tarkenton; at the end he competed with Wade Wilson. Under Denny Green in the 1990s, there was never time for controversy as the Vikings went from Gannon (with some Sean Salisbury) to Jim McMahon to Warren Moon to Brad Johnson to Randall Cunningham to Jeff George to Culpepper over a nine-year span.

College affiliation: Oregon has been represented by George Shaw and Bob Berry; Florida State by Brad Johnson and Bill Cappleman; Wisconsin by Ron Vanderkelen and Brooks Bollinger.

Ones who got away: Rich Gannon later became league MVP in Oakland. Steve Bono and Jay Fiedler developed into starters elsewhere as well.

Has beens: George Shaw, Gary Cuozzo, Norm Snead, King Hill, Bob Berry, Bob Lee, Tony Adams, Archie Manning, Steve Dils, Sean Salisbury, Gus Frerotte, Bubby Brister, and Jim McMahon.

Ruinous injuries: After 17 injury free seasons, Fran Tarkenton went down with a broken leg in 1977. Culpepper tore up his knee in the regrettable 2005 season.

Best trade: Getting two number 1's (Ron Yary and Clint Jones) and a number 2 (Bob Grim) from the Giants for Tarkenton. Getting John Charles and a number 1 (Jeff Siemens) from the Patriots for Joe Kapp. Sending Gary Cuozzo to the Cardinals for John Gilliam and a number 2.

Worst trade: Giving up two number 1's to the Saints for Gary Cuozzo. Giving up a number 2 and a number 4 to the Oilers for the washed up Archie Manning and Dave Caspar. Giving up three picks and Steve Smith to the Eagles for Norm Snead.

Title winners: None.

Hall of Famers: Fran Tarkenton and Warren Moon.

All Pro/Pro Bowl seasons: Fran Tarkenton, 7; Daunte Culpepper, 3; Warren Moon, 2; Randall Cunningham, 1; Wade Wilson, 1.

QBs as coaches: None.

Underrated: Brad Johnson and Rich Gannon both had to go elsewhere to prove they were winning quarterbacks and even faced each other in Super Bowl 37.

Overrated: Gary Cuozzo was traded three times and each time the team trading him made out much better on the deal. Cuozzo was a career backup who was better suited to being a starting dentist.

Best Nicknames: Fran "the Scrambler" Tarkenton, Bob "General" Lee and Two Minute Tommy Kramer.

Time Capsule: Tarkenton establishing scrambling as a regular approach to quarterback play. Randy Moss' coming out party against the Packers in 1998 with Randall Cunningham heaving jump balls that Moss would snatch out of the air.

What If: If the Vikings never traded Tarkenton, would they have ever reached the Super Bowl in the first place or would they have won the first one against the Chiefs?

Off the field: Culpepper's Loveboat troubles shipped him out of town. He also appeared in episodes of *George Lopez* and *Arli$$*. Fran Tarkenton was the host of *That's Incredible* and appeared in episodes of *Saturday Night Live* and *Hill Street Blues*. Sean Salisbury was in *The Benchwarmers* and *The Longest Yard* remake. Randall Cunningham was in an episode of *Martin*. Jim McMahon appeared in *Johnny Be Good* in 1987 as well as episodes of *Grounded for Life* and *Sons of Thunder*. Warren Moon appeared in *Any Given Sunday*, *Warriors of Virtue*, *Air Bud: Golden Receiver* and *Jerry Maguire* as well as an episode of *Arli$$*. Joe Kapp appeared in eight movies (including *M*A*S*H*, the original *Longest Yard*, *Semi-Tough* and *The Choirboys*), three TV movies and a dozen episodes of TV series such as *Police Woman* and *Adam-12*.

Quarterback Bibliography

Fran Tarkenton

Tarkenton, Fran, and Jack Olsen. *Better Scramble Than Lose*. New York: Four Winds Press, 1969.

Libby, Bill. *Fran Tarkenton: The Scrambler*. New York: Putnam, 1970.

Tarkenton, Fran, and Brock W. Yates. *Broken Patterns: the Education of a Quarterback*. New York: Simon and Schuster, 1971.

Klobuchar, Jim. *Tarkenton*. New York: Harper & Row, 1976.

Tarkenton, Fran. *Incredible Fran*. Franklin Springs, GA: Advocate Press, 1982.

Archie Manning *see* New Orleans Saints

Jim McMahon *see* Chicago Bears

Randall Cunningham *see* Philadelphia Eagles

33

New England Patriots

Leading Passers, by Yards

Quarterback	Years	G	Att	Comp	Pct	Yds	Y/A	Y/Cp	TD	Int	Int %	Rating
Drew Bledsoe	1993–01	124	4,518	2,544	56.3	29,657	6.6	11.7	166	138	3.05%	75.9
Steve Grogan	1975–90	149	3,593	1,879	52.3	26,886	7.5	14.3	182	208	5.79%	69.6

Quarterback	Years	G	Att	Comp	Pct	Yds	Y/A	Y/Cp	TD	Int	Int %	Rating
Tom Brady	2000–06	96	3064	1,896	61.9	21,564	7.0	11.4	147	78	2.55%	88.4
Babe Parilli	1961–67	94	2,413	1,140	47.2	16,747	6.9	14.7	132	138	5.72%	64.8
Tony Eason	1983–89	72	1,500	876	58.4	10,732	7.2	12.3	60	48	3.20%	80.6
Jim Plunkett	1971–75	61	1,503	729	48.5	9,932	6.6	13.6	62	87	5.79%	59.7
Hugh Millen	1991–92	20	612	370	60.5	4,276	7.0	11.6	17	28	4.58%	71.8
Mike Taliaferro	1968–70	32	680	305	44.9	3,920	5.8	12.9	27	44	6.47%	49.8
Butch Songin	1960–61	28	604	285	47.2	3,905	6.5	13.7	36	24	3.97%	71.7
Matt Cavanaugh	1979–82	52	385	206	53.5	3,018	7.8	14.7	19	23	5.97%	70.9
Marc Wilson	1989–90	30	415	214	51.6	2,631	6.3	12.3	9	16	3.86%	62.6
Doug Flutie	1987–89, 2005	22	305	148	48.5	1,871	6.1	12.6	11	14	4.59%	61.0

Quarterback	Rush Att	Rush Yds	Rush Avg	TD
Drew Bledsoe	270	553	2.0	2
Steve Grogan	445	2176	4.9	35
Tom Brady	239	435	1.8	3
Babe Parilli	194	949	4.9	14
Tony Eason	126	174	1.4	6
Jim Plunkett	159	817	5.1	9
Hugh Millen	48	200	4.2	1
Mike Taliaferro	23	46	2.0	0
Butch Songin	19	79	4.2	2
Matt Cavanaugh	39	190	4.9	3
Marc Wilson	12	49	4.1	0
Doug Flutie	65	308	4.7	1

Record Holders

Passing Yards, Career: 29,657 Drew Bledsoe
Passing Yards, Season: 4,555 Drew Bledsoe 1994
Completion %, Career: 61.9% Tom Brady
Completion %, Season: 63.9% Tom Brady 2004
Touchdown Passes, Career: 182 Steve Grogan
Touchdown Passes, Season: 31 Babe Parilli 1964
Interceptions, Career: 208 Steve Grogan
Interceptions, Season: 27 Babe Parilli 1964
Rating, Career: 88.4 Tom Brady
Rating, Season: 92.6 Tom Brady 2004
Rush Yards, Career: 2,176 Steve Grogan
Rush Yards, Season: 539 Steve Grogan 1978

Passers by Categories

Five best starters: Tom Brady is the best NFL quarterback since Joe Montana: smart, consistent and a great leader and teammate. Immobile Drew Bledsoe had a great arm and did lead a once-woeful franchise to the Super Bowl. Steve Grogan was a gritty leader and effective scrambling quarterback. Babe Parilli had a great arm and was very good in the AFL. Tony Eason took the Patriots to their first Super Bowl appearance.

Worst starters, career: Tom Sherman competed less than 40 percent of his passes and threw 12 touchdowns to 16 interceptions. Joe Kapp completed 44 percent of his passes and threw just 3 touchdowns to 17 interceptions in a one-season stay in Boston. Mike Taliaferro completed 45 percent of his passes, averaged 5.8 yards per pass and threw 27 touchdowns to 44 interceptions. Hugh Millen threw 17 touchdowns to 28 interceptions, and Marc Wilson threw 9 touchdowns to 16 interceptions.

Best stat line, season: With an ever-changing cast of teammates, Tom Brady had his best year in 2005, completing 63 percent of his passes for 4,110 yards and 26 touchdowns. A year after driving New England to the Super Bowl, Drew Bledsoe threw for 28 touchdowns and only 15 interceptions in 1997. Steve Grogan threw for over 3,000 yards and 28 touchdowns in 1979. Babe Parilli had career highs for yards, touchdowns and interceptions in 1964, but his best year may have been 1962 when he completed 55 percent of his passes for 18 touchdowns and only 8 interceptions while averaging 7.9 yards per pass.

Worst stat line, season: In 1965, Babe Parilli completed only 40 percent of his passes for 18 touchdowns and 26 interceptions while averaging 6.1 yards per pass. Hugh Millen threw for over 3,000 yards in 1991, but also threw just 9 touchdowns to 18 interceptions. In 1968, Mike Taliaferro completed 38 percent of his passes for 4 touchdowns and 15 interceptions while averaging 5 yards per pass. Joe Kapp's 1970 season is noted above.

Best stat line, playoffs: Tom Brady in the Super Bowl win over Carolina went 32–48, 354, 3–1; in the Super Bowl win over Philadelphia, he went 22–32, 236, 2–0; and in the AFC title win over the Steelers in 2004, he went 14–21, 207, 2–0. Tony Eason in the 1985 AFC title win over Miami went 10–12, 71, 2–0.

Worst stat line, playoffs: Tony Eason looked scared to death against Bears in the Super Bowl and went 0–6, 0, 0–0. Against the Browns in a 1994 Wildcard loss, Drew Bledsoe went 21–50, 235, 1–3, while he went 25–48, 253, 2–4 in the loss to Green Bay in the Super Bowl.

Big Days: The first passer to exceed 300 yards passing in a game was Butch Songin with 327 yards on December 18, 1960. The first to reach 400 yards was Babe Parilli with 422 on October 16, 1964. Drew Bledsoe had the biggest day in franchise history by throwing for 426 yards on November 13, 1994, and had 26 300-yard games.

Running QBs: Steve Grogan was a fearless runner who holds all the team records in this category, including scoring 35 touchdowns. He gained 103 yards rushing in a game in 1976 and gained over 500 yards rushing in 1978. Babe Parilli and Jim Plunkett were both surprisingly good at running with the ball and each averaged 4.9 yards per carry. Doug Flutie was extremely elusive when he had the ball.

Bomber: Drew Bledsoe and Babe Parilli both loved to go long whether anyone was open or not.

Most accurate: Tom Brady puts the ball where only his guy can get it.

Leader: Tom Brady is always cool under pressure.

Comeback King: Drew Bledsoe had 21 4th quarter comebacks, Steve Grogan had 19 and Tom Brady has 18 plus six in the postseason.

Highest Football IQ: Tom Brady is always in control.

Toughest: Tom Brady has a streak of 94 straight starts. Steve Grogan had a streak of 78, Drew Bledsoe started 64 straight and Babe Parilli started 58 straight.

First signal caller/T-Formation QB: 36-year-old Butch Songin from Boston College and the CFL.

First TD pass: Songin to Jim Colclough for 10 yards in the 13–10 loss to Denver in the very first AFL game on September 9, 1960.

Black QBs: Michael Bishop in 2000 and Rohan Davey in 2002–04.

Tallest QB: Marc Wilson was 6'6" while Drew Bledsoe, Scott Zolak, Hugh Millen and Vinny Testaverde were all 6'5".

Smallest QB: Doug Flutie at 5'9". Tom Yewcic and Tom Dimitroff were 5'11".

Oldest QB: Doug Flutie was 43 in 2005 as was Vinny Testaverde in 2006. Babe Parilli was still starting in 1967 at age 38. Butch Songin in 1961 and Steve Grogan in 1990 were sometime starters at 37.

Rookie sensation: Drew Bledsoe completed only half his passes as a 21-year old in 1993, but showed promise with 15 touchdowns and almost 2,500 yards. Tom Brady threw three passes as a 23-year-old rookie in 2000. In his second season, he led the team to its first Super Bowl title with 18 touchdowns and only 12 interceptions.

Late bloomer: Butch Songin got his first chance in American pro football at 36 with the 1960 Patriots. Babe Parilli got his first extended shot at age 32 the next season.

1st round picks: The Patriots have drafted a quarterback number 1 three times with no complete flops. Jim Plunkett, first in 1971, had greater success in Oakland but showed talent in New England. Tony Eason, 15th in 1983, was not great but was a professional when not facing the Chicago Bears until shoulder and elbow problems abbreviated his career. Drew Bledsoe, first in 1993, broke most of the team's passing records.

Out of position: Both Tom Yewcic and Tom Tupa were the team's punter. Receiver Stephen Starring was a quarterback in college.

Long-time subs: Steve Grogan was a long-time starter who spent his last seven seasons as mostly a relief pitcher. Tom Yewcic (five years) and Tom Owen (four years) were strictly backups.

QB controversy: There was lots of controversy regarding Grogan over the years as he competed with Jim Plunkett, Matt Cavanaugh and Tony Eason. The decision to stick with Tom Brady in 2001 after Drew Bledsoe recovered from injury was momentous and controversial.

College affiliation: Maryland gave New England such luminaries as King Corcoran, Dick Shiner and Scott Zolak. Boston College produced Butch Songin, Don Allard and Doug Flutie.

Ones who got away: It took many years, but Doug Flutie proved he could play in the NFL.

Has beens: Eddie Wilson, John Huarte, Don Trull, Kim Hammond, Mike Taliaferro, Joe Kapp, Dick Shiner, Tom Owen, Matt Cavanaugh, Marc Wilson and yes Doug Flutie and Vinny Testaverde.

Ruinous injuries: Bledsoe's Patriot career ended due to his chest injury. Tony Eason's was shortened by shoulder and elbow problems.

Best trade: Getting Babe Parilli and Billy Lott from Oakland for Dick Christy and Hal Smith. Getting three number 1's, a number 2 and Tom Owen from San Francisco for Jim Plunkett.

Worst trade: Giving a number 2 to the Chiefs for Eddie Wilson. Trading Hall of Fame linebacker Nick Buoniconti to the Dolphins for Kim Hammond and John Bramlett. Giving cornerback John Charles and a number 1 to the Vikings for Joe Kapp.

Title winners: Tom Brady 3.

Hall of Famers: None.

All Pro/Pro Bowl seasons: Drew Bledsoe, 3; Tom Brady, 3; Babe Parilli, 3; Mike Taliaferro (?!), 1.

QBs as coaches: None.

Underrated: Jim Plunkett was driven out of town but flourished elsewhere.

Overrated: How many quarterbacks had to refuse before Mike Taliaferro was chosen for the very last AFL All Star Game in 1970?

Best Nicknames: Jim "King" Corcoran, Tom "Kibby" Yewcic and Champaign Tony Eason.

Time Capsule: Tony Eason's fright night Super Bowl against the Bears. Tom Brady's timeless Super Bowl performances.

What If: If Drew Bledsoe doesn't go down to injury, does Tom Brady ever get a chance? Do the Patriots win anything? Is Bill Belichick fired within a year or two?

Off the field: King Corcoran was the high-living Joe Namath of the Continental League. Brian Dowling was the inspiration for the B.D. character in the "Doonesbury" comic strip by fellow Yalie Garry Trudeau. Damon Huard's brother Brock played quarterback for the Seahawks and Colts. Tom Brady dated actress Bridgett Moynihan for a few years and has himself appeared in episodes of *Saturday Night Live* and *Family Guy.* Drew Bledsoe appeared in *Jerry Maguire.* Jim Plunkett appeared in *Airport 1975.* Doug Flutie appeared in *Second String.* Joe Kapp appeared in eight movies, three TV movies and 12 episodes of TV series.

Quarterback Bibliography

Jim Plunkett
Plunkett, Jim, and Dave Newhouse. *The Jim Plunkett Story: the Saga of a Man Who Came Back.* New York: Arbor House, 1981.

Doug Flutie *see* Buffalo Bills

Tom Brady
Wolfe, Rich. *Tom Brady: There's No Expiration Date on Dreams.* St. Louis: Sporting News, 2002.
Greatness: The Rise of Tom Brady. Chicago: Triumph Books, 2005.
Pierce, Charles P. *Moving the Chains: Tom Brady and the Pursuit of Everything.* New York: Farrar, Strauss and Giroux, 2006.

34

New Orleans Saints

Leading Passers, by Yards

Quarterback	Years	G	Att	Comp	Pct	Yds	Y/A	Y/Cp	TD	Int	Int %	Rating
Archie Manning	1971–82	134	3,335	1,849	55.4	21,734	6.5	11.8	115	156	4.68%	67.4
Aaron Brooks	2000–05	69	2,772	1,564	56.4	19,158	6.9	12.2	120	84	3.03%	79.7
Bobby Hebert	1985–92	78	2,055	1,202	58.5	14,630	7.1	12.2	85	75	3.65%	79.1
Jim Everett	1994–96	47	1,571	958	61	10,622	6.8	11.1	60	48	3.06%	81.1
Billy Kilmer	1967–70	49	1,116	592	53	7,490	6.7	12.7	47	62	5.56%	65.1
Dave Wilson	1981–88	53	1,039	551	53	6,987	6.7	12.7	36	55	5.29%	63.8
Drew Brees	2006	16	554	356	64.3	4,418	8.0	12.4	26	11	1.99%	96.2
Steve Walsh	1990–93	22	620	336	54.2	3,879	6.3	11.5	25	22	3.55%	72.0
Ken Stabler	1982–84	25	570	326	57.2	3,670	6.4	11.3	17	33	5.79%	62.4
Billy Joe Tolliver	1998–99	17	466	249	53.4	3,343	7.2	13.4	15	20	4.29%	69.3
Bobby Scott	1973–81	41	500	237	47.4	2,781	5.6	11.7	15	28	5.60%	51.4
Ed Hargett	1969–71	30	437	205	46.9	2,727	6.2	13.3	11	10	2.29%	66.0
Wade Wilson	1993–94	18	416	241	57.9	2,629	6.3	10.9	12	15	3.61%	71.3
Richard Todd	1984–85	17	344	177	51.5	2,369	6.9	13.4	14	23	6.69%	59.4
John Fourcade	1987–90	24	313	159	50.8	2,312	7.4	14.5	14	13	4.15%	72.8
Billy Joe Hobert	1997–99	10	343	175	51	2,164	6.3	12.4	13	16	4.66%	64.1
Jeff Blake	2000–01	12	303	184	60.7	2,017	6.7	11.0	13	9	2.97%	82.4

Quarterback	Rush Att	Rush Yds	Rush Avg	TD
Archie Manning	357	2058	5.8	18
Aaron Brooks	339	1413	4.2	13
Bobby Hebert	142	150	1.1	0
Jim Everett	61	80	1.3	0
Billy Kilmer	64	299	4.7	3
Dave Wilson	45	23	0.5	2
Drew Brees	42	32	0.8	0
Steve Walsh	31	21	0.7	0
Ken Stabler	13	-19	-1.5	0
Billy Joe Tolliver	37	185	5.0	3
Bobby Scott	30	74	2.5	1
Ed Hargett	18	46	2.6	1
Wade Wilson	38	245	6.4	0
Richard Todd	28	111	4.0	0
John Fourcade	48	302	6.3	2
Billy Joe Hobert	26	96	3.7	1
Jeff Blake	58	242	4.2	1

Record Holders

Passing Yards, Career: 21,734 Archie Manning
Passing Yards, Season: 4,418 Drew Brees 2006
Completion %, Career: 64.3% Drew Brees

Completion %, Season: 64.3% Drew Brees 2006
Touchdown Passes, Career: 120 Aaron Brooks
Touchdown Passes, Season: 27 Aaron Brooks 2002
Interceptions, Career: 156 Archie Manning
Interceptions, Season: 22 Aaron Brooks 2001

Rating, Career: 96.2 Drew Brees
Rating, Season: 96.2 Drew Brees
Rush Yards, Career: 2,058 Archie Manning
Rush Yards, Season: 358 Aaron Brooks 2001

Passers by Categories

Five best starters: Archie Manning had tremendous talent and was a fine leader, but he did not have teammates to lead. Quick, strong-armed Aaron Brooks was inconsistent and made too many poor decisions. Jim Everett could throw the ball but was lacking as a leader. Bobby Hebert was a fairly efficient game manager. Fiery Billy Kilmer made the most of his limited talent in leading the even more limited talent of those surrounding him. These were the best of New Orleans until Drew Brees arrived in 2006 and gave the Crescent City its first top quarterback.

Worst starters, career: Too many to choose from: Ken Stabler and Richard Todd were washed up; Bobby Douglass never could throw the ball; the Billy Joe's — Tolliver and Hobert — were both terrible; Kerry Collins was in recovery; Dave Wilson was a flop...

Best stat line, season: Drew Brees completed 64.3 percent of his passes for 4,418 yards, 26 touchdowns and just 11 interceptions. He also averaged 8 yards per pass in leading New Orleans to a rare postseason appearance in 2006. In 1980, Archie Manning threw for a career-high 3,716 yards and 23 touchdowns. Aaron Brooks looked like he was maturing in 2003, throwing 24 touchdowns to 8 interceptions and completing 59 percent of his passes, but he soon reverted. Jim Everett threw for 3,970 yards and 26 touchdowns to 14 interceptions in 1995.

Worst stat line, season: In 1974, Archie Manning threw 6 touchdowns and 16 interceptions; he followed up the next season by completing less than 50 percent of his passes, averaging less than 5 yards per pass and throwing 7 touchdowns to 20 interceptions. As a rookie, Dave Wilson threw 1 touchdown to 11 interceptions in 1981. Ken Stabler threw 9 touchdowns to 18 interceptions in 1983, and Richard Todd matched that level in 1984 with 11 touchdowns and 19 interceptions. In 1997, while Heath Shuler was completing 52 percent of his passes for 2 touchdowns and 12 interceptions, Danny Wuerffel completed 46 percent of his passes and averaged just 5.7 yards per pass for 4 touchdowns and 8 interceptions.

Best stat line, playoffs: In a 2006 Division win over the Eagles, Drew Brees went 20–32, 243, 1–0. In a 2000 Wildcard win over the Rams, Aaron Brooks went 16–29, 266, 4–1.

Worst stat line, playoffs: In a 1987 Wildcard loss to Minnesota, Dave Wilson went 2–12, 20, 0–2 while Bobby Hebert went 9–19, 84, 1–2. In a 1990 Wildcard loss to the Bears, Steve Walsh went 6–16, 74, 0–1, while John Fourcade went 5–18, 79, 0–2.

Big Days: The first passer to exceed 300 yards passing in a game was Billy Kilmer with 345 yards on November 2, 1969. The first to reach 400 yards was Aaron Brooks with 441 on December 3, 2000. Drew Brees set the team record on November 19, 2006 with 510 yards against the Bengals. Brooks had ten 300-yard games while Archie Manning had nine. Drew Brees had eight in 2006.

Running QBs: Saints quarterbacks have had to be running quarterbacks out of necessity. The most prominent have been Aaron Brooks and Archie Manning, but Billy Kilmer, John Fourcade and Bobby Douglass could all escape the rush as well. Manning averaged 5.8 yards per carry and scored 18 touchdowns while Brooks gained 108 yards in a game in 2000.

Bomber: Drew Brees specialized in hitting the deep pass with 18 pass plays of more than 40 yards in 2006.

Most accurate: Drew Brees set the standard in 2006.

Leader: Archie Manning is still loved by the fans, but Drew Brees was a huge presence both in the huddle and the hurricane-ravaged community.

Comeback King: Aaron Brooks led 18 4th quarter comebacks while Manning led 12.

Highest Football IQ: The proof of how well Archie Manning understood the game is the performance of his sons on better teams than Archie ever saw.

Toughest: Archie Manning was regularly planted in the ground behind the line of scrimmage but never quit. Aaron Brooks had a streak of 82 straight starts.

First signal caller/T-Formation QB: Gary Cuozzo.

First TD pass: Billy Kilmer hit Flea Roberts for a 36-yard score in a 30–10 loss to the Redskins in the Saints' second game on September 24, 1967.

Black QBs: Jeff Blake and Aaron Brooks both joined New Orleans in 2000. Adrian McPherson was on the roster in 2005 and 2006 but never played. He brought suit against the Tennessee Titans after their mascot ran into him with a golf cart in the exhibition season.

Tallest QB: Jim Everett and Kerry Collins were both 6'5".

Smallest QB: Gary Wood and Edd Hargett were both 5'11". Billy Kilmer and Jeff Blake both claimed to be 6' as does Drew Brees.

Oldest QB: Ken Stabler was 37 in 1983. Jamie Martin was 36 in 2006.

Rookie sensation: Aaron Brooks threw for 1,500 yards, 9 touchdowns and 6 interceptions in 2000. Archie Manning threw for 1,100 yards for 6 touchdowns and 9 interceptions in 1972. Both ran for over 170 yards as rookies.

Late bloomer: Bobby Hebert didn't fully win the starting job till he was 27 in 1987. Billy Kilmer was 28 when he got his first shot in 1967.

1st round picks: The Saints have drafted two quarterbacks in the first round. Archie Manning, second in 1971, was as talented as expected. Dave Wilson, from the 1981 supplemental draft, was a failure.

Out of position: Guido Merkens also played defensive back and wide receiver. Ronnie South was also a punter. Bobby Douglass lined up at tightend.

Long-time subs: Bobby Scott backed up Manning for eight years, only getting a chance to start when Manning missed 1976 due to injury.

QB controversy: Dave Wilson competed with Richard Todd and then Bobby Hebert. Jeff Blake lost his job to Aaron Brooks.

College affiliation: The University of Virginia has supplied the Saints with Aaron Brooks, Bob Davis and Gary Cuozzo.

Ones who got away: Louisiana native Jake Delhomme left New Orleans and led the Panthers to the Super Bowl.

Has beens: Gary Cuozzo, Gary Wood, Jim Ninowski, Karl Sweetan, Bob Davis, Tommy Hodson, Bobby Douglass, Tommy Kramer, Wade Wilson, Guy Benjamin, Richard Todd, Ken Stabler, Billy Joe Hobert, Billy Joe Tolliver, Kerry Collins, Steve Walsh, Danny Wuerffel, Heath Shuler, Jeff Blake and Jamie Martin.

Ruinous injuries: Archie Manning was beaten down over the years of horrible offensive lines and missed 1976 due to injury. Jeff Blake broke his foot in 2000 and lost his job to Aaron Brooks.

Best trade: Getting two number 1's from the Vikings for Gary Cuozzo although the picks were wasted on Kevin Hardy and John Shinners. Getting Aaron Brooks and Lamont Hall from the Packers for K.D. Williams and a draft pick.

Worst trade: Giving up the top pick in the 1967 draft and a number 3 to the Colts for Gary Cuozzo and Butch Allison. Giving a number 1 to the Jets for Richard Todd. Giving a 1, 2 and 3 to the Cowboys for Steve Walsh.

Title winners: None.

Hall of Famers: None.

All Pro/Pro Bowl seasons: Archie Manning, 2; Drew Brees, 1.

QBs as coaches: None.

Underrated: Bobby Hebert was the first quarterback to lead the Saints to the playoffs although he could not gain a win in the postseason.

Overrated: Taking into account the extreme poverty of talented teammates, Archie Manning's numbers still are not very impressive.

Best Nicknames: Bobby "the Cajun Cannon" Hebert.

Time Capsule: None.

What If: If Archie Manning played on the Jim Mora-led Saints, would they have won a playoff game together? If the Saints had kept Jake Delhomme, would they have been more consistent than they were under Aaron Brooks in the new century?

Off the field: Billy Kilmer wasn't known as "Whiskey" for nothing. He appeared in *The Last Time I Saw Archie*—and that does not refer to Archie Manning. Ken Stabler and Richard Todd were two more notorious party boys who ended their careers in the Crescent City. Stabler appeared in *Indian Runner, The Legend of Grizzly Adams* and an episode of *Married ... with Children.* Kerry Collins drank himself out of Carolina and appeared in *Jerry Maguire*. Jim Everett appeared in an episode of *1st and Ten*. Archie Manning has two famous sons playing quarterback in the NFL. Aaron Brooks, the poor man's Michael Vick, is Vick's cousin. Greg Knafelc's father Gary played in Green Bay.

Quarterback Bibliography

Archie Manning
Manning, Archie and John Underwood. *Manning: A Father His Sons and a Football Legacy.* New York: Harper Entertainment, 2000.

Ken Stabler *see* Oakland Raiders

35

New York Giants

Leading Passers, by Yards

Quarterback	Years	G	Att	Comp	Pct	Yds	Y/A	Y/Cp	TD	Int	Int %	Rating
Phil Simms	1979–93	164	4,647	2,576	55.4	33,462	7.2	13.0	199	157	3.38%	78.5
Charlie Conerly	1948–61	161	2,833	1,418	50.1	19,488	6.9	13.7	173	167	5.89%	68.2
Kerry Collins	1999–03	72	2,448	1,435	58.6	16,678	6.8	11.6	81	69	2.82%	78.6
Fran Tarkenton	1967–71	69	1,898	1,051	55.4	13,905	7.3	13.2	103	72	3.79%	81.0
Y.A. Tittle	1961–64	54	1,308	731	55.9	10,439	8.0	14.3	96	68	5.20%	84.7
Dave Brown	1992–97	56	1,391	766	55.1	8,806	6.3	11.5	40	49	3.52%	69.3
Eli Manning	2004–06	41	1,276	690	54.1	8,049	6.3	11.7	54	49	3.84%	453
Scott Brunner	1980–83	57	986	482	48.9	6,121	6.2	12.7	28	48	4.87%	57.9
Craig Morton	1974–76	34	884	461	52.1	5,734	6.5	12.4	29	49	5.54%	60.4
Norm Snead	1972–74, 1976	32	713	416	58.3	4,644	6.5	11.2	27	45	6.31	64.2
Jeff Hostetler	1988–92	73	632	365	57.8	4,409	7.0	12.1	20	12	1.90%	81.9
Joe Pisarcik	1977–79	32	650	289	44.5	3,979	6.1	13.8	18	43	6.62%	46.3
Ed Danowski	1934–41	71	637	309	48.5	3,817	6.0	12.4	37	44	6.91%	58.1
Kent Graham	1992–99	48	648	339	52.3	3,760	5.8	11.1	20	20	3.09%	67.3
Earl Morrall	1965–67	29	477	239	50.1	3,732	7.8	15.6	32	25	5.24%	77.0
Benny Friedman	1929–31	39	348	197	56.6	3,652	10.5	18.5	36	23	6.61%	99.9
Danny Kanell	1996–98	30	653	339	51.9	3,570	5.5	10.5	23	20	3.06%	67.1
Gary Wood	1964–69	61	389	181	46.5	2,513	6.5	13.9	14	23	5.91%	55.1

Quarterback	Rush Att	Rush Yds	Rush Avg	TD
Phil Simms	349	1252	3.6	6
Charlie Conerly	270	685	2.5	10
Kerry Collins	160	220	1.4	3
Fran Tarkenton	211	1126	5.3	10
Y.A. Tittle	95	285	3.0	8
Dave Brown	177	618	3.5	7
Eli Manning	60	136	2.3	1
Scott Brunner	69	129	1.9	1

Quarterback	Rush Att	Rush Yds	Rush Avg	TD
Craig Morton	41	125	3.0	0
Norm Snead	20	37	1.9	0
Jeff Hostetler	133	704	5.3	9
Joe Pisarcik	45	131	2.9	3
Ed Danowski	435	1173	2.7	4
Kent Graham	72	314	4.4	3
Earl Morrall	26	75	2.9	1
Benny Friedman	228	1116	4.9	10
Danny Kanell	37	44	1.2	0
Gary Wood	75	425	5.7	6

Record Holders

Passing Yards, Career: 33,462 Phil Simms
Passing Yards, Season: 4,073 Kerry Collins 2002
Completion %, Career: 58.6 Kerry Collins
Completion %, Season: 61.8% Phil Simms 1993
Touchdown Passes, Career: 199 Phil Simms
Touchdown Passes, Season: 36 Y.A. Tittle 1963
Interceptions, Career: 167 Charlie Conerly
Interceptions, Season: 25 Charlie Conerly 1953
Rating, Career: 84.7 Y.A. Tittle
Rating, Season: 104.8 Y.A. Tittle 1963
Rush Yards, Career: 1,252 Phil Simms
Rush Yards, Season: 306 Fran Tarkenton 1967;
among tailbacks, Benny Friedman ran for 407
yards in 1929 and Ed Danowski ran for 335 in
1935.

Passers by Categories

Five best starters: Benny Friedman was the
first great passer in the NFL. Ed Danowski was
a very effective passing tailback in Steve Owen's
A formation. Team leader Charlie Conerly was
an unsung hero throughout the fifties. Y.A. Tittle took passing to a new level for three great seasons at the beginning of the sixties. Phil Simms
never had great receivers, but kept the Giants
offense going for almost 15 years.

Worst starters, career: The Giants used
Don Heinrich as their starter through most of
the fifties so that the regular quarterback, Charlie Conerly, could analyze the opposing defense
from the sideline. It may have extended Conerly's career, but Heinrich was never very good.
The Giants tried to use undersized Gary Wood
at quarterback in the mid-sixties, but he was a
bust. In the early to mid seventies, New York re-

lied on two washed up mediocrities: Norm
Snead and Craig Morton. The Giants had two
less-than-mediocre quarterbacks (Jerry Golsteyn
and Joe Pisarcik) fighting for the starting job in
the late seventies and had the same pointless
competition in the nineties with Dave Brown
and Kent Graham. They all stank.

Best stat line, season: When Benny Friedman threw 20 touchdowns in 1929, it was unheard of and was not topped till Cecil Isbell
threw 24 in 1942. Charlie Conerly led the NFL
in passing in his final season as a fulltime starter
in 1959, completing 58 percent of his passes, averaging 8.7 yards per pass and throwing 14
touchdowns to 4 interceptions for a 102.7 rating. In Y.A. Tittle's best season of 1963, he completed 60 percent of his passes for 3,145 yards, averaged 8.6 yards per pass and threw 36
touchdowns and only 14 interceptions. Phil
Simms closed his career in 1993 by completing
61 percent of his passes for 3,038 yards 15 touchdowns and only 9 interceptions. Kerry Collins set
a team record by passing for 4,073 yards in 2002
while completing 61 percent of his passes.

Worst stat line, season: Charlie Conerly
threw 25 interceptions to just 13 touchdowns
and averaged just 5.7 yards per pass in 1953, the
year before Vince Lombardi took over the
offense. Y.A. Tittle ended his career with a disastrous 1964 in which he threw 22 interceptions
to just 10 touchdowns and was remembered for
the famous photograph of him sitting on his
knees in the end zone without a helmet after
having been creamed by Steeler defensive end
John Baker. Gary Wood took over in 1966 and
completed 47 percent of his passes for 6 touchdowns and 13 interceptions. Jerry Golsteyn and
Joe Pisarcik combined as rookies to complete less
than 47 percent of their passes for 6 touchdowns
and 22 interceptions in 1977; the following

season, Joe Pisarcik completed 47 percent of his passes for 12 touchdowns and 23 interceptions. In 1983, Scott Brunner threw for 9 touchdowns and 22 interceptions. Dave Brown in 1996 threw 12 touchdowns to 20 interceptions while averaging just 6.1 yards per pass.

Best stat line, playoffs: In the 1933 title loss to the Bears, Harry Newman went 13–19, 201, 2–1. In the 1956 title win over the Bears, Charlie Conerly went 7–10, 195, 2–0. He followed that in the 1958 title loss to the Colts, going 10–14, 187, 1–0. Phil Simms warmed up in a 1986 Divisional game against the 49ers by going 9–19, 136, 4–0, and then in the Super Bowl against the Broncos, he went 22–25, 286, 3–0. In the 2000 NFC Conference game against the Vikings, Kerry Collins went 28–39, 381, 5–2.

Worst stat line, playoffs: Amidst gambling allegations in the 1946 title loss to the Bears, Frank Filchock went 9–26, 128, 2–6. Y.A. Tittle went 6–20, 65, 0–4 in the 1961 title loss to the Packers and 11–29, 147, 1–5 in the 1963 title loss to the Bears. Kerry Collins was overwhelmed in the Super Bowl loss to the Ravens, 15–39, 112, 0–4. Eli Manning's first playoff game was a loss to Carolina in a 2005 Wildcard game, and Manning went 10–18, 113, 0–3.

Big Days: The first passer to exceed 300 yards passing in a game was Charlie Conerly with 363 yards on December 5, 1949. The first to exceed 400 yards was Y.A. Tittle with 505 on October 28, 1962, the same day he threw 7 touchdown passes. Phil Simms had the biggest day in franchise history by throwing for 513 yards on October 13, 1985; Simms also had the most 300-yard games with 21.

Running QBs: Fran Tarkenton was the original scrambler. Gary Wood was a nifty scrambler but a weak-armed quarterback. Jeff Hostetler's running helped him guide the Giants to a Super Bowl title. Tailbacks Harry Newman, Ed Danowski and Frankie Filchock all had games in which they ran for over 100 yards in the 1930s and 1940s.

Bomber: Y.A. Tittle was the best deep passer of the early sixties, teaming with wide receiver Del Shofner.

Most accurate: Both Tittle and Phil Simms were very accurate passers.

Leader: Charlie Conerly was a former marine and a born leader.

Comeback King: Conerly had 20 4th quarter comebacks, Phil Simms had 17 and Fran Tarkenton had 15 in New York.

Highest Football IQ: Phil Simms took an analytical approach to the game.

Toughest: Charlie Conerly took a fierce beating throughout his career.

First signal caller/T-Formation QB: Tailback Jack McBride was the Giants' first signal caller. When the Giants began to switch to the T in 1948, Charlie Conerly was their rookie quarterback.

First TD pass: Jack McBride to Hinkey Haines for 28 yards in a 19–0 win over the Cleveland Bulldogs on November 1, 1925.

Black QBs: None. The Giants are the last team never to have used a black quarterback.

Tallest QB: Scott Brunner, Dave Brown, Kent Graham and Kerry Collins were all 6'5".

Smallest QB: Harry Newman and Junie Hovius were 5'8". Benny Friedman, Chris Cagle, Eddie Miller, Frank Filchock and Travis Tidwell were all 5'10". Tidwell was the only T-formation quarterback in the bunch.

Oldest QB: Conerly started some games at 40 in 1961 and 39 in 1960. He was the regular at 38 in 1959 as was Tittle at 38 in 1964.

Rookie sensation: Charlie Conerly completed 54 percent of his passes for 2,175 yards, 22 touchdowns and only 13 interceptions in 1948. Phil Simms threw for 1,745 yards, 13 touchdowns and 14 interceptions in 1979. Harry Newman led the league in attempts, completions and yards as a rookie and threw 11 touchdowns in 1933.

Late bloomer: Kerry Collins had his best years as a Giant starting in 1999 at age 27. Y.A. Tittle had his greatest years under freewheeling coach Allie Sherman starting at age 35 in 1961.

1st round picks: Travis Tidwell, 7th in 1950, could not supplant Charlie Conerly; neither could Lee Grosscup, 10th in 1959. Dave Brown, a supplemental pick in 1992, was a stiff. Phil Simms was a great pick at 7 in 1979. The jury is out on acquiring top pick Eli Manning for the Giants' pick, Philip Rivers, at 4.

Out of position: Benny Friedman was also a kicker. Frank Gifford and Tom Landry both played a little quarterback for the Giants in the fifties.

Long-time subs: Don Heinrich was Charlie Conerly's backup for six seasons in the fifties; Jeff Rutledge found himself behind Phil Simms and Jeff Hostetler for six seasons in the eighties.

QB controversy: Tittle was not initially

welcomed on the Giants because it was Conerly's team, but he won over his teammates and fans with sterling play. The oft-injured Simms had to fight the immortal Scott Brunner for the starting slot as a young player, and Jeff Hostetler as a veteran. There was a meaningless competition between Dave Brown and Kent Graham to succeed Simms, but neither could play as it turned out.

College affiliation: The University of Mississippi sent the Giants Charlie Conerly, Glynn Griffing and Eli Manning.

Ones who got away: Harry Newman only played for the Giants for three years due to contract disputes. Phillip Rivers may turn out to be the one who was given away.

Has beens: Paul Governali, Bill Mackrides, Arnold Galiffa, Ray Mallouf, Tom Dublinski, George Shaw, Ralph Guglielmi, Milt Plum, Randy Johnson, Norm Snead, Craig Morton, Dick Shiner, Jim Del Gaizo, Danny Kanell, Tommy Maddox and Kurt Warner.

Ruinous injuries: Phil Simms had trouble winning the starting job as a young player because he was getting hurt so often. Then, he was injured and lost his job to Jeff Hostetler in the Giants' second Super Bowl run. Charlie Conerly took a beating year after year. Arnold Galiffa suffered a severe back injury after the Eagles' Bucko Kilroy kneed him.

Best trade: Getting Y.A. Tittle from the 49ers for lineman Cordileone. Trading Howie Livingston to the Redskins for the rights to Charlie Conerly. Getting a number 2 (Pepper Johnson) from the Broncos for Scott Brunner. Buying the entire Detroit franchise to obtain Benny Friedman.

Worst trade: Giving up a number 1 to the Colts for George Shaw. Giving up two number 1's (Ron Yary and Clint Jones) and a number 2 (Bob Grim) to the Vikings for Fran Tarkenton. Giving up a number 1 (Randy White) to the Cowboys for Craig Morton. Giving Earl Morrall to the Colts where he became NFL MVP for Butch Allison.

Title winners: Ed Danowski, 2; Jack McBride, 1; Charlie Conerly, 1; Phil Simms, 1; Jeff Hostetler, 1.

Hall of Famers: Benny Friedman, Arnie Herber and Y.A. Tittle.

All Pro/Pro Bowl seasons: Jack McBride, 4; Benny Friedman, 3; Ed Danowski, 3; Charlie Conerly, 3, Y.A. Tittle, 3; Phil Simms, 3; Harry Newman, 2; Frank Filchock, 1.

QBs as coaches: Benny Friedman went 5–9 with the Giants and Dodgers. Frank Filchock went 7–20–1 with Denver. Doug Wycoff went 8-9-5 with Staten Island.

Underrated: Neither Charlie Conerly nor Phil Simms got the positive recognition for how good they were until the ends of their long and storied careers. Both are legitimate Hall of Fame candidates although neither is likely to make it.

Overrated: The Giants thought so highly of Norm Snead that they obtained him twice.

Best Nicknames: Eddie "Muscles" Miller, Pitchin' Paul Governali, Chuckin' Charlie Conerly, Travelin' Trav Tidwell, Y.A. "Bald Eagle" Tittle, Parkway Joe Pisarcik and Jeff "Hoss" Hostetler.

Time Capsule: The photo in *Life Magazine* of Y.A. Tittle on his knees in the endzone, looking woozy and old. Phil Simms announcing that he was "going to Disney World" after winning the Super Bowl — the first player to do so.

What If: If the Redskins had held onto the rights to Charlie Conerly as the successor to Sammy Baugh, who would have been the Giants quarterback in the 1950s?

Off the field: Benny Friedman appeared in *The Navy Way.* Frank Filchock was suspended from the NFL for not reporting a bribe attempt by some gambler friends of his before the 1946 championship game. Charlie Conerly was the original Marlboro Man in ads, and his wife Perian was a semi-regular columnist for the *New York Times.* Y.A. Tittle appeared in *Any Given Sunday.* Fran Tarkenton was the host of *That's Incredible* and appeared in episodes of *Saturday Night Live* and *Hill Street Blues.* Phil Simms appeared in episodes of *Yes, Dear* and *Buddy Faro.* Kerry Collins appeared in *Jerry Maguire.* Eli Manning's father Archie and brother Peyton were also NFL quarterbacks. Tim Hasselbeck's father Don and brother Matt also played in the NFL.

Quarterback Bibliography

Benny Friedman
Friedman, Benny. *The Passing Game.* New York: Steinfeld, 1931.

Charlie Conerly
Conerly, Charlie, and Tom Meany. *The Forward Pass.* New York: Dutton, 1960.
Conerly, Perian. *Backseat Quarterback.* Garden City, NY: Doubleday, 1963.

Y.A. Tittle

Tittle, Y.A., and Don Smith. *I Pass.* New York: Franklin Watts, 1964.

De Laet, Diane Tittle. *Giants and Heroes: A Daughter's Memories of Y.A. Tittle.* South Royalton, VT: Steerforth Press, 1995.

Lee Grosscup *see* New York Jets

Earl Morrall *see* Detroit Lions

Fran Tarkenton *see* Minnesota Viking

Phil Simms

McConley, Phil, Phil Simms, and Dick Schaap. *Simms to McConkey: Blood, Sweat and Gatorade.* New York: Crown, 1987.

Simms, Phil, and Rick Meier. *Phil Simms on Passing: Fundamentals on Throwing the Football.* New York: William Morrow, 1996.

Simms, Phil, and Vic Carucci. *Sunday Morning Quarter-back: Going Deep on the Strategies, Myths and Mayhem of Football.* New York: Harper Collins, 2004.

Jeff Hostetler

Hostetler, Jeff, and Ed Fitzgerald. *One Giant Leap.* New York: Putnam's, 1991.

Hostetler, Jeff, and Dave Hostetler. *There's No Joy in Gruntsville, But there's Plenty to Learn! : Lessons to Turn Trials into Triumphs: Grunts into Rising Stars.* Mechanicsburg, PA: Executive Books, 1995.

Hostetler, Jeff, and Dave Hostetler. *What It Takes: More than a Champion.* Sisters, OR: Multnomah Books, 1997.

Kurt Warner *see* STL

Eli Manning

Manning, Archie, and John Underwood. *Manning: A Father His Sons and a Football Legacy.* New York: Harper Entertainment, 2000.

36

New York Jets

Leading Passers, by Yards

Quarterback	Years	G	Att	Comp	Pct	Yds	Y/A	Y/Cp	TD	Int	Int %	Rating
Joe Namath	1965–76	136	3,655	1,836	50.2	27,057	7.4	14.7	170	215	5.88%	65.8
Ken O'Brien	1984–92	124	3,465	2,039	58.8	24,386	7.0	12.0	124	95	2.74%	81.0
Richard Todd	1976–83	102	2,623	1,433	54.6	18,241	7.0	12.7	110	138	5.26%	68.6
Vinny Testaverde	1998–03, 2005	66	1,854	1,094	59	12,496	6.7	11.4	77	58	3.13%	80.1
Chad Pennington	2000–06	61	1659	1,080	65.1	11,973	7.2	11.1	72	58	3.50%	634
Boomer Esiason	1993–95	43	1,302	764	58.7	8,478	6.5	11.1	49	39	3.00%	78.2
Al Dorow	1960–61	28	834	398	47.7	5,399	6.5	13.6	45	56	6.71%	58.8
Dick Wood	1963–64	25	710	329	46.3	4,502	6.3	13.7	35	44	6.20%	57.7
Pat Ryan	1978–89	127	631	354	56.1	4,222	6.7	11.9	31	31	4.91%	72.6
Neil O'Donnell	1996–97	21	648	369	56.9	3,943	6.1	10.7	21	14	2.16%	76.7
Al Woodall	1969–74	31	503	246	48.9	2,970	5.9	12.1	18	23	4.57%	60.3
Matt Robinson	1977–79	35	351	161	45.9	2,503	7.1	15.5	15	26	7.41%	53.4
Browning Nagle	1991–93	18	403	199	49.4	2,361	5.9	11.9	7	17	4.22%	55.9
Frank Reich	1996	10	331	175	52.9	2,205	6.7	12.6	15	16	4.83%	68.9
Glenn Foley	1994–98	18	352	189	53.7	2,186	6.2	11.6	10	16	4.55%	63.2
Ray Lucas	1997–00	36	320	186	58.1	1,939	6.1	10.4	14	11	3.44%	76.0

Quarterback	Rush Att	Rush Yds	Rush Avg	TD
Joe Namath	67	135	2.0	7

Quarterback	Rush Att	Rush Yds	Rush Avg	TD
Ken O'Brien	170	377	2.2	0
Richard Todd	231	821	3.6	14
Vinny Testaverde	95	205	2.2	3
Chad Pennington	127	364	2.9	5
Boomer Esiason	92	191	2.1	1
Al Dorow	144	770	5.3	11
Dick Wood	16	23	1.4	2
Pat Ryan	52	158	3.0	1
Neil O'Donnell	38	66	1.7	1
Al Woodall	60	214	3.6	0
Matt Robinson	36	72	2.0	1
Browning Nagle	25	56	2.2	0
Frank Reich	18	31	1.7	0
Glenn Foley	16	33	2.1	0
Ray Lucas	58	264	4.6	1

Record Holders

Passing Yards, Career: 27,057 Joe Namath
Passing Yards, Season: 4,007 Joe Namath 1967
Completion %, Career: 65.1% Chad Pennington
Completion %, Season: 68.9% Chad Pennington 2002
Touchdown Passes, Career: 170 Joe Namath
Touchdown Passes, Season: 29 Vinny Testaverde 1998
Interceptions, Career: 215 Joe Namath
Interceptions, Season: 28 Joe Namath 1967, 1975
Rating, Career: 89.3 Chad Pennington
Rating, Season: 104.2 Chad Pennington 2002
Rush Yards, Career: 821 Richard Todd
Rush Yards, Season: 453 Al Dorow 1960

Passers by Categories

Five best starters: Quick-release king Joe Namath was larger than life and led the Jets to their only title in perhaps the most important game in NFL history. Quietly competent Ken O'Brien was not the best and not the worst of the fabled quarterback class of 1983. Chad Pennington could have had a great career if he hadn't been sidelined with multiple shoulder surgeries. Vinny Testaverde gave the Jets some of his best years. Richard Todd had some good years mixed in with some bad ones.

Worst starters, career: The Jets were originally the Titans and trotted out such dreadful quarterbacks as Johnny Green, Lee Grosscup and Galen Hall. The first "Jets" quarterback was geeky, brittle Dick Wood. He was followed by Joe Na-math whose bad knees gave playing time to such weak backups as Mike Taliaferro, Al Woodall and Bob Davis. In more recent decades Browing Nagle and Rick Mirer have stunk up the joint. Woodall and Nagle averaged less than 6 yards per pass.

Best stat line, season: In 1967, Joe Namath became the first quarterback to exceed 4,000 yards passing. Ken O'Brien averaged 8 yards per pass and threw 25 touchdowns against only 8 interceptions in 1985. Richard Todd also threw 25 touchdowns in 1981. Vinny Testaverde completed 61 percent of his passes for 29 touchdowns and just 7 interceptions in 1998. Chad Pennington completed 68.9 percent of his passes for 3,120 yards and 22 touchdowns to just six interceptions in 2002.

Worst stat line, season: Johnny Green threw 10 touchdowns to 18 interceptions in 1962. Galen Hall was given a chance in 1963 and completed 38 percent of his passes, averaged 5.2 yards per pass and threw 3 touchdowns to 9 interceptions. In 1964, Dick Wood completed 47 percent of his passes and threw 17 touchdowns to 25 interceptions. Mike Taliaferro tried to hold off rookie Joe Namath in 1965 by completing 38 percent of his passes, averaging 4.5 yards per pass for 3 touchdowns and 7 interceptions. Bob Davis stepped in for the injured Namath in 1971 and completed 40 percent of his passes while averaging just 5.2 yards per pass. Joe Namath finished his Jet career ignobly by averaging just 4.9 yards per pass and throwing 4 touchdowns to 16 interceptions. Browning Nagle completed less than half of his passes, averaged 5.9 yards per pass and threw 7 touchdowns to 17 interceptions in 1992.

Best stat line, playoffs: Joe Namath's

Super Bowl against the Colts was understated perfection —17–28, 206, 0–0. Pat Ryan stepped in against the Chiefs in a 1986 Wildcard game, going 16–23, 163, 3–0. In a 2002 Wildcard win over the Colts, Chad Pennington went 19–25, 222, 3–0, and followed that in a 2004 Wildcard win over the Chargers with 23–33, 279, 3–0.

Worst stat line, playoffs: In a 1969 AFL Divisional loss to the Chiefs, Joe Namath went 14–40, 164, 0–3. In a disastrous 1982 AFC Conference loss to Miami, Richard Todd looked like he was throwing the game by going 15–37, 103, 0–5.

Big Days: The first passer to exceed 300 yards passing in a game was Al Dorow with 301 yards on November 24, 1960. The first to reach 400 yards was Joe Namath with 415 on October 1, 1967. Namath had the biggest day in franchise history by throwing for 496 yards on September 24, 1972, and he had the most 300-yard games with 21.

Running QBs: Al Dorow set the club season record for rushing yards by a quarterback in 1960 with 453. The only Jet quarterback to surpass Dorow's meager career total of 770 yards was Richard Todd with 821. The Jets have not been known for having mobile quarterbacks.

Bomber: Joe Namath could throw it as far as Don Maynard could run.

Most accurate: Chad Pennington does not have the strongest arm, but he is very accurate.

Leader: Joe Namath had a whole league following him.

Comeback King: Ken O'Brien had 19 4th quarter comebacks. Namath had 15, plus one in the postseason.

Highest Football IQ: Namath knew how to cut apart a defense. Chad Pennington's brain is stronger than his arm.

Toughest: Joe Namath played a dozen years in the NFL on terrible knees. Richard Todd started 86 straight games.

First signal caller/T-Formation QB: Al Dorow, refugee from the NFL and CFL.

First TD pass: Dick Jamieson hit Art Powell for a 13-yard score in a 27–3 win over Buffalo on September 11, 1960.

Black QBs: J.J. Jones got to start a Monday Night Football game in 1975 when Joe Namath was being disciplined. Walter Briggs was a replacement player in 1987. Jeff Blake was a rookie for the Jets in 1992. Bill Parcells brought Rut-

gers' Ray Lucas with him from New England in 1997. Quincy Carter fled Bill Parcells' doghouse to join the Jets in 2004. Marquel Blackwell was on the practice squad in 2003.

Tallest QB: Dick Wood, Al Woodall, Boomer Esiason and Vinny Testaverde were all 6'5".

Smallest QB: Galen Hall and Dean Look (who later became an NFL referee) were both 5'10". Harold Stephens, Ed Chlebek and Dewing Bohling were all 5'11".

Oldest QB: Vinny Testaverde was brought back as a starter at age 41 in 2005 due to a series of injuries. Babe Parilli was a 40-year-old backup in 1969.

Rookie sensation: Joe Namath had a celebrated rookie season in which he passed for 2,220 yards 18 touchdowns and only 15 interceptions, one of only two seasons in which Broadway Joe threw more touchdowns than interceptions. Ken O'Brien did not play at all in his first season. As a second year rookie in 1984, though, he completed 57 percent of his passes for 1,401 yards.

Late bloomer: Vinny Testaverde had some very good seasons in his hometown of New York in his late thirties.

1st round picks: University of Minnesota's black quarterback Sandy Stephens was the fifth player selected in the 1962 AFL draft, but he went to Canada rather than switch positions. Joe Namath, 2nd in 1965, was a success not only for the Jets but for the AFL as a whole. Richard Todd, 6th in 1976, did not live up to expectations; he followed Namath but could not replace him. Ken O'Brien, 24th in 1983, is denigrated because he was picked ahead of Dan Marino, but he did go to two Pro Bowls. Chad Pennington, 18th in 2000, had a bright future that injuries partially eclipsed.

Out of position: Al Dorow sometimes played half back. Ray Lucas also played wide receiver. Kicker Jim Turner and punter Tom Tupa were quarterbacks in college. Tory Woodbury was shifted to wide receiver.

Long-time subs: Pat Ryan was a backup in New York for 11 of the 12 years he spent as a Jet.

QB controversy: Coming out of college a few thought that Heisman Trophy winner John Huarte would be better than fellow rookie Joe Namath. That did not last long. There was a real competition between Richard Todd and Matt Robinson for a couple of years.

College affiliation: Penn State sent New

York Bob Scrabis, Galen Hall and Pete Liske; Illinois sent Mike Taliaferro, Jack Trudeau and Tony Eason; Maryland supplied retreads Boomer Esiason, Neil O'Donnell and Frank Reich.

Ones who got away: Jeff Blake went from the Jets to the Bengals where he had his best years.

Has beens: Butch Songin, Johnny Green, Lee Grosscup, Dick Wood, Babe Parilli, Bob Davis, Marty Domres, Jack Trudeau, Mark Malone, Tony Eason, Rick Mirer, Neil O'Donnell, Bubby Brister, Frank Reich, Kliff Kingsbury, Quincy Carter and Jay Fiedler.

Ruinous injuries: Joe Namath's knee problems are well known and limited his options as a player. Chad Pennington's shoulder problems short-circuited a promising career. Bill Parcells' last season as Jets coach was waylaid by Vinny Testaverde's Achilles rupture.

Best trade: Trading the rights to Jerry Rhome to the Oilers for the 2nd pick in the 1965 AFL draft netted Joe Namath. Getting a number 1 and a number 2 plus Craig Penrose from the Broncos for Matt Robinson. Getting a number 1 from the Saints for a washed up Richard Todd.

Worst trade: With all the other failures in their history, it is strange that the Jets have never made a really bad quarterback trade.

Title winners: Joe Namath, 1.

Hall of Famers: Joe Namath.

All Pro/Pro Bowl seasons: Joe Namath, 5; Ken O'Brien, 2; Boomer Esiason, 1; Vinny Testaverde, 1.

QBs as coaches: None.

Underrated: Vinny Testaverde had to wait too long to get into a favorable situation to show the talent he had.

Overrated: Richard Todd never came close to living up to predecessor at Alabama and the Jets, Joe Namath.

Best Nicknames: Broadway Joe Namath and Browning "Nuke" Nagle.

Time Capsule: Joe Namath's white shoes, white fur coat, guarantee for Super Bowl III, and his hoisted index finger signaling "number one" after the upset win. Richard Todd throwing three picks to Dolphin linebacker A.J. Duhe in the 1982 AFC championship.

What If: If the Jets had picked Dan Marino rather than Ken O'Brien, would they have won anything?

Off the field: Joe Namath was as famous for his life off the field as his heroics on it. He made a name for himself with his drinking, the endless string of women, the bachelor pad with the llama rug, the white football shoes and white fur coat, and his bar, Bachelor's III, his ownership of which caused him to briefly retire from football. Richard Todd tried to follow in Joe's footsteps off the field, and Marty Domres had a spirited bachelor life. Namath had an active and mediocre career as an actor, appearing in eight movies such as *C.C. and Company* and *The Last Rebel*, three TV movies and over 20 episodes of popular TV series such as *The Love Boat* and *Fantasy Island*. Boomer Esiason appeared in episodes of *Spin City*, *Brother's Keeper* and *Remote Control*. Chad Pennington appeared in *The Apprentice: Martha Stewart*. Kyle Mackey's father Dee played tight end for the Jets.

Quarterback Bibliography

Joe Namath

Lipman, David. *Joe Namath: A Football Legend*. New York: Putnam, 1968.

Allen, Maury. *Joe Namath's Sportin' Life*. New York: Paperback Library, 1969.

Berger, Phil. *Joe Namath: Maverick Quarterback*. Chicago: Regnery, 1969.

Bortstein, Larry. *Super Joe: The Joe Namath Story*. New York: Grossett and Dunlap, 1969.

Devaney, John, and John Cervasio. *Broadway Joe Namath*. Greenwich, CT: Fawcett, 1969.

Fox, Larry. *Broadway Joe and His Super Jets*. New York: Coward–McCann, 1969.

Namath, Joe, and Dick Schaap. *I Can't Wait Until Tomorrow ... 'cause I Get Better Looking Every Day*. New York: Random House, 1969.

Devaney, John. *Joe Namath*. New York: Scholastic, 1972.

Namath, Joe, and Bob Oates. *A Matter of Style*. Boston: Little, Brown, 1973.

Szolnoki, Rose Namath, and Bill Kushner. *Namath: My Son Joe*. Birmingham, AL: Oxmoor House, 1975.

Burke, Jim. *Joe Willie*. New York: Belmont Tower Books, 1975.

Ralbovsky, Marty. *The Namath Effect*. Englewood Cliffs, NJ: Prentice-Hall, 1976.

Birth, Margaret, Dick Ayers, and Kevin Birth. *Joe Namath: Getting a Kick Out of Life*. San Diego, CA: Revolutionary Comics, 1992.

Britten, Kenneth. *Beaver Falls*. Charleston, SC: Arcadia Pub., 2000.

Kriegel, Mark. *Namath: A Biography*. New York: Viking, 2004.

Lee Grosscup

Grosscup, Lee. *Fourth and One*. New York: Harper and Row, 1963.

Grosscup, Lee. *Football: How to Play and Watch It*. New York: Sterling, 1963.

37

Oakland Raiders

Leading Passers, by Yards

Quarterback	Years	G	Att	Comp	Pct	Yds	Y/A	Y/Cp	TD	Int	Int %	Rating
Ken Stabler	1970–79	116	2,481	1,486	59.9	19,078	7.7	12.8	150	143	5.76%	80.2
Rich Gannon	1999–04	77	2,447	1,532	62.6	17,581	7.2	11.5	114	50	2.04%	91.2
Daryle Lamonica	1967–74	95	2,248	1,138	50.6	16,655	7.4	14.6	148	114	5.07%	76.0
Tom Flores	1960–66	84	1,887	953	50.5	13,736	7.3	14.4	112	99	5.25%	72.4
Jim Plunkett	1979–86	70	1,707	960	56.2	12,665	7.4	13.2	80	81	4.75%	75.7
Marc Wilson	1980–87	96	1,666	871	52.3	11,760	7.1	13.5	77	86	5.16%	69.0
Jeff Hostetler	1993–96	55	1,562	913	58.5	11,122	7.1	12.2	69	49	3.14%	82.1
Jay Schroeder	1988–92	64	1,394	698	50.1	10,276	7.4	14.7	66	62	4.45%	71.8
Kerry Collins	2004–05	29	1,079	591	54.8	7,254	6.7	12.3	41	33	3.06%	75.7
Cotton Davidson	1962–68	58	977	412	42.2	6,532	6.7	15.9	41	63	6.45%	52.2
Jeff George	1997–98	24	690	383	55.5	5,103	7.4	13.3	33	14	2.03%	86.6
Steve Beuerlein	1988–89	20	455	213	46.8	3,320	7.3	15.6	21	16	3.52%	72.2
Vince Evans	1987–95	44	437	240	54.9	3,313	7.6	13.8	21	21	4.81%	75.4
George Blanda	1967–75	112	235	119	50.6	1,835	7.8	15.4	23	18	7.66%	77.5

Quarterback	Rush Att	Rush Yds	Rush Avg	TD
Ken Stabler	80	137	1.7	4
Rich Gannon	259	1258	4.9	11
Daryle Lamonica	83	307	3.7	7
Tom Flores	81	307	3.8	5
Jim Plunkett	117	354	3.0	4
Marc Wilson	129	562	4.4	5
Jeff Hostetler	183	659	3.6	8
Jay Schroeder	137	464	3.4	1
Kerry Collins	34	74	2.2	1
Cotton Davidson	83	343	4.1	9
Jeff George	25	46	1.8	0
Steve Beuerlein	46	74	1.6	0
Vince Evans	66	368	5.6	1
George Blanda	3	4	1.3	0

Record Holders

Passing Yards, Career: 19,078 Ken Stabler

Passing Yards, Season: 4,689 Rich Gannon 2002

Completion %, Career: 62.6 Rich Gannon

Completion %, Season: 67.6% Rich Gannon 2002

Touchdown Passes, Career: 150 Ken Stabler

Touchdown Passes, Season: 34 Daryle Lamonica 1969

Interceptions, Career: 143 Ken Stabler

Interceptions, Season: 30 Ken Stabler 1978

Rating, Career: 91.2 Rich Gannon

Rating, Season: 103.4 Ken Stabler 1976

Rush Yards, Career: 1,258 Rich Gannon

Rush Yards, Season: 529 Rich Gannon 2000

Passers by Categories

Five best starters: Daryle Lamonica, the Mad Bomber, mastered the Oakland vertical passing attack and led the Raiders to their first Super Bowl. Left-handed Ken "Snake" Stabler pinpointed them to their first championship. Jim Plunkett was on his third team when he led the Raiders to two titles. Rich Gannon was on his fourth team when he blossomed in Jon Gruden's West Coast Offense and led the Raiders to another Super Bowl. George Blanda won a league MVP award as kicker and backup quarterback known for last minute relief heroics in 1970 at the age of 43.

Worst starters, career: Cotton Davidson was a hit-or-miss deep thrower. Marc Wilson and Todd Marinovich were first round draft choices and spectacular miscalculations. Jay Schroeder was inconsistent and mistake prone. That the untalented Vince Evans was still playing for the Raiders at age 40 — and throwing the most passes of his years under Al Davis — is a testament to how far the Raiders fell in the 1990s. Andrew Walter was a clueless victim on a pitiful dysfunctional team.

Best stat line, season: Daryle Lamonica led the AFL in touchdowns with 30 in 1967 and 34 in 1969 and threw for over 3,000 yards three years in a row, 1967–69. Ken Stabler threw 26 touchdowns to only 12 interceptions in 1974, and then in 1976 threw 27 touchdowns to 17 interceptions while completing 67 percent of his passes and averaging 9.4 yards per pass. Jeff George led the league in yards with 3,917 and threw 29 touchdowns to 9 interceptions in 1997. Rich Gannon completed 67 percent of his passes for 4,689 yards 26 touchdowns and 10 interceptions in 2002.

Worst stat line, season: Babe Parilli completed 46 percent of his passes and averaged just 5.4 yards per pass while throwing 5 touchdowns to 11 interceptions in 1960. Cotton Davidson completed 37 percent of his passes for 7 touchdowns and 23 interceptions in 1962. Snake Stabler threw just 16 touchdowns to 30 interceptions in 1978. Marc Wilson in 1981 completed just 47 percent of his passes for 14 touchdowns and 19 interceptions. Jay Schroeder completed 47 percent of his passes and threw 8 touchdowns to 13 interceptions in 1989. Todd Marinovich completed 49 percent of his passes for 5 touch-

downs and 9 interceptions in 1992. Andrew Walter threw just 3 touchdowns to 13 interceptions and averaged 6.1 yards per pass in 2006.

Best stat line, playoffs: In a 1968 AFL Divisional win over the Chiefs, Daryle Lamonica went 19–39, 347, 5–0; in a 1969 AFL Divisional win over the Oilers, he went 13–17, 276, 6–1. In the "Sea of Hands" game against the Dolphins in 1974, Ken Stabler went 20–30, 293, 3–1. In the Super Bowl win over the Eagles, Jim Plunkett went 13–21, 261, 3–0. In a 1993 Divisional win over Denver, Jeff Hostetler went 13–19, 294, 3–0. In a 2001 Wildcard win over the Jets, Rich Gannon went 23–29, 294, 2–0.

Worst stat line, playoffs: In the 1972 "Immaculate Reception" game against the Steelers, Daryle Lamonica went 6–18, 45, 0–2. In a 1974 AFC Conference loss to the Steelers, Ken Stabler went 19–36, 271, 1–3. In a 1985 Divisional loss to the Patriots, Marc Wilson went 11–27, 135, 1–3. In the 1990 AFC Conference loss to the Bills, Jay Schroeder went 13–31, 150, 0–5. In a 1991 Wildcard loss to the Chiefs, Todd Marinovich went 12–23, 140, 0–4. In the Super Bowl loss to the Bucs, Rich Gannon went 24–44, 272, 2–5.

Big Days: The first Raider to exceed 300 yards passing in a game was Tom Flores with 407 yards on December 22, 1963. The first Los Angeles Raider to reach 300 yards was Jim Plunkett with 318 yards on November 28, 1982; Jeff Hostetler was the first LA Raider to reach 400 yards with 424 on October 31, 1993 — the highest total in franchise history. Hostetler also was the first Raider to reach 300 yards after they returned to Oakland with 333 on October 8, 1995. Rich Gannon was the first to hit 400 in the second term in Oakland with 403 on September 15, 2002, and he had the most 300-yard games with 18 (including a season record 10 in 2002).

Running QBs: Traditionally, Raider quarterbacks are know for throwing the long ball, not running, but Rich Gannon was an exception and gained 529 yards rushing in 2000. Jeff Hostetler ran more as a Giant than as a Raider. Vince Evans and Marques Tuiasosopo could run better than pass. Aaron Brooks often took off running early.

Bomber: Daryle Lamonica was a terrific deep passer who had great targets. Jim Plunkett could also throw a nice deep ball.

Most accurate: Rich Gannon's accuracy was made for the West Coast Offense. Kenny Stabler was a very accurate passer in his time.

Leader: Ken Stabler was a passionate leader.

Comeback King: Stabler had 22 4th quarter comebacks, plus two in the postseason. George Blanda won an MVP award for his 4th quarter heroics.

Highest Football IQ: Stabler and Gannon both knew how to win.

Toughest: Gannon had a streak of 71 straight starts.

First signal caller/T-Formation QB: Tom Flores was the Raiders' first starter.

First TD pass: Flores threw a 13-yard score to Tony Theresa in a 37–22 loss to the Oilers on September 11, 1960.

Black QBs: Vince Evans was with the Raiders from 1987–1995. Rodney Peete was with the team in 2001, Tee Martin in 2003, and Aaron Brooks signed in 2006. The Raiders were originally called the Senors in recognition of California's Latino past, and the team employed the first Hispanic quarterback in the league with Tom Flores. He was joined by Chon Gallegos in 1962 and coached Jim Plunkett in the 1980s. They also have used a Samoan quarterback in Marques Tuiasosopo.

Tallest QB: Marc Wilson was 6'6" while Dick Wood and Andrew Walter were 6'5".

Smallest QB: Chon Gallegos was only 5'9" and Nick Papac was 5'11".

Oldest QB: George Blanda joined the Raiders as a 40-year-old in 1967 and played till he was 48 in 1975. Vince Evans was starting at age 40 in 1995. Wade Wilson was 39 in 1998, and Jim Plunkett was starting at 38 in 1986.

Rookie sensation: None.

Late bloomer: The Raiders gave Daryle Lamonica his chance to start at 26 in 1967. They gave Ken Stabler the job at 27 in 1973. They brought out a refurbished Jim Plunkett at 32 in 1980, and polished up Rich Gannon at 33 in 1999.

1st round picks: Eldridge Dickey, 25th in 1968, was converted unsuccessfully to wide receiver. Marc Wilson, 15th in 1980, was a big stiff. Todd Marinovich, 24th in 1991, was immature and lacked big league talent.

Out of position: Eldridge Dickey and Ronald Curry were college quarterbacks converted to wide receivers. George Blanda was more a kicker for the Raiders. Cotton Davidson doubled as a punter.

Long-time subs: Blanda backed up Lamonica and Stabler for nine years. Stabler backed up Lamonica for four years.

QB controversy: Lamonica and Stabler competed fiercely. Jim Plunkett had to beat out the more acclaimed veteran Dan Pastorini and then beat back younger Marc Wilson. Jeff Hostetler's problems with coach Art Shell became controversial when Shell denigrated him as just "another white quarterback."

College affiliation: Five USC Trojans have quarterbacked the Raiders—Mike Rae, Vince Evans, Todd Marinovich, Rodney Peete and Rob Johnson.

Ones who got away: None.

Has beens: Don Heinrich, M.C. Reynolds, Babe Parilli, Hunter Enis, Dick Wood, Cotton Davidson, Dan Pastorini, Vince Evans, Jay Schroeder, Billy Joe Hobert, David Klingler, Wade Wilson, Rob Johnson, Rick Mirer, Bobby Hoying, Rodney Peete, Jeff George, Kerry Collins and Aaron Brooks.

Ruinous injuries: When the Raiders traded Kenny Stabler for Dan Pastorini, they were trading one beat-up quarterback for another. Rich Gannon's revitalized career was brought to a halt by shoulder and neck injuries.

Best trade: Getting Daryle Lamonica and Glenn Bass from the Bills for Tom Flores, Art Powell, a number 2 and a number 6.

Worst trade: Giving a number 1 (Buck Buchanan) to the Chiefs for Cotton Davidson. Giving All Pro tackle Jim Lachey and two draft picks to the Redskins for Jay Schroeder.

Title winners: Jim Plunkett, 2; Ken Stabler, 1.

Hall of Famers: George Blanda

All Pro/Pro Bowl seasons: Daryle Lamonica, 4; Ken Stabler, 4; Cotton Davidson, 1; Tom Flores, 1; Jeff Hostetler, 1; George Blanda, 1 (as kicker).

QBs as coaches: Tom Flores went 97–87 with Oakland and Seattle.

Underrated: Daryle Lamonica, Jim Plunkett and Rich Gannon were all brought in as projects from other teams and had great success as Raiders.

Overrated: Jeff Hostetler and Jay Schroeder had more success elsewhere before failing under Al Davis.

Best Nicknames: Ken "Snake" Stabler and Daryle "the Mad Bomber" Lamonica.

Time Capsule: The Sea of Hands pass. The forward fumble game. The Ghost to the Post game. George Blanda in relief. Al Davis' Vertical Passing Attack.

What If: If the Raiders had not picked up Jim Plunkett from the scrap heap, would they have won anything in the 1980s?

Off the field: One thing that Snake Stabler and Dan Pastorini had in common was that they loved the nightlife. Todd Marinovich was the son of former Raider guard Marv Marinovich. Rodney Peete is married to actress Holly Robinson Peete. Stabler appeared in *Indian Runner, The Legend of Grizzly Adams* and an episode of *Married ... with Children*. Jay Schroeder appeared in *Oh No Zombie* after his football career had died.

Quarterback Bibliography

Tom Flores
Flores, Tom, and Frank Cooney. *Fire in the Iceman:*
Autobiography of Tom Flores. Chicago: Bonus Books, 1992.

George Blanda
Blanda, George, and Mickey Herskowitz. *Over 40: Feeling Great and Looking Good.* New York: Simon and Schuster, 1978
Twombly, Wells. *Blanda, Alive and Kicking: The Exclusive, Authorized Biography.* New York: Avon Books, 1973.

Ken Stabler
Stabler, Ken, and Tom La Marie. *Ken Stabler's Winning Offensive Football.* Chicago: Regnery, 1976.
Stabler, Ken, and Dick O'Connor. *Super Bowl Diary: The Autobiography of Ken Stabler.* Los Angeles: Pinnacle Books, 1977.
Stabler, Ken, and Berry Stainback. *Snake.* Garden City: Doubleday, 1986.
Libby, Bill. *Ken Stabler: Southpaw Passer.* New York: Putnam, 1977.

Jim Plunkett *see* New England Patriots

Jeff Hostetler *see* New York Giants

38

Philadelphia Eagles

Leading Passers, by Yards

Quarterback	Years	G	Att	Comp	Pct	Yds	Y/A	Y/Cp	TD	Int	Int %	Rating
Ron Jaworski	1977–86	142	3,918	2,088	53.3	26,963	6.9	12.9	175	151	3.85%	74.0
Randall Cunningham	1985–95	122	3,362	1,874	55.7	22,877	6.8	12.2	150	105	3.12%	78.7
Donovan McNabb	1999–06	104	3,259	1,898	58.2	22,080	6.8	11.6	152	72	2.21%	85.2
Norm Snead	1964–70	85	2,236	1,154	51.6	15,672	7.0	13.6	111	124	5.55%	67.7
Tommy Thompson	1941–50	88	1,396	723	51.8	10,240	7.3	14.2	90	100	7.16%	67.4
Sonny Jurgensen	1957–63	83	1,107	602	54.4	9,639	8.7	16.0	76	73	6.59%	79.1
Bobby Thomason	1952–57	68	1,113	556	50	8,124	7.3	14.6	57	80	7.19%	61.2
Norm Van Brocklin	1958–60	36	998	542	54.3	7,497	7.5	13.8	55	51	5.11%	75.7
Roman Gabriel	1973–77	53	1,185	661	55.8	7,221	6.1	10.9	47	37	3.12%	74.2
Adrian Burk	1951–56	70	960	457	47.6	6,203	6.5	13.6	55	77	8.02%	54.4
Rodney Peete	1995–98	30	756	434	57.4	4,945	6.5	11.4	17	27	3.57%	69.8
Ty Detmer	1996–97	21	645	372	57.7	4,478	6.9	12.0	22	19	2.95%	78.2
King Hill	1961–68	71	635	325	51.2	4,308	6.8	13.3	29	51	8.03%	54.8
Pete Liske	1971–72	28	407	214	52.6	2,930	7.2	13.7	14	22	5.41%	64.8
Mike Boryla	1974–76	22	514	270	52.5	2,823	5.5	10.5	20	29	5.64%	58.2

Quarterback	Years	G	Att	Comp	Pct	Yds	Y/A	Y/Cp	TD	Int	Int %	Rating
Davey O'Brien	1939–40	22	478	223	46.7	2,614	5.5	11.7	11	34	7.11%	41.8
Jim McMahon	1990–92	21	363	215	59.2	2,581	7.1	12.0	13	13	3.58%	78.1
Bobby Hoying	1997–98	15	449	242	53.9	2,534	5.6	10.5	11	15	3.34%	64.8
Bubby Brister	1993–94	17	385	232	60.3	2,412	6.3	10.4	16	6	1.56%	85.8
Roy Zimmerman	1944–46	31	311	147	47.3	2,373	7.6	16.1	21	26	8.36%	60.9

Quarterback	Rush Att	Rush Yds	Rush Avg	TD
Ron Jaworski	232	772	3.3	12
Randall Cunningham	677	4482	6.6	32
Donovan McNabb	447	2726	6.1	24
Norm Snead	99	266	2.7	13
Tommy Thompson	253	-14	-0.1	6
Sonny Jurgensen	65	112	1.7	5
Bobby Thomason	89	295	3.3	6
Norm Van Brocklin	30	5	0.2	3
Roman Gabriel	43	158	3.7	2
Adrian Burk	111	305	2.7	6
Rodney Peete	65	245	3.8	3
Ty Detmer	45	105	2.3	2
King Hill	32	94	2.9	3
Pete Liske	20	49	2.5	1
Mike Boryla	43	224	5.2	2
Davey O'Brien	208	-194	-0.9	2
Jim McMahon	31	79	2.5	1
Bobby Hoying	38	162	4.3	0
Bubby Brister	21	46	2.2	0
Roy Zimmerman	111	-93	-0.8	5

Record Holders

Passing Yards, Career: 26,463 Ron Jaworski

Passing Yards, Season: 3,875 Donovan McNabb 2004

Completion %, Career: 58.4% Donovan McNabb; 60.3% Bubby Brister (384 att).

Completion %, Season: 64% Donovan McNabb 2004

Touchdown Passes, Career: 175 Ron Jaworski

Touchdown Passes, Season: 32 Sonny Jurgensen 1961

Interceptions, Career: 151 Ron Jaworski

Interceptions, Season: 26 Sonny Jurgensen 1962

Rating, Career: 85.2 Donovan McNabb; 85.8 Bubby Brister (384 att.)

Rating, Season: 104.7 Donovan McNabb 2004

Rush Yards, Career: 4,482 Randall Cunningham

Rush Yards, Season: 942 Randall Cunningham 1990

Passers by Categories

Five best starters: Norm Van Brocklin was a Hall of Famer as a passer and as a leader and led a mediocre team to a championship in 1960. Randall Cunningham was referred to as the Ultimate Weapon for his astounding variety of talents — running, passing, punting. Donovan McNabb has tried mightily to deny what a great running quarterback he is and maintain that he is a pocket quarterback. Ron Jaworski was a smart, tough and effective quarterback for a decade in Philadelphia. The choice for five is between Sonny Jurgensen who had his greatest years in Washington and one-eyed Tommy Thompson who led the Eagles to two title wins the 1940s.

Worst starters, career: Norm Snead had a strong arm but was mistake-prone and suffered in comparison to Jurgensen whom the Eagles gave up to obtain him. King Hill was not good enough to beat out Snead. Bobby Hoying and John Reaves were both overwhelmed and outclassed by NFL defenses. Doug Pederson was a rag-armed placeholder for the first half of 1999 while Donovan McNabb learned the offense.

Best stat line, season: Tommy Thompson completed 57 percent of his passes for 25 touchdowns and just 11 interceptions in a 12-game season in 1948. Norm Van Brocklin averaged 8.7 yards per pass and threw 24 touchdowns to 13 interceptions in 1960. Sonny Jurgensen followed that in 1961 by completing 56.5 percent of his passes for 3,723 yards, an average of 9 yards per throw, and 32 touchdowns. Roman Gabriel was acquired in 1973 and led the league in attempts, completions, yards (3,219) and touchdowns (23) throwing to the Fire High Gang of tall receivers. Ron Jaworski won the league MVP in 1980 by completing 57 percent of his passes for 3,529 yards, an average of 7.8 per pass, and 27 touchdowns to only 12 interceptions. Randall Cunningham had his ultimate season in 1990 by throwing for 3,466 yards, 30 touchdowns and only 13 interceptions while rushing for 942 yards at 8 yards per carry. Donovan McNabb had his greatest season in 2004 throwing to Terrell Owens and completing 64 percent of his passes for 3,875 yards, 31 touchdowns and just 8 interceptions.

Worst stat line, season: Tommy Thompson proved he was washed up in 1950 by completing 45 percent of his passes for 11 touchdowns and 22 interceptions. Adrian Burk and Bobby Thomason were capable of having games where they threw for over 400 yards as Thomason did in 1953 or for seven touchdowns as Burk did in 1954, but they suffered from inconsistency. In 1951, Burk completed 42 percent of his passes for 14 touchdowns and 23 interceptions, while in 1955 he averaged less than 6 yards per pass and threw just 9 touchdowns to 17 interceptions. In 1956, Thomason threw just 4 touchdowns to 21 interceptions. Norm Snead averaged less than 6 yards per pass in both 1966 and 1968 while completing just 45 percent of his passes in the former year and throwing 21 interceptions in the latter year. John Reaves' rookie season of 1972 saw him complete 48 percent of his passes and throw just 7 touchdowns to 12 interceptions. Mike Boryla, who threw 6 touchdowns to 12 interceptions in 1975, still went to the Pro Bowl after *six* other NFC quarterbacks dropped out; he followed that in 1976 by averaging 5 yards per pass and throwing 9 touchdowns to 14 interceptions. Bobby Hoying was given the starting job in 1998 and threw 0 touchdowns to 9 interceptions while averaging 4.3 yards per pass.

Best stat line, playoffs: In a 1991 Wildcard win over the Saints, Randall Cunningham went 19–35, 219, 2–0. In a 1995 Wildcard win over the Lions, Rodney Peete went 17–25, 270, 3–0. Donovan McNabb went 20–30, 247, 1–0 in a 2002 Division win over Atlanta.

Worst stat line, playoffs: In winning the 1948 championship over the Cardinals during a blizzard, Tommy Thompson went 2–12, 7, 0–2. In the epochal 1980 defeat of the Cowboys in the NFC Conference game, Ron Jaworski went 9–29, 91, 0–2. In the 1988 Fog Bowl loss to the Bears, Randall Cunningham went 27–54, 407, 0–4 and ended his tenure in Philadelphia in a 1995 Division loss to Dallas by going 11–26, 161, 1–1. Donovan McNabb struggled with bad protection and wimpy receivers in the 2003 Conference loss to the Panthers and went 10–22, 100, 0–3.

Big Days: The first passer to exceed 300 yards passing in a game was Davey O'Brien with 316 yards on December 1, 1940. The first to reach 400 yards was Bobby Thomason with 437 on October 8, 1953. Donovan McNabb had the biggest day in franchise history by throwing for 464 yards on December 5, 2004 and has had 18 300-yard games.

Running QBs: Jack Concannon could not throw well enough to stay on the field, but he averaged over 8 yards per carry in Philadelphia and has the fourth highest rushing total for an Eagle quarterback with 434 yards and gained 129 yards rushing in a game in 1966. Randall Cunningham is the all time NFL leader in quarterback rushing yards by a quarterback and three times gained over 100 yards rushing in a game. He gained over 500 yards in a season five times with a high of 942 in 1990 and led the team in rushing for four consecutive seasons. Donovan McNabb led the team in rushing once and twice gained over 100 yards rushing in a game, but with better running backs than Cunningham, he has relied less on his legs.

Bomber: Norm Van Brocklin and Sonny Jurgensen were noted for throwing a very accurate deep pass. Randall Cunningham had a monster arm.

Most accurate: Van Brocklin and fellow Ram-refugee Roman Gabriel were very accurate.

Leader: Norm Van Brocklin and Tommy Thompson both led the Eagles to championships.

Comeback King: Ron Jaworski had 22 4th quarter comebacks, plus one in the postseason.

Randall Cunningham had 20 with one in the playoffs. Donovan McNabb has 15 plus one in the playoffs. Norm Van Brocklin had 9 plus one in the postseason in just three seasons.

Highest Football IQ: Listen to Ron Jaworski on TV as an analyst and you will get an education.

Toughest: Jaworski started 116 straight games and racked up over 30 concussions.

First signal caller/T-Formation QB: Roger "Red" Kirkman was the first signal caller, but the first T formation quarterback was Tommy Thompson in 1941.

First TD pass: Red Kirkman hit Swede Hanson for a 30-yard touchdown in a 35–9 loss to the Packers on October 29, 1933.

Black QBs: Dick Vermeil brought Johnnie Walton in from the WFL in 1976 and he backed up Ron Jaworski for four years. Randall Cunningham was drafted in 1985 and stayed for eleven seasons. In 1988, Don McPherson was the third quarterback. Rodney Peete took the starting job from Cunningham in 1995 and Donovan McNabb took over in 1999. Jeff Blake backed up McNabb in 2004.

Tallest QB: Roman Gabriel and Dean May were both 6'5". Practice squad player Bill Troup was also 6'5".

Smallest QB: Davey O'Brien was a 5'7" passing tailback. Flippin' Foster Watkins was 5'9". Walt Masters and Allie Sherman were both 5'10". Ty and Koy Detmer both claimed to be at least 6' but were very slight of build.

Oldest QB: Jeff Garcia was a 36-year old starter in 2006. Roman Gabriel was 36 in 1976. Ron Jaworski was a 35-year old starter in 1986 as was Gabriel in 1975.

Rookie sensation: Davey O'Brien led the NFL in passing yards and average gain as a rookie in 1939 despite throwing just 6 touchdowns to 17 interceptions.

Late bloomer: Sonny Jurgensen sat on the bench for four years before getting a chance to start at 27 in 1961. Tommy Thompson didn't really get a chance to blossom till after World War II at age 31.

1st round picks: Davey O'Brien, 4th in 1939, was moderately successful in his two-year career and Donovan McNabb, 2nd in 1999, has been a star. Frank Tripucka, 9th in 1949, was waived in his rookie year, and John Reaves, 14th in 1972, was an under-prepared disaster as an Eagle.

Out of position: Kick returners John Sciarra and Brian Mitchell were college quarterbacks as was cornerback Jimmy Raye. Norm Van Brocklin, Adrian Burk, King Hill and Emmett Mortell doubled as punters; Roy Zimmerman and Dave Smukler also place-kicked.

Long-time subs: Koy Detmer and King Hill both spent eight seasons on the bench in Philadelphia.

QB controversy: Bobby Thomason and Adrian Burk shared the starting job for five years in the 1950s, with neither one ever conclusively winning the slot. Philly fans often call for the young gun on the bench when the veteran is struggling: Mike Boryla for Roman Gabriel, Randall Cunningham for Ron Jaworski, Rodney Peete for Cunningham, Ty Detmer for Peete, Bobby Hoying for Detmer, even A.J. Feeley for McNabb.

College affiliation: Five Fighting Irish quarterbacks have passed through Philadelphia without any positive effect: Emmett Mortell, Frank Tripucka, Ralph Guglielmi, John Huarte and Ron Powlus.

Ones who got away: Sonny Jurgensen went from Washington to the Hall of Fame.

Has beens: Fred Enke, Al Dorow, King Hill, Ralph Guglielmi, John Huarte, Pete Liske, George Mira, Joe Pisarcik, Dan Pastorini, Ken O'Brien, Pat Ryan, Jeff Kemp, Matt Cavanaugh, Jim McMahon, Ty Detmer, Doug Pederson, Jeff Blake, Mike McMahon.

Ruinous injuries: Randall Cunningham twice went down to season-ending injuries. Donovan McNabb has done so three times. Sonny Jurgensen's shoulder was ruined in the 1961 Playoff Bowl, and he would not be the same till he left Philadelphia.

Best trade: Getting Norm Van Brocklin from the Rams for a number 1 (Dick Bass), Buck Lansford and Jimmie Harris. Trading John Reaves and a number 2 to the Bengals for Pro Bowl tackle Stan Walters and Wayne Clark.

Worst trade: Trading Sonny Jurgensen and Jimmy Carr to the Redskins for Norm Snead and Claude Crabb. Giving the Lions two number 2's and a number 3 for Greg Barton. Giving the Bengals a 1 and 6 for Mike Boryla. Giving up a number 1 (Irv Goode) to the Cardinals for King Hill. Giving the Rams two number 1's, a number 3, Harold Jackson and Tony Baker for Roman Gabriel.

Title winners: Tommy Thompson, 2; Norm Van Brocklin, 1.

Hall of Famers: Norm Van Brocklin and Sonny Jurgensen.

All Pro/Pro Bowl seasons: Donovan McNabb, 4; Norm Van Brocklin, 3; Randall Cunningham, 3; Tommy Thompson, 3; Bobby Thomason, 3; Sonny Jurgensen, 1; Ron Jaworski, 1; Roman Gabriel, 1; Norm Snead, 1; Adrian Burk, 1; Mike Boryla, 1.

QBs as coaches: Norm Van Brocklin went 66–100–7 in Minnesota and Atlanta. John Rauch went 40–28–2 in Oakland and Buffalo. Allie Sherman went 63–59–4 with the Giants.

Underrated: Tommy Thompson is largely forgotten today, but he was just a step below his Hall of Fame contemporaries Sid Luckman and Sammy Baugh.

Overrated: The spectacular highlights of Randall Cunningham are remembered more than the postseason failures.

Best Nicknames: Davey "Slingshot" O'Brien, Flippin' Foster Watkins, Tossin' Tommy Thompson, Norm "Dutchman" Van Brocklin, Ron "Jaws" "the Polish Rifle" Jaworski, Randall "the Ultimate Weapon" Cunningham, Ty "Chicken Legs" Detmer.

Time Capsule: Randall Cunningham's series of amazing highlights running and scrambling.

What If: If Joe Kuharich had not traded Jurgensen for Snead, would the decade have been better for the Eagles? If Cunningham had received more coaching, would he have led the Eagles to the Super Bowl?

Off the field: Sonny Jurgensen was well-known for his after hours activities. Ty and Koy Detmer were the first brothers to play quarterback for the same team at the same time in 1997 although Koy was on the practice squad that year. Jeff Kemp was the son of former NFL quarterback and U.S. congressman Jack Kemp. Rick Arrington fathered sportscaster Jill Arrington. A.J. Feeley has dated soccer star Heather Mitts for years, Jeff Garcia is engaged to a former Playboy Playmate of the Year, and Rodney Peete married actress Holly Robinson. Norm Van Brocklin appeared in *The Long Gray Line, Crazy Legs* and an episode of *Red Skelton*. Jack Concannon appeared in *M*A*S*H* and the TV movie *Brian's Song*. Roman Gabriel appeared in *The Undefeated* and *Skidoo* as well as episodes of *Perry Mason, Gilligan's Island, Ironside, Rowan and Martin, Wonder Woman, Khan* and *The Misadventures of Sheriff Lobo*. Randall Cunningham appeared in an episode of *Martin*. Donovan McNabb appeared in an episode of *George Lopez*.

Quarterback Bibliography

Norm Van Brocklin *see* St. Louis Rams

Roman Gabriel *see* St. Louis Rams

Ron Jaworski
Lyon, Bill, and Cynthia Zordich. *When the Clock Runs Out: 20 NFL Greats Share their Stories of Hardship and Triumph.* Chicago: Triumph, 1999.

Randall Cunningham
Cunningham, Randall, and Steve Wattenberg. *I'm Still Scrambling.* New York: Doubleday, 1993.

Jim McMahon *see* Chicago Bears

Ty Detmer
Detmer, Ty, Brenton G. Yorgenson, and Frank Herbert. *Ty: The Ty Detmer Story.* Salt Lake City: Bookcraft, 1992.
Harmon, Dick. *Ty Detmer: The Making of a Legend.* Springville, UT: Cedar Fort, 1992.

39

Pittsburgh Steelers

Leading Passers, by Yards

Quarterback	Years	G	Att	Comp	Pct	Yds	Y/A	Y/Cp	TD	Int	Int %	Rating
Terry Bradshaw	1970–83	168	3,901	2,025	51.9	27,989	7.2	13.8	212	210	5.38%	70.9
Kordell Stewart	1995–02	114	2,107	1,190	56.5	13,328	6.3	11.2	70	72	3.42%	72.3
Neil O'Donnell	1991–95	66	1,871	1,069	57.1	12,867	6.9	12.0	68	39	2.08%	81.8
Bubby Brister	1986–92	61	1,477	776	52.5	10,104	6.8	13.0	51	57	3.86%	69.8
Bobby Layne	1958–62	55	1,156	569	49.2	9,030	7.8	15.9	66	81	7.01%	65.5
Jim Finks	1949–55	79	1,382	661	47.8	8,622	6.2	13.0	55	88	6.37%	54.7
Mark Malone	1981–87	59	1,374	690	50.2	8,582	6.2	12.4	54	68	4.95%	62.4
Ben Roethlisberger	2004–06	41	1,032	644	62.4	8,519	8.3	13.2	52	43	4.17%	87.9
Tommy Maddox	2001–05	47	1,036	603	58.2	7,139	6.9	11.8	42	40	3.86%	76.7
Mike Tomczak	1993–99	84	973	546	56.1	6,649	6.8	12.2	37	43	4.42%	71.6
Ed Brown	1962–65	55	736	339	46.1	5,821	7.9	17.2	38	50	6.79%	62.3
Bill Nelsen	1963–67	32	591	274	46.4	4,440	7.5	16.2	27	30	5.08%	66.1
Dick Shiner	1968–69	25	513	245	47.8	3,278	6.4	13.4	25	27	5.26%	62.8
Cliff Stoudt	1980–83	30	479	244	50.9	3,217	6.7	13.2	14	28	5.85%	57.9
David Woodley	1984–85	16	339	179	52.8	2,630	7.8	14.7	14	21	6.19%	66.4
Kent Nix	1967–69	25	451	217	48.1	2,597	5.8	12.0	14	33	7.32%	46.0
Terry Hanratty	1969–74	46	417	159	38.1	2,478	5.9	15.6	24	34	8.15%	43.8
Earl Morrall	1957–58	14	335	155	46.3	2,175	6.5	14.0	12	19	5.67%	56.0
Joe Gilliam	1972–75	20	331	147	44.4	2,103	6.4	14.3	9	17	5.14%	53.2
Ted Marchibroda	1953–56	23	340	157	46.2	1,931	5.7	12.3	15	24	7.06%	49.5

Quarterback	Rush Att	Rush Yds	Rush Avg	TD
Terry Bradshaw	444	2257	5.1	32
Kordell Stewart	496	2561	5.2	35
Neil O'Donnell	126	323	2.6	3
Bubby Brister	124	341	2.8	7
Bobby Layne	112	382	3.4	8
Jim Finks	118	294	2.5	12
Mark Malone	121	459	3.8	14
Ben Roethlisberger	119	311	2.6	6
Tommy Maddox	55	105	1.9	1
Mike Tomczak	65	68	1.0	0
Ed Brown	44	121	2.8	4
Bill Nelsen	45	94	2.1	1
Dick Shiner	28	108	3.9	1
Cliff Stoudt	100	553	5.5	4
David Woodley	28	85	3.0	2
Kent Nix	31	130	4.2	2
Terry Hanratty	20	98	4.9	1
Earl Morrall	45	120	2.7	2
Joe Gilliam	22	64	2.9	1
Ted Marchibroda	46	166	3.6	3

Record Holders

Passing Yards, Career: 27,989 Terry Bradshaw
Passing Yards, Season: 3,724 Terry Bradshaw 1979
Completion %, Career: 62.4% Ben Roethlisberger
Completion %, Season: 66.4% Ben Roethlisberger 2004
Touchdown Passes, Career: 212 Terry Bradshaw
Touchdown Passes, Season: 28 Terry Bradshaw 1978
Interceptions, Career: 210 Terry Bradshaw
Interceptions, Season: 25 Terry Bradshaw 1979
Rating, Career: 87.9 Ben Roethlisberger
Rating, Season: 98.6 Ben Roethlisberger 2005
Rush Yards, Career: 2,561 Kordell Stewart
Rush Yards, Season: 537 Kordell Stewart 2001

Passers by Categories

Five best starters: For a guy labeled as dumb, Terry Bradshaw has had a heck of a career as a Hall of Fame quarterback and then media superstar in television, movies and books. Bobby Layne was on the downside when he ended up in Pittsburgh but was still exciting and a winner. Ben Roethlisberger has had the best start of any Steeler quarterback in history. Neil O'Donnell was a smart game manager in the regular season. Kordell Stewart had a big arm and swift legs, but didn't always make the best decisions.

Worst starters, career: The sixties were an especially bad decade for Steeler quarterbacks. There were retread hacks like Dick Shiner and young passers who quickly proved themselves overmatched like Ron Smith, Kent Nix, Tommy Wade and Terry Hanratty. Wade threw 2 touchdowns to 13 interceptions, while Hanratty threw 14 touchdowns to 33 interceptions. Cliff Stoudt was Bradshaw's successor who, despite throwing just 14 touchdowns to 28 interceptions, landed a big contract in the USFL. We should also recall some of the wretched touchdown/interception ratios from tailbacks employed by the Steelers in single-wing days — Johnny Gildea 5/34, Ray Evans 5/17, Ed Matesic 4/16, Coley McDonough 5/20, John Grigas 6/21, Joe Gasparella 3/10, Chuck Ortman 3/13, Warren Heller 2/24, Billy Patterson 3/15, Tony Holm 2/13, John McCarthy 0/13, Dick Riffle 1/10, Whizzer White 2/18 and Bill Dudley 4/16.

Best stat line, season: Terry Bradshaw enjoyed the new rules opening up the passing game in 1978 and completed 56 percent of his passes for 28 touchdowns with a 7.9 average gain per pass. Neil O'Donnell led the Steelers to the Super Bowl in 1995 by completing 57 percent of his passes for 17 touchdowns and only 7 interceptions. Kordell Stewart's best year was 2001 when he completed 60 percent of his passes for 3,109 yards and ran for 537 more. Tommy Maddox beat out Stewart in 2002 and completed 62 percent of his passes for 20 touchdowns and 16 interceptions at 7.5 yards per pass. Ben Roethlisberger earned a 98.6 passer rating as a sophomore in 2005 by completing 62 percent of his passes, averaging 8.9 yards per pass and throwing 17 touchdowns to 9 interceptions.

Worst stat line, season: In 1955, Jim Finks ended his career by throwing just 10 touchdowns to 26 interceptions. The following season, Ted Marchibroda completed 45 percent of his passes for 12 touchdowns and 19 interceptions. The mid-to-late sixties went like this: 1964, Ed Brown completed 44 percent of his passes for 12 touchdowns and 19 interceptions; 1965, Bill Nelsen completed 44 percent of his passes for 8 touchdowns and 17 interceptions; 1966, Ron Smith completed 43 percent of his passes for 8 touchdowns and 12 interceptions; 1967, Kent Nix completed half his passes, but averaged 5.9 yards per pass and threw 8 touchdowns to 19 interceptions; after Dick Shiner managed to throw 18 touchdowns to 17 interceptions in 1968, 1969 featured Shiner completing 46 percent of his passes for 7 touchdowns and 10 interceptions while Terry Hanratty completed 41 percent of his passes for 8 touchdowns and 13 interceptions. Terry Bradshaw then opened the new decade by completing 38 percent of his passes for 6 touchdowns and 24 interceptions in his rookie year of 1970. When Cliff Stoudt replaced Bradshaw in 1983, he threw 12 touchdowns to 21 interceptions. Stoudt's successor Mark Malone ended his stint as a Steeler in 1987 by completing 46 percent of his passes and throwing 6 touchdowns to 19 interceptions.

Best stat line, playoffs: In a 1976 Divisional win over the Colts, Terry Bradshaw went 14–18, 264, 3–0. In his last two Super Bowls, Bradshaw was terrific, going 17–30, 318, 4–1 the second time against the Cowboys and going 14–21, 309, 2–3 against the Rams. In 2005, Ben

Roethlisberger followed a Wildcard win over the Bengals in which he went 14–19, 208, 3–0 with an AFC Conference win over Denver where he went 21–29, 225, 2–0.

Worst stat line, playoffs: In the 1947 Eastern Division playoff loss to the Eagles, Johnny Clement went 4–16, 52, 0–0. In the 1972 Immaculate Reception win over the Raiders, Terry Bradshaw struggled, 11–25, 175, 1–1. In the Super Bowl loss to the Cowboys, Neil O'Donnell went 28–49, 239, 1–3. In the 1997 AFC Conference loss to Denver, Kordell Stewart went 18–36, 201, 1–3. In the Super Bowl win over the Seahawks, Ben Roethlisberger went 9–21, 123, 0–2.

Big Days: The first passer to exceed 300 yards passing in a game was Jim Finks with 327 yards on September 26, 1954. The first to reach 400 yards was Bobby Layne with 409 on December 13, 1958. Tommy Maddox had the biggest day in franchise history by throwing for 473 yards on November 10, 2002 and had six 300-yard games. Neil O'Donnell had five and Terry Bradshaw and Ben Roethlisberger had four.

Running QBs: Kordell Stewart was the most consistent runner and twice exceeded 100 yards rushing in a game. Cliff Stoudt ran for 489 yards in 1983 and a young Terry Bradshaw ran for 346 in 1972. Bradshaw scored 32 times while Stewart scored 35 times on the ground and 5 times on receptions. Ted Marchibroda, David Woodley and Mark Malone were all scramblers. Despite being in his thirties by the time he reached Pittsburgh, Bobby Layne was still more mobile than most.

Bomber: Terry Bradshaw had both a great arm and two Hall of Fame receivers in Swann and Stallworth.

Most accurate: Big Ben Roethlisberger hits his targets in stride. Neil O'Donnell was pretty accurate when he wasn't throwing in the Super Bowl.

Leader: Two Blonde Bombers — Bobby Layne and Terry Bradshaw — who could fire up a team.

Comeback King: Bradshaw had 24 4th quarter comebacks, plus four in the postseason. Layne had 11 in five years.

Highest Football IQ: Ben Roethlisberger can manage a game.

Toughest: Terry Bradshaw could take a hard hit and shake it off.

First signal caller/T-Formation QB: Angelo Brovelli was the first tailback in 1933; when the Steelers became the last NFL team to switch to the T, Jim Finks was their quarterback.

First TD pass: Bill Tanguay threw an 11-yard score to Paul Moss in a 14–13 win over the Cardinals on September 27, 1933.

Black QBs: Jefferson Street Joe Gilliam was given every opportunity to win the starting job from 1972 through 1974, but lacked maturity. Tony Dungy played some emergency quarterback for the Steelers in 1977. Reggie Collier was a replacement player in 1987. Kordell Stewart had an up and down career in Pittsburgh from 1995 through 2002. Tee Martin was a third quarterback in 2002. Charlie Batch has been a backup in his hometown since 2003. Omar Jacobs was signed in 2006.

Tallest QB: Ben Roethlisberger is the first successful 6'5" quarterback for the Steelers, following Ron Smith and Kent Graham.

Smallest QB: In the days of the single-wing, Pug Vaughan was 5'7", John McCarthy was 5'8", Ed Westfall was 5'9" and Joe Geri, Frank Filchock, Billy Patterson and Walt Masters were all 5'10". The smallest quarterbacks have been Ted Marchibroda at 5'10" and Scott Campbell at 6'.

Oldest QB: Ed Brown was 37 in 1965, and Mike Tomczak was starting at 37 in 1999.

Rookie sensation: Ben Roethlisberger compiled a 118 passer rating in 2004 by completing 64 percent of his passes, averaging 8.9 yards per pass and throwing 17 touchdowns to 11 interceptions. Neil O'Donnell had a successful rookie year in 1991 by completing 54 percent of his passes for 11 touchdowns and 6 interceptions.

Late bloomer: Jim Finks was 25 and in his fourth season before he got to play quarterback because the Steelers were still playing the single-wing until then. Terry Bradshaw took a long five years to learn and fully win the starting job at 27 in 1974. Tommy Maddox had been out of the NFL for six years before the Steelers signed him on the strength of his being the MVP in XFL in 2001. He was 31 when he got his chance in 2002.

1st round picks: Ted Marchibroda, 5th in 1953, could not overcome his lack of size. Gary Glick, 1st in 1956, was shifted to defensive back where he had an eight-year professional career. Len Dawson, 5th in 1957, tried to imitate Bobby

Layne and failed. Terry Bradshaw, 1st in 1970, looked like a flop for several seasons before blossoming into a Hall of Famer. Mark Malone, 28th in 1980, is a better broadcaster than quarterback, unlike Bradshaw. Ben Roethlisberger, 11th in 2004, has been a success right from the start.

Out of position: College quarterbacks Jug Girard, Gary Glick and Tony Dungy all played defensive back in Pittsburgh. Hines Ward and Antwuan Randle El were shifted to wide receiver. Kordell Stewart played some wide receiver and runner and returner to earn the nickname Slash. Ed Brown punted and Bobby Layne kicked. Vic Eaton beat out Johnny Unitas in 1955 because he could punt.

Long-time subs: Terry Hanratty was a backup in six of seven seasons in Pittsburgh while Mike Tomczak was a backup for five of seven years as a Steeler.

QB controversy: It took Terry Bradshaw five years to beat out Terry Hanratty and Joe Gilliam. Mark Malone and David Woodley were both scramblers, but neither was very good. Kordell Stewart bred controversy. He started out pressuring Neil O'Donnell and in turn was pushed out of town by Tommy Maddox.

College affiliation: Three colleges have sent three quarterbacks each to Pittsburgh: Notre Dame — Joe Gasparella, George Izo and Terry Hanratty; Maryland — Neil O'Donnell, Dick Shiner and Jack Scarbath; Tennessee — Tee Martin, Bus Warren and Walt Slater. Plus the local institution St. Francis supplied passers Tony Bova, John McCarthy and Ed Stofka.

Ones who got away: For a team that has often lacked for quality quarterbacking, the Steelers have given a lot away. Starting with the Hall of Fame Division — Sid Luckman and Bobby Layne were traded to the Bears, Johnny Unitas was cut in training camp and Len Dawson threw 17 passes in three years before being traded to Cleveland. On to the All Pro Division — Frank Filchock was traded to Washington, Tommy Thompson ended up in Philadelphia, Jack Kemp drifted to the AFL, Earl Morrall was traded for an older Bobby Layne, and Steve Bono was released.

Has beens: Gary Kerkorian, Jack Scarbath, George Izo, Terry Nofsinger, Ron Smith, Rudy Bukich, Dick Shiner, David Woodley, Todd Blackledge, Kent Graham, Tommy Maddox and Charlie Batch.

Ruinous injuries: Bill Nelsen had such bad knees that he was practically immobile. Terry Bradshaw's career ended with his arm problems. Ben Roethlisberger has missed a number of games in his first couple of seasons and had a famous motorcycle smash in 2006.

Best trade: Getting Bobby Layne back from the Lions for Earl Morrall and a number 2. Trading Dick Shiner to the Giants for Frenchy Fuqua and Henry Davis.

Worst trade: Trading the rights to Sid Luckman to the Bears for Eggs Manske. Selling Frank Filchock to the Redskins. Trading the rights to Bobby Layne to the Bears for Ray Evans. Trading Len Dawson and Gern Nagler to the Browns for Junior Wren and Preston Carpenter. Giving the Bears a number 1 for Ed Brown. Trading Bill Nelsen and Jim Bradshaw to the Browns for Dick Shiner, Frank Parker and a number 2. Weirdest of all was obtaining Rudy Bukich from the Bears for future considerations that two years later turned out to be returning Rudy to the Bears now that they needed him.

Title winners: Terry Bradshaw, 4; Ben Roethlisberger, 1.

Hall of Famers: Terry Bradshaw, Bobby Layne, Len Dawson.

All Pro/Pro Bowl seasons: Terry Bradshaw, 3; Bobby Layne, 1; Jim Finks, 1; Kordell Stewart, 1; Ben Roethlisberger, 1.

QBs as coaches: Frank Filchock was 7–20–1 in Denver. Ted Marchibroda was 87–98–1 with the Colts and Ravens. Allie Sherman was 63–59–4 with the Giants. Ron Meyer was 54–50 in New England and Indianapolis. Tony Dungy was 114–62 in Tampa and Indianapolis.

Underrated: Jim Finks never had a lot to work with but was a talented passer in the 1950s.

Overrated: Neil O'Donnell compiled nice statistics but was not a clutch performer.

Best Nicknames: Paul "Pelican" Held, Terry "Lil' Abner" or "Ozark Ike" Bradshaw, Jefferson Street Joe Gilliam, Kordell "Slash" Stewart and Big Ben Roethlisberger.

Time Capsule: The Steelers were last team to drop the single-wing. The Immaculate Reception from Bradshaw to Franco Harris. Bradshaw's bombs to Swann and Stallworth in several Super Bowls. Slash Stewart and Antwan Randle El showed the Steeler proclivity for trick plays and versatile performers.

What If: If Vic Eaton were cut in 1955, would Johnny Unitas become a star in Pittsburgh. Would he be as successful as he was in Baltimore under Weeb Eubank? If Joe Gilliam were more mature, would Terry Bradshaw be remembered as a dopey, flakey flop?

Off the field: Bobby Layne was known for living the high life. Living the high life ended Joe Gilliam's career and life prematurely. Tailback Whizzer White served on the U.S. Supreme Court for decades. Kent Nix was the son of Giant tailback Emery Nix. Terry Bradshaw, whose brother Craig played quarterback for the Oilers, appeared in five movies including *Failure to Launch, Cannonball Run* and *Smokey and the Bandit II*, two TV movies and 15 episodes of such TV series as *Everybody Loves Raymond, Married ... with Children* and *Malcolm in the Middle.*

Quarterback Bibliography

Bobby Layne *see* Detroit Lions

Earl Morrall *see* Detroit Lions

Len Dawson *see* Kansas City Chiefs

Jack Kemp *see* Buffalo Bills

Jim Finks

Finks, Jim. *It's Been a Pleasure.* Newport Beach, CA: AMO Productions, 2003.

Terry Bradshaw

Bradshaw, Terry, and Charles Conn. *No Easy Game.* Old Tappan, NJ: F.H. Revell, 1973.

Bradshaw, Terry and David Diles. *Terry Bradshaw: Man of Steel.* Grand Rapids, MI: Zondervan, 1979.

Bradshaw, Terry, and Buddy Martin. *Looking Deep.* Chicago: Contemporary Books, 1989.

Bradshaw, Terry, and David Fisher. *It's Only a Game.* New York: Pocket Books, 2001.

Bradshaw, Terry, and David Fisher. *Keep It Simple.* New York: Atria Books, 2002.

Ben Roethlisberger

Roethlisberger: Pittsburgh's Own Big Ben. Champaign, IL: Sports Publishing, 2004.

Shribman, David, and Ed Bouchette. *Super Steelers: Pittsburgh Returns to Glory with a Championship Season.* Chicago: Triumph, 2006.

40

St. Louis Rams

Leading Passers, by Yards

Quarterback	Years	G	Att	Comp	Pct	Yds	Y/A	Y/Cp	TD	Int	Int %	Rating
Jim Everett	1986–93	107	3,277	1,847	56.4	23,758	7.2	12.9	142	123	3.75%	78.1
Roman Gabriel	1962–72	130	3,313	1,705	51.5	22,223	6.7	13.0	154	112	3.38%	74.3
Marc Bulger	2002–06	60	2,106	1,357	64.4	16,233	7.7	12.0	95	59	2.80%	91.3
Norm Van Brocklin	1949–57	104	1,897	1,011	53.3	16,114	8.5	15.9	118	127	6.69%	74.7
Kurt Warner	1998–03	54	1,634	1,087	66.5	14,105	8.6	13.0	101	64	3.92%	97.8
Bob Waterfield	1945–52	91	1,617	814	50.3	11,849	7.3	14.6	97	128	7.92%	61.6
Vince Ferragamo	1977–80, 1982–84	62	1,288	730	56.7	9,376	7.3	12.8	70	71	5.51%	74.8
Pat Haden	1976–81	65	1,363	731	53.6	9,296	6.8	12.7	52	60	4.40%	69.6
Billy Wade	1954–60	69	1,116	603	54	8,572	7.7	14.2	56	68	6.09%	70.5
Tony Banks	1996–98	44	1,263	685	54.2	8,333	6.6	12.2	36	42	3.33%	70.4
James Harris	1973–76	39	652	361	55.4	5,220	8.0	14.5	33	27	4.14%	81.2
Chris Miller	1994–95	26	722	405	56.1	4,727	6.5	11.7	34	29	4.02%	75.1

Quarterback	Years	G	Att	Comp	Pct	Yds	Y/A	Y/Cp	TD	Int	Int %	Rating
Parker Hall	1939–42	42	721	329	45.6	4,013	5.6	12.2	30	67	9.29%	38.5
Zeke Bratkowski	1961–63	30	531	279	52.5	3,559	6.7	12.8	20	35	6.59%	58.9
Bill Munson	1964–67	31	550	287	52.2	3,556	6.5	12.4	22	32	5.82%	61.6
Jamie Martin	1996, 2001–02, 2004–05	25	440	290	65.9	2,944	6.7	10.2	15	19	4.32%	78.3
John Hadl	1973–74	20	373	188	50.4	2,688	7.2	14.3	27	17	4.56%	79.3
Frank Ryan	1958–61	40	373	181	48.5	2,674	7.2	14.8	15	23	6.17%	60.1
Dieter Brock	1985	15	365	218	59.7	2,658	7.3	12.2	16	13	3.56%	82.0
Jeff Kemp	1981–85	24	353	173	49	2,395	6.8	13.8	14	9	2.55%	73.8

Quarterback	Rush Att	Rush Yds	Rush Avg	TD
Jim Everett	191	510	2.7	4
Roman Gabriel	315	1146	3.6	28
Marc Bulger	87	224	2.6	8
Norm Van Brocklin	72	35	0.5	8
Kurt Warner	78	202	2.6	1
Bob Waterfield	75	21	0.3	13
Vince Ferragamo	51	62	1.2	2
Pat Haden	124	609	4.9	6
Billy Wade	159	685	4.3	10
Tony Banks	148	554	3.7	4
James Harris	76	262	3.4	8
Chris Miller	20	100	5.0	0
Parker Hall	312	1052	3.4	6
Zeke Bratkowski	22	49	2.2	3
Bill Munson	51	288	5.6	1
Jamie Martin	29	17	0.6	0
John Hadl	25	33	1.3	0
Frank Ryan	81	326	4.0	2
Dieter Brock	20	38	1.9	0
Jeff Kemp	44	160	3.6	1

Record Holders

Passing Yards, Career: 23,758 Jim Everett
Passing Yards, Season: 4,830 Kurt Warner 2001
Completion %, Career: 66.5% Kurt Warner
Completion %, Season: 68.7% Kurt Warner 2001
Touchdown Passes, Career: 154 Roman Gabriel
Touchdown Passes, Season: 41 Kurt Warner 1999
Interceptions, Career: 128 Bob Waterfield
Interceptions, Season: 24 Bob Waterfield 1949
Rating, Career: 97.8 Kurt Warner
Rating, Season: 109.2 Kurt Warner 1999
Rush Yards, Career: 1,146 Roman Gabriel
Rush Yards, Season: 458 Parker Hall 1939 (tailback); 212 Tony Banks 1996

Passers by Categories

Five best starters: Bob Waterfield won the NFL MVP and championship as a rookie and followed that with a Hall of Fame career. He had to share the job for his last three seasons, however, because the Rams came up with another Hall of Fame quarterback in Norm Van Brocklin who could throw any pass long or short. Both were great leaders although Van Brocklin was much more abrasive and less mobile. Roman Gabriel led the team to great success in the George Allen years. Kurt Warner had a short, but magnificent career as the quarterback of the "greatest team on turf." Fifth would be either Marc Bulger or Jim Everett. Both had some big seasons statistically, but neither won anything.

Worst starters, career: Zeke Bratkowski was a decent backup, but too mistake-prone as a starter. Dieter Brock, CFL star, only lasted one season in the NFL. Tony Banks was an uninspired fumble machine for three years.

Best stat line, season: Norm Van Brocklin led the league in passing in 1950 and averaged 8.9 yards per pass and threw 18 touchdowns to 14 interceptions. Bob Waterfield averaged 8.9 yards per pass and threw 13 touchdowns to 10 interceptions in 1951. Roman Gabriel won the MVP in 1969 for throwing 24 touchdowns to just 7 interceptions. John Hadl had his best season in 1973, throwing 22 touchdowns to 11 interceptions. Vince Ferragamo threw for 3,199 yards 30 touchdowns and 19 interceptions in 1980. Jim Everett in 1989 averaged 8.3 yards per pass and threw for 4,310 yards, 29 touchdowns and 17 interceptions. Kurt Warner had two monster seasons—1999 when he threw for 4,353 yards, 41 touchdowns and 13 interceptions and 2001 when he threw for 4,830 yards, 36 touchdowns and 22 interceptions. In both seasons he averaged over 8.7 yards per pass, although he topped that in 2000 with a 9.9 average. Marc Bulger threw for 4,301 yards 24 touchdowns and 8 interceptions in 2006.

Worst stat line, season: In 1947, Bob Waterfield only completed 43 percent of his passes for 8 touchdowns and 18 interceptions while averaging 5.5 yards per pass. In 1962, Zeke Bratkowski completed half his passes for 9 touchdowns and 16 interceptions. In 1981, Dan Pastorini showed he was finished as a pro by completing 42 percent of his passes for 2 touchdowns and 14 interceptions while averaging less than 5 yards per pass. In 1993, Jim Everett ended his Ram career by completing less than half his passes for 8 touchdowns and 12 interceptions while averaging 6 yards per pass.

Best stat line, playoffs: In the 1945 title win over the Redskins, Bob Waterfield went 14–27, 192, 2–2. In the 1951 title win over the Browns, Norm Van Brocklin went 4–6, 128, 1–0 in relief. In the 1989 NFC Conference loss to the 49ers, Jim Everett went 25–44, 315, 2–1. In a 1999 Divisional win over Minnesota, Kurt Warner went 27–33, 391, 5–1 and followed that in the Super Bowl win over the Titans by going 24–45, 414, 2–0.

Worst stat line, playoffs: In the 1950 title loss to the Browns, Bob Waterfield went 12–32, 312, 1–5. In the 1955 title loss to the Browns, Norm Van Brocklin went 11–25, 166, 1–6. In the 1974 NFC Conference loss to Minnesota, James Harris went 8–24, 95, 0–2. In the 1985 NFC Conference loss to the Bears, Dieter Brock went 10–31, 66, 0–1. In a 2003 Divisional loss to Carolina, Marc Bulger went 27–46, 332, 0–3.

Big Days: The first Cleveland Ram passer to exceed 300 yards passing in a game was Bob Waterfield with 329 yards on November 22, 1945, and he was the first Los Angeles Ram, too, with 312 yards on December 1, 1946. Chris Miller was the first St. Louis Ram to do it with 326 yards on October 1, 1995. The first Ram to reach 400 yards was Jim Hardy with 406 on October 31, 1948; Tony Banks reached 401 yards for the St. Louis Rams on November 2, 1997. Norm Van Brocklin had the biggest day in franchise history by throwing for 554 yards on September 1951. Kurt Warner had 30 300-yard games.

Running QBs: Parker Hall was a single-wing tailback who was talented at running and passing; twice he gained over 100 yards rushing in a game. Among quarterbacks, Pat Haden was an elusive scrambler by necessity due to his size. By contrast, Roman Gabriel and Tony Banks were big and tough to bring down although Banks was a fumbler. Gabriel scored 28 touchdowns.

Bomber: Norm Van Brocklin was brought into the 1951 title game against Cleveland with the Rams trailing in the fourth quarter for one reason: to throw the bomb. Van Brocklin hit Tom Fears for 73 yards and the Rams were champs.

Most accurate: Kurt Warner at his peak hit his receivers in the hands while they were in motion.

Leader: Bob Waterfield was cool and calm; Norm Van Brocklin was vocal and abusive.

Comeback King: Marc Bulger had 13 4th quarter comebacks and one in the playoffs. Roman Gabriel had 12, and Waterfield had 11.

Highest Football IQ: With his intelligence, Norm Van Brocklin was destined to be a coach although his temperament was problematic.

Toughest: Sturdy Roman Gabriel had a streak of 89 consecutive starts, and Jim Everett had one of 87 games.

First signal caller/T-Formation QB: The Bears' Carl Brumbaugh opened for the new Rams franchise in 1937 although he was soon replaced by Bob Snyder. Bob Waterfield was the first T quarterback for the Rams.

First TD pass: Bob Snyder hit Johnny Drake for a 38-yard score in a 21–3 win over the Eagles on September 21, 1937.

Black QBs: James Harris came over from Buffalo in 1973. Bernard Quarles was a replacement player in 1987. Tony Banks did not fulfill his potential from 1996 to 1998.

Tallest QB: Jim Everett, Hugh Millen, Roman Gabriel and Ron Smith were all 6'5".

Smallest QB: In single-wing days, Wayne Gift was 5'8", Ken Heineman and Marty Slovak were 5'9" while Albie Riesz, Carl Brumbaugh and Ed Godard were all 5'10". The shortest T quarterbacks were Steve Nemeth and Don Klosterman at 5'10" and Pat Haden at 5'11".

Oldest QB: Chris Chandler was 39 in 2004 and Steve Bono had some starts at 36 in 1998.

Rookie sensation: Parker Hall led the NFL in attempts, completions and was second in yards in 1939. Bob Waterfield took the Rams to the title in 1945 with an MVP season of leading the NFL in yards per pass with 9.4, touchdown passes with 14 and extra points. In limited action, Norm Van Brocklin averaged 10.4 yards per pass in 1949, and Roman Gabriel completed 56 percent of his passes in 1962. Kurt Warner threw only 11 passes as a rookie in 1998, but followed that with 4,353 yards and 41 touchdowns in 1999.

Late bloomer: Kurt Warner was 28 when he finally got an opportunity to play in 1999.

1st round picks: Parker Hall, 3rd in 1939, was a great success. Bobby Thomason, 7th in 1949, was inconsistent and overshadowed by the Rams' 2nd round pick, Norm Van Brocklin. Billy Wade, 1st in 1952, washed out in Los Angeles, but succeeded with the Bears. Roman Gabriel, 2nd in 1962, won an MVP award. Terry Baker, 1st in 1963, never found a position he was comfortable in and flopped. Bill Munson, 7th in 1964, was a career backup.

Out of position: Norm Van Brocklin, Parker Hall, Zeke Bratkowski, Jim Hardy and Jack Jacobs also punted. Bob Waterfield punted and place-kicked. Terry Baker was also tried at halfback and wide receiver. Don Burroughs and Nolan Cromwell were college quarterbacks who were switched to defensive back.

Long-time subs: Jamie Martin served as a backup for the Rams for five years.

QB controversy: The Rams have been the foremost dabblers in quarterback controversies for 50 years. Bob Waterfield was challenged by Norm Van Brocklin who was challenged by Billy Wade who was challenged by Frank Ryan who was challenged by Zeke Bratkowski who was challenged by Roman Gabriel who defeated the challenge by Terry Baker and Bill Munson and was succeeded by John Hadl who was challenged by James Harris who was challenged by Pat Haden and Ron Jaworski with Haden challenged by Vince Ferragamo. Since then, there have been controversies involving Kurt Warner and Trent Green and Warner and Marc Bulger. The Rams drafted a quarterback in the first round three years in a row 1962–64 with Gabriel, Baker and Munson. Only the Redskins duplicated that strange feat.

College affiliation: Four UCLA quarterbacks became Rams: Bob Waterfield, Bernard Quarles, Tommy Maddox and Steve Bono.

Ones who got away: Frank Ryan won a championship in Cleveland. Ron Jaworski took the Eagles to the Super Bowl and Trent Green has done well in Kansas City.

Has beens: Milt Plum, Karl Sweetan, Jerry Rhome, Pete Beathard, Joe Namath, Steve Bartkowski, Bert Jones, Dan Pastorini, Chuck Long, Bob Lee, Steve Dils, Dieter Brock, Mark Herrmann, Steve Walsh, Steve Bono, Chris Miller, Mark Rypien, Chris Chandler and Gus Frerotte.

Ruinous injuries: Kurt Warner's career was derailed by thumb injuries.

Best trade: Getting a number 1 from the Redskins for Rudy Bukich. Getting a number 1 and Jack Myers from the Eagles for Bobby Thomason and Jack Zilly. Getting a number 1 from the Cardinals for Jim Hardy. Getting Harold Jackson, Tony Baker, two number 1's and a number 2 from the Eagles for Roman Gabriel. Getting two number 1's, two number 2's and a number 3 from the Packers for John Hadl.

Worst trade: Giving a number 1 and number 2 to the Colts for Bert Jones. Giving Frank Ryan and Tom Wilson to the Browns for Larry Stephens, a number 3 and a number 6.

Title winners: Bob Waterfield, 1; Norm Van Brocklin, 1; Kurt Warner, 1.

Hall of Famers: Bob Waterfield, Norm Van Brocklin, Joe Namath.

All Pro/Pro Bowl seasons: Norm Van Brocklin, 5; Bob Waterfield, 5; Roman Gabriel, 3; Kurt Warner, 3; Jim Everett, 2; Parker Hall, 2; Marc Bulger, 2; John Hadl, 1; James Harris, 1.

QBs as coaches: Bob Snyder was 6–6 with the Rams; Bob Waterfield was 9–24–1 with the Rams; Norm Van Brocklin was 66–100–7 with Minnesota and Atlanta.

Underrated: Bob Waterfield's versatility of skills is unheard of today.

Overrated: Jim Everett racked up impressive numbers but was never much of a leader.

Best Nicknames: Parker "Bullet" Hall, Bob "Buckets" Waterfield, Norm "Dutchman" Van Brocklin, Roman "the Indian" Gabriel, James "Shack" Harris and Jim "Chrissie" Everett.

Time Capsule: Clark Shaughnessy opening the T to full throttle with three receivers. Norm Van Brocklin winning the 1951 championship with a 4th quarter bomb to Tom Fears. Kurt Warner winning the Super Bowl with a 4th quarter bomb to Isaac Bruce. Mike Martz's "Greatest Show on Turf" downfield passing attack.

What If: If Trent Green didn't get hurt in 1999, would he have led the Rams to the Super Bowl? If Kurt Warner didn't hurt his thumb, does the prime of his career extend longer?

Off the field: Jeff Kemp was the son of Jack Kemp. Pat Haden was a Rhodes Scholar. Joe Namath and Dan Pastorini had their best days on the field in other cities; they probably had more success off the field in LA. They also acted. Namath appeared in eight movies, three TV movies and over 20 episodes of popular TV series, while Pastorini appeared in *Trick or Treat*, *Killer Fish* and *The Florida Connection* as well as episodes of *Voyagers!* and *Fantasy Island*. Jim Everett is most remembered for knocking over obnoxious broadcaster Jim Rome when Rome referred to Jim as "Chris" as in Chris Evert the female tennis star. He also appeared in an episode of *1st and Ten*. Jack Jacobs appeared in *Triple Threat*. Bob Waterfield was married to movie star Jane Russell and appeared in *Jungle Manhunt*, *Triple Threat* and *Crazy Legs*. Norm Van Brocklin appeared in *The Long Gray Line*, *Crazy Legs* and an episode of *Red Skelton*. Roman Gabriel appeared in *The Undefeated* and *Skidoo* as well as episodes of *Perry Mason*, *Gilligan's Island*, *Ironside*, *Rowan and Martin*, *Wonder Woman*, *Khan* and *The Misadventures of Sheriff Lobo*. Bill Munson appeared in an episode of *Perry Mason*. Vince Ferragamo appeared in the TV movie *Policewoman Centerfold* and an episode of *Dynasty*. Rudy Bukich appeared in *Spartacus* and an episode of *The Big Valley*. Jim Hardy appeared in both *Yes Sir That's My Baby* and *All American*.

Quarterback Bibliography

Kurt Warner

Warner, Kurt, and Michael Silver. *All Things Possible: My Story of Faith, Football, and the Miracle Season*. San Francisco: Harper, 2000.

Wolfe, Rich, and Bob Margeas. *Kurt Warner: And the Last Shall Be First*. Chicago: Triumph, 2002.

Norm Van Brocklin

Van Brocklin, Norm, and Hugh Brown. *Norm Van Brocklin's Football Book: Passing, Punting, Quarterbacking*. New York: Ronald Press, 1961.

Roman Gabriel

Gabriel, Roman. *Player of the Year: Roman Gabriel's Football Journal*. New York: World, 1970.

Gustkey, Earl. *Roman Gabriel: Outstanding Pro*. New York: Putnam, 1971.

Haden, Pat, and Robert Blair. *Pat Haden: My Rookie Season with the Los Angeles Rams*. New York: William Morrow, 1977.

Joe Namath *see* New York Jets

Bert Jones *see* Indianapolis Colts

Steve Bartkowski *see* Atlanta

41

San Diego Chargers

Leading Passers, by Yards

Quarterback	Years	G	Att	Comp	Pct	Yds	Y/A	Y/Cp	TD	Int	Int %	Rating
Dan Fouts	1973–87	181	5,604	3,297	58.8	43,040	7.7	13.1	254	242	4.32%	80.2
John Hadl	1962–72	154	3,640	1,824	50.1	26,938	7.4	14.8	201	211	5.80%	68.9
Stan Humphries	1992–97	71	2,350	1,335	56.8	16,085	6.8	12.0	85	73	3.11%	77.1
Drew Brees	2001–05	58	1,809	1,125	62.2	12,348	6.8	11.0	80	53	2.93%	84.9
Jack Kemp	1960–62	30	815	389	47.7	5,996	7.4	15.4	37	49	6.01%	62.6
Doug Flutie	2001–04	11	737	408	55.4	4,906	6.7	12.0	25	22	2.99%	74.8
John Friesz	1990–93	29	747	401	53.7	4,396	5.9	11.0	19	20	2.68%	68.7
Jim Harbaugh	1999–00	21	636	372	58.5	4,177	6.6	11.2	18	24	3.77%	71.9
Billy Joe Tolliver	1989–90	20	595	305	51.3	3,671	6.2	12.0	21	24	4.03%	65.5
Tobin Rote	1963–64	28	449	244	54.3	3,666	8.2	15.0	29	32	7.13%	73.2
Philip Rivers	2004–06	20	490	301	61.4	3,536	7.2	11.7	23	10	2.04%	90.5
Ed Luther	1980–84	61	460	245	53.3	3,187	6.9	13.0	12	23	5.00%	63.2
Ryan Leaf	1998–00	21	567	272	48	3,172	5.6	11.7	13	33	5.82%	48.8
Craig Whelihan	1997–98	9	557	267	47.9	3,160	5.7	11.8	14	29	5.21%	52.4
Mark Herrmann	1985–87	18	355	220	62	2,569	7.2	11.7	13	18	5.07%	75.0
Jim McMahon	1989	12	318	176	55.3	2,132	6.7	12.1	10	10	3.14%	73.5

Quarterback	Rush Att	Rush Yds	Rush Avg	TD
Dan Fouts	224	476	2.1	13
John Hadl	288	1013	3.5	15
Stan Humphries	122	240	2.0	5
Drew Brees	135	366	2.7	4
Jack Kemp	105	371	3.5	15
Doug Flutie	92	405	4.4	5
John Friesz	21	24	1.1	0
Jim Harbaugh	50	150	3.0	0
Billy Joe Tolliver	21	22	1.0	0
Tobin Rote	34	50	1.5	2
Philip Rivers	53	43	0.8	0
Ed Luther	20	-19	-1.0	0
Ryan Leaf	55	134	2.4	0
Craig Whelihan	31	67	2.2	0
Mark Herrmann	24	-3	-0.1	0
Jim McMahon	29	141	4.9	0

Record Holders

Passing Yards, Career: 43,040 Dan Fouts
Passing Yards, Season: 4,802 Dan Fouts 1981
Completion %, Career: 62.2% Drew Brees
Completion %, Season: 65.7% Mark Herrmann
   1985 (201 att.); 65.5% Drew Brees 2004

Touchdown Passes, Career: 254 Dan Fouts
Touchdown Passes, Season: 33 Dan Fouts 1981
Interceptions, Career: 242 Dan Fouts
Interceptions, Season: 32 John Hadl 1968
Rating, Career: 84.9 Drew Brees; Philip Rivers
   90.5 (490 att)
Rating, Season: 104.8 Drew Brees 2004

Rush Yards, Career: 1,013 John Hadl
Rush Yards, Season: 192 Doug Flutie 2001

Passers by Categories

Five best starters: Dan Fouts led an explosive Charger attack that scored at least 40 points 21 times in his tenure. John Hadl lived on the long ball in the wide-open AFL. Stan Humphries had a strong arm, but was more of a game manager who made the Chargers winners. Drew Brees proved himself an able quarterback, but was undone by injuries, the salary cap and a promising understudy. At the end of his long career, Tobin Rote led the Chargers to their greatest season and added an AFL title to the NFL one he won in Detroit.

Worst starters, career: Mark Herrmann, Billy Joe Tolliver and John Friesz were just generally lousy; however, Ed Luther, Craig Whelihan and Ryan Leaf were truly awful. Luther threw 23 interceptions to just 12 touchdowns. Whelihan completed 47.9 percent of his passes for 14 touchdowns and 29 interceptions while averaging 5.7 yards per pass. Ryan Leaf completed 48 percent of his passes for 13 touchdowns and 33 interceptions while averaging 5.6 yards per pass and thoroughly embarrassing the organization off the field as well.

Best stat line, season: In 1960, Jack Kemp completed 52 percent of his passes for 3,018 yards for 20 touchdowns. In 1963, Tobin Rote led the AFL by completing 59.4 percent of his passes and averaging 8.8 yards per pass while throwing 20 touchdowns. In 1966 John Hadl threw for 23 touchdowns and only 14 interceptions. Dan Fouts threw for over 4,000 yards from 1979 through 1981. In 1981, he completed 59 percent of his passes for 4,802 yards, 33 touchdowns and just 17 interceptions. In 1994, Stan Humphries completed 58 percent of his passes for 3,209 yards and 17 touchdowns to just 12 interceptions. In 2004, Drew Brees completed 65.5 percent of his passes for 27 touchdowns and just 7 interceptions.

Worst stat line, season: As a rookie in 1962, John Hadl completed 41 percent of his passes for 15 touchdowns and 24 interceptions; in 1968 he topped that interception total with 32. In Marty Domres rookie season of 1969, he completed 42 percent of his passes for 2 touch-

downs and 10 interceptions. Dan Fouts completed 45 percent of his passes as a rookie in 1973 for 6 touchdowns and 13 interceptions and followed that in 1975 by throwing 2 touchdowns to 10 interceptions. Stepping in for Fouts, Ed Luther threw 7 touchdowns and 17 interceptions in 1983. In 1998, Craig Whelihan completed 46 percent of his passes for 8 touchdowns and 19 interceptions while averaging just 5.6 yards per pass. In that same season, Ryan Leaf completed 45 percent of his passes for 2 touchdowns and 15 interceptions while averaging 5.3 yards per pass. Erik Kramer finished his career in San Diego in 1999, throwing for the familiar 2 touchdowns to 10 interceptions.

Best stat line, playoffs: In the 1963 AFL title win over the Patriots, Tobin Rote went 10–15, 173, 2–0. In the unforgettable Divisional overtime victory over the Dolphins in 1981, Dan Fouts went 33–53, 433, 3–1. In a 1982 Wildcard win over Pittsburgh, Fouts went 27–42, 333, 3–0.

Worst stat line, playoffs: In the 1960 AFL title loss to the Oilers, Jack Kemp went 21–41, 171, 0–2; he followed that in the 1961 title loss to the Oilers by going 17–32, 226, 0–4. In the 1964 AFL title loss to Buffalo, Tobin Rote went 10–26, 118, 1–2. In the 1965 AFL title loss to the Bills, John Hadl went 11–23, 140, 0–2. In a 1979 Divisional loss to the Oilers, Dan Fouts went 25–47, 333, 0–5. In a 1982 Divisional loss to the Dolphins, Fouts went 15–34, 191, 1–5. In a 1992 Divisional loss to Miami, Stan Humphries went 18–41, 140, 0–4. In a heartbreaking Divisional loss to the Patriots in 2006, Philip Rivers went 14–32, 230, 0–1.

Big Days: The first passer to exceed 300 yards passing in a game was Jack Kemp with 337 yards on September 18, 1960. The first to reach 400 yards was Dan Fouts with 444 on October 19, 1980; it was the biggest day in franchise history, and he duplicated the yardage on December 11, 1982. Fouts had 51 300-yard games and six 400-yard games.

Running QBs: The Chargers have employed several veteran quarterbacks who were adept at running in their younger years, including Tobin Rote, Bobby Douglass, Jim Harbaugh and Doug Flutie. John Hadl and Drew Brees were pretty mobile in the pocket. Jack Kemp scored 15 touchdowns in a little over two seasons as a Charger.

Bomber: Dan Fouts threw the ball downfield, but Jack Kemp, Tobin Rote and John Hadl all flourished throwing bombs to Lance Alworth in Sid Gillman's wide open attack.

Most accurate: Fouts hit his targets in stride regularly.

Leader: Dan Fouts was a forceful presence on the field.

Comeback King: Fouts had 23 4th quarter comebacks, plus three in the postseason. John Hadl had 15.

Highest Football IQ: Fouts was the son of a coach, but Doug Flutie was probably even more insightful on the field.

Toughest: John Hadl had a streak of 73 consecutive starts, and Dan Fouts reached 69 straight.

First signal caller/T-Formation QB: NFL/CFL refugee Jack Kemp.

First TD pass: Jack Kemp hit Ralph Anderson for a 46-yard score in the Los Angeles Chargers' 21–20 win over the Dallas Texans on September, 10, 1960. As a San Diego Charger, Kemp hit Dave Kocourek for 7 yards in a 34–24 win over the Oilers on September 24, 1961.

Black QBs: James Harris finished his career in San Diego from 1977–79. Cleo Lemon was on the squad but never appeared in a game in 2004.

Tallest QB: The Chargers have had several 6'5" quarterbacks throughout their existence, from Dick Wood to Steve Tensi to Cliff Olander to Sean Salisbury to Jim Everett to Craig Whelihan to Ryan Leaf to Phillip Rivers.

Smallest QB: Doug Flutie was 5'9". Jon Brittenum and Dan Henning were just 6'.

Oldest QB: Flutie was 42 in 2004, a sometime starter at 41 in 2003, 40 in 2002, and a full-time starter at 39 in 2001. Johnny Unitas started the last four games of his career at 40 in 1973.

Rookie sensation: None, although Drew Brees threw for 17 touchdowns and 3,284 yards in his second season after throwing just 27 passes as a rookie. Philip Rivers threw for 22 touchdowns and 9 interceptions and 3,388 yards in his third year after throwing just 30 passes in his first two years behind Brees.

Late bloomer: Jack Kemp was 25 in 1960 when the AFL gave him a chance. Dan Fouts didn't really catch on till he was 27 in 1978. Stan Humphries won the job at 27 in 1992.

1st round picks: Marty Domres, 9th in 1969, was a career backup. Ryan Leaf, 2nd in 1998, was a colossal flop of legendary proportions both on and off the field. Philip Rivers was obtained for Eli Manning.

Out of position: Original Charger Bob Laraba played linebacker and some quarterback. Both he and John Hadl punted as well.

Long-time subs: Several Chargers have served as backups for three years: Marty Domres, Bruce Mathison, Wayne Clark, Ed Luther, Mark Herrmann and Mark Vlasic.

QB controversy: John Hadl had to beat out Tobin Rote for the starter's job and later held off Marty Domres. San Diego has been involved in draft controversies involving both of the Manning brothers. When the Colts took Peyton, the Chargers were left with Ryan Leaf in 1998. Six years later, Eli declared he would not sign with the Chargers. They drafted him anyway and traded him to the Giants for Phillip Rivers and that drama is still playing itself out now that Drew Brees went to New Orleans and Rivers took the starting job.

College affiliation: Purdue Boilermakers who became Chargers include Mark Herrmann, Jim Everett and Drew Brees.

Ones who got away: Drew Brees will most likely continue to have a good career elsewhere.

Has beens: Bobby Clatterbuck, Johnny Unitas, Bill Munson, Bobby Douglass, Clint Longley, Bruce Mathison, Bob Gagliano, James Harris, Mark Malone, David Archer, Jim McMahon, Mark Herrmann, Todd Philcox, Sean Salisbury, Jim Everett, Erik Kramer and Billy Volek.

Ruinous injuries: An injured Jack Kemp was claimed off waivers by Buffalo because of a front office mistake. Drew Brees' shoulder problems sealed his doom as a Charger.

Best trade: Getting two number 1's (Russ Washington and Marty Domres) from Denver for Steve Tensi. Getting a number 1 (Johnny Rodgers) and John Andrews from the Colts for Marty Domres. Getting Stan Humphries from the Redskins for a number 3.

Worst trade: Losing Jack Kemp on waivers to the Bills. Giving the Bears a number 2 for Jim McMahon. Giving the Cowboys a number 1 and a number two for Clint Longley.

Title winners: Tobin Rote won an AFL title in San Diego.

Hall of Famers: Dan Fouts and Johnny Unitas.

All Pro/Pro Bowl seasons: Dan Fouts, 6; John Hadl, 5; Jack Kemp, 2; Tobin Rote, 1; Drew Brees, 1.

QBs as coaches: Kay Stephenson went 10–26 in Buffalo. Dan Henning went 38–73–1 in Atlanta and San Diego.

Underrated: Stan Humphries was a solid, professional quarterback who took the Chargers to a Super Bowl.

Overrated: Jim McMahon was washed up and obnoxious.

Best Nicknames: Mark "Pickle" Vlasic and Cryin' Ryan Leaf the Boy Blunder.

Time Capsule: The bombs to Lance Alworth. The down-the-field attack of Sid Gillman and Don Coryell. The sad end of Johnny Unitas. Fouts averaging 300 yards a game passing.

What If: If the Chargers had held onto Jack Kemp in 1962, would their history be different? If they had kept Drew Brees, would San Diego have won more games?

Off the field: Jim McMahon was rude and belligerent off the field; ten years later Ryan Leaf made McMahon look like a perfect gentleman. Dan Fouts appeared in *The Waterboy* and an episode of *The Fall Guy*. Rick Neuheisel was an advisor on the set of *Point Break*. Johnny Unitas appeared in *M*A*S*H*, *Gus* and *Any Given Sunday* as well as episodes of *The Simpsons*, *Coach* and the *Adventures of Pete and Pete*. Doug Flutie appeared in *Second String*. Jim Everett appeared in an episode of *1st and Ten*. Bill Munson appeared in an episode of *Perry Mason*. Sean Salisbury was in *The Benchwarmers* and *The Longest Yard* remake. Charlie Whitehurst's father David played quarterback for the Packers.

Quarterback Bibliography

Jack Kemp *see* Buffalo Bills

Johnny Unitas *see* Indianapolis Colts

Marty Domres *see* Indianapolis Colts

Jim McMahon *see* Chicago Bears

Doug Flutie *see* Buffalo Bills

42

San Francisco 49ers

Leading Passers, by Yards

Quarterback	Years	G	Att	Comp	Pct	Yds	Y/A	Y/Cp	TD	Int	Int %	Rating
Joe Montana	1979–92	167	4,600	2,929	63.7	35,124	7.6	12.0	244	123	2.67%	93.5
John Brodie	1957–73	201	4,491	2,469	55	31,548	7.0	12.8	214	224	4.99%	72.3
Steve Young	1987–99	132	3,648	2,400	65.8	29,907	8.2	12.5	221	86	2.36%	101.4
Jeff Garcia	1999–03	47	2,360	1,449	61.4	16,408	7.0	11.3	113	56	2.37%	88.3
Y.A. Tittle	1951–60	112	2,194	1,226	55.9	16,016	7.3	13.1	108	134	6.11%	70.0
Frankie Albert	1946–52	90	1,564	831	53.1	10,795	6.9	13.0	115	98	6.27%	73.5
Steve DeBerg	1978–80	39	1,201	670	55.8	7,220	6.0	10.8	37	60	5.00%	63.1
Steve Spurrier	1967–75	78	840	441	52.5	5,250	6.3	11.9	33	48	5.71%	61.2
Tim Rattay	2001–05	28	619	376	60.7	4,214	6.8	11.2	27	20	3.23%	82.1
Frankie Albert (NFL only)	1950–52	36	601	316	52.6	3,847	6.4	12.2	27	43	7.15%	57.7

Quarterback	Years	G	Att	Comp	Pct	Yds	Y/A	Y/Cp	TD	Int	Int %	Rating
Alex D. Smith	2005–06	25	607	341	56.2	3,765	6.2	11.0	17	27	4.45%	65.5
Jim Plunkett	1976–77	26	491	254	51.7	3,285	6.7	12.9	22	30	6.11%	62.5
Elvis Grbac	1994–96	42	430	284	66	3,098	7.2	10.9	18	16	3.72%	85.6

Quarterback	Rush Att	Rush Yds	Rush Avg	TD
Joe Montana	416	1597	3.8	20
John Brodie	235	1167	5.0	22
Steve Young	608	3581	5.9	37
Jeff Garcia	319	1561	4.9	21
Y.A. Tittle	196	637	3.3	23
Frankie Albert	329	1272	3.9	27
Steve DeBerg	38	34	0.9	1
Steve Spurrier	49	210	4.3	2
Tim Rattay	39	69	1.8	0
Frankie Albert	329	1272	3.9	27
Alex D. Smith	73	250	3.4	2
Jim Plunkett	47	166	3.5	1
Elvis Grbac	56	55	1.0	4

Record Holders

Passing Yards, Career: 35,124 Joe Montana
Passing Yards, Season: 4,278 Jeff Garcia 2000
Completion %, Career: 65.8% Steve Young
Completion %, Season: 70.3% Steve Young 1994
Touchdown Passes, Career: 244 Joe Montana
Touchdown Passes, Season: 36 Steve Young 1998
Interceptions, Career: 224 John Brodie
Interceptions, Season: 28 Y.A. Tittle 1955
Rating, Career: 101.4 Steve Young
Rating, Season: 112.8 Steve Young 1994; 112.4 Joe
  Montana 1989
Rush Yards, Career: 3,581 Steve Young
Rush Yards, Season: 537 Steve Young 1992

Passers by Categories

Five best starters: Joe Montana is generally considered one of the three top quarterbacks of all time. Steve Young followed Montana with a legendary career of his own. Throughout the 1950s, Y.A. Tittle was a great, but underappreciated quarterback because he never won a title. John Brodie had a similar career to Tittle in the 1960s and 1970s and also was underappreciated. Frankie Albert was known for being the top ball-handler of his time.

Worst starters, career: Steve Spurrier never lived up to his Heisman Trophy billing. Jim Plunkett wouldn't emerge as a top quarter-back until he was cut by San Francisco and salvaged by the Raiders across the Bay. The dreadful mid-to-late 1970s were piloted by faceless quarterbacks like Joe Reed (4 touchdowns and 13 interceptions), Scott Bull (3 touchdowns and 17 interceptions) and Tom Owen (11 touchdowns and 17 interceptions). Ken Dorsey could only complete 54 percent of his passes in what was once considered the idiot-proof West Coast offense.

Best stat line, season: Frankie Albert in 1948 led the All America Conference with 29 touchdown passes and was co-winner of the league MVP with Otto Graham. Y.A. Tittle averaged 8.2 yards per pass and threw 20 touchdowns in 1953. In a 14-game season in 1965, John Brodie threw 30 touchdowns while completing 61.9 percent of his passes for an average of 8 yards per pass. In 1970, Brodie completed 59 percent of his passes for 24 touchdowns and only 10 interceptions. Joe Montana's best years were 1984 when he completed 64.6 percent of his passes for 3,630 yards, 28 touchdowns and just 10 interceptions, a passer rating of 102.9; 1987 when he completed 66.8 percent of his passes for 3,054 yards, 31 touchdowns and just 13 interceptions, a passer rating of 102.1; and 1989 when he completed 70.2 percent of his passes for 3,521 yards, 26 touchdowns and just 8 interceptions, a passer rating of 112.4. Steve Young's best years were 1992 when he completed 66.7 percent of his passes for 3,465 yards, 25 touchdowns and just 7 interceptions, a passer rating of

107; 1994 when he completed 70.3 percent of his passes for 3,969 yards, 35 touchdowns and just 10 interceptions, a passer rating of 112.8; and 1998 when he completed 62.3 percent of his passes for 4,170 yards, 36 touchdowns and just 12 interceptions, a passer rating of 101.1. Jeff Garcia in 2000 threw for 4,278 yards and 31 touchdowns with only 10 interceptions, and followed that in 2001 with 32 touchdowns to 12 interceptions.

Worst stat line, season: Frankie Albert threw 14 touchdowns to 23 interceptions in 1950. Y.A. Tittle threw 17 touchdowns to 28 interceptions in 1955 while completing just 51 percent of his passes. Joe Reed in 1973 averaged 5.2 yards per pass and threw 2 touchdowns to 6 interceptions while completing 44.7 percent of his passes. Tom Owen in 1974 completed 47.8 percent of his passes for 10 touchdowns and 15 interceptions. In 1978, Scott Bull completed 39 percent of his passes for 1 touchdown and 11 interceptions while Steve DeBerg completed 45 percent of his passes for 8 touchdowns and 22 interceptions; neither one averaged more than 5.4 yards per throw. Alex Smith had a nightmare rookie season, throwing 1 touchdown to 11 interceptions while averaging 5.3 yards per pass.

Best stat line, playoffs: Joe Montana had a suite of great postseason games. In a 1989 Divisional win over Minnesota, he went 17–24, 241, 4–0. In the 1989 NFC Conference win over the Rams, he went 26–30, 262, 2–0. In the Super Bowl win over the Dolphins, he went 24–35, 331, 3–0. In the second Super Bowl win over the Bengals, he went 23–36, 357, 2–0. In the Super Bowl win over the Broncos, he went 22–29, 297, 5–0. Steve Young went 24–36, 325, 6–0 in the Super Bowl win over the Chargers.

Worst stat line, playoffs: In the 1971 NFC Conference loss to the Cowboys, John Brodie went 14–30, 184, 0–3. In a 1995 Divisional loss to the Packers, Steve Young went 32–65, 328, 0–2. In a 1996 Divisional loss to the Packers, Elvis Grbac went 19–36, 125, 1–3.

Big Days: The first passer to exceed 300 yards passing in a game was Y.A. Tittle with 341 yards on November 9, 1952. The first to reach 400 yards was Joe Montana with 408 on November 21, 1982. Montana had the biggest day in franchise history by throwing for 476 yards on October 14, 1990, and had 34 300-yard games. Steve Young had 28 300-yard games.

Running QBs: Steve Young has the second highest all-time rushing total among quarterbacks, including a high of 537 in 1992 and a 100-yard game in 1990. Billy Kilmer ran for 509 yards in 1961—including three 100-yard games—when the 49ers introduced the Shotgun as their primary offense, but part of that was as a halfback. The 49ers have a long history of very mobile quarterbacks from Frankie Albert to the young Y.A. Tittle to John Brodie to Joe Montana, Young and Jeff Garcia. All scored over 20 touchdowns; Steve Young topping the list with 31. This is not to mention second stringers like George Mira and Bob Waters.

Bomber: Y.A. Tittle was expert at the bomb even before he and R.C. Owens invented the "Alley Oop" or jump ball.

Most accurate: While Steve Young has a slightly higher completion percentage, no one could top Joe Montana in putting the ball where it needed to be especially in the clutch.

Leader: There has never been a cooler leader on the football field than Joe Montana.

Comeback King: Montana had 26 4th quarter comebacks, plus three in the postseason. Y.A. Tittle and John Brodie had 19 and Steve young had 17 plus one in the playoffs.

Highest Football IQ: While Young was smart, Montana was brilliant.

Toughest: Frankie Albert had a streak of 79 consecutive starts in the AAFC and NFL. Jeff Garcia started 61 straight games. Montana came back from back surgery in the same season.

First signal caller/T-Formation QB: Frankie Albert.

First TD pass: In the 49ers' first game in the All America Conference on September 8, 1946, Frankie Albert hit Len Eshmont for a 66-yard score in a 21–7 win over the New York Yankees. In their first NFL Game on September 17, 1950, Albert hit Paul Salata for a 2-yard score in a 21–17 loss to the New York Yanks.

Black QBs: Mark Stevens and Ed Blount were both replacement players in1987.

Tallest QB: Elvis Grbac and Scott Bull were both 6'5".

Smallest QB: Frankie Albert and Jesse Freitas were both 5'10". Parker Hall, Hal Ledyard, Jim Cason, Billy Kilmer, George Mira Ed Blount and Ty Detmer were all 6'.

Oldest QB: John Brodie was a 38-year old starter in 1973 as was Steve Young in 1999.

Rookie sensation: Frankie Albert threw 14 touchdowns and 14 interceptions in 1946. Jeff Garcia was thrust into the starter's role in 1999 and completed 60 percent of his passes for 11 touchdowns and 11 interceptions. Joe Montana only threw 23 passes as a rookie in 1979, but in his second season, he completed 64.5 percent of his passes for 15 touchdowns and 9 interceptions.

Late bloomer: Steve Young was blocked by Joe Montana until he was 30 in 1991. Jeff Garcia came down from Canada at 29 in 1999. Frankie Albert joined the fledgling 49ers in 1946 at 26 and was 30 when the leagues merged.

1st round picks: When the original Baltimore Colts were disbanded in 1951, their players were available to be drafted, and the 49ers grabbed Y.A. Tittle with the 3rd pick in the 1951 draft. Earl Morrall, 2nd in 1956, served as trade bait. John Brodie, 3rd in 1957, had a long, stormy yet successful career in San Francisco. Dave Baker, 5th in 1959, was converted to defensive back. Billy Kilmer, 11th in 1961, had his career derailed for several years due to a car accident. Steve Spurrier, 3rd in 1967, was the team's punter and backup quarterback. Jim Druckenmiller, 26th in 1997, was disastrously wrong for the 49ers and the NFL. Alex Smith, 1st in 2005, is a work in progress.

Out of position: Jim Cason and Billy Kilmer also played halfback. Dave Baker was converted to defensive back. Freddie Solomon and Arneaz Battle were converted to wide receiver. Frankie Albert, Earl Morrall and Steve Spurrier also punted.

Long-time subs: Steve Spurrier backed up John Brodie for six of his nine seasons by the Bay. For part of that, he overlapped with George Mira who backed up Brodie for five years.

QB controversy: Y.A. Tittle challenged Frankie Albert and was eventually challenged by John Brodie. Brodie had to beat back fan favorite backups Mira and Spurrier. The handoff from Joe Montana to Steve Young led to a messy divorce in the trading of Montana to Kansas City.

College affiliation: Five Stanford quarterbacks have played for the 49ers — Frankie Albert, John Brodie, Jim Plunkett, Guy Benjamin and Steve Stenstrom.

Ones who got away: Earl Morrall and Steve DeBerg had long careers as both starters and backups. Billy Kilmer became a grizzled leader in New Orleans and Washington.

Has beens: Arnold Galiffa, Lamar McHan, Norm Snead, Jim Plunkett, Jeff Kemp, Bob Gagliano, Mike Moroski, Rick Mirer and Trent Dilfer.

Ruinous injuries: Montana's career was interrupted twice by injury, and the second one cost him his starting job. Steve Young's career was ended by concussions.

Best trade: Getting Steve Young from the Bucs for a number 2 and a number 4. Getting Randy Beisler from the Eagles for George Mira.

Worst trade: Giving up Y.A. Tittle to the Giants for Lou Cordileone. Giving up three number 1's (Pete Brock, Tim Fox and Raymond Clayborn), a number 2 (Horace Ivory) and Tom Owen to the Patriots for Jim Plunkett.

Title winners: Joe Montana, 4; Steve Young, 1.

Hall of Famers: Y.A. Tittle, Joe Montana and Steve Young.

All Pro/Pro Bowl seasons: Joe Montana, 7; Steve Young, 7; Y.A. Tittle, 4; Frankie Albert, 4; John Brodie, 3; Jeff Garcia, 3.

QBs as coaches: Frankie Albert went 19–16–1 with the 49ers. Steve Spurrier went 12–20 in Washington.

Underrated: John Brodie played well on some very lousy 49er teams for many years.

Overrated: Jeff Garcia got a lot of benefit from the system he played in.

Best Nicknames: "Joe Cool" Montana.

Time Capsule: Y.A. Tittle and R.C. Owens invented the Alley Oop pass. Red Hickey tried to use the Shotgun as the 49er base offense in 1961. Bill Walsh perfected the West Coast Offense with the 49ers. Montana threw the pass that became The Catch for Dwight Clark. Young shook the Montana monkey off his back with 6-touchdown passes Super Bowl.

What If: If Joe Montana had been drafted by another team, would Walsh have stuck with Steve DeBerg? How much success would DeBerg have had with the 49ers?

Off the field: Billy Kilmer was in the Bobby Layne mold and appeared in *The Last Time I Saw Archie.* Ty Detmer's brother Koy also played quarterback in the NFL, as did Jeff Kemp's father Jack and John Brodie's son-in-law Chris Chandler. Frankie Albert starred in *The Spirit of Stanford.* Y.A. Tittle appeared in *Any Given Sunday.* Steve Young appeared in the

Mormon film *The Singles Ward* and in episodes of *Beverly Hills 90210, Wings, Dharma and Greg, Listen Up* and *Lois and Clark*. Rick Mirer appeared in *Jerry Maguire*. Steve DeBerg appeared in an episode of *Arli$$*.

Quarterback Bibliography

Y.A. Tittle *see* New York Giants

John Brodie
Brodie, John, and James D. Houston. *Open Field.* Boston: Houghton Mifflin, 1974.

Earl Morrall *see* Detroit Lions

Steve Spurrier
Spurrier, Steve, and Mel Larson. *It's Always Too Soon to Quit: the Steve Spurrier Story.* Grand Rapids, MI: Zondervan, 1968.
Spurrier, Steve, and Norm Carlson. *Gators: the Inside Story of Florida's First SEC Title.* Orlando, FL: Tribune Publications, 1992.
Martin, Buddy. *Down Where the Old Gators Play: How Steve Spurrier Brought Glory Home to Florida Football.* Dubuque, IA: Kendall/Hunt Publishing, 1995.
Martin, Buddy. *Reign of the Swamp Fox: Florida's Steve Spurrier Tracks the SEC Legends.* Dubuque, IA: Kendall/Hunt Publishing, 1996.
Mabe, Logan, and Mike Cobb. *Spurrier: the #1 Gator.* Lakeland, FL: The Ledger, 1996.
Chastain, Bill. *The Steve Spurrier Story: From Heisman to Head Ball Coach.* Lanham, MD: Taylor Trade, 2002.
Spurrier, Steve, and Gene Frenette. *Quotable Spurrier: the Nerve, Verve and Victorious Words of and About Steve Spurrier, America's Most Scrutinized Football Coach.* Nashville, TN: TowleHouse, 2002.

Jim Plunkett *see* OAK

Marty Domres *see* IND

Joe Montana
Montana, Joe, and Bob Raissman. *Audibles: My Life in Football.* New York: W. Morrow, 1986.
Schleicher, Paul, Bill O'Neill, and Bob Dignan. *Joe Montana.* Massapequa, NY: Personality Comics, 1991.
Manner, Michael, Kris Renkewitz, and Mike Smith. *Super-Joe: the Comeback Kid.* Melville, NY: Personality Comics, 1992.
Parrish, Kenneth, and Dick Ayers. *The Joe Montana Story.* San Diego, CA: Revolutionary Comics, 1992.
Montana, Joe, and Dick Schaap. *Montana.* Atlanta: Turner Publications, 1995.
Joe Montana. New York: House of Collectibles, 1995.
Montana, Joe, and Richard Weiner. *Joe Montana's Art and Magic of Quarterbacking.* New York: Henry Holt, 1997.
Hetz, Stanley. *Joe Montana: Just Another Player.* ?: Xlibris, 2000.

Steve Young
Harmon, Dick. *Steve Young: Staying in the Pocket.* Salt Lake City: Black Moon Publications, 1995.
Livesey, Laury. *The Steve Young Story.* Rocklin, CA: Prima Publications, 1996.

43

Seattle Seahawks

Leading Passers, by Yards

Quarterback	Years	G	Att	Comp	Pct	Yds	Y/A	Y/Cp	TD	Int	Int %	Rating
Dave Krieg	1980–91	129	3,576	2,096	58.6	26,132	7.3	12.5	195	148	4.14%	82.3
Jim Zorn	1976–84	126	2,992	1,593	53.3	20,122	6.7	12.6	107	133	4.45%	67.9
Matt Hasselbeck	2001–06	87	2,547	1,539	60.4	18,222	7.2	11.8	112	73	2.87%	85.0
Rick Mirer	1993–96	55	1,523	814	53.4	9,094	6.0	11.2	41	56	3.68%	65.2
Jon Kitna	1997–00	39	1,128	658	58.3	7,552	6.7	11.5	49	45	3.99%	76.4

Quarterback	Years	G	Att	Comp	Pct	Yds	Y/A	Y/Cp	TD	Int	Int %	Rating
Warren Moon	1997–98	25	786	458	58.3	5,310	6.8	11.6	36	24	3.05%	81.3
John Friesz	1995–98	22	416	228	54.8	2,971	7.1	13.0	16	12	2.88%	78.3
Trent Dilfer	2001–04	23	356	196	55.1	2,560	7.2	13.1	13	14	3.93%	73.7
Kelly Stouffer	1988–92	22	437	225	51.5	2,333	5.3	10.4	7	19	4.35%	54.5
Jeff Kemp	1987–91	31	249	130	52.2	1,735	7.0	13.3	9	18	7.23%	56.6

Quarterback	Rush Att	Rush Yds	Rush Avg	TD
Dave Krieg	294	1090	3.7	10
Jim Zorn	308	1491	4.8	17
Matt Hasselbeck	197	792	4.0	5
Rick Mirer	178	880	4.9	6
Jon Kitna	113	259	2.3	2
Warren Moon	33	50	1.5	1
John Friesz	29	6	0.2	0
Trent Dilfer	22	40	1.8	0
Kelly Stouffer	30	75	2.5	0
Jeff Kemp	34	166	4.9	0

Record Holders

Passing Yards, Career: 26,132 Dave Krieg
Passing Yards, Season: 3,841 Matt Hasselbeck 2003
Completion %, Career: 60.4% Matt Hasselbeck
Completion %, Season: 65.6% Dave Krieg 1991
Touchdown Passes, Career: 195 Dave Krieg
Touchdown Passes, Season: 32 Dave Krieg 1984
Interceptions, Career: 148 Dave Krieg
Interceptions, Season: 27 Jim Zorn 1976
Rating, Career: 85.1 Matt Hasselbeck
Rating, Season: 98.2 Matt Hasselbeck 2005
Rush Yards, Career: 1,491 Jim Zorn
Rush Yards, Season: 343 Rick Mirer 1993

Passers by Categories

Five best starters: Matt Hasselbeck mastered the West Coast Offense and led the 2005 Seahawks to the Super Bowl. Dave Krieg was a solid starter throughout the most consistently positive period in team history. Ageless Warren Moon was a Hall of Famer who came back to site of his college heroics late in his career. Jim Zorn had the unenviable task of being the starting quarterback on an expansion team and filled the role better than could be expected. Game manager Jon Kitna was more of a backup than a starter.

Worst starters, career: Steve Myer, Stan Gelbaugh, Jeff Kemp, Kelly Stouffer and Dan McGuire were each right around a touchdown pass to interception ratio of 1–2, totaling 31 touchdowns and 69 interceptions. Rick Mirer averaged just 6 yards per pass while throwing 41 touchdowns to 56 interceptions.

Best stat line, season: Jim Zorn threw for 3,661 yards and 20 touchdowns in 1979. Dave Krieg completed 60 percent of his passes and averaged 8.9 yards per pass in 1983 and threw 32 touchdowns in 1984. Warren Moon came home to Seattle in 1997 and threw for 3,678 yards and 25 touchdowns. Jon Kitna threw for 3,346 yards and 23 touchdowns in 1999. Matt Hasselbeck threw for 3,841 yards and 26 touchdowns in 2003 and 3,459 yards, 24 touchdowns and only 9 interceptions in 2005.

Worst stat line, season: Jim Zorn's rookie year in 1976 was not pretty, completing 47 percent of his passes, averaging 5.9 yards per pass and throwing 27 interceptions and just 12 touchdowns. Steve Myer threw 6 touchdowns and 12 interceptions in 1977. Jeff Kemp threw 4 touchdowns to 12 interceptions in 1991. Kelly Stouffer completed 48 percent of his passes, averaged 4.7 yards per pass and threw 3 touchdowns to 9 interceptions in 1992. That same season, Stan Gelbaugh completed 47 percent of his passes, averaged 5.1 yards per pass and threw 6 touchdowns to 11 interceptions. Rick Mirer averaged 5.8 yards per pass and threw 5 touchdowns to 12 interceptions in 1996.

Best stat line, playoffs: In a 1983 Wild-card win over the Raiders, Dave Krieg went 12–13, 200, 3–0. In the 2005 NFC Conference win over Carolina, Matt Hasselbeck went 20–28, 219, 2–0.

Worst stat line, playoffs: In the 1983 AFC Conference loss to the Dolphins, Dave Krieg went 3–9, 12, 0–3. In a 1999 Wildcard loss to Miami, Jon Kitna went 14–30, 162, 1–2.

Big Days: The first passer to exceed 300 yards passing in a game was Jim Zorn with 329 yards on September 3, 1978. The first to reach 400 yards was Dave Krieg with 406 on November 25, 1984. Matt Hasselbeck had the biggest day in franchise history by throwing for 449 yards on December 29, 2002 and had 12 300-yard games. Krieg had 11 and Zorn had 9.

Running QBs: Jim Zorn, Rick Mirer, and Matt Hasselbeck have all been scramblers. Dave Krieg and Jeff Kemp were mobile in the pocket.

Bomber: Warren Moon was still a bomber late in his career in Seattle.

Most accurate: Matt Hasselbeck.

Leader: Matt Hasselbeck is an exuberant leader on the field.

Comeback King: Dave Krieg had 22 4th quarter comebacks, plus one in the postseason.

Highest Football IQ: Zorn took his knowledge and went into coaching.

Toughest: Hasselbeck is pretty solid.

First signal caller/T-Formation QB: Dallas Cowboy reject Jim Zorn.

First TD pass: Zorn to Sam McCullum for 15 yards in a 30–24 loss to the Cardinals on September 12, 1976.

Black QBs: Warren Moon from 1997–98 and Seneca Wallace from 2003 on.

Tallest QB: Dan McGwire was 6'8" and the tallest quarterback in NFL history.

Smallest QB: Seneca Wallace is only 5'11". Jeff Kemp was 6' and Dave Krieg was 6'1".

Oldest QB: Warren Moon was still starting at 41 in 1998 and 40 in 1997.

Rookie sensation: Rick Mirer showed promise in 1993 by throwing for 2,833 yards and running for 343 more, but he never developed, and those two figures would be his career highs.

Late bloomer: Matt Hasselbeck was 26 in 2001 when he escaped from being Brett Favre's backup in Green Bay.

1st round picks: Both quarterbacks the Seahawks have taken in the first round have flopped: Dan McGwire, 16th in 1991, and Rick Mirer, 2nd in 1993.

Out of position: Seneca Wallace also plays some receiver.

Long-time subs: Trent Dilfer backed up Hasselbeck for four years. Jeff Kemp and Kelly Stouffer spent four of five seasons in Seattle as backups.

QB controversy: Jim Zorn and Dave Krieg competed hard for the starting job. Trent Dilfer had his supporters while Matt Hasselbeck was growing into the job. If Seattle had picked first in 1993, local support would have been with Drew Bledsoe over Rick Mirer.

College affiliation: Matt Hasselbeck and Glenn Foley played at Boston College while Warren Moon and Brock Huard starred locally at the University of Washington.

Ones who got away: None.

Has beens: Bill Munson, Bruce Mathison, Stan Gelbaugh, Jeff Kemp, Glenn Foley, Gino Torretta and Trent Dilfer.

Ruinous injuries: Dave Krieg was not a big man and took a beating.

Best trade: Getting a number 1 from the Bears for Rick Mirer. Getting Hasselbeck and a number 3 from the Packers for a first round position switch.

Worst trade: Giving up a number 1 (Joe Wolf) and a number 5 to the Cardinals for Kelly Stouffer.

Title winners: None.

Hall of Famers: Warren Moon.

All Pro/Pro Bowl seasons: Dave Krieg, 5; Matt Hasselbeck, 2; Warren Moon, 1; Jim Zorn, 1.

QBs as coaches: None.

Underrated: Dave Krieg was a fumbler but he was a very good quarterback for a decade in Seattle.

Overrated: Jim Zorn was exciting but threw too many interceptions.

Best Nicknames: Dave "Mudbone" Krieg and John "Deep" Friesz.

Time Capsule: After winning the overtime coin flip in a playoff game against the Packers, Hasselbeck announced to national television, "We'll take the ball and we're going to score." He threw a game-ending interception to Al Harris.

What If: If a couple of questionable penalties had gone the other way, Hasselbeck could have won a Super Bowl.

Off the field: Matt Hasselbeck's brother Tim and father Don played in the NFL. Brock Huard's brother Damon was also a quarterback for the Washington Huskies and in the NFL. Jeff Kemp was the son of Jack Kemp. Dan McGwire was the brother of baseball star Mark McGwire. Rick Mirer appeared in *Jerry Maguire*. Warren Moon appeared in *Any Given Sunday, Warriors of Virtue, Air Bud: Golden Receiver* and *Jerry Maguire* as well as an episode of *Arli$$*.

Bill Munson appeared in an episode of *Perry Mason*.

Quarterback Bibliography

None.

44

Tampa Bay Buccaneers

Leading Passers, by Yards

Quarterback	Years	G	Att	Comp	Pct	Yds	Y/A	Y/Cp	TD	Int	Int %	Rating
Vinny Testaverde	1987–92	76	2,160	1,126	52.1	14,820	6.9	13.2	77	112	5.19%	64.4
Trent Dilfer	1994–99	79	2,038	1,117	54.8	12,969	6.4	11.6	70	80	3.93%	69.4
Doug Williams	1978–82	67	1,890	895	47.4	12,648	6.7	14.1	73	73	3.86%	66.2
Brad Johnson	2001–04	52	1,685	1,041	61.8	10,950	6.5	10.5	64	41	2.43%	83.2
Steve DeBerg	1984–87, 1993	64	1,414	813	57.5	9,439	6.7	11.6	61	62	4.38%	73.9
Craig Erickson	1992–94	37	882	473	53.6	6,094	6.9	12.9	34	31	3.51%	73.8
Shaun King	1999–03	6	654	368	56.3	4,064	6.2	11.0	26	20	3.06%	75.4
Brian Griese	2004–05	17	510	345	67.6	3,768	7.4	10.9	27	19	3.73%	91.4
Jack Thompson	1983–84	19	475	274	57.7	3,243	6.8	11.8	20	26	5.47%	69.8
Steve Young	1985–86	19	501	267	53.3	3,217	6.4	12.0	11	21	4.19%	63.1
Chris Simms	2004–06	19	492	291	59.1	3,087	6.3	10.6	12	17	3.46%	71.2
Bruce Gradkowski	2006	13	328	177	54.0	1,661	5.1	9.4	9	9	2.74%	65.9
Steve Spurrier	1976–76	14	311	156	50.2	1,628	5.2	10.4	7	12	3.86%	57.1

Quarterback	Rush Att	Rush Yds	Rush Avg	TD
Vinny Testaverde	172	905	5.3	5
Trent Dilfer	155	650	4.2	5
Doug Williams	203	879	4.3	13
Brad Johnson	82	206	2.5	3
Steve DeBerg	47	80	1.7	3
Craig Erickson	53	163	3.1	1
Shaun King	104	424	4.1	5
Brian Griese	43	29	0.7	0
Jack Thompson	31	62	2.0	0
Steve Young	114	658	5.8	6
Chris Simms	30	52	1.7	1
Bruce Gradkowski	41	161	3.9	0
Steve Spurrier	12	48	4.0	0

Record Holders

Passing Yards, Career: 14,820 Vinny Testaverde
Passing Yards, Season: 3,811 Brad Johnson 2003
Completion %, Career: 67.6% Brian Griese
Completion %, Season: 69.3% Brian Griese 2004
Touchdown Passes, Career: 77 Vinny Testaverde
Touchdown Passes, Season: 26 Brad Johnson 2003
Interceptions, Career: 112 Vinny Testaverde
Interceptions, Season: 35 Vinny Testaverde 1988
Rating, Career: 91.4 Brian Griese
Rating, Season: 97.5 Brian Griese 2004
Rush Yards, Career: 905 Vinny Testaverde
Rush Yards, Season: 425 Steve Young 1986

Passers by Categories

Five best starters: Brad Johnson led the Bucs to their only championship. Doug Williams would have his Super Bowl success elsewhere, but was a pioneer for his race in Tampa. Trent Dilfer was never great, but did enough to post a winning record in Tampa. Brian Griese played pretty well for two seasons until succeeded by Chris Simms who showed potential before suffering a season-ending and life-threatening spleen injury in 2006.

Worst starters, career: Steve Spurrier was washed up when he came to Tampa. Steve Young and Vinny Testaverde were overmatched and undercoached as inexperienced pros. Jack Thompson could not beat out Steve DeBerg. Bruce Gradkowski displayed a rag arm as a rookie in 2006.

Best stat line, season: Doug Williams threw for over 3,500 yards and 19 touchdowns in 1981. Steve DeBerg did the same in 1984 while completing 60 percent of his passes. Trent Dilfer threw for 21 touchdowns and only 11 interceptions in 1997. In the 2002 championship year, Brad Johnson completed 62 percent of his passes for over 3,000 yards, 22 touchdowns and only 6 interceptions. In 2004, Brian Griese completed 69 percent of his passes for 20 touchdowns and 12 interceptions.

Worst stat line, season: In their inaugural 1976 season, the Bucs featured Steve Spurrier who averaged 5.2 yards per pass and threw 7 touchdowns and 12 interceptions backed up by Parnell Dickinson who completed 38 percent of his passes for 1 touchdown and 5 interceptions.

Even worse was 1977 with Gary Huff completing 48 percent of his passes for 3 touchdowns and 13 interceptions, Jeb Blount completing 41 percent of his passes for 0 touchdowns and 7 interceptions, and Randy Hedberg completing 28 percent of his passes for 0 touchdowns and 10 interceptions while averaging 2.7 yards per pass. Doug Williams, Steve Young and Vinny Testaverde all had dreadful second seasons in the NFL. Williams completed 41 percent of his passes for 18 touchdowns and 24 interceptions in 1979. Young threw 8 touchdowns and 13 interceptions in 1986. Testaverde completed 47 percent of his passes for 13 touchdowns and 35 interceptions in 1988. Bruce Gradkowski averaged just 5.1 yards per pass and 9.4 yards per completion in 2006.

Best stat line, playoffs: In the 2002 NFC Conference win over the Eagles, Brad Johnson went 20–33, 259, 1–1. In the Super Bowl win over the Raiders, Johnson went 18–34, 215, 2–1.

Worst stat line, playoffs: In the 1979 NFC Conference loss to the Rams Mike Rae was 2–13, 42, 0–0 and Doug Williams was 2–13, 12, 0–1. Williams had similar problems in a 1981 Divisional loss to Dallas, going 10–29, 187, 0–4 and in a 1982 Wildcard loss to Dallas, going 8–28, 113, 1–3. In a 1997 Divisional loss to Green Bay, Trent Dilfer went 11–36, 200, 0–2. In a 2001 Wildcard loss to Philadelphia, Brad Johnson went 22–36, 202, 0–4.

Big Days: The first passer to exceed 300 yards passing in a game was Doug Williams with 311 yards on October 1, 1978. The first to reach 400 yards was Williams with 486 on November 16, 1980, and that was the biggest day in franchise history. Vinny Testaverde had 12 300-yard games in Tampa.

Running QBs: Steve Young gained more yards rushing than any quarterback except for Randall Cunningham. Shaun King had to run to survive. Doug Williams and Vinny Testaverde were both surprisingly mobile in their younger days; Testaverde even had a 100-yard rushing game in 1990.

Bomber: Doug Williams completed less than half his passes as a Buc, but he had a big arm and liked to go deep.

Most accurate: Both Brad Johnson and Brian Griese are very accurate within the West Coast Offense.

Leader: Maligned Brad Johnson kept his head and won a Super Bowl.

Comeback King: Doug Williams had 13 4th quarter comebacks, and Trent Dilfer had 11.

Highest Football IQ: Brad Johnson doesn't make many mistakes.

Toughest: Mentally and physically, Doug Williams, hands down.

First signal caller/T-Formation QB: Steve Spurrier finished up his undistinguished playing career in Tampa.

First TD pass: On October 17, 1976, Louis Carter threw a one-yard halfback option pass to Morris Owens in a 13–10 loss to Seattle. The first touchdown pass by a quarterback didn't come until the Bucs' seventh game on October 24th when Parnell Dickinson hit Morris Owens for an 18-yard score in a 23–20 loss to the Dolphins.

Black QBs: Parnell Dickinson in 1976. Doug Williams, who was the first regular black quarterback in the NFL, from 1978 through 1982. Shaun King from 1999 through 2003, and Joe Hamilton in 2000.

Tallest QB: Vinny Testaverde and Brad Johnson were both 6'5".

Smallest QB: Joe Hamilton was 5'10". Shaun King and Mike Hold were 6'. Casey Weldon was 6'1".

Oldest QB: Joe Ferguson was 39 in 1989 and 38 in 1988. Steve DeBerg was 39 in 1993. Brad Johnson was the oldest starter at 36 in 2004.

Rookie sensation: None.

Late bloomer: Brad Johnson led the Bucs to the Super Bowl at 34.

1st round picks: Doug Williams, 17th in 1978, led the lowly Bucs to the playoffs. Steve Young, 1984 USFL draft, flopped in Tampa Bay before becoming a legend in San Francisco. Vinny Testaverde, 1st in 1987, flopped in Tampa before becoming a solid starter in Cleveland, Baltimore and New York. Trent Dilfer, 6th in 1994, never played up to that level, but was a decent backup quarterback.

Out of position: Steve Spurrier and Tom Tupa were better at punting than passing.

Long-time subs: Casey Weldon four years.

QB controversy: When the Bucs wouldn't meet Doug Williams's contract demands he jumped to the USFL, but he did not have much fan backing. The Bucs traded a number one pick to replace him with Jack Thompson in 1983, and when that failed they obtained Steve DeBerg who was succeeded a year later by Steve Young.

Later, Tampa was divided by Trent Dilfer and Shaun King factions in 1999, with King winning out. Under Jon Gruden, Brad Johnson had to compete with first Rob Johnson and then Brian Griese. Griese then lost his battle with Chris Simms after getting hurt.

College affiliation: The Bucs have supported local talent. Vinny Testaverde, Craig Erickson and Steve Walsh were all Miami Hurricanes; Brad Johnson, Casey Weldon and Gary Huff were all Florida State Seminoles; Steve Spurrier, John Reaves and Bob Hewko were all Florida Gators. If you add in Kerwin Bell, who never actually appeared in a game as a Buc, then Florida wins.

Ones who got away: Steve Young is the most obvious choice, but Vinny Testaverde, Trent Dilfer and Doug Williams went on to greater success elsewhere also.

Has beens: Steve Spurrier, Terry Hanratty, Larry Lawrence, Mike Boryla, Gary Huff, Mike Rae, Chuck Fusina, Jerry Golsteyn, Jack Thompson, Jeff Komlo, John Reaves, Joe Ferguson, Chris Chandler, Jim Zorn, Casey Weldon, Eric Zeier, Steve Walsh, Rob Johnson, Luke McCown and Tim Rattay.

Ruinous injuries: Brian Griese went out for the season in 2005, and Chris Simms did so well that Griese moved on to the Bears in 2006. Then, Simms went down in 2006.

Best trade: Getting Steve DeBerg from the Broncos for a number 2 and number 4.

Worst trade: Trading Steve Young to the 49ers for a number 2 and a number 4. Giving the Bengals a number 1 for Jack Thompson. Giving the Colts a number 1 (Quentin Coryat) for Chris Chandler. Giving the Colts a number 1 for Craig Erickson.

Title winners: Brad Johnson, 1.

Hall of Famers: Steve Young.

All Pro/Pro Bowl seasons: Brad Johnson, 1; Trent Dilfer, 1.

QBs as coaches: Steve Spurrier went 12–20 in Washington.

Underrated: Brad Johnson is very smart and very effective, the essence of a game manager, and he led the Bucs to a Super Bowl but was still out of a job two years later.

Overrated: Laid back Rob Johnson never panned out for any team.

Best Nicknames: Steve "Suitcase" DeBerg.

Time Capsule: Doug Williams being the

first black quarterback selected in the first round of the NFL draft.

What If: If Steve Young or Vinny Testaverde had received better coaching and more support, how much success would the Bucs have achieved in the 1980s?

Off the field: John Reaves once had drug problems. Brain Griese had some publicized misadventures off the field and was the son of Hall of Fame quarterback Bob Griese. Chris Simms is the son of Phil Simms. Steve Young appeared in the Mormon film *The Singles Ward* and in episodes of *Beverly Hills 90210,* *Wings, Dharma and Greg, Listen Up* and *Lois and Clark.*

Quarterback Bibliography

Doug Williams
Williams, Doug, and Bruce Hunter. *Quarterblack: Shattering the NFL Myth.* Chicago: Bonus Books, 1990.

Steve Spurrier *see* San Francisco 49ers

Steve Young *see* San Francisco 49ers

Brian Griese *see* Denver Broncos

45

Tennessee Titans

Leading Passers, by Yards

Quarterback	Years	G	Att	Comp	Pct	Yds	Y/A	Y/Cp	TD	Int	Int %	Rating
Warren Moon	1984–93	141	4,546	2,632	57.9	33,685	7.4	12.8	196	166	3.65%	80.4
Steve McNair	1995–05	141	3,871	2,306	59.6	27,190	7.0	11.8	156	102	2.63%	83.4
George Blanda	1960–66	98	2,784	1,347	48.4	19,149	6.9	14.2	165	189	6.79%	62.5
Dan Pastorini	1971–79	125	2,768	1,426	51.5	16,864	6.1	11.8	96	139	5.02%	61.0
Ken Stabler	1980–81	29	742	458	61.7	5,190	7.0	11.3	27	46	6.20%	69.0
Pete Beathard	1967–69	31	822	379	46.1	5,128	6.2	13.5	26	51	6.20%	51.2
Chris Chandler	1995–96	25	676	409	60.5	4,559	6.7	11.1	33	21	3.11%	83.9
Cody Carlson	1988–94	45	659	370	56.1	4,469	6.8	12.1	21	28	4.25%	70.0
Don Trull	1964–69	70	556	249	44.8	3,538	6.4	14.2	29	21	3.78%	67.6
Billy Volek	2001–05	23	517	312	60.3	3,504	6.8	11.2	26	13	2.51%	86.9
Jacky Lee	1960–63, 1966–67	68	409	210	51.3	3,291	8.0	15.7	25	30	7.33%	68.2
Gifford Nielsen	1978–83	55	498	273	54.8	3,255	6.5	11.9	20	22	4.42%	70.0
Neil O'Donnell	1999–03	26	367	215	58.6	2,664	7.3	12.4	16	11	3.00%	83.2
Oliver Luck	1983–86	20	413	233	56.4	2,544	6.2	10.9	13	21	5.08%	64.1
Charley Johnson	1970–71	24	375	190	50.7	2,244	6.0	11.8	10	19	5.07%	57.0
Vince Young	2006	15	357	184	51.5	2,199	6.2	12.0	12	13	3.64%	66.7

Quarterback	Rush Att	Rush Yds	Rush Avg	TD
Warren Moon	439	1541	3.5	21
Steve McNair	614	3439	5.6	36
George Blanda	41	28	0.7	4

Quarterback	Rush Att	Rush Yds	Rush Avg	TD
Dan Pastorini	204	656	3.2	8
Ken Stabler	25	-25	-1.0	0
Pete Beathard	69	299	4.3	5
Chris Chandler	56	171	3.1	2
Cody Carlson	81	217	2.7	4
Don Trull	104	393	3.8	11
Billy Volek	23	57	2.5	2
Jacky Lee	26	54	2.1	0
Gifford Nielsen	29	89	3.1	0
Neil O'Donnell	38	23	0.6	0
Oliver Luck	44	237	5.4	1
Charley Johnson	7	3	0.4	0
Vince Young	83	552	6.7	7

Record Holders

Passing Yards, Career: 33,685 Warren Moon
Passing Yards, Season: 4,690 Warren Moon 1991
Completion %, Career: 61.7% Ken Stabler
Completion %, Season: 64.7% Warren Moon 1992
Touchdown Passes, Career: 196 Warren Moon
Touchdown Passes, Season: 36 George Blanda 1961
Interceptions, Career: 189 George Blanda
Interceptions, Season: 42 George Blanda 1962
Rating, Career: 86.9 Billy Volek (517 att.); 83.4 Steve McNair
Rating, Season: 100.4 Steve McNair 2003
Rush Yards, Career: 3,439 Steve McNair
Rush Yards, Season: 674 Steve McNair 1997

Passers by Categories

Five best starters: Warren Moon overcame the obstacles thrown in his path to become a Hall of Famer. George Blanda is in the Hall of Fame mostly for his point scoring and longevity, but he did have several exciting seasons quarterbacking in Houston. Steve McNair and Dan Pastorini were both tough as nails and led their teams to the playoffs. Chris Chandler played pretty well for two seasons and mentored McNair as Steve gradually took over.

Worst starters, career: Pete Beathard was the quarterback for two Oiler playoff teams in the late 1960s, but he was awful, completing just 46 percent of his passes for 26 touchdowns and 51 interceptions. Don Trull was thought to be the quarterback of the future in the 60s, but completed only 44.8 percent of his passes and could

never win the job. Oliver Luck threw just 13 touchdowns to 21 interceptions. Charley Johnson looked to be washed up in Houston, averaging 6 yards per pass and throwing 10 touchdowns to 19 interceptions, before resurrecting his career in Denver.

Best stat line, season: In 1961, George Blanda threw for 3,330 yards, averaged 9.2 yards per pass and threw 36 touchdowns to 22 interceptions. He also scored 112 points placekicking that year. In 1990, Warren Moon threw for 4,689 yards, averaged 8 yards per pass and threw 33 touchdowns to 13 interceptions. Steve McNair in 2003 completed 62 percent of his passes for 3,215 yards, averaged 8 yards per pass and threw 24 touchdowns to 7 interceptions.

Worst stat line, season: George Blanda completed 47 percent of his passes for 27 touchdowns and 42 interceptions in 1962. He also threw 30 interceptions in 1965 and averaged 27 interceptions a year for his Oiler career. In 1969, Pete Beathard completed 48 percent of his passes for 10 touchdowns and 21 interceptions. In Dan Pastorini's rookie season of 1971, Dan completed 47 percent of his passes for 7 touchdowns and 21 interceptions, and two years later averaged just 5.1 yards per pass while throwing 5 touchdowns and 17 interceptions. Ken Stabler came over from Oakland for Pastorini in 1980 and completed 64 percent of his passes but threw just 13 touchdowns to 28 interceptions.

Best stat line, playoffs: In the 1960 AFL title win over the Chargers, George Blanda went 16–31, 301, 3–0. In a 1978 Divisional win over New England, Dan Pastorini went 12–15, 200, 3–1. In a 1991 Divisional loss to the Broncos, Warren Moon went 27–36, 325, 3–1 while the following year, he watched his defense collapse in a wildcard loss to Buffalo even though Moon himself went 36–50, 371, 4–2. In a 2002 Divisional win over Pittsburgh, Steve McNair went 27–44, 338, 2–2. In the Super Bowl against the Rams, McNair went 22–36, 214, 0–0.

Worst stat line, playoffs: In the 1961 AFL title win over San Diego, George Blanda went 18–40, 160, 1–5 and followed that in the 1962 title loss to the Dallas Texans by going 23–46, 261, 1–5. In a Divisional loss to the Raiders in 1969, Pete Beathard went 18–46, 209, 1–3. In the 1978 AFC Conference loss to the Steelers, Dan Pastorini went 15–26, 96, 0–5. In a 1988 Wildcard loss to Cleveland, Warren Moon went 16–26, 213, 1–3. In the Music City Miracle win over Buffalo in 1999, Steve McNair was 13–24, 76, 0–1.

Big Days: The first Oiler passer to exceed 300 yards passing in a game was George Blanda with 366 yards on November 13, 1960; Steve McNair was the first to do this in Tennessee with 341 yards on September 12, 1999. The first Oiler to reach 400 yards was Jacky Lee with 457 on October 13, 1961, and again McNair was the first to do so in Tennessee with 421 on October 12, 2003. Warren Moon had the biggest day in franchise history by throwing for 527 yards on December 16, 1990, and he had 37 300-yard games.

Running QBs: Steve McNair ran for over 500 yards two seasons in a row and scored 36 touchdowns. Vince Young ran for 552 yards as a rookie in 2006 in less than a full season. Warren Moon and Dan Pastorini were mobile early in their careers, and Moon scored 21 touchdowns. Pete Beathard and Don Trull were both scramblers.

Bomber: George Blanda liked to throw the ball deep.

Most accurate: Warren Moon.

Leader: Steve McNair was the ultimate football warrior, going out Sunday after Sunday despite strains, sprains and breaks.

Comeback King: Warren Moon had 23 4th quarter comebacks plus two in the postseason. McNair had 18 and two more in the playoffs.

Highest Football IQ: Warren Moon had talent and guile.

Toughest: Both McNair and Dan Pastorini played through many very painful injuries, both even donning flak jackets at times.

First signal caller/T-Formation QB: George Blanda.

First TD pass: Blanda to Charlie Hennigan for 43 yards in a 37–22 win over Oakland on September 11, 1960.

Black QBs: With Vince Young arriving as Steve McNair departed, the Titans franchise has been as well represented by black quarterbacks as any team aside from the Eagles: Warren Moon, 1984–93, McNair, 1995–2005, and now Young. Don McPherson, Reggie Slack and Brian Ransom never made it onto the field for the franchise.

Tallest QB: Both Vince Young and Craig Bradshaw were 6'5".

Smallest QB: Both Bob Naponic and Jerry Rhome were 6'. Jacky Lee, Don Trull, Pete Beathard, Bucky Richardson and Guido Merkens were all 6'1".

Oldest QB: Dave Krieg was a backup at 40 in 1998 and 39 in 1997. George Blanda was still starting at 39 in 1966.

Rookie sensation: Warren Moon came down from Canada in 1984 and threw for over 3,300 yards while completing 57 percent of his passes. Vince Young took over an 0–5 team and led it to an 8–8 record by throwing for over 2,000 yards and running for over 500 in 2006.

Late bloomer: While Moon was a rookie in 1984, he was 27 years old by then. George Blanda got a second start in the AFL with the Oilers at age 33 in 1960.

1st round picks: The franchise has never had a flop drafting quarterbacks in the first round. Dan Pastorini, 3rd in 1971, led the Oilers to the playoffs in back-to-back seasons. Jim Everett, 3rd in 1986, was traded for three draft picks and two players when the Oilers couldn't sign him. Steve McNair, 3rd in 1995, was the face of the franchise for a mostly successful decade until the salary cap led to an ugly end. Since Vince Young was also selected with the 3rd pick in 2006, the omens look good for him.

Out of position: Guido Merkens also played wide receiver and defensive back. Charley Milstead also played safety. George Blanda kicked and punted, while Dan Pastorini punted.

Long-time subs: Jacky Lee and Don Trull both spent six years in two terms as backups in Houston. Cody Carlson was a backup for six of seven seasons with the Oilers.

QB controversy: In the same draft that the Oilers picked Pastorini in round one, they picked Lynn Dickey in round three. If Dickey had not been so injury-prone, he might have beaten out the mistake-prone young Dante. The end of the Steve McNair era in Tennessee came when he was locked out of team facilities because they couldn't risk being saddled with his cap number if he got injured. It made business sense, but was a cold way to deal with a warrior like McNair.

College affiliation: Buddy Humphrey, Don Trull and Cody Carlson all were Baylor Bears from Waco, Texas.

Ones who got away: Lynn Dickey proved his arm was strong in Green Bay.

Has beens: Buddy Humphrey, Jerry Rhome, Pete Beathard, Charley Johnson, Kent Nix, John Hadl, John Reaves, Archie Manning, Ken Stabler, Dave Krieg, Mike Moroski, Billy Joe Tolliver, Neil O'Donnell and Kerry Collins.

Ruinous injuries: Both Dan Pastorini and Steve McNair took a pounding that diminished their effectiveness while demonstrating their toughness.

Best trade: Trading the rights to the unsigned Jim Everett to the Rams for two number 1's, a number 5, William Fuller and Kent Hill. Sending Jacky Lee to the Broncos on a two-year loan in return for Bud McFaddin and a number 2.

Worst trade: Trading the number 1 pick in the 1965 AFL draft (Joe Namath) to the Jets for the rights to Jerry Rhome who signed with the Cowboys. Then, the Oilers traded for the mediocre Rhome a second time by sending Dallas a number 3 (Charlie Waters) for him.

Title winners: George Blanda won the first two AFL titles

Hall of Famers: George Blanda and Warren Moon.

All Pro/Pro Bowl seasons: Warren Moon, 6; George Blanda, 3; Steve McNair, 2; Vince Young, 1; and Dan Pastorini, 1.

QBs as coaches: None.

Underrated: Steve McNair took much too long to gain respect.

Overrated: Dan Pastorini was a tough leader with a great arm, but was not very effective.

Best Nicknames: Commander Cody Carlson and Steve "Air" McNair.

Time Capsule: The Run and Shoot Offense was first established in Houston. The McNair to Kevin Dyson completion that fell inches short on the last play of the Super Bowl.

What If: If Lynn Dickey had beaten out Dan Pastorini, would the Oilers have had enough firepower to get past the Steelers in the late 1970s?

Off the field: Craig Bradshaw's brother was Terry. Kent Nix's father Emery played quarterback for the Giants. Archie Manning's sons are Peyton and Eli. Chris Chandler's father-in-law was John Brodie who once signed a contract with the Oilers to jump ship from the 49ers, but that was later nullified in the league merger. John Reaves had drug problems. Dan Pastorini loved fast cars and women. He was married to June Wilkinson, a former Playboy Playmate and sexy actress who was 10 years his senior. Dan appeared in *Trick or Treat, Killer Fish* and *The Florida Connection* as well as episodes of *Voyagers!* and *Fantasy Island*. The Oilers traded the fast-living Pastorini for the rowdy Ken Stabler who appeared in *Indian Runner, The Legend of Grizzly Adams* and an episode of *Married ... with Children*. Warren Moon appeared in *Any Given Sunday, Warriors of Virtue, Air Bud: Golden Receiver* and *Jerry Maguire* as well as an episode of *Arli$$*.

Quarterback Bibliography

George Blanda *see* Oakland Raiders
Ken Stabler *see* Oakland Raiders
Archie Manning *see* New Orleans Saints

46

Washington Redskins

Leading Passers, by Yards

Quarterback	Years	G	Att	Comp	Pct	Yds	Y/A	Y/Cp	TD	Int	Int %	Rating
Joe Theismann	1974–85	167	3,602	2,044	56.7	25,206	7.0	12.3	160	138	3.83%	77.4
Sonny Jurgensen	1964–74	135	3,155	1,831	58	22,585	7.2	12.3	179	116	3.68%	83.9
Sammy Baugh	1937–52	165	2,995	1,693	56.5	21,886	7.3	12.9	187	203	6.78%	72.2
Mark Rypien	1988–93	77	2,207	1,244	56.4	15,928	7.2	12.8	101	75	3.40%	80.2
Billy Kilmer	1971–78	82	1,791	953	53.2	12,352	6.9	13.0	103	75	4.19%	76.9
Gus Frerotte	1994–98	52	1,422	744	52.3	9,769	6.9	13.1	48	44	3.09%	72.7
Norm Snead	1961–63	42	1,092	531	48.6	8,306	7.6	15.6	46	71	6.50%	61.2
Eddie LeBaron	1952–53, 1955–59	82	1,104	539	48.8	8,068	7.3	15.0	59	88	7.97%	57.8
Jay Schroeder	1985–87	36	1,017	517	50.8	7,445	7.3	14.4	39	37	3.64%	72.6
Brad Johnson	1999–00	28	883	543	61.5	6,510	7.4	12.0	35	28	3.17%	84.0
Mark Brunell	2004–06	35	951	542	57	6,033	6.3	11.1	38	20	2.10%	80.6
Patrick Ramsey	2002–05	34	863	481	55.7	5,652	6.5	11.8	34	29	3.36%	74.9
Doug Williams	1986–89	21	617	345	55.9	4,350	7.1	12.6	27	20	3.24%	79.1
Trent Green	1997–98	16	510	278	54.5	3,441	6.7	12.4	23	11	2.16%	81.7
Frankie Filchock	1938–41, 1944–45	58	431	224	52	3,266	7.6	14.6	32	47	10.90%	62.1
Harry Gilmer	1948–54	57	411	178	43.3	2,850	6.9	16.0	17	38	9.25%	42.3

Quarterback	Rush Att	Rush Yds	Rush Avg	TD
Joe Theismann	355	1815	5.1	17
Sonny Jurgensen	116	381	3.3	10
Sammy Baugh	324	325	1.0	9
Mark Rypien	110	151	1.4	8
Billy Kilmer	70	87	1.2	3
Gus Frerotte	81	118	1.5	3
Norm Snead	77	157	2.0	8
Eddie LeBaron	157	480	3.1	8
Jay Schroeder	79	197	2.5	4
Brad Johnson	48	89	1.9	3
Mark Brunell	74	207	2.8	0
Patrick Ramsey	45	83	1.8	2
Doug Williams	17	5	0.3	2
Trent Green	42	117	2.8	2
Frankie Filchock	362	1087	3.0	5
Harry Gilmer	178	837	4.7	1

Record Holders

Passing Yards, Career: 25,206 Joe Theismann
Passing Yards, Season: 4,109 Jay Schroeder 1986
Completion %, Career: 61.5% Brad Johnson

Completion %, Season: 70.3% Sammy Baugh 1945
Touchdown Passes, Career: 187 Sammy Baugh
Touchdown Passes, Season: 31 Sonny Jurgensen 1967

Interceptions, Career: 203 Sammy Baugh
Interceptions, Season: 27 Norm Snead 1963
Rating, Career: 84 Brad Johnson
Rating, Season: 109.9 Sammy Baugh 1945; 111.6 Frankie Filchock 1939 (89 att.)
Rush Yards, Career: 1,815 Joe Theismann
Rush Yards, Season: 413 single-wing tailback Frankie Filchock 1939; 365 quarterback Harry Gilmer 1953. However, Gilmer also played half back that year so let's note Joe Theismann's 314 yards rushing in 1984.

Passers by Categories

Five best starters: Sammy Baugh is still arguably the greatest quarterback in history. Another sidearmer, Sonny Jurgensen, is also in the Hall of Fame for being such a peerless passer on some terrible Redskin teams. Billy Kilmer wasn't a pretty passer, but knew how to lead a team to victory. Joe Theismann was smart, vocal and mobile with a decent enough arm to star at quarterback despite a lack of size. Hulking Mark Rypien won a Super Bowl.

Worst starters, career: Big-armed Norm Snead has the highest averages for yards per pass and completion in team history, but completed less than half his passes and threw 71 interceptions to 46 touchdowns. Harry Gilmer completed just 43 percent of his passes while throwing 17 touchdowns to 38 interceptions. Ralph Guglielmi topped that with 17 touchdowns to 40 interceptions while completing 47 percent of his passes. Jack Scarbath completed 37 percent of his passes for 16 touchdowns and 25 interceptions. Heath Shuler was overmatched in the pros, completing 47 percent of his passes for 13 touchdowns and 19 interceptions. Shane Matthews and Danny Wuerffel established that coach Steve Spurrier belonged back in college.

Best stat line, season: Sammy Baugh had three seasons when his passer rating was more than double the league average. The best was 1945 when he completed 70 percent of his passes for 11 touchdowns and 4 interceptions while averaging 9.2 yards per pass; his passer rating of 109.9 is 132 percent better than the league average of 38.6. In 1947, Sammy became just the second quarterback to throw as many as 25 touchdown passes in a season and exceeded 2,900

yards in a 12 game season. Frankie Filchock in 1939 only threw 89 passes but completed 61 percent and averaged 12.3 yards per pass while leading the league in touchdown passes with 11. He also led the NFL in touchdown passes in 1944 with 13. Sonny Jurgensen in 1967 threw for 3,747 yards, 31 touchdowns and only 16 interceptions and a league leading 87.3 passer rating. Joe Theismann in 1983 completed 60 percent of his passes for 3,747 yards, 29 touchdowns and 11 interceptions wile averaging 8.1 yards per pass. In 1991, Mark Rypien completed 59 percent of his passes for 3,564 yards, 28 touchdowns and 11 interceptions, an average of 8.5 yards per pass. Brad Johnson threw for 4,005 yards, 24 touchdowns and 13 interceptions in 1999.

Worst stat line, season: In 1941, Frankie Filchock completed 41 percent of his passes for 1 touchdown and 11 interceptions while averaging 4.8 yards per pass. Sammy Baugh had a rough transition to the T formation in 1946, throwing 8 touchdowns to 17 interceptions. His career was ending in 1951 when he threw 7 touchdowns to 17 interceptions and achieved his lowest ever passing completion percentage of 43 percent. Harry Gilmer completed 37 percent of his passes for 4 touchdowns and 15 interceptions in 1949. Eddie LeBaron followed a promising rookie season by completing 41 percent of his passes for 3 touchdowns and 17 interceptions in 1953. Jack Scarbath tried to replace LeBaron in 1954 by completing 40 percent of his passes for 7 touchdowns and 13 interceptions. Ralph Guglielmi threw 9 touchdowns to 19 interceptions in 1960. Norm Snead exceeded 3,000 yards in 1963 but also threw just 13 touchdowns to 27 interceptions.

Best stat line, playoffs: In the 1937 title win over the Bears, Sammy Baugh went 17–34, 358, 3–1. In the 1972 NFC Conference win over Dallas, Billy Kilmer went 14–18, 194, 2–0. In a 1982 Wildcard win over Detroit, Joe Theismann went 14–19, 210, 3–0, and went 18–23, 302, 2–0 in a 1983 Division win over the Rams. In the Super Bowl win over the Broncos, Doug Williams finished 18–29, 340, 4–1. In the Super Bowl win over the Bills, Mark Rypien went 18–33, 292, 2–1.

Worst stat line, playoffs: In the epochal 73–0 championship game loss to the Bears in 1940, the Redskins used all three passers for a combined 20–51, 226, 0–8 performance. Sammy Baugh went 9–16, 91, 0–2; Frankie Filchock went 8–23, 101, 0–4; Roy Zimmerman went 3–12, 34,

0–2. In the Super Bowl loss to the Dolphins, Billy Kilmer went 14–28, 104, 0–3. In the Super Bowl loss to the Raiders, Joe Theismann went 16–35, 243, 0–2. In a 2005 Wildcard win over the Bucs, Mark Brunell went 7–15, 41, 0–1.

Big Days: The first passer to exceed 300 yards passing in a game was Sammy Baugh with 358 yards on December 5, 1937. The first to reach 400 yards was Baugh with 446 on October 31, 1948, and that's still the biggest day in franchise history. Sonny Jurgensen had 15 300-yard games, while Joe Theismann had 13, Mark Rypien had 11 and Baugh had 8.

Running QBs: Harry Gilmer could do little well except run. Joe Theismann was small and very mobile. Frankie Filchock could run and pass as a single-wing tailback.

Bomber: Sonny Jurgensen was a master of the bomb.

Most accurate: Sammy Baugh completed 70 percent of his passes in *1945* and retired as the NFL leader in completion percentage.

Leader: Sammy Baugh was Mr. Redskin, but Billy Kilmer was a great leader.

Comeback King: Joe Theismann had 23 4th quarter comebacks, plus two in the postseason. Baugh had 19 and Jurgensen had 12.

Highest Football IQ: Sammy Baugh.

Toughest: Theismann started 71 straight games. Billy Kilmer showed his toughness by coming back and having a football career after having been in an horrific auto accident in the early 1960s.

First signal caller/T-Formation QB: Honolulu Hughes was the main passer on the 1932 Boston Braves and threw 1 touchdown to 9 interceptions, but Cliff Battles called signals. Sammy Baugh and Frank Filchock shared the quarterback position when the Redskins installed the T formation in 1946.

First TD pass: For Boston, Honolulu Hughes hit Cliff Battles for a 20-yard score in a 7–7 tie against the Bears on October 20, 1932. In Washington, Sammy Baugh hit Chuck Malone for a 25-yard touchdown in a 21–14 loss to the Cardinals on September 24, 1937.

Black QBs: Doug Williams won the Redskins a championship in his 1986–89 tenure. Tony Robinson was a replacement player in 1987. Brian Mitchell was forced to play some quarterback in the "Body Bag" game against the Eagles in 1990. Rodney Peete was a backup in

1999, and Tony Banks was the same in 2001. Jason Campbell got a chance to play in 2006.

Tallest QB: Ed Rubbert, Kent Graham and Brad Johnson were all 6'5". Sammy Baugh was considered very tall for a passer at 6'2" in the 1930s.

Smallest QB: Eddie LeBaron was 5'7" and set an unofficial record in 1960 for the shortest touchdown pass—2 inches. Bill Shepherd was 5'9". Honolulu Hughes, Phil Sarboe, George Cafego, Frank Filchock and Galen Hall were all 5'10". Sonny Jurgensen was only 5'11" and Joe Theismann claimed to be 6'.

Oldest QB: Sonny Jurgensen got some starts at 40 in 1974. Jim Hart was 40 in 1984. Billy Kilmer was still starting at 38 in 1977 and still playing at 39 in 1978. Sammy Baugh was still starting at 37 in 1951 and playing at 38 in 1952.

Rookie sensation: Sammy Baugh led the NFL in attempts, completions, yards, yards per pass, interceptions and passer rating in 1937. Eddie LeBaron threw 14 touchdowns and averaged 7.3 yards per pass in 1952. Mark Rypien averaged 8.3 yards per pass and threw 18 touchdowns in 1988. Jason Campbell threw 10 touchdowns to 6 interceptions in half a season in 2006.

Late bloomer: Billy Kilmer had shown he could play quarterback with the lowly Saints, but didn't really become a star till coming to the Redskins at 32 in 1971. Joe Theismann had to wait for Kilmer to fade before he got his chance at 29 in 1978. Trent Green took a long time to develop, but showed he had talent at 28 in 1998 before leaving immediately as a free agent.

1st round picks: The Redskins have drafted 14 passers in the first round—though only 3 were picked after founder George P. Marshall lost control of the team in the mid–1960s. Riley Smith, 2nd in the first draft of 1936, was a talented signal caller. Sammy Baugh, 6th in 1937, was the greatest passer of his time. Spec Sanders, 6th in 1942, was actually a tailback who later starred in the All America Conference. Jim Hardy, 6th in 1945, was traded to the Rams. Harry Gilmer, 1st in 1948, failed miserably in trying to push aside the aging Baugh. Larry Isbell, 7th in 1952, went to Canada and never played NFL football. Jack Scarbath, 3rd in 1953, completed less than 40 percent of his passes. Ralph Guglielmi, 4th in 1955, is part of a long line of overrated Notre Dame quarterbacks who tanked in the pros. Don Allard, 4th in 1959, played briefly in Canada and the early AFL.

Richie Lucas, 4th in 1960, signed with Buffalo and played quarterback and defensive back for two years. Norm Snead, 2nd in 1961, had a big arm and a tendency to make big mistakes. Heath Shuler, 3rd in 1994, was a disaster, but clearly not unprecedented in team history. Patrick Ramsey, 32nd in 2002, performed probably better than anyone seriously expected before departing to be a backup in New York. Jason Campbell, 25th in 2005, showed promise in 2006.

Out of position: Brian Mitchell was a college quarterback who became possibly the greatest return man in league history. Joe Theismann was stuck behind Jurgensen and Kilmer and so desperate to play that he returned punts in his early years. Gary Beban won the Heisman trophy as a quarterback but was unsuccessfully converted to runner and then receiver in Washington. Sammy Baugh and Harry Gilmer were also punters. Roy Zimmerman was also a placekicker.

Long-time subs: Harry Gilmer spent six seasons as a backup in Washington.

QB controversy: Surprisingly, there were some who called for Harry Gilmer to replace Baugh in the late 1940s. Sonny Jurgensen and Billy Kilmer somehow remained friends despite the ongoing competition for the starting nod. Kilmer was later succeeded in slow motion by Joe Theismann, with Theismann coming in for heavy criticism as he struggled to take control. The transition from Jay Schroeder to Doug Williams to Mark Rypien led to yearly controversies in the late 1980s.

College affiliation: Frank Filchock, Trent Green, Jeff George and Gibran Hamdan were all Indiana Hoosiers as was Babe Laufenberg who never actually played for the Skins.

Ones who got away: Trent Green, Stan Humphries, Rich Gannon and Roy Zimmerman all had their greatest success elsewhere.

Has beens: Tommy Mont, M.C. Reynolds, Rudy Bukich, Jim Ninowski, Dick Shiner, Frank Ryan, Randy Johnson, Mike Kruczek, Tom Flick, Kim McQuilken, Tom Owen, Jim Hart, Steve Bartkowski, David Archer, Kent Graham, Jeff Hostetler, John Friesz, Rodney Peete, Tony Banks, Jeff George, Shane Matthews, Danny Wuerffel, Tim Hasselbeck and Todd Collins.

Ruinous injuries: Joe Theismann's career ended in a horror on Monday Night Football when his leg was mangled and broken during a sack by Lawrence Taylor. Sonny Jurgensen tore

up his shoulder at the beginning of the George Allen era, and Billy Kilmer took over the starting job just when Jurgensen finally was surrounded by a quality team.

Best trade: Getting Sonny Jurgensen and Jim Carr from the Eagles for Norm Snead and Claude Crabb. Picking up Frankie Filchock from Pittsburgh for cash. Trading Jay Schroeder for All Pro tackle Jim Lachey and two draft picks. Getting Billy Kilmer from the Saints for Tom Roussel and two draft picks.

Worst trade: Trading the rights to Charlie Conerly to the Giants for Howie Livingston. Trading Adrian Burk to the Eagles for Jack Dwyer — Burk wasn't great, but had great days against Washington, including a 7-touchdown pass game in 1954.

Title winners: Sammy Baugh, 2; Joe Theismann, 1; Doug Williams, 1; Mark Rypien, 1.

Hall of Famers: Sammy Baugh and Sonny Jurgensen.

All Pro/Pro Bowl seasons: Sammy Baugh, 9; Sonny Jurgensen, 4; Frankie Filchock, 3; Eddie LeBaron, 3; Billy Kilmer, 2; Joe Theismann, 2; Mark Rypien, 2; Jay Schroeder, 1; Brad Johnson, 1; Gus Frerotte, 1; Harry Gilmer, 1.

QBs as coaches: Sammy Baugh went 18–24 with the New York Titans and Houston Oilers.

Underrated: Sammy Baugh is just a name from the past today, but he would have starred in any era.

Overrated: Mark Rypien had a strong arm, but moved around like a brontosaurus in the pocket.

Best Nicknames: Honolulu Hughes, Slingin Sammy Baugh, Flingin' Frankie Filchock, Indian Jack Jacobs, George "Bad News" Cafego, Herman "Eagle" Day, Bill "Whiskey" Kilmer, Hollywood Joe Theismann.

Time Capsule: Sammy Baugh slinging the ball sidearm. Little Eddie LeBaron among the giants. Both Baugh and Billy Kilmer hitting the goal posts with a pass in the championship game. Doug Williams in the Super Bowl. Joe Gibbs' one-back offense featuring the H-back. Joe Theismann getting his leg snapped on Monday Night Football.

What If: If George Allen had stuck with Jurgensen over Kilmer, would the Over the Hill Gang have won it all?

Off the field: Frank Filchock was banned from the NFL because of not reporting a bribe attempt before the 1946 championship game.

Sonny Jurgensen and Billy Kilmer were brothers in bellying up to the bar. Kilmer appeared in *The Last Time I Saw Archie*. Sammy Baugh and Jack Jacobs appeared in *Triple Threat,* and Sammy starred in the movie serial *King of the Texas Rangers*. Joe Theismann appeared in *Good Luck*, *The Man with Bogart's Face, Cannonball Run II, The Man from Left Field* and an episode of *B.J. and the Bear*.

Quarterback Bibliography

Sammy Baugh

Canning, Whit, and Dan Jenkins. *Sam Baugh: Best There Ever Was*. Indianapolis, IN: Masters Press, 1997.

McCann, Richard P. *Slingin' Sammy Baugh, Mr. Forward Pass*. St. Louis: Spinks, 1949.

Joe Theismann

Theismann, Joe, and Dave Kindred. *Theismann*. Chicago: Contemporary Books, 1987.

Appendix A:
Records (Through 2006)

Passing

Most Seasons Leading League

6	Sammy Baugh, Washington, 1937, 1940, 1943, 1945, 1947, 1949
	Steve Young San Francisco, 1991–94, 1996–97
4	Len Dawson, Dall. Texans; 1962; Kansas City, 1964, 1966, 1968
	Roger Staubach, Dallas, 1971, 1973, 1978–79
	Ken Anderson, Cincinnati, 1974–75, 1981–82
3	Arnie Herber, Green Bay, 1932, 1934, 1936
	Norm Van Brocklin, Los Angeles, 1950, 1952, 1954
	Bart Starr, Green Bay, 1962, 1964, 1966
	Peyton Manning, Indianapolis, 2004–06

Passer Rating

Highest Passer Rating, Career (1,500 attempts)

96.8	Steve Young, Tampa Bay, 1985–86; San Francisco, 1987–1999
94.4	Peyton Manning, Indianapolis, 1998–2006
93.8	Kurt Warner, St. Louis, 1998–2003; N.Y. Giants, 2004; Arizona, 2005–06

Highest Passer Rating, Season (Qualifiers)

121.1	Peyton Manning, Indianapolis, 2004
112.8	Steve Young, San Francisco, 1994
112.4	Joe Montana, San Francisco, 1989

Highest Passer Rating, Rookie, Season (Qualifiers)

98.1	Ben Roethlisberger, Pittsburgh, 2004
96.0	Dan Marino, Miami, 1983
88.2	Greg Cook, Cincinnati, 1969

Attempts

Most Passes Attempted, Career

8,358	Dan Marino, Miami, 1983–1999
8,223	Brett Favre, Atlanta, 1991; Green Bay, 1992–2006
7,250	John Elway, Denver, 1983–1998

Most Passes Attempted, Season

691	Drew Bledsoe, New England, 1994
655	Warren Moon, Houston, 1991
636	Drew Bledsoe, New England, 1995

Most Passes Attempted, Rookie, Season

575	Peyton Manning, Indianapolis, 1998
540	Chris Weinke, Carolina, 2001
486	Rick Mirer, Seattle, 1993

Most Passes Attempted, Game

70	Drew Bledsoe, New England vs. Minnesota, Nov. 13, 1994 (OT)
69	Vinny Testaverde, N.Y. Jets vs. Baltimore, Dec. 24, 2000
68	George Blanda, Houston vs. Buffalo, Nov. 1, 1964
	Jon Kitna, Cincinnati vs. Pittsburgh, Dec. 30, 2001 (OT)

Completions

Most Passes Completed, Career

5,021	Brett Favre, Atlanta, 1991; Green Bay, 1992–2006
4,967	Dan Marino, Miami, 1983–1999
4,123	John Elway, Denver, 1983–1998

Most Passes Completed, Season

418	Rich Gannon, Oakland, 2002
404	Warren Moon, Houston, 1991
400	Drew Bledsoe, New England, 1994

Most Passes Completed, Rookie, Season

326	Peyton Manning, Indianapolis, 1998
293	Chris Weinke, Carolina, 2001
274	Rick Mirer, Seattle, 1993

Most Passes Completed, Game

45	Drew Bledsoe, New England vs. Minnesota, Nov. 13, 1994 (OT)
43	Rich Gannon, Oakland vs. Pittsburgh, Sept. 15, 2002
42	Richard Todd, N.Y. Jets vs. San Francisco, Sept. 21, 1980
	Vinny Testaverde, N.Y. Jets vs. Seattle, Dec. 6, 1998

Most Consecutive Passes Completed

24	Donovan McNabb, Philadelphia vs. N.Y. Giants (10), Nov. 28, 2004; vs. Green Bay (14), Dec. 5, 2004
22	Mark Brunell, Washington vs. Houston, Sept. 24, 2006
22	Joe Montana, San Francisco vs. Cleveland (5), Nov. 29, 1987; vs. Green Bay (17), Dec. 6, 1987
21	Rich Gannon, Oakland vs. Denver, Nov. 11, 2002

Completion Percentage

Most Seasons Leading League

8	Len Dawson, Dall. Texans, 1962; Kansas City, 1964–69, 1975
7	Sammy Baugh, Washington, 1940, 1942–43, 1945, 1947–49
5	Joe Montana, San Francisco, 1980–81, 1985, 1987, 1989
	Steve Young, San Francisco, 1992, 1994–97

Highest Completion Percentage, Career (1,500 attempts)

65.6	Kurt Warner, St. Louis, 1998–2003; N.Y. Giants, 2004; Arizona, 2005–06 (2,508–1,645)
65.1	Chad Pennington, N. Y. Jets, 2000–06 (1,659–1,080)
64.4	Marc Bulger, St. Louis, 2002–06 (2,106–1,357)

Highest Completion Percentage, Season (Qualifiers)

70.55	Ken Anderson, Cincinnati, 1982 (309–218)
70.33	Sammy Baugh, Washington, 1945 (182–128)
70.28	Steve Young, San Francisco, 1994 (461–324)

Highest Completion Percentage, Rookie, Season (Qualifiers)

66.44	Ben Roethlisberger, Pittsburgh, 2004 (295–196)

58.45 Dan Marino, Miami, 1983 (296–173)
57.18 Byron Leftwich, Jacksonville, 2003 (418–239)

Highest Completion Percentage, Game (20 attempts)

91.30 Vinny Testaverde, Cleveland vs. L.A. Rams, Dec. 26, 1993 (23–21)
90.91 Ken Anderson, Cincinnati vs. Pittsburgh, Nov. 10, 1974 (22–20)
90.48 Lynn Dickey, Green Bay vs. New Orleans, Dec. 13, 1981 (21–19)

Yards Gained

Most Seasons Leading League

5 Sonny Jurgensen, Philadelphia, 1961–62; Washington, 1966–67, 1969
   Dan Marino, Miami, 1984–86, 1988, 1992
4 Sammy Baugh, Washington, 1937, 1940, 1947–48
   Johnny Unitas, Baltimore, 1957, 1959–1960, 1963
   Dan Fouts, San Diego, 1979–1982
3 Arnie Herber, Green Bay, 1932, 1934, 1936
   Sid Luckman, Chi. Bears, 1943, 1945–46
   John Brodie, San Francisco, 1965, 1968, 1970
   John Hadl, San Diego, 1965, 1968, 1971
   Joe Namath, N.Y. Jets, 1966–67, 1972

Most Yards Gained, Career

61,361 Dan Marino, Miami, 1983–1999
57,500 Brett Favre, Atlanta, 1991; Green Bay, 1992–2006
51,475 John Elway, Denver, 1983–1998

Most Seasons, 3,000 or More Yards Passing

15 Brett Favre, Green Bay, 1992–2006
13 Dan Marino, Miami, 1984–1992, 1994–95, 1997–98
12 John Elway, Denver, 1985–1991, 1993–97

Most Yards Gained, Season

5,084 Dan Marino, Miami, 1984
4,830 Kurt Warner, St. Louis, 2001
4,802 Dan Fouts, San Diego, 1981

Most Yards Gained, Rookie, Season

3,739 Peyton Manning, Indianapolis, 1998
2,931 Chris Weinke, Carolina, 2001
2,833 Rick Mirer, Seattle, 1993

Most Yards Gained, Game

554 Norm Van Brocklin, Los Angeles vs. N.Y. Yanks, Sept. 28, 1951
527 Warren Moon, Houston vs. Kansas City, Dec. 16, 1990
522 Boomer Esiason, Arizona vs. Washington, Nov. 10, 1996

Most Games, 400 or More Yards Passing, Career

13 Dan Marino, Miami, 1983–1999
7 Joe Montana, San Francisco, 1979–1990, 1992; Kansas City, 1993–94
   Warren Moon, Houston, 1984–1993; Minnesota, 1994–96; Seattle, 1997–98; Kansas City, 1999–2000
   Peyton Manning, Indianapolis, 1998–2006
6 Dan Fouts, San Diego, 1973–1987
   Drew Bledsoe, New England, 1993–2001; Buffalo, 2002–04

Most Games, 400 or More Yards Passing, Season

4 Dan Marino, Miami, 1984
3 Dan Marino, Miami, 1986
2 By many players

Most Games, 300 or More Yards Passing, Career

63 Dan Marino, Miami, 1983–1999
51 Dan Fouts, San Diego, 1973–1987
49 Warren Moon, Houston, 1984–1993; Minnesota, 1994–96; Seattle, 1997–98; Kansas City, 1999–2000

Most Games, 300 or More Yards Passing, Season

10	Rich Gannon, Oakland, 2002
9	Dan Marino, Miami, 1984
	Warren Moon, Houston, 1990
	Kurt Warner, St. Louis, 1999
	Kurt Warner, St. Louis, 2001
8	Dan Fouts, San Diego, 1980
	Kurt Warner, St. Louis, 2000
	Trent Green, Kansas City, 2004

Longest Pass Completion (All TDs except as noted)

99   Frank Filchock (to Farkas), Washington
vs. Pittsburgh, Oct. 15, 1939
George Izo (to Mitchell), Washington
vs. Cleveland, Sept. 15, 1963
Karl Sweetan (to Studstill), Detroit vs.
Baltimore, Oct. 16, 1966
Sonny Jurgensen (to Allen), Washington vs. Chicago, Sept. 15, 1968
Jim Plunkett (to Branch), L.A. Raiders
vs. Washington, Oct. 2, 1983
Ron Jaworski (to Quick), Philadelphia
vs. Atlanta, Nov. 10, 1985
Stan Humphries (to Martin), San Diego
vs. Seattle, Sept. 18, 1994
Brett Favre (to Brooks), Green Bay vs.
Chicago, Sept. 11, 1995
Trent Green (to Boerigter), Kansas City
vs. San Diego, Dec. 22, 2002
Jeff Garcia (to Davis), Cleveland vs.
Cincinnati, Oct. 17, 2004

Average Gain

Most Seasons Leading League

7   Sid Luckman, Chi. Bears, 1939–1943,
1946–47
5   Steve Young, San Francisco, 1991–94,
1997
3   Arnie Herber, Green Bay, 1932, 1934,
1936
Norm Van Brocklin, Los Angeles, 1950,
1952, 1954
Len Dawson, Dall. Texans, 1962; Kansas City, 1966, 1968
Bart Starr, Green Bay, 1966–68
Kurt Warner, St. Louis, 1999–2001

Highest Average Gain, Career (1,500 attempts)

8.63   Otto Graham, Cleveland, 1950–55
(1,565–13,499)
8.42   Sid Luckman, Chi. Bears, 1939–1950
(1,744–14,686)
8.21   Kurt Warner, St. Louis, 1998–2003;
N.Y. Giants, 2004; Arizona, 2005–06
(2,508–20,591)

Highest Average Gain, Season (Qualifiers)

11.17   Tommy O'Connell, Cleveland, 1957
(110–1,229)
10.86   Sid Luckman, Chi. Bears, 1943 (202–
2,194)
10.55   Otto Graham, Cleveland, 1953 (258–
2,722)

Highest Average Gain, Rookie, Season (Qualifiers)

9.411   Greg Cook, Cincinnati, 1969 (197–1,854)
9.409   Bob Waterfield, Cleveland, 1945 (171–
1,609)
8.88   Ben Roethlisberger, Pittsburgh, 2004
(295–2,621)

Highest Average Gain, Game (20 Attempts)

18.58   Sammy Baugh, Washington vs. Boston,
Oct. 31, 1948 (24–446)
18.50   Johnny Unitas, Baltimore vs. Atlanta,
Nov. 12, 1967 (20–370)
17.71   Joe Namath, N.Y. Jets vs. Baltimore,
Sept. 24, 1972 (28–496)

Touchdowns

Most Seasons Leading League

4   Johnny Unitas, Baltimore, 1957–1960
Len Dawson, Dall. Texans, 1962; Kansas City, 1963, 1965–66
Steve Young, San Francisco, 1992–94,
1998
Brett Favre, Green Bay, 1995–97, 2003
3   Arnie Herber, Green Bay, 1932, 1934,
1936

Sid Luckman, Chi. Bears, 1943, 1945–46

Y.A. Tittle, San Francisco, 1955; N.Y. Giants, 1962–63

Dan Marino, Miami, 1984–86

Peyton Manning, Indianapolis, 2000, 2004, 2006

Most Touchdown Passes, Career

420	Dan Marino, Miami, 1983–1999
414	Brett Favre, Atlanta, 1991; Green Bay, 1992–2006
342	Fran Tarkenton, Minnesota, 1961–66, 1972–78; N.Y. Giants, 1967–1971

Most Touchdown Passes, Season

49	Peyton Manning, Indianapolis, 2004
48	Dan Marino, Miami, 1984
44	Dan Marino, Miami, 1986

Most Touchdown Passes, Rookie, Season

26	Peyton Manning, Indianapolis, 1998
22	Charlie Conerly, N.Y. Giants, 1948
20	Dan Marino, Miami, 1983

Most Touchdown Passes, Game

7	Sid Luckman, Chi. Bears vs. N.Y. Giants, Nov. 14, 1943
	Adrian Burk, Philadelphia vs. Washington, Oct. 17, 1954
	George Blanda, Houston vs. N.Y. Titans, Nov. 19, 1961
	Y.A. Tittle, N.Y. Giants vs. Washington, Oct. 28, 1962
	Joe Kapp, Minnesota vs. Baltimore, Sept. 28, 1969

Most Games, Four or More Touchdown Passes, Career

21	Dan Marino, Miami, 1983–1999
19	Brett Favre, Atlanta, 1991; Green Bay, 1992–2006
17	Johnny Unitas, Baltimore, 1956–1972; San Diego, 1973

Most Consecutive Games, Touchdown Passes

47	Johnny Unitas, Baltimore, 1956–1960
36	Brett Favre, Green Bay, 2002–2004
30	Dan Marino, Miami, 1985–87

Had Intercepted

Most Consecutive Passes Attempted, None Intercepted

308	Bernie Kosar, Cleveland, 1990–91
294	Bart Starr, Green Bay, 1964–65
279	Jeff George, Indianapolis, 1993; Atlanta, 1994

Most Passes Had Intercepted, Career

277	George Blanda, Chi. Bears, 1949, 1950–58; Baltimore, 1950; Houston, 1960–66; Oakland, 1967–1975
273	Brett Favre, Atlanta, 1991; Green Bay, 1992–2006
268	John Hadl, San Diego, 1962–1972; Los Angeles, 1973–74; Green Bay, 1974–75; Houston, 1976–77

Most Passes Had Intercepted, Season

42	George Blanda, Houston, 1962
35	Vinny Testaverde, Tampa Bay, 1988
34	Frank Tripucka, Denver, 1960

Most Passes Had Intercepted, Game

8	Jim Hardy, Chi. Cardinals vs. Philadelphia, Sept. 24, 1950
7	Parker Hall, Cleveland vs. Green Bay, Nov. 8, 1942
	Frank Sinkwich, Detroit vs. Green Bay, Oct. 24, 1943
	Bob Waterfield, Los Angeles vs. Green Bay, Oct. 17, 1948
	Zeke Bratkowski, Chicago vs. Baltimore, Oct. 2, 1960
	Tommy Wade, Pittsburgh vs. Philadelphia, Dec. 12, 1965
	Ken Stabler, Oakland vs. Denver, Oct. 16, 1977

Steve DeBerg, Tampa Bay vs. San Francisco, Sept. 7, 1986

Ty Detmer, Detroit vs. Cleveland, Sept. 23, 2001

Lowest Percentage Intercepted

Most Seasons Leading League, Lowest Percentage, Passes Had Intercepted

5   Sammy Baugh, Washington, 1940, 1942, 1944–45, 1947

3   Charlie Conerly, N.Y. Giants, 1950, 1956, 1959

Bart Starr, Green Bay, 1962, 1964, 1966

Roger Staubach, Dallas, 1971, 1977, 1979

Ken Anderson, Cincinnati, 1972, 1981–82

Ken O'Brien, N.Y. Jets, 1985, 1987–88

Lowest Percentage, Passes Had Intercepted, Career (1,500 attempts)

2.11   Neil O'Donnell, Pittsburgh, 1991–95; N.Y. Jets, 1996–97; Cincinnati, 1998; Tennessee, 1999–2003 (3,229–68)

2.21   Donovan McNabb, Philadelphia, 1999–2006 (3,259–72)

2.31   Mark Brunell, Green Bay, 1994; Jacksonville, 1995–2003; Washington, 2004–06 (4,594–106)

Lowest Percentage, Passes Had Intercepted, Season (Qualifiers)

0.66   Joe Ferguson, Buffalo, 1976 (151–1)

0.90   Steve DeBerg, Kansas City, 1990 (444–4)

1.16   Steve Bartkowski, Atlanta, 1983 (432–5)

Lowest Percentage, Passes Had Intercepted, Rookie, Season (Qualifiers)

1.98   Charlie Batch, Detroit, 1998 (303–6)

2.03   Dan Marino, Miami, 1983 (296–6)

2.10   Gary Wood, N.Y. Giants, 1964 (143–3)

Times Sacked

Times Sacked has been compiled since 1963.

Most Times Sacked, Career

516   John Elway, Denver, 1983–1998

494   Dave Krieg, Seattle, 1980–1991; Kansas City, 1992–93; Detroit, 1994; Arizona, 1995; Chicago, 1996; Tennessee, 1997–98

484   Randall Cunningham, Philadelphia, 1985–95; Minnesota, 1997–99; Dallas, 2000; Baltimore, 2001

Most Times Sacked, Season

76   David Carr, Houston, 2002

72   Randall Cunningham, Philadelphia, 1986

68   David Carr, Houston, 2005

Most Times Sacked, Game

12   Bert Jones, Baltimore vs. St. Louis, Oct. 26, 1980

Warren Moon, Houston vs. Dallas, Sept. 29, 1985

Fumbles

Most Fumbles, Career

161   Warren Moon, Houston, 1984–1993; Minnesota, 1994–96; Seattle, 1997–98; Kansas City, 1999–2000

153   Dave Krieg, Seattle, 1980–1991; Kansas City, 1992–93; Detroit, 1994; Arizona, 1995; Chicago, 1996; Tennessee, 1997–98

137   John Elway, Denver, 1983–1998

Most Fumbles, Season

23   Kerry Collins, N.Y. Giants, 2001

Daunte Culpepper, Minnesota, 2002

21   Tony Banks, St. Louis, 1996

David Carr, Houston, 2002

18   Dave Krieg, Seattle, 1989

Warren Moon, Houston, 1990

Most Fumbles, Game

7   Len Dawson, Kansas City vs. San Diego, Nov. 15, 1964

6   Sam Etcheverry, St. Louis vs. N.Y. Giants, Sept. 17, 1961

     Dave Krieg, Seattle vs. Kansas City, Nov. 5, 1989

     Brett Favre, Green Bay vs. Tampa Bay, Dec. 7, 1998

     Kurt Warner, St. Louis vs. N.Y. Giants, Sept. 7, 2003

     Chad Pennington, N.Y. Jets vs. Kansas City, Sept. 11, 2005

5   Paul Christman, Chi. Cardinals vs. Green Bay, Nov. 10, 1946

     Charlie Conerly, N.Y. Giants vs. San Francisco, Dec. 1, 1957

     Jack Kemp, Buffalo vs. Houston, Oct. 29, 1967

     Roman Gabriel, Philadelphia vs. Oakland, Nov. 21, 1976

     Randall Cunningham, Philadelphia vs. L.A. Raiders, Nov. 30, 1986 (OT)

     Willie Totten, Buffalo vs. Indianapolis, Oct. 4, 1987

     Dave Walter, Cincinnati vs. Seattle, Oct. 11, 1987

     Dave Krieg, Seattle vs. San Diego, Nov. 25, 1990 (OT)

     Andre Ware, Detroit vs. Green Bay, Dec. 6, 1992

     Steve Beuerlein, Carolina vs. San Francisco, Nov. 8, 1998

     Patrick Ramsey, Washington vs. Green Bay, Oct. 20, 2002

Most Fumbles Recovered, Career, Own and Opponents'

56   Warren Moon, Houston, 1984–1993; Minnesota, 1994–96; Seattle, 1997–98; Kansas City, 1999–2000 (56 own)

47   Dave Krieg, Seattle, 1980–1991; Kansas City, 1992–93; Detroit, 1994; Arizona, 1995; Chicago, 1996; Tennessee, 1997–98 (47 own)

45   Boomer Esiason, Cincinnati, 1984–1992, 1997; N.Y. Jets, 1993–95; Arizona, 1996 (45 own)

Appendix B:
Extended Passing Data

League Passing Rates

Year	G	P Att/G	P Yds/G	P TD/G	Int Rate	Pass Rating
1932	58	18	91.4	0.7	9.40%	27.2
1932	*58*	*18*	*91.4*	*0.7*	*9.40%*	*27.2*
1933	57	28.6	155.8	1	15.30%	26.3
1934	60	26.8	118.6	0.9	12.80%	18.8
1935	53	30.8	159.5	1.2	14.60%	25.4
1936	54	30.7	165.9	1.2	13.00%	28.9
1937	55	33	185.9	1.6	11.30%	34.5
1938	55	36.9	211.7	1.7	10.90%	35.5
1939	55	40.7	257.6	1.8	9.30%	39.7
1940	55	41	250.7	1.8	9.90%	38.6
1941	55	40.2	243.6	1.8	9.90%	39.6
1942	55	40.9	247.4	2	9.70%	40.3
1943	40	43.3	282.7	2.9	10.50%	48.6
1944	50	42.3	258.5	2.3	11.10%	42.1
1945	50	42.2	287.5	2.2	9.10%	47.4
1933–45	*694*	*36.4*	*214.5*	*1.7*	*11.10%*	*36.4*
1946	55	42.6	287.9	2.3	9.00%	48
1947	60	49.9	361.2	3.1	8.40%	57.6
1948	60	51.9	347.9	3.3	7.40%	60
1949	60	54.6	357.3	2.8	7.50%	53.9
1950	78	55.2	372.4	2.8	8.00%	52.9
1951	72	53.9	367.8	2.8	7.40%	55.6
1952	72	55.9	372	3	7.10%	56.7
1953	72	59.3	387.8	2.6	7.20%	53.7
1954	72	58.8	422.2	3	6.90%	62.1
1955	72	53.1	351.2	2.5	6.80%	57.1
1956	72	45.6	322.8	2.3	7.30%	59.6
1957	72	46.4	343.7	2.4	6.90%	63.2
1958	72	54.9	392.9	2.9	6.20%	65.3
1959	72	51.6	373.9	2.7	6.00%	66.9
1946–59	*961*	*52.6*	*363.1*	*2.7*	*7.20%*	*58.2*
1946a	56	40.3	269.2	2.4	8.30%	55.4
1947a	56	41.1	295.6	2.6	7.10%	64.5
1948a	56	50.1	353.1	3	6.70%	64.2

Year	G	P Att/G	P Yds/G	P TD/G	Int Rate	Pass Rating
1949a	42	46.7	331.5	2.5	7.30%	58.4
AAFC	*210*	*44.4*	*311*	*2.6*	*7.30%*	*60.9*
1960	78	52.7	381.4	2.8	6.70%	64.2
1961	98	54	404	2.9	6.30%	68.5
1962	98	54.7	429.2	3.1	6.10%	72.5
1963	98	55.3	426	3.1	5.60%	72.5
1964	98	55.5	397.1	2.8	5.10%	70.6
1965	98	55.2	411.7	3.1	5.10%	73.5
1966	105	58.2	402.1	2.7	5.20%	67.4
1967	112	57.6	400	2.9	5.70%	66.6
1968	112	53.5	375.8	2.9	5.50%	69.6
1969	112	56.7	395.8	2.9	4.90%	71.6
1970	182	53.8	362.1	2.3	5.20%	65.6
1971	182	51.7	347.5	1.6	5.80%	58.6
1972	182	49.5	337.5	2.2	5.30%	66.3
1973	182	48.6	318.7	2.1	5.30%	64.9
1974	182	52.8	342.8	2.1	5.20%	64.2
1975	182	54.8	365.9	2.4	5.30%	65.8
1976	196	52.3	346.9	2.2	4.80%	67
1977	196	49.9	324.5	2	5.70%	61.2
1960–77	*2493*	*53.2*	*367*	*2.4*	*5.40%*	*66.6*
1960a	56	66.1	436.4	3.3	5.90%	62.1
1961a	56	64.8	434.6	3.3	6.40%	59.1
1962a	56	61.7	419.9	3.1	7.00%	57.9
1963a	56	63.2	399.3	3.4	6.00%	62
1964a	56	67	471.9	3.4	6.40%	62.6
1965a	56	65.2	415.2	2.9	5.60%	58
1966a	63	63.2	430.6	3.2	5.40%	63
1967a	63	61.6	412.2	3	5.90%	61.6
1968a	70	57.7	398.8	2.7	5.60%	62.6
1969a	70	57.6	400.7	2.8	5.80%	64.5
AFL	*602*	*62.5*	*420.9*	*3.1*	*6.00%*	*61.4*
1978	224	52.8	355.2	2.1	5.40%	65
1979	224	57.9	398.1	2.4	4.60%	70.4
1980	224	56.7	428.3	2.7	4.90%	79.4
1981	224	63.3	445.2	2.6	4.30%	72.9
1982	126	63	441.7	2.5	4.40%	73.4
1983	224	62.7	450.5	2.8	4.40%	75.9
1984	224	64	456.4	2.7	4.10%	76.1
1985	224	64.4	453.2	2.7	4.20%	73.5
1986	224	64.6	451.5	2.6	4.00%	74.1
1987	210	64.2	446.8	2.9	4.00%	75.2
1988	224	63.1	435.9	2.5	3.90%	72.9
1989	224	64	457.4	2.6	3.90%	75.6
1990	224	60.3	422.8	2.6	3.60%	77.3
1991	224	62.3	429	2.3	3.50%	76.2
1992	224	59.9	410.8	2.3	3.90%	75.3
1993	224	64.3	430.8	2.3	3.30%	76.7
1978–93	*3472*	*61.7*	*431.8*	*2.5*	*4.10%*	*74.5*
1994	224	67.2	454.8	2.6	3.10%	78.4
1995	240	69.6	471.1	2.8	3.10%	79.2
1996	240	66.5	444.5	3	3.40%	79
1997	240	65.5	438.7	2.6	3.00%	77.2
1998	240	64.5	442	2.7	3.30%	78.3
1999	248	67.6	456.7	2.7	3.40%	77.3
2000	248	66	444.1	2.6	3.20%	77.8
2001	248	65.2	442.1	2.6	3.40%	78.5
2002	256	67.5	453.9	2.7	3.10%	80.4

Year	G	P Att/G	P Yds/G	P TD/g	Int Rate	Pass Rating
2003	256	64.4	427.6	2.6	3.30%	78.3
2004	256	63.9	450.5	2.8	3.20%	82.6
2005	256	64.3	406.9	2.5	3.10%	78.2
2006	256	64	409.6	2.5	3.20%	78.5
1994–06	*3208*	*65.8*	*441.4*	*2.7*	*3.20%*	*78.8*
1932–06	*11698*	*58.3*	*397.7*	*2.5*	*4.70%*	*70.4*

Basic League Passing Data

Year	G	Att	Comp	%	Yards	Y/Att	Y/Comp	TD	Ints	300-Yd Gms
1932	58	1044	372	35.6%	5300	5.1	14.2	42	98	0
1932	*58*	*1044*	*372*	*35.6%*	*5300*	*5.1*	*14.2*	*42*	*98*	*0*
1933	57	1631	576	35.3%	8878	5.4	15.4	57	249	0
1934	60	1606	505	31.4%	7117	4.4	14.1	56	206	0
1935	53	1630	552	33.9%	8453	5.2	15.3	64	238	0
1936	54	1656	604	36.5%	8960	5.4	14.8	67	216	0
1937	55	1815	697	38.4%	10227	5.6	14.7	90	206	1
1938	55	2030	824	40.6%	11641	5.7	14.1	93	221	0
1939	55	2238	952	42.5%	14168	6.3	14.9	99	209	0
1940	55	2254	968	42.9%	13788	6.1	14.2	100	223	1
1941	55	2210	978	44.3%	13397	6.1	13.7	99	219	0
1942	55	2249	986	43.8%	13608	6.1	13.8	108	219	1
1943	40	1732	769	44.4%	11308	6.5	14.7	114	182	2
1944	50	2114	906	42.9%	12925	6.1	14.3	117	234	0
1945	50	2111	958	45.4%	14375	6.8	15.0	109	193	1
1933–45	*694*	*25276*	*10275*	*40.7%*	*148845*	*5.9*	*14.5*	*1173*	*2815*	*6*
1946	55	2342	1050	44.8%	15836	6.8	15.1	126	211	1
1947	60	2991	1407	47.0%	21670	7.2	15.4	188	250	8
1948	60	3116	1498	48.1%	20871	6.7	13.9	196	232	2
1949	60	3275	1527	46.6%	21436	6.5	14.0	168	247	8
1950	78	4307	2008	46.6%	29050	6.7	14.5	220	343	6
1951	72	3881	1809	46.6%	26482	6.8	14.6	200	288	5
1952	72	4024	1863	46.3%	26781	6.7	14.4	218	287	3
1953	72	4267	2020	47.3%	27925	6.5	13.8	189	306	12
1954	72	4232	2135	50.4%	30397	7.2	14.2	216	294	5
1955	72	3820	1829	47.9%	25285	6.6	13.8	180	258	5
1956	72	3282	1656	50.5%	23242	7.1	14.0	162	240	2
1957	72	3339	1685	50.5%	24745	7.4	14.7	170	231	2
1958	72	3951	1953	49.4%	28291	7.2	14.5	211	243	6
1959	72	3714	1858	50.0%	26922	7.2	14.5	197	221	5
1946–59	*961*	*50541*	*24298*	*48.1%*	*348933*	*6.9*	*14.4*	*2641*	*3651*	*70*
1946a	56	2255	1091	48.4%	15073	6.7	13.8	133	187	0
1947a	56	2301	1128	49.0%	16551	7.2	14.7	147	164	1
1948a	56	2805	1370	48.8%	19772	7.0	14.4	167	187	7
1949a	42	1963	930	47.4%	13921	7.1	15.0	104	143	5
AAFC	*210*	*9324*	*4519*	*48.5%*	*65317*	*7.0*	*14.5*	*551*	*681*	*13*
1960	78	4114	2064	50.2%	29753	7.2	14.4	221	274	8
1961	98	5292	2759	52.1%	39591	7.5	14.3	285	332	18
1962	98	5356	2851	53.2%	42057	7.9	14.8	300	325	19
1963	98	5415	2791	51.5%	41746	7.7	15.0	302	302	21
1964	98	5436	2794	51.4%	38914	7.2	13.9	278	276	11
1965	98	5407	2774	51.3%	40349	7.5	14.5	307	277	16
1966	105	6108	3149	51.6%	42225	6.9	13.4	280	318	13
1967	112	6451	3292	51.0%	44801	6.9	13.6	324	366	19
1968	112	5997	3093	51.6%	42095	7.0	13.6	324	327	6
1969	112	6345	3340	52.6%	44324	7.0	13.3	323	311	12
1970	182	9796	5008	51.1%	65904	6.7	13.2	427	510	13

Year	G	Att	Comp	%	Yards	Y/Att	Y/Comp	TD	Ints	300-Yd Gms
1971	182	9412	4788	50.9%	63253	6.7	13.2	289	544	11
1972	182	9011	4659	51.7%	61425	6.8	13.2	404	480	8
1973	182	8845	4603	52.0%	58009	6.6	12.6	378	470	10
1974	182	9609	5041	52.5%	62391	6.5	12.4	376	500	11
1975	182	9973	5231	52.5%	66595	6.7	12.7	433	533	16
1976	196	10260	5351	52.2%	67990	6.6	12.7	432	497	13
1977	196	9786	5022	51.3%	63594	6.5	12.7	388	562	5
1960–77	*2493*	*132613*	*68610*	*51.7%*	*915016*	*6.9*	*13.3*	*6071*	*7204*	*230*
1960a	56	3699	1795	48.5%	24437	6.6	13.6	186	219	12
1961a	56	3630	1699	46.8%	24336	6.7	14.3	182	232	9
1962a	56	3456	1644	47.6%	23515	6.8	14.3	176	242	6
1963a	56	3539	1722	48.7%	22358	6.3	13.0	192	213	11
1964a	56	3750	1838	49.0%	26428	7.0	14.4	190	239	16
1965a	56	3652	1653	45.3%	23253	6.4	14.1	163	203	6
1966a	63	3982	1842	46.3%	27128	6.8	14.7	199	217	13
1967a	63	3878	1846	47.6%	25969	6.7	14.1	190	227	14
1968a	70	4037	1916	47.5%	27914	6.9	14.6	189	227	17
1969a	70	4032	2006	49.8%	28046	7.0	14.0	194	233	12
AFL	*602*	*37655*	*17961*	*47.7%*	*253384*	*6.7*	*14.1*	*1861*	*2252*	*116*
1978	224	11829	6278	53.1%	79557	6.7	12.7	468	639	15
1979	224	12979	7022	54.1%	89170	6.9	12.7	538	597	44
1980	224	12705	7699	60.6%	95935	7.6	12.5	606	627	54
1981	224	14180	7745	54.6%	99721	7.0	12.9	591	609	57
1982	126	7933	4474	56.4%	55657	7.0	12.4	320	349	35
1983	224	14047	7993	56.9%	100922	7.2	12.6	625	620	65
1984	224	14325	8076	56.4%	102233	7.1	12.7	615	584	68
1985	224	14423	7911	54.8%	101518	7.0	12.8	598	602	66
1986	224	14469	8014	55.4%	101128	7.0	12.6	586	581	60
1987	210	13491	7396	54.8%	93822	7.0	12.7	611	540	58
1988	224	14131	7670	54.3%	97635	6.9	12.7	556	553	52
1989	224	14338	8000	55.8%	102456	7.1	12.8	582	559	66
1990	224	13516	7572	56.0%	94700	7.0	12.5	575	480	42
1991	224	13951	8003	57.4%	96100	6.9	12.0	511	488	53
1992	224	13408	7705	57.5%	92011	6.9	11.9	516	519	43
1993	224	14414	8351	57.9%	96490	6.7	11.6	517	469	37
1978–93	*3472*	*214139*	*119909*	*56.0%*	*1499055*	*7.0*	*12.5*	*8815*	*8816*	*815*
1994	224	15056	8739	58.0%	101884	6.8	11.7	583	474	64
1995	240	16699	9717	58.2%	113069	6.8	11.6	663	512	79
1996	240	15967	9199	57.6%	106691	6.7	11.6	726	540	50
1997	240	15729	8844	56.2%	105288	6.7	11.9	617	479	46
1998	240	15489	8766	56.6%	106086	6.8	12.1	658	509	53
1999	248	16760	9567	57.1%	113254	6.8	11.8	675	562	73
2000	248	16372	9497	58.0%	110131	6.7	11.6	634	531	65
2001	248	16181	9542	59.0%	109639	6.8	11.5	635	545	71
2002	256	17292	10314	59.6%	116201	6.7	11.3	694	528	79
2003	256	16493	9695	58.8%	109467	6.6	11.3	654	538	59
2004	256	16354	9772	59.8%	115338	7.1	11.8	722	524	80
2005	256	16465	9790	59.5%	104174	6.3	10.6	645	506	68
2006	256	16388	9796	59.8%	104861	6.4	10.7	648	520	62
1994–06	*3208*	*211245*	*123238*	*58.3%*	*1416083*	*6.7*	*11.5*	*8554*	*6768*	*849*
1932–06	*11698*	*681837*	*369182*	*54.1%*	*4651933*	*6.8*	*12.6*	*29708*	*32285*	*2099*

Career Relative Passer Rating

Name	Pass Rating	League Pass Rating	Relative Pass Rating
Bob Monnett	64.4	28.6	225%

Name	Pass Rating	League Pass Rating	Relative Pass Rating
Keith Molesworth	52.7	27	195%
Cecil Isbell	72.6	38.6	188%
Bernie Masterson	57.2	32.4	177%
Ed Danowski	58.1	33.4	174%
Sid Luckman	75.2	47.6	158%
Sammy Baugh	72.2	47.4	152%
Otto Graham	86.6	57.6	150%
Arnie Herber	50.1	34	147%
Ray Mallouf	75	52.5	143%
Harry Newman	33.5	23.5	143%
Dutch Clark	40.3	28.5	141%
Greg Cook	88.3	64.5	137%
Frank Filchock	58	42.4	137%
Tommy Thompson	66.5	49.5	134%
Glenn Presnell	33	25.1	131%
Ace Parker	53.2	40.7	131%
Len Dawson	82.6	63.8	129%
Frankie Albert	73.5	57.6	128%
Roger Staubach	83.4	65.5	127%
Norm Van Brocklin	75.1	59.2	127%
Steve Young	96.8	76.5	127%
Sonny Jurgensen	82.6	66.9	123%
Joe Montana	92.3	75.3	123%
George Ratterman	70.4	57.9	122%
Tony Romo	95.1	78.4	121%
Fran Tarkenton	80.4	66.5	121%
Bart Starr	80.5	67.2	120%
Peyton Manning	94.4	78.9	120%
Kurt Warner	93.8	78.9	119%
Johnny Lujack	65.3	55.4	118%
Y.A. Tittle	74.3	63.3	117%
Johnny Unitas	78.2	66.9	117%
Ken Anderson	81.9	70.1	117%
Bob Berry	77.2	66.1	117%
Daryle Lamonica	72.9	63.2	115%
Daunte Culpepper	90.8	79	115%
Bob Griese	77.1	67.1	115%
Marc Bulger	91.3	79.6	115%
Carson Palmer	91.5	79.8	115%
Bert Jones	78.2	68.8	114%
Charlie Conerly	68.2	60.1	113%
Philip Rivers	90.5	79.8	113%
Dan Marino	86.4	76.4	113%
Bob Waterfield	61.6	54.5	113%
Frank Ryan	77.6	68.8	113%
Charley O'Rourke	63.6	56.4	113%
Chad Pennington	89.3	79.2	113%
Jay Cutler	88.5	78.5	113%
Danny White	81.7	72.5	113%
Carl Brumbaugh	32.1	28.5	113%
Dan Fouts	80.2	71.3	112%
Butch Songin	67.1	59.8	112%
Tom Brady	88.4	79.2	112%
Roman Gabriel	74.3	66.6	112%
Neal Lomax	82.7	74.3	111%
Trent Green	87.5	78.7	111%
Earl Morrall	74.1	66.7	111%

Name	Pass Rating	League Pass Rating	Relative Pass Rating
Jim Kelly	84.4	76.5	110%
Ben Roethlisberger	87.9	79.8	110%
Tom Flores	67.6	61.4	110%
Drew Brees	87.5	79.5	110%
Billy Volek	86.8	79.2	110%
Jeff Garcia	86.4	79	109%
Joe Theismann	77.4	71	109%
Rich Gannon	84.7	77.7	109%
Ken Stabler	75.3	69.2	109%
Brett Favre	85	78.3	109%
Bobby Thomason	62.9	58.1	108%
Damon Huard	85.2	78.9	108%
Craig Morton	73.5	68.1	108%
Donovan McNabb	85.2	79	108%
Bill Munson	71.5	66.3	108%
Davey O'Brien	41.8	38.8	108%
Matt Hasselbeck	85.1	79	108%
Billy Kilmer	71.6	66.5	108%
Bob Snyder	42.3	39.3	108%
John Brodie	72.3	67.2	108%
Don Meredith	74.8	69.6	107%
Bill Wade	72.2	67.2	107%
Bernie Kosar	81.8	76.2	107%
Brian Griese	84.5	78.9	107%
Brian Sipe	74.8	70	107%
Mark Brunell	84.2	78.8	107%
Jacky Lee	65.6	61.4	107%
Dave Krieg	81.5	76.3	107%
Ken O'Brien	80.4	75.3	107%
Rob Johnson	83.6	78.3	107%
Paul Governali	59.5	55.8	107%
Greg Landry	72.9	68.5	106%
Virgil Carter	69.9	65.7	106%
Jake Delhomme	84	79	106%
Boomer Esiason	81.1	76.3	106%
Randall Cunningham	81.5	76.7	106%
John Hadl	67.4	63.5	106%
Tony Eason	79.7	75.1	106%
Gary Danielson	76.6	72.5	106%
Warren Moon	80.9	76.6	106%
Steve McNair	83.2	78.8	106%
Brad Johnson	83.1	78.8	105%
Troy Aikman	81.6	77.4	105%
Steve Bartkowski	75.4	71.8	105%
Neil O'Donnell	81.8	78	105%
James Harris	67.3	64.2	105%
Bill Nelsen	70.2	67	105%
Jaime Martin	82.3	78.6	105%
Jeff Hostetler	80.5	76.9	105%
Phil Simms	78.5	75	105%
Milt Plum	72.2	69	105%
John Elway	79.9	76.4	105%
Don Strock	74.9	71.7	104%
Tim Rattay	82.6	79.2	104%
Steve Beuerlein	80.3	77.5	104%
Terry Bradshaw	70.9	68.5	104%
Jeff George	80.4	77.7	103%

Name	Pass Rating	League Pass Rating	Relative Pass Rating
Bobby Layne	63.4	61.3	103%
Charley Johnson	69.2	67.1	103%
Bill Kenney	77	74.8	103%
Jim McMahon	78.2	76.1	103%
Jim Everett	78.6	76.5	103%
Joe Namath	65.5	63.8	103%
Mark Rypien	78.9	76.9	103%
Bobby Hebert	78	76.2	102%
Paul Christman	54.8	53.8	102%
Elvis Grbac	79.6	78.2	102%
Clyde LeForce	58.1	57.1	102%
Lynn Dickey	70.9	69.7	102%
Chris Chandler	79.1	77.8	102%
Turk Schonert	75.6	74.5	101%
Byron Leftwich	80.5	79.4	101%
Ron Jaworski	72.8	72	101%
Jim Harbaugh	77.6	77	101%
Roy Zimmerman	46.7	46.4	101%
Rudy Bukich	66.6	66.3	100%
Kelly Holcomb	79.9	79.6	100%
Glenn Dobbs	61	60.9	100%
Charlie Batch	78.6	78.9	100%
Pat Haden	69.6	69.9	100%
Jeff Blake	78	78.4	99%
Aaron Brooks	78.5	79	99%
George Blanda	60.6	61	99%
Wade Wilson	75.6	76.1	99%
Steve DeBerg	74.2	74.7	99%
Don Trull	61.6	62.1	99%
Tommy Kramer	72.8	73.4	99%
David Garrard	78.9	79.6	99%
Erik Kramer	76.6	77.4	99%
Steve Bono	75.3	76.5	98%
Doug Flutie	76.3	77.6	98%
Drew Bledsoe	77.1	78.6	98%
Stan Humphries	75.8	77.3	98%
Babe Parilli	59.6	60.8	98%
Chris Miller	74.9	76.5	98%
Parker Hall	38.5	39.4	98%
Norm Snead	65.5	67.1	98%
Jay Fiedler	77.1	79	98%
Jim Finks	54.7	56.1	98%
Jason Campbell	76.5	78.5	97%
Mike Livingston	63.3	65	97%
J.P. Losman	77.4	79.8	97%
Tommy O'Connell	57.5	59.3	97%
Scott Mitchell	75.3	77.8	97%
Vinny Testaverde	75.2	77.7	97%
Jon Kitna	76.1	78.7	97%
Archie Manning	67.1	69.4	97%
Vince Ferragamo	70.1	72.6	97%
Hugh Millen	73.5	76.2	96%
Jim Hart	66.6	69.1	96%
Jim Hardy	53.1	55.1	96%
Jim Plunkett	67.5	70.1	96%
Seneca Wallace	75.4	78.4	96%
Gary Hogeboom	71.9	74.9	96%

Name	Pass Rating	League Pass Rating	Relative Pass Rating
Eddie LeBaron	61.4	64.1	96%
Steve Grogan	69.6	72.7	96%
Tim Couch	75.1	78.5	96%
Craig Erickson	74.3	77.7	96%
Gus Frerotte	75.3	78.8	96%
Jim Miller	75.2	78.7	96%
Shane Matthews	75	78.5	96%
Ty Detmer	74.7	78.2	96%
Steve Pelluer	71.6	75	95%
Frank Reich	72.9	76.4	95%
Al Dorow	53.8	56.4	95%
Tobin Rote	56.8	59.6	95%
Michael Vick	75.7	79.5	95%
Bob Lee	63.7	67	95%
Don Majkowski	72.9	76.7	95%
Pete Liske	60.4	63.6	95%
Jay Schroeder	71.7	75.5	95%
David Carr	75.5	79.6	95%
Doug Williams	69.4	73.2	95%
Jake Plummer	74.6	78.7	95%
Joe Ferguson	68.4	72.3	95%
Matt Leinart	74	78.5	94%
Al Woodall	60.3	64	94%
Bubby Brister	72.3	76.8	94%
Patrick Ramsey	74.9	79.6	94%
Steve Fuller	70.1	74.5	94%
Johnny Green	56.7	60.3	94%
Jeff Kemp	70	74.5	94%
Richard Todd	67.6	72	94%
Rodney Peete	73.3	78.1	94%
Sean Salisbury	72.9	77.8	94%
Ed Brown	62.8	67.2	93%
Steve Tensi	59	63.2	93%
John Friesz	72.3	77.6	93%
George Shaw	58.8	63.2	93%
Jack Kemp	57.3	61.6	93%
Jim Zorn	67.3	72.4	93%
Kerry Collins	73.2	78.8	93%
Pat Ryan	69.2	74.5	93%
Shaun King	73.4	79.2	93%
Charlie Frye	72.3	78.4	92%
Eric Hipple	68.7	74.5	92%
Dick Shiner	61.3	66.5	92%
Gary Cuozzo	62.1	67.4	92%
Adrian Burk	52.2	56.7	92%
Cody Carlson	70	76.1	92%
Tony Banks	72.4	78.8	92%
Tommy Maddox	72.4	78.8	92%
Eli Manning	73.2	79.8	92%
Steve Spurrier	60.1	65.7	91%
Steve Ramsey	58.9	64.5	91%
Rex Grossman	72.4	79.4	91%
Frank Tripucka	52.2	57.4	91%
Josh McCown	72.1	79.6	91%
Trent Dilfer	71.3	78.8	90%
Mickey Slaughter	55.4	61.4	90%
Cotton Davidson	54.9	60.9	90%

Name	Pass Rating	League Pass Rating	Relative Pass Rating
Marc Wilson	67.7	75.1	90%
Mike Tomczak	68.9	76.5	90%
Kordell Stewart	70.8	78.8	90%
Mike Boryla	58.1	64.7	90%
Quincy Carter	71.7	80	90%
A.J. Feeley	71.1	79.5	89%
Kyle Boller	71	79.4	89%
Todd Collins	70.4	78.8	89%
Chris Simms	71.2	79.8	89%
Kent Graham	69	77.8	89%
Johnny Clement	47	53.1	89%
Dennis Shaw	56.8	64.2	88%
Steve Dils	65.8	74.4	88%
Billy Joe Tolliver	67.8	77.4	88%
Dan Pastorini	59.1	67.5	88%
Paul McDonald	65.7	75.1	87%
Dave Brown	67.9	77.7	87%
Cade McNown	67.7	77.5	87%
David Woodley	65.7	75.3	87%
Dick Wood	52.9	60.8	87%
Timm Rosenbach	66	76.1	87%
Irv Comp	41.6	48.3	86%
Chuck Long	64.5	75	86%
Dave Wilson	63.8	74.3	86%
Steve Walsh	66.4	77.4	86%
Billy Joe Hobert	67	78.2	86%
Mark Herrmann	64.3	75.1	86%
Joey Harrington	68.1	79.6	86%
Vince Young	66.7	78.5	85%
Jack Thompson	63.4	74.8	85%
Anthony Wright	66.9	79	85%
Vince Evans	63	74.5	85%
Harry Gilmer	48	56.8	85%
Scott Hunter	55	65.1	84%
Mike Pagel	63.3	75.2	84%
Bruce Gradkowski	65.9	78.5	84%
David Klingler	65.1	77.7	84%
Alex Smith	65.5	78.2	84%
Randy Johnson	55.1	65.8	84%
Jack Trudeau	63.3	76.2	83%
Marty Domres	53.8	64.8	83%
David Archer	61.9	74.7	83%
David Whitehurst	59.2	71.6	83%
Mark Malone	61.9	74.9	83%
Jack Concannon	54.8	66.4	83%
Randy Wright	61.4	74.4	83%
Jeff Rutledge	61.4	74.9	82%
Fred Enke	46.2	56.4	82%
Rick Mirer	63.5	78	81%
Jack Jacobs	42.9	52.7	81%
Joe Kapp	55.1	68	81%
Todd Blackledge	60.2	74.8	80%
Doug Pederson	62.3	77.5	80%
Derek Anderson	63.1	78.5	80%
Danny Kanell	63.2	78.7	80%
Bob Hoernschemeyer	48.9	60.9	80%
Zeke Bratkowski	54.3	67.7	80%

Name	Pass Rating	League Pass Rating	Relative Pass Rating
Jim Ninowski	55.4	69.3	80%
Pete Beathard	49.9	63.2	79%
Mike Phipps	52.6	67.4	78%
Cliff Stoudt	58.3	75	78%
Billy Shepherd	26.6	34.3	78%
Chris Weinke	61.4	79.5	77%
Bob Avellini	54.8	71.2	77%
Lamar McHan	50.3	65.9	76%
John Reaves	51.4	68.3	75%
Bobby Scott	51.4	68.5	75%
Scott Brunner	56.3	75.3	75%
Joe Pisarcik	53.9	72.2	75%
Mike Taliaferro	46.1	62.9	73%
Joe Reed	48.1	65.8	73%
Gary Huff	46.8	64.7	72%
Boley Dancewicz	40.1	55.8	72%
King Hill	49.3	69.3	71%
Karl Sweetan	48.3	67.9	71%
Andrew Walter	55.8	78.5	71%
Matt Robinson	50.2	70.7	71%
Ralph Guglielmi	46.5	66.3	70%
Heath Shuler	54.2	78.5	69%
Craig Whelihan	52.4	77.7	67%
Kent Nix	44.3	65.8	67%
John Gildea	20.7	31.4	66%
Bobby Douglass	48.5	74.5	65%
Ryan Leaf	50	78.2	64%
John McCormick	37.6	61.4	61%
John Grigas	27	45.5	59%

Won-Lost Records (40+ wins since 1950 and all active quarterbacks)

Name	Win	Losses	Ties	Percentage	Name	Win	Losses	Ties	Percentage
Elway, John	148	82	1	0.643	Tittle, Y.A.	87	70	3	0.553
Favre, Brett	147	90	0	0.620	Hart, Jim	87	87	5	0.500
Marino, Dan	147	93	0	0.613	Staubach, Roger	86	29	0	0.748
Tarkenton, Fran	125	106	6	0.540	Gabriel, Roman	86	65	7	0.566
Unitas, John	119	57	4	0.672	Fouts, Dan	86	83	1	0.509
Montana, Joe	117	47	0	0.713	Layne, Bobby	84	60	4	0.581
Bradshaw, Terry	107	51	0	0.677	Cunningham, Randall	82	52	1	0.611
Graham, Otto	103	17	4	0.847	Hadl, John	82	78	9	0.512
Moon, Warren	102	100	0	0.505	Morton, Craig	81	60	1	0.574
Kelly, Jim	101	59	0	0.631	Esiason, Boomer	80	93	0	0.462
Krieg, Dave	98	77	0	0.560	Conerly, Charlie	79	52	2	0.602
Bledsoe, Drew	98	95	0	0.508	Ferguson, Joe	79	92	0	0.462
Stabler, Ken	96	49	1	0.661	Brunell, Mark	78	72	0	0.520
Griese, Bob	95	56	3	0.627	Theismann, Joe	76	48	0	0.613
Dawson, Len	95	58	8	0.615	Gannon, Rich	76	56	0	0.576
Simms, Phil	95	64	0	0.597	Van Brocklin, Norm	75	45	4	0.621
Young, Steve	94	49	0	0.657	Grogan, Steve	75	60	0	0.556
Starr, Bart	94	59	5	0.611	Plunkett, Jim	73	69	0	0.514
Aikman, Troy	94	71	0	0.570	Jaworski, Ron	72	69	1	0.511
Manning, Peyton	92	52	0	0.639	Johnson, Brad	71	51	0	0.582
Anderson, Ken	91	81	0	0.529	Brodie, John	71	71	6	0.500
McNair, Steve	89	58	0	0.605	Brady, Tom	70	24	0	0.745
Testaverde, Vinny	88	119	1	0.425	Plummer, Jake	69	67	0	0.507

Name	Win	Losses	Ties	Percentage	Name	Win	Losses	Ties	Percentage
Jurgensen, Sonny	68	74	7	0.480	Griese, Brian	39	33	0	0.542
McMahon, Jim	67	30	0	0.691	Culpepper, Daunte	39	45	0	0.464
Chandler, Chris	67	85	0	0.441	Kitna, Jon	39	56	0	0.411
Lamonica, Daryle	66	15	6	0.793	Vick, Michael	38	28	1	0.575
Kemp, Jack	66	37	3	0.637	Brooks, Aaron	38	52	0	0.422
Harbaugh, Jim	66	74	0	0.471	Fiedler, Jay	37	23	0	0.617
Collins, Kerry	66	82	0	0.446	Bulger, Marc	36	24	0	0.600
McNabb, Donovan	65	33	0	0.663	Delhomme, Jake	36	26	0	0.581
Everett, Jim	64	89	0	0.418	Frerotte, Gus	36	42	1	0.462
Kilmer, Billy	63	50	1	0.557	Banks, Tony	35	43	0	0.449
White, Danny	62	30	0	0.674	Pennington, Chad	31	22	0	0.585
Schroeder, Jay	62	37	0	0.626	Roethlisberger, Ben	29	11	0	0.725
Johnson, Charley	62	56	8	0.524	Palmer, Carson	25	20	0	0.556
Morrall, Earl	61	40	2	0.602	Leftwich, Byron	24	20	0	0.545
Bartkowski, Steve	59	67	0	0.468	Harrington, Joey	23	43	0	0.348
Waterfield, Bob	58	26	4	0.682	Batch, Charlie	22	27	0	0.449
Dilfer, Trent	57	50	0	0.533	Carr, David	22	53	0	0.293
Ryan, Frank	56	27	3	0.669	Manning, Eli	20	19	0	0.513
Hebert, Bobby	56	44	0	0.560	Boller, Kyle	18	16	0	0.529
Green, Trent	56	51	0	0.523	Grossman, Rex	17	6	0	0.739
Sipe, Brian	56	54	0	0.509	Rivers, Philip	14	2	0	0.875
Pastorini, Dan	56	65	1	0.463	Orton, Kyle	10	5	0	0.667
Plum, Milt	55	41	6	0.569	Garard, David	10	8	0	0.556
O'Donnell, Neil	55	45	0	0.550	McCown, Josh	10	12	0	0.455
Namath, Joe	55	62	3	0.471	Ramsey, Patrick	10	14	0	0.417
Brown, Ed	54	32	4	0.622	Huard, Damon	9	4	0	0.692
Kramer, Tommy	54	56	0	0.491	Smith, Alex	9	14	0	0.391
Kosar, Bernie	53	54	1	0.495	Losman, J.P.	9	16	0	0.360
Blanda, George	53	60	2	0.470	Young, Vince	8	5	0	0.615
DeBerg, Steve	53	86	1	0.382	Wright, Anthony	8	11	0	0.421
Albert, Frankie	52	30	3	0.629	Holcomb, Kelly	8	13	0	0.381
Hostetler, Jeff	51	32	0	0.614	Feeley, A.J.	7	6	0	0.538
Rote, Tobin	51	67	2	0.433	Simms, Chris	7	8	0	0.467
Snead, Norm	51	101	7	0.343	Collins, Todd	7	10	0	0.412
O'Brien, Ken	50	59	1	0.459	Romo, Tony	6	4	0	0.600
Stewart, Kordell	48	34	0	0.585	Frye, Charlie	6	12	0	0.333
Todd, Richard	48	60	1	0.445	Rattay, Tim	5	13	0	0.278
Humphries, Stan	47	29	0	0.618	Martin, Jamie	4	4	0	0.500
Rypien, Mark	47	31	0	0.603	Leinart, Matt	3	7	0	0.300
Hasselbeck, Matt	47	33	0	0.588	Volek, Billy	3	8	0	0.273
Parilli, Babe	47	41	10	0.531	Gradkowski, Bruce	3	8	0	0.273
Jones, Bert	47	49	0	0.490	McMahon, Mike	3	11	0	0.214
Lomax, Neil	47	52	2	0.475	Hutchinson, Chad	3	11	0	0.214
Beuerlein, Steve	47	55	0	0.461	Wallace, Seneca	2	2	0	0.500
Meredith, Don	46	32	1	0.589	Cutler, Jay	2	3	0	0.400
George, Jeff	46	78	0	0.371	Campbell, Jason	2	5	0	0.286
Peete, Rodney	45	42	0	0.517	Walter, Andrew	2	6	0	0.250
Dickey, Lynn	45	60	1	0.429	Dorsey, Ken	2	8	0	0.200
Garcia, Jeff	44	48	0	0.478	Johnson, Doug	2	9	0	0.182
Landry, Greg	44	53	3	0.455	Weinke, Chris	2	17	0	0.105
Warner, Kurt	43	31	0	0.581	Rosenfels, Sage	1	1	0	0.500
Wade, Bill	43	47	2	0.478	Lemon, Cleo	0	1	0	0.000
Zorn, Jim	43	62	0	0.410	Tuiasosopo, Marques	0	2	0	0.000
Tomczak, Mike	42	31	0	0.575	Jackson, Tarvaris	0	2	0	0.000
Grbac, Elvis	40	30	0	0.571	Fitzpatrick, Ryan	0	3	0	0.000
Nelsen, Bill	40	31	3	0.561	Anderson, Derek	0	3	0	0.000
Brees, Drew	40	34	0	0.541					

Estimated Won-Lost Records (10+ wins; pre–1950 players)

Name	Wins	Losses	Ties	Percentage	Name	Wins	Losses	Ties	Percentage
Baugh, Sammy	94	50	7	0.646	Comp, Irv	27	13	1	0.671
Herber, Arnie	81	41	6	0.656	Sanders, Spec	27	13	2	0.667
Luckman, Sid	72	23	2	0.753	Mercer, Ken	27	13	10	0.640
Driscoll, Paddy	70	36	13	0.643	Ernst, Jack	27	20	2	0.571
Dunn, Red	68	27	8	0.699	Kelly, Wild Bill	26	25	9	0.508
Smyth, Lou	57	26	9	0.668	Lujack, John	25	11	0	0.694
Friedman, Bennie	56	30	5	0.643	Zimmerman, Roy	25	26	3	0.491
Brumbaugh, Carl	55	18	3	0.743	Pollard, Fritz	23	22	13	0.509
Leemans, Tuffy	53	27	8	0.648	Nevers, Ernie	23	29	6	0.448
Presnell, Glenn	48	20	6	0.689	Dobbs, Glenn	21	32	1	0.398
McBride, Jack	48	39	11	0.546	Wilson, Wildcat	20	12	5	0.608
Molesworth, Keith	45	10	8	0.778	Clement, Johnny	20	24	2	0.457
Danowski, Ed	45	20	5	0.679	Newman, Harry	19	8	0	0.704
Monnett, Bob	45	25	2	0.639	Geri, Joe	16	18	2	0.472
Stockton, Hust	44	20	7	0.669	Hall, Parker	16	26	2	0.386
Thompson, Tommy	44	35	2	0.556	O'Rourke, Charley	14	12	2	0.536
Isbell, Cecil	41	12	2	0.764	Dudley, Bill	14	17	1	0.453
Masterson, Bernie	38	16	3	0.693	Jacobs, Jack	14	20	1	0.414
Clark, Dutch	38	16	6	0.683	Gildea, John	14	21	0	0.400
Lambeau, Curly	36	19	8	0.635	Matesic, Ed	12	22	0	0.353
Christman, Paul	36	23	1	0.608	Mallouf, Ray	11	1	0	0.917
Filchock, Frank	36	26	3	0.577	Fenenbock, Chuck	10	9	1	0.525
Parker, Ace	33	20	5	0.612	Hoernschemeyer, Bob	10	28	4	0.286

4th Quarter Game Winning Drives (10+ comebacks and all active quarterbacks)

Name	Regular Season	Post-Season	Total	Name	Regular Season	Post-Season	Total
Elway, John	42	6	48	Brady, Tom	18	6	24
Marino, Dan	42	4	46	Bartkowski, Steve	23	1	24
Unitas, John	37	2	39	McNair, Steve	21	2	23
Tarkenton, Fran	36	1	37	Staubach, Roger	21	2	23
Moon, Warren	35	2	37	Layne, Bobby	22	1	23
Favre, Brett	33	2	35	Sipe, Brian	23	0	23
Montana, Joe	29	5	34	Collins, Kerry	22	0	22
Testaverde, Vinny	33	0	33	DeBerg, Steve	22	0	22
Krieg, Dave	31	1	32	Hart, Jim	21	0	21
Bledsoe, Drew	31	0	31	Starr, Bart	19	1	20
Kelly, Jim	29	1	30	Conerly, Charlie	20	0	20
Manning, Peyton	28	1	29	Harbaugh, Jim	20	0	20
Johnson, Brad	29	0	29	Kramer, Tommy	19	1	20
Plummer, Jake	29	0	29	Williams, Doug	19	1	20
Bradshaw, Terry	24	4	28	Griese, Bob	18	1	19
Stabler, Ken	25	2	27	Dawson, Len	17	2	19
Fouts, Dan	23	3	26	Baugh, Sammy	19	0	19
Brunell, Mark	25	1	26	Morton, Craig	19	0	19
Cunningham, Randall	23	2	25	Grogan, Steve	19	0	19
Theismann, Joe	23	2	25	Van Brocklin, Norm	17	2	19
Tittle, Y.A.	24	0	24	Plunkett, Jim	18	1	19
Esiason, Boomer	24	0	24	Brodie, John	19	0	19
Ferguson, Joe	24	0	24	Green, Trent	19	0	19
Jaworski, Ron	23	1	24	O'Donnell, Neil	18	1	19

Name	Regular Season	Post-Season	Total	Name	Regular Season	Post-Season	Total
Snead, Norm	19	0	19	Luckman, Sid	10	1	11
O'Brien, Ken	19	0	19	Waterfield, Bob	11	0	11
Dickey, Lynn	19	0	19	Plum, Milt	11	0	11
Young, Steve	17	1	18	Grbac, Elvis	11	0	11
Gannon, Rich	18	0	18	Brister, Bubby	10	1	11
Lamonica, Daryle	18	0	18	Fiedler, Jay	10	1	11
George, Jeff	18	0	18	Roethlisberger, Ben	10	1	11
Brooks, Aaron	18	0	18	Leftwich, Byron	11	0	11
Simms, Phil	17	0	17	Couch, Tim	11	0	11
Anderson, Ken	16	1	17	Kemp, Jack	10	0	10
Hadl, John	17	0	17	Jones, Bert	10	0	10
Johnson, Charley	17	0	17	Wade, Bill	10	0	10
Kosar, Bernie	16	1	17	Tomczak, Mike	10	0	10
Blake, Jeff	17	0	17	Brees, Drew	10	0	10
Kitna, Jon	17	0	17	Flutie, Doug	10	0	10
Aikman, Troy	15	1	16	Avellini, Bob	10	0	10
Gabriel, Roman	16	0	16	Carr, David	10	0	10
Chandler, Chris	15	1	16	Pennington, Chad	8	1	9
McNabb, Donovan	15	1	16	Griese, Brian	9	0	9
Schroeder, Jay	14	2	16	Batch, Charlie	9	0	9
White, Danny	14	2	16	Warner, Kurt	7	1	8
Hebert, Bobby	16	0	16	Vick, Michael	8	0	8
Namath, Joe	15	1	16	Palmer, Carson	8	0	8
Jurgensen, Sonny	15	0	15	Frerotte, Gus	7	0	7
McMahon, Jim	15	0	15	Harrington, Joey	7	0	7
Everett, Jim	14	1	15	Collins, Todd	6	0	6
Kilmer, Billy	15	0	15	Manning, Eli	5	0	5
Pastorini, Dan	14	1	15	Boller, Kyle	5	0	5
Beuerlein, Steve	15	0	15	Huard, Damon	5	0	5
Humphries, Stan	13	2	15	Young, Vince	5	0	5
Garcia, Jeff	13	2	15	Feeley, A.J.	5	0	5
Delhomme, Jake	14	1	15	Martin, Jamie	5	0	5
Graham, Otto	11	3	14	Grossman, Rex	3	1	4
Dilfer, Trent	14	0	14	Rivers, Philip	4	0	4
Blanda, George	14	0	14	McCown, Josh	4	0	4
Todd, Richard	13	1	14	Smith, Alex	4	0	4
Lomax, Neil	14	0	14	Garard, David	3	0	3
Hasselbeck, Matt	13	1	14	Losman, J.P.	3	0	3
Peete, Rodney	14	0	14	Holcomb, Kelly	3	0	3
Bulger, Marc	13	1	14	Wright, Anthony	3	0	3
LeBaron, Eddie	14	0	14	Simms, Chris	3	0	3
Wilson, Marc	14	0	14	Romo, Tony	3	0	3
Brown, Ed	13	0	13	McMahon, Mike	3	0	3
Hostetler, Jeff	11	2	13	Gradkowski, Bruce	3	0	3
Zorn, Jim	13	0	13	Ramsey, Patrick	2	0	2
Culpepper, Daunte	13	0	13	Orton, Kyle	1	0	1
Kramer, Erik	13	0	13	Frye, Charlie	1	0	1
Majkowski, Don	13	0	13	Rattay, Tim	1	0	1
Morrall, Earl	10	2	12	Volek, Billy	1	0	1
Stewart, Kordell	12	0	12	Leinart, Matt	1	0	1
Rypien, Mark	12	0	12	Weinke, Chris	1	0	1
Phipps, Mike	12	0	12	Campbell, Jason	1	0	1
Manning, Archie	12	0	12	Wallace, Seneca	1	0	1
Miller, Chris	11	1	12	Fitzpatrick, Ryan	1	0	1

Comeback Leaders by Decades

1920s and 1930s	Reg. Season	Post-Season	Total
Benny Friedman	8	0	8
Red Dunn	7	0	7
Arnie Herber	7	0	7
Dutch Clark	7	0	7
Ed Danowski	5	1	6
Paddy Driscoll	5	0	5
Hust Stockton	5	0	5
Lou Smyth	5	0	5

1940s	Reg. Season	Post-Season	Total
Sammy Baugh	12	0	12
Bob Waterfield	8	0	8
Sid Luckman	7	1	8
Paul Christman	7	0	7
Ace Parker	6	0	6
Johnny Clement	5	0	5
Glenn Dobbs	4	0	4
Bob Hoernschemeyer	4	0	4
Tommy Thompson	3	1	4
George Ratterman	3	1	4

1950s	Reg. Season	Post-Season	Total
Y.A. Tittle	19	0	19
Charlie Conerly	14	0	14
Bobby Layne	14	1	15
Eddie Lebaron	13	0	13
John Unitas	11	2	13
Norm Van Brocklin	11	1	12
Otto Graham	9	2	11
Jim Finks	8	0	8
Lamar McHan	7	0	7
Tobin Rote	6	1	7

1960s	Reg. Season	Post-Season	Total
John Unitas	23	0	23
Fran Tarkenton	18	0	18
Bart Starr	17	1	18
Charley Johnson	13	0	13
John Brodie	12	0	12
Sonny Jurgensen	10	0	10
Ed Brown	10	0	10
Norm Snead	10	0	10
Don Meredith	9	0	9
Roman Gabriel	8	0	8
Bill Wade	8	0	8
Frank Ryan	8	0	8

1960s AFL	Reg. Season	Post-Season	Total
Len Dawson	10	2	12
John Hadl	11	0	11
Jack Kemp	10	0	10
Daryle Lamonica	10	0	10

1960s AFL	Reg. Season	Post-Season	Total
Joe Namath	9	1	10
Tom Flores	8	0	8

1970s	Reg. Season	Post-Season	Total
Roger Staubach	21	2	23
Ken Stabler	20	2	22
Terry Bradshaw	16	4	20
Fran Tarkenton	18	1	19
Jim Hart	14	0	14
Dan Pastorini	13	1	14
Joe Ferguson	13	0	13
Bob Griese	12	1	13
Brian Sipe	12	0	12
Craig Morton	12	0	12
Ken Anderson	12	0	12
Mike Phipps	12	0	12
Steve Bartkowski	11	1	12
Archie Manning	11	0	11
Joe Theismann	10	0	10

1980s	Reg. Season	Post-Season	Total
Joe Montana	21	2	24
John Elway	17	3	20
Ron Jaworski	17	0	17
Dan Marino	16	1	17
Dan Fouts	14	3	17
Steve DeBerg	16	0	16
Dave Krieg	15	1	16
Tommy Kramer	14	1	15
Joe Theismann	13	2	15
Neil Lomax	14	0	14
Marc Wilson	14	0	14
Ken O'Brien	14	0	14
Lynn Dickey	14	0	14
Bernie Kosar	13	1	14
Doug Williams	13	1	14
Warren Moon	12	2	14

1990s	Reg. Season	Post-Season	Total
Dan Marino	26	3	29
John Elway	25	3	28
Warren Moon	23	0	23
Jim Kelly	21	1	22
Jim Harbaugh	19	0	19
Drew Bledsoe	18	0	18
Jeff George	18	0	18
Neil O'Donnell	17	1	18
Dave Krieg	16	0	16
Brett Favre	15	1	16
Vinny Testaverde	15	0	15
Troy Aikman	14	1	15
Stan Humphries	13	2	15
Steve Young	13	1	14
Mark Brunell	13	1	14

2000s	Reg. Season	Post- Season	Total		2000s	Reg. Season	Post- Season	Total
Tom Brady	18	6	24		Jeff Garcia	13	1	14
Peyton Manning	20	1	21		Matt Hasselbeck	13	1	14
Brett Favre	18	1	19		Marc Bulger	13	1	14
Jake Plummer	18	0	18		Vinny Testaverde	13	0	13
Steve McNair	16	2	18		Drew Bledsoe	13	0	13
Kerry Collins	17	0	17		Aaron Brooks	13	0	13
Trent Green	17	0	17		Jon Kitna	13	0	13
Brad Johnson	15	0	15		Daunte Culpepper	13	0	13
Jake Delhomme	13	1	14		Mark Brunell	12	0	12
Donovan McNabb	13	1	14					

Postseason Data for All Passers, by Yards

QB	Att	Comp	Percent	Yards	Yds/Att	Yds/C	TD	Int	Int%	Rating
Montana, Joe	732	463	63.3%	5772	7.9	12.5	44	20	2.73	96.3
Elway, John	650	355	54.6%	4964	7.6	14	14	25	21	3.23	78.8
Favre, Brett	663	401	60.5%	4902	7.4	12.2	34	26	3.92	84
Marino, Dan	687	385	56.0%	4512	6.6	11.7	32	24	3.49	77.1
Kelly, Jim	545	322	59.1%	3863	7.1	12	21	28	5.14	72.3
Aikman, Troy	502	320	63.7%	3849	7.7	12	24	17	3.39	89
Bradshaw, Terry	456	261	57.2%	3832	8.4	14.7	30	26	5.70	83
Manning, Peyton	475	290	61.1%	3495	7.4	12.1	18	15	3.16	83.1
Young, Steve	471	292	62.0%	3326	7.1	11.4	20	13	2.76	85.8
Brady, Tom	486	295	60.7%	3217	6.6	10.9	20	10	2.06	85.4
Moon, Warren	403	259	64.3%	2836	7	10.9	17	14	3.47	84.5
Staubach, Roger	410	224	54.6%	2827	6.9	12.6	24	19	4.63	76.5
Stabler, Kenny	351	203	57.8%	2641	7.5	13	13	17	15	4.27	80
McNabb, Donovan	412	245	59.5%	2524	6.1	10.3	17	12	2.91	78.8
Cunningham, Randall	365	192	52.6%	2426	6.6	12.6	13	10	2.74	74.1
Plunkett, Jim	272	162	59.6%	2296	8.4	14.2	10	12	4.41	80.8
White, Danny	359	206	57.4%	2284	6.4	11.1	15	16	4.46	71.8
Warner, Kurt	268	169	63.1%	2221	8.3	13.1	15	10	3.73	92.3
Graham, Otto	301	159	52.8%	2101	7	13.2	14	17	5.65	67.2
Fouts, Dan	286	159	55.6%	1991	7	12.5	12	18	6.29	65.2
Lamonica, Daryle	263	117	44.5%	1928	7.3	16.5	19	10	3.80	77.9
Kosar, Bernie	270	152	56.3%	1927	7.1	12.7	14	10	3.70	80.6
Kreig, Dave	282	144	51.1%	1895	6.7	13.2	11	10	3.55	70.9
Brunell, Mark	307	156	50.8%	1833	6	11.8	11	11	3.58	66.3
Tarkenton, Fran	292	149	51.0%	1803	6.2	12.1	10	17	5.82	57.5
Hasselbeck, Matt	260	150	57.7%	1788	6.9	11.9	9	6	2.31	80.7
Theismann, Joe	211	128	60.7%	1782	8.4	13.9	11	7	3.32	91.4
Rypien, Mark	234	126	53.8%	1776	7.6	14.1	8	10	4.27	72.2
McNair, Steve	311	184	59.2%	1764	5.7	9.6	5	11	3.54	65.6
Starr, Bart	213	130	61.0%	1753	8.2	13.5	15	4	1.88	102.9
O'Donnell, Neil	275	159	57.8%	1705	6.2	10.7	9	8	2.91	74.9
Gannon, Rich	240	154	64.2%	1691	7	11	11	9	3.75	84.6
Simms, Phil	279	157	56.3%	1679	6	10.7	10	6	2.15	77
Unitas, Johnny	226	120	53.1%	1676	7.4	14	6	10	4.42	67.6
Jaworski, Ron	270	126	46.7%	1669	6.2	13.2	10	10	3.70	63.6
Delhomme, Jake	178	104	58.4%	1541	8.7	14.8	10	5	2.81	93.9
Dawson, Len	188	107	56.9%	1497	8	14	7	9	4.79	75.2
Griese, Bob	208	112	53.8%	1467	7.1	13.1	10	11	5.29	70.3
Johnson, Brad	224	125	55.8%	1403	6.3	11.2	7	12	5.36	62.8
Humphries, Stan	228	118	51.8%	1347	5.9	11.4	6	13	5.70	54.8
Plummer, Jake	197	122	61.9%	1340	6.8	11	7	9	4.57	74.8
Bledsoe, Drew	252	129	51.2%	1335	5.3	10.3	6	12	4.76	54.9

QB	Att	Comp	Percent	Yards	Yds/Att	Yds./C	TD	Int	Int%	Rating
Testaverde, Vinnie	190	115	60.5%	1329	7	11.6	6	5	2.63	81.2
Wilson, Wade	185	99	53.5%	1322	7.1	13.4	7	6	3.24	75.6
Anderson, Ken	166	110	66.3%	1321	8	12	9	6	3.61	93.5
Collins, Kerry	199	115	57.8%	1275	6.4	11.1	13	10	5.03	77.8
Morton, Craig	227	91	40.1%	1235	5.4	13.6	9	16	7.05	42
Ferragamo, Vince	188	92	48.9%	1228	6.5	13.3	8	11	5.85	59.9
Roethlisberger, Ben	147	89	60.5%	1210	8.2	13.6	10	8	5.44	86.8
Blanda, George	189	89	47.1%	1190	6.3	13.4	7	17	8.99	42.4
Pennington, Chad	178	107	60.1%	1166	6.6	10.9	7	4	2.25	83.2
Garcia, Jeff	178	103	57.9%	1149	6.5	11.2	6	5	2.81	76.7
Everett, Jim	176	87	49.4%	1120	6.4	12.9	7	11	6.25	57
McMahon, Jim	155	82	52.9%	1112	7.2	13.6	5	5	3.23	73.4
Williams, Doug	169	68	40.2%	1110	6.6	16.3	9	11	6.51	53.6
Kemp, Jack	160	78	48.8%	1106	6.9	14.2	2	10	6.25	49.6
Kilmer, Billy	178	92	51.7%	1060	6	11.5	8	7	3.93	68.6
Hostetler, Jeff	115	72	62.6%	1034	9	14.4	7	0	0.00	112
Todd, Richard	140	78	55.7%	1026	7.3	13.2	4	12	8.57	52.9
George, Jeff	129	71	55.0%	1002	7.8	14.1	9	3	2.33	93.9
Waterfield, Bob	126	57	45.2%	984	7.8	17.3	6	12	9.52	48.6
Culpepper, Daunte	134	73	54.5%	980	7.3	13.4	8	5	3.73	82.3
Brodie, John	133	71	53.4%	973	7.3	13.7	4	7	5.26	65.1
Dilfer, Trent	135	59	43.7%	970	7.2	16.4	4	4	2.96	66
Pastorini, Dan	116	74	63.8%	954	8.2	12.9	4	8	6.90	72.3
Bulger, Marc	113	68	60.2%	944	8.4	13.9	4	5	4.42	80.4
Brees, Drew	123	78	63.4%	916	7.4	11.7	5	2	1.63	92.7
Harbaugh, Jim	163	83	50.9%	906	5.6	10.9	6	5	3.07	67.2
Tomczak, Mike	143	74	51.7%	884	6.2	11.9	2	9	6.29	49.4
Tittle, Y.A.	157	70	44.6%	874	5.6	12.5	4	14	8.92	33.8
Kramer, Tommy	140	71	50.7%	874	6.2	12.3	3	7	5.00	56.7
Baugh, Sammy	101	55	54.5%	847	8.4	15.4	7	8	7.92	72.5
Nelsen, Bill	132	68	51.5%	839	6.4	12.3	3	8	6.06	53.8
Kramer, Erik	102	72	70.6%	838	8.2	11.6	5	3	2.94	99.2
Kapp, Joe	101	61	60.4%	835	8.3	13.7	3	6	5.94	72
Ferguson, Joe	120	58	48.3%	814	6.8	14	6	9	7.50	56
Morrall, Earl	103	50	48.5%	806	7.8	16.1	3	7	6.80	56.5
Conerly, Charley	90	47	52.2%	793	8.8	16.9	4	3	3.33	83.2
Bartkowski, Steve	111	53	47.7%	792	7.1	14.9	5	8	7.21	56.6
Schroeder, Jay	158	72	45.6%	791	5	11	5	8	5.06	50.4
Reich, Frank	114	67	58.8%	783	6.9	11.7	7	3	2.63	89.2
Grossman, Rex	133	69	51.9%	783	5.9	11.3	4	4	3.01	67.3
Stewart, Kordell	142	69	48.6%	744	5.2	10.8	1	8	5.63	43.3
Luckman, Sid	86	45	52.3%	732	8.5	16.3	6	4	4.65	85
Chandler, Chris	97	59	60.8%	728	7.5	12.3	4	4	4.12	80.6
Haden, Pat	123	55	44.7%	728	5.9	13.2	4	12	9.76	35.3
Grbac, Elvis	133	75	56.4%	718	5.4	9.6	3	6	4.51	60.3
Van Brocklin, Norm	95	46	48.4%	686	7.2	14.9	4	7	7.37	55.9
Maddox, Tommy	96	54	56.3%	667	6.9	12.4	5	3	3.13	82.2
Fiedler, Jay	110	59	53.6%	655	6	11.1	3	8	7.27	50.4
Hebert, Bobby	102	58	56.9%	648	6.4	11.2	3	7	6.86	57.1
Woodley, David	81	48	59.3%	645	8	13.4	5	6	7.41	74.4
Namath, Joe	117	50	42.7%	636	5.4	12.7	3	4	3.42	54.6
Vick, Mike	103	58	56.3%	609	5.9	10.5	3	3	2.91	71.2
Esiason, Boomer	87	51	58.6%	600	6.9	11.8	4	3	3.45	80.6
Dickey, Lynn	59	36	61.0%	592	10	16.4	5	3	5.08	101.8
Rote, Tobin	60	32	53.3%	571	9.5	17.8	7	2	3.33	111.2
Grogan, Steve	95	48	50.5%	571	6	11.9	3	7	7.37	49.1
Layne, Bobby	97	46	47.4%	568	5.9	12.3	2	12	12.37	33.3
Eason, Tony	72	42	58.3%	561	7.8	13.4	7	0	0.00	115.6

QB	Att	Comp	Percent	Yards	Yds/Att	Yds/C	TD	Int	Int%	Rating
Brooks, Aaron	77	46	59.7%	561	7.3	12.2	6	3	3.90	92
Malone, Mark	71	40	56.3%	558	7.9	14	4	3	4.23	83
Strock, Don	64	39	60.9%	558	8.7	14.3	4	3	4.69	90.5
Meredith, Don	77	38	49.4%	551	7.2	14.5	3	5	6.49	59
Ryan, Frank	72	35	48.6%	534	7.4	15.3	6	4	5.56	78.1
DeBerg, Steve	72	45	62.5%	511	7.1	11.4	3	3	4.17	80.3
O'Brien, Ken	67	45	67.2%	504	7.5	11.2	2	4	5.97	74.5
Thompson, Tommy	82	45	54.9%	503	6.1	11.2	4	7	8.54	54.1
Flutie, Doug	67	32	47.8%	494	7.4	15.4	2	3	4.48	63.9
Hart, Jim	81	40	49.4%	491	6.1	12.3	2	4	4.94	56.1
King, Shaun	92	45	48.9%	491	5.3	10.9	1	3	3.26	55.1
Parilli, Babe	65	28	43.1%	489	7.5	17.5	2	2	3.08	66.8
Miller, Chris	62	35	56.5%	469	7.6	13.4	3	5	8.06	63.2
Holcomb, Kelly	43	26	60.5%	429	10	16.5	3	1	2.33	107.6
Herber, Arnie	58	24	41.4%	425	7.3	17.7	3	8	13.79	44.8
Ratterman, George	76	37	48.7%	420	5.5	11.4	6	6	7.89	59.1
Hadl, John	66	27	40.9%	416	6.3	15.4	1	6	9.09	29.6
Filchock, Frank	63	25	39.7%	401	6.4	16	4	12	19.05	43.3
Jones, Bert	62	29	46.8%	399	6.4	13.8	1	2	3.23	59.8
Brunner, Scott	51	25	49.0%	386	7.6	15.4	6	3	5.88	89.2
Lomax, Neil	51	32	62.7%	385	7.5	12	2	2	3.92	82.6
Lee, Bob	67	33	49.3%	382	5.7	11.6	1	3	4.48	53.2
Frerotte, Gus	74	34	45.9%	375	5.1	11	1	3	4.05	49.1
Walsh, Steve	59	32	54.2%	373	6.3	11.7	2	4	6.78	56.7
Beathard, Pete	86	34	39.5%	368	4.3	10.8	2	4	4.65	41.2
Kitna, Jon	70	38	54.3%	359	5.1	9.4	2	4	5.71	54.4
Brister, Bubby	62	34	54.8%	356	5.7	10.5	1	0	0.00	77.1
Harris, James	49	21	42.9%	343	7	16.3	2	5	10.20	41
Ryan, Pat	51	32	62.7%	340	6.7	10.6	5	1	1.96	106.7
Gabriel, Roman	63	33	52.4%	336	5.3	10.2	3	2	3.17	70.6
Danowski, Ed	48	22	45.8%	325	6.8	14.8	3	5	10.42	49.7
Green, Trent	54	32	59.3%	319	5.9	10	2	2	3.70	73
Phipps, Mike	59	25	42.4%	300	5.1	12	1	7	11.86	24.6
Peete, Rodney	32	20	62.5%	298	9.3	14.9	3	0	0.00	124.2
Fuller, Steve	41	22	53.7%	298	7.3	13.5	2	1	2.44	83.2
Hipple, Eric	38	22	57.9%	298	7.8	13.5	1	2	5.26	69.8
Cuozzo, Gary	52	22	42.3%	286	5.5	13	2	5	9.62	33.5
McDonald, Paul	37	18	48.6%	281	7.6	15.6	1	0	0.00	83.3
Manning, Eli	45	26	57.8%	274	6.1	10.5	2	4	8.89	53.4
Beuerlein, Steve	31	16	51.6%	271	8.7	16.9	1	2	6.45	65.4
Trudeau, Jack	33	21	63.6%	251	7.6	12	2	1	3.03	94.4
Bratkowski, Zeke	40	22	55.0%	248	6.2	11.3	0	2	5.00	52.9
Danielson, Gary	38	24	63.2%	236	6.2	9.8	0	5	13.16	41
Isbell, Cecil	26	13	50.0%	235	9	18.1	2	1	3.85	91
Salisbury, Sean	44	14	31.8%	234	5.3	16.7	0	3	6.82	22.3
Rivers, Philip	32	14	43.8%	230	7.2	16.4	0	1	3.13	55.5
Tobin Rote	30	16	53.3%	214	7.1	13.4	1	1	3.33	73.5
Wright, Anthony	37	20	54.1%	214	5.8	10.7	1	2	5.41	57.7
Kubiak, Gary	19	16	84.2%	212	11.2	13.3	0	0	0.00	113.2
Majkowski, Don	23	14	60.9%	206	9	14.7	3	2	8.70	93.5
Albert, Frank	41	17	41.5%	204	5	12	2	2	4.88	53.3
Newman, Harry	19	13	68.4%	201	10.6	15.5	2	1	5.26	116.3
Kanell, Danny	32	16	50.0%	199	6.2	12.4	1	1	3.13	67.1
Simms, Chris	38	25	65.8%	198	5.2	7.9	0	2	5.26	56.7
Lujack, Johnny	29	15	51.7%	193	6.7	12.9	0	3	10.34	33.3
Zolak, Scott	44	21	47.7%	190	4.3	9	0	1	2.27	50.4
Romo, Tony	29	17	58.6%	189	6.5	11.1	1	0	0.00	89.6
Stoudt, Cliff	20	10	50.0%	187	9.4	18.7	1	1	5.00	78.5

QB	Att	Comp	Percent	Yards	Yds/Att	Yds/C	TD	Int	Int%	Rating
Mitchell, Scott	54	23	42.6%	183	3.4	8	1	5	9.26	19.3
Sipe, Brian	40	13	32.5%	183	4.6	14.1	0	3	7.50	17
Pagel, Mike	25	17	68.0%	179	7.2	10.5	2	1	4.00	98.6
Leftwich, Byron	31	18	58.1%	179	5.8	9.9	0	1	3.23	61.1
Avellini, Bob	25	15	60.0%	177	7.1	11.8	1	4	16.00	55.3
Kemp, Jeff	37	18	48.6%	173	4.7	9.6	0	1	2.70	50.8
Carlson, Cody	33	16	48.5%	165	5	10.3	2	1	3.03	70.9
Hogeboom, Gary	29	14	48.3%	162	5.6	11.6	2	2	6.90	59.8
Carter, Quincy	36	21	58.3%	154	4.3	7.3	0	1	2.78	56.9
Johnson, Rob	23	11	47.8%	152	6.6	13.8	0	0	0.00	69.5
Hunter, Scott	24	12	50.0%	150	6.3	12.5	0	1	4.17	52.4
Detmer, Ty	21	14	66.7%	148	7	10.6	0	2	9.52	47.4
Owen, Tom	22	12	54.5%	144	6.5	12	1	1	4.55	71
Leemans, Tuffy	25	7	28.0%	143	5.7	20.4	1	8	32.00	24.7
Marinovich, Todd	23	12	52.2%	140	6.1	11.7	0	4	17.39	31.3
Weese, Norris	26	12	46.2%	140	5.4	11.7	0	0	0.00	63
Wade, Bill	31	10	32.3%	138	4.5	13.8	0	1	3.23	34.1
Bono, Steve	27	13	48.1%	137	5.1	10.5	1	3	11.11	36.1
Wilson, Marc	27	11	40.7%	135	5	12.3	1	3	11.11	29.6
Zorn, Jim	28	14	50.0%	134	4.8	9.6	2	2	7.14	57.7
Plum, Milt	25	12	48.0%	134	5.4	11.2	0	4	16.00	24.8
Masterson, Bernie	17	4	23.5%	131	7.7	32.8	2	2	11.76	58.8
Nielsen, Gifford	24	13	54.2%	129	5.4	9.9	1	2	8.33	48.8
Vlasic, Mark	20	9	45.0%	124	6.2	13.8	1	4	20.00	42.5
Panciera, Don	25	7	28.0%	116	4.6	16.6	0	3	12.00	6.8
Brock, Dieter	53	16	30.2%	116	2.2	7.3	0	2	3.77	24
O'Rourke, Charley	6	4	66.7%	110	18.3	27.5	0	0	0.00	109.7
Hoying, Bobby	16	8	50.0%	107	6.7	13.4	0	2	12.50	32
Kenney, Bill	16	8	50.0%	97	6.1	12.1	0	0	0.00	69
Brown, Ed	20	8	40.0%	97	4.9	12.1	0	1	5.00	34.8
Sanders, Spec	17	7	41.2%	89	5.2	12.7	0	1	5.88	33.7
Detmer, Koy	14	7	50.0%	88	6.3	12.6	0	1	7.14	40.2
Parker, Ace	18	8	44.4%	81	4.5	10.1	0	1	5.56	34.7
Still, Jim	18	6	33.3%	80	4.4	13.3	1	2	11.11	27.3
Blackledge, Todd	21	12	57.1%	80	3.8	6.7	0	2	9.52	26
Fourcade, John	18	5	27.8%	79	4.4	15.8	0	2	11.11	5.8
Jurgensen, Sonny	12	6	50.0%	78	6.5	13	0	3	25.00	31.3
Cafego, George	11	3	27.3%	76	6.9	25.3	0	3	27.27	16.3
Van Every, Hal	6	2	33.3%	75	12.5	37.5	0	1	16.67	42.4
Comp, Irv	10	3	30.0%	74	7.4	24.7	1	3	30.00	51.7
Garrard, David	8	3	37.5%	68	8.5	22.7	0	0	0.00	68.8
Palmer, Carson	1	1	100.0%	66	66	66	0	0	0.00	118.8
Matthews, Shane	17	8	47.1%	66	3.9	8.3	0	2	11.76	17.9
Heinrich, Don	17	6	35.3%	65	3.8	10.8	0	2	11.76	7.8
Carter, Virgil	20	7	35.0%	64	3.2	9.1	0	1	5.00	23.8
O'Connell, Tommy	8	4	50.0%	61	7.6	15.3	0	2	25.00	35.9
Snyder, Bob	13	5	38.5%	57	4.4	11.4	0	0	0.00	52.4
Hanratty, Terry	10	5	50.0%	57	5.7	11.4	0	0	0.00	67.5
Brown, Dave	10	6	60.0%	56	5.6	9.3	0	1	10.00	35.8
Christman, Paul	14	3	21.4%	54	3.9	18	0	2	14.29	3.6
Jackson, Jarious	10	5	50.0%	54	5.4	10.8	0	0	0.00	66.3
Clement, Johnny	16	4	25.0%	52	3.3	13	0	0	0.00	40.6
Landry, Greg	12	5	41.7%	48	4	9.6	0	0	0.00	53.5
Huard, Damon	16	5	31.3%	46	2.9	9.2	0	0	0.00	40.6
Kruczek, Mike	6	5	83.3%	44	7.3	8.8	0	0	0.00	97.2
Munson, Bill	8	2	25.0%	44	5.5	22	0	1	12.50	10.4
Rae, Mike	13	2	15.4%	42	3.2	21	0	0	0.00	40.5
Buivid, Ray	11	3	27.3%	41	3.7	13.7	0	1	9.09	4.7

QB	Att	Comp	Percent	Yards	Yds/Att	Yds/C	TD	Int	Int%	Rating
Canadeo, Tony	2	1	50.0%	40	20	40	0	1	50.00	56.3
Matte, Tom	12	5	41.7%	40	3.3	8	0	0	0.00	50.7
Miller, Ed	6	3	50.0%	40	6.7	13.3	0	1	16.67	31.9
Yewcic, Tom	8	3	37.5%	39	4.9	13	0	1	12.50	14.1
Mallouf, Ray	7	3	42.9%	35	5	11.7	0	0	0.00	58.6
Zimmerman, Roy	12	3	25.0%	34	2.8	11.3	0	2	16.67	0
Ninowski, Jim	15	3	20.0%	31	2.1	10.3	0	1	6.67	11.8
Van Pelt, Alex	10	4	40.0%	27	2.7	6.8	1	0	0.00	81.3
Evans, Vince	8	2	25.0%	26	3.3	13	0	1	12.50	1
Monnett, Bob	9	3	33.3%	24	2.7	8	0	1	11.11	2.8
Rutledge, Jeff	1	1	100.0%	23	23	23	0	0	0.00	118.8
Nix, Emery	10	2	20.0%	23	2.3	11.5	0	0	0.00	39.6
Miller, Jim	5	3	60.0%	23	4.6	7.7	0	1	20.00	31.7
Wilson, Dave	12	2	16.7%	20	1.7	10	0	2	16.67	0
Huard, Brock	5	4	80.0%	17	3.4	4.3	0	0	0.00	80.8
Reichow, Jerry	3	1	33.3%	16	5.3	16	1	0	0.00	91.7
Ware, Andre	9	4	44.4%	15	1.7	3.8	0	1	11.11	12
Garrett, Jason	2	2	100.0%	14	7	7	0	0	0.00	95.8
Johnson, Doug	1	1	100.0%	14	14	14	0	0	0.00	118.8
Schonert, Turk	1	1	100.0%	14	14	14	0	0	0.00	118.8
Holly, Bob	2	2	100.0%	13	6.5	6.5	0	0	0.00	93.8
Wilhelm, Erik	5	1	20.0%	12	2.4	12	0	0	0.00	39.6
Domres, Marty	11	2	18.2%	9	0.8	4.5	1	2	18.18	30.3
Collins, Todd	4	1	25.0%	7	1.8	7	0	0	0.00	39.6
Musgrave, Bill	1	1	100.0%	6	6	6	0	0	0.00	91.7
Cavanaugh, Matt	2	1	50.0%	3	1.5	3	0	0	0.00	56.3
Banks, Tony	3	0	0.0%	0	0	0	0	0	0.00	39.6
Lorenzen, Jared	0	0	#DIV/0!	0	0	0	0	0	0	0
Ramsey, Patrick	1	1	100.0%	-1	-1	-1	0	0	0.00	79.2

Playoff Rushing by Quarterbacks
(50+ rushing yards by rushing yards)

QB	Rush Attempts	Yards	Ave	Rush TDs	QB	Rush Attempts	Yards	Ave	Rush TDs
Young, Steve	96	535	5.6	7	Wilson, Wade	23	105	4.6	0
Elway, John	94	461	4.9	6	Esiason, Boomer	19	105	5.5	0
Staubach, Roger	76	432	5.7	0	Dawson, Len	21	103	4.9	0
McNabb, Donovan	63	362	5.7	3	Anderson, Ken	19	101	5.3	0
Graham, Otto	73	362	5.0	6	Woodley, David	17	101	5.9	1
McNair, Steve	55	355	6.5	6	Unitas, Johnny	19	98	5.2	1
Montana, Joe	64	300	4.7	2	Hostetler, Dave	24	98	4.1	0
Bradshaw, Terry	51	288	5.6	3	Plunkett, Jim	28	97	3.5	0
Cunningham, Randall	46	254	5.5	1	Theismann, Joe	19	95	5.0	0
Stewart, Kordell	45	250	5.6	2	Leemans, Tuffy	41	93	2.3	0
Vick, Mike	28	239	8.5	0	Garcia, Jeff	17	86	5.1	1
Kelly, Jim	44	161	3.7	0	Aikman, Troy	31	84	2.7	1
Kapp, Joe	27	160	5.9	1	Griese, Bob	13	84	6.5	0
Brunell, Mark	39	147	3.8	0	Haden, Pat	18	81	4.5	1
Culpepper, Daunte	17	140	8.2	1	McMahon, Jim	20	77	3.9	3
Layne, Bobby	33	120	3.6	1	Favre, Brett	50	73	1.5	1
Harbaugh, Jim	30	119	4.0	0	Fiedler, Jay	13	71	5.5	0
Moon, Warren	35	114	3.3	0	Tarkenton, Fran	25	70	2.8	1
Roethlisberger, Ben	28	112	4.0	2	Weese, Norris	7	69	9.9	0
Gannon, Rich	29	111	3.8	1	Simms, Phil	30	68	2.3	0
Hasselbeck, Matt	44	107	2.4	1	Brady, Tom	36	66	1.8	1

QB	Rush Attempts	Yards	Ave	Rush TDs	QB	Rush Attempts	Yards	Ave	Rush TDs
Plummer, Jake	25	66	2.6	0	Brooks, Aaron	15	55	3.7	0
Thompson, Tommy	22	64	2.9	0	Grogan, Steve	9	54	6.0	0
Luckman, Sid	14	61	4.4	2	Grbac, Elvis	15	52	3.5	0
Plum, Milt	6	59	9.8	0	Phipps, Mike	9	50	5.6	1
Clement, Johnny	14	59	4.2	0	Stoudt, Cliff	9	50	5.6	0
Matte, Tom	12	57	4.8	0					

Head to Head Matchups of Top Five Quarterbacks

%	Quarterback	Wins	Opponent	Wins	Ties
0.900	Tommy Thompson	4	Bob Waterfield	0	1
0.875	John Elway	7	Warren Moon	1	0
0.857	Troy Aikman	6	Brett Favre	1	0
0.833	Brett Favre	5	Steve Young	1	0
0.800	Red Dunn	4	Bennie Friedman	1	0
0.800	Bobby Layne	4	Otto Graham	1	0
0.778	Sid Luckman	7	Cecil Isbell	2	0
0.750	John Elway	6	Bernie Kosar	2	0
0.750	Bob Griese	3	Terry Bradshaw	1	0
0.727	Otto Graham	8	Frankie Albert	3	0
0.714	Dan Fouts	5	Ken Anderson	2	0
0.679	Norm Van Brocklin	9	Y.A. Tittle	4	1
0.667	Jim Kelly	14	Dan Marino	7	0
0.667	Tom Brady	6	Peyton Manning	3	0
0.667	Joe Montana	6	Phil Simms	3	0
0.667	Bart Starr	4	Y.A. Tittle	2	0
0.667	Warren Moon	4	Dan Marino	2	0
0.667	Daryle Lamonica	4	Joe Namath	2	0
0.667	Jim Kelly	4	John Elway	2	0
0.667	Ben Roethlisberger	4	Carson Palmer	2	0
0.600	Sid Luckman	6	Sammy Baugh	4	0
0.600	Boomer Esiason	3	Jim Kelly	2	0
0.600	Ken Stabler	3	Bob Griese	2	0
0.583	Ed Danowski	3	Sammy Baugh	2	1
0.571	Y.A. Tittle	8	Bobby Layne	6	0
0.571	Troy Aikman	4	Steve Young	3	0
0.571	Ken Stabler	4	Terry Bradshaw	3	0
0.565	Bobby Layne	13	Norm Van Brocklin	10	0
0.563	Terry Bradshaw	9	Ken Anderson	7	0
0.556	Randall Cunningham	5	Phil Simms	4	0
0.556	Y.A. Tittle	5	John Unitas	4	0
0.500	John Unitas	8	Bart Starr	8	0
0.500	Len Dawson	6	Daryle Lamonica	6	2
0.500	Otto Graham	5	Charlie Conerly	5	1
0.500	Warren Moon	4	Jim Kelly	4	0
0.500	Bob Waterfield	3	Sid Luckman	3	1
0.500	Roger Staubach	3	Fran Tarkenton	3	0
0.500	Joe Montana	3	John Elway	3	0

300-Yard Games (10+ games and all active players)

Name	300 Yards	400 Yards	500 Yards	Name	300 Yards	400 Yards	500 Yards
Marino, Dan	63	13	1	Fouts, Dan	51	6	

Name	300 Yards	400 Yards	500 Yards
Moon, Warren	49	6	1
Favre, Brett	48	1	
Manning, Peyton	39	7	
Montana, Joe	38	7	
Bledsoe, Drew	37	6	
Elway, John	36	2	
Warner, Kurt	36	2	
Collins, Kerry	30		
Testaverde, Vinny	30	3	
Esiason, Boomer	29	4	1
Green, Trent	29	2	
Young, Steve	28	3	
Brunell, Mark	26	2	
Kelly, Jim	26	1	
Unitas, John	26	1	
Everett, Jim	25	1	
Jurgensen, Sonny	25	3	
Gannon, Rich	24	1	
Bulger, Marc	22	3	
DeBerg, Steve	21		
Namath, Joe	21	3	
Simms, Phil	21	3	1
Anderson, Ken	19	2	
Culpepper, Daunte	19	2	
Kramer, Tommy	19	3	
Blanda, George	18	2	
Cunningham, Randall	18	3	
George, Jeff	18		
Krieg, Dave	18	3	
McNabb, Donovan	18	1	
Sipe, Brian	18	1	
Dickey, Lynn	16	1	
Griese, Brian	16		
Hadl, John	16		
Johnson, Charley	16	2	
Lomax, Neil	16	2	
O'Brien, Ken	16	2	
Tittle, Y.A.	16	1	1
Brady, Tom	15	1	
Brees, Drew	15	1	1
Garcia, Jeff	15	2	
Johnson, Brad	15	1	
Kenney, Bill	15	1	
Aikman, Troy	13	1	
Hart, Jim	13		
Hasselbeck, Matt	13	3	
Rypien, Mark	13	2	
Snead, Norm	13	1	
Tarkenton, Fran	13	1	
Theismann, Joe	13	1	
Bartkowski, Steve	12	1	
Beuerlein, Steve	12	1	
Blake, Jeff	12		
Graham, Otto	12	1	
Grogan, Steve	12	1	
Jaworski, Ron	12		
Miller, Chris	12		
O'Donnell, Neil	12		
Grbac, Elvis	11	1	1
Manning, Archie	11		
McNair, Steve	11	1	
Plunkett, Jim	11		
Williams, Doug	11	2	
Brooks, Aaron	10	1	
Ferguson, Joe	10	1	
Kosar, Bernie	10	2	
Lamonica, Daryle	10		
Layne, Bobby	10	1	
Plummer, Jake	10	2	
Wilson, Wade	10		
Kitna, Jon	9	1	
Delhomme, Jake	8		
Palmer, Carson	7	1	
Frerotte, Gus	6	1	
Dilfer, Trent	5		
Pennington, Chad	5		
Carr, David	4		
Holcomb, Kelly	4	1	
Leftwich, Byron	4		
Manning, Eli	4		
Roethlisberger, Ben	4	1	
Batch, Charlie	3	1	
Harrington, Joey	3		
McCown, Josh	3		
Ramsey, Patrick	3		
Romo, Tony	3		
Stewart, Kordell	3		
Volek, Billy	3	2	
Feeley, A.J.	2		
Losman, J.P.	2		
Rivers, Philip	2		
Vick, Michael	2		
Boller, Kyle	1		
Bollinger, Brooks	1		
Bouman, Todd	1		
Collins, Todd	1		
Grossman, Rex	1		
Huard, Damon	1		
Leinart, Matt	1	1	
Martin, Jamie	1		
Rattay, Tim	1	1	
Simms, Chris	1		
Weinke, Chris	1	1	
Wright, Anthony	1		

Black Quarterbacks (by Yards)

Name	Att	Comp	%	Yards	Y/Att	Y/Comp	TD	Int	Sacks	Rating
Moon, Warren	6823	3988	58.4%	49325	7.2	12.4	291	233	458	80.9
McNair, Steve	4339	2600	59.9%	30191	7.0	11.6	172	115	243	83.2
Cunningham, Randall	4289	2429	56.6%	29979	7.0	12.3	207	134	484	81.5
McNabb, Donovan	3259	1898	58.2%	22080	6.8	11.6	152	72	255	85.2
Blake, Jeff	3241	1827	56.4%	21711	6.7	11.9	134	99	248	78.0
Culpepper, Daunte	2741	1759	64.2%	21091	7.7	12.0	137	89	249	90.8
Brooks, Aaron	2963	1673	56.5%	20261	6.8	12.1	123	92	235	78.5
Williams, Doug	2507	1240	49.5%	16998	6.8	13.7	100	93	84	69.4
Peete, Rodney	2346	1344	57.3%	16338	7.0	12.2	76	92	244	73.3
Banks, Tony	2356	1278	54.2%	15315	6.5	12.0	77	73	227	72.4
Stewart, Kordell	2358	1316	55.8%	14816	6.3	11.3	77	84	170	70.8
Vick, Michael	1730	930	53.8%	11505	6.7	12.4	71	52	187	75.7
Batch, Charlie	1423	801	56.3%	9801	6.9	12.2	55	41	152	78.6
Evans, Vince	1390	704	50.6%	9485	6.8	13.5	52	74	118	63.0
Leftwich, Byron	1344	789	58.7%	9042	6.7	11.5	51	36	76	80.5
Harris, James	1113	592	53.2%	7866	7.1	13.3	44	58	92	67.3
Carter, Quincy	960	542	56.5%	6337	6.6	11.7	32	37	80	71.7
King, Shaun	738	415	56.2%	4566	6.2	11.0	27	24	61	73.4
Wright, Anthony	595	328	55.1%	3547	6.0	10.8	20	25	55	66.6
Garrard, David	539	313	58.1%	3543	6.6	11.3	18	13	41	78.9
Lucas, Ray	483	280	58.0%	3029	6.3	10.8	18	17	29	74.3
Smith, Akili	461	215	46.6%	2212	4.8	10.3	5	13	59	52.8
Young, Vince	357	184	51.5%	2199	6.2	12.0	12	13	25	66.7
Gilliam, Joe	331	147	44.4%	2103	6.4	14.3	9	17	12	53.2
Briscoe, Marlin	224	93	41.5%	1589	7.1	17.1	14	13	0	62.9
Campbell, Jason	207	110	53.1%	1297	6.3	11.8	10	6	7	76.5
Ware, Andre	161	83	51.6%	1112	6.9	13.4	5	8	27	63.5
Mays, Dave	156	80	51.3%	937	6.0	11.7	7	11	9	55.4
Wallace, Seneca	141	82	58.2%	927	6.6	11.3	8	7	14	76.2
Taliaferro, George	160	47	29.4%	843	5.3	17.9	6	15	0	22.5
Taliaferro, George	124	45	36.3%	790	6.4	17.6	4	14	0	30.0
Wynn, Spergon	152	70	46.1%	585	3.8	8.4	1	7	23	39.5
Jackson, Tarvaris	81	47	58.0%	475	5.9	10.1	2	4	8	62.5
Lemon, Cleo	68	38	55.9%	412	6.1	10.8	2	1	5	77.6
Lillard, Joe	95	27	28.4%	372	3.9	13.8	2	19	0	10.8
Pollard, Fritz	64	31	48.4%	366	5.7	11.8	5	5	0	59.8
Walton, Johnnie	65	31	47.7%	338	5.2	10.9	3	3	1	59.6
Gray, Quinn	36	21	58.3%	266	7.4	12.7	2	0	2	100.0
Moore, Shawn	34	17	50.0%	232	6.8	13.6	0	3	6	35.4
Dickinson, Parnell	39	15	38.5%	210	5.4	14.0	1	5	14	25.5
Burris, Henry	51	18	35.3%	207	4.1	11.5	3	5	4	28.4
Collier, Reggie	22	12	54.5%	206	9.4	17.2	3	3	4	86.6
Jones, John	57	16	28.1%	181	3.2	11.3	1	5	7	9.6
Totten, Willie	33	13	39.4%	155	4.7	11.9	2	2	5	49.4
Robinson, Tony	18	11	61.1%	152	8.4	13.8	0	2	2	48.6
Jackson, Jarious	22	11	50.0%	114	5.2	10.4	0	1	2	46.4
Davey, Rohan	19	8	42.1%	88	4.6	11.0	0	0	0	56.5
Bishop, Michael	9	3	33.3%	80	8.9	26.7	1	1	0	64.4
Martin, Tee	16	6	37.5%	69	4.3	11.5	0	1	1	25.3
Lewis, Dave	14	6	42.9%	57	4.1	9.5	0	0	4	54.8
Stevens, Mark	4	2	50.0%	52	13.0	26.0	1	0	0	135.4
Dungy, Tony	8	3	37.5%	43	5.4	14.3	0	2	0	16.1
Mitchell, Brian	6	3	50.0%	40	6.7	13.3	0	0	1	71.5
Quarles, Bernard	3	1	33.3%	40	13.3	40.0	1	1	0	81.9
Craig, Dameyune	8	4	50.0%	34	4.3	8.5	0	0	2	61.5

Name	Att	Comp	%	Yards	Y/Att	Y/Comp	TD	Int	Sacks	Rating
Walker, Jay	2	2	100.0%	31	15.5	15.5	0	0	0	118.8
Gillus, Willie	5	2	40.0%	28	5.6	14.0	0	0	3	58.8
Thrower, Willie	8	3	37.5%	27	3.4	9.0	0	1	0	7.8
Miller, Larry	6	1	16.7%	2	0.3	2.0	0	1	1	0.0
Richardson, Wally	2	1	50.0%	1	0.5	1.0	0	0	0	56.3
Briggs, Walter	2	0	0.0%	0	0.0	0	0	1	0	0.0
Blount, Ed	0	0	0	0	0	0	0	0	0	0
Brackins, Charlie	2	0	0	0	0	0	0	0	0	39.6
Jordan. Homer	0	0	0	0	0	0	0	0	0	0
McPherson, Don	0	0	0	0	0	0	0	0	0	0
Slack, Reggie	0	0	0	0	0	0	0	0	0	0
Tipton, Greg	0	0	0	0	0	0	0	0	0	0
White, Ted	0	0	0	0	0	0	0	0	0	0
Ransom, Brian	0	0	0	0	0	0	0	0	0	0
Bonner, Sherdrick	0	0	0	0	0	0	0	0	0	0
Shockley, D.J.	0	0	0	0	0	0	0	0	0	0
Printers, Casey	0	0	0	0	0	0	0	0	0	0
Jacobs, Omar	0	0	0	0	0	0	0	0	0	0
Woodbury, Tory	0	0	0	0	0	0	0	0	0	0
Boyd, Shane	0	0	0	0	0	0	0	0	0	0
Hamilton, Joe	0	0	0	0	0	0	0	0	1	0

Running Quarterbacks (1,500+ Rushing yards, by rushing yards)

Name	Pass Yards	Y/Att	TD	Rating	Rush Att	Rush Yards	Avg	TD
Cunningham, Randall	29979	7.0	207	81.5	775	4928	6.4	35
Young, Steve	33124	8.0	232	96.8	722	4239	5.9	43
Vick, Michael	11505	6.7	71	75.7	529	3859	7.3	21
Tarkenton, Fran	47003	7.3	342	80.4	675	3674	5.4	32
McNair, Steve	30191	7.0	172	83.2	659	3558	5.4	37
Elway, John	51475	7.1	300	79.9	774	3407	4.4	33
Rote, Tobin	18850	6.5	148	56.8	635	3128	4.9	37
Stewart, Kordell	14816	6.3	77	70.8	560	2874	5.1	38
Harbaugh, Jim	26288	6.7	129	77.6	560	2787	5.0	18
McNabb, Donovan	22080	6.8	152	85.2	447	2726	6.1	24
Landry, Greg	16052	7.0	98	72.9	430	2655	6.2	21
Douglass, Bobby	6493	5.5	36	48.5	410	2654	6.5	22
Culpepper, Daunte	21091	7.7	137	90.8	464	2496	5.4	30
Layne, Bobby	26768	7.2	196	63.4	611	2451	4.0	25
Gannon, Rich	28743	6.8	180	84.7	521	2449	4.7	21
Brunell, Mark	31826	6.9	182	84.2	509	2433	4.8	15
Staubach, Roger	22700	7.7	153	83.4	410	2264	5.5	20
Bradshaw, Terry	27989	7.2	212	70.9	444	2257	5.1	32
Anderson, Ken	32838	7.3	197	81.9	397	2220	5.6	20
Manning, Archie	23911	6.6	125	67.1	384	2197	5.7	18
Grogan, Steve	26886	7.5	182	69.6	445	2176	4.9	35
Blake, Jeff	21711	6.7	134	78	418	2027	4.8	14
Garcia, Jeff	20385	6.9	136	86.4	395	1878	4.8	24
Plummer, Jake	29253	6.7	161	74.6	428	1853	4.3	17
Theismann, Joe	25206	7.0	160	77.4	355	1815	5.1	17
Unitas, Johnny	40239	7.8	290	78.2	450	1777	3.9	13
Favre, Brett	57500	7.0	414	85	526	1774	3.4	13
Moon, Warren	49325	7.2	291	80.9	543	1736	3.2	22
Montana, Joe	40551	7.5	273	92.3	457	1676	3.7	20
Testaverde, Vinny	45281	6.9	270	75.2	421	1639	3.9	15
Flutie, Doug	14715	6.8	86	76.3	338	1634	4.8	10
McMahon, Jim	18148	7.1	100	78.2	338	1631	4.8	16

Name	Pass Yards	Y/Att	TD	Rating	Rush Att	Rush Yards	Avg.	TD
Brooks, Aaron	20261	6.8	123	78.5	362	1534	4.2	13
Isbell, Cecil	5945	7.3	61	72.6	422	1522	3.6	10
Kilmer, Billy	20495	6.9	152	71.6	362	1509	4.2	21
Zorn, Jim	21115	6.7	111	67.3	322	1504	4.7	17
Esiason, Boomer	37920	7.3	247	81.1	447	1598	3.6	7

Appendix C:
Drafts, Trades, Awards, Numbers

Quarterbacks and Passing Tailbacks Drafted in the First Round

Year	Slot	Name	Team	Year	Slot	Name	Team
1936	2	Riley Smith	Redskins	1952	4	Vito (Babe) Parilli	Packers
1937	6	Sammy Baugh	Redskins	1952	7	Larry Isbell	Redskins
1938	4	Byron (Whizzer) White	Steelers	1952	12	Harry Agganis	Browns
1938	7	Cecil Isbell	Packers	1953	3	Jack Scarbath	Redskins
1939	2	Sid Luckman	Bears	1953	5	Ted Marchibroda	Steelers
1939	3	Parker Hall	Rams	1954	1	Bobby Garrett	Browns
1939	4	Davey O'Brien	Eagles	1954	2	Lamar McHan	Cardinals
1940	1	George Cafego	Cardinals	1954	5	Cotton Davidson	Colts
1942	1	Bill Dudley	Steelers	1955	1	George Shaw	Colts
1942	6	Orban (Spec) Sanders	Redskins	1955	4	Ralph Guglielmi	Redskins
1942	10	Frankie Albert	Bears	1956	1	Gary Glick	Steelers
1943	3	Glenn Dobbs	Cardinals	1956	2	Earl Morrall	49ers
1943	4	Paul Governali	Dodgers	1957	3	John Brodie	49ers
1944	1	Angelo Bertelli	Yanks	1957	5	Len Dawson	Steelers
1944	4	Otto Graham	Lions	1958	1	King Hill	Cardinals
1945	1	Charley Trippi	Cardinals	1959	1	Randy Duncan	Packers
1945	8	Jim Hardy	Redskins	1959	4	Don Allard	Redskins
1946	1	Frank (Boley) Dancewicz	Yanks	1959	5	Dave Baker	49ers
1946	4	Johnny Lujack	Bears	1959	10	Lee Grosscup	Giants
1947	6	Ernie Case	Packers	1960	2	George Izo	Cardinals
1948	1	Harry Gilmer	Redskins	1960	4	Richie Lucas	Redskins
1948	3	Bobby Layne	Bears	1961	2	Norm Snead	Redskins
1948	6	Y.A. Tittle	Lions	1961	11	Billy Kilmer	49ers
1948	7	Earl (Jug) Girard	Packers	1962	2	Roman Gabriel	Rams
1949	2	Johnny Rauch	Lions	1962	10	John Hadl	Lions
1949	5	Stan Heath	Packers	1963	1	Terry Baker	Rams
1949	7	Bobby Thomason	Rams	1964	5	Pete Beathard	Lions
1949	9	Frank Tripucka	Eagles	1964	7	Bill Munson	Rams
1950	2	Adrian Burk	Colts	1965	5	Craig Morton	Cowboys
1950	7	Travis Tidwell	Giants	1965	12	Joe Namath	Cardinals
1951	2	Bob Williams	Bears	1966	16	Randy Johnson	Falcons
1951	3	Y.A. Tittle	49ers	1967	3	Steve Spurrier	49ers
1952	1	Billy Wade	Rams	1967	4	Bob Griese	Dolphins

Year	Slot	Name	Team	Year	Slot	Name	Team
1967	25	Don Horn	Packers	1991	24	Todd Marinovich	Raiders
1968	11	Greg Landry	Lions	1992	6	David Klingler	Bengals
1968	25	Eldridge Dickey	Raiders	1992	25	Tommy Maddox	Broncos
1969	5	Greg Cook	Bengals	1993	1	Drew Bledsoe	Patriots
1969	9	Marty Domres	Chargers	1993	2	Rick Mirer	Seahawks
1970	1	Terry Bradshaw	Steelers	1994	3	Heath Shuler	Redskins
1970	3	Mike Phipps	Browns	1994	6	Trent Dilfer	Buccaneers
1971	1	Jim Plunkett	Patriots	1995	3	Steve McNair	Oilers
1971	2	Archie Manning	Saints	1995	5	Kerry Collins	Panthers
1971	3	Dan Pastorini	Oilers	1997	26	Jim Druckenmiller	49ers
1972	11	Jerry Tagge	Packers	1998	1	Peyton Manning	Colts
1972	14	John Reaves	Eagles	1998	2	Ryan Leaf	Chargers
1973	2	Bert Jones	Colts	1999	1	Tim Couch	Browns
1975	1	Steve Bartkowski	Falcons	1999	2	Donovan McNabb	Eagles
1976	6	Richard Todd	Jets	1999	3	Akili Smith	Bengals
1977	19	Steve Pisarkiewicz	Cardinals	1999	11	Daunte Culpepper	Vikings
1977	27	Tommy Kramer	Vikings	1999	12	Cade McNown	Bears
1978	17	Doug Williams	Buccaneers	2000	18	Chad Pennington	Jets
1979	3	Jack Thompson	Bengals	2001	1	Michael Vick	Falcons
1979	7	Phil Simms	Giants	2002	1	David Carr	Texans
1979	23	Steve Fuller	Chiefs	2002	3	Joey Harrington	Lions
1980	15	Marc Wilson	Raiders	2002	32	Patrick Ramsey	Redskins
1980	28	Mark Malone	Steelers	2003	1	Carson Palmer	Bengals
1981	6	Rich Campbell	Packers	2003	7	Byron Leftwich	Jaguars
1982	4	Art Schlichter	Colts	2003	19	Kyle Boller	Ravens
1982	5	Jim McMahon	Bears	2003	22	Rex Grossman	Bears
1983	1	John Elway	Colts	2004	1	Eli Manning	Chargers
1983	7	Todd Blackledge	Chiefs	2004	4	Philip Rivers	Giants
1983	14	Jim Kelly	Bills	2004	11	Ben Roethlisberger	Steelers
1983	15	Tony Eason	Patriots	2004	22	J.P. Losman	Bills
1983	24	Ken O'Brien	Jets	2005	1	Alex D. Smith	49ers
1983	27	Dan Marino	Dolphins	2005	24	Aaron Rodgers	Packers
1986	3	Jim Everett	Oilers	2005	25	Jason Campbell	Redskins
1986	12	Chuck Long	Lions	2006	3	Vince Young	Titans
1987	1	Vinny Testaverde	Buccaneers	2006	10	Matt Leinart	Cardinals
1987	6	Kelly Stouffer	Cardinals	2006	11	Jay Cutler	Broncos
1987	13	Chris Miller	Falcons	1981supp	0	Dave Wilson	Saints
1987	26	Jim Harbaugh	Bears	1984usfl	0	Steve Young	Buccaneers
1989	1	Troy Aikman	Cowboys	1985supp	0	Bernie Kosar	Browns
1990	1	Jeff George	Colts	1989supp	0	Steve Walsh	Cowboys
1990	7	Andre Ware	Lions	1989supp	0	Timm Rosenbach	Cardinals
1991	16	Dan McGwire	Seahawks	1992supp	0	Dave Brown	Giants

Table of Quarterback Trades

Hyphenated numbers indicate year and round of a draft pick included as part of a trade. When the team took a player with that pick in the draft, the name of the draftee appears in parentheses; otherwise only the year and round of the draft pick are given. As indicated, some players were picked up on waivers, were part of a cash-based transaction ($) or were part of a trade involving other concessions. Quarterbacks are listed in italics. Team abbreviations are listed in the preface. Example:

1999 MIN *Brad Johnson*   WSH   99-1 (*Daunte Culpepper*) & 99-2 & 00-3

In 1999, the Vikings traded Brad Johnson to the Redskins for Washington's first and second round picks in the 1999 draft as well as their third round pick in the 2000 draft. The

Vikings used the first round pick to draft Daunte Culpepper, and the second and third round picks were traded away in later deals.

Year	Team A	Gave	Team B	Gave
1926	ARZ	*Paddy Driscoll*	CHI	$
1929	NYG	Bought Detroit Bulldog Franchise	DBD	*Bennie Friedman*
1938	CHI	Ed Manske	PIT	39-1 (*Sid Luckman*)
1939	PIT	*Frank Filchock*	WSH	$
1940	ARZ	*George Cafego* and Ben Kish	XBRK	Joe Kuharich and Ed Beinor
1942	ARZ	*Johnny Clement* & Bill Daddio	PIT	Mal Kutner
1943	WSH	*Roy Zimmerman*	PHL	Jack Smith & Ken Haydn
1946	WSH	*Frank Filchock*	NYG	Paul Stenn & *Tom Mont*
1946	WSH	*Jim Hardy*, Bob Hoffman & Walt Ziemba	STL	*Jack Jacobs*
1947	GBP	Bob Nussbaumer	WSH	*Jack Jacobs*
1947	PHL	Jim Kekeris & Charles Hoover	DET	*Roy Zimmerman*
1947	PIT	*Bill Dudley* & Jack Duggers	DET	Bob Cifers & Bob Chappuis & Paul White & 48-1
1947	XBOS	*Paul Governali*	NYG	Bill Paschal & rights to George Connor
1948	NYG	Howie Livingston	WSH	*Charlie Conerly*
1948	PIT	Rights to *Bobby Layne*	CHI	Ray Evans
1948	XBOS	*John Grigas*	DET	*Roy Zimmerman*
1949	CHI	*Bobby Layne*	XNYB	50-1 (Chuck Hunsinger)
1949	PHL	*Frank Tripucka*	DET	Waiver
1949	STL	*Jim Hardy*	ARZ	50-1 (Ralph Pasquariello)
1950	CHI	*George Blanda*, Bob Perina, Ernie Zalejski, Jim Crawford & Bob Jensen	ZBAL	Dick Barwegen
1950	DET	Bob Mann	XNYB	*Bobby Layne*
1950	DET	*Frank Tripucka*	ARZ	Jim Cain, Clarence Self & Ray Stackhouse
1950	DET	*Bill Dudley*	WSH	Dan Sandifer
1950	GBP	?	ARZ	*Paul Christman*
1950	ZBAL	$	CHI	*George Blanda*
1951	NYY	52-5 (Mel Sinqufield)	PHL	*John Rauch*
1951	STL	*Bobby Thomason*	GBP	Conditional 52-1 & 52-2
1951	WSH	*Adrian Burk*	PHL	Jack Dwyer
1952	ARZ	*Jim Hardy*	DET	Art Murakowski & Bob Momsen
1952	DET	*Fred Enke*	PHL	John Thomas
1952	PHL	Piggy Barnes & John Rauch	PIT	Frank Wydo
1952	STL	53-1 (Donn Moomaw) & Jack Myers	PHL	*Bobby Thomason* & Jack Zilly
1952	XNYY	*George Ratterman*	CLE	Stanley Williams & Herschel Forrester
1953	CHI	*Steve Romanik*	ARZ	S.J. Whitman
1953	CLE	*Harry Agganis*, Don Shula, Bert Rechichar, Carl Taseff, Ed Sharkey, Gern Nagler, Dick Batten, Stu Sheets, Art Spinney & Elmer Willhoite	BAL	Mike McCormack, Don Colo, Tom Catlin, John Petitbon & Herschell Forester
1953	GBP	*Arnold Galiffa*	NYG	54-1 (Veryl Switzer) & Val Joe Walker
1954	GBP	*Babe Parilli* & Bob Fleck	CLE	*Bob Garrett*, John Bauer, Jack Miller, Chester Gierula
1954	NYG	*Arnold Galiffa*	SFF	Bob Vandover & Jim Monachino & Searcy Miles
1957	DET	Ollie Spencer, Norm Masters, Jim Salsbury, Don McIlhenny	GBP	*Tobin Rote* & Val Joe Walker
1957	DET	*Jack Kemp* & Dave Liddick	PIT	58-9 (Jim Loftin) & 58-18 (Bill Austin)
1957	GBP	*Bob Garrett* & Roger Zatkoff	CLE	Babe Parilli, John Petitbon, Carl Massey,

Year	Team A	Gave	Team B	Gave
				Sam Palumbo, Bill Kinard, John Macerelli
1957	SFF	*Earl Morrall*	PIT	Marv Matuszak
1957	STL	*Rudy Bukich* & Ray Shiver	WSH	58-1 (Lou Michaels)
1957	WSH	58-3 (Bill Anderson)	PHL	*Al Dorow*
1958	PIT	*Earl Morrall* & 59-2 (Mike Rabold) & 60-4 (Roger Brown)	DET	*Bobby Layne*
1958	STL	59-1 (Dick Bass) & Buck Lansford & Jimmy Harris	PHL	*Norm Van Brocklin*
1959	GBP	60-3 (Charley Elizey)	ARZ	*Lamar McHan*
1959	IND	*George Shaw*	NYG	60-1
1960	ARZ	*M.C. Reynolds*	WSH	61-3 (Billy Wilson)
1960	CHI	*Rudy Bukich*	PIT	Rudy Bukich
1960	DET	Bob Long & 61-1 (Bobby Crespino)	CLE	*Jim Ninowski*
1960	PIT	*Len Dawson* & Gern Nagler	CLE	Jr. Wren & Preston Carpenter
1960	WSH	*Eddie LeBaron*	DAL	61-1 (*Norm Snead*) & 61-6 (Joe Krakoski)
1961	ARZ	62-1 (Irv Goode)	PHL	*King Hill*
1961	CHI	Erich Barnes & *Zeke Bratkowski*	STL	*Bill Wade*
1961	GBP	*Lamar McHan*	IND	62-5 (Chuck Morris)
1961	GBP	62-3 (John Furman)	CLE	*John Roach*
1961	MIN	62-5 (Bookie Bolin)	NYG	*George Shaw*
1961	OAK	*Babe Parilli* & Billy Lott	NEP	Dick Christy & Hal Smith
1961	SDC	Duane Leopard	NEP	*Tom Greene*
1961	SFF	*Y.A. Tittle*	NYG	Lou Cordileone
1961	WSH	*Ralph Guglielmi*	ARZ	*George Izo*
1962	ARZ	*Ralph Guglielmi*	NYG	Bill Triplett
1962	CHI	*Ed Brown*	PIT	63-1 (Dave Behrman)
1962	DET	*Jim Ninowski*, Bill Glass, Howard Cassady	CLE	*Milt Plum*, Dave Lloyd, Tom Watkins
1962	KCC	*Cotton Davidson*	OAK	63-1 (Buck Buchanan)
1962	NEP	*Butch Songin*	NYJ	Dick Felt
1962	NYJ	*Al Dorow*	BUF	*Johnny Green* & Billy Atkins
1962	SDC	*Jack Kemp*	BUF	Waivers
1962	STL	*Frank Ryan* & Tom Wilson	CLE	Larry Stephens & 63-3 (Johnny Baker) & 63-6 (Terry Monaghan)
1963	DAL	*Buddy Humphrey*	ARZ	Hugh McInnis
1963	GBP	Ken Iman	STL	*Zeke Bratkowski*
1963	NYG	*Ralph Guglielmi* & conditional draft pick	SFF	Eddie Dove
1963	PHL	*Sonny Jurgenson* & Jimmy Carr	WSH	*Norm Snead* & Claude Crabb
1964	KCC	*Eddie Wilson*	NEP	67-2 (Jim Lynch) & $
1964	NYJ	Draft rights to *Jerry Rhome*	TEN	65-1 (*Joe Namath*)
1964	PHL	Ted Dean & *Bob Berry*	MIN	Ray Poage & Don Hultz & Chuck Lamson & Terry Kosens
1964	TEN	*Jacky Lee* (2-year loan)	DEN	64-2 (Charley Taylor) & Bud McFadin
1965	DET	*Earl Morrall*	NYG	Mike Lucci, Darrell Dess and 66-4 (Doug Van Horn)
1965	NYJ	*Pete Liske*	BUF	John Sklopan
1965	PIT	*Terry Nofsinger*	ARZ	Ken Kortas
1965	PIT	*Ed Brown*	IND	Bob Wade
1965	WSH	*George Izo* & Ted Karras	DET	Darrell Dess
1966	BUF	*George Wilson*	MIA	67-13 (Howard Finley)
1966	NYJ	*John Huarte*	NEP	Jim Colclough & Jim Waskiewicz
1967	ARZ	*Terry Nofsinger*	ATL	68-4 (Don Fitzgerald)
1967	BUF	*Daryle Lamonica* & Glenn Bass & 67-3 (Bill Fairband) & 67-6 (Rick		

Year	Team A	Gave	Team B	Gave
		Egloff)	OAK	*Tom Flores* & Art Powell & 67-2 (Jim LeMoine) & 67-6 (Bill Wilkerson)
1967	CHI	Mike Ditka	PHL	*Jack Concannon*
1967	CLE	*Jim Ninowski*	WSH	*Dick Shiner* & 68-3 (Reece Morrison)
1967	GBP	*Kent Nix*	PIT	68-5 (Steve Duich)
1967	IND	*Gary Cuozzo* and Butch Allison & 67-17 (Billy Bob Stewart)	NOS	67-1 (Bubba Smith) & Bill Curry & 67-3 (Norman Davis)
1967	KCC	*Pete Beathard*	TEN	Ernie Ladd & 68-1 (George Daney) & *Jacky Lee*
1967	MIA	*John Stofa*	CIN	68-1 (Doug Crusan) & 68-2 (Jim Cox)
1967	MIN	*Fran Tarkenton*	NYG	68-1 (Ron Yary) & 67-1 (Clint Jones) & 67-2 (Bob Grim)
1967	SDC	*Steve Tensi*	DEN	68-1 (Russ Washington) & 69-1 (*Marty Domres*)
1967	TEN	*Don Trull*	NEP	67-9 (Bob Robertson)
1968	DET	*Milt Plum*, Pat Studstill, Tom Watkins & 69-1 (Larry Smith)	STL	*Bill Munson* & 69-3 (Jim Yarbrough)
1968	DET	*Karl Sweetan*	NOS	Walter Roberts
1968	MIN	68-1 (Kevin Hardy) & 69-1 (John Shinners)	NOS	*Gary Cuozzo*
1968	NEP	*Babe Parilli*	NYJ	*Mike Taliaferro*
1968	NYG	*Earl Morrall*	IND	Butch Wilson
1968	PHL	69-3 (Bill Bradley)	MIN	*King Hill*
1968	PIT	*Bill Nelsen* & Jim Bradshaw	CLE	*Dick Shiner* & Frank Parker & 69-2 (Warren Bankston)
1969	DAL	*Jerry Rhome*	CLE	70-3
1969	MIA	*Kim Hammond* & John Bramlett & 70-5 (Bob Olson)	NEP	Nick Buoniconti
1969	NOS	*Karl Sweetan*	STL	70-5 (*Steve Ramsey*) & 71-4 (Don Morrison)
1969	PHL	Randy Beisler	SFF	*George Mira*
1969	STL	*Milt Plum*	NYG	69-3
1970	ARZ	*Charley Johnson* & Robert Atkins	TEN	*Pete Beathard* & Miller Farr
1970	BUF	*Virgil Carter*	CIN	71-6 (Bill McKinley)
1970	CLE	*Jerry Rhome*	TEN	70-3
1970	MIA	70-1 (*Mike Phipps*)	CLE	Paul Warfield
1970	MIN	*Joe Kapp*	NEP	John Charles & 72-1 (Jeff Siemen)
1970	PIT	*Dick Shiner*	NYG	John Fuqua & Henry Davis
1971	GBP	*Don Horn* & 71-1 (Marv Montgomery)	DEN	Alden Roche and 71-1 (John Brockington)
1971	GBP	72-3 (Bart Buetow)	MIN	*Zeke Bratkowski*
1971	MIA	*John Stofa*	DEN	71-7 (Bill Adams)
1971	MIN	*Norm Snead*	PHL	Steve Smith & 71-2 (Hank Allison) & 71-6 (Wyck Neely) & 72-3 (Bobby Majors)
1972	MIN	*Norm Snead*, Bob Grim, Vince Clements & 72-1 (Larry Jacobson) & 73-2 (Brad Van Pelt)	NYG	*Fran Tarkenton*
1971	NOS	*Billy Kilmer*	WSH	Tom Roussel & 73-2 (Steve Baumgartner) & 72-4 (Joe Federspiel)
1971	NOS	*Steve Ramsey*	DEN	71-4 (DAL Tim Kearney)
1971	NYG	*Dick Shiner*	ATL	*Randy Johnson*
1971	PHL	71-2 (Dave Thompson) & 72-2 (ATL — Pat Sullivan) & 72-3 (Ken Sanders)	DET	*Greg Barton*
1971	PHL	72-5 (Jim Kreig)	DEN	*Pete Liske*
1972	MIN	*Gary Cuozzo*	ARZ	John Gilliam & 73-2 (Jackie Wallace)

Year	Team A	Gave	Team B	Gave
1972	SDC	*Marty Domres*	IND	John Andrews & 72-1 (Johnny Rodgers)
1972	TEN	*Charley Johnson*	DEN	72-3
1973	GBP	*Zeke Bratkowski*	CHI	74-6 (Don Woods)
1973	GBP	74-2 (Fred Solomon) & 75-2 (Andre Tillman)	MIA	*Jim Del Gaizo*
1973	IND	*John Unitas*	SDC	$
1973	MIN	*Bob Lee* & Lonnie Warwick	ATL	*Bob Berry* & 74-1 (Fred McNeil)
1973	PHL	Harold Jackson & Tony Baker & 74-1 (John Cappaletti) & 75-1 (Dennis Harrah) & 75-3 (Dan Nugent)	STL	*Roman Gabriel*
1973	SDC	*John Hadl*	STL	Coy Bacon & Bobby Thomas
1974	DAL	*Craig Morton*	NYG	75-1 (Randy White)
1974	GBP	75-1 (Mike Fanning) & 76-1 (Dennis Lick) & 75-2 (Monte Jackson) & 76-2 Pat Thomas) & 75-3 (Geoff Reese)	STL	*John Hadl*
1974	MIA	*Joe Theismann*	WSH	76-1 (Larry Gordon)
1974	NYG	*Norm Snead*	SFF	75-3 (Danny Buggs) & 76-4 (Gordon Bell)
1974	PHL	76-1 (Billy Brooks) & 75-6 (*Tom Shuman*)	CIN	*Mike Boryla*
1974	SFF	*Joe Reed*	DET	76-5 (Anthony Leonard)
1975	GBP	*Jim Del Gaizo*	NYG	76-3 (Gary Barbaro)
1975	GBP	76-3 (Gary Barbaro)	KCC	*Dean Carlson*
1975	PHL	*John Reaves* & 76-2 (Glenn Bujnoch)	CIN	Stan Walters & *Wayne Clark*
1976	DAL	*Clint Longley*	SDC	77-1 & 77-2 Both picks used in trade for Tony Dorsett draft rights
1976	GBP	*John Hadl*, Ken Ellis, 77-3 (Tim Wilson) & 76-4 (Steve Largent)	TEN	*Lynn Dickey*
1976	IND	*Marty Domres*	SFF	76-5 (Frank Myers)
1976	NEP	*Jim Plunkett*	SFF	76-1 (Pete Brock) & 76-1 (Tim Fox) & 77-1 (Raymond Clayborn) & 77-2 (Horace Ivory) & *Tom Owen*
1976	SFF	*Steve Spurrier*	TBB	Bruce Elia, Willie McGee & 76-2 (Eddie Lewis)
1977	CHI	*Mike Phipps*	CLE	78-1 (Ozzie Newsome) & 77-4 (Robert Sims)
1977	NYG	*Craig Morton*	DEN	*Steve Ramsey* & 78-5 (Brian DeRoo)
1977	PHL	Charley Young	STL	*Ron Jaworski*
1977	STL	*James Harris*	SDC	77-2 (Billy Waddy) & 77-3 (Ed Fulton)
1978	STL	*Jeff Rutledge*	NYG	Announced as 78-6 & 78-7
1979	DET	*Greg Landry*	IND	80-3 (Mike Friede) & 79-4 (Ulysses Norris) & 79-5 (Walt Brown)
1980	MIA	*Guy Benjamin*	NOS	81-4 (Sam Greene)
1980	NYJ	*Matt Robinson*	DEN	80-1 (Lam Jones) & 80-2 (Ralph Clayton) and *Craig Penrose*
1980	PHL	81-6 (Edward O'Neal)	NYG	*Joe Pisarcik*
1980	TEN	*Dan Pastorini*	OAK	*Ken Stabler*
1981	SFF	*Steve DeBerg*	DEN	83-4
1982	IND	*Bert Jones*	STL	82-1 (*Art Schlichter*) and 82-2 (Rohn Stark)
1982	NEP	*Tom Owen*	WSH	*Tom Flick*
1982	NOS	*Archie Manning*	TEN	Leon Gray
1983	CIN	*Jack Thompson*	TBB	84-1
1983	IND	*John Elway*	DEN	*Mark Herrmann* & Chris Hinton & 84-1 (Ron Solt)
1984	BUF	*Joe Ferguson*	DET	86-7 (Mark Pike)
1984	DEN	*Steve DeBerg*	TBB	85-2 & 84-4 (Randy Robbins)

Year	Team A	Gave	Team B	Gave
1984	MIA	*David Woodley*	PIT	84-3
1984	MIN	84-2 & 84-4 (Patrick Allen)	TEN	*Archie Manning* & Dave Caspar
1984	NYG	*Scott Brunner*	DEN	84-4 (Gary Reasons)
1984	NYJ	*Richard Todd*	NOS	84-1 (Ron Faurot)
1985	BUF	Rights to *Bernie Kosar* in Supplemental Draft	CLE	85-1 & 85-3 (Hal Garner) & 85-5
1985	DET	*Gary Danielson*	CLE	86-3 (Joe Millinichik)
1985	GBP	86-6 (Orson Mobley)	DEN	*Scott Brunner*
1985	GBP	*Scott Brunner*	ARZ	86-6 (Burnell Dent)
1985	IND	*Mark Herrmann*	SDC	86-10 (Pete Anderson)
1985	STL	*Vince Ferragamo*	BUF	86-5 (Kevin Greene) & Tony Hunter
1986	DAL	*Gary Hogeboom*	IND	Draft pick switch
1986	IND	*Mike Pagel*	CLE	87-9 (Bob Ontko)
1986	PHL	86-3 (Tim McKyer) & 87-2 (Jeff Bragel)	SFF	*Matt Cavanaugh*
1986	TEN	*Jim Everett*	STL	87-1 (Haywood Jeffries) & 88-1 & 87-5 (Spencer Tillman) & Kent Hill & William Fuller
1987	CHI	*Doug Flutie*	NEP	88-8 (David Tate)
1987	SFF	*Jeff Kemp*	SEA	88-5
1987	TBB	*Steve Young*	SFF	88-2 (Jamel Tate) & 88-4 (Monte Robbins)
1988	ARZ	*Kelly Stouffer*	SEA	89-1 (Joe Wolf) & 89-5 (David Edeen) & 88-5 (Chris Gaines)
1988	IND	*Stan Humphries*	WSH	Clarence Verdin
1988	KCC	*Todd Blackledge*	PIT	88-4 (J.R. Ambrose)
1988	PIT	*Mark Malone*	SDC	88-8 (Mike Hiant)
1988	TBB	*Steve DeBerg*	KCC	Mike Robinson & 88-4 (John Bruhin)
1988	WSH	*Jay Schroeder*	OAK	Jim Lachey & 89-4 (Erik Affholter) & 89-5 (Lybrant Robinson)
1989	CHI	*Jim McMahon*	SDC	90-2 (Ron Cox)
1989	DAL	*Scott Secules*	MIA	90-5
1990	DAL	*Steve Walsh*	NOS	91-1 & 92-2 & 91-3 (Erik Williams)
1990	IND	*Chris Chandler*	TBB	91-1 (Quentin Coryatt)
1990	IND	Andre Rison & Chris Hinton	ATL	*Jeff George* draft rights
1991	KCC	*Steve DeBerg*	TBB	Waivers
1991	OAK	*Steve Beuerlein*	DAL	91-5 & 91-7
1991	TBB	*Chris Chandler*	ARZ	Waivers
1992	GBP	92-1	ATL	*Brett Favre*
1992	WSH	*Stan Humphries*	SDC	93-3 (Ed Bunn)
1993	CIN	*Boomer Esiason*	NYJ	93-3 (Steve Tovar)
1993	SFF	*Joe Montana* & David Whitmore & 94-3 (Lake Dawson)	KCC	93-1
1994	DEN	*Tommy Maddox*	STL	95-4 (Ken Brown)
1994	IND	*Jeff George*	ATL	96-1 (Marvin Harrison) & 94-1 & 94-3 Traded for 94-1 (Trev Alberts)
1994	TEN	*Warren Moon*	MIN	94-4 (Michael Davis) and 95-3 (Rodney Thomas)
1995	GBP	*Mark Brunell*	JAX	95-3 (William Henderson) & 95-5 (Travis Jervey)
1995	TBB	*Craig Erickson*	IND	96-1 (Marcus Jones)
1997	CHI	97-1	SEA	*Rick Mirer*
1997	TEN	*Chris Chandler*	ATL	97-4 (Derrick Mason) & 97-6 (NOS Nicky Savoie)
1997	WSH	*Heath Shuler*	NOS	98-5 (Jamel Williams)
1998	CAR	*Kerry Collins*	NOS	Waivers
1998	GBP	99-7 (Chris Akins)	STL	*Steve Bono*
1998	IND	*Jim Harbaugh*	BAL	98-3 (E.G. Green) & draft slot switch

Year	Team A	Gave	Team B	Gave
1998	IND	*Paul Justin*	CIN	98-5 (Anthony Jordan)
1998	JAX	*Rob Johnson*	BUF	98-1 (Fred Taylor) & 98-4 (Tavian Banks)
1999	BAL	*Eric Zeier*	TBB	99-6 (Talance Sawyer)
1999	BAL	*Jim Harbaugh*	SDC	Announced as 2000-5
1999	DEN	*Jeff Lewis*	CAR	99-3 (Chris Watson) & 2000-4 (Cooper Carlisle)
1999	DET	*Scott Mitchell*	BAL	Announced as 99-3
1999	GBP	*Rick Mirer*	NYJ	2000-4 (traded to SFF in position exchange)
1999	MIN	*Brad Johnson*	WSH	99-1 (*Daunte Culpepper*) & 99-2 & 00-3
1999	NYJ	*Glenn Foley*	SEA	99-7 (Ryan Young)
1999	PHL	*Bobby Hoying*	OAK	2000-6 (John Frank)
1999	PHL	*Rodney Peete*	WSH	2000-6 (John Romero)
1999	SFF	*Jim Druckenmiller*	MIA	2000-7 (Brian Jennings)
1999	STL	*Tony Banks*	BAL	99-5 (Cameron Spikes)
2000	GBP	*Aaron Brooks* & Lamont Hall	NOS	KD Williams & 2001-3 (position exchange with 49ers)
2001	ATL	2001-1 (LaDainian Tomlinson), 2001-3 (Tay Cody) & 2001-2 (Reche Caldwell)	SDC	2001-1 (*Michael Vick*)
2001	GBP	*Matt Hasselbeck* & 2001-1 (Steve Hutchinson)	SEA	2001-1 (Jamal Reynolds) & 2001-3 (Torrance Marshall)
2001	STL	*Trent Green* & 2001-5 (Derrick Blaylock)	KCC	2001-1 (Damione Lewis)
2002	CHI	*Cade McNown* & 2002-7 (Leonard Henry)	MIA	2002-6 (Adrian Peterson)
2002	HOU	*Danny Wuerffel*	WSH	Jerry DeLoach
2002	NEP	*Drew Bledsoe*	BUF	2003-1 (Ty Warren)
2002	SEA	*Brock Huard*	IND	2004-5 (Rocky Bernard)
2002	WSH	*Sage Rosenfels*	MIA	2002-7 (*Gibran Hamdan*)
2004	HOU	*Drew Henson*	DAL	2005-3 (Vernand Morency)
2004	JAX	*Mark Brunell*	WSH	2004-3 (GBP Donnell Washington)
2004	NYG	Draft Rights to *Philip Rivers*	SDC	Draft Rights to *Eli Manning*
2004	PHL	*A.J. Feeley*	MIA	2005-2 (Reggie Brown)
2005	CLE	*Luke McCown*	TBB	2005-6 (Andrew Hoffman)
2005	MIA	*A.J. Feeley* & 2006-6 (Kurt Smith)	SDC	*Cleo Lemon*
2005	SFF	*Tim Rattay*	TBB	2006-6 (Hudson Marcus)
2006	CIN	*Dave Ragone*	STL	Conditional 2007-7
2006	MIN	*Daunte Culpepper*	MIA	2006-2 (Ryan Cook)
2006	SFF	*Ken Dorsey*	CLE	*Trent Dilfer* & Conditional Draft
2006	TEN	*Steve McNair*	BAL	2007-4 (Chris Davis)
2006	WSH	*Patrick Ramsey*	NYJ	2006-6 (Reed Doughty)

Quarterback Award Winners

Most Valuable Player

1939	Parker Hall[a]	1942		1945	Bob Waterfield[a]
1940	Ace Parker[a]	1943	Sid Luckman[a]	1946	Glenn Dobbs[x]
1941		1944		1947	Otto Graham[x]

[a]Joe F. Carr Award 1938-46   [b]UPI Player of the Year 1953-69; UPI NFC/AFC Player of the Year 1970-96   [c]AP Player of the Year 1957-06   [d]Sporting News Player of the Year 1954-06   [e]Bert Bell Trophy from the Maxwell Club 1959-06
[f]PFW/PFWA Player of the Year 1968-06   [x]All America Conference MVP 1946-48

1948 Otto Graham[x] Frankie Albert[x]
1949
1950
1951
1952
1953 Otto Graham[b]
1954
1955 Otto Graham[b,d]
1956
1957 Y.A. Tittle[b]
1958
1959 John Unitas[b,d,e] Charlie Conerly[c]
1960 Norm Van Brocklin[b,c,d,e]
1961 George Blanda[b]
1962 Y.A. Tittle[b,d]
1963 Y.A. Tittle[c,d]
1964 John Unitas[b,c,d,e]
1965
1966 Bart Starr[b,c,d] Don Meredith[e]
1967 John Unitas[b,c,d,e] Daryle Lamonica[b]
1968 Earl Morrall[b,c,d,f] Joe Namath[b,f]
1969 Roman Gabriel[b,c,d,e,f] Daryle Lamonica[b,f]
1970 John Brodie[b,c,d,f] George Blanda[b,d,e]
1971 Roger Staubach[d,e] Bob Griese[d]
1972 Earl Morrall[d]
1973 John Hadl[b,d]
1974 Jim Hart[b,f] Ken Stabler[b,c,d]
1975 Fran Tarkenton[b,c,d,e,f]
1976 Bert Jones[b,c,f] Ken Stabler[d,e,f]
1977 Craig Morton[b,d] Bob Griese[e]

1978 Archie Manning[b,d] Terry Bradshaw[c,e]
1979 Dan Fouts[b,d]
1980 Ron Jaworski[b,e] Brian Sipe[b,c,d,f]
1981 Ken Anderson[b,c,d,e,f]
1982 Dan Fouts[b,f] Joe Theismann[e]
1983 Joe Theismann[c,f]
1984 Dan Marino[b,c,d,e,f]
1985
1986
1987 John Elway[b]
1988 Boomer Esiason[b,c,d,f] Randall Cunningham[e]
1989 Joe Montana[b,c,d,e,f]
1990 Randall Cunningham[b,e,f] Warren Moon[b] Joe Montana[c]
1991 Mark Rypien[b]
1992 Steve Young[b,c,d,e,f]
1993 John Elway[b]
1994 Steve Young[b,c,d,e,f] Dan Marino[b]
1995 Brett Favre[b,c,d,e,f]
1996 Brett Favre[b,c,d,e,f]
1997 Brett Favre[c,d]
1998 Randall Cunningham[e]
1999 Kurt Warner[c,d,e,f]
2000 Rich Gannon[e]
2001 Kurt Warner[c]
2002 Rich Gannon[c,d,e]
2003 Peyton Manning[c,d,e] Steve McNair[c]
2004 Peyton Manning[c,d,e,f]
2005
2006

Rookies

1965 Joe Namath[A]
1969 Greg Cook[A,D]
1970 Dennis Shaw[A,B,C,D]
1971 Jim Plunkett[A,C,D]
1975 Steve Bartkowski[C,D]

1982 Jim McMahon[A]
1983 Dan Marino[C]
1993 Rick Mirer[A]
2004 Ben Roethlisberger[D]
2006 Vince Young[B,C,D]

[A]UPI 1955-96   [B]AP 1967-06   [C]Sporting News 1955-06   [D]PFW 1969-06

Uniform Numbers of Top Passers

Note: This table includes tailbacks (TB) and fullbacks (FB) from the first quarter-century of NFL history, when those positions were the primary passers. Hall of Famers are in **boldface.**

	Best Player/HOFers	Most Seasons	Most Teams
0	Johnny Clement (TB)	Johnny Clement 3	Johnny Clement 1
1	**Jim Conzelman**		
	Paddy Driscoll (TB)		
	Benny Friedman (TB)		
	Curly Lambeau (TB)		
	Warren Moon		
	Fritz Pollard	Warren Moon 17	**Warren Moon** 4
2	**Paddy Driscoll**		
	Charley Trippi (TB)		
		Aaron Brooks	
		Anthony Wright 7	Anthony Wright 3
3	**Bill Dudley** (TB)		

Best Player/HOFers	Most Seasons	Most Teams
Daryle Lamonica	Bobby Hebert 11	Ralph Guglielmi 3
		Rick Mirer 3
4 Brett Favre		
Ernie Nevers (FB)		
Tuffy Leemans (FB)	Brett Favre 16	Jim Harbaugh 4
5 Donovan McNabb	Terry Hanratty 8	
	Kerry Collins 8	
	Donovan McNabb 8	Kerry Collins 3
		Jeff Garcia 3
6 **Benny Friedman** (TB)	Bubby Brister 14	Bubby Brister 5
7 **Dutch Clark** (TB)		
John Elway		
Ace Parker		
Bob Waterfield		
Boomer Esiason		
Bert Jones		
Ben Roethlisberger		
Joe Theismann		
Michael Vick	**John Elway** 16	Steve Beuerlein 5
8 **Troy Aikman**		
Steve Young	**Steve Young** 15	Mark Brunell 3
		Tommy Maddox 3
9 **Sonny Jurgensen**		
Fritz Pollard		
Drew Brees		
Jim McMahon		
Steve McNair		
Carson Palmer	**Sonny Jurgensen** 18	Rodney Peete 4
10 **Fran Tarkenton**		
Steve Bartkowski		
Marc Bulger		
Trent Green	**Fran Tarkenton** 18	Rudy Bukich 4
11 Norm Van Brocklin		
Ernie Nevers (TB)		
Phil Simms		
Tommy Thompson		
Danny White	Greg Landry 15	Mark Rypien 4
		Mike Quinn 4
12 **Terry Bradshaw**		
Dutch Clark (TB)		
Bob Griese		
Arnie Herber (TB)		
Jim Kelly		
Joe Namath		
Roger Staubach		
Tom Brady		
John Brodie		
Randall Cunningham		
Rich Gannon		
Ken Stabler	John Brodie 17	Gus Frerotte 6
13 **Dan Marino**		
Frank Ryan		
Kurt Warner	**Dan Marino** 17	Steve Bono 4
14 **Dan Fouts**		
Otto Graham		
Curly Lambeau (TB)		
Y.A. Tittle		
Ken Anderson		

	Best Player/HOFers	Most Seasons	Most Teams
	Steve Grogan		
	Brad Johnson		
	Eddie LeBaron	Ken Anderson 16	Brian Griese 3
			Brad Johnson 3
			Neil O'Donnell 3
15	**Jimmy Conzelman**		
	Bart Starr	**Bart Starr** 16	Gary Cuozzo 4
16	**George Blanda**		
	Len Dawson		
	Arnie Herber (TB)		
	Joe Montana		
	Bart Starr		
	Jim Plunkett	**George Blanda** 23	Norm Snead 5
17	**Benny Friedman** (TB)		
	Jim Hart		
	Cecil Isbell (TB)		
	Billy Kilmer		
	Dave Krieg		
	Don Meredith		
	Brian Sipe	Dave Krieg 19	Steve DeBerg 6
18	**Len Dawson**		
	Roman Gabriel		
	Peyton Manning		
	Tobin Rote	Roman Gabriel 15	
		Mike Tomczak 15	Mike Tomczak 4
19	**Dutch Clark** (TB)		
	Arnie Herber (TB)		
	Joe Montana		
	John Unitas		
	Bernie Kosar	**John Unitas** 18	Cotton Davidson 3
20	**Arnie Herber** (TB)		
	Paddy Driscoll (TB)	George Taliaferro 5	George Taliaferro 3
21	**Benny Friedman** (TB)		
	John Hadl	John Hadl 16	John Hadl 4
22	**George Blanda**		
	Bobby Layne		
	Ed Danowski (TB)	**Bobby Layne** 15	**Bobby Layne** 3
23	Johnny Clement (TB)	George Cafego 2	na
24	**Whizzer White** (TB)	Fred Enke 3	na
25	**Norm Van Brocklin**	**Norm Van Brocklin** 3	Hugh McCullough 2
26	**Benny Friedman** (TB)		
	Arnie Herber (TB)	Benny Friedman 3	
		Jack McBride 3	
		Albie Riesz 3	na
27	Jack Jacobs	Jack Jacobs 3	na
28	Bobby Thomason	na	na
29	Roy Zimmerman	na	na
30	Frank Filchock	Frank Filchock 6	na
31	**Ace Parker**	Larry Weldon 2	na
32	Parker Hall		
	Johnny Lujack	Parker Hall 4	
		Johnny Lujack 4	na
33	**Sammy Baugh**		
	Bernie Masterson	**Sammy Baugh** 16	na
34	Jimmy German	Jimmy German 1	na
35	**Bill Dudley** (TB)	Bill Dudley 3	
		Riley Smith 3	na
36	Dwight Sloan	Dwight Sloan 3	Dwight Sloan 2

Best Player/HOFers	Most Seasons	Most Teams
37 Young Bussey	Young Bussey 2	na
38 **Arnie Herber** (TB)	**Arnie Herber** 6	na
39 Bill Mackrides	Bill Mackrides 5	na
40 Frank Filchock	na	na
41 **Arnie Herber** (TB)	**Arnie Herber** 2	
	Paul Governali 2	na
42 **Sid Luckman**		
Curly Lambeau (TB)		
Charlie Conerly	Charlie Conerly 14	na
43 Jack Jacobs	Jack Jacobs 2	na
44 Paul Christman		
Ernie Nevers (FB)	Paul Christman 4	na
45 Arnie Herber (**TB**)	na	na
46 Fred Enke	Bob Scrabis 3	na
47 Fred Benners	na	na
48 Charlie O'Rourke	Chuck Fenenbock 2	
	Joe Gasparella 2	na
49 Charley Eikenberg	na	na
50 Bob Monnett (TB)	na	na
51 Irv Comp (TB)	Irv Comp 7	na
52 Harry Gilmer	Harry Gilmer 4	na
53 Bev Wallace	na	na
55 Frank Filchock	na	na
56 Coley McDonough	Coley McDonough 2	na
57 Billy Patterson	Billy Patterson 1	na
58 Warren Plunkett	Warren Plunkett 1	na
60 **Otto Graham**	**Otto Graham** 6	na
61 George Ratterman	George Ratterman 3	na
62 Cliff Lewis	Cliff Lewis 6	na
63 Frankie Albert		
Y.A. Tittle	Frankie Albert 6	na
64 **Y.A. Tittle**	Bev Wallace 3	Bud Schwenk 2
65 Glenn Dobbs	Norm Cox 2	na
66 Charlie O'Rourke	Charlie O'Rourke 3	Charlie O'Rourke 2
		Al Dekdebrun 2
67 Sam Vacanti	na	na
68 **Arnie Herber** (TB)	na	na
69 Sam Vacanti	Sam Vacanti 2	Sam Vacanti 2
72 Johnny Clement (TB)	na	na
76 Frankie Sinkwich	na	na
77 Frankie Sinkwich	Tommy Mont 3	na
78 Ray Mallouf	na	na
80 Tom Hearden	na	na
81 Spec Sanders (TB)	Spec Sanders 4	Spec Sanders 2
84 Parker Hall	na	na
86 Al Dekdebrun	na	na
87 Jesse Freitas	na	na
88 **Ace Parker**	na	na
90 Glenn Dobbs		
Bob Hoernschemeyer (TB)	Bob Hoernschemeyer 3	Bob Hoernschemeyer 2
93 George Taliaferro	Chuck Fennenbock 3	na
95 Glenn Dobbs	Glenn Dobbs 2	na
98 Ray Mallouf	na	na
99 Bob Chappuis (TB)	Bob Chappuis 2	Bob Chappuis 2

Bibliography

Books

Allen, George, with Ben Olan. *Pro Football's 100 Greatest Players: Rating the Stars of Past and Present.* Indianapolis: Bobbs-Merrill, 1982.

Ashe, Arthur. *A Hard Road to Glory: A History of the African-American Athlete.* New York: Warner Books, 1988. 3v.

Carroll, Bob. *When the Grass Was Real: Unitas, Brown, Lombardi, Sayers, Butkus, Namath and All the Rest: The Ten Best Years of Pro Football.* New York: Simon and Schuster, 1993.

Carroll, Bob, Michael Gershman, David Neft, and John Thorn. *Total Football: The Official Encyclopedia of the National Football League.* New York: Harper Collins, 1999.

Carroll, Bob, Pete Palmer and John Thorn. *The Hidden Game of Football: The Next Edition.* New York: Total Sports, 1998.

_____, _____ and _____. *Total Quarterbacks.* New York: Total Sports, 1998.

Chalk, Ocania. *Pioneers of Black Sport: The Early Days of the Black Professional Athlete in Baseball, Basketball, Boxing, and Football.* New York: Dodd, Mead, 1975.

Cohen, Richard M., Jordan A. Deutsch, Roland T. Johnson, and David S. Neft. *The Scrapbook History of Pro Football.* Indianapolis, IN: Bobbs-Merrill, 1976.

Cope, Myron. *The Game That Was: An Illustrated Account of the Tumultuous Early Days of Pro Football.* New York: Crowell, 1974.

Curran, Bob. *Pro Football's Rag Days.* Englewood Cliffs, NJ: Prentice-Hall, 1969.

Daly, Dan, and Bob O'Donnell. *The Pro Football Chronicle: The Complete (Well Almost) Record of the Best Players, the Greatest Photos, the Hardest Hits, the Biggest Scandals, and the Funniest Stories in Pro Football.* New York: Collier, 1990.

DeVito, Carlo. *The Ultimate Dictionary of Sports Quotations.* New York: Facts on File, 2001.

Fleder, Rob, ed. *Sports Illustrated: The Football Book.* New York: Time Inc. Home Entertainment, 2005.

Garraty, John A., and Mark C. Carnes, general editors. *American National Biography.* New York: Oxford University Press, 1999.

Gillette, Gary, Matt Silverman, Pete Palmer, Ken Pullis and Sean Lahman. *The ESPN Pro Football Encyclopedia.* New York: Sterling, 2006.

Golenbock, Peter. *Cowboys Have Always Been My Heroes: The Definitive Oral History of America's Team.* New York: Warner, 1997.

Herskowitz, Mickey. *The Golden Age of Pro Football: NFL Football in the 1950s.* Dallas: Taylor, 1990.

_____. *The Quarterbacks: The Uncensored Truth About the Men in the Pocket.* New York: Morrow, 1990.

King, Peter. *Football: A History of the Professional Game.* New York: Bishop [Time. Inc. Home Entertainment], 1997.

_____. *Greatest Quarterbacks.* New York: Bishop [Time. Inc. Home Entertainment], 1999.

Leuthner, Stuart. *Iron Men: Bucko, Crazy Legs, and the Boys Recall the Golden Days of Professional Football.* New York: Doubleday, 1988.

Maikovich, Andrew J., and Michele D. Brown. *Sports Quotations: Maxims, Quips, and Pronouncements for Writers and Fans.* Jefferson, NC: McFarland, 2000.

Maule, Tex. *The Game: The Official Picture History of the NFL and AFL.* New York: Random House, 1967.

Merchant, Larry. *...And Every Day You Take Another Bite.* Garden City, New York: Doubleday, 1971.

Neft, David S., Richard M. Cohen and Richard Korch. *The Football Encyclopedia: The Complete History of Professional Football from 1892 to the Present.* New York: St. Martin's, 1994.

Olderman, Murray. *The Pro Quarterback.* Englewood Cliffs, NJ: Prentice-Hall, 1966.

Peterson, Robert. *Pigskin: The Early Years of Pro Football.* New York: Oxford University Press, 1997.

Porter, David L., ed. *Biographical Dictionary of American Sports: Football.* New York: Greenwood, 1987.

_____. *Biographical Dictionary of American Sports: 1989–1992 Supplement for Baseball, Football, Basketball, and Other Sports.* New York: Greenwood, 1992.

_____. *Biographical Dictionary of American Sports: 1992–1995 Supplement for Baseball, Football, Basketball, and Other Sports.* New York: Greenwood, 1995.

Pruyne, Terry W. *Sports Nicknames: 20,000 Professionals Worldwide.* Jefferson, NC: McFarland, 2002.

Rand, Jonathan. *The Gridiron's Greatest Quarterbacks.* Champaign, IL : Sports Publishing, 2004.

Rathet, Mike, and Don R. Smith. *Their Deeds and Dogged Faith.* New York: Rutledge, 1984.

Rhoden, William C. *Third and a Mile: The Trials and Triumph of the Black Quarterback.* New York: ESPN Books, 2007.

Riffenburgh, Beau. *Great Ones: NFL Quarterbacks from Baugh to Montana.* New York: Viking, 1989.

Ross, Charles K. *Outside the Lines: African Americans and the Integration of the National Football League.* New York: New York University Press, 1999.

Schaap, Dick. *Quarterbacks Have All the Fun: The Good Life and Hard Times of Bart Johnny, Joe, Francis, and Other Great Quarterbacks.* Chicago: Playboy Press, 1974.

75 Seasons: The Complete Story of the National Football League 1920–1995. Atlanta, GA: Turner, 1994.

Smith, Myron J. *Pro Football: The Official Pro Football Hall of Fame Bibliography.* Westport, CT: Greenwood, 1993.

_____. The *Pro Football Bio-Bibliography.* West Cornwall, CT: Locust Hill Press, 1989.

Smith, Ron. *The Sporting News Selects Football's 100 Greatest Players: A Celebration of the 20th Century's Best.* St. Louis, MO: Sporting News, 1999.

_____. *Sporting News Books Presents Pro Football's Heroes of the Hall.* St. Louis, MO: Sporting News, 2003.

_____. *The Sporting News Selects Pro Football's Greatest Quarterbacks.* St. Louis, MO: Sporting News, 2005.

Whittingham, Richard. *What a Game They Played.* New York: Harper and Row, 1974.

Zimmerman, Paul. *The New Thinking Man's Guide to Pro Football.* New York: Simon and Schuster, 1984.

Newspapers and Magazines

New York Times   *Los Angeles Times*
Washington Post   *Sport*
Chicago Tribune   *Sports Illustrated*

Web Sites

College Football Hall of Fame (http://collegefootball. org/)

Current Team Histories (http://www.jt-sw.com/football/pro/teams.nsf)

databaseFootball.com (http://www.databasefootball. com/)

Draft History (http://www.drafthistory.com/index. php)

Ghosts of the Gridiron (http://www.geocities.com/ ghostsofthegridiron/)

NFL History Network (http://nflhistory.net/)

NFL.com (http://www.nfl.com/)

Pro Football Hall of Fame (http://www.profootball hof.com/)

Pro-Football-Reference.com (http://www.pro-football-reference.com/index.htm)

Professional Football Researchers Association (http:// www.footballresearch.com/)

Index

Adams, Bud 122
Adams, Tony 33, 233, 234, 241
Adderley, Herb 220
Agannis, Harry 13, 28, 30, 208
Aikman, Troy 17, 18, 24, 25, 36, 41, 43, 58, 64, 65, 70, 152, 164, 165, 167, 177, 210–13
Akron Pros 13, 81
Albert, Frankie 11, 13, 20, 42, 45, 49, 67, 74, 103–106, 115, 202, 278–81
Alexander, Charles 193
All America Football Conference (AAFC) 2, 11–13, 21, 27, 32, 38, 45, 50, 51, 59, 65, 102–107, 111, 113, 129, 187, 202, 208, 219, 224, 278, 293
Allard, Don 27, 28, 245, 293
Allen, George 54, 67, 68, 133, 138, 141, 146, 270, 294
Allen, Gerry 142
Allen, Marcus 71
Allison, Butch 229, 248, 252
Alworth, Lance 7, 277
American Football League (AFL) 2, 18, 20, 26, 27, 31, 32, 49, 59, 65, 66, 70, 103, 122–32, 133, 135, 142–44, 219, 228, 234, 235, 245, 255, 258, 268, 275–76, 289, 293
American Professional Football Association (APFA) 6, 80–82
Anderson, Derek 12, 208
Anderson, Gary 175
Anderson, Ken 16, 19, 28, 35, 40, 46, 51, 63, 65, 66, 70, 134, 145, 147, 156, 159, 161, 204–6
Anderson, Ralph 276
Andrews, John 276
Angsman, Elmer 110, 186
Archer, David 190, 276, 294
Arena League 34, 176
Arizona Cardinals 11, 13, 23, 26–29, 32, 33, 40, 84, 90, 94, 95, 97, 99–101, 108, 110, 111, 113, 114, 116–118, 120, 122, 133, 136, 141, 147, 148, 159, 163, 171, 173, 176, 181, 185–89, 202, 211, 222, 224, 241, 262, 272, 283, 293
Armstrong, Johnny 82
Arrington, Jill 264
Arrington, LaVar 43
Arrington, Rick 264
Atkins, Doug 44
Atlanta Falcons 8, 23, 52, 141, 156, 160, 165, 166, 171, 173–75, 179, 180, 189–91, 211, 215, 227, 229, 262, 264, 272, 277
Autry, Alan see Carlos Brown
Avellini, Bob 200

Bachelors III 17
Bacon, Coy 31
Baker, Dave 28, 280
Baker, John 250
Baker, Ralph 131
Baker, Terry 13, 26, 27, 41, 138, 272
Baker, Tony 30, 263, 272
Baltimore Colts (AAFC) 27, 103–106
Baltimore Colts (NFL 1950) 31, 113, 114, 202, 280
Baltimore Colts (NFL 1953) see Indianapolis Colts
Baltimore Ravens 18, 32, 57, 173, 177, 178, 188, 192–94, 251, 268, 286, 293
Banks, Tony 17, 173, 193, 226, 270–72, 294
Barnes, Erich 202
Barnes, Gary 190
Bartkowski, Steve 18, 23, 24, 55, 65, 134, 149, 150, 152, 156, 157, 159–61, 189–91, 272, 277, 294
Barton, Greg 219, 220, 263
Barwegan, Dick 31, 202
Bass, Dick 263
Bass, Glen 31, 196, 259
Batch, Charlie 175, 218, 219, 267, 268
Battle, Arneaz 280
Battles, Cliff 293
Baugh, Sammy 12, 18, 21, 26, 35, 36, 38, 40, 41, 43, 45, 46, 54, 63–66, 70, 71, 73, 75, 76, 90, 94–101, 108–110, 115, 205, 222, 264, 291–95
Baylor University 290
Beathard, Pete 20, 23, 27, 61, 123, 127, 130, 188, 219, 233, 234, 272, 288–90
Beban, Gary 294
Beisler, Randy 280
Belichick, Bill 8, 17, 245
Bell, Bert 41, 121
Bell, Kerwin 286
Benjamin, Guy 238, 248, 280
Berry, Bob 189–91
Bertelli, Angelo 25, 26, 104, 105
Beuerlein, Steve 163, 176, 179, 187, 188, 198, 199, 212, 215, 216, 231
Bishop, Michael 244
Blackledge, Todd 152, 158, 161, 164, 233, 234, 268
Blackwell, Marquel 255
Blake, Jeff 29, 32, 38, 56, 167, 181, 187, 188, 193, 201, 202, 204, 205, 248, 255, 256, 263
Blanda, George 18, 21, 22, 28, 31, 32, 40, 41, 45, 46, 50, 52, 54, 59, 63, 65, 66, 74, 75, 108, 112, 117, 119, 123–25, 127, 128, 130, 132, 144, 149, 202, 203, 258–60, 288–90
Bledsoe, Drew 12, 19, 26, 30, 38, 39, 42, 43, 58, 67, 152, 168, 170, 171, 173, 178, 179, 181, 195–97, 212, 213, 243–45, 283
Blount, Ed 279
Blount, Jeb 150, 285
Blundin, Matt 219, 234
Boerigter, Marc 178
Bohling, Dewey 255
Boller, Kyle 28, 129, 192, 193
Bollinger, Brooks 241
Bono, Steve 160, 166, 176, 199, 223, 233, 234, 241, 268, 272
Booty, Josh 73
Borton, John 208
Boryla, Mike 23, 36, 205, 262–64, 286

Boston Braves *see* Washington Red-skins

Boston College 13, 25, 202, 244, 245, 283

Boston Patriots *see* New England Patriots

Boston Red Sox 13, 28

Boston Redskins *see* Washington Redskins

Boston Yanks 26, 28, 90, 100, 104, 110

Bova, Tony 268

Boyd, Bob 229

Boynton, Benny 81

Brackins, Charlie 14, 118, 223

Bradshaw, Craig 269, 289, 290

Bradshaw, Jim 268

Bradshaw, Terry 17–19, 36, 39, 41, 44, 55, 56, 58, 62, 63, 65–67, 69, 70, 73, 74, 77, 134, 144, 146, 148, 149, 152, 154, 155, 157, 158, 202, 266–69

Brady, Tom 16–19, 25, 28, 37, 38, 42, 43, 55, 56, 58, 66, 68, 73, 74, 170, 177–80, 182, 198, 243–45

Bramlett, John 238, 245

Branch, Cliff 7

Bratkowski, Zeke 29, 41, 43, 117, 135, 136, 140, 200–2, 223, 270–72

Breaux, Don 216

Brees, Drew 12, 27, 32, 178, 182, 246–49, 274–77

Briggs, Walter 255

Briscoe, Marlin 12, 14, 123, 131, 196, 215, 216, 237

Brister, Bubby 32, 73, 161, 168, 216, 241, 256

Brittenum, Jon 276

Brock, Dieter 33, 160, 270–72

Brock, Pete 280

Brodie, John 22, 23, 32, 42, 74, 76, 120, 122, 134, 136, 138–40, 144, 147, 2778–81, 290

Brohm, Jeff 48

Brooklyn Dodgers (AAFC) 105, 106, 187

Brooklyn Dodgers (NFL) 88, 94, 101, 102, 252

Brooklyn Tigers *see* Brooklyn Dodgers (NFL)

Brooks, Aaron 20, 36, 56, 170, 177, 223, 246–49, 258, 259

Brooks, Robert 172

Brovelli, Angelo 267

Brown, Carlos 46, 224

Brown, Dave 26, 64, 167, 173, 187, 188, 250–52

Brown, Ed 30, 41, 45, 61, 108, 117, 119, 140, 200–2, 229, 266–68

Brown, Jim 50, 137, 140, 207

Brown, Paul 6, 19, 39, 41, 42, 44, 50, 102, 108, 117, 118, 131, 135–37, 156, 205, 209

Bruce, Isaac 176, 273

Brumbaugh, Carl 201, 202, 271, 272

Brunell, Mark 17, 20, 67, 170–72, 223, 224, 230–32, 293

Brunner, Scott 156, 187, 251, 252

Bryan, Johnny 202

Buchanan, Buck 234, 254

Buffalo Bills 8, 22, 23, 30–32, 55, 65, 123, 126–32, 149, 152, 163–68, 175, 179, 194–98, 209, 211, 215, 231, 233, 234, 237, 258, 259, 264, 271, 275–77, 2889, 292

Buffalo Bills (AAFC) 28, 103, 105, 106

Bukich, Rudy 23, 25, 41, 42, 108, 116, 139, 140, 201–3, 268, 272, 273, 294

Bulger, Marc 29, 31, 35, 42, 62, 179, 270–72

Bull, Scott 12, 278, 279

Buoniconti, Nick 238, 245

Burford, Chris 234

Burk, Adrian 41, 46, 64, 73, 108, 113, 114, 117, 119, 262–64, 294

Burris, Henry 201, 202, 223

Burroughs, Don 272

Burt, Jim 43

Bussey, Young 201

BYU 25, 219

Caddell, Ernie 219

Cafego, George 26, 187, 293, 294

Cagle, Chris 11, 251

Cahill, Ron 99, 187

California Polytechnic Institute 28

Camp, Walter 5

Campbell, Jason 182, 293, 294

Campbell, Rich 157, 223

Campbell, Scott 73

Canadian Football League (CFL) 12, 14, 20, 21, 23, 26, 27, 29, 32, 33, 36, 37, 39, 47, 66, 103, 114, 117, 136, 141, 157, 159, 160, 175, 176, 196, 215, 218, 220, 223, 234, 255, 270, 276, 280, 289, 293

Cannon, Billy 124

Canton Bulldogs 82, 83

Cappleman, Bill 241

Carlisle Indian Institute 5

Carlson, Cody 289, 290

Carmichael, Al 124, 125

Carolina Panthers 32, 34, 52, 55, 172, 173, 175, 176, 178, 179, 197–99, 244, 258, 251, 262, 271, 282

Carpenter, Preston 268

Carr, David 26, 52, 64, 170, 179, 225, 226

Carr, Jimmy 263, 294

Carr, Joe 81, 84

Carson, Bud 133

Carter, Louis 286

Carter, Quincy 73, 178, 211, 212, 255, 256

Carter, Virgil 7, 144, 204,-6

Casares, Rick 237

Case, Ernie 13, 27, 273

Case, Stoney 193, 219

Cason, Jim 279

Caspar, Dave 241

Cavanaugh, Matt 245, 263

CBS 119

Celeri, Bob 12, 114, 115

Chamberlin, Guy 82, 84

Chandler, Chris 24, 30, 163, 170,

174, 180, 187–91, 201, 202, 272, 280, 286, 288, 290

Chappuis, Bob 27

Charles, John 241, 245

Chicago Bears 6, 11–13, 16, 18, 23, 29–32, 40–44, 54, 59, 81, 82, 84, 87, 90–94, 96–99, 104, 108, 109–112, 116, 117, 119, 133, 135, 136, 138–40, 145, 146, 150, 160, 161, 182, 188, 196, 198–203, 209, 223, 234, 244, 245, 247, 251, 262, 268, 271, 276, 292

Chicago Cardinals *see* Arizona Cardinals

Chicago Hornets *see* Chicago Rockets (AAFC)

Chicago Rockets (AAFC) 105, 106

Chicago Staleys *see* Chicago Bears

Chlebek, Ed 255

Choboian, Max 129, 216

Christman, Paul 27, 76, 90, 101, 110, 111, 113, 186–88, 223–24

Christy, Dick 245

Cincinnati Bengals 7, 16, 19, 23, 26, 29, 43, 58, 123, 131, 144, 147, 152, 156, 157, 160, 174, 180, 182, 188, 203–6, 220, 256, 263, 266, 279, 286

Cincinnati Reds 91–93

Claridge, Dennis 223

Clark, Brian 73

Clark, Dutch 20, 50, 54, 67, 88, 90, 93, 95, 218–220

Clark, Dwight 55, 280

Clark, Wayne 205, 263, 276

Clatterbuck, Bobby 276

Clayborn, Raymond 280

Clement, Johnny 106, 186, 187, 266

Clements, Tom 33, 234

Cleveland Browns 6–8, 16, 19, 26, 28, 30–32, 40, 42, 45, 51, 54, 55, 64, 102–106, 113, 114, 116–118, 120, 135–42, 144, 150, 156, 168, 173, 180, 181, 196, 206–9, 211, 215, 216, 218, 220, 223, 228, 244, 271, 272, 286

Cleveland Bulldogs 83, 85, 86

Cleveland Rams *see* St. Louis Rams

Coffee, Pat 94, 187

Colclough, Jim 244

Cole, Terry 73

College of the Pacific 12, 28

Collier, Blanton 40, 138, 207

Collier, Reggie 212, 267

Collins, Kerry 12, 17, 32, 36, 76, 170, 172, 175, 176, 178, 180, 198, 199, 247, 248, 250–52, 259, 290

Collins, Todd 24–25, 172, 195, 294

Comp, Irv 36, 75, 90, 100, 224

Concannon, Jack 20, 201–3, 219, 223, 224, 262, 264

Conerly, Charlie 16, 22, 31, 35, 36, 41, 42, 45, 46, 49, 54, 55, 59, 66–68, 79, 108, 111, 112, 119, 134, 136, 250–53, 294

Conerly, Perian 252

Conrad, Bobby Joe 187

Continental Football League 245

Conzelman, Jimmy 82, 83, 201, 202

Cook, Greg 7, 11, 24, 36, 43, 65, 67, 123, 132, 147, 204–6
Cooper, Gary 16
Corcoran, King 17, 245
Cordileone, Lou 31, 252, 280
Coryat, Quentin 286
Coryell, Don 7, 40, 147, 148, 152, 154, 155, 277
Couch, Tim 26, 28, 64, 176, 177, 180, 207, 208
Coughlin, Tom 232
Crabb, Claude 263, 294
Craig, Dameyune 198
Cromwell, Nolan 272
Csonka, Larry 146
Culpepper, Daunte 12, 20, 27, 28, 76, 170, 176, 178, 236, 239–42
Cunningham, Randall 14, 17, 18, 20, 21, 32, 40, 42, 45, 56, 65, 66, 72, 152, 153, 160–68, 175, 178, 193, 194, 212, 213, 240–42, 261–64, 285
Cunningham, Sam 72
Cuozzo, Gary 23, 43, 139, 188, 229, 240–42, 248
Curry, Bill 229
Curry, Ronald 259
Cutler, Jay 182, 215

Dale Carnegie Institute 218
Dallas Cowboys 11, 12, 20, 23, 31, 40, 41, 44, 54, 55, 74, 123, 133, 135, 137, 139–45, 149, 150, 154, 163, 164, 167, 168, 172, 180–82, 190, 201, 210–13, 215, 218, 222, 279, 285, 292
Dallas Texans (AFL) *see* Kansas City Chiefs
Dallas Texans (NFL 1952) 115
Dancewicz, Boley 11, 26, 109, 110
Daney, George 234
Danielson, Gary 28, 33, 150, 155, 163, 218, 219
Danowski, Ed 20, 38, 43, 90, 92, 93, 98, 250–52
Darius, Donovan 231
Darragh, Dan 131, 195
Davey, Rohan 244
Davidson, Ben 42
Davidson, Cotton 30, 32, 61, 117, 123–26, 131, 228, 233, 234, 258, 259
Davis, Al 7, 122, 258, 260
Davis, Andre 180
Davis, Bob 248, 254, 256
Davis, Henry 268
Davis, Mouse 8
Dawson, Len 16, 18, 24, 25, 32, 39, 40, 42, 46, 59, 63, 65, 70, 120, 123, 125, 129, 132, 134, 149, 209, 233–35, 267–69
Day, Eagle 294
Dayton Triangles 81, 88
DeBerg, Steve 23, 29, 32, 36, 45, 46, 55, 56, 153–55, 157, 159, 163, 165, 167, 190, 191, 216, 233, 235, 237, 238, 279–81, 285, 286
Decatur Staleys *see* Chicago Bears
Dekdebrun, Al 11
Del Bello, Jack 116, 229

Del Gaizo, Jim 13, 17, 223, 238, 252
Delhomme, Jake 16, 28, 32, 34, 52, 55, 62, 176, 179, 182, 198, 199, 248
Denver Broncos 14, 16, 23, 31, 32, 43, 48, 52, 125–27, 129, 131, 150, 156–58, 161, 162, 174–76, 179, 188, 196, 199, 207, 213–16, 228, 229, 231, 251, 252, 256, 267, 268, 279, 288, 290, 292
Detmer, Koy 17, 23, 224, 263, 264, 280
Detmer, Ty 23, 25, 32, 208, 209, 219, 223, 224, 263, 264, 279, 280
Detroit Lions 16, 23, 27, 29, 31, 32, 39, 41, 42, 49, 50, 54, 88, 90, 93, 99, 100, 108, 110–113, 115–120, 133, 135, 137, 138, 140–42, 175, 194, 207, 217–20, 222, 234, 262, 263, 268, 275, 292
Detroit Wolverines 31, 86, 202
Devine, Dan 57, 223
Diaz, Cameron 224
Dickey, Eldridge 14, 123, 131, 259
Dickey, Lynn 24, 28, 42, 43, 45, 56, 62, 134, 145, 150, 152, 160, 221–24, 289, 290
Dickinson, Parnell 285, 286
Dilfer, Trent 18, 31, 32, 57, 59, 170–74, 177, 178, 181, 192–94, 209, 280, 283, 285–87
Dils, Steve 191, 240, 241, 272
Dilweg, Anthony 73, 164
Dilweg, Lavie 73
Dimitroff, Tom 244
Ditka, Mike 164, 194, 202
Dobbs, Glenn 12, 21, 27, 38, 47, 103–106, 187
Dole, Bob 197
Domres, Marty 17, 23, 74, 216, 227, 229, 230, 256, 275–77, 281
Doran, Jim 54, 116, 212, 220
Dorow, Al 27, 77, 117, 123–26, 196, 254–56, 263
Dorsett, Tony 212
Dorsey, Ken 209, 278
Douglass, Bobby 13, 20, 38, 63, 64, 143, 146, 154, 200–2, 223, 247, 248, 275, 276
Douglass, Hugh 43
Dowling, Brian 224, 224, 245
Doxzon, Todd 237
Drake, Johnny 271
Driscoll, Paddy 46, 67, 73, 84–86, 186–88, 201, 202
Druckenmiller, Jim 48, 174, 280
Dubenion, Elbert 196
Dublinski, Tom 219, 252
Dudley, Bill 266
Duffek, Don 72
Duffek, Joe 72
Duhe, A.J. 256
Duke University 25, 59
Duluth Eskimos 188, 202
DuMoe, Billy 223
Duncan, Randy 26–28, 223, 234
Dungy, Tony 267, 268
Dunn, Perry Lee 191, 212
Dunn, Red 54, 71, 80, 83–88, 188
Dyson, Kevin 290

Ealey, Chuck 14
Eason, Bo 72
Eason, Tony 72, 152, 158, 160, 161, 165, 234, 243–45, 256
Eaton, Vic 118, 268
Ebding, Harry 219
Elway, John 16–21, 23, 28, 31, 36, 39–41, 45, 46, 48, 51, 55, 56, 63, 60, 73, 74, 152, 153, 158–61, 167, 168, 170, 174, 175, 207, 214–16, 227, 229, 234, 235
Enis, Hunter 216, 259
Enke, Fred 111, 116, 228, 229, 263
Erickson, Craig 23, 24, 229, 238, 286
Ernst, Jack 84
Eshmont, Len 279
Esiason, Boomer 12, 13, 32, 39, 51, 152, 159, 160, 168, 173, 174, 187, 188, 204–6, 255, 256
Etchevery, Sam 33, 136
Evans, Ray 19, 111, 202, 266
Evans, Vince 34, 52, 53, 200–2, 258, 259
Everett, Jim 12, 18, 161, 171, 174, 247, 248, 270–73, 276, 277, 289, 290
Evert, Chris 273
Ewbank, Weeb 38, 40, 126, 269

Fanning, Mike 223
Farkas, Andy 96
Fasani, Randy 198
Fassell, Jim 63
Favre, Brett 13, 16, 19, 23, 28, 40, 44, 51, 52, 65, 66, 70, 75, 152, 166, 167, 170–74, 180, 181, 191, 221–24, 231, 283
Fears, Tom 114, 271, 273
Feeley, A.J. 180, 236, 238, 263, 264
Fenenbock, Chuck 219
Ferguson, Joe 18, 45, 67, 147, 149, 150, 153, 159, 165, 195–97, 219, 228, 229, 286
Ferragamo, Vince 33, 41, 150, 156, 157, 160, 161, 195, 196, 223, 224, 271–73
Fiedler, Arthur 232, 238
Fiedler, Jay 28, 32, 232, 236, 237, 241, 256
Filchock, Frank 18, 20, 33, 38, 41, 64, 75, 90, 95–97, 99, 100, 109, 113, 215, 251, 252, 267, 268, 292–94
Finks, Jim 43, 44, 108, 112, 115, 118, 266, 267
Fitzpatrick, Ryan 35, 181
Flaherty, Ray 40, 102, 106
Flick, Tom 294
Flores, Tom 28, 36, 40, 52, 123, 124, 126, 130–32, 196, 234, 235, 258, 259
Florida State 25, 241, 286
Flowers, Dick 228
Flutie, Darren 72
Flutie, Doug 12, 20, 28, 32–34, 46, 67, 72, 161, 175, 178, 181, 195–97, 201–3, 244, 245, 275–77
Foley, Glenn 171, 283
Fontes, Wayne 219, 220

Football Outsiders 1
Forester, Hersch 209
Fourcade, John 72, 247
Fourcade, Keith 72
Fouts, Dan 16, 18, 19, 25, 27, 40, 45, 51, 56, 59, 62, 63, 70, 74–77, 134, 147, 149, 150, 152, 154–57, 162, 274–77
Fox, Tim 280
Francis, Wallace 191
Frankford Yellow Jackets 80, 83, 84
Freitas, Jesse, Sr. 11, 279
Frerotte, Gus 23, 32, 53, 171, 205, 216, 217, 241, 272, 294
Friedman, Bennie 11, 17, 21, 31, 46, 54, 65, 70, 71, 80, 85–88, 91, 250–52
Friesz, John 165, 275, 283, 294
Frye, Charlie 181
Fuller, Steve 155, 159, 202, 233, 234
Fuller, William 290
Fuqua, Frenchy 146, 268
Furrer, Will 13
Fusina, Chuck 34, 223, 286

Gabriel, Roman 12, 27, 30, 32, 39, 41, 76, 122, 134, 137, 139, 141, 147, 150, 262–64, 270–73
Gagliano, Bob 158, 219, 276, 280
Galiffa, Arnold 25, 42, 252, 280
Gallegos, Chon 259
Gannon, Rich 16, 20, 32, 43, 45, 162, 168, 170, 176–80, 233–35, 240–42, 257–60, 294
Garcia, Jeff 22, 28, 32, 33, 37, 42, 74, 170, 176, 180, 208, 209, 219, 263, 264, 278–81
Garrard, David 179, 231
Garrett, Bobby 30, 208, 223
Garrett, Jason 23, 26, 34, 46, 72, 212
Garrett, John 72
Garrison, Gary 7
Gasparella, Joe 12, 266, 268
Gelbaugh, Stan 34, 52, 282, 283
George, Bill 44
George, Jeff 17, 26, 32, 165, 171, 173, 174, 178, 189–91, 227–29, 240, 241, 258, 259, 294
Geri, Joe 267
Gibbs, Joe 7, 152, 294
Gibbs, Sonny 12, 212, 219
Gifford, Frank 71, 251
Gift, Wayne 272
Gilbride, Kevin 168
Gilchrist, Cookie 128
Gildea, John 266
Gilliam, Joe 14, 18, 41, 146, 148, 267–69
Gilliam, John 188, 241
Gillman, Sid 7, 8, 18, 40, 117, 122, 126, 133, 152, 155, 276, 277
Gillus, Willie 223
Gilmer, Harry 23, 26, 111, 219, 220, 292–94
Girard, Jug 27, 73, 223, 268
Glanville, Jerry 8, 152, 162, 165, 191
Glasglow, Bill 219
Glick, Gary 26, 267, 268

Godard, Ed 272
Golsteyn, Jerry 250, 286
Goode, Irv 188, 263
Governali, Paul 109–111, 252
Gradkowski, Bruce 182, 285
Graham, Kent 25, 167, 187, 188, 250–52, 267, 268, 293, 294
Graham, Otto 6, 16, 18, 19, 22, 27, 35, 38, 39, 42–45, 49, 51, 54, 56, 57, 59, 63, 65, 66, 68–70, 103–106, 108, 113, 116–118, 180, 202, 207–9, 219, 278
Grambling 14, 196
Grange, Red 84, 85, 88
Grant, Bud 24, 33
Gray, Leon 31
Gray, Quinn 231
Graziani, Tony 13, 191
Grbac, Elvis 18, 24, 32, 171, 177, 178, 193, 194, 233–35, 279
Green, Dennis 241
Green, Johnny 124, 196, 254, 256
Green, Trent 28–30, 32, 43, 54, 62, 170, 174, 176–78, 182, 233–35, 272, 273, 293, 294
Green Bay Packers 14, 16, 18, 27, 30, 36, 41–44, 49, 52, 55, 58, 73, 79, 80, 82, 83, 85–88, 94–96, 100, 110, 112–116, 118, 121, 123, 129, 130, 132, 133, 135–38, 140–42, 152, 158, 161, 165, 167, 172–74, 176, 179, 186, 188, 202, 211, 216, 220–24, 228, 231, 240, 242, 244, 248, 251, 272, 279, 283, 285, 290
Greene, Cornelius 14
Griese, Bob 12, 17, 20, 22, 25, 40, 44, 62, 66, 70, 123, 130, 134, 144, 146, 147, 149, 152, 156, 203, 236–38, 287
Griese, Brian 25, 62, 74, 176, 177, 181, 182, 202, 203, 214, 216, 238, 285–87
Griffing, Glynn 252
Grigas, John 20, 99, 187
Grim, Bob 241, 252
Grogan, Steve 20, 22, 55, 61, 62, 134, 149, 152–54, 165, 243–45
Grosscup, Lee 17, 28, 251, 254, 256
Grossman, Rex 24, 28, 73, 179, 201, 202
Grossman, Rex, Sr. 73
Groza, Lou 51
Gruden, Jon 176, 178, 286
Gudmundson, Scott 11
Guglielmi, Ralph 25–27, 118, 188, 252, 263, 292, 293

Haden, Pat 12, 25, 33, 36, 38, 39, 41, 150, 154, 155, 157, 271–73
Hadl, John 18, 30, 31, 36, 40, 41, 45, 54, 65, 70, 123, 126–28, 145, 147, 148, 150, 219, 223, 271, 272, 274–77, 290
Haines, Hinkey 251
Halas, George 6, 41, 81, 86, 87, 201, 202
Hall, Galen 254–56, 293
Hall, Lamont 248
Hall, Parker 20, 90, 96–99, 270–73, 279

Hamdan, Gibran 12, 294
Hamer, Tex 83
Hamilton, Joe 286
Hammond, Kim 238, 245
Hammond Pros 201
Handley, Ray 166
Hanratty, Terry 23, 25, 41, 143, 266, 268, 286
Hanson, Swede 263
Harbaugh, Jim 28, 55, 162, 171, 177, 193, 194, 200–2, 227–29, 275
Harder, Pat 110
Hardy, Bruce 237
Hardy, Jim 23, 108–110, 112, 113, 115, 186, 188, 219, 271–73, 293
Hardy, Kevin 248
Hargett, Edd 248
Harley, Chic 81
Harrington, Joey 26, 52, 53, 170, 179, 218, 219, 238
Harris, Al 283
Harris, Franco 146, 268
Harris, James 14, 41, 62, 123, 132, 148, 157, 196, 271–73, 276
Harris, Jimmy 30, 263
Harrison, Marvin 178, 229
Hart, Jim 28, 40, 42, 45, 49, 51, 65, 141, 148, 152, 159, 186–88, 294
Hartenstine, Mike 42
Hartsell, Mark 202
Harvard University 181
Hasselbeck, Don 224, 252, 283
Hasselbeck, Matt 62, 73, 176, 178, 181, 182, 223, 224, 252, 282, 283
Hasselbeck, Tim 73, 224, 252, 283, 294
Havrilak, Sam 229
Heath, Stan 27, 36, 112, 222, 223
Hebert, Bobby 18, 28, 34, 160, 165, 189, 191, 247, 248
Hedberg, Randy 150, 285
Heidi 131
Heineman, Ken 272
Heinrich, Don 23, 41, 49, 108, 212, 250, 251, 259
Heisman Trophy 12, 13, 26, 28, 128, 138, 189, 255, 278, 294
Held, Paul 223, 268
Heller, Warren 266
Hennigan, Charley 289
Henning, Dan 276, 277
Henson, Drew 25, 73, 212, 226
Herber, Arnie 31, 41, 43, 45, 50, 54, 59, 63–65, 68, 70, 75, 87, 88, 90, 92–97, 100, 101, 222, 224, 252
Herring, George 125, 214
Herrmann, Mark 52, 158, 216, 227, 229, 272, 274–76
Hewitt, Bill 91, 99
Hewko, Bob 286
Hickey, Red 136, 280
Hilger, Rusty 218, 219
Hill, King 23, 26, 120, 138, 187, 188, 241, 261, 263
Hinton, Chris 158, 191, 216, 229
Hipple, Eric 156, 217, 219, 220
Hobert, Billy Joe 247, 248, 259
Hodson, Tommy 165, 248
Hoernschemeyer, Bob 71, 104, 105, 106

Hogeboom, Gary 64, 156, 188, 211, 213, 229
Holcomb, Kelly 207, 208
Hold, Mike 286
Holloway, Condredge 14
Holly, Bob 191
Holm, Tony 266
Holmgren, Mike 23, 40
Holy Cross 99
Horn, Don 141, 214, 216, 222, 223
Hornung, Paul 71, 138, 223
Horvath, Les 25
Hostetler, Jeff 42, 43, 59, 159, 165, 166, 179, 251, 252, 258–60, 294
Houston Gamblers 8
Houston Oilers *see* Tennessee Titans
Houston Texans 212, 225, 226
Hovius, Junie 252
Howard University 234
Howell, Jim Lee 117
Hoying, Bobby 175, 259, 261–63
Huard, Brock 245, 283
Huard, Damon 34, 237, 245, 283
Huarte, John 25, 128, 234, 245, 255, 263
Huff, Gary 150, 200, 285, 286
Huffine, Ken 81
Hufnagel, John 46
Hughes, Honolulu 293, 294
Hull, Kent 290
Humm, David 13, 196, 229
Humphrey, Buddy 290
Humphries, Stan 164, 168, 171, 275–77, 294
Hunsinger, Chuck 202
Hunt, Lamar 122, 135
Hunter, Scott 24, 145, 191, 219
Hutchinson, Chad 73, 179, 201, 202, 212
Hutson, Don 18, 93, 98, 222, 224

Indianapolis Colts 13, 14, 16, 23, 26, 28–31, 40, 43, 45, 52, 55, 73, 74, 116, 118, 120, 121, 131, 133, 135, 139, 140, 142–46, 149, 158, 171, 175, 178, 180, 181, 186, 188, 191, 193, 194, 202, 204, 207, 208, 216, 226–30, 233, 245, 248, 251, 252, 255, 266, 268, 269, 286
Irsay, Robert 229
Isbell, Cecil 20, 38, 41, 44, 46, 64–67, 90, 95, 96, 98, 99, 222–24, 250
Isbell, Larry 26, 27, 293
Ivory, Horace 280
Izo, George 25, 27, 138, 187, 188, 219, 268

Jackson, Alfred 191
Jackson, Harold 30, 263, 272
Jackson, Jarious 215
Jackson, Monte 223
Jackson, Tarvaris 241
Jacksonville Jaguars 172, 173, 176, 196, 223, 230–32, 237
Jacobs, Jack 47, 110, 222, 224, 272, 294, 295
Jacobs, Omar 267
Jamieson, Dick 255
Jaworski, Ron 31, 41–45, 55, 148,

155, 159, 160, 164, 238, 261–64, 272, 291, 293, 294
Jensen, Jim 237
Johnson, Brad 12, 18, 28, 31, 32, 56, 170, 171, 176, 178, 240–42, 285, 286
Johnson, Charley 18, 38, 39, 42, 134, 136, 140, 141, 144, 149, 186–88, 214, 216, 288, 290
Johnson, Doug 73
Johnson, Pepper 252
Johnson, Randy 38, 52, 54, 141, 149, 189–91, 223, 252, 294
Johnson, Rob 23, 172, 195, 196, 231, 259, 286
Joiner, Charley 123
Jones, Bert 24, 30, 36, 38, 73, 74, 134, 147, 149, 152, 155, 157, 158, 227–30, 272, 273
Jones, Clint 241, 252
Jones, Dub 208
Jones, John 255
Jones, June 8, 191
Jones, Matt 231
Jones, Ralph 6, 87
Jordan, Randy 231
Jurgensen, Sonny 9, 18, 22–25, 27, 30, 31, 40, 42, 43, 46, 49, 54, 59, 64, 65, 70, 74, 75, 134, 136, 138–42, 145, 261–64, 291–95
Justin, Paul 205

Kalmanir, Tommy 228
Kanell, Danny 216, 252
Kansas City Chiefs 16, 30, 32, 57, 75, 122, 123–26, 129, 131–33, 135, 143, 154, 163, 165, 167–69, 171, 177–79, 195, 232–35, 242, 245, 255, 258, 259, 272, 276, 289
Kapp, Joe 17, 28, 32, 33, 141, 143, 144, 240–45
Karr, Bill 91
Karras, Alex 138
Kelly, Jim 8, 24, 27, 28, 34, 35, 37, 45, 55, 59, 65, 152, 158, 161, 164, 166, 170, 173, 195–97, 234
Kemp, Jack 7, 18, 22, 28, 32, 33, 46, 59, 65, 70, 120, 123–28, 130–32, 195–97, 220, 268, 269, 275–77, 284
Kemp, Jeff 263, 264, 273, 280, 282–84
Kennedy, Tom 36
Kenney, Bill 73, 234
Kerkorian, Gary 115, 228, 268
Kern, Rex 25
Kiick, Jim 146
Kilmer, Billy 9, 16, 17, 20, 27, 42, 67, 74, 136, 145, 146, 152, 154, 247, 248, 279, 280, 292–95
Kilroy, Bucko 252
King, Peter 67
King, Rip 81
King, Shaun 176, 187, 285, 286
Kingsbury, Kliff 256
Kirkland, Mike 227, 229
Kirkman, Red 263
Kitna, Jon 34, 56, 77, 170, 204, 217, 282
Kittner, Kurt 34

Klingler, David 52, 167, 204, 206, 259
Klosterman, Don 272
Knafelc, Gary 249
Knafelc, Greg 73, 249
Kocourek, Dave 276
Kofler, Matt 158
Komlo, Jeff 155, 217, 286
Kosar, Bernie 12, 17, 24, 26, 38, 54, 67, 152, 153, 160, 161, 168, 173, 207–9, 212, 237, 238
Kozar, Heather 209
Kramer, Erik 32, 33, 162, 176, 191, 200–2, 218, 219, 275, 276
Kramer, Tommy 150, 165, 240, 242, 248
Krieg, Dave 32, 39, 42, 65, 76, 152, 153, 156, 158, 160, 167, 187, 188, 201, 202, 214, 217, 219, 220, 234, 282–84, 290
Kruczek, Mike 294
Kubiak, Gary 23, 215, 216
Kuharich, Joe 30, 264
Kupp, Craig 73

Lachey, Jim 259, 294
Ladd, Ernie 234
Lambeau, Curly 6, 41, 46, 71, 79–83, 85, 86, 116, 222–24
Lambert, Jack 43
Lamonica, Daryle 7, 18, 22, 25, 31, 50, 56, 61, 63, 65, 74, 76, 123, 127, 129–32, 147, 196, 197, 257–60
Landry, Greg 12, 20, 34, 38, 142, 159, 202, 218–20, 229
Landry, Tom 8, 39–41, 117, 133, 135, 145, 163, 167, 211, 212, 224, 251
Lane, Gary 46
Lansford, Buck 30, 263
Laraba, Bob 276
Larson, Paul 187
Laufenberg, Babe 211, 212, 294
Lavelli, Dante 104
Lawrence, Larry 286
Layne, Bobby 9, 16, 17, 19, 20, 23, 29, 31, 38–42, 44, 45, 49, 54, 59, 65, 69, 70, 73, 75–77, 108, 111–113, 116–120, 134, 137, 202, 203, 217–20, 266–69
Leaf, Ryan 17, 26, 36, 52, 77, 175, 177, 178, 211, 212, 229, 275–77
LeBaron, Eddie 11, 12, 33, 41, 55, 67, 108, 115–117, 135, 137, 138, 210–212, 292–294
LeBeau, Dick 152
Ledyard, Hal 279
Lee, Bob 23, 28, 190, 191, 241, 242, 272
Lee, Jacky 31, 123, 124, 127, 132, 214, 216, 234, 289, 290
Leemans, Tuffy 90, 94, 98
LeForce, Clyde 36, 110, 219
Leftwich, Byron 12, 24, 28, 179, 182, 231
Leinart, Matt 13, 182, 187
Lemm, Wally 125
Lemon, Cleo 237, 276
Levy, Marv 154, 155
Lewellen, Vern 86, 87
Lewis, Cliff 45, 208

Lewis, D.D. 44
Lewis, Dave 205
Lewis, Jeff 199
Lewis, Ray 18
Lick, Dennis 223
Lillard, Joe 13, 73, 91, 106, 187
Lilly, Bob 20
Limbaugh, Rush 13
Lincoln, Keith 7
Lisch, Rusty 188, 202
Liske, Pete 33, 46, 47, 214, 216, 256, 263
Livingston, Howie 31, 252, 294
Livingston, Mike 75, 134, 233, 234
Lofton, James 222
Lomax, Neil 8, 43, 67, 157, 159, 163, 186–88
Lombardi, Vince 7, 24, 40, 41, 58, 117, 119–121, 133, 135, 141, 152, 223, 224, 250
Long, Chuck 52
Longley, Clint 23, 212, 276
Look, Dean 46, 73, 235
Lorenzen, Jared 12, 13
Los Angeles Chargers *see* San Diego Chargers
Los Angeles Dons (AAFC) 13, 104–106
Los Angeles Raiders *see* Oakland Raiders
Los Angeles Rams *see* St. Louis Rams
Los Angeles Times 19
Losman, J.P. 28, 180, 196
Lott, Billy 245
Lowe, Paul 7
LSU 19, 25
Lucas, Ray 178, 236–38, 255
Lucas, Richie 27, 196, 294
Luck, Oliver 288
Luckman, Sid 16, 18, 23, 35, 38, 41–43, 46, 50, 54, 57–59, 61–63, 65, 66, 69, 70, 90, 96–99, 104, 108–110, 112, 113, 200–3, 222, 264, 268
Lujack, John 20, 23, 25, 28, 41–43, 105, 108, 111–114, 200–2
Lumpkin, Father 219
Luther, Ed 275, 276

Mackey, Dee 238, 250
Mackey, Kyle 73, 250, 256
Mackrides, Bill 252
Maddox, Tommy 34, 41, 167, 179, 266–68, 272
Mahrt, Al 81
Majkowski, Don 24, 28, 55, 162, 164, 165, 167, 219, 222–24, 229
Mallouf, Ray 111, 186–88, 252
Malone, Chuck 293
Malone, Mark 53, 156, 256, 266–68, 276
Mann, Bob 31, 220
Manning, Archie 23, 26, 28, 31, 52, 64, 65, 134, 145, 149, 150, 157, 159, 241, 246–49, 252, 290
Manning, Eli 26, 28, 31, 52, 180, 251–53, 276, 290
Manning, Peyton 2, 12, 16, 18, 19, 26, 35, 44, 45, 52, 55, 66, 68, 73,

74, 170, 175, 178–80, 182, 227–30, 252, 290
Manske, Eggs 202, 268
Manueal, Lionel 64
Mara, Tim 121
Marangi, Gary 195
Marchibroda, Ted 12, 116, 187, 188, 266–68
Marino, Dan 16, 18, 19, 27, 28, 35, 36, 38–41, 44–46, 49, 51, 55, 56, 59, 61, 63, 65, 69, 70, 73–75, 152, 158–63, 168, 170–72, 176, 180, 234, 236–38, 255, 256
Marinovich, Marv 260
Marinovich, Todd 13, 18, 53, 73, 166, 258–60
Marquadt, Rube 187
Marshall, George P. 88, 94, 293
Martin, Charles 42, 161
Martin, Jamie 23, 248, 272
Martin, Tee 259, 267, 268
Martin, Tony 171
Martz, Mike 7, 176, 273
Masters, Walt 187, 263, 267
Masterson, Bernie 12, 93, 94, 96, 97, 201–3
Matesic, Ed 266
Mathison, Bruce 160, 195, 196, 276, 283
Mathys, Charlie 223
Matte, Tom 43, 139, 228, 229
Matthews, Shane 200, 202, 292, 294
Mauldin, Stan 111
May, Dean 263
Maynard, Don 124, 131, 255
Mays, Dave 196, 208
McBride, Jack 71, 84, 85, 251, 252
McCarthy, John 187, 266–68
McClure, Brian 12, 196
McConkey, Phil 64
McCormick, John 129, 214, 216
McCown, Josh 179
McCown, Luke 286
McCullough, Hugh 97
McCullum, Sam 283
McDonald, Paul 13, 156, 207
McDonald, Tommy 16
McDonough, Coley 266
McFadin, Bud 31, 127, 216, 290
McGee, Max 140
McGwire, Dan 12, 166, 237, 282–84
McGwire, Mark 284
McHan, Lamar 17, 26, 36, 38, 52, 54, 61, 108, 117, 118, 138, 186, 187, 223, 229, 280
McMahon, Jim 17, 24, 25, 32, 38, 42, 65, 67, 158–61, 164, 166, 168, 173, 188, 200–3, 223, 241, 242, 263, 264, 276, 277
McMahon, Mike 53, 218, 263
McNabb, Donovan 12, 13, 20, 24, 26, 28, 36, 170, 176, 177, 179, 180, 182, 209, 261–64
McNair, Steve 20, 21, 67, 170, 172, 174, 175, 192–94, 288–90
McNeil, Fred 191
McNown, Cade 17, 28, 176–78, 201, 203

McPherson, Adrian 248
McPherson, Don 72, 263, 289
McPherson, Miles 72
McQuilken, Kim 190, 294
Meadows, Ed 42, 119
Mercer, Ken 80
Meredith, Don 17, 18, 27, 40 41, 53, 67, 74, 134, 135, 137, 139, 140, 142, 211–213, 224
Meredith, Michael 213
Merkens, Guido 248, 289
Metzelaars, Pete 198
Meyer, Ron 268
Meyers, Jack 272
Miami Dolphins 16, 19, 23, 32, 36, 40, 41, 54, 60, 65, 127, 130, 133, 144–47, 156, 157, 159, 161, 178, 180, 195, 205, 208, 235–38, 244, 245, 255, 258, 275, 279, 283, 293
Miami Seahawks (AAFC) 104, 129, 208
Michigan State 13, 201
Mildren, Jack 229
Millen, Hugh 191, 215, 243, 244, 272
Miller, Billy 225
Miller, Chris 28, 43, 52, 162, 181, 190, 191, 216, 271, 272
Miller, Eddie 251, 252
Miller, Jim 32, 43, 172, 202
Miller, Larry 241
Milstead, Charley 289
Milwaukee Badgers 202
Minneapolis Marines 187
Minnesota Vikings 19, 23, 24, 30, 32, 33, 52, 55, 134–36, 141, 143, 146, 147, 168, 171, 175, 190, 191, 211, 212, 219, 236, 239–42, 245, 247, 248, 251, 252, 264, 271, 272, 279
Miodszewski, Ed 116
Mira, George 22, 237, 238, 263, 279
Mirer, Rick 26, 30, 52, 63, 65, 168, 202, 254, 256, 259, 280–84
Mitchell, Bobby 137, 138, 207
Mitchell, Brian 42, 263, 293, 294
Mitchell, Scott 12, 13, 32, 34, 165, 171, 193, 194, 204, 205, 217–20, 237, 238
Mitts, Heather 238, 264
Molenda, Bo 88
Molesworth, Keith 73, 201, 202
Monnett, Bob 41, 90, 94, 95
Mont, Tommy 294
Montana, Joe 16, 18, 19, 23, 25, 27, 30, 35, 37, 42, 43, 41, 55–58, 61, 63, 64, 66, 68–70, 74, 152, 153, 155, 156, 159, 161–66, 168–71, 233–35, 243, 278–81
Moon, Warren 14, 16, 27, 29, 33, 37, 46, 51, 55, 58, 59, 66, 69, 70, 74, 76, 152, 159, 161, 162, 165, 166, 171, 174, 177, 234, 235, 240–42, 282–84, 288–90
Moore, Nat 237
Moore, Shawn 41, 167, 215
Mora, Jim, Jr. 17
Mora, Jim, Sr. 17, 248

Moreno, Moses 72
Moreno, Zeke 72
Moroski, Mike 191, 280, 290
Morrall, Earl 22, 23, 26, 29, 31, 40, 45, 46, 65, 67, 74, 76, 118, 120, 134, 138, 140, 142, 144–46, 149, 218–20, 227–30, 236, 238, 268, 269, 280, 281
Morris, Mercury 146
Mortell, Emmett 263
Morton, Craig 12, 30, 31, 39–41, 46, 54, 62, 74, 134, 140, 143–45, 150, 152, 211, 212, 214–16, 250, 252
Moss, Paul 267
Moss, Randy 119, 175, 240, 242
Moynihan, Bridgett 245
Munson, Bill 27, 41, 42, 134, 139, 141, 142, 150, 155, 196, 218–220, 272, 273, 276, 277, 283, 284
Musgrave, Bill 216
Myer, Steve 282

Nagle, Browning 166, 191, 229, 254, 256
Nagler, Gern 268
Nagurski, Bronko 88, 91
Namath, Joe 17–19, 24, 25, 27, 30, 31, 35, 38, 40–44, 57, 59, 61, 63–66, 70, 73, 75–77, 123, 128–32, 142, 144–47, 149, 150, 187, 245, 254–56, 272, 273, 290
Naponic, Bob 289
National Basketball League 51
Naval Academy 16, 143
Navarre, John 12, 25
NBC 34, 128
NCAA 5
Neale, Greasy 8, 29, 40
Nelsen, Bill 24, 25, 40, 94, 134, 138, 140–42, 146, 207–9, 266, 268
Nemeth, Steve 272
Neuheisel, Rick 162, 277
Nevers, Ernie 71, 73, 80, 85
New England Patriots 8, 12, 16, 26, 30, 32, 33, 52, 55, 125, 126, 144, 156, 160, 171, 173, 178–82, 196, 215, 228, 234, 241–45, 258, 268, 275, 278
New Mexico State 136
New Orleans Saints 23, 26, 30, 31, 141, 150, 156, 157, 165, 171, 174, 182, 191, 198, 212, 229, 241, 246–50, 262, 276, 280
New York Bulldogs 112–115, 202, 220, 279
New York Giants 8, 11–13, 16, 18, 19, 23, 30, 31, 41–43, 49, 55, 59, 74, 84, 86–88, 91–93, 95, 96, 98–100, 108, 109, 111–113, 117, 119, 120, 136–38, 140, 141, 152, 155, 159, 161, 165, 166, 168, 173, 176, 180, 187, 203, 212, 215, 216, 228, 229, 240, 241, 249–53, 268, 276, 294
New York Jets 17, 23, 27, 30, 32, 74, 124, 126–28, 130–32, 142, 145, 156, 163, 168, 173, 187, 207, 216, 227, 231, 233, 237, 238, 248, 253–56, 258, 286, 290, 294
New York Titans *see* New York Jets

New York Yankees (AAFC) 102, 104–106, 113, 279
New York Yanks (NFL) *see* New York Bulldogs
Newman, Harry 11, 20, 38, 43, 90–92, 251, 252
Newsome, Ozzie 202, 209
NFL Europe 34
NFL Films 67
NFL Network 17, 170
NFL Sunday Ticket 170
Nielsen, Gifford 25
Ninowski, Jim 23, 41, 42, 108, 120, 135, 137, 207, 208, 218, 219, 248, 294
Nix, Emery 269, 290
Nix, Kent 141, 202, 266, 269, 290
Nofsinger, Terry 191, 268
Noll, Chuck 17, 39
Nori, Reino 187
Northwestern 50
Northwestern State, Louisiana 28
Norton, Rick 27, 52, 129, 130, 223, 236, 237
Norwood, Scott 165
Notre Dame 25–28, 57, 80, 84, 104, 105, 202, 215, 234, 263, 268, 293
Nott, Mike 234

Oakland Raiders 14, 16, 22, 30–32, 40, 42, 43, 52, 65, 74, 122, 123, 125, 126, 130–32, 141, 146–50, 155–58, 163, 172, 174, 176–78, 180, 193, 195, 196, 207–9, 233, 234, 241, 245, 257–60, 264, 267, 278, 282, 285, 288, 289, 293
O'Brien, Davey 11, 12, 16, 46, 52, 90, 96, 97, 262–64
O'Brien, Ken 36, 74, 153, 158–61, 168, 234, 254–56, 263
O'Connell, Tommy 116, 118, 124, 196, 202, 207
O'Donnell, Neil 75, 166, 173, 179, 256, 266–68, 290
Ohio State 25, 190, 219
Olander, Cliff 276
Olderman, Murray 67, 68
Oliphant, Elmer 81
O'Malley, Tom 113, 222
Orlovsky, Dan 219
O'Rourke, Charley 41, 75, 98, 104, 105, 202
Orr, Jimmy 229
Ortman, Chuck 266
Orton, Kyle 181
Osiecki, Sandy 234
Owen, Steve 42, 112, 117, 250, 279
Owen, Tom 30, 156, 244, 245, 278, 280, 294
Owens, Morris 286
Owens, R.C. 119, 279, 280
Owens, Terrell 8, 13, 180, 209, 262

Pagel, Mike 54, 63, 64, 158, 209, 227, 228
Palmer, Carson 19, 28, 36, 43, 58, 170, 180, 182, 204, 205
Palmer, Jesse 25
Panciera, Don 106
Papac, Nick 259

Parcells, Bill 8, 40, 152, 255, 256
Parilli, Babe 27, 30, 32, 33, 45, 49, 63, 115, 116, 118, 123–28, 132, 208, 209, 222, 223, 243–45, 255, 258, 259
Parker, Ace 25, 27, 35, 59, 64–66, 73, 90, 94, 99, 103, 104
Parker, Buddy 39, 40, 119, 120
Parker, Frank 209, 268
Pastorini, Dan 17, 21, 24, 26, 28, 31, 36, 42, 44, 51, 55, 63, 74, 134, 145, 155, 157, 158, 259, 263, 271–73, 288–90
Pastrana, Al 214
Patrick, Frank 12, 223
Patterson, Billy 201, 266, 267
Payton, Sean 162, 202
Payton, Walter 71
Pearson, Drew 55, 212
Pederson, Doug 34, 168, 207, 209, 223, 261, 263
Peete, Holly Robinson 199, 200, 260, 264
Peete, Rodney 18, 25, 32, 38, 39, 164, 198, 199, 212, 217, 219, 220, 259, 260, 263, 264, 293, 294
Pelluer, Scott 72
Pelluer, Steve 72, 159, 211
Penn State 25, 255
Pennington, Chad 24, 37, 177, 179, 254–56
Penrose, Craig 216, 256
Philadelphia Eagles 7, 8, 11, 13, 16, 22, 23, 26, 29–31, 39–41, 43, 58, 65, 91, 95, 99–102, 110–112, 114, 117, 119–121, 133, 135, 136, 139, 150, 154–56, 166–78, 175, 179, 180, 186, 201, 202, 205, 208, 209, 218, 220, 223, 240, 244, 247, 258, 260–64, 267, 268, 272, 285, 293, 294
Philcox, Todd 205, 276,
Phillips, Wade 168
Phipps, Mike 30, 134, 144, 149, 150, 201, 202, 207–9, 238
Pickens, Carl 205
Pisarcik, Joe 154, 250–52, 263
Pisarkiewicz, Steve 187, 223
Pittsburgh Pirates *see* Pittsburgh Steelers
Pittsburgh Steelers 12, 17, 22, 29–31, 39–41, 43, 58, 65, 91, 95, 99–102, 107, 110–112, 115, 116, 118, 120, 121, 133, 138, 142, 144, 148, 149, 152, 154, 155, 172, 174, 175, 178–81, 193, 202, 204, 209, 211, 219, 220, 240, 244, 258, 265–69, 275, 284, 294
Plum, Milt 27, 41, 42, 108, 120, 135–40, 143, 207–9, 218–20, 252, 272
Plummer, Jake 1, 17, 18, 20, 32, 55, 56, 170, 174, 176, 179, 180, 187, 188, 214–16
Plunkett, Jim 7, 26, 28, 30–32, 39, 40, 46, 62, 65, 74, 134, 145, 149, 150, 154, 156, 158, 159, 161, 244, 245, 258–60, 278, 280, 281
Podolak, Ed 234
Pollard, Fritz 13, 67, 81

Pool, Hampton 16, 41, 108
Porter, Quinton 226
Portland State University 8
Portsmouth Spartans *see* Detroit Lions
Pottstown Firebirds 17
Pottsville Maroons 84
Powell, Art 31, 124, 196, 255, 259
Powlus, Ron 263
Prairie View 14
Presnell, Glenn 88, 93, 220
Printers, Casey 234
Providence Steam Roller 86, 202
Purdue 25, 28, 276
Purdy, Pid 85
Pyle, C.C. 84

Quarles, Bernard 271, 272
Quick, Mike 160
Quinn, Jonathan 12, 201, 231, 234

Rabb, Warren 124
Rae, Mike 259, 285, 286
Ragone, Dave 13, 34, 226
Ramsey, Patrick 27, 179, 294
Ramsey, Steve 214, 216
Ramsey, Tom 229
Rand, Jonathan 67
Randle, Sonny 187
Randle El, Antwaan 72, 268
Ransom, Brian 289
Rattay, Tim 12, 286
Ratterman, George 17, 23, 28, 45, 103, 105, 106, 113, 114, 117, 118, 208, 209
Rauch, John 219, 264
Raye, Jimmy 263
Reagan, Ronald 197
Reaves, John 52, 146, 205, 206, 261–63, 286, 287, 290
Red Grange's New York Yankees 85
Redman, Chris 193
Reed, Joe 145, 219, 278, 279
Reese, Geoff 223
Reeves, Dan 39, 41, 63, 71, 167, 212
Reich, Frank 23, 55, 160, 167, 195–99, 219, 256
Reichow, Jerry 219, 241
Reinhard, Bill 72
Reinhard, Bob 72
Reisz, Albie 11, 272
Retzlaff, Pete 16
Reynolds, M.C. 195, 196, 259, 294
Rhome, Jerry 12, 30, 31, 140, 208, 209, 212, 256, 272, 289, 290
Rice, Jerry 64
Richardson, Bucky 289
Richardson, Wally 193
Riffle, Dick 266
Riggins, John 157
Rison, Andre 191, 229
Rivers, Philip 12, 28, 31, 37, 170, 180, 182, 251, 252, 274, 276
Roach, John 212, 223
Robbins, Jack 95
Roberts, Flea 248
Robinson, Matt 23, 42, 156, 196, 216, 255, 256
Robinson, Tony 293
Rochester Royals 51

Rock Island Independents 202
Rockne, Knute 6, 80
Rodgers, Aaron 181, 223
Rodgers, Johnny 276
Roethlisberger, Ben 12, 27, 28, 35, 38, 65, 170, 180–82, 266–69
Rome, Jim 273
Romo, Tony 28, 180, 182, 211, 212
Ronzani, Gene 41, 202
Roosevelt, Theodore 5
Root, Jim 116
Rosenbach, Tim 26, 164, 186–88
Rosenfels, Sage 226
Rote, Kyle 224
Rote, Tobin 7, 18, 20, 21, 23, 27, 32, 33, 36, 39, 41, 45, 49, 59, 108, 113–116, 119, 126, 127, 215, 216, 218–24, 275–77
Roussel, Tom 294
Rozelle, Pete 60, 173
Rubbert, Ed 35, 293
Rubley, T.J. 223
Russell, Doug 95
Russell, JaMarcus 25
Rutkowski, Ed 131, 195, 196
Rutledge, Jeff 24, 251
Ryan, Buddy 8, 40, 152, 168
Ryan, Dave 219
Ryan, Frank 17, 31, 40, 50, 53, 120, 134, 137–42, 144, 207–9, 272, 294
Ryan, Pat 23, 255, 263
Rymkus, Lou 125
Rypien, Mark 35, 36, 65, 163, 166, 209, 228, 229, 272, 292, 294

Saban, Lou 127
Sacca, Tony 187
St. Francis College 268
St. Louis Cardinals *see* Arizona Cardinals
St. Louis Gunners 29
St. Louis Rams 6, 8, 16, 18, 19, 22, 23, 26, 27, 29, 31, 32, 38, 40, 41, 43, 49, 51, 54, 74, 90, 94, 98–101, 107–109, 111–116, 119, 120, 123, 132, 133, 136–39, 141, 143, 147, 148, 150, 151, 156–58, 169, 172, 176–79, 190, 196, 201, 202, 207, 209, 211, 220, 222–24, 229, 234, 240, 247, 263, 266, 269–73, 279, 289, 290
Salata, Paul 279
Salisbury, Sean 228, 240–42, 276, 277
San Diego Chargers 7, 16, 23, 26, 28, 31, 39, 40, 45, 74, 124–28, 147, 152, 155–57, 164, 171, 177, 178, 182, 191, 196, 202, 212, 229, 236, 238, 255, 274–77, 279, 288
San Francisco 49ers 7, 11, 13, 20, 23, 26, 30, 31, 40, 55, 57, 60, 61, 74, 102–106, 113, 114, 119, 120, 135, 136, 138, 140, 144, 150, 152, 154–56, 159, 162–68, 171, 172, 204, 211, 215, 218, 222, 240, 245, 251, 252, 277–81, 286
San Jose State 28
Sanders, Spec 27, 104, 105, 293
Sarboe, Phil 187, 293, 268, 292, 293

Saunders, Al 194
Sayers, Gale 140
Scarbath, Jack 26, 27, 116, 117
Schaub, Matt 23, 191
Schlichter, Art 18, 158, 227–30
Schmidt, Joe 118
Schnelker, Bob 241
Schonert, Turk 23, 205
Schroeder, Jay 17, 53, 61, 62, 73, 152, 160, 161, 163, 188, 205, 258, 259, 291, 294
Schwenk, Bud 36, 98, 104
Sciarra, John 263
Scott, Bobby 248
Scrabis, Bob 256
Seattle Seahawks 65, 149, 158, 174, 178, 181, 182, 187, 196, 198, 201, 202, 212, 223, 234, 245, 259, 266, 281–84, 286
Seifert, George 164
Shanahan, Mike 40, 63
Shapiro, Jack 11
Sharpe, Shannon 194
Shaughnessy, Clark 6, 11, 90, 96, 112, 273
Shaw, Buck 102
Shaw, Dennis 36, 65, 144, 195
Shaw, George 23, 26, 118, 126, 215, 216, 227–29, 241, 252
Shell, Art 259
Shepherd, Billy 20, 218–20, 293
Sherman, Allie 11, 13, 251, 263, 264, 268
Sherman, Tom 243
Shiner, Dick 29, 191, 209, 245, 252, 266, 268, 294
Shinners, John 248
Shockley, D. J. 190
Shofner, Del 251
Shula, David 72
Shula, Don 22, 39–41, 133, 139, 144, 146, 168, 229, 237
Shula, Mike 72
Shuler, Heath 46, 53, 171, 174, 247, 248, 292, 294
Shurmur, Fritz 8
Siemens, Jeff 241
Simms, Chris 13, 180, 285–87
Simms, Phil 8, 17, 35, 40, 42, 43, 64, 66, 152, 153, 155, 157, 159–61, 165, 166, 168, 250–53, 287
Simpson, Jessica 213
Simpson, O.J. 134, 149, 195, 196
Sinkwich, Frankie 20, 90, 99, 218, 219
Sipe, Brian 16, 28, 55, 56, 148, 150, 156–58, 207–9
Siragussa, Tony 43
Slack, Reggie 289
Slater, Walt 268
Slaughter, Mickey 127, 214, 215
Sloan, Dwight 11, 95, 187, 219, 220
Sloan, Steve 24
Slovak, Marty 272
Smiley, Tom 205
Smith, Akili 26, 52, 73, 176, 177, 179, 204, 205
Smith, Alex 26, 28, 181, 279, 280
Smith, Bubba 23, 229
Smith, Don 60–61

Smith, Hal 245
Smith, Jackie 154, 187
Smith, Riley 26, 293
Smith, Ron 12, 266–68, 272
Smith, Steve 241
Smith, Troy 25
Smukler, Dave 263
Smyth, Lou 82
Snead, Norm 12, 23, 27, 29–31, 52, 134, 136, 139, 141, 149, 240, 241, 250, 256, 261, 262, 280, 292, 294
Snyder, Bob 41, 90, 97, 202, 271, 272
Solomon, Freddie 237, 280
Songin, Butch 124, 125, 244, 245, 256
Sorgi, Jim 228
South, Ronnie 248
Speedie, Mac 208
Sporting News 67
Sports Illustrated 20, 67, 165
Sprinkle, Ed 42
Spurrier, Steve 22, 23, 134, 141, 149, 278, 280, 285–87, 292
Stabler, Ken 13, 17–19, 24, 31, 50, 52, 55, 66, 74, 134, 144, 147–49, 152, 155, 157, 159, 247–49, 257–60, 288, 290
Stagg, Amos Alonzo 5, 6, 12
Stallworth, John 19, 58, 267, 268
Stanford University 11, 115, 205
Starr, Bart 16, 18, 19, 24, 25, 28, 40, 43, 55, 57, 58, 62, 69, 70, 73, 108, 118, 134–35, 139–45, 221–24
Starring, Stephen 244
Stasica, Leo 72
Stasica, Stan 72
Staten Island Stapletons 11, 252
Staubach, Roger 16, 19, 20, 27, 28, 39–41, 43, 45, 46, 50, 55, 62, 63, 67, 70, 73, 74, 134, 140, 143, 145–47, 149, 150, 152, 154, 155
Stenstrom, Steve 202, 280
Stephens, Harold 255
Stephens, Larry 209, 272
Stephens, Sandy 27, 255
Stephenson, Kay 131, 196, 277
Sternaman, Dutch 72, 201, 202
Sternaman, Joey 72, 202
Stevens, Mark 279
Stevens, Matt 234
Stewart, Kordell 17, 20, 21, 170, 172, 174, 175, 178, 179, 181, 193, 201, 202, 237, 266–69
Stockton, Hust 84, 86
Stockton, John 84
Stofa, John 23, 129, 205, 237, 238
Stofka, Ed 268
Stoudt, Cliff 188, 266, 267
Stouffer, Kelly 28, 163, 187, 282, 283
Stram, Hank 17, 39, 40, 122, 125, 133
Streeter, Jimmy 14
Strock, Don 8, 12, 22, 23, 39–41, 147, 157, 208, 209, 236, 237
Studstill, Pat 141
Stydahar, Joe 108
Sullivan, Pat 146, 189, 190
Super Bowl 8, 17, 20, 22, 23, 30, 32, 34, 36, 48, 51, 55, 57, 58, 60, 65, 66, 69, 70, 73, 123, 129–33, 140–44, 146, 148–50, 154–68, 171–82, 188, 207, 214, 216, 224, 229, 233, 234–36, 238, 240, 243–45, 255, 256, 258, 292
Sutherland, Jock 111
Swann, Lynn 19, 44, 58, 149, 267, 268
Sweetan, Karl 141, 248, 272

Tagge, Jerry 146, 223
Taliaferro, George 13, 27, 106, 115, 116, 228, 229
Taliaferro, Mike 30, 127, 144, 146, 243–45, 254, 256
Tampa Bay Buccaneers 14, 18, 23, 30, 149, 150, 154, 159, 163, 172–74, 176, 178, 181, 188, 205, 220, 229, 258, 284–87, 293
Tanguay, Bill 267
Tarkenton, Fran 12, 17, 19, 20, 26, 27, 30, 31, 39, 42, 44–46, 49, 51, 55, 59, 62, 63, 65, 69, 70, 134, 136, 141, 146, 148–50, 152, 154, 172, 239–42, 250–53
Tarr, Jerry 216
Tate, Charlie 11
Tatum, Jack 146
Taylor, John 55, 64
Taylor, Lawrence 43, 160
Tennessee Oilers *see* Tennessee Titans
Tennessee State 14
Tennessee Titans 8, 14, 23, 26, 29, 31, 40, 42, 51, 55, 122, 124, 125, 127, 130, 144, 150, 152, 157, 162, 165, 167, 168, 174–76, 188, 191, 194–97, 224, 233, 234, 237, 241, 248, 256, 258, 271, 275, 276, 287–90, 294
Tensi, Steve 12, 23, 123, 131, 214–16, 276
Terlep, George 11, 208
Testaverde, Vinny 12, 19, 20, 23, 24, 26, 28, 36, 40, 45, 51, 152, 162–64, 168, 180, 181, 192–94, 208, 209, 211, 244, 245, 254–56, 284–87
Theismann, Joe 12, 20, 23, 25, 28, 33, 43, 45, 56, 74, 76, 134, 145, 148, 152, 158, 160, 291–95
Theofiledes, Harry 12
Theresa, Tony 259
Thomas, Bobby 31
Thomas, Pat 223
Thomason, Bobby 31, 41, 112, 114, 119, 223, 262, 264, 272
Thompson, Jack 19, 23, 52, 204–6, 285, 286
Thompson, Kevin 208
Thompson, Lex 112
Thompson, Tommy 16, 29, 40, 90, 97–99, 108, 110, 111, 113, 261–64, 268
Thorpe, Jim 81, 86
Thrower, Willie 13, 116, 201, 203
Tidwell, Travis 12, 251, 252
Tillman, Pat 180
Tinsely, Gaynell 94, 95

Tipton, Gregg 187
Tittle, Y.A. 18, 19, 22, 27, 31, 35, 36, 42, 43, 45, 46, 49, 54, 57, 59, 62–65, 67, 70, 74, 75, 103, 105, 106, 108, 111, 113, 114, 118–120, 134, 136, 138, 219, 250–53, 278–81
Todd, Richard 17, 18, 24, 30, 42, 77, 150, 152, 156, 160, 247, 248, 254–56
Tolliver, Billy Joe 54, 64, 164, 191, 247, 248, 275, 290
Tomczak, Mike 23, 25, 32, 76, 200, 202, 209, 223, 267, 268
Tomlinson, Ladainian 72
Torretta, Gino 24, 283
Totten, Willie 196
Trippi, Charlie 73, 110, 114, 186, 187
Tripucka, Frank 26, 31–33, 52, 112, 115, 123–26, 188, 214–16, 263
Trocano, Rick 208
Troup, Bill 12, 223, 228, 263
Trudeau, Gary 245
Trudeau, Jack 64, 76, 77, 161, 227, 228, 256
Trull, Don 127, 245, 288–90
Trumpy, Bob 205
Tuiasosopo, Marques 73, 258–59
Tupa, Tom 21, 187, 244, 255, 286
Turner, Jim 255
Turner, Norv 7
Turner, Ricky 228

UCLA 13, 25, 272
Underwood, Carrie 213
Unitas, John 2, 8, 16, 19, 22, 23, 26, 27, 29, 35, 39, 40, 43–46, 49, 55, 56, 59, 62, 65, 66, 68, 70, 73–76, 108, 118, 120, 134, 135, 139, 142–47, 149, 179, 180, 209, 227–30, 268, 276, 277
United States Congress 46, 134, 197
United States Football League (USFL) 8, 14, 26, 33, 34, 37, 48, 103, 158, 160–62, 196, 266
United States Supreme Court 46, 269
University of Alabama 24–26, 57, 111
University of Arkansas 95, 229
University of California 25
University of Chicago 5, 6, 90
University of Eastern Illinois 28
University of Florida 286
University of Illinois 84, 202, 256
University of Indiana 294
University of Iowa 25
University of Kentucky 115
University of Louisiana, Lafayette 28
University of Maryland 25, 205, 245, 256, 268
University of Miami 11, 24, 212, 229, 238, 286
University of Michigan 11, 24–25, 91, 193
University of Minnesota 27, 255
University of Mississippi 252
University of Missouri 187
University of Nebraska 25, 160, 195, 196, 223

University of Northern Iowa 28
University of Oregon 13, 25, 26, 187, 216, 241
University of Pennsylvania 121
University of Pittsburgh 267
University of Southern Illinois 28
University of Tennessee 205, 268
University of Tulsa 25, 29, 30, 219
University of Utah 219
University of Virginia 25, 248
University of Washington 14, 25, 29, 283
University of Wisconsin 241
USC 25, 259
Utah State 219

Vacanti, Sam 11, 105
Van Brocklin, Norm 16–19, 22, 25, 27, 30, 31, 41, 42, 49, 61, 62, 69, 70, 74, 108, 112–114, 117–120, 134, 135, 261–64, 270–73
Vanderbilt University 115
Vander Kelen, Ron 240, 241
Van Oelhoffen, Kimo 43
Van Pelt, Bradlee 73
Vaughn, Pug 267
Vermeil, Dick 263
Vick, Marcus 237
Vick, Michael 122, 13, 17, 20, 23, 26, 58, 1778, 180–82, 189–91, 249
Vlasic, Mark 276, 277
Volek, Billy 276, 288

Wade, Bill 18, 31, 41, 42, 74, 108, 115, 118, 136, 138, 139, 194, 200–3, 272
Wade, Tommy 266
Walker, Jay 241
Wallace, Seneca 12, 283
Walquist, Laurie 82, 201, 202
Walsh, Bill 7, 23, 40, 57, 61, 144, 152, 155–57, 163, 206
Walsh, Steve 18, 23, 24, 26, 41, 164, 165, 169, 202, 212, 229, 247, 248, 272, 286
Walter, Andrew 182, 258, 259
Walters, Stan 205, 263
Walton, Johnny 33, 263
Ward, Arch 102
Ward, Hines 268
Ware, Andre 165, 219
Warfield, Paul 209, 238
Warner, Glenn "Pop" 5, 6
Warner, Kurt 17, 18, 28, 34, 42, 43, 67, 170, 176–81, 186, 188, 224, 252, 253, 270–73
Warren, Bus 268
Warren, Dewey 205, 206

Warwick, Lonnie 191
Washington, Russ 216, 276
Washington Redskins 6, 7, 11, 14, 16, 23, 26, 27, 29–32, 40–43, 54, 55, 74, 88, 90, 94–97, 99–102, 109, 111, 116–118, 133, 136, 137, 139, 145, 146, 148, 152, 157, 158, 161, 163, 166, 168, 173, 176, 190, 195, 201, 215, 224, 240, 248, 252, 259, 261, 263, 268, 271, 272, 280, 291–95
Washington State 25
Waterfield, Bob 16, 18, 22, 25, 27, 35, 38, 40–42, 49, 54, 68, 70, 74, 77, 90, 101, 108–115, 270–73
Waters, Bob 136, 279
Waters, Charlie 290
Watkins, Foster 263, 264
Watts, J.C. 14
Weese, Norris 20, 33, 215
Weinke, Chris 36, 52, 73, 178, 182, 198
Weldon, Casey 48, 286
Welk, Lawrence 30, 223
Wells, Mike 205, 241
Wells, Warren 7
Werblin, Sonny 126, 128
Westbrook, Bryan 8
Westfall, Bob 219, 220
Westfall, Ed 267
Whelihan, Craig 174, 275, 276
White, Danny 21, 33, 39–40, 50, 73, 74, 134, 150, 155, 163, 210–12
White, Randy 212, 252
White, Reggie 180
White, Ted 234
White, Whizzer 46, 95, 266, 269
Whitehurst, Charlie 224, 277
Whitehurst, David 222, 224, 277
Whitmore, David 30
Wilhelm, Erik 13, 205
Wilkinson, June 290
Williams, Aeneas 43
Williams, Bob 25, 114, 202
Williams, Doug 14, 34, 36, 56, 62, 67, 152, 154, 162–64, 285–87, 292, 294
Williams, Jerry 133
Williams, K.D. 248
Williams, Stan 209
Willis, Peter Tom 165
Wilson, Butch 229
Wilson, Camp 220
Wilson, Dave 26, 157, 247, 248
Wilson, Eddie 234, 245
Wilson, George, Jr. 73, 129, 236, 237
Wilson, George, Sr. 119, 238

Wilson, Larry 133
Wilson, Marc 12, 25, 156, 243–45, 258, 259
Wilson, Tom 209, 272
Wilson, Wade 28, 157, 189, 190, 212, 240–42, 248, 259
Wilson, Wildcat 86
Wolf, Joe 283
Wood, Dick 12, 44, 126, 129, 228, 236–38, 254–56, 259, 276
Wood, Gary 20, 248, 250, 251
Wood, Willie 129, 223
Woodall, Al 12, 254, 255
Woodbury, Tory 255
Woodley, David 41, 50, 53, 156, 157, 236, 237, 267, 268
Workman, Hoge 83
World Football League (WFL) 28, 33, 37, 47, 103, 148–50, 263
World War II 13, 90, 101–102, 107
World Wrestling Federation (WWF) 34
Wren, Junior 268
Wright, Anthony 193, 205, 212
Wright, Randy 52, 54, 222
Wuerffel, Danny 174, 247, 248, 292, 294
Wyche, Sam 188, 205, 219, 220
Wycoff, Doug 252
Wynn, Spergon 208, 241

XFL 34, 48, 179

Yale University 5
Yary, Ron 241, 252
Yepremian, Garo 146
Yewcic, Tom 73, 244, 245
Young, Charlie 31
Young, Steve 17, 18, 20–26, 31, 34, 36, 39, 42, 43, 46, 58, 64, 69, 70, 74, 152, 160, 162, 163, 166–68, 171, 176, 231, 235, 278–81, 285–87
Young, Vince 20, 65, 182, 276, 289, 290

Zatkoff, Roger 30
Zeier, Eric 172, 286
Zilly, Jack 272
Zimmerman, Paul 61, 67
Zimmerman, Roy 75, 90, 97, 219, 263, 292, 294
Zolak, Scott 167, 237, 244, 245
Zorn, Jim 13, 23, 28, 42, 149, 157, 162, 223, 282, 283, 286
Zuppke, Bob 6